CompuServe
from A to Z

Second Edition

CompuServe
from A to Z
Second Edition

Charles Bowen

RANDOM HOUSE
ELECTRONIC PUBLISHING
New York

With love, to Pamela
In our 25th year together!

Acknowledgments

Thanks to the many friends at CompuServe Inc. for continued support and encouragement, especially Rich Baker, Doug Branstetter and Michelle Moran. Also thanks, as always, to the great team at Random House—Mike Roney, Kenzi Sugihari, and Jean Davis Taft, and to Katinka Matson and Irv Wiener at Brockman Inc.

Preface

CompuServe has grown up.

Ten years ago this book was not yet necessary. CompuServe was still an infant in the early 1980s with considerably fewer features than today's 1,800 or so. Subscribers, then, had quite predictable expectations. In fact, many computer hobbyists logged on simply to *see* CompuServe, because the system already was recognized as the best in this new world of modems and telecomputing.

Many people still become CompuServe subscribers for the experience itself, like hitting the road to become seasoned travelers. But far more have begun turning to CompuServe, and for thousands of different reasons. In the past decade, it has become a remarkably cosmopolitan information service, supporting interests from Apple and astronomy to Zenith and zoology.

Therein lies a problem, but it's a good kind of problem to have: there is *too much* information. Data overload. It is the same world-weariness that stymies many first-time visitors to New York or Los Angeles or Chicago.

The scope and variety of our questions illustrate just how far CompuServe has come. Nowadays we ask, for instance:

- Is there a place online where I can get help researching my family tree?

- Do Vietnam veterans have a meeting place? (What about lawyers and doctors, gardeners and journalists, broadcasters and science lovers, police and firefighters, students and teachers?)

- I use an orphaned computer. The company that made it has gone out of business. Can someone on CompuServe help with my technical questions?

- Where can I talk to somebody about cars? Can the system help me with some comparison shopping if I'm in the market for a new one?

- Is there some place to get information on stocks and bonds, current market quotes and historical stock prices, analysts' reports and company profiles, and all that?

- Can I use CompuServe to get information about cancer? About diabetes? AIDS? Attention Deficient Disorder. Rare diseases and illnesses, and common ones too?

- Can I search back issues of magazines, journals, and newspapers? And what about today's news? Is it possible to use CompuServe like a kind of electronic newspaper?

- What if I get really lost while I'm trying to use this new software that my company spent hundreds of dollars for? Are there features on CompuServe that can help me get more out of this program? And, while we're at it, what about some help with our mysterious desktop publishing system?

- Can I make airline reservations? Hotel reservations? Car rentals?

- Can I access an electronic encyclopedia? Is there an online dictionary?

- Can I browse through and buy products by keyboard?

Yes. Yes to these and thousands of other questions. *If* you know where to look. And that's where this book comes in. *CompuServe from A to Z* is the first of its kind: a CompuServe companion, the way an atlas is a companion for the road.

This book complements rather than competes with the rapidly growing number of tutorial books about CompuServe. These have been boom years for tutorial books about America's largest computer information service, mainly because there are suddenly so many *different* CompuServes to see. The last few years have witnessed the arrival of scores of powerful and sophisticated communications programs which are designed to interact exclusively with features of CompuServe. Many of the programs were created by long-time travelers who have innovative ideas for getting the most out of the system. And now CompuServe itself has entered this exciting new software arena. Programmers at its Columbus, Ohio, headquarters have produced various versions of the company's popular CompuServe Information Manager program, for IBM-DOS computers, Windows-based units, and Apple Macintosh users. Each dedicated communications program—those from CompuServe as well as the myriad of imaginative third-party efforts—presents its own screen interface and its own navigation structure (with and without menus, with and without icons, and so on). This has kept the tutorial writers hopping just to keep up with an ever-more-diverse CompuServe subscriber community.

But because this new brand of software takes much of the mystery out of *how* to travel CompuServe, *CompuServe from A to Z* moves on to the next important question: *where* to find the good stuff.

Since its first edition in 1991, *CompuServe from A to Z* has established itself as the next generation of CompuServe books and the ultimate "where-to-find-it" resource. Like its predecessor, this completely updated edition offers an encyclopedic approach to the thousands of things that are CompuServe, listing and cross-referencing its features and services. Written for new and long-time subscribers alike, it is intended to reside in that cozy place next to the computer, within easy reach of the keyboard.

Woven into its alphabetic structure are three kinds of entries. Specific *topic* articles range in length from a paragraph or two to several pages, depending on the subject. *Overviews* give general roundups on subjects such as hardware and software forums, games, financial services, investment analysis tools, travel, news, and more. Tying them all together are thousands of short *cross-references*, by name, subject, people, and so on.

Cross-referencing is the heart of this enterprise. It also enables readers to tap into some of CompuServe's nifty out-of-the-way places—specialized resources that might not always be apparent from their names or locations on the system. For instance, if you were an adoptee searching for your natural parents, you probably would think to check into CompuServe's popular Genealogy Forum for some guidance, but you might *not* know that another feature, called the IBM Special Needs Forum, offers similar help. Or if you were a pipe smoker, would you know that a service called the Bacchus Wine Forum has a section of its message board just for you? Suppose you needed a copy of the U.S. Constitution or the Declaration of Independence. Nothing in CompuServe's own online index would tell you that you can get both from Grolier's *Academic American Encyclopedia*. Or while you might turn to the encyclopedia for articles about the American Civil War, this book will tell you that if you want to talk to other Civil War buffs, you really ought to drop by the Military Forum as well. This list goes on and on. Looking for prime time television schedules from 20 or 30 years ago? Want to know about terrorism in a country you're thinking of visiting? Want to talk about Rush Limbaugh? Or UFOs? Or computerdom's "fuzzy logic" technology? Or soap operas? Or health care? Or fonts for your laser printer? Well, you've come to the right place.

This book should save you money, too, because it allows you to research CompuServe topics of interest at your own pace, without having to log on. It also will speed up your search, because it anticipates how you look for subjects. You can start with a general idea and search for specific features, or start with a specific feature you already know and use this information to locate related services that are available.

Most of CompuServe's features are mentioned in several different places in the book. For instance, the New Car/Truck Showroom is an online area used by computerists wanting to compare new automobiles. It is discussed in detail in the book's "N" section under "New Cars." It also is mentioned in the "S" section under "Shopping Features" and under "C" in the general article about "Cars." Along the way, if you follow the cross references, you can learn about related online features that may be of interest, such as the electronic version of *Consumer Reports* magazine's automobile reviews; car-oriented forums, car stores, and services in the Electronic Mall; relevant databases that can be accessed; car magazines that can be electronically searched; and more.

Two kinds of cross references are used. One directs you to other sections of the book for additional information and related topics; others refer to parts of CompuServe itself, providing specific commands that can be entered on the system to reach the features. A typical short entry looks like this:

FCC (Federal Communications Commission)   is discussed in the Broadcasters and Engineers Forum (GO BPFORUM). For more information, see Broadcasters and Broadcast Engineers.

Also:
- FCC Daily Digest and FCC Week databases may be searched through the IQuest gateway (GO IQUEST). See IQuest. The resource also can be searched through the Business Database Plus (GO BUSDB), as can *FCC Report*. See Business Database.

Both kinds of cross references are represented here:

1. "(GO BPFORUM)," "(GO IQUEST)," and "(GO BUSDB)" are the commands on CompuServe to reach the services referred to. GO and an *address* (or page number) can be entered at virtually any point on CompuServe to reach a feature, whether you're using CIM or CompuServe's plain-text interface. Almost all the book's entries provide one or more such direct access addresses to use when you go online.

2. The example also points to other portions of the book for additional information and background. Looking in the "I" section, you'll find a longer article on the powerful IQuest gateway. See the "B" section for "Business Database Plus" and for "Broadcasters." Also in the latter you will see references to other features covering related interests, such as the Journalism Forum, the Ham Radio Forum, access to back issues of related magazines, and so forth.

Some features are cited many times in this book. Hundreds of references are made to IQuest, the powerful gateway provided by Telebase Systems. When it was introduced in 1985, this important surcharged service virtually doubled the number of topics covered for CompuServe subscribers. Today, hundreds of databases are accessible through IQuest and they are cataloged here. Also there are scores of references to spin-off gateways of IQuest, including the Business Management InfoCenter, Marketing/Management Research Center, the legal and medical research centers, and the Patent Research Center. For an overview of these gateways, see Telebase Systems as well as IQuest.

Also, you will find hundreds of references to databases provided by magazine publisher Ziff-Davis Co. A few years ago, Ziff Communications launched its surcharged Computer Database Plus to enable users to search back issues of important computer-oriented magazines. After the success of that project, Ziff led the way in making other major magazines searchable on the system, through related gateways, including Magazine Database Plus, Health Database Plus, and Business Database Plus. Not only that, Ziff has started entire networks of forums and related services so its readers can communicate with its editors by telecomputing. For an overview of Ziff-Davis' formidable presence online, see ZiffNet.

These are just some of the massive electronic resources on which this book reports. To provide the most comprehensive coverage possible, we have made revisions right up to time of printing. That said, it's important also to recognize that change is as natural to CompuServe as it is to any other living thing. People and features come and go online just as they do in your own community. Occasionally, you'll discover that a service reported in the book is no longer available. Even more likely, you'll find features that have been brought online since these pages were published. Fortunately, the book will continue to be useful because CompuServe itself has become so adept at keeping us subscribers up to date. These days, if you try to GO to a feature no longer online—such as a little shop in the corner of the system's large Electronic Mall—CompuServe might report that while that particular feature is no longer available, you might be interested in several others that offer similar services.

That simple innovation allows you to use this book on a higher plane. If you're old hand at CompuServe, it can lead you to examine areas of the system outside your usual stomping grounds. And if you are new to these parts, you can use the book in concert with CompuServe itself as starting point for your own exploration. Either way, as you begin to research your favorite subjects, make notes in the margins of changes you find, especially the additions. Over the years, CompuServe has added more than it has removed.

Finally, if you get stuck, don't be shy about asking for directions. Start with CompuServe's own extensive assistance. It is covered here under "Help." If you're still confused, ask us. Just drop a line by CompuServe Mail at 71635,1025. If we don't know the answer, we'll find someone who does.

It has been a privilege to have gone along for the ride in the first decade of CompuServe's phenomenal expansion. And by all indications, the journey's just begun.

A+ **(magazine)** articles are searchable through Computer Database Plus (GO COMPDB). See Computer Database Plus. The magazine was incorporated into *InCider* in June 1989.

ABA Banking Journal **(magazine)** is searchable in the Business Database Plus (GO BUSDB). See Business Database.

Abacus products are supported in the Windows 3rd-Party C Forum (GO WINAPC). See Microsoft Software.

ABC Europe **(business database)** may be searched through the IQuest gateway. See IQuest.

ABC Systems products are supported in the Windows 3rd-Party D Forum (GO WINAPD). See Microsoft Software.

ABC Worldwide Hotel Guide (GO ABC) provides hotel data for travelers. For details, see Hotel Information.

ABI/INFORM **(business database)** is accessible through the Marketing/Management Research Center (GO MKTGRC). See Marketing/Management. The database also is accessible through IQuest (GO IQUEST) and through the Knowledge Index (GO KI). See Knowledge Index and see IQuest.

Abisch, Barry (71333,3066) is the sysop of the New York Newslink Forum (GO NEWYORK). See New York Newslink.

Above Software products are supported in the IBM PC Vendor D Forum (GO PCVEND). See IBM Computers.

Abstracts of Tropical Agriculture **(database)** may be searched through the IQuest gateway. See IQuest.

Academic American Encyclopedia, Grolier's (GO ENCYCLOPEDIA)

is an electronic encyclopedia that is updated and revised four times a year. It has more than 33,000 articles, fact boxes, bibliographies, and tables. In print, it would be a 21-volume work containing some 10 million words. This is one of the system's basic services, meaning those signed up under the Standard Pricing Plan (see Billing) have unlimited access to the feature.

AAE also is:

- Searchable by keywords. You may enter something quite general, like CIVIL WAR, and then zero in on the specific subject by examining the menu of articles it retrieves; or you may start by entering something like GETTYSBURG and get right to heart of the matter.

- Quickly readable because of the way complex subjects are presented. If you ask AAE for its article on ENGLAND, it produces an outline with a menu that lets you jump directly into the middle to portions dealing with "Land," "People," "Economic Activity," "Government," and so on.

- Thoughtfully organized. Some topics are broken down even further. Under the "Land" section usually is a submenu to take you to the discussions of soils, climate, vegetation, animal life, resources, and so on.

To Search for data, access the encyclopedia and enter a keyword at the search prompt. Then the service sorts its entries and displays in menu form a list of titles matching the term.

Keywords With most searches, the encyclopedia finds all entries beginning with the letters you enter, so DOG finds DOG, DOG DAYS, DOGBANE, DOGE, DOGFISH, DOGGER BANK, DOGGEREL, DOGWOOD, and so on. If you enter only one or two characters, the feature will locate articles that match these letters exactly. For instance, if you enter ID, it searches for *id* only. Enter three or more characters, and the service finds all articles that begin with those letters.

Statistics also are included in the encyclopedia. Many AAE articles are accompanied by summary "fact boxes." They are supplied with all articles about countries, continents, states, Canadian provinces, and U.S. presidents. Several hundred entries also display statistics tables such as sports records, awards and prizes, and industry production data. If an article has an accompanying table, the system calls your attention to it on a menu displayed before the text begins.

See also Dictionary.

Academic Index (database) may be searched through the IQuest gateway (GO IQUEST) and through the Knowledge Index (GO KI). See Knowledge Index and see IQuest.

Academy Award winners from 1928 to the present are listed in the Entertainment Encyclopedia, which is part of the Hollywood Hotline (GO HOLLYWOOD). See Hollywood Hotline.

Accent on Living   is searchable in the Health Database Plus (GO HDPLUS). See Health.

Access Advisor   electronic version is available in the Data Based Advisor Forum (GO DBADVISOR). See Data Based Advisor.

Access Phone Numbers   (GO PHONE) provides numbers for hundred of locations. The database lets you list all the numbers, accessible from anywhere in the U.S. and Canada, by a specific baud rate or locate a number in a specific city or area code. See Phone, CompuServe Access. For details on connect rates, see Billing information.

Access Reports/Freedom of Information **(government regulatory agency database)** may be searched through the IQuest gateway. See IQuest.

Access Softek Software Products   are supported in Windows 3rd-Party Forum A (GO WINAPA). See Microsoft Software.

Access Software   software is regularly discussed in The Game Publishers B Forum (GO GAMBPUB). See Gaming Forums.

Accolade Software   is regularly discussed in The Game Publishers B Forum (GO GAMBPUB). See Gaming Forums.

Accounting   features are covered in the Financial Services section. See Financial. Also:

- Searchable in the Business Database Plus (GO BUSDB) are a number of related magazines, including *Accounting and Finance, Accounting Today, Journal of Accountancy, CMA—the Management Accounting Magazine, The National Public Accountant*, and *World Accounting Report*. See Business Database.

- Relevant databases on IQuest (GO IQUEST) include ABI/INFORM, American Banker Fulltext, Corporate EFT Report, EFT Report, Financial Services Report, Management Contents, and POS News. See IQuest.

- Accounting and taxes also are discussed in the Working From Home Forum (GO WORK). See Working From Home.

ACCPAC   accounting software is supported in the CAI Forums (GO CAI) operated by Computer Associates International. See CAI.

Acer America **(computer systems)** products are supported in PC Vendor F Forum (GO PCVENF). For details, see IBM Computers.

Aces on Bridge, The, **(column)** is among the syndicated columns provided by United Features (GO COLUMNS). See Columnists.

ACI US Software: The ACI US Forum (GO ACIUS) is designed to support all of the products from ACI US. Primary sysops are Thom Hickey (70760,2475) and Chip Paige (76270,2131). Assisting are Lee Hinde, Tony Oppenheim, Lou Benjamin, Rich Gay, and David Batton.

ACKnowledge The Window Letter (magazine) can be searched through Computer Database Plus (GO COMPDB). See Computer Database Plus.

ACM Computing Surveys   (computer publications on databases, graphics, math software, office information services, programming languages and more) are searchable (abstracts) in Database Plus (GO COMPDB). See Computer Database Plus.

Acronyms   and abbreviations often are used in the daily conversations on CompuServe, in the real-time conferencing of the forums and the CB Simulator, and in the messages in the forums and on electronic mail. Some of the more frequently used acronyms—sometimes referred to as "slanguage"—are:

ASAP	As soon as possible.
BBS	Computer "bulletin board system," usually a private dial-up service.
BCNU	Be seein' you.
BFN	Bye for now.
BRB	Be right back.
BTW	By the way.
CIM	CompuServe Information Manager
CIS	CompuServe Information Service
CO	conference, used to refer to real-time conferencing, either as a noun ("At the CO...") or a verb ("When we CO...")
config	configuration
CP	copy protection
CU	See you, as in "CU tomorrow."
DOSCIM	IBM/DOS version of the CompuServe Information Manager
DBMS	database management system
FB	Files busy.
FUBAR	Fouled up beyond all recognition.
FWIW	For what it's worth.
FYI	For your information.
GR&D	Grinning, running, and ducking.
IAE	In any event.
IMO	In my opinion.
IMHO	In my humble opinion.
IOW	In other words.
MacCIM	Apple Macintosh version of CompuServe Information Manager

NBD	No big deal.
OIC	Oh, I see.
OTOH	On the other hand.
OZCIS	OZCIS terminal program (see OzCIS)
params	parameters, that is, communications settings
p.d.	public domain (usually referring to software)
PDQ	Pretty darn quick.
PITA	Pain in the acronym.
PKZIP	PKZIP archiving utility, popular in the IBM computing community (See Files, Compressed.)
PPN	Programmer Project Number, now called "User ID."
prog.	program
ROF,L	Rolling on floor, laughing.
RSN	Real soon now.
RTFM	Read the fine/funny/feckless manual (or message).
SNAFU	Situation normal, all fouled up.
Sysop	system operator, one who runs the forums.
TTFN	Ta ta for now.
TIA	Thanks in advance.
TSR	Terminate and stay resident (in-memory program).
WinCIM	IBM Windows version of the CompuServe Information Manager
WizOp	wizard sysop, the primary administrator of a forum
w.p.	word processor
WYSIWYG	What you see is what you get.
xfer	transfer, as in file transfer

In addition to these acronyms, the online talking world has come up with "emoticons," the online equivalent of facial expressions. For newcomers, emoticons in messages look like cryptic codes; in fact, they are a clever way to express the emotions of normal voice communication. Figures created with symbols on the keyboard, emoticons should be read with your head tilted to the left. Use them to tell others the spirit of your message. Here is a sampling of favorite emoticons:

:-)	smiley face
:-(	Boo hoo
:-<	Really sad
:->	Hey hey
|-)	Hee hee
|-D	Ho ho
;-)	Winking
:-@	Screaming

```
>:-<    Mad
:-|)    smiley face with a mustache
:-o     user singing national anthem
:-)8    well-dressed user
:-x     "my lips are sealed"
:-o     shock (or surprise)
:-&     user who is tongue-tied
*<|:-)  Santa Claus (Ho Ho Ho)
```

Across the Board (magazine) is searchable in the Business Database Plus (GO BUSDB). See Business Database.

Acting is a subject in the ShowBiz Forum (GO SHOWBIZ). Also, the IQuest gateway allows access to the Backstage database. See IQuest. See also Entertainment.

ActionMedia products are supported in the Ultimedia Hardware Plus Forum (GO ULTIHW). See Ultimedia.

Activision/Infocom software is supported in the Game Publishers B Forums (GO GAMBPUB) and in the Macintosh Vendor A Forum (GO MACAVEN). See Apple Computers.

Actrix computers are supported in the Computer Club (GO CLUB). See Computer Club.

Ad Week (magazine) is searchable in the Business Database Plus (GO BUSDB). See Business Database.

Adhemix (French glue industry database) can be searched through IQuest (GO IQUEST). The resource is in French. See IQuest.

Ada is supported in the Computer Language Forum (GO CLMFORUM). See Computer Language. It also is supported in the Portable Programming Forum (GO CODEPORT). See Programmers Support.

Adam Computer is one of the systems supported in CompuServe's Computer Club Forum (GO CLUB). See Computer Club.

Addiction & Recovery and **The Addiction Letter** are searchable in the Health Database Plus (GO HLTBD), as is *Brown University Digest of Addiction Theory and Application*. See Health.

   Addiction and recovery also is a topic of the Health & Fitness Forum (GO GOODHEALTH). See Health.

Address change   can be recorded online for billing purposes by entering GO AD-DRESS. For related topics, see Help Online.

AddStor   products are supported in the IBM PC Vendor E Forum (GO PCVENE). See IBM Computers.

Adhesives Age (magazine) is searchable through the Business Database Plus (GO BUSDB). See Business Database.

ADIS DrugNews   (health database) may be searched through the IQuest gateway. See IQuest. See also Pharmaceuticals.

Adler, Noel D.   (76703,264) is sysop of the Legal Forum (GO LAWSIG). See Legal Forum.

Administrative Management (magazine) can be searched through Computer Database Plus (GO COMPDB) and Business Database Plus (GO BUSDB). See Computer Database and Business Database.

Adobe Software: The Abode Forum (GO ADOBE) is operated by the Adobe Technical support staff to provide online support for users, dealers, service bureaus, third-party developers, and others.

   The data libraries include utilities, technical support notes, PostScript files, and text files of information about Adobe and non-Adobe Software products, printers and other hardware, desktop publishing, training, press releases, and new product announcements.

   The sysop is Michael Shahamatdoust (76704,21) assisted by members of technical support, engineering, and marketing.

Adoption searches   is a topic of the Genealogy Forum (GO ROOTS). The feature is intended to those who are adopted and have little or no knowledge of who their birth parents are. See Genealogy. Also the IBM Special Needs Forum (GO IBMSPECIAL) has a section for discussing the topic.

ADSTAR Distributed Storage Manager   (software) is supported in the IBM Storage Systems Division Forum (GO IBMSTORAGE). See IBM Storage Systems.

Advanced Ceramics Report, Advanced Coatings & Surface Technology, Advanced Composites Bulletin, Advanced Manufacturing Technology, Advanced Metals Technology, Advanced Military Computing, Advanced Office Technologies Report, Advanced Recovery Week, and **Advanced Wireless Communications** are magazines that can be searched through the Business Database Plus (GO BUSDB). See Business Database.

Advanced Gravis products are supported in the IBM PC Vendor B Forum (GO PCVENB). See IBM Computers.

Advanced Logic Research products (GO ALRINC) are supported in the PC Vendor G Forum (GO PCVENG). See IBM.

Advanced Program-to-Program Communications is covered in the APPC Info Exchange (GO APPC). For more details, see IBM Computers.

Advanced Software products are supported in the Mac D Vendor Forum (GO MACDVEN). See Apple Computers.

Advanced Support Group (**office automation software tools**) is supported by the Office Automation Vendor Forum (GO OAFORUM). See Office Automation.

Advanced Telenet is supported in the **SunSelect Forum** (GO SUNSELECT). See SunSelect.

Advanced Wireless Communications covering personal communications from cellular phones to digital radios, can be searched through IQuest (GO IQUEST). See IQuest.

Advantage (**magazine**) is searchable through the Business Database Plus (GO BUSDB). See Business Database.

Advantis remote mail system users can receive mail from CompuServe. See Mail, CompuServe.

Adventure, Classic (**game**) (GO CLADVENT) is the first text adventure from which all other adventures, both micro and mainframe, evolved. The game understands English words and phrases. The player explores a cave, finds treasures, and deposits them in the building. A perfect score is 350 points. If this is your first adventure, you should use HELP and INFO when the game begins. The system also offers Enhanced Adventure (GO ENADVENT). Both games are intended for players age 12 and up. Both games are among the system's basic services, meaning those signed up under the Standard Pricing Plan (see Billing) have unlimited access to the features. For information on other games, see Games.

Adventures in Food (GO AIF) is a store in the Electronic Mall (GO MALL) that offers gourmet food items. See Electronic Mall.

Adventures in Travel (GO AIT) is a travel column. A single article runs for two weeks; earlier articles also may be reviewed. The articles aim to cover all aspects of travel. Also, you may leave a question or comment for Foster, by choosing another menu item. For other travel-related features, see Travel.

Advertisements, classified: Users may read and place online ads in the Classifieds Service (GO CLASSIFIEDS). Reading messages is free; posting an ad is surcharged. See Classifieds Service.

Advertising in *CompuServe Magazine* is the topic of Online Inquiry (GO OLI). You can leave your names and addresses at the prompts supplied and further information will be sent to you. You also can add specific comments or special requests to the inquiry, if you like. Requests are filed electronically and are accessible only by the advertisers you specify.

Advertising industry is covered in a number of magazines searchable through the Business Database Plus (GO BUSDB), including *Ad Solutions Report, AdWeek (Eastern Edition, Western Advertising News, and Marketing Week News),* and *International Journal of Advertising* and *Journal of Advertising.* See Business Database.

Also, relevant IQuest databases (see IQuest) include Academic Index, Boomer Report, Business Week, Campaign, Cellular Sales, and Marketing, D&B—Donnelley Demographics, FINDEX: Directory of Market Research Reports, FINIS: Financial Industry Information Service, Market Research Reports from MSI, Marketing, Marketing Surveys Index, Media Week, PR Week, PTS F&S Indexes (1980 to present), PTS International Forecasts, PTS MARS, PTS New Product Announcements, PTS Newsletter Database, PTS PROMT, PTS U.S. Forecasts, PTS U.S. Time Series, Super Marketing, and Video Marketing News.

See also Public Relations, Marketing, and Demographics.

AECO **(French and international business database)** can be searched through the IQuest gateway. The resource is in French. See IQuest.

Aerospace Financial News **(magazine)** can be searched through the Business Database Plus (GO BUSDB). See Business Database. See also Aviation, Space, and Defense.

After Dark **(software)** is supported in Windows 3rd-Party Forum C (GO WINAPC). See Microsoft Software.

Africa, news: IQuest provides access to Africa News On-line, South African Focus, Africa Telecommunications Report, and Southscan/Southern Africa. See IQuest.

Also, *ESP-Business Opportunities in Africa & the Middle East, Executive Briefing Service Middle East & North Africa,* and *Sub-Saharan Monitor* can be searched through the Business Database Plus (GO BUSDB). See Business Database.

Africa/Middle East also is a topic in the International Trade Forum (GO TRADE) and the Travel Forum (GO TRAVSIG). See Travel and International Trade.

African American issues are topics in the Issues Forum (GO ISSUESFORUM). See Issues.

Age issues are covered in several features:

- Ageline (database) may be searched through the IQuest gateway (GO IQUEST) and through the Knowledge Index (GO KI). See Knowledge Index and see IQuest.
- *Aging* (magazine) articles are searchable through Magazine Database Plus (GO MDP). For details see Magazine Database.
- The Seniors Forum (GO SENIORS). See Senior Citizens.

Agence France Presse is a French news service that is searchable through Comtex Scientific Inc.'s NewsGrid database. For details, see NewsGrid. The newswire reports from 1985 to present, which are updated daily, also can be searched through IQuest (GO IQUEST). See IQuest.

For related topics, see French News.

Agenda (**software**) is supported in the Lotus Words & Pixels Forum (GO LOTUSB). See Lotus Software.

Agri-Commodities (GO ACI) covers general commodity information. See Commodities.

Agriculture Among the databases searchable through IQuest (see IQuest) are Abstracts of Tropical Agriculture, Agribusiness U.S.A., Agricola, Agris International, Biobusiness, Biological & Agricultural Index, Biosis Previews, CAB Abstracts, Cendata, Coffeeline, Current Research Information/USDA, Fearless Taster, Food Channel, Food Science and Technology Abstracts, Foods Adlibra, Ialine, Ice Cream Reporter, Nation's Restaurant News, Restaurant Business Magazine, Super Marketing, and Washington Beverage Insight.

Through the Business Database Plus (GO BUSDP) are several agricultural magazines, including *Agexporter*, *Agra Europe*, *Fertilizer International*, and *Agribusiness Worldwide*. See Business Database.

Through the Knowledge Index (GO KI), you can search AGRICOLA, The Agrochemicals Handbook, CAB Abstracts 1984–present, CAB Abstracts 1972–1983. See Knowledge Index.

Agriculture also is discussed in the White House Forum (GO WHITEHOUSE). See White House.

See also Farming, Food and Cooking, Pets and Animals, and Gardening Forum.

AIDS (Acquired Immune Deficiency Syndrome) information is supplied in several databases:

- The Comprehensive Core Medical Library (GO AIDSNEWS). This surcharged database includes the full text of AIDS-related articles from leading medical reference books, textbooks, and general medical journals such as *the New England Journal of Medicine, Science,* and *Nature*. Information available for an article includes author, title, publication, and publication date and references if included in the article, as well as the full text of the article. You may retrieve articles by entering subject words, author, publication, or publication year as your search criteria. The CCML's AIDS Articles carry these surcharges: A standard search which retrieves up to 10 titles, $5. Additional titles (in groups of 10), $5. Full reference, with abstract where available (selected from the titles), $5 each. There is a $1 charge for a search that retrieves no titles.

- AIDSLine, the National Library of Medicine's database of clinical, research and health care policy information on AIDS contains more than 80,000 references, selected from more than 4,000 sources dating from 1980, that discuss AIDS and related topics. This is part of the Paperchase (GO PAPERCHASE) medical database. See Paperchase. AIDSLine also is searchable through the Knowledge Index (GO KI). See Knowledge Index.

- Rare Disease Database (GO NORD), made up of reports by the National Organization for Rare Disorders, a nonprofit, voluntary health agency, includes an AIDS Update section. See Rare Disease Database.

- Also, searchable on IQuest (GO IQUEST) are the AIDS Database with articles from 1982 to present, updated monthly; the AIDS Knowledge Base, updated monthly, with information on treatment, pathogenesis, diagnosis, as well as social and psychological implications; and AIDS Weekly, featuring the latest 12 months of the international newsletter. See IQuest.

- Searchable through the Business Database Plus (GO BUSDB) are *AIDS Therapies* and *AIDS Weekly*. See Business Database.

- Through the Health Database Plus (GO HLTBD) you can search *AIDS Alert* and *AIDS Weekly* (formerly *CDC AIDS Weekly*). Abstracts of *Journal of Acquired Immune Deficiency Syndromes* can be searched there. See Health.

- AIDS and social/ethical issues are a topic in the MedSIG Forum (GO MEDSIG). See Health.

AI Expert magazine: The AI Expert Forum (GO AIEXPERT) covers artificial intelligence. The magazine's staff use the AI Forum to interact with readers and would-be readers on topics such as languages like LISP and Turbo Prolog, expert systems in general, reviews, and utilities.

Running the forum is Susan Shepard (76703,4326) who writes regularly for the magazine. She is an AI consultant for private business and educational institutions on intelligent applications. Among her assistants are Marc Rettig, Jeff Jacobs, Jim Freeman, and Larry O'Brien.

And *AI Expert* magazine also can be searched through Database Plus (GO COMPDB). See Computer Database Plus.

AIMplus   is searchable in the Health Database Plus (GO HLTBD). See Health.

AIMS products   are supported in the PC Vendor G Forum (GO PCVENG). See IBM.

AimTech   products are supported in the Multimedia Vendor Forum (GO MULTIVEN). See Multimedia. They also are supported in the Ultimedia Tools Forum A (GO ULTIATOOLS). See Ultimedia.

AIN Report   (**magazine**) can be searched through the Business Database Plus (GO BUSDB). See Business Database.

Air Cargo World and **Air Transport World**   (**magazines**) are searchable through the Business Database Plus (GO BUSDB). See Business Database.

Air Conditioning, Heating & Refrigeration News   (**magazine**) is searchable through the Business Database Plus (GO BUSDB). See Business Database.

Aircraft & Adventure Factory   (**software**) is supported in the Game Publishers B Forum (GO GAMPUB). See Gaming Forums.

Air France   (GO AF) is a store in the Electronic Mall (GO MALL) that offers tour booking, information on sights and scenery. See Electronic Mall.

Airline Financial News and **Commuter/Regional Airline News International**   (**business databases**) may be searched through the IQuest gateway. See IQuest.

Airlines   (GO FLIGHTS) are the topic of several different electronic air travel reservation services, including:

- Eaasy Sabre (GO SABRE), a flight reservation service by American Airlines. See Eaasy Sabre.
- Travelshopper (GO PARS), a service provided by PARS Travel Information Systems, features a discount fare finder, has information for the frequent flight bonus programs, and offers national and international scheduling. See Travelshopper.
- Official Airline Guides/Electronic Edition (GO OAG), the oldest airline information service of its kind and still is praised by many as the most extensive air-schedule database around. See Official Airline Guides.

Note that Eaasy Sabre and Travelshopper are part of the basic services (meaning those signed up under the Standard Pricing Plan have unlimited access to the feature), while OAG is part of the extended service. (See Billing.)

The Travel Forum (GO TRAVSIG) has added a message section on "Airlines" for a discussion of ways to make air travel less costly and less annoying, if not downright enjoyable.

See also Travel and Aviation.

Airports **(newsletter),** focusing on airport operations, can be searched through IQuest. See IQuest.

Air safety is the topic of a number of resources searchable on IQuest, including Air Safety Week Accident/Incident Log, Air Safety Week Newsletter, and Air Safety Week Regulatory Log. See IQuest. Air Safety Week also can be searched through the Business Database Plus (GO BUSDB). See Business Database.

Air Toxics Report **(magazine)** can be searched through the Business Database Plus (GO BUSDB). See Business Database. See also Toxic, Hazardous Materials, and Safety.

Air Traffic Controller **(game)** (GO ATCONTROL) is a game based on cooperation among players. It simulates an air traffic controller's duties and you are responsible for all planes within a sector of air space. You guide the planes safely through your assigned sector of airspace or to a nearby airport. New planes arrive from other sectors and from the airports. You can influence other sectors by delaying planes or sending them out with inadequate fuel. You also may send messages to other players to notify them of planes you send into their sectors. If everyone cooperates, you all score better. If there are no other players, you still can play, though you receive only computer-generated planes. If other people are playing, you can get additional planes from them. You have direct contact with as many as four other players, to the north, south, east, and west. Several levels of difficulty are available and score is kept for each 10- to 12-minute "shift" you play. The game is intended for those 12 and up.

Incidentally, if you use an IBM-compatible system, you might be interested in using a graphics interface. The program is called ATC Scope in Library 14 ("Other Games") of the MultiPlayer Games Forum (GO MPGAMES). See the file called ATSCPX.ZIP. It provides a graphics, front-end interface for the game.

For information on other games, see Games.

Air/Water Pollution Report **(databases)** may be searched through the IQuest gateway. See IQuest. The resource also can be searched through the Business Database Plus (GO BUSDB). See Business Database. See also Environmental.

AISB products are supported in the Desktop Publishing Vendor Forum (GO DTPVENDOR). For details, see Desktop Publishing.

AI Week **(magazine)** is searchable in the Business Database Plus (GO BUSDB). See Business Database.

Akron (OH) Beacon Journal   **(newspaper)** is searchable through Telebase System's News Source USA (GO NEWSUSA) and through the Knowledge Index (GO KI). See Knowledge Index and see News Source.

Alabama   **(news)** is included in the daily Southeast regional reports from United Press International. See Executive News Service for details.

Also, *Birmingham Business Journal* can be searched through the Business Database Plus (GO BUSDB). See Business Database.

Aladdin Systems   **(software),** including StuffIt and ShortCut, is supported in Mac C Vendor Forum (GO MACCVEN). For details, see Apple Computers.

Alaska   **(news)** is covered in the Anchorage Daily News, searchable through Telebase System's News Source USA (GO NEWSUSA). See News Source.

Alaska Business Monthly   **(magazine)** is searchable through the Business Database Plus (GO BUSDB). See Business Database.

AlaskaNet   logon instructions (GO LGN-29); to log on to CompuServe using AlaskaNet:

1. Dial the AlaskaNet network telephone access number, listen for the modem tone, and connect your communications equipment.
2. At the "PLEASE ENTER YOUR TERMINAL IDENTIFIER" prompt, enter A. Do *not* press the Enter or Return key afterward.
3. At the "PLEASE LOG IN" prompt, enter COMPUSERVE, and press Return.
4. When the network displays "Host Name:" enter CIS and press Return.
5. At the "User ID:" prompt, enter your User ID number and you will next be prompted for your password.

Costs   AlaskaNet surcharges (rates charged in addition to CompuServe's basic rates) are $11.70 an hour.

Alaska Peddler   (GO ALASKA) is a store in the Electronic Mall (GO MALL) that calls itself a "venture to the last frontier." See Electronic Mall.

Albany (NY) Times-Union   **(newspaper)** is searchable through Telebase System's News Source USA (GO NEWSUSA). See News Source.

Alberta Business   **(magazine)** is searchable through the Business Database Plus (GO BUSDB). See Business Database.

Alcoholics Anonymous   has representatives on the Health and Fitness Forum (GO GOODHEALTH). See Health.

Alcoholism is a topic in a number of publications searchable through the Health Database Plus (GO HLTBD), including *Alcohol Health & Research World*, *Alcoholism & Addiction Magazine*, *Alcoholism & Drug Abuse Week*, *Alcoholism & Drug Abuse Weekly*, *The Alcoholism Report*, and *American Journal of Drug and Alcohol Abuse*. See Health.

Alcom products are supported in the IBM Vendors H Forum (GO PCVENH). See IBM Computers.

Aldus Magazine **(magazine abstracts)** can be searched through Computer Database Plus (GO COMPDB). See Computer Database Plus.

Aldus Software: Aldus Forum (GO ALDUS) supports the company's publishing software, including Aldus PageMaker for the Apple Macintosh, IBM PC/AT, and AT-compatible computers, as well as Aldus FreeHand, Persuasion, PhotoStyler, and PrePrint. The forum is managed by the Aldus technical support staff. The sysop is Reuben Lam (76703,4357) assisted by company officials in technical support, and engineering and marketing departments. Message areas have been set aside for both novice and expert users and the data libraries contain technical support notes, design formats (templates) for publications, and utility programs. Assisting in running the forum are Darwin Terry, Sean Baird, Eldor Gemst, Ian Wright, John Cornicello, Sam Merrell, Dennis Holmes, Tom Delaney, Dave Saunders, Don Picard, Moe Rubenzahl, Sheridan Slater, Mike Farrell, Olav Kvern, and Nick Allison.

The feature offers Aldus Special Programs Forum (GO ALDUSSP) and provides public areas such as the "Developer's Corner" for TIFF information and support, and "Additions Dev." for Aldus Additions questions. Assisting Lam are Andy Commons and Mike Mitchell.

Alexander, Keith (76711,1223) is the sysop of the Intersolv Forum (GO INTERSOLV). See Intersolv.

"All My Children" **(television)** summaries on the latest shows are available in Soap Opera Summaries (GO SOAPS). See Soap Opera.

Allen Communications products are supported in the Ultimedia Tools Forum A (GO ULTIATOOLS). See Ultimedia.

Allentown (PA) Morning Call **(newspaper)** is searchable through Telebase System's News Source USA (GO NEWSUSA). See News Source.

Allied & Alternative Medicine **(newsletter)** can be searched through IQuest. See IQuest. See also Medicine.

Allied Telesis products are supported in the PC Vendor I Forum (GO PCVENI). See IBM Computers.

All Music Guide   (GO ALLMUSIC) provides data and discussion on more than 200,000 albums, covering most known forms of music. The All Music Guide Forum (GO AMGPOP) provides a discussion area. See Music.

Alpha AXP platform   is supported in the Digital NT Support Forum (GO DEC4WNT). See Digital Equipment forums.

Alpha Books   computer books are supported in the Prentice Hall Computer Publishing Forum (GO PHCP). See Prentice Hall.

Alpha Software   products are supported in the IBM PC Vendor E Forum (GO PCVENE). See IBM Computers.

Alternative Energy Digests and **Alternative Energy Network Online Today** (**magazines**) can be searched through the Business Database Plus (GO BUSDB). See Business Database. See also Energy.

Alternatives   (**magazine**) can be searched in the Magazine Database Plus (GO MDP). See Magazine Database.

Altium   products are supported in the CADD/CAM/CAE Vendor Forum (GO CADDVEN). See CAD/CAM.

Altizer, Dorr   (76702,402) is sysop of the TrainNet Forum (GO TRAINNET). See TrainNet.

Altsys Corporation products   are supported in the Mac B Vendor Forum (GO MACBVEN). See Apple Computers.

Aluminium Industry Abstracts (**database**) can be searched through IQuest. See IQuest.

Alysis   products are supported in the Macintosh C Vendor Forum (GO MACCVEN). See Apple Computer.

AMAZE   (**software**) is supported in Delrina Technology Forum (GO DELRINA). See Delrina.

Ambulance operation   is discussed in the Safetynet Forum (GO SAFETY). See Safety.

America: History and Life   (**history scholarship**) can be searched through IQuest and through the Knowledge Index (GO KI). See IQuest and see Knowledge Index.

Americana Clothing   (GO AC) is a store in the Electronic Mall (GO MALL) that offers Levi Strauss & Co. products. See Electronic Mall.

American Artist (**magazine**) can be searched in the Magazine Database Plus (GO MDP). See Magazine Database.

American Banker (**newsletter**) can be searched through a number of resources. See Banking.

American Cybernetics Inc. products are supported in the IBM PC Vendor E Forum (GO PCVENE). See IBM Computers.

American Express (GO AE), the credit card firm, operates a kiosk in the Electronic Mall (GO MALL) for Travelers Cheques and Gift Cheques. See Electronic Mall.

American Family Physician is searchable in the Health Database Plus (GO HLTBD). See Health.

American Heritage Dictionary (GO DICTIONARY) is searchable online. See Dictionary.

American Libraries (**database**) may be searched through the IQuest gateway (GO IQUEST). See IQuest.

American Marketplace can be searched through IQuest. See IQuest.

American Medical Informatics Association sponsors MedSig (GO MEDSIG), a health-related forum. For details, see Health.

American Power Conversion products are supported in the IBM PC Vendor E Forum (GO PCVENE). See IBM Computers.

American Spectator (**magazine**) can be searched in the Magazine Database Plus (GO MDP). See Magazine Database.

America's Cup is discussed in the Sailing Forum (GO SAILING). See Sports and Recreation.

Ami and **Ami Pro** (**software**) are supported in the Lotus Word Processing Forum (GO LOTUSWP). See Lotus Software.

Amiga computers: The system offers the Amiga Arts Forum (GO AMIGAARTS) and the Amiga Vendor Forum (GO AMIGAVENDOR). See Commodore computers.

Amnesty International officials are sometimes represented in the Issues Forum (GO ISSUES). See Issues.

Amortization tables   for mortgages and other loans can be created with the Mortgage Calculator (GO HOM-17). See Mortgage Calculator.

Amstrad computers   are supported in the Computer Club (GO CLUB). See Computer Club. It also is supported in the UK Computing Forum (GO UKCOMP). See UK Computing.

Amusement Business   (**magazine**) is searchable through the Business Database Plus (GO BUSDB). See Business Database.
 See also Entertainment.

Analyst   (**software**) is supported in the Ventura Software Forum (GO VENTURA). See Ventura.

Analytical Abstracts   (**database**) may be searched through the IQuest gateway (GO IQUEST) and through the Knowledge Index (GO KI). See IQuest and see Knowledge Index.

Analyzer, Company   (GO ANALYZER) provides a menu of financial services with fundamental and technical data on a company. See Company Reports.

Anchorage (AK) Daily News   (**newspaper**) is searchable through Telebase System's News Source USA (GO NEWSUSA). See News Source.

Anderson, Jack,   (**column**) is among the syndicated columns provided by United Features (GO COLUMNS). See Columnists.

Anderson, Ron   (72241,113) is the sysop of the Windows Sources Forum (GO ZNT:WINSOU). See Windows Sources.

Anderson, Tony   (76703,4062) is a sysop in TandyNet (GO TANDYNET). For details, see Tandy Computers.

Andress, Frank   (76711,176) is sysop in the IBM OS/2 forums. See IBM Computers.

Andrew Seybold's Outlook on Professional Computing (**magazine**) is searchable (abstracts) through Computer Database Plus (GO COMPDB). See Computer Database Plus. Seybold publications also are accessible through the Seybold/ZiffNet Information Connection (GO ZNT:SEYBOLD). See ZiffNet.

Andyne Computing Ltd.   (**products**) are supported in the Windows 3rd-Party Forum (GO WINAPD). See Microsoft Software.

Animals and animal rights   are discussed in the Pets and Animals Forum (GO PETS). See Pets and Animals Forum. Also of interest, see Fish (Tropical) and the Humane Society Forum (GO HSUS). See Humane Society and Earth Forum (GO EARTH). See Earth.
 Animal pictures are featured in several of the graphics forums. See Graphics.

Animated Software   (computer graphics products) is supported in the Graphics B Vendor Forum (GO ANISOFT). See Graphics.

Animation   is discussed in the Comics and Animation Forum (GO COMICS). See Comics. It also is a topic in the Multimedia Forum (GO MULTIMEDIA) and in the Sight & Sound Forum (GO SSFORUM). See Multimedia.

Animotion   (products) are supported in the MIDI A Vendor Forum (GO MIDIAVEN). See Music.

"Another World"   (television) summaries on the latest shows are available in Soap Opera Summaries (GO SOAPS). See Soap Opera.

Anthony, Karl   (76702,1206) is a sysop in the Ventura Software Forum (GO VENTURA). See Ventura.

Antitrust FOIA Log   (database) may be searched through the IQuest gateway. See IQuest. The resource also can be searched through the Business Database Plus (GO BUSDB). See Business Database.

Antiviral Agents Bulletin   (magazine) can be searched through the Business Database Plus (GO BUSDB). See Business Database.

AP (Associated Press)   is a major news wire accessible through a number of CompuServe news services. For details, see Associated Press.

APE   (software) is supported in Windows 3rd-Party Forum A (GO WINAPA). See Microsoft Software.

Apilit   (energy database) may be searched through the IQuest gateway. See IQuest.

APL   (programming language) is supported in the Portable Programming Forum (GO CODEPORT). See Programmer's Support.

Appian Technology Inc.   software is supported in the Graphics A Vendor Forum (GO GRAPHAVEN). See Graphics.

Applause   (software) is supported in the Borland Applications Forum (GO BORAPP). See Borland.

Apple Computers: The Micronetworked Apple Users Groups (GO MAUG) is administered by New York writer/editor Neil Shapiro (76703,401). MAUG is made up of forums serving everything from early systems like the Apple II and the Apple III to the latest versions of the Apple Macintosh. The scope of the forums ranges from new users and entertainment software to advanced applications such as hypercard.

Shapiro is assisted by a large staff of assistants, headed by Bill Cook (76703,1030), the Macintosh executive sysop and library manager, and Shawn Goodin (76703,1034), Apple II executive sysop. Also assisting, in the Mac-oriented forums, are Lofty Becker, Dennis Brothers, Binky Melnik, Anne Peck, David Ramsey, David S. Rose, Robert Seaver, Marty Silbernik, Bill Steinberg, Russ Wetmore, and David Winograd; and, in the Apple II forums, Peter Chin, Jason Harper, and Joe Walters.

For the Macintosh (GO MACINTOSH), there are:

- Hypertext Forum (GO MACHYPER), devoted to Hypertext, Apple's Hyper-Card program.
- Mac Applications Forum (GO MACAP), covering word processing, spread-sheets, paint and draw programs, accounting and financial packages, and so on.
- The Mac Community Clubhouse Forum (GO MACCLUB), the "lobby" where you will find all sorts of informal discussions ranging from views on Apple's corporate policies to current events.
- Mac Communications Forum (GO MACCOMM), to discuss ways that the Mac can be used to communicate with other Macs, other computers, and Fax machines.
- Mac Developers' Forum (GO MACDEV), concerned with all of the ways and techniques to program Macintosh computers. Here you find special sections on languages such as Pascal and C and a section on utilizing the Inside Macintosh guidelines. Developers will find a special section for themselves, as will novices.
- Macintosh Entertainment Forum (GO MACFUN), where all kinds of enter-tainment uses for the Macintosh are covered and discussed.
- Mac Hardware Forum (GO MACHW), discussing equipment for the Apple systems.
- Mac Multimedia Forum (GO MACMULTI), devoted to CD-ROM/sound/graphic systems designed for the Mac.
- Mac New Users and Help Forum (GO MACNEW), a place intended to help new users get the most out of their online experience.
- Mac Systems Software Forum (GO MACSYS), focusing on system software and the hardware side of the Macintosh, such as system/finder and utilities.

For other Apple systems use the following:

- Apple Newton/PIE Forum (GO NEWTON or GO APPLEPIE), to support the company's new Newton MessagePad pen-based personal communicator, which Shapiro co-sysops with Ron Luks (76703,254), who also manages the Palmtop Forum and the Atari forums. This forum covers Newton and Pie technology as it relates to all computer systems. It has sections on IBM PC, Macintosh, and other connectivity issues, as well as simply using these devices on their own. Assisting in the management of the forum are Marty Mankins and Jeff Goldman, as well as the usual Apple forum staff.

- Newton Developers Forum (GO NEWTDEV), where members discuss the various aspects of Newton Technology and how to design software and hardware for this technology.
- Apple II Programmers' Forum (GO APPROG), designed to help users learn to take their Apple II through all of its paces, from programming in BASIC, Pascal, and machine language to accessing the easy-to-use, graphic interface of HyperStudio on the IIgs.
- Apple II Users' Forum (GO APPUSER), covering word processing, spreadsheets, databases, educational, and entertainment programs. It also serves the Apple IIGS, with its extended graphic interface.

Apple vendors forums, where third-party companies provide support for their products:

- Apple II Vendor Forum (GO APIIVEN) supports products from Applied Engineering, 1st Class Peripherals, Stone Edge Technology, Beagle Brothers, InTrec Software, On Three Inc., Seven Hills Software, and TMS Peripherals.
- Mac A Vendor Forum (GO MACAVEN) provides support for products from CE Software, DeltaPoint, Mainstay, Survivor Software, (Sitka) TOPs, Articulate Systems, Activision, TENpointO, Daystar Digital Inc., MicroMat, Portfolio Systems, Paragon Concepts, and Connectix.
- Mac B Vendor Forum (GO MACBVEN) supports products from GCC Technologies, Altsys Corp., Jasik Designs, Software Ventures, T/Maker Inc., Working Software, Microseeds Publishing, Hyperpress Publishing, Opcode Systems, Radius Inc., Deneba Software, SuperMac Technology, Olduvai Corp., TACTIC Software, and Berkeley Systems.
- Mac C Vendor Forum (GO MACCVEN) supports products from Aladdin Systems, which supports StuffIt and ShortCut; Baseline Publishing, which supports Talking Moose, INIT Manager, and other products; Inline Designs, which supports Darwin's Dilemma, Tesserae, and other products; Avatar Corp.; CoStar; TMS Peripherals; Iomega Corp.; Softsync Inc.; Farallon; Alysis; Mirror Technologies, and Virtus Corp.
- Mac D Vendor Forum (GO MACDVEN) discussing products from MacTech Magazine, Atticus Corp., Teknosys Inc., TidBITS Magazine, Mercury Systems, Digital Eclipse, MicroNet Technology, Advanced Software, and Helix Technologies.

In addition, the Macintosh File Finder (GO MACFF) is an online comprehensive searchable database of file descriptions from MAC related forums. It provides quick, easy reference to some of the best programs and files available in related forums, including Adobe, the Macintosh forums, Aldus, Borland forums, MicroSoft forums, WordPerfect Support Groups, Symantec, and Lotus forums. You may search by keyword or keywords, submission date of file, forum name, file type, file extension, filename, or file submitter's user ID number. Once a file is located, you are told where the file is located, the library name, and the filename. If you select a file from the menu, you are shown the filename, forum, library name and number, submitter's user ID number, date the file was uploaded, size of the file in characters, the number of times the file was has been accessed, the file's keywords, and a short description of the contents.

MAUG is a registered trademark owned by MCU Incorporated of Bethpage, New York. The organization also provides a voice help line daily between 10 a.m. and 5 p.m. (Eastern Time) at (516) 735-6924. You also can send U.S. Mail to the group at MCU Inc., P.O. Box 520, Bethpage, NY 11714 or send CompuServe Mail to 76703,401.

Also:

- ZiffNet/Mac (GO ZMAC) is magazine publisher Ziff Davis Company's collection of services for Apple Macintosh users, part of its massive ZiffNet gateway. See ZiffNet/Mac and see ZiffNet.

- A category in the CompuServe Classifieds lets you read and post ads regarding Apple and Macintosh computers and software. See Classifieds Service.

- Apple News Clips (GO APPLENEWS) is a surcharged clipping folder for seeing news stories about Apple clipped from various news sources including AP, UPI, and The Washington Post. See Executive News Service for details.

- Also, Apple science is a topic in the Science/Math Education Forum (GO SCIENCE). See Science.

AppleWorks   (software) is supported in the Claris Corp. Forum (GO CLARIS). For more information, see Claris.

Appliance and **Appliance Manufacturer**   (magazines) are searchable through the Business Database Plus (GO BUSDB). See Business Database.

Applied Engineering Software   is supported in the Apple II Vendor Forum (GO APIIVEN). See Apple Computers.

Applied Genetics   (publication) can be searched through IQuest. See IQuest.

Applied Mathematics and Computation   (magazine) is searchable (abstracts) through Database Plus (GO COMPDB). See Computer Database Plus.

Applied Science and Technology Index (database) can be searched through IQuest. See IQuest.

Appraisal Journal   (magazine) is searchable through the Business Database Plus (GO BUSDB). See Business Database.

Apricot computers   are supported in the Computer Club (GO CLUB). See Computer Club.

APS Diplomat publications (Fate of the Arabian Peninsula, News Service, Operations in Oil Diplomacy, Recorder, Redrawing the Islamic Map, and Strategic Balance in the Middle East) can be searched through the Business Database Plus (GO BUSDB). See Business Database.

APS/Maintenance Workbench is supported in the Intersolv Forum (GO INTERSOLV). See Intersolv.

APS Review publications (Downstream Trends, Gas Market Trends, and Review Oil Market Trends) can be searched through the Business Database Plus (GO BUSDB). See Business Database.

AQUALINE, Aquaculture, and **Aquatic Sciences and Fisheries Abstracts** (databases) may be searched through the IQuest gateway. See IQuest. See also Fish.

Aquaria and Fish Forum (GO AQUAFORUM) is operated by FISHNET. See Fish (Tropical).

Arabesque Software products are supported in Windows 3rd-Party Forum A (GO WINAPA). See Microsoft Software.

Arab Information Bank (international database) may be searched through the IQuest gateway. See IQuest. See also Middle East.

.ARC, as an extension on filenames in forum libraries, usually means the program is in a *compressed/packed* form. See Files, Compressed.

Arcade and cartridge games are regular topics in the Gamers' Forum (GO GAMERS). See Gaming Forums.

Archimedes Software (products) are supported in the Windows 3rd-Party Forum (GO WINAPD). See Microsoft Software.

Architecture Database and **Avery Architecture Index** (databases) may be searched through the IQuest gateway. See IQuest.
  Also, *Progressive Architecture* magazine can be searched through the Business Database Plus (GO BUSDB). See Business Database. See also Buildings and Art and see Homing Instinct Forum.

Archive utilities are programs that compress and pack software for economic storage online. See Files, Compressed.

Arc-Info and **Arc-CAD** is supported in the CADD/CAM/CAE Vendor Forum (GO CADDVEN). See CAD/CAM.

Arcnet is supported in the Standard Microsystem Forum (GO SMC) and in the Thomas-Conrad Support Forum (GO TCCFORUM). See Standard Microsystem and see Thomas-Conrad.

ARCTIC **(ARChimedes Terminal Interface to CompuServe)** **(automated software)** for Risc-OS systems is supported in the UK Computing Forum (GO UKCOMP). See Automated Terminal.

Aristosoft products are supported in the Windows 3rd-Party C Forum (GO WINAPC). See Microsoft Software.

Arithmetic: The Science/Math Forum (GO SCIENCE) is a gathering place for teachers, students, and other subscribers with an interest in science and math. See Science/Math Forum.

Arizona Republic/Phoenix Gazette **(newspaper)** is searchable through Telebase System's News Source USA (GO NEWSUSA) and through the Knowledge Index (GO KI). See News Source and see Knowledge Index.
    Also:

 • Selected reports from Arizona are included in the Western regional reports from United Press International. See Executive News Service.

 • *Arizona Business*, *Arizona Business Gazette*, and *The Business Journal—Serving Phoenix & the Valley of the Sun* can be searched through the Business Database Plus (GO BUSDB). See Business Database.

.ARJ, as an extension on filenames in forum libraries, usually means the program is in a *compressed/packed* form. See Files, Compressed.

Arkansas **(news)** is included in the daily Southwest regional reports from United Press International. See Executive News Service for details. And *Arkansas Business* is searchable through the Business Database Plus (GO BUSDB). See Business Database.

Arnett, Nick (75300,1324) is a sysop of the Multimedia Forum (GO MULTIMEDIA). For details, see Multimedia.

Art is covered in a number of IQuest databases (see IQuest), including Academic Index, Architecture Database, Art Index, Art Literature International, Artbibliographies Modern, Arts & Humanities Search, and Avery Architecture Index.
    Computer art and reductions of fine art are the subject of the forums of Graphics Net (GO GRAPHICS). See Graphics and Computer Art.
    American Artist magazine can be searched in the Magazine Database Plus (GO MDP). See Magazine Database.
    Through the Knowledge Index (GO KI), you can search Art Bibliographies Modern and Art Literature International (RILA). See Knowledge Index.

In addition, drawing is a topic of Comics/Animation Forum (GO COMICS). See Comics.

Art is a topic of the Education Forum (GO EDFORUM). See Education. And it is a topic in the Mensa Forum (GO MENSA). See Mensa. Art also is discussed in the Students' Forum (GO STUFO). See Students.

Enter GO ARTS to reach the mail arts/music/literature menu.

Also Arts, Music, and Video are the topics of a number of shops in the Electronic Mall (GO MALL), including BMG Compact Disc Club (GO CD), Columbia House Music (GO CH), The Laser's Edge (GO LE), Justice Records (GO JR), Metropolitan Museum of Art (GO MMA), McGraw-Hill Book Company (GO MH), and Music Alley Online (GO MAO).

See Electronic Mall and also Humanities.

Arthritis Today is searchable in the Health Database Plus (GO HLTBD). Also *Arthritis and Rheumatism* abstracts are searchable in the same resource. See Health.

Articulate Systems products are supported in the Macintosh Vendor A Forum (GO MACAVEN). See Apple Computers.

Artificial intelligence is the subject of the AI Expert Forum (GO AIEXPERT). See AI Expert Magazine.

Artisoft Forum (GO ARTISOFT) is dedicated to the discussion of the LANtastic Network Operating System, including LANtastic for Windows, LANtastic for Netware, and LANtastic for Macs. The forum's message sections and libraries will also support Ethernet and NetMedia products, as well as the Artisoft Sounding Board, Artisoft's Articom–Communications software, and the new Netmedia Products. The sysop is Rick Roth (75600,1377), a senior tech support representative with Artisoft, Inc. He is author of several LANtastic utilities and articles on the LANtastic. He is assisted by Curtis Hertwig and Kenneth Elliott.

Asahi News Service (**Japanese database**) can be searched through IQuest. See IQuest.

As-Easy-As (**software**) is supported in the UK Shareware Forum (GO UKSHARE). See UK Shareware.

Asbestos & Lead Abatement Report (**database**) may be searched through the IQuest gateway. See IQuest. Also *Asbestos Abatement Report* and *Asbestos Control Report* can be searched through the Business Database Plus (GO BUSDB). See Business Database. See also Safety.

.ASC, as an extension on filenames in forum libraries, usually means ASCII (text) format. See Files, Extensions.

ASDG Products are supported in the Amiga Vendor Forum (GO AMIGAVENDOR). See Commodore Computers.

Ashlar Inc. software is supported in the CADD/CAM/CAE Vendor Forum (GO CADDVEN).

Ashton-Tate Software, originally produced by Ashton-Tate Inc., now is supported by the Borland Forums. (GO BORLAND). See Borland.

Asian America issues are topics in the Issues Forum (GO ISSUESFORUM). See Issues.

Asian news is provided in several IQuest databases, including Asahi News Service, Asia-Pacific, Asian Economic News, Asian Political News, and D&B—Asia-Pacific Dun's Market Identifiers. See IQuest. Also, Asian Economic News and Asian Political News can be searched through the Business Database Plus (GO BUSDB), as can ESP–Business Opportunities in Asia & the Pacific, Executive Briefing Service Asia & the Pacific, Market Asia Pacific, and Power in Europe. See Business Database. For related services, see Japan.

   Asia also is a topic in the International Trade Forum (GO TRADE) and in the Travel Forum (GO TRAVSIG). See Travel and International Trade. See also Japan Forum.

Ask3Com Information Service (GO THREECOM) is operated by 3Com Corporation to support its software. See 3Com Software.

ASP (Association of Shareware Professionals) operates the ASP/ Shareware Forum (GO ASPFORUM). For details, see Shareware.

Aspect software is supported in the Datastorm Forum (GO DATASTORM). See Procomm.

Assembler/Microsoft Editor (software) is supported in the Microsoft Languages Forum (GO MSLANG). See Microsoft Software.

Assembly and **Assembly Engineering** (magazines) are searchable through the Business Database Plus (GO BUSDB). See Business Database.

Asset Sales Report (magazine) can be searched through the Business Database Plus (GO BUSDB). See Business Database.

Assistance, Member: CompuServe maintains a database of answers to frequently asked questions about billing, forums, electronic mail, logons, real-time conferencing, and so on (GO QUESTIONS). See Help On-line.

Associated Press (news) (GO APO): Through AP Online, Associated Press provides a specially edited report, usually containing between 250 and 300 stories that make up the top national, international, Washington, financial, and sports news of the day. One option offers summaries of the top stories of the hour. The feature is transmitted around the clock every day. This is one of the system's basic services, meaning those signed up under the Standard Pricing Plan (see Billing) have unlimited access to the feature.

Sports news also is available, news stories about assorted sports, including baseball, football, basketball, hockey, soccer, tennis, golf, college, and scoreboards. This is an extra cost service from the Associated Press that is surcharged at $15 an hour. Enter GO APN-1 to see the sports menu. See Sports and Recreation.

AP news also is available in the Executive News Service (for more information, see Executive News Service).

Association of Shareware Professionals, a nonprofit group dedicated to educating computer users about the "try before you buy" software marketing concept, operates the ASP/Shareware Forum (GO ASPFORUM). For details, see Shareware.

Associations are listed in a number of IQuest databases. See Foundations.

AST Research products are supported in the Novell Vendor Forum A (GO NVENA). See Novell Software.

Astrology is covered in the New Age Forum (GO NEWAGE). For more information, see New Age Forum.

Astrology Charting (game) (GO ASTROLOGY) casts conventional horoscopes. It asks for your birth date, birth time, time zone in effect, and birthplace expressed as latitude and longitude. For information on other games, see Games.

Astronomy Forum (GO ASTROFORUM) is devoted to skywatching as a profession and as a hobby. The forum is administered by NASA research scientist Dick DeLoach (76703,303), who is assisted by J. Kelly Beatty, senior editor of *Sky and Telescope* magazine. The publication maintains a regular presence in the forum, where editors upload the computer programs that appear in their magazine. They also provide timely news updates between issues. Enter GO SKYTEL to access a number of special features the editors share in addition to their forum contributions. Also assisting are Conrad Kirksey, Steve Mastellotto, and Alan Higgins.

The forum also is frequented by representatives of a number of major astronomy equipment manufacturers for answering visitors' questions. And professional astronomers and serious amateurs also find the Astronomy Forum a stimulating place, discussing such advanced topics as comet ephemeris calculations, special photographic techniques, and satellite orbital elements. The forum is visited by a number of observatory and planetarium officers who routinely discuss observations reported here and other subjects of interest.

For related topics, see also the Space Forum.

Also, *Astronomy* magazine can be searched in the Magazine Database Plus (GO MDP). See Magazine Database.

Asymetrix   products are supported in the Windows 3rd-Party Forum A (GO WINAPA) and in the Multimedia Vendor Forum (GO MULTIVEN). See Microsoft Software and Multimedia. They also are supported in the Ultimedia Tools Forum A (GO ULTIATOOLS). See Ultimedia.

Asystem   **(products)** are supported in the MIDI C Vendor Forum (GO MIDICVEN). See Music.

"As the World Turns"   **(television)** summaries on the latest shows are available in Soap Opera Summaries (GO SOAPS). See Soap Opera.

Atari Computers   (GO ATARINET): New Yorker Ron Luks is well known in the Atari computing world. Since 1982, Luks, who uses the ID number 76703,254, has built the Atari Users Network from a single section in a general computing forum into a network of separate forums. Assisting him in operating the assorted forums are Mike Schoenbach, Bill Aycock, Dan Rhea, Don LeBow, Keith Joins, Bob Puff, Bob Retelle, Brad Hill, Jeff Kovach, B.J. Gleason, Judy Hamner, and Marty Mankins.

The Atari forums are:

- Atari Gaming Forum (GO ATARIGAMING), specializing in current and future Atari game products. The feature formerly was the Atari 8-Bit Forum, and still offers programs and information pertaining to the 8-bit series of computers.

- Atari Portfolio Forum (GO APORTFOLIO) devoted to the support and exchange of information pertaining to the Atari Portfolio Computer System, a set of communication tools.

- Atari ST Arts Forum (GO ATARIARTS), specializing in graphics and entertainment-related programs and information pertaining to the Atari 16-bit (ST) series of computers.

- Atari ST Productivity Forum (GO ATARIPRO), specializing in productivity-related programs and information pertaining to the Atari 16-bit (ST) series of computers.

- Atari Vendors Forum (GO ATARIVEN), which provides support for commercial hardware and software by participating vendors. A number of companies are responsible for the maintenance of sections in the Atari Vendors Support Forum, including Double Click, Maxwell CPU, Gribnif Software, Lexicor Software, Supra Corporation, Intersect Software, ICD Incorporated, Michtron Inc., Atari Explorer, SoftLogik, Gadgets by Small, CodeHead Software, ISD Marketing, and OXXI/Precision Software.

Also of interest to Atari users is the Atari File Finder (GO ATARIFF), a special database containing information on all important files from the Atari forums. The File Finder allows you to search for a filename or keyword or use a variety of search methods that help you locate files of interest in any of the forums.

Atari Explorer products are supported in the Atari Vendors Forum (GO ATARIVEN). See Atari Computers.

ATI Technologies products are supported in the Graphics A Vendor Forum (GO ATITECH). See Graphics.

Atlanta news is covered in Business Atlanta magazines, which can be searched through the Business Database Plus (GO BUSDB). See Business Database.

Atlanta Constitution/Atlanta Journal **(newspaper)** is searchable through Telebase System's News Source USA (GO NEWSUSA) and through the Knowledge Index (GO KI). See News Source, and see Knowledge Index.

Atlantic **(magazine)** is searchable through Magazine Database Plus (GO MDP). For details see Magazine Database.

Atlantic Business and **Atlantic Economic Journal** **(magazines)** are searchable through the Business Database Plus (GO BUSDB). See Business Database.

AT&T Mail subscribers can be reached through CompuServe Mail. See Mail, CompuServe.

AT&T, Report on **(business database)** may be searched through the IQuest gateway. See IQuest. The resource also can be searched through the Business Database Plus (GO BUSDB). See Business Database.

AT&T Technical Journal and **Edge on & about AT&T** **(magazines)** are searchable through Computer Database Plus (GO COMPDB). See Computer Database Plus.

AT&T Online Store (GO DP) is offered through the Electronic Mall (GO MALL), marketing DataPort fax modems. See Electronic Mall.

Attention Deficit Disorder Forum (GO ADD) discusses various aspects of the condition in children and adults. It features discussions among doctors, people who are diagnosed with ADD, and those who live with ADD sufferers. Many members of the National Association for Children and adults with ADD (CH.A.D.D.) visit the forum. In addition, the forum also includes a section for discussion of other "neurobehavioral disorders," such as Tourette's Syndrome. Thom Hartmann (76702,765) is the primary sysop. He is assisted by Dave deBronkart, Dr. Dale

Hammerschmidt, Ann Linden, Hal Meyer, Cj Bowman, Janie Bowman, Carla Nelson, and Wendy Hoechstetter.

The topic also is discussed in the Education Forum (GO EDFORUM). See Education.

Atticus Corp. products are supported in the Mac D Vendor Forum (GO MACDVEN). See Apple Computers.

Audio (magazine) can be searched in the Magazine Database Plus (GO MDP). See Magazine Database.

Audio Engineering Society (GO AESNET) is a backer of the Broadcasters and Broadcast Engineers Forum (GO BPFORUM). For details, see Broadcasters.

Audiotex Update (database) may be searched through the IQuest gateway. See IQuest. It also can be searched through the Business Database Plus (GO BUSDB), as can *Audiotex Now*. See Business Database.

Audio Week (database) may be searched through the IQuest gateway. See IQuest. It also can be searched through the Business Database Plus (GO BUSDB). See Business Database.

Audubon (magazine) can be searched in the Magazine Database Plus (GO MDP). See Magazine Database.

Austad's (GO AU) offers a store in the Electronic Mall (GO MALL) that sells golf equipment and accessories. See Electronic Mall.

Austin Business Journal (magazine) is searchable through the Business Database Plus (GO BUSDB). See Business Database.

Australia topics are discussed in the Pacific Forum (GO PACFORUM). For details, see Pacific Forum.

Australian/New Zealand Company Library (GO ANZCOLIB) promises an in-depth directory and news information on more than 95,000 public and private businesses in the Pacific area. The data can be compiled from D&B-Australian and New Zealand Dun's Market Identifiers (updated quarterly), Reuter Textline (updated continuously), and the Asia-Pacific databases (updated every two weeks).

Austrian Economy, Report on the (magazine) can be searched through the Business Database Plus (GO BUSDB). See Business Database.

Authority software is supported in the IBM PC Vendor C Forum (GO PCVENC). See IBM Computers.

Author of the Week Forum (GO TWEP) features weekly visits with authors published by Time Warner Trade Publishing. See Time Warner's.

Authorware products are supported in the Multimedia Vendor Forum (GO MULTIVEN). See Multimedia.

Autodesk Software: The Autodesk Forums (GO ADESK) are devoted to computer-aided design/computer-aided manufacturing (CAD/CAM). Its members include engineers, architects, facilities managers, consultants, designers, and others.

The forums are the Autodesk AutoCAD Forum (GO ACAD), devoted exclusively to AutoCAD and its companion products AME and AutoShade; the Autodesk Software Forum (GO ASOFT), supporting Autodesk's multimedia and New Science series software; and the Autodesk Retail Products Forum (GO ARETAIL) for the support of its Mass Market CADD and CADD related products, including Generic CADD (PC and Mac), AutoSketch, Generic 3D, GenCADD, and the HOME series.

The primary sysop of the AutoCAD and Software forums is Jeffrey Pike (76702,531) of Autodesk's product support center, and managing the Retail forum is C. Scott van der Linden (76702,533). They are assisted by specialists in the company's software, quality control, and marketing divisions.

Autodesk products also are supported in the Ultimedia Tools Forum A (GO ULTIATOOLS). See Ultimedia.

CAM/CAD also is discussed in other forums. See CAD/CAM.

Autograph collecting is discussed in the Collectibles Forum (GO COLLECT). See Collectibles.

AutoLISP is supported in the Cadence Forum (GO CADENCE). See Cadence.

Automap products are supported in the UK Computing Forum (GO UKCOMP). See UK Computing.

Automated Design products are supported in the Windows 3rd-Party D Forum (GO WINAPD). See Microsoft Software.

Automated Medical Payments News (newsletter) can be searched through IQuest. See IQuest. It also can be searched through the Business Database Plus (GO BUSDB). See Business Database.

Automated terminal software are programs designed to work intimately with major features of CompuServe, such as forums and electronic mail. They fully automate many tasks. Typically, users of such software start offline making selections from a menu to tell the program what tasks to perform, such as checking news in specific forums, retrieving CompuServe Mail messages, and so on. Once the user has laid out the jobs, the program automatically logs on and, like a faithful assistant, carries out the assignments, quickly saving new messages to disk files as it goes. The user later reads the saved files at his or her leisure, composes replies offline, and instructs the program to log on again and post them.

These days, a number of public domain and shareware terminal programs, available for an assortment of computers, are custom-built to communicate with CompuServe. Here are some of the popular automated programs:

ARCTIC (ARChimedes Terminal Interface to CompuServe), an offline reader and CompuServe access program for the Acorn Archimedes, created by Richard Proctor of Waveney Games in Dorset, England. The program is fully Risc-OS compliant and can run on any machine with at least 2MB of RAM and one floppy disk drive. It will run on any Acorn Archimedes Computer running Risc-OS, including A4, A310, A410, A440, A3000, A3010, A3020, A4000, A5000, and A540. ARCTIC also needs Clib version 3.75 (or higher), which is available in the UK Computing Forum (GO UKCOMP). The program can be obtained in Section 5, "Archie/Beeb/Z88," in the UK Computing Forum. The ARCTIC supports messaging, mail, conferencing, and libraries. At this writing, the necessary files were ARCTIC.ARC and RUNIMG.ARC from Library 5, "Archie/Beeb/Z88."

AutoPilot a shareware program for the Amiga, was created by veteran sysop Steve Ahlstrom of Denver, Colorado, who has been an administrator in the Amiga forums for several years now. AutoPilot requires that you have, in addition to OS 2.04 or later, at least 2MB of memory and at least 5MB of free space on a hard drive. The disk font library you must have is version 37 or later. You must not use PowerPacker or other programs on AutoPilot, which would alter the code in any way. At this writing, a demo version of AutoPilot found in Library 9 of the Amiga Vendor Forum (GO AMIGAVENDOR) is fully functional for basic work on the CompuServe Amiga Forums and CompuServe Mail, but many of its special features are disabled. These will be turned on after you have the program working and after you send your $69.95 registration fee.

AutoSig for IBM and compatibles, written by Don Watkins, Vernon Buerg, Frank Lipschutz, Howard Benner, and others. It is a free, public domain program. AutoSig runs on an IBM PC, XT, AT, PS/2 (not the 50Z), or close compatible with at least 256K of available memory. It needs a minimum of 250K of disk space and a Hayes command-set-compatible modem that is auto-dial-capable. Optional are a hard disk (recommended for speed) and a mouse (MS and Logitech compatible are supported). Any monitor will work; graphics are not used. DOS 3.0 or later is recommended. DESQview and Double DOS environments are supported. AutoSig does not work with Novell netware loaded. All files needed can be downloaded from the "AutoSig" Library (Library 1) of the IBM Communications Forum (GO IBMCOM). At this writing, the files were ATOSIG.REQ (a description of the hardware and software requirements), ATOSIG.EXE (the executable program itself and a script to get started) and ATODOC.EXE, the user's manual.

CompuServe Navigator for Apple Macintosh by Mike O'Connor. The $79.95 program is supported by the free Navigator Support Forum (GO MNAVSUP). You also can find help in the Macintosh Communications Forum (GO MACCOM). The program requires two double-sided 800K disk drives, or one double-sided 800K disk drive and a hard disk and a total of 650K of available memory. System 4.1 is the minimum required, although System 6.0.1 or higher is needed to use some of the features. You can download Navigator online (GO CISSOFT).

CompuServe Navigator, Windows version is the relatively new IBM/compatible version of the successful Macintosh program. At this writing, the software requires an 80386SX processor (or higher) and at least 2MB of RAM memory, Microsoft Windows Version 3.1, running in enhanced mode, and an IBM EGA or higher resolution monitor compatible with the Microsoft Windows graphical environment. Also needed is 4MB of free hard-disk space (with Windows installed) and one high-density floppy drive. The software is supported in the WinNav Support Forum (GO WNAVSUPPORT).

Copilot for Apple IIgs computers was written by Kenneth I. Gluckman, as a $25 shareware program. At this writing, the latest online version is an evaluation copy of version 2.0.2, which has some nonessential features disabled. On payment of a $25 fee you will be told how to activate all features. (The update is $10 for registered users of 1.x.) Users have contributed supporting scripts and programs. To find the latest Copilot and supporting files, search for COPILOT in Library 12 ("Telecommunications") in the Apple II/III Users Forum (GO APPUSER).

Golden CommPass is a commercial automated program for an IBM OS/2 link with CompuServe. The program is published by Creative Systems Programming Corp., a Mount Laurel, New Jersey, firm operated by Larry B. Finkelstein, an assistant sysop in the IBM OS/2 Users Forum (GO OS2USER). Golden CommPass operates on IBM PC 286, 386, 386sx, 486, 486sx, or other machine capable of running OS/2. Three to four megabytes of RAM are the minimum advised. It needs 1.5MB of hard disk space. It also needs OS/2 1.21, OS/2 1.3, or OS/2 2.0 to operate. Golden CommPass is available on a single 3.5-inch low density (720K) or 5.25-inch high density (1.2MB) diskette. The software is discussed in the Golden CommPass Support Forum (GO GCPSUPPORT). See Golden CommPass.

Email8 (also called EM8SIG) for Tandy Models 100 and 102 was written by Marvin M. Miller, who supported it and constantly upgraded it until his death in late 1987. After that, Stan Wong undertook the work, with George Sherman writing the documentation. The public domain program can be retrieved from Library 3 ("Telecom") of the Model 100 Forum (GO TANDYLAPTOP). For the latest version, search the keyword EM8SIG.

OzCIS for IBM and compatibles was written by Steve Sneed. This is a public domain program intended for higher level systems. An IBM AT-compatible computer (80286 or better processor, 10MHz or faster) or IBM PS/2 MicroChannel computer with a 286 or better processor, and at least 1MB of RAM. A minimum of 486K of free conventional memory must be available when OzCIS loads; 520K to 550K or more is strongly recommended. OzCIS simply won't run on XT-class machines (8086/8088). At least 1MB of EMS/XMS memory is recommended, a hard disk with at least 1.5MB free. OzCIS is available for downloading in the OzCIS Forum (GO OZCIS). At this writing, version 2 files were located in library 2 (OzCIS Ver. 2) and version 1.2a files were available in library 9 (OzCIS V1). See OzCIS.

QuickCIS, also public domain, runs on Atari ST computers. It was written by Jim Ness and is available in the Atari Productivity Forum (GO ATARIPRO) Telecommunications Library (Library 2). To find the latest version, Search with the keyword QUICKCIS. At this writing, the latest version, 1.71, was in QWKCIS.PRG. However, a beta file of version 1.72 was being tested.

TapCIS is a $79 shareware program for IBM PCs and compatibles, written by Howard Benner. TapCIS is designed for an IBM PC/XT, -/AT, -/PS/2, or a close compatible. It runs in 384K of RAM and will operate as a DOS application under Windows, Desqview, and OS/2. A hard disk is recommended for desktop use, and twin 720K 3.5-inch floppies for portable operation. TapCIS can be run on a single 720K floppy, but the user will need to manage remaining disk space very carefully. TapCIS is stored in Library 1 of the TapCIS Forum (GO TAPCIS) as TAP.EXE (the program) and TAPDOC.EXE (documentation).

Whap! for Commodore Amiga, a $39.95 shareware program, was written by Jim Nangano and Steve Ahlstrom. It is possible to use Whap! on a 512K Amiga, but it will perform much better if you have 1MB of memory. Hard disks are not necessary, but the system should have two disk drives. You'll find Whap! in Library 9 of Amiga Vendor Forum (GO AMIGAVENDOR). Search with the keyword WHAP to get the latest version. This is a demo version, but is fully working. You can use the demo as much as you want before you register.

WigWam is a Windows navigation program for CompuServe designed and supported by Ashmount Research Ltd. of London. Including its help system, it requires Windows 3.0 or 3.1, 2MB RAM and about 2MB of hard disk space. It is available for downloading in Library 10, "WigWam/TP," of the U.K. Computing Forum (GO UKCOMP).

WinCIS is another Windows-based program, using a script template language that can be modified to customize the program. It requires at least a 386 20MHz or better system, with at least 4MB of memory and Windows 3.1. It can be downloaded from the Windows Users Group Network Forum (GO WUGNET). See Library 12 files WC094*.ZIP and VBUN*.*.

XC is an automated communications program for Unix and Xenix, supporting shell escapes and has BREAK capability, a dialing directory, a script language that includes shell command, and variable support. You'll find the source code for XC in two files in the Library 4 of the Unix Forum (GO UNIXFORUM). XC.TAZ is the compressed source code for XC . XC.SHK is the self-extracting ASCII file for the XC source code.

Automation   (**magazine**) is searchable through the Business Database Plus (GO BUSDB). See Business Database.

Automenu   (**software**) is supported in the PC Vendor A Forum (GO PCVENA). See IBM Computers.

Automobile Forum (GO CARS) covers all facets of the car world, from buying that first car to selling your last one, from fixing the one you have to what future cars will be like. The primary sysop is Atlanta writer/software designer Shel Hall (76701,103), a veteran online personality. Formerly associated with Crosstalk Communications, he founded the Crosstalk Forum on CompuServe, was a sysop on the Earthquake Forum, the Persian Gulf Crisis Forum, the Soviet Union Crisis Forum, and the Hurricane Forum. Assisting him is Judy Russell, the forum's archivist and librarian. See also Cars.

Automobile Information Center (GO AI) is a service in the Electronic Mall (GO MALL) that offers wholesale and retail car prices from 1978. For more automobile-related features, see Cars.

Automotive Engineering, Automotive Industries, Automotive Parts International, Autoparts Report, and ***Automotive Marketing*** **(magazines)** are searchable through the Business Database Plus (GO BUSDB). See Business Database.
   For more automobile-related features, see Cars.

AutoPilot, a shareware system navigation program for the Amiga computers, was created by Steve Ahlstrom of Denver, Colorado. A demo version of AutoPilot can be found in Library 9 of the Amiga Vendor Forum (GO AMIGAVENDOR). For more information, see Automated Terminal Software.

AutoQuot-R (GO AQ) is a store in the Electronic Mall (GO MALL) that offers vehicle price quotes. See Electronic Mall.
   For more automobile-related features, see Cars.

AutoSig: A popular public domain communications program for IBM and compatible PCs that can be retrieved from the IBM Communications Forum (GO IBMCOM). See Automated Terminal Software and IBM Computers.

Autovantage Online (GO AV) is a store in the Electronic Mall (GO MALL) that offers new and used car information. See Electronic Mall.

Avantos products are supported in the Windows 3rd-Party D Forum (GO WINAPD). See Microsoft Software.

Avatar Corp. products are supported in the Macintosh C Vendor Forum (GO MACCVEN). See Apple Computers.

Avery Dennison products are supported in the IBM PC Vendor F Forum (GO PCVENF). See IBM Computers.

Aviation is the topic of a number of online services, including the following:

- *Aerospace Financial News, Aircraft Value Newsletter, Airline Business, Airline Financial News, Business & Commercial Aviation, Commuter-Regional Airline News,* and *World Airline News* magazines can be searched through the Business Database Plus (GO BUSDB). See Business Database.

- Airplane modeling is discussed in the Model Forum (GO MODELNET). See ModelNet.

- Aviation Forum (GO AVSIG), one of the older forums on CompuServe, deals with all topics relating to airplanes and flying, including weather, navigation, air traffic control, safety, maintenance, legal issues, and so on. The forum is managed by Bob Kaputa (76701,300), who is assisted by Alan Bose, Irv Siegel, Andy Dulay, Rick Cremer, Johnny Sewell, Wally Roberts, Mike Busch, John Haverland, and Leo G. Janssens.

- Aviation Safety Institute (GO ASI) allows you to read about hazards to aviation in the Aviation Safety Institute's Monitor, report hazards to the folks who will do something about them, check service difficulty reports, and more.

- CompuServe Aviation Briefings offers a simplified approach: You don't need to know airport three-letter identifiers; you may specify airports by city name. The edited briefing saves time over direct access to the NWS reports. The flight plan format and content are ideal for many users. These flight plans are not as optimized as the EMI product, nor can they be automatically filed. The cost: 4 tenths of a cent per nautical mile, with a minimum charge of 25 cents. There is no charge for looking up airports, using the route entry to find distances between airports and along airways, or receiving a sample briefing from the Sample menu.

- EMI Flight Planning/Aviation Weather Briefings (GO EMI) enables pilots to specify a route or let EMI choose the best one. Times en route are corrected for forecast winds. Weather briefings are tailored. Flight planning carries a surcharge of 13 cents per nautical mile (a minimum of $2.50, a maximum of $6). An additional 50 cents is charged for each plan using registered aircraft data, though the maximum remains $6. Other charges: en route weather briefing is 4 cents a nautical mile (a minimum of 50 cents, maximum of $2); digital Radar maps are 50 cents per session; and an abbreviated local summary is available for 25 cents. EMI Aerocorp also offers flight planning, weather briefing, and flight plan filing services via fax. Pilots can dial a U.S. toll-free telephone number, speak with an EMI Direct representative, and pull requested flight plans and weather briefings from any fax machine without using a computer. The toll-free number is 800/951-0006 from the contiguous United States. In Canada, dial 314/727-9600.

- Jeppesen DUAT, a gateway that provides access to Jeppesen Dataplan's Direct User Access Terminal (DUAT) service. DUAT is an FAA-sponsored service consisting of weather briefings and IFR flight plans that you have prepared and filed yourself. The basic service is free of connect and network charges.

- NWS Aviation Weather, including weather reports of every variety as issued by the U.S. National Weather Service. They can be used as the raw material for a self-customized weather briefing. A 25-cent surcharge is levied for retrieving data from this database. There is no extra charge for viewing menus, help, LIST, or any data from the Public menu. You may retrieve as many reports as you wish for a single surcharge, as long as you remain within the Public or Aviation Weather menus.

- Several relevant databases also are searchable through the IQuest gateway (see IQuest), including Airports, Aviation Week and Space Technology, Commuter/Regional Airline News International, Compendex Plus, Defense Marketing International, Flightline, Helicopter News, Military Robotics 1989 Sourcebook, Mobile Satellite News, Modem Users News, Navy News and Undersea Technology, Performance Materials, Periscope—Daily Defense News Capsules, PTS Aerospace/Defence Markets and Technology, PTS Newsletter Database, Satellite Week, Space Business News, Space Calendar, Space Daily, Space Exploration Technology, Space Station News, and Weekly of Business Aviation.

See also Defense and Space.

Avionics Report (magazine) is searchable through the Business Database Plus (GO BUSDB). See Business Database.

A-V Online (educational database) may be searched through the IQuest gateway (GO IQUEST) and through the Knowledge Index (GO KI). See IQuest and see Knowledge Index.

Ayre, Rick (72241,215) is chief sysop of ZiffNet (GO ZIFFNET). See ZiffNet.

Ayre, Sue (72241,234) is the sysop of the Public Brand Software Arcade (GO ZNT:PBSARCADE) and the Public Brand Software Applications Forum (GO ZNT:PBSAPPS). See Public Brand.

B

Bacchus Wine Forum (GO WINEFORUM) covers all aspects of wine with experts as well as those who simply enjoy wine. See Wine Forum.

Backgammon (game) in the Entertainment Center (GO ECENTER) enables players to compete with others from around the world. The game currently requires an IBM PC-compatible computer with EGA or better graphics capability. Members can download the software to play either of these games from the Entertainment Center Main Menu for a nominal fee. See also Games and see Entertainment Center.

Back Letter is searchable in the Health Database Plus (GO HLTBD). See Health.

Backpacker (magazine) can be searched in the Magazine Database Plus (GO MDP). See Magazine Database.

Backstage (theatre magazine) may be searched through the IQuest gateway. See IQuest. It also can be searched through Business Database Plus (GO BUSDB). See Business Database.
   See also Entertainment.

Baha'i is discussed in the Religion Forum (GO RELIGION). See Religion.

Bailey, Richard D. (76702,1637) operates Worldwide Car Network Forum (GO WWCAR). See Worldwide Car.

Bakery Production and Marketing (magazine) can be searched through the Business Database Plus (GO BUSDB). See Business Database. For related topics, see Food.

Baldeck, Charles M. (76703,2005) administers the SafetyNet Forum (GO SAFETYNET). See Safety.

Balkans and **Baltic Republics** are topics of the Global Crisis Forum (GO CRISIS). See Global Crisis.

Baltic Business Report **(newsletter)** can be searched through IQuest. See IQuest.

Baltimore Business Journal **(magazine)** can be searched through the Business Database Plus (GO BUSDB). See Business Database.

Baltimore Sun **(newspaper)** is searchable through Telebase System's News Source USA (GO NEWSUSA) and through the Knowledge Index (GO KI). See News Source and see Knowledge Index.

Banking is covered by a number of magazines searchable through the Business Database Plus (GO BUSDB), including *Bank Automation News*, *Bank Loan Report*, *Bank Management*, *Bank Marketing*, *Bank Network News*, *Bankers Monthly*, *ABA Banking Journal*, *Mortgage Banking*, *United States Banker*, and *World Bank Watch*. World Bank International Business Opportunities and Bank Automation News can be searched through the IQuest gateway. See IQuest. In addition, *Computers in Banking* magazine is searchable through Computer Database Plus (GO COMPDB). See Computer Database Plus.

Also, the famed *American Banker* magazine is accessible through:

- The Legal Research Center (GO LEGALRC). For details, see Legal Research.
- IQuest (GO IQUEST). See IQuest.
- Business Database Plus (GO BUSDB). See Business Database.

And for other business-oriented features, see Financial Services and see Investment Analysis Tools.

Banksia Information Technologies products are supported in the **Pacific Vendors Forum** (GO PACVENDOR). See Pacific.

Banner Blue Software products are supported in the PC Vendor I Forum (GO PCVENI). See IBM Computers.

Banyan Software is supported in the Banyan Forum (GO BANFORUM), including VINES and related products. The forum is administered by Scott Sharkey, John Allen, Peter Thomas, and Alan Smith, with assistance from Bill Posner, Judith Gordon, and Laura Zuromsky. Also in the network are the Banyan Patchware Forum (GO BANPATCH), the Banyan Vines 4.x Patch Forum (GO VINES4), and the Banyan Vines 5.x Patch Forum (GO VINES5).

BAO software products   are supported in the Flight Simulation Forum (GO FSFORUM). See Gaming Forums.

Barefoot/Hybrid   (products) are supported in the MIDI A Vendor Forum (GO MIDIAVEN). See Music.

Barr, Chris   (72241,13) is among the editors and writers associated with the PC Magazine forums. See PC Magazine.

Bartering,   trading, and swapping are pastimes in almost all CompuServe forums that involve a hobby or a product. Some of the notable ones are Automobile Forum (GO CARS), Consumer Electronics Forum (GO CEFORUM), Crafts Forum (GO CRAFTS), DEC PC Forum (GO DECPC), Desktop Publishing Forum (GO DTPFORUM), Gardening Forum (GO GARDEN), League of Engineering Automation Productivity Forum (GO LEAP), PDP-11 Forum (GO PDP11), Photography Forum (GO PHOTOFORUM), TrainNet Forum (GO TRAINNET), Travel Forum (GO TRAVSIG), and UK Forum (GO UKFORUM).

.BAS,   as an extension on filenames in forum libraries, means a program written in Basic. See Files, Extensions.

Baseball   is a regular topic in the Sports Forum (GO FANS). For more on this and related subjects, see Sports.

Baseball card collecting   is discussed in the Collectibles Forum (GO COLLECT). See Collectibles.

Baseline Publishing   (software) is supported in Mac C Vendor Forum (GO MACCVEN). For details, see Apple Computers. It also is supported in the Windows 3rd-Party D Forum (GO WINAPD). See Microsoft Software.

BASIC   (Microsoft) is supported in the Microsoft Languages Forum (GO MSLANG). See Microsoft Software. Also *Inside Microsoft BASIC, Inside Visual BASIC,* and *Inside QuickBASIC* are among the publications supported in the Cobb Group Programming Forum (GO ZNT:COBBPROG). See Cobb Group. See also Programmers Support.

BASIS International Software   is supported in the BASIS International Forum (GO BASIS). The feature supports the firm's BBxProgression software for DOS, UNIX, and Xenix platforms. Operating the forum are Gary McClellan (76702,1440) and Teresa Dominquez, with help from Kurt Williams and Edie Downs. Also, BASIS President/CEO Thom Olson frequents the forum.

Basketball is a regular topic in the Sports Forum (GO FANS) and in the NCAA Collegiate Sports Network (GO NCAA). For more on this and related subjects, see Sports and Recreation.

Baton Rouge Business Report (magazine) can be searched through the Business Database Plus (GO BUSDB). See Business Database.

Battery & EV Technology (industry database) may be searched through the IQuest gateway. See IQuest. It also can be searched through the Business Database Plus (GO BUSDB). See Business Database.

BattleChess (software) by InterPlay is supported in the National Modem-to-Modem Game Players' Challenge Board (GO CHALLENGE). See Modem-to-Modem Games.

Baya, Harry (76702,513) administers CODEPORT, The Portable Programming Forum (GO CODEPORT). See Programmers Support.

BBI Newsletter can be searched through the Business Database Plus (GO BUSDB). See Business Database.

BBC Summary of World Broadcasts (database) may be searched through the IQuest gateway. See IQuest.

BBS (bulletin board system) software and operations are supported in a number of CompuServe forums:

- Those running or interested in running IBM compatible BBSes should check out the IBM BBS Forum (GO IBMBBS), which contains programs, utilities, door programs, and a discussion of issues concerning bulletin board operators and users. See IBM Computers.
- Apple Macintosh communications issues, including BBSes, are covered in the Mac Communications Forum (GO MACCOMM). See Apple Computers.
- For other BBS-related matter, you might check out the Telecommunication Issues Forum (GO TELECOM). See Telecommunication Issues.
- For other BBS software, visit the forums supporting that particular hardware. Most have sections on their message boards covering telecommunications and some specifically invite BBS discussions.
- Other forums with BBS sections include CP/M Users Group Forum (GO CPMFORUM), Color Compuer (CoCo) Forum (GO COCO), Commodore Applications Forum (GO CBMAPP), Epson Forum (GO EPSON), Modem Games Forum (GO MODEMGAMES), OS-9 Forum (GO OS9), and Texas Instruments Forums (GO TIFORUM).

See also Telecomputing.

BBxProgression (software) is supported in the BASIS International Forum (GO BASIS). See BASIS International Software.

BC Business (magazine) can be searched through the Business Database Plus (GO BUSDB). See Business Database.

BCD Associates products are supported in the Multimedia Vendor Forum (GO MULTIVEN). See Multimedia.

Beagle Brothers Software is supported in the Apple II Vendor Forum (GO APIIVEN). See Apple Computers.

Beatty, J. Kelly (75706,3371) is a sysop in the Astronomy Forum (GO ASTROFORUM). See Astronomy.

Beck, Marilyn (Hollywood columnist) (GO BECK) provides five-day-a-week reports from Hollywood, from the inner offices of the studios and from the personalities, producers, and other power players in the film industry. This is similar to the Beck column that is syndicated in newspapers by the Tribune Media Services and to her ETV Hollywood reports. Each column averages eight to ten news reports. She is assisted in the reports by Stacy Jenel Smith. See also Hollywood.

Bechtel SEC Filings Index (business database) may be searched through the IQuest gateway. See IQuest.

Bed & Breakfast Database (GO INNS) from Lanier Publishing provides access to data on more than 9000 inns in the United States and Canada. The resource contains location and phone number for the inns, as well as listings of amenities, types of meals served, accessibility for the handicapped, accomodation of children and pets, and price range. Also of interest is the associated Inn Forum (GO INNFORUM).

Beer and home-brewing are topics in the Wine Forum (GO WINEFORUM). See Wine for details. Also, Cook's Online Forum (GO COOKS) has sections on beverages. See Cooks.

Belgium: Economic and Commercial Information (magazine) can be searched through the Business Database Plus (GO BUSDB). See Business Database.

Bendata Forum (GO ZNT:BENDATA) supports users of the HEAT and FLS products. See ZiffNet.

Benelux Developers Forum, Microsoft (GO MSBEN), offers information in English and Dutch on Microsoft products. See Microsoft.

Benn, John R. (76703.4256) is FISHNET manager, associated with the Aquaria and Fish Forum (GO AQUAFORUM). See Fish (Tropical). He also heads the Pets and Animals Forum (GO PETS). See Pets.

Benner, Howard, was a programmer who popularized a form of communications program called "automated software." As a CompuServe subscriber, Benner was instrumental in three such programs. In 1983 he wrote the public domain SUPER.SIG for the Tandy Model 1000. Later he assisted in the creation of a similar program called AutoSig for the IBM PC, also public domain. Then, working with Turbo Pascal for his next creation, he wrote TAPCIS, a shareware program for IBM PC and compatible computers. Benner opened the TAPCIS Forum (GO TAPCIS) in early 1988, where registered users could have access to special private areas.

For more on Benner's work, see TAPCIS. For details on this style of programming, see Automated Terminal Software.

Bennett, Steve (76702,1071) is a sysop in the Amiga forums (GO AMIGA). See Commodore.

Bentley Systems Inc. products are supported in the Microstation Forum (GO MSTATION). See Microstation.

Berkeley Systems Software products are supported in the Macintosh Vendor B Forum (GO MACBVEN). See Apple Computers. They also are supported in Windows 3rd-Party Forum C (GO WINAPC). See Microsoft Software.

Bernoulli Box is supported in the IBM PC Vendor E Forum (GO PCVENE). See IBM Computers.

Best of "GO Graphics," a printed guide to the "stars" of the world's largest online collection of computer artwork, is available from PRC Database Publishing (GO PRC), a store in the Electronic Mall (GO MALL). See also Graphics.

Best Photo Labs products are supported in the CD-ROM Vendors Forum (GO CDVEN). See CD-ROM.

Best Power products are supported in the Novell Vendor Forum A (GO NVENA). See Novell Software.

Best's Review (**magazine**) Life-Health Insurance Edition and Property-Casualty Insurance Edition can be searched through the Business Database Plus (GO BUSDB). See Business Database.

See also Insurance.

Bestways (**magazine**) is searchable in the Health Database Plus (GO HLTBD). See Health.

Bethesda Softworks   products are supported in the Game Publishers A Forum (GO GAMAPUB). See Gaming Forums.

Better Homes and Gardens   (**magazine**) can be searched in the Magazine Database Plus (GO MDP). See Magazine Database.

Beverage World   (**magazine**) can be searched through the Business Database Plus (GO BUSDB). See Business Database.
   See also Wine.

"Beverly Hills 90210"   (**television**) summaries on the latest shows are available in Soap Opera Summaries (GO SOAPS). See Soap Opera.

Bible   (**King James Version**) may be searched through the IQuest gateway (GO IQUEST) and through the Knowledge Index (GO KI). See IQuest and see Knowledge Index. For related topics, see Religion.

Bicycling   (**magazine**) articles are searchable through Magazine Database Plus (GO MDP). For details see Magazine Database.

Biener, Terry A.,   is best known in the CompuServe CB world by her handle, "Cupcake." She is the author of the regular Cupcake's CB Society (GO CUP), which reports the news and events of one of the system's most popular features. For related topics, see CB.

Biermann, Bruce   (71333,1077) is the sysop of the Canopus Research Forum (GO CANOPUS). See Canopus.

Big-D products   are supported in the Graphics A Vendor Forum (GO BIGD). See Graphics.

Big Noise   (**products**) are supported in the MIDI A Vendor Forum (GO MIDIAVEN). See Music.

Billing information   (GO BILLING) is provided online on a multifunction menu that allows you to look at your own latest charges, to check news on surcharges, and so on. You can review your current charges online in the billing area (free of access connect charges). To do that, enter GO CHARGES which takes you to a menu where you can choose from:

1. Explanation, which explains what information is offered in each report and defines the billing processes.
2. Account Balance, providing the most current billing information available. This information is usually 48 hours old.

3. Billing History. Each Sunday your charges for that week are compiled and the sum then becomes part of billing history. The billing history option allows you to examine charges, payments, and adjustment details on your account for up to 90 days (excluding current activity).

4. Current Activity, which includes the activity on your account before charges are compiled each week. You will see a series of chronologically ordered items describing your usage activity. This includes the date you logged on, a description of your activity (baud rate, network, premium programs accessed, etc.), the time you logged on, the number of minutes you were online, and the amount of charges you accrued for that session.

5. Previous Activity, including all activity for up to 90 days excluding Current Activity (above). The report is identical in format to Current Activity as described above (option 4). You will be provided with a list of the weeks available and their totals. You should then select the desired week that you wish to see by entering the number that appears to the left of that week-ending date. You will then be able to see the date, time, and description of your logons within that week.

6. Mail Hardcopy. You are provided with the opportunity to mail detailed hardcopy of your charges to your account address. There is a $3.50 fee associated with that service. For rate information, enter GO RATES at any ! prompt.

CompuServe offers two pricing options, the Standard Plan and the Alternative Plan. For online details, enter GO RATES.

Standard Pricing Plan Under the Standard Pricing Plan, you pay a flat monthly fee of $8.95, which allows unlimited access to scores of primary services, and a special deal on electronic mail. (Reading the mail is free, except for Internet messages; and users may send up to the equivalent of about 60 three-page messages per month at no additional charge.) New members are not charged the membership fee until the second month. When you are using CompuServe's U.S. and Canadian networks, these services are free of communication (network) charges. Supplemental network charges still apply outside of the U.S. and Canada. Enter GO RATES for more information. Use of features outside this core group (that is, in the "Extended Services") is billed by connect time minute. These services are indicated by a "+" or "$" next to the menu choice.

- Services marked with a "+" are charged at the CompuServe charge depending on the modem speed.
- Services marked with a "$" are charged at an additional rate.

For additional information on premium surcharges, enter GO TRANSACTION online.

The services included in the unlimited-access, basic services area (GO BASIC) are:

- In News, Sports, and Weather: Associated Press Online (hourly news summaries, sports, entertainment, business news, today in history), U.S. News & World Report Online Accu-Weather Maps and Reports, National Weather Service, UK news clips, sports clip, weather, syndicated columns, and Deutsche Presse-Agentur Kurnachrichtendienst.

- In the Reference Library: American Heritage Dictionary, Grolier's Academic American Encyclopedia, Consumer Reports, Consumer Reports Complete Drug Reference, Peterson's College Database, Healthnet, Handicapped Users' Database, Rehabilitation Database.

- In Shopping: The Electronic Mall and Shopper's Advantage discount shopping club.

- In Money Talks: Basic Current Stock Quotes, FundWatch Online by Money Magazine, Issue/Symbol Reference, Mortgage Calculator.

- Games and Entertainment: Science Trivia Quiz, The Grolier Whiz Quiz, ShowBizQuiz, CastleQuest, Black Dragon, Classic Adventure, Enhanced Adventure, Hangman, Hollywood by Marilyn Beck/Stacy Smith, Hollywood Hotline, and Soap Opera Summaries.

- In Communications Exchange: CompuServe Mail (Enter GO MAILRATES for additional details), Classified Ads (to read; placement costs extra), DOS CIM Support Forum, Macintosh CIM Support Forum, WINCIM Support Forum, Navigator Support Forums, Practice Forum, Help Forum, Directory of Members, Ask Customer Service.

- In Travel and Leisure: Travelshopper and Eaasy Sabre (airline, hotel, rental car information, and reservation services) plus other travel information, including Department of State Advisories, Visa Advisors, Zagat Restaurant Survey, Travel Britain Online, Bed & Breakfast Database, and Golf Online Database.

CompuServe's billing period runs Sunday through Saturday. The billing month ends on the last Saturday of each month, so your $8.95 charge will be applied to your CompuServe account on the last Saturday of each month.

You may access the basic services at any baud rate. Access to extended services, as well as all usage (except FREE areas) for members on the Alternative Pricing Plan, will be billed at an hourly rate based on the speed at which you access.

Alternative Pricing Plan Most users prefer the Standard Pricing Plan. However, if you plan only specialized or generally limited access to the system, you might prefer the Alernative Pricing Plan. Under it, you are charged a monthly $2.50 membership support fee which supports unlimited use of the online Membership Support services free of connect-time charges. All other usage is billed at the hourly connect rates based on baud rate, plus any applicable network charges and premium surcharges. Hourly connect-time charges are billed in one-minute increments, with a one-minute minimum charge per session.

To change from one plan to another, enter GO CHOICES. This provides a menu with details of the plans, commonly asked questions, and so on, as well as options for changing the billing. There is no fee to change from one pricing plan to the other.

Hourly Rates Connect-time rates apply for all usage of extended services for members on the Standard Pricing Plan. For members on the Alternative Pricing Plan, hourly connect-time charges are in effect at all times except in the Free services (GO FREE). Based on modem speed, the rates are:

For connection at:	Standard Plan	Alternative Plan
300bps	$4.80 an hour	$6.30 an hour
1200 to 2400bps	$4.80 an hour	$12.80 an hour
9600 to 14400bps	$9.60 an hour	$22.80 an hour

Connect time is billed in one-minute increments, with a minimum of one minute per session. Connect time rates do not include communications (network) charges or premium surcharges, which are billed in addition to hourly connect-time charges. (For details on network surcharges, enter GO BIL-74.)

Free Services Regardless of which pricing plan you accept, some features, called the Member Support Services, are always free of connect-time rates. (Applicable network charges are still effective in these areas for all members. Enter GO RATES for current information on network rates.) If you are on the alternative pricing plan, the free areas are identified by a "FREE" banner on each menu page. The free services include the Electronic Mall (GO MALL), What's New Articles (GO NEW), Access Phone Numbers (GO PHONES), Logon Instructions (GO LOGON), Billing Information (GO BILLING), Review Charges (GO CHARGES), Electronic Funds Transfer Amount (GO BILL), Change Your Password (GO PASSWORD), Change Your Billing (GO BILLING), Change Your Phone or Address (GO ADDRESS), Service Terms & Rules (GO RULES), Online Settings (GO PROFILE), Subject Index (GO INDEX), Online Questions & Answers (GO QUESTIONS), Online Ordering (GO ORDER), Summary of Commands (GO COMMAND), Practice Forum (GO PRACTICE), CompuServe Help Forum (GO HELPFORUM), Rates Information (GO RATES), Online Tour (GO TOUR), Membership Directory (GO DIRECTORY), Feedback (GO FEEDBACK).

Also, Member Support Services for European Members (in addition to the services already listed) include Access Phone Numbers (GO EUROPHONES), Logon Instructions (GO EUROLOGON), Online Questions, and Answers (GO EUROQUESTIONS).

Executive Service Option CompuServe offers an Executive Service Option that allows you to receive access to exclusive databases (most of them financial in nature), merchandise offers, and discounts. Executive Option users have:

- Access to exclusive databases, including Company Analyzer, Disclosure II, Executive News Service, SuperSite, Institutional Broker's Estimate System, Securities Screening, Return Analysis, and Company Screening. Many of these reports are designed to take full advantage of 80-character screens.
- Volume discounts on information retrieval from selected transaction price financial databases.
- A six-month storage period for personal files without charge (30 days is standard).
- A 10 percent discount on the purchase of most CompuServe products. This does not include sale items.
- A 50 percent increase in the amount of online storage available in your Personal File Area, along with an opportunity to purchase additional storage space at a reduced weekly rate.

Executive Option users are subject to a $10 monthly minimum usage level. Your monthly $8.95 CompuServe basic membership on the Standard Pricing Plan, or the $2 membership support fee under the Alternative Pricing Plan is applied to this minimum.

Billing options Most CompuServe subscribers have their charges billed to a credit card, either VISA, MasterCard, Discover Card, Diners Club, or American Express. Credit card accounts are billed weekly, directly to the credit card account. The system also supports Electronic Funds Transfer billing. CompuServe also offers business accounts. Users obtain an application and agreement form from CompuServe's customer service ordering department, Box L-477, Columbus, Ohio 43220, or through the online Feedback service after subscribing. You can convert to a business account from MasterCard, VISA, American Express, or Checkfree billing. A one-time $39.95 charge is levied for setting an initial business account user ID number, which includes a $25 usage credit for new users. For online details on various billing options, enter GO BILOPT.

Network surcharges Besides basic connect charges, some users are billed for network communication surcharges when accessing the system through alternative networks. Besides the CompuServe rates, network surcharges are levied, depending on how you access the system, through CompuServe's own connections or a carrier network. These rates are subject to change; the latest at the time of this publication were:

- CompuServe Network, 30 cents per hour.
- Sprintnet/Tymnet $1.70 per hour, evening and weekends; $11.70 per hour daytime for contiguous U.S. The Non-prime rate for Alaska and Hawaii is $11.70 an hour.
- AlaskaNet, $11.70 per hour.

- LATA Networks (where available), $1.70 per hour, evenings and weekends; $.70 per hour daytime.

To check latest rates and to compare rates for networks outside the U.S., enter GO NETWORKS and select the Communications Surcharges option from the resulting menu.

Premium charges Some services carry extra, "premium" surcharges. The actual costs vary from feature to feature. The surcharges generally are based on the number of minutes of connect time used in accessing them, the amount of data retrieved from them, or both. You are billed the surcharge in addition to the connect-time charges and applicable network charges. For the latest amounts of premium charges, enter GO TRANSACTIONS.

Here are some online addresses for news about the bill. For:

- General billing information, GO BILL or GO CHARGES.
- Information on various billing options, GO BILOPT.
- Data on storage charges, GO STORAGE.
- The news on connect time and other rates, GO CONNECT and GO RATES.
- Specifics on surcharge and transaction program charges, GO SURCHARGES and GO TRANSACTION.
- Miscellaneous billing charges, GO MISC.

For a related topic, see Executive Option. For specific CompuServe Mail surcharges (such as communicating with remote systems), see Mail, CompuServe.

BindView products are supported in the Novell Vendor Forum A (GO NVENA). See Novell Software.

Biographies: Marquis's Who's Who (GO BIOGRAPHY) includes biographical information describing key North American professionals. See Marquis's Who's Who.

Also, relevant databases on IQuest (GO IQUEST) include Biography Index, Biography Master Index, L'Elite et les Institutions Sovietiques, and Standard & Poor's Register—Biographical. See IQuest.

Biology is a topic in the Science/Math Education Forum (GO SCIENCE). For details, see Science. See also Life Sciences.

Biorhythms **(game)** (GO BIORHYTHM) plots personalized charts for any year. You may print an individual month or several months. Enter the name of the person for whom you want a chart, then enter the date of his or her birth, the year to chart, beginning month, and number of months to chart. The biorhythm chart also provides text for appropriate days in any given month. This program should be used with an 80-column printer. The game is intended for those age 12 and up. For information on other games, see Games.

BioScience   (magazine) is searchable through Magazine Database Plus (GO MDP). For details see Magazine Database.

Biotechnology   is covered in a number of IQuest databases (see IQuest), including Applied Genetics News, Biobusiness, Biological & Agricultural Index, Biosis Previews, Biotech Business, Biotechnology Newswatch, Comline Japan Daily: Biotechnology, Compendex Plus, Current Biotechnology Abstracts, and PTS Newsletter Database.

   And searchable on the Business Database Plus (GO BUSDB) are *Biomedical Market Newsletter*, *Biomedical Materials (incorporating Biomedical Polymers)*, *Bioprocessing Technology*, *Biotech Business*, *Biotech Patent News*, *Biotechnology Business News*, and *Biotechnology Investment Opportunities*. See Business Database.

   Through the Knowledge Index (GO KI) you can search Current Biotechnolgy Abstracts, Life Sciences Collection, and Current Biotechnolgy Abstracts. See Knowledge Index.

   See also Life Sciences and Medicine.

Birds   are regularly discussed in the Pets and Animals Forum (GO PETS). For details, see Pets. Birding also is a topic of the Outdoors Forum (GO OUTDOORFORUM). See Sports and Recreation. And *Audubon* magazine can be searched in the Magazine Database Plus (GO MDP). See Magazine Database.

Birmingham Business Journal   (magazine) can be searched through the Business Database Plus (GO BUSDB). See Business Database.

Bitnet   users can receive mail from CompuServe. See Mail, CompuServe, under the Internet section.

Bitstream   products are supported in the Desktop Publishing Vendor Forum (GO DTPVENDOR). For details, see Desktop Publishing.

Biz*File   (GO BIZFILE) provides access to names, addresses, and phone numbers for companies through the United States and Canada. See Phone Directories, Yellow Pages.

Black Belt Systems   products are supported in the Amiga Vendor Forum (GO AMIGAVENDOR). See Commodore Computers.

BlackDragon   (game) (GO BLACKDRAGON) is a fantasy role-playing game set in a ten-level maze. The object is to accumulate treasure and, by converting gold into experience points, to gain strength. To win, you must be strong enough to conquer the "Arch Demon" on the final level. Skill, experience, and some luck are required. The game is intended for those age 12 and up. This is one of the system's basic services, meaning those signed up under the Standard Pricing Plan (see Billing) have unlimited access to the feature. For information on other games, see Games.

Blindness is discussed in the Disabilities Forum (GO DISABILITIES). See Disabilities.

BLOC Publishing products are supported in the IBM PC Vendor D Forum (GO PCVEND). See IBM Computers.

Blood magazine abstracts are searchable in the Health Database Plus (GO HLTBD). See Health.

Blue Lance products are supported in the Novell Vendor Forum A (GO NVENA). See Novell Software.

Blue Ribbon products are supported in the MIDI C Vendor Forum (GO MIDICVEN). See Music.

Blues music is discussed in the Music/Arts Forum (GO MUSICARTS). See Music.

Blyth Software Forum (GO BLYTH) provides news and support for its Omnis line of database products. Its current flagship product, Omnis 5, provides a relational database development environment for Mac and Windows, as well as optional front-end support for major SQL databases. Blyth technical support staffers and software engineers participate daily on the forum; and Blyth's technical notes and program updates are available from the forum's libraries. The sysop is Rick Moen (76711,243), an MIS engineer in Foster City, California.

BMD Monitor (defense business database) can be searched through IQuest. See IQuest.

BMG Compact Disc Club (GO CD) is a store in the Electronic Mall (GO MALL) that offers CD recordings. See Electronic Mall.

BNA Daily News (database on regulatory issues) can be searched through IQuest (GO IQUEST) and through the Knowledge Index (GO KI). See IQuest and see Knowledge Index.

BNH (Business of New Hampshire) (magazine) can be searched through the Business Database Plus (GO BUSDB). See Business Database.

Boating is the topic of the Sailing Forum (GO SAILING). For more on this and related topics, see Sports. In addition, *Boating* magazine can be searched through the Magazine Database Plus (GO MDP) and Business Database Plus (GO BUSDB), which also provides access to *Boating Industry* magazines. See Magazine Database and see Business Database.

Also, boat and ship model-building is discussed in the Model Forum (GO MODELNET). See ModelNet.

Bobbin (magazine) can be searched through the Business Database Plus (GO BUSDB). See Business Database.

Boca Research (modem equipment) is supported the Modem Vendor Forum (GO MODEMVEN). See Modem Vendor.

BocaSoft products are supported in the OS/2 Vendor Forum (GO OS2AVEN). See IBM Computers.

BOC Week (magazine) can be searched through the Business Database Plus (GO BUSDB). See Business Database.

BODACC (French business database) may be searched through the IQuest gateway. See IQuest.

"Bold and the Beautiful, The" (television) summaries on the latest shows are available in Soap Opera Summaries (GO SOAPS). See Soap Opera.

Boling, Douglas (72241,217) is among the editors and writers associated with the PC Magazine forums. See PC Magazine.

Bond Buyer Fulltext (database) may be searched through the IQuest gateway. See IQuest.

Bonds Listing (GO BONDS) displays all active bonds for a company. The report displays the ticker symbols, CUSIP numbers, issue descriptions, yield, and current selling price for each bond. In addition, a quality rating is provided, expressed by both Standard & Poor's and Moody's. For related services, see Stock Symbols; and for an overview of other money-oriented features, see Financial and see Investment Analysis Tools.

Book collecting of all kinds is covered in the Coin and Stamp Forum (GO COINS or GO STAMPS). See Coin and Stamp Forum.

BookManager (software) is supported in the Software Solutions Forum (GO SOFSOL). See Software Solutions.

Booknet (GO ZNT:BOOKNET) offers computer and technical books from Ziff-Davis Press at a 20 percent discount. The feature offers the "How It Works" services, the PC Learning Labs series, the "Help!" services, the "Take It to the Edge" series, and the Techniques and Utilities book/disk packages. See also ZiffNet.

Book of the Month Club (GO BOM) offers nine different clubs that can be joined online through the Electronic Mall (GO MALL). See Electronic Mall.

Book Review Digest (GO BRD) is a database produced by the H.W. Wilson Co. It is available directly or through IQuest (see IQuest). The database provides references to more than 26,000 fiction and nonfiction English language books, and is updated twice weekly. It goes back to April 1983. Reviews are drawn from 80 American, Canadian, and British periodicals covering general and social sciences, humanities, and general reference. The service is searchable by subject, title, author, or person named as subject. The surcharge is $2 for the first 10 titles located, $2 for each additional 10 titles, and $2 for each full-text article retrieved. There is a $1 charge for a search that retrieves no titles.

Book Review Digest and Book Review Index (databases) also may be searched through the IQuest gateway. See IQuest.

Books are the topic of the Literary Forum (GO LITFORUM), which hosts discussions for writers and readers of fiction, poetry, and nonfiction. See Literature. The Science Fiction and Fantasy Forum (GO SCIFI) caters to sci-fi of all kinds, including books. See Science Fiction for more information. Book collecting is discussed in the Collectibles Forum (GO COLLECT). See Collectibles.

Also, books and periodicals are sold in a number of stores in the Electronic Mall (GO MALL), including Book of the Month Club (GO BOM), Books in Print (GO BOOKS), Compubooks (GO CBK), Computer Shopper (GO CS), Harpercollins Online (GO HAR), Macmillan Publishing (GO MMP), MacUser (GO MC), McGraw-Hill Book Co. (GO MH), Microsoft Press (GO MSP), PC Computing (GO PCC), PC Magazine (GO PM), Quality Paperback Book Club (GO QPB), Small Computer Book Club (GO BK), VNR Bookstore Cafe (GO VNR), and Wiley Professional Books (GO JW). See Electronic Mall.

And Booknet (GO ZNT:BOOKNET) offers computer and technical books from Ziff-Davis Press at a 20 percent discount. See Booknet.

Also, Time Warner's Author of the Week Forum (GO TWEP) features weekly visits with authors published by Time Warner Trade Publishing, the home of Little, Brown and Company and of Warner Books, Inc. See Time Warner's.

Books File, Library of Congress MARC (database) may be searched through the IQuest gateway. See IQuest.

Books in Print (GO BOOKS) is a Telebase Systems Incorporated gateway that lists most books currently in print at U.S. trade publishers. It also lists books currently out of print and those slated for publication.

Data includes bibliographic references and descriptions of books distributed in the United States for single- or multiple-copy purchase, those currently in print and those to be published in the next six months, and those that went out-of-print or out-of-stock during the last two years. Most records include author, title, publisher, date of publication, edition, binding (e.g., "paperback"), list price, and subject as published by R.R. Bowker Co.

The cost is $2 for the first 10 titles located, $2 for each additional 10 titles, and $2 for each reference retrieved. A charge of $1 is made for searches that retrieve no titles.

This resource also can be searched through the Knowledge Index (GO KI). See Knowledge Index.

For information on other Telebase gateways, see Telebase Systems Incorporated.

Books on Tape   (GO BOT) is a store in the Electronic Mall (GO MALL) that offers audio books. See Electronic Mall.

Boomer Report   (**marketing database**) may be searched through the IQuest gateway. See IQuest. See also Demographics.

Borland Software: The Borland International Forums (GO BORLAND) support the company's various programs, including Turbo Pascal, SideKick, SuperKey, Turbo Lightning, and Turbo Prolog. Borland operates several forums. All the forums offer teams of experienced users in a number of areas of specialization. The names of the team members and their user IDs are displayed in the bulletin areas of the respective forums.

The forums include:

- Borland Applications Forum (GO BORAPP) for help with Sidekick and utilities. Among the operators are Andrew Morrow, Bob Rucinski, Don Schubert, James Walker, Jim Wetzel, Ken Getz, Scotte Meredith, and Tim Colling.
- Borland Development Tools Forum (GO BDEVTOOLS) for help with ObjectVision, Paradox Engine, Interbase, Brief, and Sourcerer's Apprentice. The administrators are Jennifer Dunvan, Jason Sprenger, Charlie Calvert, Mike Starrett, Bill Tello, Rich Damon, and Mike Fitz-Enz.
- Borland C++/DOS Forum (GO BCPPDOS) for help with Borland C++, TC++, TC, TD, and Tools. The sysops include Greg Macdonald, Steve Barnette, Mike Starrett, Rich Wesson, Ed James-Beckham, Tom Orsi, Jim Hartley, Bill Kirby, Evan Scott, and Peter Williams.
- Borland C++/Windows Forum (GO BCPPWIN), discussing Borland's programming language products, Borland C++, Turbo C++, and Turbo C. Sysops include Bill Dunlap, Bruneau Babet, Dave Wilhelm, Gary Johnson, Lar Mader, Pete Williams, Peter Yueh, Shea Anderson, Steve Barnette, and Tommy Hui.
- Borland dBASE Forum (GO DBASE), supporting the famed spreadsheet Borland acquired with the acquisition of Ashton-Tate several years ago. The sysops are Abe Cohen, Charles Miedzinski, Debbie Runkle, Ed Hoskins, Hanh Nguyen, Patrick Kennedy, Paul Powers, Steve Koterski, and Yvonne Arinduque.
- Borland Deutschland Forum (GO BORGER) for German-speaking users.

- Borland Paradox/DOS Forum (GO PDOXDOS) for help with Paradox and Reflex. Sysops are Bill Curtis, Dan Bernstein, David Orriss Jr., Jeff Meyer, John Hawklyn, Josh Evans, Keith Bigelow, Scott Arnett, Tayward Wong, Tina Grubbe, Weylan Wang, and Mike Fitz-Enz.
- Borland Paradox/Windows Forum (GO PDOXWIN) for assistance in using the Windows version of Paradox. Operating the forum are Ben Holton, Brian Reed, David Orriss, Ellie Moradeshagh, Jeff Meyer, Jose Correa, Ken Merson, Kip Obenauf, Mark Mateus, Mike Justus, Mike Prestwood, Quinn Wildman, Randy Sell, Randy Spitz, Robert Ramirez, Scott Arnett, Sean Schnoor, Stephanie Haas, Steve Neverve, Steve Trefethen, Tarik Ghbeish, Weylan Wang, and Mike Fitz-Enz.
- Borland Pascal Forum (GO BPASCAL). Administrators include Jason Sprenger, Charlie Calvert, Xavier Pacheco, Rich Jones, and Lester Jackson.
- Borland Quattro Pro Forum (GO QUATTROPRO) for both DOS and Windows. The forum's managers are Eric Nelson, Sandy Nakazono, Andy Chittum, Jason Hanashi, Leslie Creach, Bob Porporato, Emil Gallant, Rich Wilkman, Ralph Galantine, John Aylesworth, and Mike Fitz-Enz.

Also available on the GO BORLAND menu are company announcements, a suggestion box for the research and development department, and even an online area for bulletins about work opportunities at Borland.

Bose Express Music (GO BEM) operates a store in the Electronic Mall (GO MALL) selling cassettes, CDs, records, and gifts. See Electronic Mall.

Bosnia is a topic of the Global Crisis Forum (GO CRISIS). See Global Crisis.

B.O.S.S. computers are supported in the Palmtop Forum (GO PALMTOP). See Palmtop.

Boston Audio Society is represented in the Consumer Electronics Forum (GO CEFORUM). See Electronics.

Boston Business Journal (**magazine**) can be searched through the Business Database Plus (GO BUSDB). See Business Database.

Boston (MA) Globe (**newspaper**) is searchable through Telebase System's News Source USA (GO NEWSUSA) and through the Knowledge Index (GO KI). See News Source and see Knowledge Index.

Bottomline (**magazine**) can be searched through the Business Database Plus (GO BUSDB). See Business Database.

Bowdish, David (76711,143) operates the NeXT Forum (GO NEXTFORUM), supporting NeXT computers. See NeXT.

Bowen, Charles, is the author of this book and he invites your CompuServe Mail. Send questions, comments, and suggestions to 71635,1025.

Bowen, Richard (76711,1153) is the sysop of the CTOS/Open Forum (GO CTOS). See CTOS.

Bowers, Rich (71333,1114), executive director of the Optical Publishing Association, is a sysop in the CDROM Forum (GO CDROM). See CD.

Bowker (Reed) Electronic Publishing products are supported in the CD-ROM Vendors Forum (GO CDVEN). See CD-ROM.

Bowker Co., R. R., publisher of *Books in Print* is featured in the Books in Print database. See Books in Print.

   Also Bowker's International Serials Database and Bowker Biographical Directory (databases) can be searched through the IQuest gateway. See IQuest.

Bowne Digest—Corp/SEC Article Abstracts (law database) may be searched through the IQuest gateway. See IQuest.

Boxing is a topic of the Sports Forum (GO FANS). See Sports and Recreation.

B Protocol, CompuServe is a binary protocol supported by CompuServe for sending and receiving files in forums, electronic mail, and so on. See Files, Transfer.

BP Report (magazine) can be searched through the Business Database Plus (GO BUSDB). See Business Database.

Brady Books computer books are supported in the Prentice Hall Computer Publishing Forum (GO PHCP). See Prentice Hall.

Braille access technology is a topic in the IBM/Special Needs Forum (GO IBMSPECIAL). See Handicapped.

Brain (magazine) abstracts are searchable in the Health Database Plus (GO HLTBD). See Health.

Brain, David (76703,401) is the sysop of the European Community Telework Forum (GO ECTF). See European Community.

Branch Automation News (database) may be searched through the IQuest gateway. See IQuest.

Brandon, Bill (76701,256) is a sysop in the Computer Training Forum (GO DPTRAIN). See Computer Training. He also is sysop of ASSIST Journal On-Line Forum (GO ASSIST) on ZiffNet (see ZiffNet).

Brazil Service (magazine) can be searched through the Business Database Plus (GO BUSDB). See Business Database.

Breton Harbor Baskets Company (GO BH) is a store in the Electronic Mall (GO MALL) that offers gift baskets, gourmet foods, skin care, and more. See Electronic Mall.

Brewery Age, Modern (magazine) can be searched through the Business Database Plus (GO BUSDB). See Business Database.

Bridge (software) is supported in Windows 3rd-Party Forum B (GO WINAPB). See Microsoft Software.

Bridge, The Aces on, (column) is among the syndicated columns provided by United Features (GO COLUMNS). See Columnists.

Brightwork Development products are supported in the IBM PC Vendor D Forum (GO PCVEND). See IBM Computers.

Britain is served in a number of features, including:

- The UK Forum (GO UKFORUM), for general UK interest. See UK Forum.
- The UK Computing Forum (GO UKCOMP). For details, see UK Computing.
- The UK Shareware Forum (GO UKSHARE). See UK Shareware.
- The PC Magazine UK Forum (GO PCMAGUK). See Ziff.

British business reports and news are covered in several IQuest databases, including Daily and Sunday Telegraph, Financial Times & The Economist, Financial Times, Guardian, International News, Times and Sunday Times, UK News, British Company Directory, Key British Enterprises, British Company Financial Datasheets, Infocheck, Kompass UK, British Medical Association's Press Cuttings, Campaign, ICC British Company Directory, ICC British Company Financial Datasheets, Jordans Registered Companies, and Super Marketing. See IQuest.
Also:

- The Business Database Plus (GO BUSDB) provides access to *British Plastics & Rubber*, *British Telecom World*, and *UK Venture Capital Journal*. See Business Database.
- News/business/reference products are included in British Trade Marks (GO UKTRADEMARK), U.K. Marketing Library (GO UKMARKETING), U.K. Newspaper Library (GO UKPAPERS), U.K. News/Weather/Sports (GO UKNEWS), and U.K. Company Library (GO UKLIB).
- ICC British Company Directory can be searched through the Knowledge Index (GO KI). See Knowledge Index.

- Quotes from British stock exchanges also are available (GO UKPRICES). See Stock Quotes (Historical), UK for details.

British Legends   (game) (GO LEGENDS) is a multi-player game that has rolling pastures, dense forests, misty graveyards, and evil beings lurking in the shadows. Some, but not all, of the creatures you encounter are computer-controlled; others are real people who are also playing at the same time you are. You must conquer more than unknown countryside. You also must battle other players. Your goal is to progress from warrior (400 points) to a witch or a wizard (102,400 points) by solving some of the game's more than 200 puzzles. As the game starts, your charter begins in an Elizabethan tea room where you can chat with the natives, ask for help, maybe find a friend. To talk it up, enter CONVERSE; anything you enter after that is treated as a message. To cancel conversation mode, enter an asterisk. Also helpful for a newcomer, you can request a tour before you get down to some serious gaming; enter WISH,TOUR and witch or a wizard will take you in hand. The game is intended for those age 12 and up. To find other British Legends enthusiasts for advice and companionship, visit the Multi-Player Games Forum (GO MPFORUM). For more on other games, see Games.

British Medical Association's Press Cuttings   (database) may be searched through the IQuest gateway. See IQuest.

British Medical Journal   is searchable in the Health Database Plus (GO HLTBD). See Health.

British science fiction   in various media is discussed in the ScienceFiction & Fantasy Forum (GO SCI-FI). See Science Fiction.

Broadband Networking News   (magazine) can be searched through the Business Database Plus (GO BUSDB). See Business Database.

Broadcasters and Broadcast Engineers Forum   (GO BPFORUM) is operated by John Hoffman (76703,1036), a broadcast engineer at the NBC Television Network in New York. He also presents an electronic magazine called *InCue OnLine*. The forum is open to individuals and companies involved in radio, television, cable television, professional audio and video communications, and so on. It also provides online services for two professional organizations, the Audio Engineering Society and the Society of Broadcast Engineers.

Assisting him are Joe Bartlett, Chris Hays, John Reiser, Jonathan Kramer, Chip Morgan, Jay Trachman, Jim Jordan, John MacPherson, Jerry Whitaker, Ken Hoehn, and Jeff Noah.

Also of interest:

- *Broadcasting* magazine can be searched through the Business Database Plus (GO BUSDB). See Business Database. It also can be search through IQuest. See IQuest.

- HamNet (Ham Radio) Forum (GO HAMNET), devoted to amateur radio. See HamNet.
- News broadcasting is discussed in the Journalism Forum (GO JFORUM). See Journalism and for other related features, see News, General.
- Public Broadcasting Report can be searched through IQuest. See IQuest.

And for more related topics, see Television.

Broadway theater and musicals are a topic of the Music/Art Forum (GO MUSICARTS). See Music.

Broderbund software has a kiosk in the Electronic Mall which can be reached by entering GO BB. See Electronic Mall.

Brokerages, stock: The system supports several online stock brokers (GO BROKERAGE). See Stock Brokerages.

Brooks Brothers (GO BR) is a store in the Electronic Mall (GO MALL) that offers men's and women's apparel. See Electronic Mall.

Brothers, Dr. Joyce, American psychologist, is featured in the Human Sexuality Information and Advisory Service, a database provided in the Human Sexuality Forums (GO HSX). Dr. Brothers offers practical advice to parents on a variety of delicate problems that arise in dealing with children and teenagers. See Sex.

Brown Bag Software products are supported in the PC Vendor G Forum (GO PCVENG). See IBM.

Brown, Edward (71154,674) is sysop of the Holistic Health Forum (GO GO HOLISTIC). See Holistic.

Browning, Joey (76702,1365) is the administrator of the Online With Hayes Forum (GO HAYES). See Hayes Microcomputer Products Inc.

BRS (**Bibliographic Retrieval Service)** of Latham, New York, is a major database vendor accessible through the IQuest gateway (GO IQUEST). See IQuest.

Bruce, Tracy (76702,1051) is sysop of the WordStar Forum (GO WORDSTAR). For details, see WordStar Software.

Bruner, Al (72662,102) is a sysop of the Prentice Hall Computer Publishing Forum (GO PHCP). See Prentice Hall.

BT Catalyst (**magazine)** can be searched through the Business Database Plus (GO BUSDB). See Business Database.

Buerg, Vern   (70007,1212) is a sysop of the IBM Users Network (GO IBMNET). See IBM Computers.

Buffalo (NY) News   **(newspaper)** is searchable through Telebase System's News Source USA (GO NEWSUSA). See News Source.
   Also *Business First of Buffalo* magazine can be searched through the Business Database Plus (GO BUSDB). See Business Database.

BugBase for Windows   **(software)** is supported in the Windows 3rd-Party Forum (GO WINAPD). See Microsoft Software.

Buick Magazine   (GO BU) is a store in the Electronic Mall (GO MALL) that offers car information, customer service. See Electronic Mall. For other automobile-related features, see Cars.

Building and construction   are covered in an assortment of magazines that are searchable through the Business Database Plus (GO BUSDB), including *Buildings, Building Design & Construction, Building Supply Home Centers, Professional Builder and Remodeler,* and *Professional Builder.* See Business Database.
   See also Architecture and see Construction.

Bulletin Board Systems   are discussed in a number of CompuServe forums. For details, see BBS.

Bureau of Electronic Publishing   products are supported in the CD-ROM Vendors Forum (GO CDVEN). See CD-ROM.

Burnes, Barbara   (76711,1246) is a sysop of the Ideas, Inventions & Innovations Forum (GO INNOVATION). See Ideas.

Business   features abound. For an online overview, enter GO BUSINESS. For further information, see Financial Services and see Investment Analysis Tools. Also see Industry.

Business Climate Indicators, International   **(database)** may be searched through the IQuest gateway. See IQuest.

Business Computer and Business Software Database   **(database)** may be searched through the IQuest gateway. See IQuest.

Business Daily, Commerce   (GO COMBUS) is published by the U.S. Commerce Department, includes the full text of U.S. Commerce Department publications listing contracts, requests for proposals, and other data related to government contracts. See Commerce Business Daily.

Business Database Plus   (GO BUSDB) is sponsored by magazine publisher Ziff Communications and contains business-related articles from more than 500 publications, including those on industries such as agriculture, retailing, and telecommunications. The resources access two collections of articles: Business and trade journals (for in-depth coverage of products and companies) and industry newsletters (for timely, industry-oriented news). Coverage for most titles in the first group goes back five years, while the second group spans a year. Most are updated weekly. Every article contains full text.

This surcharged feature provides seven methods to locate articles, methods that can be used singly or in any combination. The service is menu-driven but, for those experienced with information retrieval services, it provides shortcuts around many of the menus.

The surcharge is $15 an hour plus $1.50 for each article retrieved (either viewed on the screen or downloaded). You will be charged only once for each article you view. You may return to the Article Citation menu or jump from article to article and be charged only once for each article; you will not incur additional retrieval charges. Note, though, that if you return to the Search Summary menu and then display an article again, you will be charged again. You can find a user guide and the latest publication list for the feature in the Ziff Support Forum (GO ZIFFHELP) in Library 8 ("Business DB Plus"). See file BDPUSR.TXT for the user guide, BDPPUB.TXT for the publication list.

The feature's search methods fall into two broad categories:

- General searches let you look for articles based on individual words occurring in articles, so they are useful when you aren't sure exactly where to look in an article for the occurrence of a word.

- Specific searches let you look for articles based on specific kinds of words or phrases, such as a subject heading or publication name. For specific searches, a search term can be composed of letters, numerals, and spaces.

Among the specific search methods supported are:

1. Key Words (in article titles, subject headings, featured names, etc.).

2. Subject Headings, words or phrases selected from a controlled list of terms to best describe the primary focus of an article.

3. Company Names, included only when a company is significantly covered in an article, rather than merely mentioned.

4. Publication Names, without the word "the" if it occurs at the beginning. You may obtain a complete list by typing "??" when asked for a publication name.

5. Publication Dates in the format "month day, year", "day month year", "month year", with or without a comma before the year.

As you search, the feature generates a menu of actual search terms that match the (partial) search term you supply. You then make one or more selections from the menu.

Techniques for searching this resource are the same as those used with all of the ZiffNet gateways. For specifics, see ZiffNet Databases.

The database also allows for downloading of articles (as well as displaying them on the screen). Selecting the download option from a menu causes the database to display a File Transfer Protocol list. The first option on the menu is explicitly for users of the CompuServe Information Manager. Users of other terminal programs can select a different protocol. See Files, Transfer.

The magazines searchable through the Business Database Plus include:

ABA Banking Journal
Accounting and Finance
Accounting Today
Across the Board
Ad Solutions Report
Adhesives Age
Administrative Management
Advanced Coatings & Surface Technology
Advanced Ceramics Report
Advanced Composites Bulletin
Advanced Manufacturing Technology
Advanced Metals Technology
Advanced Military Computing
Advanced Office Technologies Report
Advanced Recovery Week
Advanced Wireless Communications
Advantage
ADWEEK Eastern Edition
ADWEEK Western Advertising News

Adweek's Marketing Week
Aerospace Financial News
Affluent Markets Alert
Aftermarket Business
Agexporter
Agra Europe
Agribusiness Worldwide
AIDS Therapies
AIDS Weekly
AIN Report
Air Cargo World
Air Conditioning Heating & Refrigeration News
Air Safety Week
Air Toxics Report
Air Transport World
Air Water Pollution Report
Aircraft Value Newsletter
Airline Business
Airline Financial News
AIWeek
Alaska Business Monthly
Alberta Business
Alternative Energy Digests
Alternative Energy Network Online Today

American City & County
American Demographics
American Federationist
American Forests
American Machinist
American Medical News
American Paint & Coatings Journal
American Papermaker
American Printer
American Salesman
American Shipper
Amusement Business
Antitrust Freedom of Information Log
Antiviral Agents Bulletin
Appliance
Appliance Manufacturer
Applied Genetics News
Appraisal Journal
APS Diplomat publications (Fate of the Arabian Peninsula, News Service, Operations in Oil Diplomacy, Recorder, Redrawing the Islamic Map, and Strategic Balance in the Middle East)

APS Review publications
(Downstream Trends,
Gas Market Trends,
and Review Oil
Market Trends)
Arizona Business
Arizona Business Gazette
Arkansas Business
Asbestos Abatement
Report
Asbestos Control Report
Asian Economic News
Assembly
Assembly Engineering
Asset Sales Report
Atlantic Business
Atlantic Economic
Journal
Audio Week
Audiotex Now
Audiotex Update
Austin Business Journal
Automated Medical
Payments News
Automation
Automotive Engineering
Automotive Industries
Automotive Marketing
Automotive Parts Inter-
national
Autoparts Report
Avionics Report
Back Stage
Bakery Production and
Marketing
Baltimore Business
Journal
Bank Automation News
Bank Loan Report

Bank Management
Bank Marketing
Bank Network News
Bankers Monthly
Baton Rouge Business
Report
Battery & EV Technol-
ogy
BBI Newsletter
BC Business
Best's Review—Life-
Health Insurance
Edition
Best's Review—Property-
Casualty Insurance
Edition
Beverage World
Beverage World Peri-
scope Edition
Biomedical Market
Newsletter
Biomedical Materials
(incorporating Bio-
medical Polymers)
Bioprocessing Technol-
ogy
Biotech Business
Biotech Patent News
Biotechnology Business
News
Biotechnology Invest-
ment Opportunities
Birmingham Business
Journal
BNH (Business of New
Hampshire)
Boating
Boating Industry
Bobbin
BOC Week

Boston Business Journal
Bottomline
BP Report
Brazil Service
British Plastics & Rubber
British Telecom World
Broadband Networking
News
Broadcasting
BT Catalyst
Building Design &
Construction
Building Supply Home
Centers
Buildings
Business America
Business & Commercial
Aviation
Business & Health
Business & the Environ-
ment
Business Atlanta
Business Credit
Business Economics
Business First of Buffalo
Business First—Colum-
bus
Business First—Louisville
Business Journal—
Milwaukee
Business Journal of New
Jersey Magazine
Business Journal—
Portland
The Business Journal—
San Jose
The Business Journal—
Serving Phoenix & the
Valley of the Sun

The Business Journal
 Serving Charlotte and
 the Metropolitan Area
The Business Journal
 Serving Greater
 Sacramento
Business Law Brief
The Business Month
Business North Carolina
Business Perspectives
Business Publisher
Business Quarterly
Business Record (Des
 Moines)
Business Tech Romania
Buyouts
Cable Television Business
CAD/CAM Update
California Business
California Management
 Review
California Public Finance
Canadian Business
Canadian Business
 Review
Canadian Chemical News
Canadian Dimension
Canadian Labour
Canadian Machinery and
 Metalworking
Canadian Occupational
 Health & Safety News
Cancer Weekly
Canmaking & Canning
 International
Cap Weekly
Capital District Business
 Review
Card News

Cardfax
Caribbean Update
Case Strategies
CCI—Canmaking &
 Canning International
CD Computing News
CD ROM Databases
CD-ROM Librarian
CD-ROM Professional
Cellular Business
Central America Update
Ceramic Industry
Chain Drug Review
Chain Store Age Execu-
 tive
Challenge
Channelmarker Letter
Chemical Business
Chemical Marketing
 Reporter
Chemical Monitor
Chemical Process Safety
 Report
Chemical Week
Chemistry and Industry
Children's Business
Chlor-Alkali Marketwire
CIM Strategies
Cincinnati Business
 Courier
CIS Economics &
 Foreign Trade
City Business—Minne-
 apolis–St. Paul
Clean Air Network
 Online Today
CMA—The Manage-
 ment Accounting
 Magazine

Coal & Synfuels Tech-
 nology
Coal Outlook
Colorado Business
 Magazine
Columbia Journal of
 World Business
COMLINE: Transporta-
 tion Industry of Japan
Common Carrier Week
Communication World
Communications Daily
Communications Inter-
 national
Communications News
Community & Worker
 Right-To-Know News
Commuter—Regional
 Airline News
Compensation and
 Benefits Review
Composites & Adhesives
 Newsletter
Composites Industry
 Monthly
Computer & Communi-
 cations Decisions
Computer Audit Update
Computer Dealer News
Computer Decisions
Computer Fraud &
 Security Bulletin
Computergram Interna-
 tional
Computer Industry
 Report
Computer Pictures
Computer Product
 Update

Computer Protocols

Computer Workstations

Computers in Libraries

Congressional Research Report

Construction Equipment Consultant

Consumer Electronics

Control and Instrumentation

Cornell Hotel & Restaurant Administration Quarterly

Corporate Cashflow Magazine

Corporate EFT Report

Corporate Report— Kansas City

Corporate Report— Minnesota

Cosmetic World News

Cosmetics International

Cosmetics and Toiletries

Cosmetics & Toiletries & Household Products Marketing News in Japan

Country Forecast Tables

The CPA Journal

Crain's Cleveland Business

Credit

Credit Card News

Credit Risk Management Report

Currency Quarterly

Dairy Foods

Dairy Industries International

Dallas Business Journal

Dallas–Fort Worth Business Journal

Data Broadcasting Report

Data Channels

Data Storage Report

Database

Database Searcher

Datamation

DataTrends Report on DEC & IBM

Dealing with Technology

Defense & Aerospace Electronics

Defense Cleanup

Defense Daily

Defense Electronics

Defense Marketing International

Defense Technology Business

Defense Week

Delaney Report

Denver Business

Denver Business Journal

Derivatives Engineering & Technology

Diagnostics Business Matters

Diesel Progress

Diesel Progress Engines & Drives

Direct Marketing

Discount Store News

Distribution

Document Image Automation Update

Drug & Cosmetic Industry

Drug Store News

Drug Topics

E&P Environment

East European Insurance Report

East European Markets

Eastern European & Former Soviet Telecom Report

Eastern European Energy Report

EBRD Watch

EC Energy Monthly

EC&M Electrical Construction & Maintenance

Eco-Log Week

Economic Journal

Economic Progress Report

Economic Review

The Economist

EDGE

EDI in Finance

EDI News

Education Technology News

Educational Marketer

EFT Report

800-900 Review

Electric Light & Power

Electro Manufacturing

Electronic Business

Electronic Chemicals News

Electronic Imaging Report

Electronic Materials & Processing

Electronic Materials Technology News

Electronic Messaging News

Electronic News

Electronic Office

Electronic Services Update

En Route Technology

Energy Alert

Energy & Environment

Energy Conservation News

Energy Daily

Energy Economics & Climate Change

Energy Report

Energy User News

E-MJ—Engineering & Mining Journal

Engineering Economist

Enhanced Energy Recovery News

Enhanced Recovery Week

Enhanced Services Outlook

Enterprise Integration Strategies

Entertainment Marketing Letter

Environment Watch (East Europe, Russia & Eurasia, Latin America, Western Europe)

Environment Week

Environmental Business Journal

Environmental Compliance Update

ESP Business Opportunities (in Africa & the Middle East, in Asia & the Pacific, in Latin America & the Caribbean)

EuroBusiness

Euromarketing

Euromoney

Europe 2000

Europe Energy

Europe Environment

Europe 92

European Cosmetic Markets

European Energy Report

European Polymers Paint & Colour Journal

European Report

European Rubber Journal

European Social Policy

European Venture Capital Journal

Evans-Novak Political Report

Exchange

Executive Briefing Service

Export Control News

Facts on File World News Digest

Fairfield County Business Journal

FCC Daily Digest

FCC Report

FCC Week

FDA Enforcement Report

FDA Medical Bulletin

FDIC Watch

Federal & State Insurance Week

Federal Industry Watchdog

Fertilizer International

Fiber Optics News

Finance & Finland

Financial Management

Financial Market Trends

The Financial Post

Financial Services Report

Financial Technology Insight

Financial World

Finmeccanica News

Finnish Trade Review

Flame Retardancy News

Flight International

Floor Covering Business

Florida Trend

Folio: The Magazine for Magazine Management

Food & Beverage Marketing

Food & Drink Daily

Food Channel
Food Chemical News
Food Cosmetics & Drug
　Packaging
Food Engineering
Food Engineering
　International
Food in Canada
Food Labeling News
Food Manufacture
Food Processing
Footwear News
Forest Industries
Foundry Management &
　Technology
411 Newsletter
Free Trade Advisory
Frohlinger's Marketing
　Report
Frozen and Chilled Foods
Frozen Food Digest
FTC Freedom of Infor-
　mation Log
FTC Watch
Fujitsu Weekly
Fusion Power Report
Futurehome Technology
　News
Futures: Magazine of
　Commodities &
　Options
The Futurist
FW
FX Week
Gas Daily
Gas World
General Accounting
　Office Reports &
　Testimony

Genesis Report
Genetic Technology
　News
German Business Scope
Gifts & Decorative
　Accessories
Global Communications
Global Environmental
　Change Report
Global Guaranty
Global Telecom Report
Global Trade
Global Warming Net-
　work Online Today
Going Public: The IPO
　Reporter
GPS Report
Green Marketing Report
Grocery Marketing
Ground Water Monitor
GUI Program News
Gulf Business Report
Gulf Reconstruction
　Report
Hardware Age
Hawaii Business
Hazardous Waste
　Network Online
　Today
Hazardous Waste News
Hazmat Transport News
HazNews
HDTV Report
Health & Human
　Services News
Health Business
Health Care Competition
　Week

Health Care Manage-
　ment Review
Health Industry Today
Health Legislation &
　Regulation
Health Manager's Update
Healthcare Financial
　Management
Healthcare Technology
　& Business Opportu-
　nities
Heating, Piping, Air
　Conditioning
Helicopter News
HFD—The Weekly
　Home Furnishings
　Newspaper
High Performance
　Plastics
High Performance
　Textiles
High Tech Ceramics
　News
High Tech Separations
　News
High Technology
　Business
High Yield Report
Highway & Heavy
　Construction
Hitachi Weekly
Home Media Technol-
　ogy News
Home Video Publisher
Hospital & Health
　Services Administra-
　tion
Hospitals

Housewares
Houston Business Journal
HRMagazine
Hydraulics & Pneumatics
Hydrocarbon Processing
IBM Japan Weekly
ICEN
IDC Japan Report
IDP Report
Illinois Business Review
Imaging News
Imaging Update
Implement & Tractor
Improved Recovery
    Week
Inc.
Independent Telco News
Indiana Business Maga-
    zine
Indonesian Investment
    Highlights
Industrial Bioprocessing
Industrial Communica-
    tions
Industrial Distribution
Industrial Engineering
Industrial Environment
Industrial Finishing
Industrial Health &
    Hazards Update
Industrial Management
Industrial Relations
Industrial Specialties
    News
Industries in Transition
Industry Week
Information Executive
Information Technology
    and Libraries

Information Today
Infosystems
Ingram's
Innovation
Innovator's Digest
Inside DOT & Transpor-
    tation Week
Inside IVHS
Inside Market Data
Inside R&D
Institutional Distribution
Institutional Investor
Insurance Review
Integrated Circuits
    International
Intelligent Network
    News
Intelligent Software
    Strategies
Inter Press Service
Interior Design
Internal Auditor
International Coal Report
International Gas Report
International Journal of
    Advertising
International Manage-
    ment
International Product
    Alert
International Reports
International Solar
    Energy Intelligence
    Report
International Trade
    Finance
International Trade
    Forum

Investment Management
    Technology
ISDN News
Israel Business
Israel High-Tech Report
Jacksonville Business
    Journal
JAMA
The Journal of the
    American Medical
    Association
Japan Computer Industry
    Scan
Japan Consumer Elec-
    tronics Scan
Japan Energy Scan
Japan Policy & Politics
Japan Report Biotechnol-
    ogy
Japan Report Information
    Technology
Japan Report Telecom-
    munications
Japan Science Scan
Japan Semiconductor
    Scan
Japan Transportation
    Scan
Japan Weekly Monitor
Japanese Government
    Weekly
Japanese New Materials
    Advanced Alloys &
    Metals
Japanese New Materials
    Advanced Plastics
Japanese New Materials
    Electronic Materials

Japanese New Materials High-Performance Ceramics

Jewelers Circular Key-stone

Journal of Accountancy

Journal of Advertising

Journal of the American Planning Association

The Journal of Coatings Technology

Journal of Common Market Studies

Journal of Consumer Affairs

Journal of Consumer Research

Journal of Electronic Defense

Journal of Finance

Journal of International Business Studies

Journal of Marketing

Journal of Marketing Research

Journal of Retailing

Junk Bond Reporter

Just-In-Time & Quick Response News

The Kansas City Business Journal

Korea Economic Daily

Kyodo

LA-C Business Bulletin

Lagniappe Letter

Lagniappe Quarterly Monitor

LAN Product News

The Lancet

Land Mobile Radio News

Laserdisk Professional

Latin America Opportunity Report

Latin American Business News Wire

Latin American Telecom Report

Law Office Technology Review

Lawn & Garden Marketing

LDC Debt Report

Legal Publisher

LI Business News

Liability Week

Library Software Review

Library Workstation Report

Licensing Letter

Link-Up

Lodging Hospitality

Long Distance Outlook

The Long-Distance Letter

Long Term Care Management

Los Angeles Business Journal

Louisiana Industry Environmental Alert

Machine Design

Mainframe Computing

Managed Care Law Outlook

Managed Care Outlook

Managed Care Week

Management Matters

Management Review

Management Today

The Management of World Wastes

Manitoba Business

Manufacturing Automation

Manufacturing Automation News

Manufacturing Chemist

Manufacturing Technology

Market Asia Pacific

Market Europe

Market Research Europe

Marketing

Marketing Computers

Marketing & Media Decisions

Marketing News

Marketing Research Review

Marketing to Women

Marketletter

Material Handling Engineering

Materials Engineering

Matsushita Weekly

Mechanical Engineering—CIME

Medical Economics

Medical Laboratory Observer

Medical Research Funding News

Medical Textiles
Medical Utilization
  Review
Medical Waste News
Medical World News
Medicine & Health
MEED Middle East
  Business Weekly
MEED Middle East
  Economic Digest
Membrane and Separa-
  tion Technology News
Memphis Business
  Journal
Mergers & Acquisitions
  Report
Metallurgia
Metalworking News
Mexico Business Monthly
Mexico Service
Michigan Business
Microcell Report
Micronesian Investment
  Quarterly
Microwave Journal
Mid-Atlantic Journal of
  Business
Mid East Business Digest
Middle East News
  Network
Mideast Markets
The Milbank Quarterly
Military & Commercial
  Fiber Business
Military Robotics
Military Space
Milling & Baking News

MIN Media Industry
  Newsletter
Mine Regulation Re-
  porter
Mini-Micro Systems
Minneapolis–St. Paul
  City Business
Minority Markets Alert
Mississippi Business
  Journal
MM&M Medical Mar-
  keting & Media
Mobile Communications
Mobile Data Report
Mobile Phone News
Mobile Satellite News
Mobile Satellite Reports
Modem User News
Modern Brewery Age
Modern Casting
Modern Machine Shop
Modern Materials
  Handling
Modern Office Technol-
  ogy
Modern Paint and
  Coatings
Modern Power Systems
Modern Tire Dealer
Money Laundering Alert
Montana Business
  Quarterly
Mortgage Banking
Mortgage Marketplace
Mortgage-backed
  Securities Letter
Motor Age

Motor Report Interna-
  tional
Multichannel News
Multimedia Publisher
Multimedia Week
Multimedia & Videodisc
  Monitor
Multinational Environ-
  mental Outlook
Multinational Service
The Music Trades
Nashville Business and
  Lifestyle
Nation's Business
Nation's Cities Weekly
Nation's Restaurant
  News
National Food Review
National Petroleum
  News
The National Public
  Accountant
National Real Estate
  Investor
National Report on
  Computers & Health
National Underwriter
  Life & Health
National Underwriter
  Property & Casualty
Navy News & Undersea
  Technology
NDT Update
NEC Weekly
Netline
Network Management
  Systems & Strategies

Network Monitor
Networks Update
New England Business
New Era Japan
New Food Products in
Japan
New Jersey Industry
Environmental Alert
New Materials Japan
New Media Markets
New Mexico Business
Journal
New Technology Week
Newsbytes News Network
Nitrogen
Nonwovens Industry
North American Report
on Free Trade
North Sea Letter
Northern Ontario
Business
NOTISUR—South
American & Caribbean
Political Affairs
NTIS Alert Foreign
Technology
NTIS Foreign Technology Newsletter
NTT Topics
NTT Weekly
Nuclear Waste News
Nursing Homes
Nursing Homes and
Senior Citizen Care
Oakland Business
Monthly
Occupational Hazards

Occupational Health &
Safety Letter
Ocean Industry
Octane Week
OECD Economic
Outlook
Ohio Business
Ohio Industry Environmental Advisor
Oil Express
The Oil and Gas Journal
Oil Price Information
Service
Oil Spill Intelligence
Report
Oil Spill US Law Report
Oilweek
Online
Online Libraries &
Microcomputers
Online Magazine
Online Newsletter
Online Product News
Open OSI Product &
Equipment News
Open Systems Communication
Open Systems Report
Optical Information
Systems
Optical Materials &
Engineering News
Optical Memory News
Orange County Business
Journal
Oregon Business
Orlando Business Journal
OTC Market Report
Update USA

OTC News & Market
Report
Oxy-fuel News
Ozone Depletion Network Online Today
Pacific Business News
Packaging
Packaging Week
Paper
Paper, Film and Foil
CONVERTER
Party and Paper Retailer
PC Business Products
PC Week
PCN News
PCS News
Pennsylvania Industry
Environmental
Advisor
Pension World
Periscope Daily Defense
News Capsules
Personal Computer
Markets
Personnel
Perspectives
Pesticide & Toxic
Chemical News
Petroleum Economist
Petroleum Independent
Petroleum Times
Pets-Supplies-Marketing
Pharmaceutical Business
News
Philadelphia Business
Journal
Phosphorous and Potassium

Photonics Spectra
Physician and
    Sportsmedicine
Pipe Line Industry
Pipeline
Pittsburgh Business
    Times
Planning
Plant Engineering
Plastics Engineering
Plastics Technology
Plastics World
Playthings
Political Risk Letter
Polymers Paint & Colour
    Journal
POS News
Potato Markets
Power in Asia
PR Newswire
Prepared Foods
Private Placement
    Reporter
Privatisation Interna-
    tional
Process Engineering
Process Industries
    Canada
Product Alert
Production
Productivity Software
Professional Builder
Professional Builder and
    Remodeler
Progressive Architecture
Progressive Grocer
PRS Automotive Service
PSA Journal

Public Broadcasting
    Report
Public Finance Washing-
    ton Watch
Public Relations Journal
Public Relations Review
Public Roads
Public Works
Puget Sound Business
    Journal
Pulp & Paper
Pulp & Paper Journal
Pulp and Paper Interna-
    tional
Purchasing
Purchasing World
Quarterly Review of
    Economics and
    Business
Quick Frozen Foods
    International
Quick Response News.
Railway Age
RBOC Update
Real Estate Today
Regulatory Compliance
    Watch
Report on AT&T
Report on the Austrian
    Economy
Report on Defense Plant
    Wastes
Report on IBM
Research Alert
Restaurant Business
    Magazine
Restaurant Hospitality

Restaurant-Hotel Design
    International
Restaurants & Institu-
    tions
Rig Market Forecast
Risk Management
Royal Bank of Scotland
    Review
RQ
RTC Watch
Rubber Trends
Rubber World
Russia Express Contracts
Russia Express–
    Perestroika: Executive
    Briefing
Russian Aerospace &
    Technology
Sales & Marketing
    Management
Sales Prospector
San Antonio Business
    Journal
San Diego Business
    Journal
San Francisco Business
    Times
Sarasota Magazine
Satellite Communications
Satellite News
Satellite TV Finance
Satellite Week
Screen Digest
Screen Finance
SDI Monitor
Security Management
Semiconductor Industry
    & Business Survey

Sensor Business Digest
Sensor Technology
Shooting Industry
Shopper Report
Skiing Trade News
Sludge
Small Computers in
    Libraries
SMT Trends
Soap Perfumery &
    Cosmetics
Soap-Cosmetics-Chemi-
    cal Specialties
Software Industry Report
Software Markets
Solid State Technology
Solid Waste Report
Sourcemex Economic
    News & Analysis on
    Mexico
South Dakota Business
    Review
South Magazine
Southern California
    Business
Southern Economic
    Journal
Southwest Journal of
    Business & Economics
Soviet Aerospace
Space Business News
Space Commerce Week
Space Exploration
    Technology
Space Station News
Special Libraries
Spectrum Report

St. Louis Business Journal
State Environment
    Report
State Telephone Regula-
    tion Report
STN
Skiing Trade News
Sub-Saharan Monitor
Successful Farming
Sulphur
Super Collider News
Superconductor Week
Superfund
Superfund Week
Supermarket Business
    Magazine
Supermarket News
Surface Modification
    Technology News
Survey of Current
    Business
swissBusiness
Systems Integration
Tactical Technology
Tampa Bay Business
    Journal
Tea and Coffee Trade
    Journal
Tech Europe
Technical Computing
Technology Access
    Report
Technology Alert
Technology Review
Tele-Service News
Telecom Markets
Telecommunications

Telecommunications
    Alert
Telephone IP News
Telephone News
Telephone Week
Telephony
Television Digest
Testing Technology
Texas Business Review
Texas Industry Environ-
    mental Alert
Thomson's International
    Banking Regulator
Thrift Liquidation Alert
Thrift Regulator
Tooling & Production
Topics in Health Care
    Financing
Toshiba Weekly
Toxic Materials News
Trading Systems Tech-
    nology
Traffic Management
Training & Development
    Journal
Training: the Magazine
    of Human Resources
    Development
Transport Europe
Travel Weekly
U.S. Distribution Journal
UK Venture Capital
    Journal
United States Banker
UNIX Update
Urban Transport News
US ITC Update

US Oil Week
US Rail News
USSR Economics &
   Foreign Trade
Utility Reporter Fuels
   Energy & Power
Venture Capital Journal
Video Marketing News
Video Marketing News-
   letter
Video Technology News
Video Week
Videonews International
ViewText
Voice Technology News
Wall Street Network
   News
Wall Street Transcript
   Digest

Ward's Auto World
Washington Beverage
   Insight
Washington Business
   Journal
Waste Information
   Digests
Waste Treatment
   Technology News
Week in Germany
Westchester County
   Business Journal
Wines & Vines
Wing Newsletter (Japan's
   Aerospace & Aviation
   Weekly)
Women's Wear Daily
World Accounting
   Report

World Airline News
World Bank Watch
World Economic Out-
   look
World Environment
   Report
World Insurance Corpo-
   rate Report
World Insurance Report
World Oil
World Tax Report
World Wood
Worldwide Biotech
Worldwide Databases
Worldwide Energy
Worldwide Telecom
Worldwide Videotex
   Update
Youth Markets Alert

Business Dateline   (GO BUSDATE) is a financial service that includes full text of articles from more than 115 regional business publications in the U.S. and Canada. See Company Reports. This service also is searchable through the IQuest gateway; see IQuest.

Business Demographics   (GO BUSDEM), based upon information from the U.S. Census Bureau and developed by a firm called Market Statistics, and intended to help businesses analyze their markets. Two types of reports are available:

- Business to Business Report includes information on all broad Standard Industrial Classification (SIC) categories, including the total number of employees in each category for a designated geographical area.
- Advertisers' Service Report includes data on businesses which comprise the SICs for Retail Trade.

Each report breaks down the total number of businesses for each specified geographical unit in relation to company size and may be requested by ZIP code, county, state, Metropolitan area, ADI (Arbitron TV Markets), DMA (Nielsen TV Markets), or the entire U.S. Reports are $10 for any geographical unit.

   For related services, see Demographics.

Business Directory, American,   can be searched through IQuest. See IQuest.

Business Economics   (**magazine**) articles are searchable through Magazine Database Plus (GO MDP) and through Business Database Plus. For details, see Magazine Database and Business Database.

Business and the Environment   (**database**) may be searched through the IQuest gateway. See IQuest.

Business & Health   (**magazine**) is searchable in the Health Database Plus (GO HLTBD). See Health.

Business Horizons   (**magazine**) is searchable through Magazine Database Plus (GO MDP). See Magazine.

Business Incorporating Guide (GO INC) is a store in the Electronic Mall (GO MALL) that offers nationwide incorporating. See Electronic Mall.

Business Link   (**magazine**) can be searched through the Business Database Plus (GO BUSDB). See Business Database.

Business Management InfoCenter, IQuest   (GO IQBUSINESS) is a Telebase Systems Incorporated gateway to specific information from databases covering management research, marketing studies, company ownership, mergers and acquisitions, and so on.

This is a surcharged gateway to bibliographic and full-text business information provided from magazines, books, and other published sources, and may be obtained from single-database or multi-database SmartSCAN searches.

Many of the references also are searchable through IQuest. In addition, searching of the research centers is similar to IQuest's procedure. (See IQuest.) And for information on other Telebase gateways, see Telebase Systems Incorporated.

The surcharge is $9 for the first 10 titles located, $9 for each additional 10 titles, and $3 for each abstract retrieved. A "SmartScan" for the databases costs $5. There is a $1 charges for a search that retrieves no titles.

Among the specialized services available are:

- ABI/INFORM, with abstracts dealing primarily with company, corporate, and industry management applications. ABI/INFORM, notes Schoenbrun, is a popular choice of those working in the insurance and personnel management fields.
- The full text of the Harvard Business Review, one of the most prestigious scholarly business journals in the world. The emphasis in this database is on applicable and theoretical management and is ideal for the practicing manager as well as the undergraduate or graduate business school student.

- PTS PROMT, considered to be one of the best sources of international business information anywhere, with more than 1,500 international business journals that offer summary abstracts online. Every facet of information is covered, including projections, market and industry share data, corporate structure and news, and trade literature.

Business Opportunities, Business Periodicals Index, and **Business Publisher** (databases) may be searched through the IQuest gateway. See IQuest.

Business Opportunities, ESP (in Africa & the Middle East, in Asia & the Pacific, in Latin America & the Caribbean) can be searched through the Business Database Plus (GO BUSDB). See Business Database.

Business Perspectives, Business Quarterly, Business Record (Des Moines), Business Month, Business Publisher, and **Journal of International Business Studies** (magazines) can be searched through Business Database Plus (GO BUSDB). See Business Database.

Business startups are discussed in the Working From Home Forum (GO WORK). See Working From Home.

Business 20 Plus Companies, American, can be searched through IQuest. See IQuest.

Business Week (magazine) may be searched through the IQuest gateway. See IQuest. It can also be searched through News Source USA (GO NEWSUSA); see News Souce. Article abstracts also can be searched through Computer Database Plus (GO COMPDB). See Computer Database Plus.

Business Wire (news) (GO TBW): Throughout each business day, the Business Wire brings online press releases, news articles, and other information from the world of business. Information on hundreds of different companies is transmitted daily. And for other business-related features, see Financial Services and see Investment Analysis Tools.

This resource also may be searched through IQuest (see IQuest) and through Newsgrid (see Newsgrid).

ButtonWare Incorporated Software is supported in the PC Vendor A Forum (GO PCVENA). See IBM Computers.

Buyer's Guide to Micro Software (database) may be searched through the IQuest gateway. See IQuest.

Buyer's Market from Ziff (GO BMC) is a store in the Electronic Mall (GO MALL). See Electronic Mall.

Buyouts **(magazine)** can be searched through the Business Database Plus (GO BUSDB). See Business Database.

Buzzworm: *The Environmental Journal* **(magazine)** can be searched in the Magazine Database Plus (GO MDP). See Magazine Database.

Byte **(magazine)** is searchable (abstracts) through Computer Database Plus (GO COMPDB). See Computer Database Plus.

C

C **(Microsoft software)** is supported in the Microsoft Languages Forum (GO MSLANG), the Borland C++ Forum (GO BCPPDOS), and Borland C++/Windows Forum (GO BCPPWIN). See Microsoft Software and see Borland. Also, *C Users Journal* can be searched through Computer Database Plus (GO COMPDB). See Computer Database Plus. And *Microsoft C, C++ Developers' Journal* and *Inside Turbo C++* are among the publications supported in the Cobb Group Programming Forum (GO ZNT:COBBPROG). See Cobb Group. Also C programming sections are supported in the Amiga Tech Forum (GO AMIGATECH) and in the Apple II Programmers Forum (GO APPROG). See Commodore and see Apple Computers. It also is supported in the Portable Programming Forum (GO CODEPORT). See Programmers Support.

Ca **(formerly Ca—A Cancer Journal for Clinicians)** is searchable in the Health Database Plus (GO HLTBD). See Health.

CAB Abstracts **(agriculture database)** may be searched through the IQuest gateway (GO IQUEST) and through the Knowledge Index (GO KI). See IQuest and see Knowledge Index.

Cable television issues are discussed in the Broadcast Professionals Forum (GO BPFORUM). See Broadcast. Also, it is a topic in the Consumer Electronics Forum (GO CEFORUM). See Electronics.

Cabletron Systems (GO CTRON) offers information and the corporate background on Cabletron, a manufacturer of computer networking hardware and network management software, including a list of sales offices, information about training and presentations, and the Cabletron Systems Forum (GO CTRONFORUM). Managing the forum are Dave Norton, Christine Marquis, Robert Tuohey, and David Turner.

Cactus Development Company **(products)** are supported in the Game Publishers C Forum (GO GAMCPUB). See Gaming Forums.

CAD/CAM (computer-aided design/manufacturing) is covered in a variety of features including:

- *CAD/CAM International* (magazine) is searchable (abstracts) through Computer Database Plus (GO COMPDB), as can *Cadcam* magazine. See Computer Database Plus. Also, the CAD/CAM Update (database) may be searched through the IQuest gateway. See IQuest. The resource also can be searched through the Business Database Plus (GO BUSDB). See Business Database.
- CADD/CAM/CAE Vendor Forum (GO CADDVEN), managed by the League for Engineering Automation Productivity, service supports computer-aided engineering, design, and manufacturing of hardware and software. The forum provides technical support, information on product upgrades, and new product announcements on companies such as Evolution Computing, ISICAD, Ashlar Inc., Intergraph/Bentley Systems, Cadkey Inc., ESRI, Altium, and Universal Technical Systems. Sysops of the forum include Evan Yares, Joe MacRae, and Brad Holtz.
- IBM CAD/CAM Information Exchange Forum (GO IBMENG) which is a link to the IBM CAD/CAM Technical Support team. Visitors are encouraged to ask any questions about managing their installations or the use of CADAM or CATIA. The primary sysop is Jerry Odell (72662,74) of the IBM engineering solutions technical support unit. See also CAM/CAD and see IBM computers.

Also, CAM/CAD is discussed in the Autodesk Forum (GO ADESK). See Autodesk Software, Cadence Forum (GO CADENCE) and Engineering Automation Forum (GO LEAP).

Cadence Forum (GO CADENCE) operated by *Cadence* magazine, a publication for the professional AutoCAD user. The forum is an electronic supplement of the magazine and an area for exchanging ideas and information on Autodesk's AutoCAD applications. The libraries contain Cadence code, AutoCAD utilities, product news, user tutorials, a user group exchange, and more. The message sections provide access to Cadence editors and writers, as well as other AutoCAD users and special guest experts. The primary sysop is Susan Shepard (76703,4326).

For related services, see CAD/CAM.

CADKEY Inc. (**software**) is supported in the CADD/CAM/CAE Vendor Forum (GO CADDVEN). See CAD/CAM.

CADVANCE is supported in the CADD/CAM/CAE Vendor Forum (GO CADDVEN). See CAD/CAM.

CadWare products are supported in the OS/2 Vendor Forum (GO OS2AVEN). See IBM Computers.

CAI ColorAge products are supported in the Desktop Publishing Vendor Forum (GO DTPVENDOR). For details, see Desktop Publishing.

CAI Forums   (GO CAI) operated by Computer Associates International to support its assorted products such as database management systems, business applications, and applicaton development software, including programs for mainframes, minis, and PCs. Among the company's PC systems are Clipper, a database management tool, the SuperCalc spreadsheet, the Cricket graphics programs, and the ACCPAC accounting packages. The sysop is Steve Silverwood (76703,3035), assisted by Steve Gilliard, Chiunglin Lin, Larry Eiss, Jim Jankay, Luiz Quintela, David Morgan, Clayton Neff, Larry Dysert, Glenn Scott, Don Caton, Tad Frysinger, Kent Kingery, Larry Rappaport, Steve Kolterman, Steven Rainess, Michael Duncan, Ranjit Ramakrishan, and Kevin Long. The forums include:

- Applications Development Forum (GO CAIDEV) for assort utilities and projects.
- The CA Clipper Forum (GO CLIPPER) to support the Clipper database management system, including the database language application development system for PC and PC-LAN installations.
- CA—Clipper Germany Forum (GO CLIPGER) for German-speaking users.
- CA Micro Germany Forum (GO CAMICRO) for the general computing needs of a Germany-speaking audience.
- CA—Simply Forum (GO CASIMPLY), supporting users of the firm's CA-Simply series of software applications.
- Productivity Solutions Forum (GO CAIPRO), support Cricket graphics, as well as SuperCalc, and other products.

Calera Recognition Systems Inc.   (products) are supported in the Windows 3rd-Party Forum (GO WINAPD). See Microsoft Software.

California   (news) is covered in the Fresno Bee, the Los Angeles Daily News, the Los Angeles Times, the Sacramento Bee, the San Francisco Chronicle, the San Francisco Examiner and the San Jose Mercury News, all searchable through Telebase System's News Source USA (GO NEWSUSA). See News Source.

Also, selected reports from California are included in the Western regional reports from United Press International. See Executive News Service. And through the Business Database Plus (GO BUSDB), you can search *The Business Journal Serving Greater Sacramento, The Business Journal—San Jose, California Business, California Management Review, California Public Finance, Los Angeles Business Journal, Oakland Business Monthly, Orange County Business Journal, San Diego Business Journal, San Francisco Business Times,* and *Southern California Business.* See Business Database.

California Forum   (GO CALFORUM) discusses California's history and future, sports and recreation, tourism, politics, and the arts. There are also message sections devoted to the northern and southern regions of the state, as well as the San Diego, San Francisco Bay, and Los Angeles basin areas. The forum is managed by Linda Woeltjen (76711,1142) and Bill Eastburn (70007,1657), with help from Lindsey Rush, Terese Gaugh, and Gretchen Beck.

California Public Finance (financial database) can be searched through IQuest. See IQuest. It also can be searched through the Business Database Plus (GO BUSDB). See Business Database.

CAM/CAD (computer-aided manufacturing/design) is discussed in various features. See CAD/CAM.

Camcorders, their purchase and their use, are discussed in the Consumer Electronics Forum (GO CEFORUM). See Electronics Forum.

Cameron, Jim (76703,3010) is sysop of the Journalism Forum (GO JFORUM). See Journalism and, for related features, see News, General.

CA Micro Germany Forum (GO CAMICRO) provides computer support for German-speaking users.

Campaign (British marketing database) may be searched through the IQuest gateway. See IQuest.

Campbell Services products are supported in the Windows 3rd-Party C Forum (GO WINAPC). See Microsoft Software.

Camping, hunting, and fishing are discussed in the Great Outdoors Forum (GO OUTDOORFORUM). See Sports and Recreation. Also, the Recreational Vehicle Forum (GO RVFORUM) discusses camping in tent trailers, travel trailers, fifth-wheels, and motor homes. See Recreational Vehicle.

Canada is a topic in the Travel Forum (GO TRAVSIG). See Travel.

Canada, Access from: For logon instruction on Canada's DataPac network, see DataPac.

Canadian business is covered in several areas:

- Business Database Plus (GO BUSDB) offers access to an assortment of business magazines, including *Canadian Business, Canadian Business Review, Canadian Chemical News, Canadian Dimension, Canadian Labour, Canadian Machinery and Metalworking, Canadian Occupational Health & Safety News, Industrial Relations (Canadian), Mergers & Acquisitions in Canada, Process Industries Canada.* Also available are: *Alberta Business, Food in Canada, Manitoba Business,* and *Northern Ontario Business.* See Business Database.

- Canadian Business and Current Affairs can be searched through the Knowledge Index (GO KI). See Knowledge Index.

- Canadian Datasystems and Computing Canada magazines are searchable through Computer Database Plus (GO COMPDB). See Computer Database Plus.

- IQuest databases are Cancorp, ICC Canadian Corporation Database, Canadian Business and Current Affairs, D&B—Canadian Dun's Market Identifiers, Sales Prospector/Canada (business databases), Canadian Business and Current Affairs, and BBC Summary of World Broadcasts. See IQuest.

Canadian history and ancestry are topics of the Genealogy Forum (GO ROOTS). See Genealogy.

Canadian Medical Association Journal abstracts are searchable in the Health Database Plus (GO HLTBD). See Health.

Cancer information is provided in a forum, while several databases provide information about cancer in its many forms:

- The Cancer Forum (GO CANCER) shares information and provides support for cancer patients and their friends and relatives. The forum is administered by John Ross (76703,551). His assistants are Gene Feaster, Roger Honkanen, John Deakin, Barbara L. Stone, and Jon Manchester. Support on the forum is also provided by the volunteers of the Cancer Hot Line in Kansas City.

- CancerLit, the National Cancer Institute's database of cancer information, includes more than 950,000 references and abstracts about cancer, with more than 7,000 new references being added each month. This is part of the Paperchase (GO PAPERCHASE) medical database. See Paperchase. This resource also can be searched through the Knowledge Index (GO KI). See Knowledge Index.

- Physicians Data Query (GO PDQ-1) is a collection of four surcharged databases copyrighted and published by the National Cancer Institute. The Consumer Cancer Information File contains material written for the laymen covering more than 80 forms of cancer, treatment alternatives, stage expectations, and general prognoses. Information is retrieved by entering the cancer name. The Professional Cancer Information File is written for the health care providers and contains current information on most major cancers. The information usually includes prognosis, stage-of-growth classifications with treatment options, and extensive bibliographies for further research. Information is retrieved by entering the cancer name. The Directory File is an organization directory that lists the name, address, parent, and subsidiary organizations of approximately 1,500 institutions having National Cancer Institute–designated cancer centers or other career-approved programs. The physicians directory contains names, addresses, and phone numbers of some 12,000 cancer specialists. The fourth database, The Protocol File, has data on 1,000 protocols for cancer treatment. The surcharges for the Consumer and Professional Cancer Information Files are $5 for the first 10 titles located, $5 for each additional 10 titles; for the Directory File, $7.50 for the first 10 titles located, $7.50 for each additional 10 titles; for the Protocol File, $2 for the first 10 titles located, $2 for each additional 10 titles and $2 for Full record selected from the headings. In each, there is a $1 for each search that retrieves no titles.

- Through IQuest gateway, searchable are Cancer Research Weekly and Cancerlit. See IQuest. *Cancer Weekly* also can be searched through the Business Database Plus (GO BUSDB). See Business Database. And *Cancer News*, *Cancer Weekly*, and *NCI Cancer Weekly* are searchable in the Health Database Plus (GO HLTBD), which also has abstracts of *Cancer* magazine and *Journal of the National Cancer Institute*.

See also Health and Medical references.

Canning industry is covered in *CCI—Canmaking & Canning International* magazine, which is searchable through the Business Database Plus (GO BUSDB). See Business Database.

Canon Support Forum (GO CANON) is operated by the firm to provide technical support for Canon brand printers, scanners, and other related products. It also offers information on product promotions, new product releases, and regional sales office and service facility telephone numbers and addresses.

The forum fields questions on product specifications, escape/error code information, and helpful product operation techniques from its data libraries, device driver files on Canon printers and scanners, and so on.

Administering the forum are Tim Venettozzi (76702,1473) and Cindy Lowell.

Canopus Research Forum (GO CANOPUS) is for discussion of information industry trends, technologies, and products. It also serves as an online newsletter (Canopus Report) with analysis, commentary, and reviews written by Canopus Research President William F. Zachmann (76004,3657). The forum's primary sysops are Bruce Biermann (71333,1077) and John Love (71333,1267), who are helped by Ken Parker.

Canter, Sheryl (72241,510) is sysop of the PC Magazine's Programming Forum (GO ZNT:PROGRAMMING). See PC Magazine.

Canyon Software Corp. products are supported in the OS/2 Vendor Forum (GO OS2AVEN). See IBM Computers.

Capital District Business Review (magazine) can be searched through the Business Database Plus (GO BUSDB). See Business Database.

Cap Weekly (magazine) can be searched through the Business Database Plus (GO BUSDB). See Business Database.

Cardfax (magazine) can be searched through the Business Database Plus (GO BUSDB). See Business Database.

Cardiology, American Journal of, is searchable in the Health Database Plus (GO HLTBD). See Health.

Card News (credit card industry database) may be searched through the IQuest gateway. See IQuest. It also can be searched through Business Database Plus (GO BUSDB). See Business Database.

Career Placement Registry (database) may be searched through the IQuest gateway. See IQuest.
    See also Employment.

Careers and the workplace are among the topics discussed in Information USA (GO INFOUSA). See Information.

Careertrack (GO CT) is a service provided through the Electronic Mall (GO MALL) that offers career and personal training programs. See Electronic Mall.

Care Management, Long Time (database) can be searched through IQuest. See IQuest. Also *Brown University Long-Term Care Letter*, *Brown University Long-Term Care Quality Letter*, and *Journal of Health Care Marketing* are searchable in the Health Database Plus (GO HLTBD). See Health.

Carey, Theresa W. (72241,237) is the sysop of the Computer Shopper Forum (GO ZNT:COMPSHOPPER). See Computer Shopper.

Caribbean Update (magazine) can be searched through the Business Database Plus (GO BUSDB), as well as *ESP—Business Opportunities in Latin America & the Caribbean* and *NOTISUR—South American & Caribbean Political Affairs*. See Business Database. The Caribbean is a topic in the Travel Forum (GO TRAVSIG). See Travel.

Carpal tunnel syndrome is the topic of the RSINews database, which can be searched through IQuest. See IQuest.

Carry Associates products are supported in the OS/2 Vendor Forum (GO OS2AVEN). See IBM Computers.

Cars are the topic of a number of services, from products by specific car makers to services that review and compare automobiles, including the Automobile Forum (GO CARS), see Automobile, and the Worldwide Car Network Forum (GO WWCAR), see Worldwide Car.
    Also, the New Car/Truck Showroom (GO NEWCAR) is a surcharged service that lets you view and compare features of passenger cars, vans, and trucks to help you make buying decisions. See New Car/Truck Showroom.
    Consumer Reports (GO CSR) also has automobile-related reviews (GO CRAUTO) prepared by the Consumers Union staff that publishes *Consumer Reports* magazine. See Consumer Reports.
    Also of interest are several stores in the Electronic Mall (GO MALL), including:

- Automobile Information Center (GO AI), wholesale/retail prices from 1978.

- Autoquot-R (GO AQ), vehicle price quotes.
- Autovantage Online (GO AV).
- Buick Magazine, which that offers car information, customer service, and so on.
- Ford Cars & Trucks (GO FD) for car and truck information, dealer locations, and so on.
- Ford Motor Co. (GO FMC), which offers car and truck information, dealer locator, and so on.
- Lincoln/Mercury Showroom (GO LM), for model information, location of dealers, etc.

See Electronic Mall.

Automobile information is also offered by a variety of other services:

- Some airline travel services provide information on rental cars. See Airlines.
- A category in the CompuServe Classifieds lets you read and post ads regarding cars and recreational vehicles. See Classifieds Service.
- On the subject of car racing, the Motor Sports Forum (GO RACING) invites visitors to talk about past races and learn about upcoming races throughout the world. For details, see Sports and Recreation.
- Recreational vehicles (RVs) are a topic of the Recreational Vehicle Forum (GO RVFORUM). See Recreational Vehicle.
- The Detroit Free Press Forum (GO DETROIT), is a resource for international automative information and photography. See Detroit Free Press.
- IQuest provides access to several car-related databases, including Autoparts Report, Battery & EV Technology, PRS World Automotive News Service, and SIS Automotive Industry Abstracts. See IQuest.
- *Car and Driver, Motor Trend, Off Road,* and *Road & Track* (magazines) are searchable through Magazine Database Plus (GO MDP). For details see Magazine Database. See also Cars.
- *Battery & EV Technology* and *Ward's Auto World* can be searched through the Business Database Plus (GO BUSDB), as can *PRS Automotive Service.* See Business Database.
- Model-car building is discussed in Model Forum (GO MODELNET). See ModelNet.

Cartooning is a topic of the Comics/Animation Forum (GO COMICS). See Comics. Cartoons also are featured in several of the graphics forums. See Graphics.

CASE DCI Forum (GO CASEFORUM), sponsored by Digital Consulting, Inc. is an independent information exchange. The central issues of the forum are methods and tools used to improve the quality of software development. The primary sysop is Warren Keuffel (76702,525), assisted by Rich Cohen and Mark Weisz.

CA Search (chemical database) may be searched through the IQuest gateway. See IQuest.

CASE Strategies (database) may be searched through the IQuest gateway. See IQuest. It also can be searched through the Business Database Plus (GO BUSDB). See Business Database.

CASE ToolWorks software is supported in the Computer Language Forum (GO CLMFORUM). See Computer Language.

Casio systems are supported in the Palmtop Forum (GO PALMTOP). See Palmtop.

Castlequest (game) (GO CQUEST) challenges you to search the castle, find the master, and deal with him as needed, while looting the castle of its treasures. You get points for depositing the treasures in the vault. The game is intended for those age 12 and up. This is one of the system's basic services, meaning those signed up under the Standard Pricing Plan (see Billing) have unlimited access to the feature. For information on other games, see Games.

Casting, Modern (magazine) can be searched through the Business Database Plus (GO BUSDB). See Business Database.

Cats are regularly discussed in the Pets and Animals Forum (GO PETS). For details, see Pets.

Caves, wrecks, and (underwater) caverns are topics in the Scuba Forum (GO DIVING). See Sports and Recreation.

CB Forum (GO CBFORUM) is an online bulletin board/library for regulars on the real-time CB Simulator. It specializes in teaching people how to use the CompuServe real-time talk medium. The sysop is Pat Phelps, a/k/a LooLoo in the CBing world (70006,522).

CB Simulator (GO CB) enables those online to "talk" to each other in real-time by typing their messages on the keyboard and reading replies on the screen. CB provides three "bands" of numbered channels (the General CB Band, Adult I CB Band and Adult II CB Band) where talkers identify themselves by handles. In addition, the system automatically assigns each talker a *job number* that can be used with paging and other commands, such as those for private group talks. Users may talk and listen on one channel and monitor the conversations on one or two additional channels. To talk on the CB channels, simply enter a message and press RETURN. When someone types a message and presses RETURN, it appears to the other users logged on or monitoring that channel as something like this: "(3-205,Bluegrass) Hi folks. Good to see all of you!" The first number is the channel number (1-36), then the *job number* assigned by the system, the talkers's handle, and his or her message.

The CompuServe Information Manager platforms provide special split-screen displays to facilitate CB talking along with pull-down menus or icons for various functions such as getting lists of other users online, sending private talk requests, squelching incoming message for specific other users, and so on. See your users manual for details on conferencing with CIM. For non-CIM users, to enter commands, precede them with a slash (/) in the first position of a new line. All conferencing commands may be abbreviated to the slash and the first three letters.

When visiting CB, you are greeted by an introductory menu, then a subsequent message prompts you to enter your handle. Your handle may be up to 19 characters, but may not include either an asterisk (*) or a pound sign (#). After you have entered your choice, the system checks its files to make sure your handle has not already been reserved by someone else. If it finds a problem, it asks you to pick another name.

Once you have entered an accepted handle, the system reports how many people are on the 36 channels and asks what channel you wish to visit. Some channels are loosely dedicated for specific uses. Channel 1 is called the adult channel, channel 6 is "The French Connection," channel 7 is for young adults, channel 9 is "The Summit," channel 13 is the "gender alternatives" channel, channel 15 is called "Habla Espanol," channel 16 is "The Flamingo Lounge," channel 17 is the youth center, channel 22 is for seniors, channel 23 is "the Knights of Olde" channel (for CB'ing old-timers), channel 29 is the poetry corner, channel 33 is the "alternative lifestyles" channel—primarily for gays, and channel 34 is called "The Porch." All others are unassigned.

When you enter the number the channel to which you wish to tune, you begin seeing incoming messages from others already talking there.

Acronyms Many of the messages on the conferencing use abbreviations for standard phrases. For more on this, see Acronyms.

CB Club A favorite handle may be reserved so that you are the only CB Simulator visitor who can ever use it. The option is a feature of CompuServe's "CB Club," which also provides regulars with an optional pricing plan. To join the club, you pay a monthly fee. To check out details, enter GO CBCLUB. See Entertainment Center.

CIM Users Sending a message requires merely typing in the special split screen and pressing RETURN. The transmitted message appears in the upper screen along with those coming in from others on the channel. Other options on your CIM desktop provide commands for monitoring and tuning to other channels, squelching other talkers so that you don't see their messages, getting lists of other CBers on your channel or on the entire band, talking privately with other CBers, and more. Specific procedures for these and related functions vary depending on which CIM platform and which version of the software you are using. See your users manual for the specifics.

Non-CIM Commands If you are using a non-CIM terminal package, you can enter /HELP on any channel for a list of the latest commands.

CB Society News
(GO CUP), also known as Cupcake's CB Society, is the CB Simulator's society pages. Cupcake, a New York CB enthusiast named Terry A.

Biener, has been writing monthly columns for years about all the CB goings-on. On her menu, you can read the current issue and back issues, take part in surveys, and tell her your own news. To reach it, enter GO CUP from any CompuServe ! prompt (or /GO CUP from one of the CB channels).

cc:Mail   **(software)** is supported in the Lotus Communication Forum (GO LOTUSCOMM). See Lotus.

CCML AIDS articles (GO AIDSNEWS) is supplied in the Comprehensive Core Medical Library (GO AIDSNEWS). See AIDS.

CD **(compact disk)** technology is the topic of several features.

The CDROM Forum (GO CDROM) is the gathering place for fans as well as those who are merely curious about the technology. The forum is operated by the Optical Publishing Association of Columbus, Ohio, in cooperation with Metatec/ Discovery Systems, a CD-ROM mastering and replication facility located in Dublin, Ohio. Rich Bowers (71333,1114), executive director of the Optical Publishing Association, is a sysop. He is assisted by Steve Luper (also known as "Lupes," which is pronounced "Loops").

Also, the CD-ROM Vendors Forum (GO CDVEN) supports various makers and sellers of CD-ROM products. Vendors include Creative Multimedia Corp., Bureau of Electronic Publishing, Bowker Electronic Publishing (becoming known as Reed Reference Electronic Publishing), Trantor Systems, Meridian Data, Nimbus Information Systems, Online Computer Systems, Monitor Information Services, Multimedia Monitor (Future Systems Inc.), One-Off CD Shops, Best Photo Labs, QuickScan, ZCI Inc., and Compton's NewMedia.

Also:

- CD Computing News and CD-ROM Databases are searchable through IQuest. See IQuest. They also can be searched through the Business Database Plus (GO BUSDB), as can CD-ROM Librarian and CD-ROM Professional. See Business Database.

- CD-ROM Store (GO RS) is a store in the Electronic Mall (GO MALL) that offers CD-ROM drives and accessories. See Electronic Mall.

- Kodak CD Forum (GO KODAK) is devoted to that company's CD products and technology, and other closely related products. See Kodak.

- Multimedia Forum (GO MULTIMEDIA) covers video, audio, animation, interface design, music, hypertext, entertainment, and more. See Multimedia.

Celex   **(European business database)** may be searched through the IQuest gateway. See IQuest.

Cellular phones are covered in the Telecommunications Forum (GO TELECOM) and the Consumer Electronics (GO CEFORUM) Forum. See Telecommunications. For related topics, visit the Broadcast Professionals Forum (GO BPFORUM). See Broadcast.

Cellular Sales and Marketing (database) may be searched through the IQuest gateway. See IQuest. Also, *Cellular Business* magazine can be searched through the Business Database Plus (GO BUSDB). See Business Database. See also Telelocator Bulletin.

Censorship is a topic of the Literary Forum (GO LITFORUM) and in the ShowBiz Forum (GO SHOWBIZ). See Literature and Showbiz.

Census data (GO CENDATA) is a nonsurcharged service of the U.S. Census Bureau that includes reports on population, manufacturing, foreign trade, agriculture, business, and so on. It is menu-driven. CENDATA is a frequently updated service that also provides a "what's new" feature, accessible from the main menu, to help you keep up on the latest additions. The Cendata database also is accessible through IQuest (GO IQUEST). See IQuest.

For other demographics services, see Demographics.

Center for Electronic Art products are supported in the Multimedia Vendor Forum (GO MULTIVEN). See Multimedia.

Central America Update (magazine) can be searched through the Business Database Plus (GO BUSDB), as can *Executive Briefing Service North & Central America*. See Business Database. Central American also is a topic in the International Trade Forum (GO TRADE). See International Trade. Central America also is a topic in the Travel Forum (GO TRAVSIG). See Travel.

Central Coast Software products are supported in the Amiga Vendor Forum (GO AMIGAVENDOR). See Commodore Computers.

Central Point Software Forums (GO CENTRAL) support the software published by that Beaverton, Oregon, firm, including PC Tools Deluxe, Mac Tools Deluxe, Central Point Backup, and Copy II. The forums operated by the company's technical support department are:

- Central Point DOS Forum (GO CPSDOS) for Central Point Software DOS applications.
- Central Point Win/Mac Forum (GO CPSWINMAC) for Central Point Software Windows and Macintosh applications.

Sections are divided by product line, with support sections for each product plus sections for suggesting enhancements and communicating with the customer service department. The sysop of the forums is Larry Beck (75300,1172), who is helped by Sam Guidice, Kim Ritchey, Kim Sell, and Eric Watson.

Ceramics News, High Tech (database) may be searched through the IQuest gateway. See IQuest. The resource also can be searched through the Business Database Plus (GO BUSDB), as can *Ceramic Industry*, *Advanced Ceramics Report*, and *Japanese New*

Materials High-Performance Ceramics. See Business Database.
  Ceramics also are discussed in Crafts Forum (GO CRAFTS). See Crafts.

Ceranski, Mike   (71333,11) is sysop of the Dvorak Development Forum (GO DVORAK). See Dvorak Development.

CE Software is supported in the Mac A Vendor Forum (GO MACAVEN). See Apple Computers.

Chain Store Age (database) may be searched through the IQuest gateway. See IQuest. It also can be searched through Business Database Plus (GO BUSDB). See Business Database.

Challenge (magazine) can be searched through the Business Database Plus (GO BUSDB). See Business Database.

Challenge Board, The National Modem-to-Modem Game Players' (GO CHALLENGE) was created to allow owners of modem-to-modem computer games to find opponents in their local calling area. See Modem-to-Modem Games.

Changing Times (magazine) is searchable through Magazine Database Plus (GO MDP). For details see Magazine Database.

Channelmarker Letter (magazine) can be searched through the Business Database Plus (GO BUSDB). See Business Database.

Chapman, Michael   (76004,2310) is the primary sysop of the Quarterdeck Office Systems Forum (GO QUARTERDECK). See Quarterdeck.

Charges, CompuServe   (GO RATES) provides a multifunction menu that allows you to look at your latest charges, to check news on surcharges, and so on. See Billing Information.

Charlotte (NC) Observer   (newspaper) is searchable through Telebase System's News Source USA (GO NEWSUSA) and through the Knowledge Index (GO KI). See News Source and see Knowledge Index.
  Also, *The Business Journal Serving Charlotte and the Metropolitan Area* magazine can be searched through the Business Database Plus (GO BUSDB). See Business Database.

Chart   (software) is supported in the Microsoft Application Forum (GO MSAPP). See Microsoft Software.

Checkbook Balancer Program   (GO CHECKBOOK) provides a way to keep your checkbook accounting system online, entering debits and credits. You may read the documentation about the program online or obtain printed documentation for the program at current line printer charges.

Checkfree Corporation (GO CF) is a store in the Electronic Mall (GO MALL) that offers an electronic payment service. See Electronic Mall. For Checkfree billing information (putting your CompuServe expenses on that system), enter GO CHECKFREE.

Checkmate and **Checkmate-GL** (software) is supported in the PC Vendor A Forum (GO PCVENA). See IBM Computers.

Checkwrite Plus (software) is supported in the Meca Software Forum (GO MECA). See Meca.

Chef's Catalog (GO CC) is a store in the Electronic Mall (GO MALL) that offers cookware and kitchen accessories. See Electronic Mall.

Chemistry is a topic in the Science/Math Education Forum (GO SCIENCE). For details, see Science/Math.

Also:

- Through IQuest (see IQuest), a number of databases provide chemical identification, including Analytical Abstracts, CA Search, Chapman and Hall Chemical Database, Chemname, Chemplant Plus, Chemsearch, Claims/Compound Registry, Hazardline, Janssen, Kirk-Othmer Encyclopedia of Chemical Technology, Merck Index Online, TOXLINE, and TSCA Chemical Substances Inventory.

- Also on IQuest are these additional databases related to chemistry and chemical engineering: Chemical Abstracts Source Index, Chemical Business Newsbase, Chemical Engineering, Chemical Engineering & Biotechnology Abstracts (CEBA), Chemical Industry Notes, Chemical Monitor, Chemical Safety Newsbase, CIM, Comline Japan Daily: Chemicals, East European Monitor—The Chemical Industry Database, Engineered Materials Abstracts, European Chemical News, Food Science and Technology Abstracts, KOSMET, PASCAL, TSCA Chemical Substances Inventory, and World Surface Coatings Abstracts.

- Through the Business Database Plus (GO BUSDB), several relevant magazines are searchable, including Chemical Business, Chemical Marketing Reporter, Chemical Monitor, Chemical Process Safety Report, Chemical Week, Chemistry and Industry, Electronic Chemicals News, Manufacturing Chemist, and Pesticide & Toxic Chemical News. See Business Database.

- Through the Knowledge Index (GO KI) you can search Analytical Abstracts, The Agrochemicals Handbook, Chapman and Hall Chemical Database, Chemical Business Newsbase, Chemical Engineering and Biotechnology Abstracts, and Kirk-Othmer Online. See Knowledge Index.

Cheque-It-Out (software) is supported in the PC Vendor C Forum (GO PCVENC). See IBM Computers.

Chess Forum (GO CHESSFORUM) provides casual matches as well as tournaments. Also in the forum, the U.S. Chess Federation is offering rated games to members who join the USCF on a six-month trial basis for $9.95 (regularly $30 per year). For related topics, see Games. The chief sysop is Patricia Fitzgibbons (76703,657), also known on the system as "Nightshift." She is also sysop of the games forum (GO GAMERS). She is assisted by John Rummel and Chris Thibodeau. The forum also has a staff of online chess coaches to help visitors with the game.

Chess games also are played in the Entertainment Center (GO ECENTER). See Entertainment Center.

Chest magazine is searchable in the Health Database Plus (GO HLTBD). See Health.

Cheyenne Software products are supported in the IBM PC Vendor G Forum (GO PCVENG). See IBM Computers.

Chicago (magazine) can be searched in the Magazine Database Plus (GO MDP). See Magazine Database. Also, The Chicago Tribune is searchable through Telebase System's News Source USA (GO NEWSUSA) and through the Knowledge Index (GO KI). See News Source and see Knowledge Index.

Child Abuse and Neglect, published by the U.S. Department of Health and Human Services, is accessible through the Legal Research Center (GO LEGALRC). For details, see Legal Research. This resource also may be searched through IQuest. See IQuest.

Child behavior is covered in *Brown University Child and Adolescent Behavior Letter* and *Brown University Child Behavior and Development Letter*, searchable in the Health Database Plus (GO HLTBD). See Health.

Child development and parenting is a topic of the Education Forum (GO EDFORUM). See Education.

Child Health Alert is searchable in the Health Database Plus (GO HLTBD), as is *Pediatric Report's Child Health Newsletter*. Also searchable there are abstracts from *American Journal of Diseases of Children* and *Archives of Diseases in Childhood*. See Health.

Children, Missing: Missing Children Database, an effort by the National Child Safety Council, is the oldest and largest U.S. nonprofit organization entirely dedicated to the safety of children and is supported in the free Missing Children Forum (GO MISSING). The forum, part of CompuServe's graphics forum network (see Graphics), contains descriptions and computerized pictures of missing children. If you can identify a person in this database, you are asked to call National Child Safety Council, 800-222-1464 (in Michigan, call 517-764-6070).

Children's Business (magazine) can be searched through the Business Database Plus (GO BUSDB). See Business Database.

Children Today (magazine) can be searched in the Magazine Database Plus (GO MDP). See Magazine Database.

Chinese news is the specialty of Xinhua, an international news service that is searchable through Comtex Scientific Inc.'s NewsGrid database. For details, see NewsGrid.

    Also, Patent Abstracts of China may be searched through the IQuest gateway. See IQuest.

ChipSoft Support Forum (GO CHIPSOFT) supports that firm's line of DOS, Windows, and Macintosh products. The forum is operated by Linda Payne (76004,3107), with the assistance of Renard Wynn and Roy Army.

Chiropractic, Journal of abstracts are searchable in the Health Database Plus (GO HLTBD). See Health. Also, chiropractic medicine is discussed in the Holistic Health Forum (GO HOLISTIC). See Holistic Health.

Chlor-Alkali Marketwire (magazine) can be searched through the Business Database Plus (GO BUSDB). See Business Database.

Christian Education is a topic in the IBM/Special Needs Forum (GO IBMSPECIAL). See Handicapped.

Christianity is regularly discussed in the Religion Forum (GO RELIGION). See Religion.

Christian Science Monitor (newspaper) is searchable through Telebase System's News Source USA (GO NEWSUSA) and through the Knowledge Index (GO KI). See News Source and see Knowledge Index.

Church News International (database) may be searched through the IQuest gateway. See IQuest. See also Religion.

CIC (software) is supported in the Pen Technology Forum (GO PENFORUM). For more information, see Pen Technology.

Cigars and pipes are among topics discussed in the Bacchus Wine Forum (GO WINEFORUM). See Wine.

CIM Support Forums (GO CIMSUPPORT, GO MCIMSUP, and GO WCIMSUP) are free forums that serve users of the CompuServe Information Manager software. See CompuServe Information Manager.

CIM (database on hydraulic binders, cements, chalks and lime, plaster, and allied fields) can be searched through IQuest. See IQuest. The resource also can be searched through the Business Database Plus (GO BUSDB). See Business Database.

CIME (magazine) is searchable (abstracts) through Computer Database Plus (GO COMPDB). See Computer Database Plus.

Cincinnati/Kentucky Post (newspaper) is searchable through Telebase System's News Source USA (GO NEWSUSA). See News Source.

Also, *Cincinnati Business Courier* magazine can be searched through the Business Database Plus (GO BUSDB). See Business Database.

Cinema, Magill's Survey of (GO MAGILL) contains descriptions of most major films from 1902 to the present. See Magill's Survey of Cinema. See also Reviews, Movies.

CIS Economics & Foreign Trade (magazine) can be searched through the Business Database Plus (GO BUSDB). See Business Database.

Cititronics (GO CTR) is a store accessible through the Electronic Mall (GO MALL) that offers computer memories. See Electronic Mall.

Citizen Emergency Center maintains the The U.S. Department of State's Travel Advisory Service (GO STATE) as a continuously updated information service to Americans traveling abroad. See U.S. Government Information.

City & County, American (magazine) is searchable in both Magazine Database Plus (GO MDP) and Business Database Plus (GO BUSDB). For details, see Magazine Database and see Business Database.

Civil Engineering is covered in some databases on IQuest (GO IQUEST) including Compendex Plus, Engineered Materials Abstracts, and Engineering News Record. See IQuest.

See also Engineering.

Civil War is a topic of the Military Forum (GO MILITARY) managed by long-time Civil War enthusiast David Woodbury. Also, the Civil War also is a favorite topic in the Genealogy Forum (GO ROOTS).

Claims and patent data are searchable in several IQuest resources, including Claims/Citation (1971 to the present), Claims/Compound Registry, Claims/Reassignment & Reexamination, Claims/Reference, Claims/U.S. Patent Abstracts, and Claims/U.S. Patent Abstracts Weekly. See IQuest. Also see Patents.

Clarion Software Forum (GO CLARION) offers technical support for the firm's products such as Clarion Database Developer V3.x, Clarion Professional Developer V2.x, the TopSpeed Compilers (C, C++, Modula 2, Pascal), Report Writer, Personal Manager (Personal Developer), and all the Clarion LEMs (Language Extension Modules).

Also supported are discussion topics covering Clarion's products as well as suggestions for the company's Research & Development area, sales and service inquiries, and third-party vendors. Libraries include extended documentation, technical bulletins, program samples and examples, demos, and utilities.

The sysops are Greg Whitaker (76711,1035) and Paul Schomaker (76711,1034). Assisting them are Scott Ferrett, Steve Bellamy and David Buchler.

Clarion Tech Journal is supported in the IBM PC Vendor D Forum (GO PCVEND). See IBM Computers.

Claris Corp. forums (GO CLARIS) supports the company's application software titles for Macintosh and other operating systems. Among them are FileMaker, ClarisWorks, HyperCard, MacWrite, MacProject/SF, Resolve, AppleWorks, and more. These areas are an excellent resource when looking for files, technical support, or discussion about products from Claris. The features are Claris Macintosh Forum (GO MACCLARIS) and the Claris Windows Forum (GO WINCLARIS), covering cross-platform issues. The feature also offers the TechInfo Database (GO CLATECH) for searchable information. The primary sysop of the forums is Lydia Nicholson (76004,1614). She is assisted by Peter Haase and Akilan Kapilan.

Clark, Ron (76702,1601) is the primary sysop of the Dell Forum (GO DELL). See Dell.

Clark, Spencer (76702,1713) is a sysop of McAfee Virus Help Forum (GO VIRUSFORUM). See McAfee.

Classic Quotes (game) (GO TMC-45) part of the Multiple Choice trivia games. For information on other games, see Games.

Classical music is a subject of the Music/Performing Arts Forum (GO MUSICARTS). See Music.

Classifieds Service (GO CLASSIFIEDS) is a classified advertisement section, where users may buy, sell, swap, or give away goods and services. This is one of the system's basic services, meaning those signed up under the Standard Pricing Plan (see Billing) have unlimited access to the feature. Reading messages is free; posting an ad is surcharged.

To read existing ads, start by selecting from these categories:

1. Employment/Education
2. Job Search (E-Span)
3. DOS Computer/Software/Accessories
4. Apple/Mac Computers/Software
5. Other Computers/Software
6. Business Services/Investments
7. Travel
8. Real Estate
9. Cars/Boats/Planes/RVs/Cycles
10. Electronics/Hobbies/Collectibles
11. Occasions/Announcements/Reunion
12. Miscellaneous Info/Merchandise

Each is further divided into subsections. Real Estate, for instance, is broken down into business/commercial, residential, and vacation homes. Employment/education has specific areas dedicated to positions wanted, computer-related positions, other positions open, employment services, educational opportunities, and positions at CompuServe.

After you have selected a subtopic, you are shown a menu of available ads with a 40-character subject description. Read the accompanying text, and then you can immediately send a reply or make a note of the classifieds number for responding later with the "Reply to an Ad" option from the main menu. Either way, your comments or questions will be sent to the poster's CompuServe Mail box.

To enter a classified ad, select "Submit an Ad" from the main menu. Pick the category and subcategory that best matches your entry, and you are prompted for the subject used by readers in the Browse mode. The ad itself is limited to 25 lines.

The cost depends on the size of the message and the length of time it will be on display. A one-line ad (70 characters) for seven days is priced at $1, while 14 days is $1.50.

Also, a part of Classifieds is **E-Span JobSearch** (GO ESPAN), an employment advertising network that provides job listings for a variety of career fields and geographic locations. For details, see E-Span. See also Bartering.

Classroom Computer Learning (magazine) is searchable through Computer Database Plus (GO COMPDB). See Computer Database Plus.

Clay working is a topic of the Crafts Forum (GO CRAFTS). See Crafts.

Clean Air Network Online Today (magazine) can be searched through the Business Database Plus (GO BUSDB). See Business Database.

Clean Tech News and Policy Outlook (database on cleanser industry) can be searched through IQuest. See IQuest.

Clean-up (software) is supported in the McAfee Virus Help Forum (GO VIRUSFORUM). See McAfee.

Clear & Simple Inc. products are supported in the OS/2 Vendor Forum (GO OS2AVEN). See IBM Computers.

Cleveland, Ohio, news is covered in the Cleveland (OH) Plain Dealer, searchable through Telebase System's News Source USA (GO NEWSUSA). See News Source. Business news is reported in *Crain's Cleveland Business* magazine, which can be searched through the Business Database Plus (GO BUSDB). See Business Database.

Clipper (database software) is supported in the CAI Forums (GO CAI) operated by Computer Associates International. See CAI.

Clipper Advisor Magazine is supported in the Data Based Advisor Forum (GO DBADVISOR). See Data Based Advisor.

Clipping folder (electronic) is the computer term for a service that allows you to have the system automatically save information for you as it comes in from a news wire service or database. You set up the clipping folder by specifying keywords for the subjects in which you are interested as well as the specific wires you wish monitored. The system then "clips" and saves stories for you while you are not online so that you may examine them during a later session. Such clipping folders are supported in the Executive News Service (GO ENS). See Executive News for details.

Clothing products are offered for sale in some Electronic Mall stores (GO MALL), including Americana Clothing (GO AC), Brooks Brothers (GO BR), JC Penney Online Catalog (GO JCP), Lands' End (GO LA), L'eggs Hanes Store (GO LEGGS), Patagonia (GO PG), and Paul Fredrick Shirt Co. (GO PFS). See Electronic Mall.

Clubs and memberships are offered in a number of Electronic Mall stores (GO MALL), including Columbia House Music (GO CH) and Shoppers Advantage Club (GO SAC) for discount shopping. See Electronic Mall for more information.

Clyman, John (72241,1365) is one of the editors and writers associated with the PC Magazine forums. See PC Magazine.

CMC products are supported in the Music Vendor Forum (GO MUSICVEN). See Music.

.CNF, .CO, or .CON as extensions on filenames in forum libraries, usually stand for a conference transcript, discussions that occurred in the real-time conferencing section of the system. For related topics, see Files, Extensions.

Coal & Synfuels Technology and **Coal Outlook** (databases) may be searched through the IQuest gateway. See IQuest. They also can be searched through Business Database Plus (GO BUSDB), as can *International Coal Report*. See Business Database. See also Energy.

Coatings and surface technology is reported in several journals in the Business Database Plus (GO BUSDB), including *The Journal of Coatings Technology*, *Advanced Coatings & Surface Technology*, *American Paint & Coatings Journal* and *Modern Paint and Coatings*. See Business Database.

COBAL (Microsoft software) is supported in the Microsoft Languages Forum (GO MSLANG). See Microsoft Software. For related topics, see Programmers Support. Cobal also is discussed in the Micro Focus Forum (GO MICROFOCUS). See Micro Focus.

Cobb Group Forums, provided through ZiffNet (see ZiffNet), offer a variety of computer technical support. The forums include:

- Cobb Applications Forum (GO ZNT:COBBAPP), built on information from five print publications, including *The 1-2-3 User's Journal, Inside 1-2-3 Version 3.1, The DOS Authority, Inside DOS*, and *Inside Microsoft Windows*. The forum offers technical support, information services, and downloadable software. The sysop is Chris Kinsman (76701,154), assisted by Lotus 1-1-3 expert Bob Quinn and DOS/Windows experts Doug Chamberlin and Dan Crawford.

- Cobb Group Programming Forum (GO ZNT:COBBPROG) provides access to all of the code listings that appear in the Cobb programming journals. Kinsman also is the sysop there. Cobbs Group journals covered in this forum include *Inside Turbo C++, Microsoft C, C++ Developers' Journal, Inside Microsoft BASIC, Inside Visual BASIC, Inside QuickBASIC, Inside Turbo Pascal, Inside Turbo C, Paradox Users' Journal, Paradox Developers' Journal*, and *The DOS Authority*. Code listings can be downloaded from any of six libraries organized by programming language (BASIC, C/C++, Pascal, and so forth).

Cockwell, Steve (76711,563) is sysop of the Corel Forum (GO COREL). See Corel.

Coda Music Technology (products) are supported in the MIDI B Vendor Forum (GO MIDIBVEN). See Music.

CodeHead Software products are supported in the Atari Vendors Forum (GO ATARIVEN). See Atari Computers.

CODEPORT, The Portable Programming Forum (GO CODEPORT) is sponsored by USUS, the UCSD Pascal System Users' Society for discussion of topics related to Pascal, Apple Pascal, Modula-2, and similar software systems. See Programmers Support.

Coffee Anyone ??? (GO COF) is a store in the Electronic Mall (GO MALL) that offers coffee shipped within 48 hours. See Electronic Mall. See also Green Mountain Coffee Roasters (GO GMR).

Coffeeline (database) may be searched through the IQuest gateway. See IQuest. See also Food.

Cogent Data Technologies products are supported in the IBM PC Vendor G Forum (GO PCVENG). See IBM Computers.

Cognetics products are supported in the Multimedia Vendor Forum (GO MULTIVEN). See Multimedia.

Coin collecting is a topic in the Collectibles Forum (GO COLLECT). See Collectibles.

Colburn, Don (76703,4160) is sysop of the CSI Forth Net (GO FORTH). See Programmers Support.

COLD (**Antarctic region database**) may be searched through the IQuest gateway. See IQuest.

Collectibles Forum (GO COLLECT) covers some of the country's faster growing hobbies. Coin and stamp collecting are major topics here, but the forum actually is devoted to all kinds of collectibles, including baseball cards, autographs, books, and more. Stamp dealer Dave Cunningham (76702,453), the administrator, operates a computer business and a stamp and coin store. Assisting is Errol Osteraa, with section leaders Dudley Bauerlein (stamps), Russell Freeland (nonsports and comics), Bob Foppiano and Bijan Anvar (coins and currency), Jim Gallucci (sports card trading), Ron Abler (other collectibles), Robin O'Hair (books and media), Matt Mrowicki (autographs), Ron Szypajlo and Kevin Daly (sports memorabilia), Carolyn Andre (music collectibles), Craig Clarke (dolls and figurines), and Harold J. Day (ANA money bytes).

In addition, a category in the CompuServe Classifieds lets you read and post ads regarding collectibles. See Classifieds Service.

College Database, Peterson's (GO PETERSON) contains descriptions of more than 3,400 accredited or approved U.S. and Canadian colleges that grant associate and/or bachelor's degrees. See Peterson's. And for other education-related services, see Education and Students' Forum.

Collegiate Sports Network, NCAA (GO NCAA) provides by menu collections of sports statistics, scores, men's and women's basketball schedule information, assorted news releases and sports polls, as well as information on the NCAA visitors center and other news from the college sports world. See also Sports and Recreation.

Colonel Video & Audio (GO CVA) is a store in the Electronic Mall (GO MALL) specializing in home electronics of all kinds.

Colorado (**news**) is covered in the Denver Rocky Mountain News, searchable through Telebase System's News Source USA (GO NEWSUSA). See News Source.

Also:

- Selected reports from Colorado are included in the Southwest regional reports from United Press International. See Executive News Service.
- Colorado Business Magazine can be searched through the Business Database Plus (GO BUSDB). For details, see Business Database.
- Denver Business Journal also can be searched through the Business Database Plus (GO BUSDB). See Business Database.

ColorAge, CAI products are supported in the Desktop Publishing Vendor Forum (GO DTPVENDOR). For details, see Desktop Publishing.

Color Computer (**Tandy Corp.**) CompuServe has forums that support this Tandy Corp. machine (GO COCO). See Tandy Corp. Computers.

ColorLab (**software**) is supported in Windows 3rd-Party Forum B (GO WINAPB). See Microsoft Software.

ColorPro (**software**) is supported by the Ventura Software Forum (GO VENTURA). See Ventura.

ColoRIX for DOS (**software**) is supported in the Graphics A Vendor Forum (GO RIXSOFT). See Graphics.

Columbia House Music (GO CH) is a store in the Electronic Mall (GO MALL) that offers memberships for CDs and tapes. See Electronic Mall.

Columbia Journal of World Business (**magazine**) can be searched through the Business Database Plus (GO BUSDB). See Business Database.

Columbia (SC) State (**newspaper**) is searchable through Telebase System's News Source USA (GO NEWSUSA). See News Source.

Columbus (OH) Dispatch (**newspaper**) is searchable through Telebase System's News Source USA (GO NEWSUSA) and through the Knowledge Index (GO KI). See News Source and see Knowledge Index.

Also, *Business First—Columbus* magazine can be searched through the Business Database Plus (GO BUSDB). See Business Database.

Columnists, Syndicated Newspaper, (GO COLUMNS), from United Features are accessible online. They include daily and weekly columns from Jack Anderson, Marilyn Beck/Stacy Smith, Miss Manners, Alan Dershowitz and Harvey MacKay, as well as The Aces on Bridge, Miss Manners, The Housing Scene, The Medical Advisory, Tune in Tonight and You be the Critic.

Combat games are featured in Flight Simulator Forum (GO FSFORUM). See Gaming Forums. War games are also a topic of the Mac Fun/Entertainment Forum (GO MACFUN). See Apple.

Comedy is a topic in the ShowBiz Forum (GO SHOWBIZ). See ShowBiz.

Comics and Animation Forum (GO COMICS) covers topics ranging from collecting comics to learning more about the world of comic books, comic strips, sequential art of all kinds, and animation. In addition to comics and animation fans, there are more than two dozen professionals in the forum. Incidentally, the forum has one rule: If you're posting a message about a new movie or book that others on the forum may not have seen and there's a chance that reading your message will spoil the ending for them, you must put the word SPOILER in the subject of your message. (That will alert these folks not to read your message and ruin the experience for themselves.)

Also, some followers of the late Wit*Sig Forum, a humor forum that folded a few years ago, have taken up residence in a private area of this forum. Post a message to *SYSOP to request admission to your special message section and library.

Doug Pratt (76703,3041) of Washington, D.C., is the primary sysop. He is assisted by Steve Bennett.

Comics and humor also are topics in the Literary Forum (GO LITFORUM). For details, see Literature. Also comic collecting is covered in the Collectibles Forum (GO COLLECT). See Collectibles.

Comline Japan Daily (**databases**) (on various topics, including computers, electronics, biotechnology, industry automation, telecommunications, transportation, and others) may be searched through the IQuest gateway. See IQuest. *COMLINE: Transportation Industry of Japan* also can be searched through the Business Database Plus (GO BUSDB). See Business Database.

Command HQ (**modem game**) is supported in the Modem-to-Modem Gaming Lobby (GO MTMLOBBY). See Modem-to-Modem Games.

CommandPost (**software**) is supported in Windows 3rd-Party Forum A (GO WINAPA). See Microsoft Software.

Commands: A newer generation of CompuServe subscribers use sophisticated "front-end" communications software, such as CompuServe's own CompuServe Information Manager, for communicating with the system. Such dedicated terminal programs use windows, icons, and light-bar cursors for command processing, translating the user's desires into commands that the system will understand, using an agreed-upon protocol. Meanwhile, other CompuServe users log on with third-party communications software and communicate with the system just as they would with other ASCII-based online services. This second group of subscribers uses various letter commands for navigation, message-writing, visiting forums, and so on. This section contains summaries of commands used with such general software.

NOTE: CIM users also occasionally have use for the commands listed in this section, because not all of CompuServe supports the protocol at work in the CompuServe Information Manager. When accessing these unsupported sections of the service, the CIM software automatically goes into "terminal emulation" mode, which is the same as an ASCII-based terminal program. In CIM's terminal emulation mode, the commands listed in this section are used.

Navigation commands are the same almost everywhere in the system. (In the few services using special or addition commands, online help messages explain them to you.) Here are the commands that can be entered at the bottom of any menu or at an abbreviated prompt.

T—TOP menu page. From virtually anywhere in the system, this command takes you directly to the first page of CompuServe.

M—previous Menu. This command goes back to the menu page that points to the current page.

GO *n*—Go to *n*. The GO command takes you directly to page *n* which is an address, as in G OLT. These days the GO command is used more often with a quick reference word, as in GO IBMNEW and GO PHONES.

H or ?—HELP gives elaboration from the system on the current command.

S *n*—Scroll from *n*. This continuously outputs pages until the last page in a series is reached. If you are at a menu page, you can use S in connection with a menu item, as in S 1 to scroll item 1.

N—(Next) can be entered at any prompt within related pages of information. This selects the next menu item from the most recently used menu without re-displaying the menu.

OFF or BYE—disconnects you from the service immediately.

F—(Forward) moves you forward a page; that is, it displays the next page in a series of pages. A single carriage return (the RETURN or ENTER key) will do the same thing.

B—(Backward) returns to the page preceding the current page.

P—(Previous) goes to the previous item from the last menu selected. For example, if 5 was the last choice, the P command will display item 4.

R—(Resend) re-displays the current page. This is useful if the current page has scrolled off the screen or after a HELP command.

FIND—follow this by a keyword and you can locate other features on the system. For instance, FIND IBM would cause the system to locate any features it has on file that deal with IBM. FIND builds a special menu for you, from which you can access any of the features found by simply entering a numbered option.

For an online review of commands, enter (GO COMMAND).

Control codes control the display of data on your screen. They are entered by holding down the control key on your keyboard and pressing a specific letter key. (Most keyboards these days have a key labelled "CONTROL" or "CTRL." If yours doesn't, consult your users manual. Some computers require a sequence of alternate keys to signal the CONTROL function.) In online messages about control functions, the system often uses the character ^, as in "^C Interrupt."

The control codes most often used on CompuServe are listed below.

Pausing

CONTROL A temporarily freezes the display at the end of the current line. CONTROL Q resumes the display.

CONTROL S temporarily freezes the display like CONTROL A, but unlike CONTROL A, this freezes the output immediately, even in the middle of a line. Again, CONTROL Q resumes the display.

Resuming

CONTROL Q resumes the display after either a CONTROL S or A. (CONTROL W is an alternate version of CONTROL Q).

Full Stops

CONTROL C interrupts the display so that you can enter another menu selection or command. Often it results in the display of a ^C Interrupt Menu from which you can cancel the current operation, continue at the point before the CONTROL C was enter, or go to the previous menu or prompt.

CONTROL O stops the display immediately. (Unlike CONTROLs A and S, this one can't be resumed; instead, you are taken to a prompt, from which you can enter a new command.)

CONTROL P interrupts the display of a file and returns you to the command prompt. Unlike CONTROL O, it does not display any Interrupt menu.

Typed Lines

CONTROL U deletes the line which you are typing. This is similar to pressing the Backspace key repeatedly. It removes all characters that you have typed (though they remain displayed on your screen) on the current line and does not send them to CompuServe when you press RETURN.

CONTROL V re-displays a partial line and allows you to continue typing it. This is really helpful when using the CB Simulator or conferencing in the forums if you are being bombarded by others' messages such that you aren't sure of what you have typed so far.

Others

CONTROL H backspaces, deleting the character that was there. (The character may not disappear from your screen, but it is no longer recognized by the system after you have used CONTROL H.)

CONTROL G sounds a "bell tone," if your computer supports the function. Generally, this isn't used in "real-time" applications. However, some users like to have enter CONTROL G as their "prompt character" in the forums' OPTIONS section so that they receive a bell tone at major prompts in the navigation of the forums.

CONTROL I tabs on the current line being typed.

CONTROL J issues a line feed, advancing the current line up one. In most terminal software, this acts as a carriage return.

CONTROL K is a vertical tab.

CONTROL L is a form feed and clears the screen on most terminals.

CONTROL M is a carriage and a line feed.

Command Software Systems products are supported in the IBM PC Vendor F Forum (GO PCVENF). See IBM Computers.

Commentary (magazine) can be searched in the Magazine Database Plus (GO MDP). See Magazine Database.

Commerce Business Daily (GO COMBUS) is a Telebase Systems Incorporated gateway. The database, published by the U.S. Commerce Department, includes the full text of U.S. Commerce Department publications listing contracts, requests for proposals, and other data related to government contracts. The data includes listings from the printed publication of the same name, as well as from the printed "DMS Bluetops," published by the Office of the Assistant Secretary of Defense. It is updated daily and includes only listings from the most recent 90 days.

The information includes a summary that usually describes the contract/procurement, contracting agency, the "Section Heading" or category of needed product/service, and date of issue. You may retrieve listings by entering subject words, sponsoring agency, or ZIP code of the sponsoring agency as your search criteria.

The cost is $2 for the first 10 titles located, $2 for each additional 10 titles, and $2 for each full listing retrieved. There is a $1 charge for a search that retrieves no titles.

For information on other Telebase gateways, see Telebase Systems Incorporated.

Commerce Department is discussed in the White House Forum (GO WHITEHOUSE). See White House.

Also National Technical Information Service (GO NTIS) is a gateway to a database published by the U.S. Department of Commerce. See National Technical Information.

Commodity Markets (GO COMMODITIES) provides historical information on futures contracts and cash prices along with newsletters offering news, features, and analysis:

- Agri-Commodities (GO ACI) includes Futures Focus and the Futures Tutor and covers general commodity information and educational material, market indicators, trade recommendations, fundamental trading news, commodity industry news, long-term trade assessments, and technical indicator reviews. The service is updated weekly and is surcharged at $20 an hour in weekday, daytime hours and $15 an hour in evenings and on weekends.

- Commodity Pricing (GO CPRICE) is the pricing history for one contract. It presents historical performance by day, week, or month for the requested commodity contract (or optionally the contract nearest delivery). The data displayed includes open, high, low, and setting prices along with volume and open interest. Also available are aggregated volume and open interest for all contracts for the requested commodity along with the cash market price for the commodity. The program is updated daily at 6:00 p.m. Eastern Time. The feature is surcharged at 5 cents per quote/contract.

- Menu of Available Commodities (GO CSYMBOL), which covers available such commodity groups as foods, grains, metals, financial, petroleum, fibers, currencies, and indexes. Access symbols, active contracts, exchange (where traded), and commodity descriptions are shown for each commodity. There is no surcharge on this feature.

- News-A-Tron (GO NAT), a product of Herman Communications, offers daily market commentary and analysis on the commodity markets. Some limited market price quotations are also available. The feature covers markets in grains, precious metals, foreign exchange, petroleum products, and analysis of major market indices. Two general categories are offered: (1) Market reports with news, features, and cash quotes for selected commodities, interest rates, and financial instruments and (2) stock indices analysis and news reports which offer analyses and quotes for the major stock market indicies. It is updated twice a day. The market reports and indexes are each surcharged at $1.25.

See Stock Quotes (Historical), and for an overview of other money-related features, see Financial Services and see Investment Analysis Tools.

Commodore computers are supported in the Commodore Users Network (GO CBMNET). Commodore computers always have had a big following on CompuServe and users these days have seven forums at their disposal.

The newest of the Commodore forums serve the newest computer, the colorful, musical Amiga. These include:

- Amiga Arts Forum (GO AMIGAARTS) for those with an interest in the creative aspects of the Amiga.
- Amiga Technical Forum (GO AMIGATECH) for programming and other technical issues.
- Amiga Users Forum (GO AMIGAUSER) for general questions and discussion.

The forums are operated by Steve Ahlstrom, Don Curtis, Larry Phillips, Betty Clay, Steve Pietrowicz, Steve Bennett, John Toebes, David Art, Michael Gerard, Bob Rakosky, and John Wiederhirn.

Also of interest will be the Amiga Vendor Forum (GO AMIGAVENDOR), which is operated for selected vendors who are using this electronic medium as customer support, where possible. The forum is supported by the following vendors: Brown-Wagh, Avant-Garde, Impulse, Syndesis, Transactor (for the Amiga), MicroIllusions, New Horizons, ProWrite, ProScript, M2S, Black Belt Systems, NewTek, and Softwood.

Also for Amiga computerists is the Amiga File Finder (GO AMGFF), a special database containing information on major files in the Amiga forums. The File Finder allows you to search on a filename or keyword or use a variety of search methods that help you locate files of interest in any of the forums.

And for users of others Commodore machines, there are:

- Betty Knight's Commodore Arts and Games Forum (GO CBMART), serving a variety of Commodore 8-bit machines, including the Commodore 64, C128, the VIC-20, the Pet, the C-16, the Plus 4, and the B-128. Knight (76703,4037) has been a mainframe computer programmer/systems analyst since 1960. She is assisted by Todd Heimarck, Joe Buckley.

- The Commodore Application Forum (GO CBMAPP), the place to be if you're a Commodore 8-bit programmer or you're interested in discussions concerning hardware, utilities, and application software for your C64 or C128. The forum maintains a large set of file libraries. Gary Farmaner (76703,3050) is administrator of the forum. He is assisted by Marte Brengle, Malcolm O'Brien, Jim Russell, Bill Roberson, and Joe Buckley.

All of these forums are independent of Commodore International. Meanwhile, the company does have an online presence itself. Its staff maintains the Commodore Service Forum (GO CBMSERVICE), which is operated by the company's Telecommunications Department along with in-house engineers, customer support, and service staff members. All staff members are located in the Commodore's headquarters in West Chester, Pennsylvania. The sysops are Greg Givler (76702,647) of Commodore and Mike Jacobus.

To stay up on the latest from Commodore itself, you might be interested in the company's online newsletter (GO CBMNEWS), which provides announcements, information on education resources, user group information, a directory of service centers and conferences, updates on software, and so on.

Also, Commodore Science is a topic in the Science/Math Education Forum (GO SCIENCE).

Common Carrier Week (database) may be searched through the IQuest gateway. See IQuest. The resource also can be searched through the Business Database Plus (GO BUSDB). See Business Database.

Common Cause is discussed in the Political Debate Forum (GO POLITICS). See Political.

Common Market Studies, Journal of can be searched through the Business Database Plus (GO BUSDB). See Business Database.

Communications Daily, Communications Week, and Communications Week International (databases) may be searched through the IQuest gateway. See IQuest. They also can be searched through Business Database Plus (GO BUSDB). See Business Database.

In addition, abstracts of *Communications Week* can be searched through Computer Database Plus (GO COMPDB). See Computer Database Plus.

Communications, Global (magazine) can be searched through the Business Database Plus (GO BUSDB) as can *Industrial Communications*. See Business Database.

Communications News (magazine) is searchable through Computer Database Plus (GO COMPDB). See Computer Database Plus. It also can be searched through Business Database Plus (GO BUSDB). See Business Database.

Comp Presentations Software Products are supported in Windows 3rd-Party Forum B (GO WINAPB). See Microsoft Software.

Compact Disc Club (GO CD) is a store in the Electronic Mall (GO MALL) that offers compact disks and club memberships. See Electronic Mall. For related topics, see CD.

Company Corporation (GO CO) is a store in the Electronic Mall (GO MALL) that provides online incorporating. If you are a business owner, note that this service enables you to incorporate online for as little as $45 plus state filing fees. See Electronic Mall.

Company names lookup: For finding stock symbols for other financial services, see Issue and Symbol Lookup (GO SYMBOLS). See Stock Symbols, Lookup.

Company Reports (GO COMPANY) is a collection of financial services that provide the latest information about all aspects of American and foreign corporations and businesses. All of the databases carry surcharges. They include:

- Business Dateline (GO BUSDATE), including full text of articles from more than 115 regional business publications in the U.S. and Canada. Coverage includes local economic conditions, retailing, real estate, people and management, financial institutions, transportation, and electronics. Articles from 1985 to the present are included in the database. The information includes the article's author, title, publication, date of publication, the dateline, as well as the complete text of the article. Articles may be retrieved by subject words, author name, company name, geographic location, or publication date. The surcharge is $7.50 for the first five titles located, $7.50 for each additional five titles, and $7.50 for each full-text article retrieved. There is a $1 charge for a search that retrieves no titles.

- Citibank's Global Report (GO GLOREP), launched by Citibank in 1987, brings together 12 respected financial and news services. See Global Report.

- Company Analyzer (GO ANALYZER) provides a menu of financial services with fundamental and technical data on a company. (At this writing, only those who sign up for the Executive Option have access to this feature. See Executive Option.) The surcharged feature searches the financial products' databases and, for easy access, "bundles" several of the products containing information on the company you select within one menu. (Note: The surcharges are waived for retrieving H&R Block data, ticker symbol HRB. CompuServe encourages you to use the HRB ticker symbol to try this and various other financial products). Automatically displayed is a current quote that costs 1.5 cents, and a menu from which you can choose one or more of the following:

  1. Descriptive company information from S&P Online at $1, Disclosure's "Company Name & Address" at no surcharge, or Disclosure's "Company Profile" at $5.

2. Daily, weekly, or monthly pricing history at 5 cents a quote displayed.

3. Dividend history at 15 cents per dividend displayed.

4. A pricing Statistics report for the last 52 weeks at $1.25.

5. A detailed Issue Description at $1.25.

6. A report of the available bonds for 5 cents per bond displayed.

7. An Options Profile report at $1.25.

8. A Return on $1,000 Invested report at 15 cents.

9. A Management Discussion report from Disclosure at $5.

10. Disclosure's "Officers, Directors, and Salaries" report at $5.

11. Ownership reports from Disclosure, ranging in price from $5 to $10.

12. Price Volume Graphs for $1 each.

13. Any current news at $15 per hour.

14. Earnings/Growth Forecasts including Value Line's forecast at $1.60, an I/B/E/S "Detailed Earnings Report" at $2, and an I/B/E/S "Summary Earnings Discussion" at 50 cents.

15. Financial Reports from Value Line at 40 cents per year displayed, or all Disclosure financial reports on a company for $10.

- Corporate Affiliations (GO AFFILIATIONS), covering most large U.S. public and private companies and their affiliates. The database includes all companies and affiliates from the New York Stock Exchange and the American Stock Exchange and any company from the OTC Exchange that has affiliates. The information available for a company or affiliate includes company name, address, phone number, business description, executive names, and its place in the corporate family hierarchy. You may retrieve company references by entering the company's name or ticker symbol, city, state, ZIP code, or telephone area code; as well as executive name or executive position title, or board of directors member. The surcharge is $7.50 for the first five titles located, $7.50 for each additional five titles, and $7.50 for each full-text article retrieved. There is a $1 charge for a search that retrieves no titles.

- D&B Dun's databases (GO DUNS) includes material published and copyrighted by Dun's Marketing Services Inc. and made available by Dialog Information Services Inc. It is offered on CompuServe through a joint effort with Telebase Systems Inc. The databases are similar to IQuest's procedure. (See IQuest.) And for information on other Telebase gateways, see Telebase Systems Incorporated. All are charged at $7.50 for the first five references retrieved, $7.50 for the next five, $7.50 for each full reference, and $1 for all searches that produce no hits. The databases include:

1. Dun's Market Identifiers (GO DMI-9), a directory on more than 6.7 million U.S. establishments, both public and private. The information on a com-

pany includes the name, address, and telephone number, and company characteristics such as sales figures, number of employees, corporate family relationships, and executive names. An individual reference may not include all of this information. You may retrieve records by entering as your search criteria the company name, geographic location, product or service, executive name, number of employees, or sales.

2. Canadian Dun's Market Identifiers (GO CMI-1), a similar database of information on about 350,000 Canadian companies.

3. Dun's International Market Identifiers (GO DII-1), a directory information on approximately 2.1 million public, private, and government-controlled companies in 120 countries, including Asia, Africa, Europe, the Middle East, South America, Australia, and the Pacific Rim.

- DISCLOSURE II (GO DISCLOSURE), which is a compilation of various information of publicly owned companies in files required by the Securities and Exchange Commission. Detailed reports on more than 10,500 publicly traded corporations contain fundamental company and ownership information, including the names, holdings, and recent transactions of the principal insiders and institutions. This includes the 10K management discussions, detailed financial statements, business segment data, five-year financial summaries, company name and address, a list of SEC filings, a business description, officers and directors, a list of subsidiaries and insider owners, institutional owners, and owners of 5 percent or more of the company's stock. Also included are the President's Letter to Shareholders and the Footnotes to Financial Statements, as well as a new Cash Flow Report. The service has expanded its offering of annual balance-sheet and income-statement reports for the past eight years. It is updated every Sunday with market prices updated nightly. The surcharge is $5 each for company profiles, reports on management discussion, officers and directors and president's letter; $11 for financial statements; $10 for footnotes; and $17 for a package of all of these. Also available is an ownership and subsidiary summary ($5), and for $10 each reports on 5-percent owners, insider holdings, and institutional holdings (or $25 for all of these). You can try out the service with no surcharge by entering the ticker symbol HRB (H&R Block). (At this writing, only those who sign up for the Executive Option have access to this feature. See Executive Option.)

- International Company Information (GO COINT) for data on companies in the U.S., Canada, Europe, Germany, the UK, and Pacific region.

- InvesText (GO INVTEXT), featuring two years of reports by analysts in more than 50 Wall Street, regional and international, brokerage houses and research firms. Individual company reports are available for more than 8,200 U.S. public companies and more than 2,300 publicly held foreign companies. Company reports include historical information such as company profiles, revenues, earnings, and other financial operating results and stock performance. The reports also may include the brokerage's recommendations along with analyses and forecasts of the company's future performance. Industry reports are available for some 50 predefined industry groups, including assorted high-technology fields, consumer goods and services, energy and natural resources, and finance, construction, and real estate services. Industry reports are comprised of information on trends and conditions in the industry, new technology, and product development, as well as competition and market share. Many reports contain analysis as well as descriptive text and statistics. InvesText offers four ways of searching. You may access:

1. Company reports by entering the company name or ticker symbol to retrieve all of the Company Reports on the entered company.

2. Industry reports by entering an industry group name to retrieve all of the Industry Reports for the entered industry.

3. By topic, individual report PAGES containing topics of interest to you. To retrieve them, enter a word or phrase describing the subject. The search retrieves all pages in which the entered word or phrase appears. Searches may include company, industry, and product names.

4. Reports by number, using a report's unique, six-digit InvesText code. The report number usually is obtained from previous searches in InvesText. Searching by InvesText Report Number retrieves complete industry or company reports.

The surcharge is $7.50 for the first five titles located, $7.50 for each additional five titles, and $7.50 for each full-text article retrieved. There is a $1 charge for a search that retrieves no titles.

- S&P Online (GO S&P), from Standard & Poor's Corporation, which offers data on about 4,700 companies, including business summaries, earnings outlooks, historical earnings and dividends, and summaries of product lines. All information is dated to indicate when it was last reviewed. The S&P Master List has buy recommendations for various investments. S&P investment "Ideas" present stocks that the analysts expect will out-perform the market over the next 12 months. Surcharges are $1 for basic company information, $2 for a master list, and $2 for investment ideas.

- Thomas Companies and Products Online (GO THOMAS) which includes two databases. The surcharge on both databases is $5 for the first 10 titles located, $5 for each additional 10 titles, $5 for each full-text article retrieved, and $1 for a search that retrieves no titles. The resources are:

1. Thomas Register Online, which has data on almost 150,000 U.S. and Canadian manufacturers and service providers and is updated annually. The information includes the company name, address, telephone number, and products or services provided. Also available for some companies are trade

names with descriptions, TELEX and cable address, asset rating, number of employees, exporter status, names of parent or subsidiary companies, and executive names and titles. You may retrieve company records by entering the company name, words from a description of its business, SIC code, product, trade name, city, state, ZIP code, or telephone area code.

2. Thomas New Industrial Products, which contain the latest technical information on new industrial products introduced by U.S. (and some non-U.S.) manufacturers and sellers. The database is updated weekly. Various industrial products are covered, with each database record supplying key technical data including features, attributes, and performance specifications. The data in each record includes the product name, any applicable product synonyms, SIC codes, trade name, model number, product use, attributes and specifications, plus manufacturer name, address, and telephone number. (An individual record may not contain all of this information.)

For other money-related features, see Financial Services and see Investment Analysis Tools.

- TRW Business Credit Profiles (GO TRWREPORT), which includes credit and business information on more than 13 million organizations. Use this database to find actual account information for over 70 million business account relationships as reported by participating corporations. Available are credit histories, financial information, and ratios; key business facts such as size, ownership, and products; UCC filings, tax liens, judgments, bankruptcies, and an executive summary. Reports may be retrieved by entering a company name and either the state or ZIP code of the specific company location. If no company name exactly matches the name you entered, it will try to retrieve and display up to 24 companies with similar names. Likewise, if you enter a ZIP code it will also retrieve similarly named companies from adjacent ZIP areas. The surcharge is $9 for the first 24 company locations, $34 for the full report selected from the locations, and $9 each for up to four additional full reports (selected from the locations). To view more than five full reports you must re-enter the search and pay an additional $9 search charge plus applicable full-report charges, including another $34 "First full-report" charge.

Company Screening (GO COSCREEN) is a financial service that lets you search the DISCLOSURE II database by menu and based on your own guidelines, produce a list of companies that meet your criteria. See Investment Analysis Tools.

Compaq Connection (GO COMPAQ) is operated by Compaq Computer Corp.'s technical support staff. It is set up to discuss laptops, notebooks, portables, desktops, towers, networking, and software. The file libraries contain downloadable diagnostic and setup tools, drivers, utilities, software solutions, press releases, product information, and more. Included is Compaq Forum (GO CPQFORUM) which provides users with access to Compaq technical support and downloadable files, drivers, utilities, and software solutions. The sysops are Larry Edington (75300,3533) and Richard Hunsinger (75300,3531).

Compendex Plus (database) may be searched through the IQuest gateway (GO IQUEST) and through the Knowledge Index (GO KI). See IQuest and see Knowledge Index.

Compensation and Benefits Review (magazine) can be searched through the Business Database Plus (GO BUSDB). See Business Database.

Complementary Solutions Inc. products are supported in the IBM PC Vendor D Forum (GO PCVEND). See IBM Computers.

Complete PC and Computer Peripherals products are supported in the Modem Vendor Forum (GO MODEMVEN). See Modem Vendor.

Composites Bulletin, Advanced (magazine) can be searched through the Business Database Plus (GO BUSDB), as can *Composites & Adhesives Newsletter* and *Composites Industry Monthly*. See Business Database.

Comprehensive Core Medical Library (database) may be searched through the IQuest gateway. See IQuest.

Compton's NewMedia is supported by the CD-ROM Vendor Forum (GO CDVEN). See CD.

CompuAdd Forum (GO COMPUADD) serves those wishing to communicate with CompuAdd's technical support, its engineering staff, or with each other. Topic areas include all CompuAdd systems such as desktops, laptops, notebooks, towers and Sparc-compatible CPUs. Forum libraries store the complete collection of diagnostic and setup utilities shipped with CompuAdd systems, as well as press releases, retail information, and timely "how-to" instructions. The forum is managed by Lisa Johnson (75300,2751).

Compubooks (GO CBK) is a store in the Electronic Mall (GO MALL) that offers discount computer books. See Electronic Mall.

CompuServe Information Manager (software) is a front-end program CompuServe itself produced for IBM PC (DOS and Windows versions) and Apple Macintosh users. The interface features pull-down menus, dialog boxes, icons, mouse support, and so on, giving a new look to features such as the forums, CB, securities quotations, and CompuServe Mail.

The software, which can be downloaded online (GO CIMSOFT) or ordered online (GO ORDER), features error-free data transmission using CompuServe's B+ Protocol, local/offline message editing, integrated local address book for mail and forum messages, familiar desktop metaphor for messages, "Favorite Places" menu for quick access, message maps that graphically represent forum conversations, electronic Conferencing Support with split screen and multiple windows, and Graphic Interchange Format (GIF) Support. The programs support a modem of 300 baud or higher (ideally, a Hayes-compatible) and an optional printer.

IBM/compatible CIM comes in three versions:

- For the minimum configuration is CIM version 1, which will work on an IBM or compatible with at least 640K of random access memory and at least 470K free when the program is started. MS-DOS 3.1 or higher is required. The program is compatible with color and monochrome monitors and a variety of video adapters (Hercules, EGA, MCGA, VGA, and so on). The version will work on a system without hard disk; the minimum disk configuration is two low-density (360K) 5.25-inch floppy drives, though a hard disk with at least 500K of free space is recommended. Mouse is optional.

- For advanced DOS systems, there is CIM version 2.x. It is recommended for a system with an 80286 or faster processor, a hard disk drive with at least 1.5MB available, at least 500K of available RAM, and either a color or monochrome monitor. Mouse is optional.

- The Windows version for IBM or compatibles with a 80386SX processor or higher requires at least 2MB of RAM memory, Microsoft Windows Version 3.0 or higher (though Version 3.1 or higher is recommended), an IBM EGA or higher resolution monitor compatible with the Microsoft Windows graphical environment, a hard disk with 4MB of space available with Windows installed, a high-density floppy drive, and a mouse (or other pointing device) that is compatible with Microsoft Windows.

The Apple Macintosh version is compatible with a Macintosh Plus or later model with at least 1MB of RAM, System 6.0.4 or later, and a hard drive and at least one 800K floppy disk drive. (CompuServe recommends either two drives or a hard disk and one floppy drive).

Support forums   CompuServe offers several forums to aid users of the CompuServe Information Manager. The forums, which are staffed by CompuServe Customer Service representatives and members of CompuServe's Software Development team, can be used without charge. The forums are among the system's basic services, meaning those signed up under the Standard Pricing Plan (see Billing) have unlimited access to the features. The forums are:

- IBM DOSCIM Support Forum (GO CIMSUPPORT), providing support to users of the IBM PC and compatible version.

- WinCIM Support Forum (GO WCIMSUPPORT) supports users of the IBM Windows version of the program.

- Macintosh CIM Support Forum (GO MCIMSUP), for supporting users of the Macintosh versions of the program.

CompuServe, Jobs at   is a topic in the Classifieds section of the system (GO CLASSIFIED) under the Employment/Education section. See Classifieds.

CompuServe Magazine is a monthly publication produced by CompuServe and mailed free to all the service's online users. The magazine features stories about how to get more out of your CompuServe usage. It also has regular features about your fellow subscribers, announces of new products, reviews and views, and more.

For information about advertising in *CompuServe Magazine*, see Online Inquiry (GO OLI). You may leave your name and addresses at the prompts supplied and further information will be sent to you. You may also add specific comments or special requests to the inquiry if you like. The requests are filed electronically and are accessible only by the advertisers you specify.

CompuServe Magazine also operates a daily electronic edition called Online Today (GO OLT) featuring news and views from the computing world and around the online neighborhoods. See Online Today.

Abstracts of the magazine (formerly called *Online Today*) can be searched through Database Plus (GO COMPDB). See Computer Database Plus.

CompuServe Mail (GO MAIL) provides each subscriber with a private mailbox where electronic letters can be received and sent online around the clock. For details, see Mail, CompuServe.

Computamart, an Australian distributor of the Soundblaster range, is covered in the Pacific Vendors Forum (GO PACVENDOR). For details, see Pacific.

Computer Associates International operates the CAI Forums (GO CAI). See CAI.

Computer books and magazines are sold in many of the stores in the Electronic Mall (GO MALL). For details, see Books.

Computer Audit Update (magazine) can be searched through the Business Database Plus (GO BUSDB). See Business Database.

Computer Club Forum (GO CLUB): One of the oldest forums on CompuServe, the Computer Club has the distinction of being the starting place for many other forums. In fact, the entire Atari User Network and the IBM Users Network have their roots in this special interest group, each starting out as just single subtopics on this forum. These days, the club has evolved into a major source of information about so-called orphaned computers. The primary sysop is Dave Yaros (76703,4332) of Cincinnati, Ohio (who also manages the group's Eagle computer section).

At this writing, the forum provides discussion areas and data libraries for the following systems: Adam, managed by Tim Nunes and Rob Friedman; Eagle, overseen by Dave Yaros; Kaypro, handled by John Deakin; Ohio Scientific Instruments; Panasonic, overseen by Anthony Gonzalez; Sanyo, directed by John Jacobs; and Timex/Sinclair, for which Dave Rothman is responsible.

Computer Communications and **Computer & Communications Decisions** (magazines) are searchable through Computer Database Plus (GO COMPDB). See Computer Database Plus. They also can be searched through Business Database Plus (GO BUSDB). See Business Database.

Computer Conference Analysis Newsletter can be searched through Computer Database Plus (GO COMPDB). See Computer Database Plus.

Computer Consulting (GO CONSULT): The Computer Consultant's Forum is the electronic arm of the Independent Computer Consultants Association (ICCA), a St. Louis group that, since its inception in 1976, has grown from 11 member firms to more than 2,300, representing more than 5,000 data-processing professionals.

   Administering the forum is primary sysop David Moskowitz (76701,100) with the assistance of Guy Scharf, Martin Schiff, Larry Finkelstein, and Dorothy Creswell.

Computer Database Plus (GO COMPDB) is sponsored by Information Access Company in conjunction with magazine publisher Ziff Communications. It contains full text and summaries of computer-related articles in more than 230 magazines, newspapers and journals, covering hardware, software, electronics, engineering, communications, and the application of technology. Articles cover companies, people, products, trends, corporate finances, case histories on the use of computer products, industry projections, programming, and computer design.

   The database carries a surcharge of $15 an hour. In addition, you are charged $2.50 for each complete record (abstract and full-text) viewed or downloaded, $1 for abstracts only, and if, no abstract is available, the $2.50 charge is reduced to $1.50. You may read about how to use the system before accessing the database.

   Computer Database Plus is menu-driven. Selecting the option called Access Computer Database Plus brings you to the main menu. From there you begin your search. Most searchers begin with the "Words Occurring Anywhere" option. Subsequent menus give you the opportunity to narrow or broaden your search field. When you are ready to see the selected stories, an option allows you to request a menu. The database allows you to call up the entire text of more than 70 percent of indexed articles. Most coverage begins with the January 1987 issues. The database is updated weekly with material from current issues of the publications.

   The feature's search methods fall into two broad categories:

- General searches, which let you look for articles based on individual words occurring in articles; they are useful when you aren't sure exactly where to look in an article for the occurrence of a word.

- Specific searches let you look for articles based on specific kinds of words or phrases, such as a subject heading or publication name. For specific searches, a search term can be composed of letters, numerals, and spaces. Specific search methods include keywords (words in titles, subject headings, company or product names), subject headings (words or phrases selected from a controlled list of terms), company names, product names, publication names (you can obtain a complete list by typing ?? when asked for a publication name), publication dates, article types (enter ?? for a list), or words in the article text.

   As you search, the feature generates a menu of actual search terms that match the (partial) search term you supply. You then make one or more selections from the menu.

You can find a user guide and the latest publication list for the feature in the Ziff Support Forum (GO ZIFFHELP) in Library 9 ("Computer DB Plus"). See file CDPUSR.TXT for the user guide, CDPPUB.TXT for the publication list.

Techniques for searching this resource are the same as those used with all of the ZiffNet gateways. For specifics, see ZiffNet Databases.

The database also allows for downloading of articles (as well as displaying them on the screen). Selecting the download option from a menu causes the database to display a File Transfer Protocol list. The first option on the menu is explicitly for users of the CompuServe Information Manager. Users of other terminal programs can select a different protocol. See Files, Transfer.

The publications available for full-text searching include:

A+
ACKnowledge The Window Letter
Administrative Management
AI Expert
C Users Journal
Cadcam
CAD-CAM International
Canadian Datasystems
Classroom Computer Learning
Communications of the ACM
Communications News
Computer-Aided Engineering
Computers in Banking
Computer & Communications Decisions
Computer Conference Analysis Newsletter
Computer Design
Computer Graphics World
Computers in Healthcare
Computer Language
Computer Shopper

Computer & Software News
Computer Weekly
Computergram International
Computing Canada
Data Based Advisor
Datamation
DBMS
DEC Professional
DEC User
DG Review
Digital Media
Digital News & Review
Digital Systems Journal
Dr. Dobb's Journal
EDGE: on & about AT&T
EDGE: Work-Group Computing Report
EDN
Electronic Business
Electronic Design
Electronic Learning
Electronic News
Electronics Weekly

ESD: The Electronic System Design Magazine
EXE
Government Computer News
Hewlett-Packard Journal
High Technology Business
HP Professional
IBM System User
IDP Report
I&CS (Instrumentation & Control Systems)
Industrial Computing
Industrial Engineering
Information Executive
Infosystems
InfoWorld
Journal of Systems Management
LAN Computing
LAN Magazine
LAN Technology
Lasers & Optronics
Lotus
MacUser

MacWEEK

Microprocessor Report

Microsoft Systems Journal

MIDRANGE Systems

Mini-Micro Systems

MIS Week

Modern Office Technology

Networking Management

Optical Information Systems

PC/Computing

PC Magazine

PC Sources

PC Tech Journal

PC User

PC Week

Personal Computing

Personal Workstation

Rainbow

Release 1.0

Robotics Today

The Seybold Report on Desktop Publishing

The Seybold Report on Publishing Systems

Soft-Letter

Software Magazine

SuperGroup Magazine

Systems Integration

Systems Integration Business

T H E Journal (Technological Horizons in Education)

Tech PC User

TECH Specialist

Tech Street Journal

Technology & Learning

Telecommunications

Telecommuting Review: The Gordon Report

Teleconnect

Telephony

3D

TPT—Networking Management Magazine

UNIX Review

VAX Professional

Wall Street Computer Review

Wall Street & Technology

Which Computer?

Windows—DOS Developer's Journal

Windows Sources

Wordperfect Magazine

In addition, abstracts of articles in many other computer-oriented publications can be searched, including:

ACM Computing Surveys

Aldus Magazine

Andrew Seybold's Outlook on Professional Computing

Applied Mathematics and Computation

AT&T Technical Journal

Business Week

Byte

CIME

CommunicationsWeek

Computer

Computer-Aided Design

Computer Communications

Computer Reseller News

Computer Security Journal

Computer Systems News

Computer Vision

Computers in Biology and Medicine

Computers in Mechanical Engineering

Computers & Operations Research

Computerworld

Corporate Computing

CSN

CVGIP: Graphical Models and Image Processing

CVGIP: Image Understanding

Database Programming & Design

Data Base Monthly

Data Communications

Data Management

Desktop Communications

Educational Technology

80 Micro

Electronic Engineering Times

Electronics

Federal Computer Week

Forbes

Fortune

Graphics Image & Processing

Hardcopy

High Technology

IBM Journal of Research and Development

IBM Systems Journal

IEE publications

Image and Vision Computing

Incider

Information Week

InTech

Journal of the ACM

Journal of the Association for Computing Machinery

Journal of Computers in Mathematics and Science Teaching

Journal of Object-Oriented Programming

The Journal of Systems and Software

LAN Times

Lasers and Applications

Lawyer's PC

Library Hi Tech

Los Angeles Times

Macworld

M.D. Computing

Micro Marketworld

Microprocessors and Microsystems

Mini-Micro Software

MIS Quarterly

NetWare Technical Journal

Network World

The New York Times

Newsbytes

Nibble

The Office

Office Technology Management

Online Today

Patricia Seybold's Office Computing Report

PC World

Proceedings of the IEEE

Publish!

San Jose Mercury News

Science of Computer Programming

Seybold Outlook on Professional Computing

Simulation

Small Computers in Libraries

Software News

Systems & Network Integration

Telecommunication Journal

Theoretical Computer Science

Today's Office

UNIX World

The Wall Street Journal

Workgroup Computing Report

Computer Database Plus also incorporates a feature called Computer Buyer's Guide (GO COMPBG) that provides information on more than 75,000 computer hardware and software products sold in North America. Updated monthly, the directory may be used to pinpoint an exact product or group of products, and encompasses information on software packages, computer systems (micro-mainframe), peripherals, and data and telecommunications products. It is surcharged at $15 an hour plus $1 per menu of matching products or manufacturers and 25 cents for each full-product or manufacturer listing displayed.

Computer Decisions and **Computer Design** (magazines) are all available for full-text searchable through Computer Database Plus (GO COMPDB). See Computer Database Plus.

Computer Dealer News (magazine) can be searched through the Business Database Plus (GO BUSDB). See Business Database.

Computer Directory (GO COMPDIR) provides information on more than 75,000 computer hardware and software products sold in North America. The directory is updated monthly. See Computer Database Plus.

Computer Express (GO CE) is a store in the Electronic Mall (GO MALL) that offers Apple, IBM, MAC, Amiga software. See Electronic Mall.

ComputerEyes products supported in the Graphics A Vendor Forum (GO DIGVIS). See Graphics.

Computergram International (magazine) is searchable through Computer Database Plus (GO COMPDB). See Computer Database Plus. The resource also can be searched through the Business Database Plus (GO BUSDB). See Business Database.

Computer Graphics World (magazine) is available for full-text searchable through Computer Database Plus (GO COMPDB). See Computer Database Plus.

Computer Index, National (database) may be searched through the IQuest gateway. See IQuest.

Computer industry databases (IQuest) are legion on CompuServe. Some of those accessible through the IQuest gateway (see IQuest) include:

- For computer science and general computing: Business Computer, CAD/CAM Update, Campaign, CASE Strategies, CD Computing News, CD-ROM Databases, Comline Japan Daily: Computers, Communications Week, Communications Week International, Compendex Plus, Computer ASAP, Computer Database, Computer Decisions, Computer News Fulltext, Computer Protocols, Computer Reseller News, Computer Workstations, Computergram International, Data Channels, Data Communications, Datamation, EDI News, Electronic Design, Electronic Services Update, GUI Program News, Imaging

Update, Information & Interactive Svcs. Report, Information Week, INSPEC, Japan Computer Industry Scan, Japan Semiconductor Scan, Microcomputer Index, Microcomputer Resources, Microsearch, Modem Users News, Multimedia Monitor, Newsbytes News Network, Online Products News, Open Systems Communication, PC Business Products, PC Magazine, PC Week, PTS Newsletter Database, Report on AT&T, Report on IBM, Technical Computing, Telephone Week, Terry Shannon on DEC, Turing Institute Bibliographic Database, Voice Technology News, and Worldwide Databases.

- For new products: Communications: Week International, Computer ASAP, Computer Database, Computer News Fulltext, Electronic Design, Electronic News, Friday Memo, Microcell Report, Online Newsletter, Online Products News, PC Business Products, PC Magazine, PC Week, PTS Newsletter Database, and Voice Technology News.

- For software information: Business Computer, Business Software Database, Buyer's Guide to Micro Software (SOFT), Computer ASAP, Computer Database, Electronic News, Heller Report on Educational Technology & Telecommunications, Intelligent Software Strategies, Microcomputer Software Guide, and Windows Magazine.

Also searchable through the Knowledge Index (GO KI) are Business Software Database, Computer Database, Computer News Fulltext, INSPEC, Microcomputer Index, Microcomputer Software Guide, and Micro Software Directory (SOFT). See Knowledge Index.

Computer Industry Report (magazine) can be searched through the Business Database Plus (GO BUSDB). See Business Database.

Computerized Engineering Index (GO COMPENDEX) contains abstracts of articles from significant engineering and technological literature, including journals, publications of engineering societies and organizations, papers from the proceedings of conferences, selected government reports, and books from around the world. See Engineering.

Computer Language Magazine: Computer Language Magazine Forum (GO CLMFORUM) is built around a magazine that invites advanced computerists to discuss languages such as C and FORTH, to upload and download public domain utilities, and to swap programming tips and techniques.

The forum also provides an outlet for distributing the programs mentioned in the magazine's monthly "Public Domain Software Review" column. In effect, it is building a public database of utilities for virtually all major operating systems. Sysops include Jim Kyle, Jeff Brenton, Chip Rabinowitz, Warren Keuffel, Mark Magnus, and J.D. Hildebrand.

The magazine also is available for full-text searching through Computer Database Plus (GO COMPDB). See Computer Database Plus.

For related topics, see Programmers Support.

Computer Pictures (**magazine**) can be searched through the Business Database Plus (GO BUSDB). See Business Database.

Computer products are sold in a number of stores and kiosks in the Electronic Mall (GO MALL), including Cititronics (GO CTR), offering computer memories; Computer Express (GO CE), for Apple, IBM, MAC, Amiga software; Computer Shopper (GO CS) publication; Dalco Computer Electronics (GO DA); Digital's PC Store (GO DD); Direct Micro (GO DM) discounts on accessories; Heath Co. (GO HTH) build-it-yourself kits, etc.; JDR Microdevices (GO JDR); Macuser (GO MC) supporting Macintosh owners; Macwarehouse (GO MW) for Macintosh supplies; Mac Zone/PC Zone (GO MZ); Microsoft Press (GO MSP); Microwarehouse (GO MCW), for assorted hardware, software and accessories; Mission Control Software (GO MCS); Parsons Technology (GO PA); PC Catalog (GO PCA); PC Computing (GO PCC) publication; PC Magazine (GO PM) publication; PC Sources (GO PC); Penny Wise Office Products (GO PW); Safeware Computer Insurance (GO SAF); Shareware Depot (GO SD); Sierra Online (GO SI), for computer games and accessories; Small Computer Book Club (GO BK); Softdisk Publishing (GO SP); and Wiley Professional Books (GO JW), for technical and professional books. See Electronic Mall.

Computer Product Update and **Computer Protocols** (**magazines**) can be searched through the Business Database Plus (GO BUSDB). See Business Database.

Computer Security Association, National is represented in the McAfee Virus Help Forum (GO VIRUSFORUM). See McAfee.

Computer Security Journal (**magazine**) is searchable (abstracts) through Computer Database Plus (GO COMPDB). See Computer Database Plus.

Computers in Banking and **Computers in Healthcare** (**magazines**) are searchable through Computer Database Plus (GO COMPDB). See Computer Database Plus.

Computers & Health, National Report on can be searched through the Business Database Plus (GO BUSDB). See Business Database.

Computers in Libraries (**magazine**) can be searched through the Business Database Plus (GO BUSDB). See Business Database.

Computer Shopper (GO CS) is a store in the Electronic Mall (GO MALL) that offers discount computer products. See Electronic Mall. The resource also can be searched through Computer Database Plus (GO COMPDB). See Computer Database Plus. Also, the Computer Shopper Forum (GO ZNT: COMPSHOPPER) is accessible on ZiffNet. It is an online companion to the print publication for direct buyers. The forum invites visitors to communicate with editors, columnists, writers, and others. The sysop is Theresa W. Carey (72241,237).

Computer & Software News and **Computer-Aided Engineering** (magazines) are searchable through Computer Database Plus (GO COMPDB). See Computer Database Plus.

Computer Training Forum (GO DPTRAIN) is sponsored by the Ziff Institute of Cambridge Mass., and the Association for Computer Training & Support. It is part of a national effort to improve the quality and effectiveness of computer training. For ACTS membership information, call 1-800-34-TRAIN. The sysops are Elliott Masie (76703,4375) and Bill Brandon (76701,256). Assisting are Rhonda Rosenof, John Warne, and Bob Mosher.

Computer Tyme products are supported in the Novell Vendor Forum A (GO NVENA). See Novell Software.

Computer Weekly (magazine) can be searched through Computer Database Plus (GO COMPDB). See Computer Database Plus.

Computer Workstations (magazine) can be searched through the Business Database Plus (GO BUSDB). See Business Database.

Computerworld (magazine) is searchable through Computer Database Plus (GO COMPDB). See Computer Database Plus.

Computing Canada (magazine) is searchable (abstracts) through Computer Database Plus (GO COMPDB). See Computer Database Plus.

COMSTATION modems and others from PSI Integration are supported in the Modem Vendor Forum (GO MODEMVEN). See Modem Vendor.

Comtex Scientific Corporation is a Stamford, Connecticut, firm that provides the news database, NewsGrid. For details, see NewsGrid.

Concord Direct (GO CA) is a store in the Electronic Mall (GO MALL) that offers free catalogs and information. See Electronic Mall.

Conferences and trade shows are covered in several IQuest databases (GO IQUEST), including Meeting and Eventline. See IQuest. Also Conference Papers Index database may be searched through the IQuest gateway. See IQuest.

Congress is discussed in the Political Debate Forum (GO POLITICS). See Political.

Congress, Letters to: CongressGram is a feature of CompuServe Mail (GO MAIL), allowing you to automatically send mail to members of the Senate and House of Representatives. For details, see Mail, CompuServe.

Congress, Members of: A database that provides the names of congressional representatives, the president and vice president. To use the database, enter GO FCC-1 at a prompt. This service provides a state-by-state listing of all members in the House of Representatives and the Senate. Each listing includes the name, party affiliation, Washington telephone number, hometown, and committee memberships. For related information, see Mail, CompuServe.

Congressional Activities, Congressional Information Service, and **Congressional Record Abstracts** (**databases**) may be searched through the IQuest gateway. See IQuest. Also, *Congressional Research Report* (magazine) can be searched through the Business Database Plus (GO BUSDB). See Business Database.

Connecticut (**news**) is included in the daily Northeast regional reports from United Press International. See Executive News Service for details.

Connectivity is a term that has come to mean all forms of computer communications, from logging on to services like CompuServe and private computer bulletin board systems to linking an office full of computers with a local area network. A number of CompuServe services cover connectivity issues. To see an overview online, select the Connectivity Services option from the Communications menu, GO COMMUNI-CATE. See Telecomputing.

Connell, John, (72662,1370) is sysop of the Homing Instinct Forum (GO HOM-ING). See Homing Instinct.

Connectix products are supported in the Macintosh Vendor A Forum (GO MACAVEN). See Apple Computers.

Connect Software (**publishers of E-Mail Connection**) is supported in a section of the Windows Vendor B Forum (GO EMCONNECT). See Microsoft Software.

Connect Times (**database**) may be searched through the IQuest gateway. See IQuest.

Connolly, Tammy (72241,1650) is the sysop of the ZiffNet Bendata Forum (GO ZNT:BENDATA). See ZiffNet.

Conover, Harry (76701,220) is primary sysop of the Sports Forum (GO FANS). See Sports and Recreation.

Conroy, Cathryn (70007,417) is senior writer and frequent contributor to *CompuServe Magazine* and to the daily news section of Online Today (GO OLT). See CompuServe Magazine and see Online Today.

Conservationist (**magazine**) can be searched in the Magazine Database Plus (GO MDP). See Magazine Database.

Conspiracy theories are discussed in the Political Debate Forum (GO POLI-TICS). See Political.

Constitution, U.S. can be retrieved and searched in Grolier's Academic American Encyclopedia, Grolier's (GO ENCYCLOPEDIA). Enter CONSTITUTION at the search prompt and select "U.S. Constitution" from the subsequent menu. A resulting menu provides each article of the document. See Academic American.

Construction business is covered in *Construction Equipment*, *EC&M Electrical Construction & Maintenance*, and *Highway & Heavy Construction* magazines, which can be searched through the Business Database Plus (GO BUSDB). See Business Database.

Also, Construction Claims Citator, a legal database, may be searched through the IQuest gateway. See IQuest. See also Building.

Consultant (**magazine**) can be searched through the Business Database Plus (GO BUSDB). See Business Database. The resource also can be searched through the Health Database Plus (GO HLTDB). See Health.

Consulting (**computer**): CompuServe's Computer Consultant's Forum (GO CONSULt) supports those teaching computing. See Computer Consulting.

Consumer Affairs, Journal of, and Journal of Consumer Research (**magazines**) can be searched through the Business Database Plus (GO BUSDB). See Business Database.

Consumer Electronics (**database**) may be searched through the IQuest gateway. See IQuest. It also can be searched through Business Database Plus (GO BUSDB). See Business Database.

Consumer Electronics Forum (GO CEFORUM), covers audio, video, software, and more. See Electronics Forum, Consumer.

Consumerism and **consumer information** are specialties of Matthew Lesko's Information USA (GO INFOUSA). See Information USA.

Consumer Reports (GO CSR) allows you to search reports prepared by the Consumers Union staff. The reports are similar to what you find in *Consumer Reports* magazine, modified slightly for placement in this electronic database. This is one of the system's basic services, meaning those signed up under the Standard Pricing Plan (see Billing) have unlimited access to the feature.

Reports are listed in categories—such as appliances, automobiles, electronics/cameras, home—and are alphabetized in each category. The reports generally cover products and services that cost $50 or more, or lower-priced products and services that are typically bought frequently or in bulk.

Most reports are divided into four sections: introduction/overview, what to look for, recommendations, and models tested/ratings. Occasionally, other choices, such as features/specifications or article updates, are available. A guide explains ratings symbols and a full description of each characteristic. Generally, the ratings system is:

[*****]	Excellent
[****]	Very Good
[***]	Good
[**]	Fair
[*]	Poor

Of particular interest to many is the automobile section (GO CRAUTO), which covers most popular cars, small vans, and sport and utility vehicles sold in the United States. Information is taken from New-Car Ratings, Summary Judgments, Frequency-of-Repair Records, and Road Test Reports developed by Consumers Union. The information is organized and presented by vehicle, making available for review all of the current information for an individual model. Begin a search by choosing a search criterion in either (1) Model Year, (2) Make/Manufacturer, (3) Size/Type, (4) Reliability, (5) Recommended by Consumers Union, (6) Gas Mileage, and (7) Model. Narrow a search by specifying additional criteria or broaden it by adding criteria. The vehicles you retrieve must match all criteria.

Consumer Reports also can be searched through the Knowledge Index (GO KI). See Knowledge Index.

Also:

- Articles from Consumer Reports and Consumer Reports Travel Letter are searchable through Magazine Database Plus (GO MDP). For details, see Magazine Database. Consumer Reports also may be searched through IQuest; see IQuest.
- Information from The Consumer Reports Complete Drug Reference (GO DRUGS) is searchable. See Drug.
- Consumer Reports Health Letter is searchable in the Health Database Plus (GO HLTBD). See Health.

Consumers Digest and **Consumers' Research Magazine** (magazines) can be searched in the Magazine Database Plus (GO MDP). See Magazine Database.

Contact Lens Supply Inc. (GO CL) is a store in the Electronic Mall (GO MALL) that offers contact lenses and supplies. See Electronic Mall.

Continental Insurance (GO CIC) is a store accessible through the Electronic Mall (GO MALL) that is an online source for insurance. See Electronic Mall.

Contract information and worldwide bids (tenders) is the subject of Tenderlink (GO TENDERLINK). For more information, see Tenderlink.

Control Codes control the display of data on your screen. They are entered by holding down the control key on your keyboard and pressing a specific letter key. (Most keyboards these days have a key labeled "CONTROL" or "CTRL." If yours doesn't, consult your users manual. Some computers require a sequence of alternate keys to signal the CONTROL function.) For an overview of control codes, see Commands.

Control and Instrumentation (magazine) can be searched through the Business Database Plus (GO BUSDB). See Business Database.

Convention Center (GO CONVENTION) allows a large number of subscribers to gather and listen to a prescheduled real-time presentation, such as an electronic lecture or a panel discussion. The service was launched in March 1987 with a convention where nearly 300 subscribers gathered to read the real-time transcript of the words of then Apple Computer President John Sculley and others who were appearing on-stage in Los Angeles to announce the latest in the Apple Macintosh line of computers.

These electronic conventions usually are sponsored by a particular forum, but the actual conference runs outside of the forum.

An introductory menu offers instructions and lets you make reservations for upcoming gatherings. If a scheduled convention already is going on at the time you access the feature, an additional option says, "ENTER A CONFERENCE IN SESSION."

There are three kinds of conventions:

- A roundtable, which permits open chatter throughout the duration of the conference by all participants.
- A more formal "moderated" conference, in which the guest speaker makes an opening statement, then members of the audience may ask questions in turn. The Convention Center software prevents listeners from transmitting questions except when the moderator authorizes it.
- A lecture conference, the most formal of the three, which permits no open chatter or questions during the event.

Those conventions that permit questions "from the floor" use some simple commands that are described in the "Instructions" section of the main menu. Some of the commands are tailored to the event. For instance, in a moderated conference, the moderator exercises control over who can transmit and when. Speaking is permitted by only one audience member at a time. In those conventions, if you want to ask a question, enter /QUESTION. You are then notified when it is your turn. To see how many questioners are still ahead of you, enter /LOOK. For details of other special convention commands, see the "Instructions" option on the main conference menu.

Some particularly popular conventions require advanced registration to attend. You can read about upcoming conventions by regularly checking the main menu's "List Conferences/Make Reservations" option. Some require a fee to attend; that bulletin will identify any such surcharged features.

Cook, Bill (76703,1030) is the Macintosh executive sysop and library manager in the Micronetworked Apple Users Groups, (GO MAUG). See Apple Computers.

Cook's Online Forum (GO COOKS) is for everyone who has an interest in food and cooking. Members exchange their favorite recipes, cooking tips, and information on new products. The forum's libraries are filled with hundreds of recipes as well as several programs for storing and maintaining recipes. Larry Wood (76703,704) is forum administrator. The sysop is Jenee Burns (70007,3367). They are assisted by Judy Gruhn (nutrition, soups and salads), Lon Hall (outdoor cooking), Nicole Novak (breads and ethnic foods), Chris Mitchell (vegetarian and vegetables), Nancy Blum (vegetarian), Michael Aichlmayr (herbs and spices), and Neil Spinner (tools and books).

Cooking also is a topic in Gardening Forum (GO GARDENING). See Gardening. For related topics, see Food.

Cool Shoes Software (products) are supported in the MIDI B Vendor Forum (GO MIDIBVEN). See Music.

Coordinator Software is supported in the DaVinci Forum (GO DAVINCI). See DaVinci.

Copilot (software) for Apple IIgs computers is automated terminal program written by Kenneth I. Gluckman. The $25 shareware program can be retrieved in the Apple II/III Productivity Forum (GO APPRODUCT). For related subjects, see Automated Terminal Software.

Copy II (software) is supported in the Central Point Software Forum (GO CENTRAL). See Central Point.

Copyright, CompuServe rules of (GO RULES) are displayed online, along with an elaboration on the policy (GO COPYRIGHT). For a copy of the operating rules agreement all subscribers sign, see Rules, CompuServe Operating.

Corel Support Forum (GO COREL) supports the firm's line of graphics and SCSI products. Among the supported products is Corel DRAW! 3.0. The sysop is Steve Cockwell (76711,563), assisted by Paul Coffin.

Corporate Cashflow Magazine (magazine) can be searched through the Business Database Plus (GO BUSDB). See Business Database.

Corporate Computing (magazine abstracts) can be searched through Computer Database Plus (GO COMPDB). See Computer Database Plus.

Corporate Computing Forum (GO ZNT:CORPORATE)

Corporate EFT Report (magazine) can be searched through the Business Database Plus (GO BUSDB). See Business Database.

Corporate information: Corporate Affiliations (GO AFFILIATIONS) is a financial service covering most of the large, U.S. public and private companies and their affiliates. See Company Reports.

Also, a number of IQuest databases (see IQuest) are relative to the topic, American Business Directory, including American Business 20 Plus Companies, Business Dateline, Business Week, Corporate Affiliations, Corptech, D&B—Dun's Market Identifiers, D&B—Million Dollar Directory, Disclosure Database, Disclosure/Spectrum Ownership, IDD M&A Transactions, M & A Filings, Media General Plus, Moody's Corporate News U.S., Moody's Corporate Profiles, PR Newswire,

Standard & Poor's Corporate Descriptions plus News, Standard & Poor's Register—Biographical, Standard & Poor's Register—Corporate and TRW Business Credit Database.

Cosmetics business is covered in some magazines that can be searched through the Business Database Plus (GO BUSDB), including Cosmetic World News, Cosmetics International, Cosmetics and Toiletries, Cosmetics & Toiletries & Household Products Marketing News in Japan, Food Cosmetics & Drug Packaging, Soap Perfumery & Cosmetics, and Soap-Cosmetics-Chemical Specialties. See Business Database.

Also, the KOSMET database may be searched through the IQuest gateway (GO IQUEST). See IQuest.

Cosmology is discussed in the Astronomy Forum (GO ASTROFORUM). See Astronomy.

Cosmopolitan (magazine) is searchable through Magazine Database Plus (GO MDP). For details see Magazine Database.

CoStar products are supported in the Macintosh C Vendor Forum (GO MACCVEN). See Apple Computers.

Country Forecast Tables (magazine) can be searched through the Business Database Plus (GO BUSDB). See Business Database.

Country Living (magazine) can be searched in the Magazine Database Plus (GO MDP). See Magazine Database.

Country music is a subject of the Music/Performing Arts Forum (GO MUSICARTS). See Music.

Courier modems from U.S. Robotics are supported in the Modem Vendor Forum (GO MODEMVEN). See Modem Vendor.

Court Reporters Forum (GO CRFORUM) hosts members of the the National Court Reporters Association and the Journal of Court Reporting, as well as students, schools, vendors, and anyone interested in the court reporting profession. The forum is operated by Richard A. Sherman (71154,61), assisted by Kent L. Carter, Walter R. Ledge, Phil R. Lassiter, Terry Lee, Kelda Ytterdal, Jennie Voorhis, Martha Reifschneider, Gary Robson, Claire Ryder, and Alex Morelli.

See also Legal Forum.

Covox (products) are supported in the MIDI B Vendor Forum (GO MIDIBVEN). See Music.

CPA Journal (magazine) can be searched through the Business Database Plus (GO BUSDB). See Business Database.

CPI-C is supported in the APPC Info Exchange Forum (GO APPCFORUM). See IBM Computers.

CP/M (software) is supported in CP/M Users Group Forum (GO CPMFORUM). See Programmers Support.

.CPT as an extension on filenames in forum libraries, usually means the program is in a *compressed/packed* form. See Files, Compressed.

Crafts Forum (GO CRAFTS) for those interested in any of the broad spectrum of crafts from knitting and weaving to wood-carving and jewelry-making. The forum features specific sections and libraries on knitting and crocheting, weaving and spinning, sewing and quilting, stitchery, surface design, and woodworking. Discussion topics have included such things as armor-making, doll houses, mirroring, and blown glass. Running the forum are Susan Lazear (76702,1664) and Kathy Morgret (76702,1665). They are assisted by Anne Brown, Linda Bryant, Margaret Copeland, Helen Feddema, Mary Beth Finnerty, Debra Freisleben, Teresa Gregory, Vicki Jacobs, Colleen Kozlowski, Sherry London, Ginger Luters, Gerry Phibbs, Debbie Rindfleisch, Laura Sawyer, Kathy Sheldrake, Jack Turley, Katy Ulrich, and Susan Vazquez.

Crandall, Paul (76702,366) is sysop of The Intel Forum (GO INTELFORUM). See Intel.

Crater, Zeke (76711,773) is the sysop of the Advanced Program-to-Program Communications Forum (GO APPC). See IBM Computers for details.

Creative Anachronisms, Society of, is discussed in the Science Fiction & Fantasy Forum (GO SCI-FI). See Science Fiction.

Creative Labs' User Support Forum (GO BLASTER) supports the firm's Sound Blaster line of audio cards for PCs, as well as CD-ROM drives and the Video Spigot and Video Blaster capture cards. The forum provides direct access to company representatives who can answer your questions, and who will listen to recommendations and suggestions for improvements. Operating the forum is Jennifer Smith (72662,1602), who works in Creative Labs' technical services department in Stillwater, Oklahoma. She is assisted by Chris Owens, Paul Fletcher and Marcel Evans.

Creative Multimedia Corp. products are supported in the CD-ROM Vendors Forum (GO CDROMVEN). See CD-ROM.

Creative Solutions Inc. sponsors the Forth Forum (GO FORTH). See Programmer Support.

Creative Systems Programming products are supported in the OS/2 Vendor Forum (GO OS2AVEN). See IBM Computers.

Credit (**magazine**) can be searched through the Business Database Plus (GO BUSDB), as can *Credit Card News* and *Credit Risk Management Report*. See Business Database.

Credit information: TRW Business Credit Profiles (GO TRWREPORT) is a financial service that includes credit and business information on more than 13 million organizations. See Company Reports.

   Also, searchable through IQuest are Credit Card News, Credit Risk Management Report, and Creditreform. See IQuest.

Cricket graphics programs is supported in the CAI Forums (GO CAI) operated by Computer Associates International. See CAI.

Criminal Justice Periodical Index and **National Criminal Justice Reference Service** are accessible through the Legal Research Center (GO LEGALRC). For details, see Legal Research. These resources also may be searched through IQuest. See IQuest.

Critics' Choice Video (GO CCV) is a store in the Electronic Mall (GO MALL) that features videos of all kinds. See Electronic Mall.

Crocheting is one of the topics discussed in the Crafts Forum (GO CRAFTS). See Crafts.

Cross System Product (**software**) is supported in the Software Solutions Forum (GO SOFSOL). See Software Solutions.

Crosstalk (**software**) is supported in the Crosstalk Forum (GO XTALK). The company operates this forum as a support facility for CompuServe subscribers for Crosstalk, Crosstalk XVI, Crosstalk Mk. 4, Transporter, and Remote2. The data libraries contain utilities, script files, and information about DCA products, and so forth. The message boards are used to answer general and technical questions.

   Managing the forum are Steve Johnson (76702,1216) and Ed Girou (76702,542), assisted by Philip R. Mann and Maria Forrest.

   For related topics, see Telecomputing.

Crutchfield (GO CFD) is a store in the Electronic Mall (GO MALL) that specializes in various electronics, including home audio, car stereo, computers, video, and telephones. See Electronic Mall.

CrystalGraphics products are supported in the Graphics B Vendor Forum (GO GRAPHBVEN). See Graphics.

CSI Forth Software is supported in the Forth Forum (GO FORTH). See Programmers Support.

CSN (**magazine abstracts**) can be searched through Computer Database Plus (GO COMPDB). See Computer Database Plus.

CTOS/Open Forum (GO CTOS), operated by Unisys Corp., supports and provides instruction about the CTOS operating system, the CTOS Workstation family, and its Client/Server technology. Information includes press releases, application tips, upcoming CTOS events, CTOS training schedules, documentation listings, and more. The primary sysop is Richard Bowen (76711,1153). He is assisted by Mary Erickson.

Ctrlalt Associates products are supported in the IBM PC Vendor A Forum (GO PCVENA). See IBM Computers.

Cruise vacations are offered by Rosenbluth Vacations (GO CRUISE) is a store in the Electronic Mall (GO MALL). See Rosenbluth.

Cruising is discussed in the Sailing Forum (GO SAILING). See Sports and Recreation. Cruises also are a topic in the Travel Forum (GO TRAVSIG). See Travel.

Cuadra Directory of Online Databases (database) may be searched through the IQuest gateway. See IQuest.

Cumulus Corp. (computer products) are supported in the PC Vendor D Support Forum (GO PCVEND). See IBM Computers.

Cunningham, Dave (76702,453) is sysop of the Collectibles Forum (GO COLLECT). See Collectibles.

Cupcake's CB Society (GO CUP) is the CB Simulator's society pages. For more information, see CB Society.

Currency conversion service is provided in the Travelshopper (GO PARS) airline service. See Travelshopper.

Currency Quarterly (magazine) can be searched through the Business Database Plus (GO BUSDB). See Business Database.

Current (IBM software) is supported in the IBM Desktop Software Forum (GO IBMDESK). See IBM Computers.

Current (magazine) can be searched in the Magazine Database Plus (GO MDP). See Magazine Database.

Current Biotechnology Abstracts (scientific database) can be searched through IQuest. See IQuest.

Current Day Quotes (GO QQUOTE) are available on a 20-minute delayed basis. For details, see Stock Quotes, Current.

Current events are debated in the Issues Forum (GO ISSUESFORUM). And for related features, see News, General.

Current Market Snapshot (GO SNAPSHOT) is a surcharged area that gives a quick overview of current stock market trends by displaying key indicators in a one-page statistical report. The page contains highlights of current trading trends by displaying the highest, lowest, and latest values for the Dow Jones 30, Standard and Poor's 500, and NASDAQ Composite indices. The strength of the trend is displayed in a summary of New York Stock Exchange activity, including the percent of change and the number of shares traded in current session. Advancing and declining issues, separated into up and down volumes, are presented. Snapshot also presents the value of the U.S. dollar in gold, yen, deutsche marks, and pounds. For information on other money-related features, see Financial Services and see Investment Analysis Tools. The feature is surcharged at 10 cents per report.

Current Research Information/USDA (food and agriculture database) may be searched through the IQuest gateway. See IQuest.

Current Technology Index (database) may be searched through the IQuest gateway. See IQuest.

CU Services (credit union software) is supported by the Office Automation Vendor Forum (GO OAFORUM). See Office Automation.

CUSIP lookup: For finding stock symbols for other financial services, see Issue and Symbol Lookup (GO SYMBOLS). See Stock Symbols, Lookup.

Custom Technologies software is supported in the PC Vendor A Forum (GO PCVENA). See IBM Computers.

Customer Support Professionals, Association for, is a sponsor of the General Computing Forum (GO GENCOM). See General Computing.

CVGIP: Graphical Models and Image Processing and **CVGIP: Image Understanding** (magazine abstracts) can be searched through Computer Database Plus (GO COMPDB). See Computer Database Plus.

Cyberdreams software is supported in the Game Publishers A Forum (GO GAMAPUB). See Gaming Forums.

CyberForum (GO CYBERFORUM) focuses on the "new edge of technology." Topics range from virtual reality to how computers influence the visual arts, entertainment, music and literature. Library files demonstrate virtual reality and other techniques, and offer tips for experimentation. Neil Shapiro (76703,401) is the chief sysop, assisted by John Eagan, Robert Wiggins, and Harry Baya.

CyberCorp products, like Cyberdesk, are supported in the Windows 3rd-Party Forum (GO WINAPD). See Microsoft Software.

Cycle World (magazine) can be searched in the Magazine Database Plus (GO MDP). See Magazine Database.

D

DacEasy Software is supported in the PC Vendor B Forum (GO PCVENB). See IBM Computers.

Dairy Foods and **Dairy Industries International** (**magazines**) can be searched through the Business Database Plus (GO BUSDB). See Business Database.

Dalco Computer Electronics (GO DA) is a store in the Electronic Mall (GO MALL) that offers PC components and supplies. See Electronic Mall.

Dallas Business Journal and **Dallas-Fort Worth Business Journal** (**magazines**) can be searched through the Business Database Plus (GO BUSDB). See Business Database.

Darling, Kevin (76703,4227) is sysop in OS-9 Forum (GO OS9). For details, see Tandy Computers.

Darwin's Dilemma (**software**) is supported in Mac C Vendor Forum (GO MACCVEN). For details, see Apple Computers.

Data Access Corp. Forum (GO DACCESS) supports the firm's software products, including DataFlex (Relational 4GL DBMS), Office Works (Group Productivity Software), FlexQL (Relational Report Writer-SQL), C Source & Library (C Interface to DataFlex 4GL), and others. The forum is operated by Doug Goldner (76702,1257), Katie Schepman (76702,1256), and Pat Kloepfer (76702,1330).

Database and **Database Searcher** (**magazines**) can be searched through the Business Database Plus (GO BUSDB), as can *Worldwide Databases*. See Business Database.

Data Based Advisor Forum   (GO DBADVISOR) is operated by the magazine of the same name and is dedicated to informing buyers and users about different databases.

The forum is divided among product types and contains sections for subscriber information and access to the magazine's editors. The libraries contain code to assist in developing a custom application using various database packages. The sysop of the forum is David Frier (76702,1417). Assisting are John Mueller, Holly Covell, Bill House, Warren Keuffel, and Aldene Yeo.

Available are electronic version of three magazines, including Data Based Advisor, Foxpro Advisor, and Access Advisor.

Also:

- Data Based Advisory has a kiosk in the Electronic Mall which can be reached by entering GO DB. Also see Electronic Mall.

- It is available for full-text searching through Computer Database Plus (GO COMPDB). See Computer Database Plus.

Data Base Monthly and **Database Programming & Design** (**magazine abstracts)** can be searched through Computer Database Plus (GO COMPDB). See Computer Database Plus.

Databases, Worldwide   (database) may be searched through the IQuest gateway. See IQuest.

Databook   computers are supported in the Palmtop Forum (GO PALMTOP). See Palmtop.

Data Broadcasting Report (magazine) can be searched through the Business Database Plus (GO BUSDB). See Business Database.

Data Channels   (database) may be searched through the IQuest gateway. See IQuest. The resource also can be searched through the Business Database Plus (GO BUSDB). See Business Database.

Data Communications (magazine) may be searched through the IQuest gateway (see IQuest) and through Computer Database Plus (GO COMPDB). See Computer Database Plus.

DataEase International Forum   (GO DATAEASE) supports the firm's family of database products, including DataEase for DOS and OS/2 as well as DataEase Express for Windows. The forum also has sections for the DataEase Query Language, client-server issues, third-party add-ons, and user groups. The primary sysop is Chris Griffith (76702,2017), who is assisted by Mark Fien, Shelby Smith, Lee Drake, Kevin Witty, David Gray, and Greg Evans.

DataFlex (software) is supported in the Data Access Corp. Forum (GO DACCESS). For details, see Data Access.

Datamation (magazine) is searchable through Computer Database Plus (GO COMPDB), the Business Database Plus (GO BUSDB), and IQuest (GO IQUEST).

DataPac (Canada) log-on instructions (GO LOG-41):

1. Dial the DataPac telephone access number and make the modem connection.
2. Enter one period (.) for 300bps access, two periods (..) for 1200bps, or three periods (...) for 2400pbs access.
3. When your screen displays "<Datapac dial port address), enter 29400138.
4. At the subsequent "Host Name:" prompt, enter CIS.
5. You then will be prompted to enter "User ID:" and "Password:".

Costs DataPac surcharges (rates charged in addition to CompuServe's basic rates) are $8 an hour for 300 to 2400bps access, $20 an hour for 9600bps. (Important note: Datapac doesn't distinguish between baud rates, so if you connect through one of Datapac's 9600bps access numbers you will be charged the 9600bps surcharge, *regardless of your actual modem speed*.)

DataPerfect (software) is supported by the WordPerfect Support forums. See WordPerfect Software.

Datapoint products are supported in the IBM PC Vendor H Forum (GO PCVENH). See IBM Computers.

Data processing newsletters (GO DPNEWS) are accessible through a Telebase Systems Incorporated gateway. For details, see PTS Newsletter Database/Communications.

Dataquest Online (GO DATAQUEST) is a feature operated by Dataquest Incorporated, a 21-year-old global market research and consulting firm serving the high-technology and financial communities. Dataquest provides worldwide market coverage on the communications, computer systems, document management, semiconductor, services, and software sectors of the information technology industry.

A key feature is Dataquest Alert, an event-driven collection of Dataquest's analyses of the most significant product, corporate, and governmental activities across all of the industries that Dataquest serves. Also in the service is Dataquest Service Industry News and related topics. Reports also can be packaged with other Dataquest services to meet specific needs. Dataquest's Direct Products Group can match your information requirements to the proper Dataquest study.

The Dataquest services are surcharged at $15 an hour.

Datasoft products are supported in the UK Computing Forum (GO UKCOMP). See UK Computing.

DataSolve of London is a major database vendor accessible through the IQuest gateway (GO IQUEST). See IQuest.

Datastar of Switzerland is a major database vendor accessible through the IQuest gateway (GO IQUEST). See IQuest.

Data Storage Report (magazine) can be searched through the Business Database Plus (GO BUSDB). See Business Database.

Datastorm Software is supported in the Datastorm Forum (GO DATA STORM). See Procomm (software).

DataTimes of Oklahoma City, is a major database vendor, accessible through the IQuest gateway (GO IQUEST). See IQuest.

DataTrends Report on DEC & IBM (magazine) can be searched through the Business Database Plus (GO BUSDB). See Business Database.

DAUGAZ (energy database) may be searched through the IQuest gateway. See IQuest.

DaVinci Forum (GO DAVINCI) supports its MHS-based electronic mail products, eMAIL for DOS, eMAIL for Windows, MacAccess, The Coordinator Software, and assorted utilities. The primary sysop is Michelle Vickery (76702,1054), who is assisted by Dana Berenson (76711,1121). Both are technical support representatives at DaVinci Systems.

Day, Wayne (76703,376) is administrator of the TandyNet forums (GO TANDYNET). See Tandy Corp. Computers.

DAYO (accounting software) is supported in the Office Automation Vendor Forum (GO OAFORUM). See Office Automation.

"Days of Our Lives" (television) summaries on the latest shows are available in Soap Opera Summaries (GO SOAPS). See Soap Opera.

Daystar Digital Inc. products are supported in the Macintosh Vendor Forum A (GO MACAVEN). See also Apple Computers.

Dayton (OH) Daily News (newspaper) is searchable through Telebase System's News Source USA (GO NEWSUSA). See News Source.

dBASE software is supported in the dBASE Forum (GO DBASE). See Borland.

D&B Dun's Market Identifiers (GO DUNS), **D&B Dun's Canadian Market Identifiers** (GO DBCAN), and **D&B International Dun's Market Identifiers** (GO DBINT) are financial directories on millions of establishments, public and private. See Company Reports. Some of these resources also can be searched on IQuest (see IQuest), and through Business Database Plus (see Business Database).

DBMS Magazine Forum (DBMSFORUM) is built around a monthly magazine devoted to database management systems programming, client-server systems, front-ends to databases, and other technical DBMS hardware and software issues. The main purpose of the forum is to make available in electronic form the programming code published every month in the pages of the magazine, as well as to stimulate discussion between readers, editors, and authors, and to serve as a clearinghouse for information of interest to the database industry. The primary sysop is Tom Genereaux (76703,4265). He assisted by Steve Wilent, who is managing editor of the magazine.

Also *DBMS* magazine is searchable through Computer Database Plus (GO COMPDB). See Computer Database Plus.

dBXL (**software**) is supported in the PC Vendor C Forum (GO PCVENC). See IBM Computers.

Deafness and hearing problems are discussed in the Disabilities Forum (GO DIS-ABILITIES). See Disabilities.

Deakin, John (76702,310) is a sysop in CP-MIG (GO CPMFORUM). See Programmers Support.

Dealing with Technology (**magazine**) can be searched through the Business Database Plus (GO BUSDB). See Business Database.

DEC computers: The system has two forums supporting DEC systems, The DEC PC Forum (GO DECPC), and the PDP-11 Forum (GO PDP11). See Digital Equipment Forums.

Declaration of Independence and the text of other historical documents can be retrieved and searched in Grolier's Academic American Encyclopedia, Grolier's (GO ENCYCLOPEDIA). See Academic American.

DEC Professional and ***DEC User*** are both available for searching through Computer Database Plus (GO COMPDB). See Computer Database Plus.

Decorating is covered in *Interior Design* magazine, which can be searched through the Business Database Plus (GO BUSDB). See Business Database. Also of interest is HFD—The Weekly Home Furnishings Newspaper, which may be searched through IQuest (GO IQUEST), as well as Business Database Plus.

Defense is discussed in the Political Debate Forum (GO POLITICS) and in the White House Forum (GO WHITEHOUSE). See Political and White House.

Defense and aerospace are covered in a variety of resources: *Defense & Aerospace Electronics, Defense Cleanup, Defense Daily, Defense Electronics, Defense Marketing International, Defense Technology Business,* and *Defense Week* magazines can be searched through the Business Database Plus (GO BUSDB), as well as *Report on Defense Plant Wastes.* See Business Database.

Also, relevant databases on IQuest (GO IQUEST) include:

Aerospace Electronic Business	Pac-Rim Defense Marketing
Aviation Week and Space Technology	Periscope—Daily Defense News Capsules
Compendex Plus	PTS Aerospace/Defence Markets and Technology
Defense/Aerospace Business Digest	PTS Newsletter Database
Defense Marketing International	Satellite Week
Defense Technology Business	SDI Intelligence Report
DMS Contractors	Soviet Aerospace and Technology
EI Engineering Meetings	Space Business News
Flightline	Space Calendar
Helicopter News	Space Commerce Bulletin
Japanese Aviation News: Wing	Space Daily
Military Robotics 1989 Sourcebook	Space Exploration Technology
Mobile Satellite News	Space Station News
Navy News and Undersea Technology	

See also IQuest and Space and see Military.

Default, in computer parlance, means an action that takes place unless you specify another action. For instance, your account on CompuServe may be set up to "default" to displaying 80-character lines, but you can charge it to display a different display, such as 64-character lines. These *defaults* (GO DEFALT) (screen sizes and characteristics for your CompuServe account) are automatically set in many of the modern communications programs, such as the CompuServe Information Manager platforms. (See CompuServe Information Manager.) On the other hand, if you are using a general third-party terminal program and viewing CompuServe in its ASCII version, you can set your defaults manually in the Terminal Settings area of the system. See Terminal.

Delaney Report (magazine) can be searched through the Business Database Plus (GO BUSDB). See Business Database.

Delaware (news) is included in the daily Northeast and Mid-Atlantic regional reports from United Press International. See Executive News Service for details.

Dell Computer Forum (GO DELL) provides access to the firm's technical support representatives and users, product and company information, and first access to the latest driver and flash BIOS files for immediate downloading. The primary sysop is Ron Clark (76702,1601). Assisting him are John Webb, Kerry Harrison, Sandy Willyard, Graham Keen, and Alison Davison.

Also, Dell computers are represented in the Novell Vendor Forum A (GO NVENA). See Novell Software.

DeLoach, Dick (76703,303) who has been a CompuServe forum administrator since 1982, is the sysop of the Space Forum (GO SPACEFORUM). See Space Forum. He also administers the Astronomy Forum (GO ASTROFORUM). For details on that, see Astronomy.

Delrina Technology Forum (GO DELRINA) supports a variety of products, including its family of form processing software, PerFORM PRO and PerFORM, and its fax products for the DOS and Windows environments, WINFAX PRO and DOSFAX PRO. You'll also find support for Delrina's new line of calendars from Amaze, including the Far Side and Cathy calendars. The sysops are Line Robichaud (72120,2676), Wayne Beyea (72262,1165), Wendy Schreiber (73424,2261), and Kevin Quinn (72410,2273). The Consumer Division sysop is John Brumett (75270,1126).

DeltaPoint Software is supported in the Mac A Vendor Forum (GO MACAVEN). See Apple Computers. It also is supported in the Windows 3rd-Party D Forum (GO WINAPD). See Microsoft Software.

Democratic Party Forum (GO DEMOCRATS) is overseen by the Democratic National Committee. It includes a hotline for national political updates. The forum's libraries contain the party platform, press releases, lists of candidates, speeches, and more. The sysops, all of whom are with the Democratic National Committee in Washington, are Dick Bell (71333,2523), Robin Bachman (71333,2522), and Kim Callinan.

See also Politics.

Demographics (GO DEMOGRAPHICS) are covered in a variety of business and personal services:

- *American Demographics* (**magazine**) is searchable through the Business Database Plus (GO BUSDB). See Business Database.
- Business Demographics (GO BUSDEM) is intended to help businesses analyze their markets with several types of reports. See Business Demographics.
- CENDATA (GO CENDATA) is a non-surcharged service of the U.S. Census Bureau. See CENDATA.
- D&B—Donnelley Demographics (database) may be searched through the IQuest gateway. See IQuest.

- Neighborhood Reports (GO NEIGHBOR) has information organized by age, income, occupation and household statistics, searching by ZIP code, county, or state. See Neighborhood Reports.
- SUPERSITE (GO SUPERSITE) provides a wide variety of demographics for the United States as a whole as well as every individual state, county, and assorted industry groups. See SUPERSITE.

See also Ecomonics.

Deneba Software is supported in the Mac B Vendor Forum (GO MACBVEN). See Apple Computers.

Dennis Publishing Ltd. sponsors UK Computer Shopper Forum (GO UKSHOPPER). For details, see UK Computer.

Dental Association, Journal of the American abstracts are searchable in the Health Database Plus (GO HLTBD). See Health.

Dental issues issues are a topic in the MedSIG Forum (GO MEDSIG). See Health.

Denver (CO) Rocky Mountain News (newspaper) is searchable through Telebase System's News Source USA (GO NEWSUSA). See News Source. Also, Denver Business Journal (magazine) can be searched through the Business Database Plus (GO BUSDB). See Business Database.

DePaoli, Marilyn (76702,1626) is sysop of the Telecommunication Issues Forum (GO TELECOM). See Telecommunication Forum.

Department of Health and Social Security (database) may be searched through the IQuest gateway. See IQuest.

Derivatives Engineering & Technology (magazine) can be searched through the Business Database Plus (GO BUSDB). See Business Database.

Dermatology, Journal of American abstracts are searchable in the Health Database Plus (GO HLTBD). See Health.

Dershowitz, Alan, (column) is among the syndicated columns provided by United Features (GO COLUMNS). See Columnists.

DeScribe products are supported in the IBM PC Vendor A Forum (GO PCVENA). See IBM Computers.

Designer (software) is supported in Windows 3rd-Party Forum A (GO WINAPA). See Microsoft Software.

DesignWare products are supported in the Graphics B Vendor Forum (GO GRAPHBVEN). See Graphics.

DeskMan/2 is supported in the OS/2 Vendor Forum (GO OS2AVEN). See IBM Computers.

Desktop Communications (**magazine abstracts**) can be searched through Computer Database Plus (GO COMPDB). See Computer Database Plus.

Desktop Publishing is the topic of these forums:

- Desktop Publishing Forum (GO DTPFORUM), supported by The Newsletter Factory, MacPrePress faxletter, High Text Graphics, HealthNote Publications, Board Room Graphics, and Computer Consulting Associates. Sysops include Thom Hartmann (76702,765), president of The Newsletter Factory, an Atlanta based company which writes, designs, layouts, typesets, and prints newsletters and magazines using desktop publishing, and Brad Walrod (76702,1043), owner of High Text Graphics. Assisting them are Don Arnoldy, Dianne Breen, Elyse Chapman, John Cornicello, Dave deBronkart, Laura Haggarty, Kathleen Tinkel, and Skye Lininger.

- Desktop Publishing Vendor Forum (GO DTPVENDOR) provides product support for desktop publishing products. The primary sysop is Thom Hartmann (76702,765), who is assisted by Laura Haggarty, John Cornicello, and Paul Solyn. Vendors offering advice and technical support in the forum include Timeworks, QMS Inc., Fontbank, Sigma Designs, CAI ColorAge, Hyphen, XChange, Scitex/SGAUA, Frame Technology, Bitstream, Electronics For Imaging, Monotype, and AISB.

Also of possible interest is the IBM Desktop Software Forum (GO IBMDESK), see IBM Computers, and FontBank Online (GO FONTBANK), see FontBank.

Des Moines news is provided in *Business Record*, searchable through the Business Database Plus (GO BUSDB). See Business Database.

DESQview (**software**) is supported in the (GO QUARTERDECK). For more details, see Quarterdeck.

Detroit Free Press Forum (GO DETROIT), operated by the Detroit Free Press newspaper, is a resource for international automotive information and photography. The forum provides news and GIF images of latest car models from North American International Auto Shows over the past 80 years. Message sections and libraries cover state and local sports, Michigan travel, lifestyles, entertainment and "how to's" covering everything from preparing a home for sale to checking your credit rating. Also, the newspaper is searchable through Telebase System's News Source USA (GO NEWSUSA) and through the Knowledge Index (GO KI). See News Source and see Knowledge Index.

Deutsche Presse-Agentur is a German news service that is searchable through Executive News Service (GO ENS) and through NewsGrid (GO NEWSGRID). For details, see Executive News Service and see NewsGrid.

Deutsches Computer Forum (GO GERNET) invites CompuServe users in Germany to discuss a range of computing and other topics. The forum is conducted in German, with sections including "Telekommunikathion," "Programmieren," "Mac/Atari/Amiga," "Datex-J," "Politik/Wirtschaft," "Press & Medien," and others. The forum is managed by Max Bold, a writer with *Bildschirmtext Magazin*.

Development Technologies products are supported in the OS/2 Vendor Forum (GO OS2AVEN). See IBM Computers.

Devich, Don (76711,725) is the sysop of the Showbiz Forum (GO SHOWBIZ). See Showbiz.

DG Review **(magazine)** is searchable through Computer Database Plus (GO COMPDB). See Computer Database Plus.

Diabetes magazine is searchable in the Health Database Plus (GO HLTBD), as are *Clinical Diabetes*, *Diabetes Forecast*, and *Diabetes in the News*. See Health.

Diabetes Forum (GO DIABOL) was created for the discussion of diabetes, hypoglycemia, and related chronic metabolic disorders in a self-help and support group setting. It was founded by diabetics with the idea that patients, their friends, families, and health care professionals should have a place to discuss the lifestyles that are crucial to their health. Forum administrator is Dave Groves (76703,4223), an insulin-dependent, type I diabetic since 1954 at the age of 9. Assisting him are Tom Arthurs, Dr. Charles Baker, Jim Beyer, Dr. John T. Carlock, Dr. Ron Dansereau, Shawn Davidson, Dr. Robert Fuentes, Belver D. Ladson, Elizabeth B. Pollard, Dr. E. Bruce MacDougall, Michael Mohle', Lisa Shifrin, Linda Wilk, and Faith Winter.

For other medical-related subjects, see Health.

Diagnostics Business Matters **(magazine)** can be searched through the Business Database Plus (GO BUSDB). See Business Database.

DiagSoft Forum (GO DIAGSOFT) supports the firm's QAPlus diagnostic programs. The forum is operated by Rudy Oakes, (75300,2515), senior technical support engineer with the company.

Dialog Information Services Inc. of Palo Alto, Calif., is the provider of the Knowledge Index (GO KI). See Knowledge Index. It also is a major database vendor accessible through the IQuest gateway (GO IQUEST). See IQuest.

Diamond Computer Systems **(compter graphics products)** is supported in the Graphics B Vendor Forum (GO DMNDONLINE). See Graphics.

Dickens, Ted (76701,272) is a primary sysop of the Hewlett-Packard PC Forum (GO HP). See Hewlett-Packard Computers.

Dictionary, American Heritage (GO DICTIONARY) from Houghton Mifflin Company, contains detailed definitions of more than 303,000 words, phrases, people, and geographic locations.

Search the database by entering the word, and if the spelling is unknown, type in the first five characters. All words and phrases beginning with those letters will be listed. If you enter a word of four characters or less, the dictionary will list only those words that match the characters exactly. In the resulting definition display, the word entry is broken into syllables with an an asterisk (*). Syllables with primary emphasis are represented by a double quote (”), while syllables with secondary emphasis are represented by a single quote, as in *ad*min”is*tra’tive*ly*.

Tips:

- Your search term can be quite specific and may contain a phrase or punctuation. For example, if you enter the idiom "over the hill," the dictionary will match on the word OVER, which has a definition of that idiom.

- You can enter compound words, such as "mother-in-law," by including the hyphens.

- However, do not enter diacritics or accented characters. Instead, enter the appropriate single- or two-character transliteration.

- Proper names can be searched in their normal or inverted form (so either George Washington or Washington George may be entered). Since many names contain middle initials or names, it is easier to search the inverted form without the middle name. Also, surnames alone can be searched.

This is one of the system's basic services, meaning those signed up under the Standard Pricing Plan (see Billing) have unlimited access to the feature.

See also Academic American Encyclopedia.

Diesel Progress (**magazine**) can be searched through the Business Database Plus (GO BUSDB). See Business Database.

Dieterich, Thom (75300,2270) is sysop of the Revelation Tech Forum (GO REVELATION). See Revelation.

Dietetic Association, Journal of the American is searchable in the Health Database Plus (GO HLTBD). See Health.

Digestive Diseases and Sciences abstracts are searchable in the Health Database Plus (GO HLTBD). See Health.

Digital Communications Associates publishes the Crosstalk communications program, which is supported in the Crosstalk Forum (GO XTALK). See Crosstalk.

Digital Eclipse products are supported in the Mac D Vendor Forum (GO MACDVEN). See Apple Computers.

Digital Equipment Forums: Several forums are concerned with computers from the Digital Equipment corporation:

- The DEC PC Forum (GO DECPC), independent of the computer maker, is dedicated to understanding and using Digital Equipment Corporation's line of personal computers, including but not limited to, the Rainbow, VT-180, DECmate, VAXmate, DECstation. The sysop here is Bill Leeman (76703,3055), a Tucson, Arizona, system manager of a seven-node VAXcluster. He is assited by Bill Mayhew and Carl Neiburger.

- DEC PC Integration Forum (GO DECPCI) is dedicated to the discussion of Digital's PC Integration products. It will be of particular interest to those using the DEC PathWORKS system, since the Digital PathWORKS support group maintains the forum. The sysops are Mitch Lichtenberg and Chris Lord.

- Digital Windows NT Support Forum (GO DEC4WNT) provides information on running Windows NT on Digital's Alpha AXP platform and other platforms. Digital's multivendor customer service staff are online to answer questions about start-up, interoperability, or peripheral devices in the NT environment. The sysops are Butch Leitz, Bob Withers, and Tim O'Donnell.

- The PDP-11 Forum (GO PDP11) is for users of the DEC PDP11 series of computers. The forum also supports the PROfessional Series Machines (325, 350, 380), as it is based on the LSI-11/PDP-11 instruction set and runs PDP11-related system software. Primary sysop is Chuck Sadoian (76703,414), assisted by Eli Willner.

- The VAX Forum (GO VAXFORUM), for discussion of the VAX 32-bit systems, VAX applications, and Digital's version of the Unix operating system known as Ultrix-32 and Ultrix-32m. The sysops are Stuart Fuller (76703,501), Doyle Myers (76703,4403), Richard Gilbert (76702,1567), and William H. Mayhew (76702,502).

Also of interest is *DataTrends Report on DEC & IBM*, which can be searched through the Business Database Plus (GO BUSDB). See Business Database.

Digitalk Forum (GO DIGITALK) supports users of Digitalk's Smalltalk/V products. The feature's libraries contain Smalltalk code, tools and applications, compilations of technical tips, Digitalk public relations announcements, and more.

Members may use the forum's message sections to keep up on the latest information about Smalltalk/V, receive answers to technical support questions, and learn how others are using Smalltalk/V development systems to create and deliver software. The primary sysop is Brenda Friederich (76711,366). Assisting are Dan Goldman and Jim Haungs.

Digital Media, Digital News & Review, and **Digital Systems Journal** (**magazines**) are searchable through Computer Database Plus (GO COMPDB). See Computer Database Plus. Digital Media also is available on Seybold Newsletters (GO ZNT:SEYBOLD) on ZiffNet. See ZiffNet.

Digital Research Inc. software is supported in the Novell Desktop Forum (GO NDESKTOP). See Novell.

Digital's PC Store (GO DD) is a store in the Electronic Mall (GO MALL) that offers computer products. See Electronic Mall.

Digital Vision products are supported in the Graphics A Vendor Forum (GO DIGVIS). See Graphics.

DigiVox products are supported in the Ultimedia Tools Forum B (GO ULTIBTOOLS). See Ultimedia.

Dinosaur Forum (GO DINO) was established by the Dinosaur Club in association with the Dinosaur Society for discussion of one of history's greatest mysteries. Among the forum's features are message sections devoted to "Entertainment," "Dinosaur Science," "News/Discoveries," "Publications," and "Dinosaur Humor." In addition, the forum's libraries include computer images of "famous" prehistoric animals such as tyrannosaurus, stegosaurus, triceratops, and more. The forum is managed by Dinamation International Society. Daily operations are performed by Bruce Hoover and the overall management and direction is being provided by Joe Donnelly (76702,204).

Diplomacy (game) enthusiasts gather in the Play-by-Mail Games Forum (GO PBMGAMES). See Games.

Diplomat, APS, publications (Fate of the Arabian Peninsula, News Service, Operations in Oil Diplomacy, Recorder, Redrawing the Islamic Map, and Strategic Balance in the Middle East) can be searched through the Business Database Plus (GO BUSDB). See Business Database.

Diogenes (health database) may be searched through the IQuest gateway. See IQuest.

Direct Marketing (magazine) can be searched through the Business Database Plus (GO BUSDB). See Business Database.

Direct Micro (GO DM) is a store in the Electronic Mall (GO MALL) that offers discount computer disks and accessories. See Electronic Mall.

Disabilities Forum (GO DISABILITIES) is open to all people interested in disabilities, from those with handicapping conditions and their families to those who assist, train, educate, or employ the disabled. The administrator is Dr. David Manning (76703,237), director of the mainstream center at The Clarke School for the Deaf in Northampton, Massachusetts. Assisting are Larry Orloff, Karen Mann, David Andrews, Merle Spector, and Richard Korejwo.

For related topics, see Handicapped Issues.

DISCLOSURE II (GO DISCLOSURE), available only with the Executive Option, is a financial service that has information from the 10K filings and other reports of publicly owned companies' files, which are required by the Securities and Exchange

Commission. See Company Reports. This also may be searched on IQuest, as can be Disclosure/Spectrum Ownership. See IQuest.

Discount Store News (database) may be searched through the IQuest gateway. See IQuest. It also can be searched through Business Database Plus (GO BUSDB). See Business Database.

Discover (magazine) is searchable through Magazine Database Plus (GO MDP). For details see Magazine Database.

Disease Database (GO NORD) is made up of the online reports by the National Organization for Rare Disorders. See Rare Disease Database.

Disney Software products are covered in Game Publishers B Forum (GO GAMBPUB). See Gaming Forums.

Disney World is a topic in the Florida Forum (GO FLORIDA). For details, see Florida.

DisplayWrite (IBM software) is supported in the IBM Desktop Software Forum (GO IBMDESK). See IBM Computers.

Dissertation Abstracts (GO DISSERTATION) is a Telebase Systems Incorporated gateway that contains bibliographic references for nearly all Ph.D. dissertations published since 1861 and for selected masters' theses. Abstracts are available for dissertations published after 1980.

Data on each dissertation includes author, title, date of publication, college, and degree for which the dissertation was submitted. Surcharges for the database are $5 for the first 10 titles located; $5 for addition titles in groups of 10; $5 for each full reference retrieved, with abstract where available; and $1 for searches that retrieve no titles.

For information on other Telebase gateways, see Telebase Systems Incorporated.

This resource also may be searched through IQuest (GO IQUEST) and through the Knowledge Index (GO KI). See IQuest and see Knowledge Index.

Distribution and **U.S. Distribution Journal** (magazines) can be searched through the Business Database Plus (GO BUSDB). See Business Database.

Dividends, Splits, and **Bond Interest** (GO DIVIDENDS) gives historical information about these events for an issue over a given period. See Stock Quotes (Historical).

Diving is discussed in the Scuba Forum (GO SCUBA). For details, see Sports.

Dixon, Beth (76702,763) administers the Lotus Word Processing Forum (GO LOTUSWP). See Lotus Software.

DMS/Fi Contract Awards (aerospace and defense database) may be searched through the IQuest gateway. See IQuest.

.DOC, as an extension on filenames in forum libraries, stands for documentation, that is, the instructions for a particular program. See Files, Extensions.

Doctors, nurses, and patients might be interested in assorted medical references available through the system. See Medical References and see Health.

Doctor's People Newsletter is searchable in the Health Database Plus (GO HLTBD). See Health.

Dr. Dobb's Journal: The Dr. Dobb's Journal Forum (GO DDJFORUM) encourages discussions on programming languages, techniques, tools, utilities, and algorithms. The forum's primary purpose is to make available in electronic form the programming code published each month in the magazine, as well as to give readers a communications link to its editors and writers.

Managing the forum is Tom Genereaux (76703,4265), who is head of systems programming for the Computer Graphics Lab at the New York Institute of Technology.

At present, the message board is subdivided into discussions on C, CP/M, ALGOL, FORTH, 68000 programming, artificial intelligence, and more.

The magazine also can be searched through Computer Database Plus (GO COMPDB). See Computer Database Plus.

For related topics, see Programmers Support.

Dr. Neuhaus Forum (modem support) (GO NEUHAUS) is a German-speaking forum that supports Dr. Neuhaus modems and other communication products, operated by the Dr. Neuhaus support staff.

The forum supports the firm's networking products, communication programs, FAXY (telefax board), FURY modems, and NICCY (ISDN) products.

"Dr. No" (television) fans often gather in the Science Fiction & Fantasy Forum (GO HOM-9). See Science Fiction.

Dr. T's (products) are supported in the MIDI C Vendor Forum (GO MIDICVEN). See Music.

Documentation, instruction books for various CompuServe features, may be ordered online. For details, enter GO ORDER.

Document Image Automation Update (magazine) can be searched through the Business Database Plus (GO BUSDB). See Business Database.

Dogs are regularly discussed in the Pets and Animals Forum (GO PETS). For details, see Pets.

Do-it-yourself projects are discussed in the Family Handyman Forum (GO HANDYMAN). See Family Handyman Forum. It also is a topic in the Homing Instinct Forum (GO HOMING). See Homing Instinct.

Doll collecting is discussed in the Collectibles Forum (GO COLLECT). See Collectibles.

Donnelly, Joe (76702,204) manages the Dinosaur Forum (GO DINOFORUM). See Dinosaur.

Donnelley Demographics, D&B **(marketing database)** may be searched through the IQuest gateway. See IQuest.

DOSFAX PRO **(software)** is supported in Delrina Technology Forum (GO DELRINA). See Delrina.

Double Click **products** are supported in the Atari Vendors Forum (GO ATARIVEN). See Atari Computers.

DoubleDisk is supported in the PC Vendor G Forum (GO PCVENG). See IBM.

Doubler **(software)** is supported in the Symantec Fifth Generation Systems Forum (GO SYMFGS). See Symantec.

Downloading covers retrieving a file (program or a text file, such as a letter or article) from CompuServe and saving it on disk for use later. For more on this subject, see Files, Transfer.

DPA-Kurznachrichtendienst Basic News Services (GO DPANEW) provides full-text articles in German. See German for other such services.

Draft Choice **(software)** is supported in the UK Shareware Forum (GO UKSHARE). See UK Shareware.

Draw **(software)** is supported in the Corel Support Forum (GO COREL). For details, see Corel Support.

DrawPerfect **(software)** is supported by the WordPerfect Support Forums. See WordPerfect Software.

DRDOS software is supported in the Novell Desktop Forum (GO NDESKTOP). See Novell.

Dreier, Harry (72662,1755) is sysop of the Intuit Forum (GO INTUIT). See Intuit.

Drew, Richard C. (76701,123) administers the Scuba Forum (GO SCUBA). See Sports and Recreation.

Dreyfuss, Joel (72241,264) is one of the editors and writers associated with the PC Magazine forums. See PC Magazine.

Dreyfus Corp. (GO DR) is a store in the Electronic Mall (GO MALL) that offers mutual funds information. See Electronic Mall.

Drug abuse is discussed in the Health and Fitness Forum (GO GOODHEALTH). See Health.

Drug Reference, The Consumer Reports Complete (GO DRUGS) is searchable by either brand or generic drug name to retrieve descriptions, proper usage guidelines, precautions, side effects, and more for prescription and over-the-counter drugs sold in the United States and Canada. Based on the Drug Reference's print version and written in everyday language, the database contains more than 700 entries, each covering a drug family or generic drug. Data includes both prescription and over-the-counter medicines as compiled by the U.S. Pharmacopeia. The database is updated quarterly. This is one of the system's basic services, meaning those signed up under the Standard Pricing Plan (see Billing) have unlimited access to the feature.

Drugs and pharmacy are topics of a number of IQuest databases, including Consumer Drug Information Database, De Haen Drug Data, Diogenes, Drug Information Fulltext, DrugNews (ADIS), Drug Topics and Druginfo, Alcohol Use and Abuse, International Pharmaceutical Abstracts, Unlisted Drugs, and Merck Index Online. See IQuest.

Also, *Drug & Cosmetic Industry*, *Drug Store News*, and *Drug Topics* are searchable through Business Database Plus (GO BUSDB). See Business Database.

In addition, *Medical Letter on Drugs and Therapeutics* abstracts are searchable in the Health Database Plus (GO HLTBD). See Health.

Searchable through the Knowledge Index (GO KI) are Consumer Drug Information Fulltext, International Pharmaceutical Abstracts, Consumer Drug Information Fulltext, and The Merck Index Online. See Knowledge Index.

For related topics, see Health/Medicine and see Pharmaceuticals.

DrumTrax (products) are supported in the MIDI C Vendor Forum (GO MIDICVEN). See Music.

DSI Software Systems products are supported in the IBM PC Vendor E Forum (GO PCVENE). See IBM Computers.

Dun's Electronic Business Directory (database) may be searched through the IQuest gateway. See IQuest.

Dun's Electronic Yellow Pages (GO DYP) is a Telebase Systems Incorporated gateway that contains directory information on more than 8.5 million businesses and professionals in the United States. It covers both public and private companies of all sizes and types.

The information for a company includes the name, address, telephone number, type of business, SIC code, number of employees, professional's name, Dun's number, industry, city population, and parent company information as compiled by Dun & Bradstreet Incorporated.

The surcharge amounts to $7.50 for the first five titles located, $7.50 for each additional five titles, and $1 for searches that retrieve no companies.

For information on other Telebase gateways, see Telebase Systems Incorporated. And for other telephone databases, see Phone Directories.

Duncan, Ray (72241,52) is among *PC Magazine*'s editors and contributors who are regulars in the publication's PC-Magnet service. See *PC Magazine*.

Dunford, Chris (76703,2002) is a sysop of the IBM Users Network (GO IBMNET). See IBM Computers.

Dungeons & Dragons and similar role-playing fantasy games are supported in the Role-Playing Games Forum (GO RPGAMES). See Gaming Forums.

Dunlea, Keith (75300,2755) is sysop of the Stac Electronics Forum (GO STACKER). See Stac Electronics.

Durrant, Scott (76702,2035) is sysop of the Intel ACCESS/Real-Time Forum (GO INTELACCESS). See Intel Corp.

Dutch users might be interested in the Microsoft Benelux Developers Forum (GO MSBEN). See Microsoft Software. Also, PCM Online (GO PCMONLINE) and the associated PCM Forum support readers of the Dutch publication, *Personal Computer Magazine*. See PCM. Also see the Dutch Personal Computer Magazine (GO VNUBPA).

Dvorak, John (72241,47) computer columnist and critic is a regular in *PC Magazine*'s online PC-Magnet service. See *PC Magazine*.

Dvorak Development products, including two offline navigational programs (NavCIS SE for Windows and NavCIS SE for DOS), are support in a section of the Dvorak Development Forum (GO DVORAK or GO NAVCIS). For system requirement information or to download, use GO WNAVCIS (for Windows) or GO DNAVCIS (for DOS). The sysops include Mike Ceranski (71333,11) and Kevin Minard (72662,736), assisted by David Holmes, Rob Seifert, Diane Jernigan, and Steve Brothers.

DynaComm (**software**) is supported in Windows 3rd-Party Forum A (GO WINAPA). See Microsoft Software.

Dynamix software is supported in the Game Publishers C Forum (GO GAMCPUB). See Gaming Forums.

E

Eaasy Sabre (GO SABRE), an electronic flight reservation service by American Airlines, enables a user to review and select from scheduled flights on all major airlines and to make reservations for hotels and car agencies in major cities. This is one of the system's basic services, meaning those signed up under the Standard Pricing Plan (see Billing) have unlimited access to the feature.

The service provides access to information on the current availability for more than 600 airlines (300 for booking), 18,000 hotel properties worldwide, and more than 45 car rental companies. You can search more than 43 million fares that are updated at a rate of a million changes daily.

First-time users are invited to select the Access EAASY SABRE option on the introductory menu and create a password to ensure the security of your reservations. When the application is complete, you can immediately begin booking privileges for flights, hotels, and cars. (A free user's guide will be mailed to you within a few weeks of applying.) This also entitles you to instant membership to AAdvantage, American Airlines' travel awards program. (If you are already an AAdvantage member, your AAdvantage number will be activated for Eaasy Sabre access upon completing the reservation. You will be mailed another passcode—different from the password you created when making reservations—to be used for checking your AAdvantage account status.)

After your signup, you can browse the feature to shop for fare, flight, car, and hotel availability, and hold a reservation with no obligation until your reservation is finalized and your tickets are purchased. Different operating procedures have been set up for users of the various CompuServe Information Manager platforms as well as for those of general third-party communications software. The Eaasy Sabre introductory menu offers specific instructions for CIM and non-CIM users for navigating the feature and selecting and reviewing the data.

Other highlights:

- You can view actual departure and arrival information—even gate numbers and baggage claim information for American Airlines flights—as well as scheduled flight information for all other airlines.

- You can see reports on current weather conditions as provided by the National Weather Bureau for more than 600 cities in the U.S. and Canada and the Caribbean.

- Regular users of the service can save time with Eaasy Sabre's built-in "Quick Path" and "Faasttrack" options, also described on the main menu.

- A Travel Club offers users a variety of discounted vacation packages, and contains instructions on obtaining exclusive membership.

- Bargain Finder enables you to automatically price your itinerary at the lowest available fare. It also saves time by minimizing the amount of research you are required to do prior to selecting your flights, letting you profile an itinerary. An online tutorial is provided.

- Eaasy Sabre also operates a phone "help desk" service for users. The numbers are 800-331-2690 inside the U.S., 817-355-2936 outside the U.S.

For other online airline reservation services, see Airline Services; for an overview of other travel-related features, see Travel.

Eagle computers are among the systems supported in CompuServe's Computer Club Forum (GO CLUB). See Computer Club.

Earnings Estimates (GO IBES). Available to subscribers of the Executive Option, this is a financial service called the Institutional Broker's Estimate System. It represents a consensus of annual and long-term forecasts from more than 2,500 analysts at 130 brokerage and institutional research firms. See Investment Analysis Tools.

Earth Forum (GO EARTH) covers environmental issues, offering discussions with environmental scientists and professionals, media and environmentally oriented organizations. The sysop is Joe Reynolds (76704,37), a Marylander, who is eastern editor for *Field & Stream* magazine, and an active participant in the environmental movement, both as a writer and an organizer at the grassroots level. Assisting Reynolds is New Yorker Les Line, editor-in-chief for 25 years of *Audubon* magazine, published by the National Audubon Society.

The forum also offers wildlife graphics in its Library 0, "Earth Graphics/GIFs," including 256-color wildlife and scenic GIF images scanned from slides by award-winning wildlife and nature photographer Norm Smith. The pictures have been published in such magazines as *Natural History, Wildlife Conservation, Animals, Arizona Highways, Modern Photography, Oceans,* and *Pacific Discovery.*

See also Environmental Issues.

Earth sciences are covered in various IQuest databases (GO IQUEST), including Academic Index, COLD, ECOMINE, General Science Index, Geoarchive, Geobanque, Geomechanics Abstracts, Georef, Meteorological and Geoastrophysical Abstracts,

National Technical Information Service, Oceanic Abstracts, PASCAL, SciSearch, Water Resources Abstracts, and Waternet. See IQuest.

See also Environmental issues, Geo studies, and Energy.

East Asia Express Contracts (database) may be searched through the IQuest gateway. See IQuest.

Eastburn, Bill (70007,1657) manages the California Forum (GO CALFORUM). See California.

East Europe is subject of several IQuest databases, including East Europe Intelligence Report, East European Monitor, the Chemical Industry Database, Eastern Europe Finance, and Eastern European & Soviet Telecom Report. See IQuest.

And searchable through the Business Database Plus (GO BUSDB) are *Eastern European & Former Soviet Telecom Report, Eastern European Energy Report, East European Insurance Report, East European Markets, Executive Briefing Service Eastern Europe,* and *Finance East Europe*. See Business Database.

Eastman, Dick (76701,263) is sysop in the Genealogy Forum (GO ROOTS). See Genealogy Forum.

East West and ***East West Natural Health*** (magazines) are searchable in the Health Database Plus (GO HLTBD). See Health.

EasyCAD is supported in the CADD/CAM/CAE Vendor Forum (GO CADDVEN). See CAD/CAM.

EasyPlex (GO MAIL) is an older name for CompuServe Mail, which provides each subscriber with a private mailbox where electronic letters can be received and sent online around the clock. For details, see Mail, CompuServe.

Ebert, Roger offers a database of movie Reviews (GO EBERT). See Roger Ebert. See also Movies. Roger Ebert also is a regular visitor in the ShowBiz Forum (GO SHOWBIZ). See Showbiz.

Ebony (magazine) is searchable through Magazine Database Plus (GO MDP). For details see Magazine Database.

EBRD Watch (magazine) can be searched through the Business Database Plus (GO BUSDB). See Business Database.

Ecology is discussed in the Earth Forum (GO EARTH). For details, see Earth. And environmental databases on IQuest include Enviroline, Environmental Bibliography, Environmental Compliance Update, and Environment Week. See IQuest.

Eco-Log Week can be searched through the Business Database Plus (GO BUSDB). See Business Database.

See also Environment.

ECOMINE (mining info database) may be searched through the IQuest gateway. See IQuest.

Economics is covered in a variety of services, including:

- Magazines are searchable through the Business Database Plus (GO BUSDB) including *CIS Economics & Foreign Trade*, *Economic Journal*, *Economic Progress Report*, *Economic Review*, *Engineering Economist*, *Quarterly Review of Economics*, and *Business and World Economic Outlook*. See Business Database.

- Economist is searchable through Magazine Database Plus (GO MDP), the Business Database Plus (GO BUSDB), and through IQuest (GO IQUEST). See, Magazine Database, Business Database, and IQuest.

- Relevant databases on IQuest (GO IQUEST) include:

  Academic Index
  AECO
  American Statistics Index
  Business Periodicals Index
  Business Week
  Cendata
  Chronicle of Latin American
     Economic Affairs
  D&B—Donnelley Demographics
  Econbase
  Economic Literature Index
  Economist
  Financial Times & The Economist
  Frost & Sullivan Political Risk
     Country Reports

  Harvard Business Review Online
  Industries in Transition
  Japan Economic Newswire Plus
  Keesing's Record of World Events
  Liquidation Alert
  PAIS International
  PTS F&S Indexes (1980 to present)
  PTS International Forecasts
  PTS U.S. Forecasts
  PTS U.S. Time Series
  Sourcemex: Economic News on
     Mexico
  Week in Germany

  See IQuest.

- Economic Literature Index can be searched through the Knowledge Index (GO KI). See Knowledge Index.

- Economy, trade, and budgets are discussed in the Political Debate Forum (GO POLITICS) and in the White House Forum (GO WHITEHOUSE). See Political and White House.

  See also Financial Services, Banking, Business, and Demographics.

Edell Health Letter is searchable in the Health Database Plus (GO HLTBD). See Health.

EDF-DOC (French economics database) may be searched through the IQuest gateway. See IQuest.

Edge: Work Group Computing Report (database) may be searched through the IQuest gateway. See IQuest. It also can be searched through Computer Database Plus (GO COMPDB) and the Business Database Plus (GO BUSDB). See Business Database and see Computer Database Plus.

EDI News (database) may be searched through the IQuest gateway. See IQuest. The resource also can be searched through the Business Database Plus (GO BUSDB), as can *EDI in Finance*. See Business Database.

Edington, Larry (75300,3533) is sysop of Compaq Forum (GO CPQFORUM). See Compaq.

Editors Only (writing database) may be searched through the IQuest gateway. See IQuest.

*EDN_* **(magazine)** is searchable through Computer Database Plus (GO COMPDB). See Computer Database Plus.

EDOC and **EPAT** (European patent databases) may be searched through the IQuest gateway. See IQuest.

Education: Online services for students and teachers range from research databases and reference books to school-oriented forums. Central to the educational features is Grolier's Academic American Encyclopedia (GO ENCYCLOPEDIA), a 10-million-word reference that is updated four times a year, and the American Heritage Dictionary (GO DICTIONARY) from Houghton Mifflin Company, which contains detailed definitions of more than 303,000 words, phrases, people, and geographic locations. For more on those, see Academic American and see Dictionary.

Other resources include the Knowledge Index (GO KI), Educational Resources Information Center (GO ERIC), Dissertation Abstracts (GO DISSERTATION), and Peterson's College Guide (GO PETERSON).

A number of forums support education, including Computer Forum Training (GO DPTRAIN), Education Forum (GO EDFORUM), Education Research Forum (GO EDRESEARCH), Foreign Language Forum (GO FLEFO), LOGO Forum (GO LOGOFORUM), Mensa Forum (GO MENSA), Science/Math Forum (GO SCIENCE), and Students' Forum (GO STUFO), as well as the Political Debate Forum (GO POLITICS), Space/Astronomy Forum (GO SPACEFORUM), and the White House Forum (GO WHITEHOUSE).

Relevant databases on IQuest (GO IQUEST) include A-V Online, Academic Index, Educational Resources Information Center, Education Daily, Education Index, Exceptional Child Education Resources, Heller Report on Educational Technology & Telecommunications, Linguistics & Language Behavior Abstracts, Mental Measurements Yearbook, Peterson's College Database, Peterson's Gradline, Rehabdata, and Report on Literacy Programs. See IQuest.

Searched through the Knowledge Index (GO KI) are Academic Index, A-V Online, ERIC, Peterson's Colege Database, and Peterson's Gradline. See Knowledge Index.

Educational Resources Information Center (ERIC)   (GO ERIC) is a Telebase Systems Incorporated gateway to ERIC, a famous educators' database. It contains abstracts of articles covering all aspects of education, including vocational education, counseling, teacher education, and testing. The data goes back to 1966 and is updated monthly. Also included are two subfiles:

- The Resources In Education (RIE) file, which contains research/technical reports, conference papers and proceedings, program descriptions, opinion papers, bibliographies, reviews, dissertations, teaching and curriculum materials, lesson plans, and guides.
- The Current Index to Journals in Education (CIJE) file, which contains abstracts of articles from 750 education-related professional journals.

The surcharge is $2 for the first 10 titles located, $2 for each additional 10 titles, and $2 for each reference retrieved. Reprints on by normal delivery are $18 each, $42 for express delivery. There is a $1 charge for searches that retrieve no titles.

This resource also can be searched through the Knowledge Index (GO KI). See Knowledge Index.

For information on other Telebase gateways, see Telebase Systems Incorporated.

Educational Technology (**magazine**) is searchable (abstracts) through Computer Database Plus (GO COMPDB). See Computer Database Plus.

Education Forum (GO EDFORUM) is operated by Chuck Lynd (76703,674), a former classroom teacher with experience in both regular and special education. He also has more than 10 years experience in education and computer-based retrieval systems. Assistants include Georgia Griffith (a Columbus, Ohio, music educator), Fran Staniec, Elvira Casal, Dr. Kurt Harper, Kevin Dohmen, Lynne Schrum, Ken and Carrie Loss-Cutler, Lawrence and Bonnie Williams, Betsy Fein, Barbara Gollon, Hal Meyer, and Cynthia Garland.

Education Research Forum (GO EDRESEARCH) is set up to share, compare, and comment on research findings in the field. Many of its regular members are associated with the American Educational Research Association. The sysop is Dr. Jean W. Pierce (76703,445), an associate professor at Northern Illinois University, and past president of the Mid-Western Educational Research Association.

Education Technology News and **Educational Marketer** (**magazines**) can be searched through the Business Database Plus (GO BUSDB). See Business Database.

Edwards, John (70007,412) is a contributing editor of *CompuServe Magazine* and a regular in the Online Today Electronic Edition (GO OLT). See Online Today.

Edwards, Paul and Sarah (76703,242) administer the Working From Home Forum (GO WORK). See Working From Home Forum.

E. F. Haskell (general ledger/accounting software) is supported by the Office Automation Vendor Forum (GO OAFORUM). See Office Automation.

EFT Report (database) may be searched through the IQuest gateway. See IQuest. It also can be searched through Business Database Plus (GO BUSDB). See Business Database.

Eicon Forum (GO EICON) provides information and technical support on products from Eicon Technology, a manufacturer of connectivity solutions for the X.25 and SNA world. Jacques Riopel (75300,3455) is the main sysop. Assisting are Steve Acosta and Dan Gill.

EI Engineering Meetings (database) may be searched through the IQuest gateway. See IQuest. See also Engineering.

Eiffel OOP products are supported in the IBM PC Vendor E Forum (GO PCVENE). See IBM Computers.

800 Flower and Gift Shoppe (GO GM) is a store in the Electronic Mall (GO MALL) that offers gifts for all occasions. See Electronic Mall.

800-900 Review (magazine) can be searched through the Business Database Plus (GO BUSDB). See Business Database.

80 Micro (magazine) is searchable (abstracts) through Computer Database Plus (GO COMPDB). See Computer Database Plus.

Elderly issues are discussed in the Seniors Forum (GO SENIORS). See also Age.

Electricity, electric industry, and **electrical engineering** are covered in magazines *Electrical Construction and Maintenance*, *Electric Light & Power*, *Electronic Business*, *Electronic News*, *Battery & EV Technology*, all of which can be searched through the Business Database Plus (GO BUSDB). See Business Database.

Relevant databases on IQuest (GO IQUEST) include:

Audio Week	Electronic Buyer's News
Battery & EV Technology	Electronic Design
Comline Japan Daily: Electronics	Electronic Engineering Times
Compendex Plus	Electronic Materials Technology
Consumer Electronics	News
Data Channels	Electronic News
EDF-DOC	Engineered Materials Abstracts
Electric and Magnetic Field	Fiber/Optics News
Keeptrack	High Fidelity
Electric Power Database	INSPEC

Japan Computer Industry Scan

Japan Consumer Electronics Scan

Japan Science Scan

Japan Semiconductor Scan

Japan Telecommunications Scan

Japan Weekly Monitor

PSN News

PTS Newsletter Database

Semiconductor Industry & Business Survey

SMT Trends

Stereo Review

Telephone Engineer and Management

Video Technology Newsletter

See also IQuest and see Energy.

Electro Manufacturing (**magazine**) can be searched through the Business Database Plus (GO BUSDB). See Business Database.

Electronic Arts software regularly is discussed in The Game Publishers A Forum (GO GAMAPUB) and in the Flight Simulation Forum (GO FSFORUM). See Gaming Forums.

Electronic Chemicals News (**magazine**) can be searched through the Business Database Plus (GO BUSDB). See Business Database.

Electronic Defense, Journal of (**magazine**) can be searched through the Business Database Plus (GO BUSDB). See Business Database.

Electronic Frontier Foundation Forum (GO EFFSIG) supports and discusses the activities of this nonprofit computer rights organization. Its message section topics include Cyberlaw, NetTech, TechnoRisks, Media Watch, and more.

EFF, intent on the "civilizing of cyberspace," which was founded by Mitchell Kapor, John Barlow, and John Gilmore, advocates system standards and open access for all information providers and consumers. EFF works to promote research and development tools to guarantee easy access to networks, and aims to stimulate creativity and an entrepreneurial spirit throughout all information networks. Administering the forum is Cliff Figallo (76711,320), formerly director of the Whole Earth Lectronic Link (The WELL).

See also Telecommunications.

Electronic Gamer (GO TEG) is an online magazine edited by Patricia Fitzgibbons and devoted to computer gaming of all types. See Gaming Publications.

Electronic Learning (**magazine**) articles are searchable through Magazine Database Plus (GO MDP). For details, see Magazine Database.

Electronic Mail (GO MAIL). CompuServe provides each subscriber with a private mailbox where electronic letters can be received and sent online around the clock. For details, see Mail, CompuServe.

Electronic Mall (GO MALL) provides merchants who offer online ordering and product information. From an introductory menu, you may examine an introduction and see directions on how to place orders. Other options list current events by the mall merchants and take you to a feedback area where you may leave messages for those who manage the service. This is one of the system's basic services, meaning those signed up under the Standard Pricing Plan (see Billing) have unlimited access to the feature.

After you select the "Enter the Mall" option, the system provides options to display the names of the mall's stores by department; the second option provides an alphabetical list of merchants; the third offers an alphabetical index of product and services available in the mall, which is especially useful for first-time users.

Other menus cause the system to display lists of product groups (such as apparel/ accessories, audio equipment, automotive, books, business services, cameras/optical equipment, children's clothes/merchandise). You are prompted to either select a group or press RETURN to see more of the index.

The Electronic Mall gives store managers a free hand to display introductory pages. Most mall merchants present visitors with a "signboard" before entering the main shopping area.

To enter a mall store, either select it through the menus or access it directly with the GO command followed by its unique address. When you arrive, you are greeted by a welcome message, followed by a general menu of options. The menu varies slightly from store to store. Most offer an introductory overview, followed by one or more catalogs (often searchable by keywords or topics). This is usually followed by ordering instructions and customer service information.

When looking through catalogs of products, you usually are shown descriptions, including a price, followed by a prompt that says, "Enter 'O' to order." If you want to order a product you have read about, enter O (the letter "o", not a zero), and the system notes it. The O command is universal in the Electronic Mall, that is, it means *order* in all the stores.

About ordering:

- You browse through a single store's database, ordering as many things as you like with the O command.

- As you exit the store, you are taken to an order area where you are asked for your name, address, phone number, and your method of payment (usually a credit card number, though the billing options vary depending on the merchant).

- There are stopping places all along the way to make corrections to the ordering information or to cancel the entire order.

- Most mall stores send you notification later by CompuServe Mail of what you have ordered, along with an order number and other pertinent information. By retrieving and filing the mail, you have a record of the order in case you need to refer to it later.

For related topics, see Shopper Features.

Electronic Materials & Processing and ***Electronic Materials Technology News*** **(magazines)** can be searched through the Business Database Plus (GO BUSDB). See Business Database.

Electronic Messaging News **(database)** can be searched through IQuest. See IQuest. The resource also can be searched through the Business Database Plus (GO BUSDB). See Business Database.

Electronic Office **(magazine)** can be searched through the Business Database Plus (GO BUSDB). See Business Database.

Electronics businesses are covered in an assortment of features; among them are:

- Dun's Electronic Business Directory, Electronic Design, Electronic Engineering Times, Electronic Materials Technology News, Electronic Messaging News, Electronic, News and Electronic Services Update, which may be searched through the IQuest gateway. See IQuest.
- Magazines such as *Electronic Business*, *Electronic News*, *Electronics*, *Electronic Design*, and *Electronic Learning*, which are searchable in Computer Database Plus (GO COMPDB). See Computer Database Plus.

See also Electricity.

Electronic Services Update **(database covering online business)** can be searched through IQuest. See IQuest. The resource also can be searched through the Business Database Plus (GO BUSDB). See Business Database.

Electronics For Imaging products are supported in the Desktop Publishing Vendor Forum (GO DTPVENDOR). For details, see Desktop Publishing.

Electronics Forum, Consumer (GO CEFORUM) covers audio, video, software, satellite systems, telephone equipment, and "interesting electronic stuff." It is directed by Dawn Gordon (76703,204) with help from Bill Rood, Marc Wielage, Andy Adler, E. Brad Meyer, Eric Carter, Steve Schechter, James Shobert, Michael Marcus, Jeff Goldman, and Roderick Woodcock.

In addition, the Consumer Electronics Vendor Forum (GO CEVENDOR) features ongoing support, information, and advice from numerous consumer electronics manufacturers and organizations. At this writing, participating vendors include Pioneer Electronics, Harman Video, and Fosgate Audionics.

For possible related topics, see Entertainment, Electronics Products, and Telecommunications.

Electronics products are featured in many stores in the Electronic Mall (GO MALL), including Bose Express Music (GO BEM), Chef's Catalog (GO CC) for kitchen items, Colonel Video & Audio (GO CVA), Crutchfield (GO CFD), Hammacher Schlemmer (GO HS), Heath Co. (GO HTH), IBMLink (GO IL), JC Penney Online Catalog (GO JCP), Laser's Edge (GO LE) for laser discs and accessories, Music Alley Online (GO

MAO), Omron (GO OMRON), Penny Wise Office Product (GO PW), and Z Best (GO ZB).

See Electronic Mall.

Electronics Scan, Japan Consumer can be searched through the Business Database Plus (GO BUSDB). See Business Database.

Electronics Workbench is supported in the IBM PC Vendor C Forum (GO PCVENC). See IBM Computers.

Electronic Yellow Pages, Dun's (GO DYP) contains directory information on nearly 8 million businesses and professionals in the United States, covering both public and private companies of all sizes and types. See Dun's Electronic Yellow Pages.

L'Elite et Res Institutions Sovietiques (database) may be searched through the IQuest gateway. See IQuest.

ELSA GmbH Forum (GO ELSA) provides German-language technical support. See German for related topics.

E-mail (electronic mail): CompuServe Mail (GO MAIL) provides each subscriber with a private mailbox that may receive electronic letters online around the clock. See Mail, CompuServe.

eMail (software) is supported in the DaVinci Forum (GO DAVINCI). See DaVinci.

E-Mail Connection (software) is supported in a section of the Windows Vendor B Forum (GO EMCONNECT). See Microsoft Software.

Email8 (software) for Tandy Models 100 and 102 is automated terminal program written by Marvin M. Miller. The public domain program can be retrieved in the Model 100 Forum (GO TANDYLAPTOP). For related subjects, see Automated Terminal Software.

Embase (medical database) may be searched through the IQuest gateway (GO IQUEST) and through the Knowledge Index (GO KI). See IQuest and see Knowledge Index.

EMCEE software is supported in the IBM PC Vendor F Forum (GO PCVENF). See IBM Computers.

Emergency medical services are discussed in the Safetynet Forum (GO SAFETY). See Safety.

Emoticons is the term some used for the figures created with symbols on the keyboard to express emotions in messages and real-time online conversation. For details, see Acronyms.

Emotional problems are discussed in the Disabilities Forum (GO DISABILI-TIES). See Disabilities.

Empire (software) by Interstel is supported in the National Modem-to-Modem Game Players' Challenge Board (GO CHALLENGE). See Modem-to-Modem Games.

Employee Benefits Infosource (EBIS) (database) may be searched through the IQuest gateway. See IQuest.

Employment and business opportunities are categories in the CompuServe Classifieds. With them, you may read and post ads regarding jobs. See E-Span and see Classifieds Service.

Also:

- Career Placement Registry, a database with resumes of more than 8,000 people seeking employment, may be searched through the IQuest gateway (see IQuest). Also searchable on IQuest are Labordoc and Laborlaw I and II.

- Careers and working conditions are among the topics discussed in Information USA (GO INFOUSA). See Information.

- International Entrepreneurs' Network (GO USEN) operates for people looking for new business opportunities. See Entrepreneurs.

In addition, some forums have special sections for job openings. For instance, the Journalism Forum (GO JFORUM) has a portion of its library set aside for job openings for photographers, editors, and writers. The Photography Forum (GO PHOTOFORUM) routinely reports assignment opportunities. Some computer-related features, such as Borland International's online feature (GO BORLAND) report job openings. When looking for employment in a specific field, it is wise to become familiar with the forums already covering that area. Career opportunities at CompuServe itself are announced in the Classifieds area of the system (GO CLAS-SIFIED). See Classified.

EMU/470 and EMU/220 (software) is supported in the IBM PC Vendor C Forum (GO PCVENC). See IBM Computers.

E-mu Systems (products) are supported in the MIDI A Vendor Forum (GO MIDIAVEN). See Music.

Emulaser products are supported in the PC Vendor GO Forum (GO PCVENG). See IBM.

Enable Software Inc. is supported in the PC Vendor A Forum (GO PCVENA). See IBM Computers.

Encyclopedia: CompuServe offers Grolier's Academic American Encyclopedia (GO ENCYCLOPEDIA) with more than 33,000 articles, fact boxes, bibliographies, and tables. See Academic American Encyclopedia.

Encyclopedia of Associations (database) may be searched through the IQuest gateway. See IQuest.

Energy is the topic of a number of magazines searchable through the Business Database Plus (GO BUSDB), including *Energy Alert, Energy Conservation News, Energy Daily, Energy Economics & Climate Change, Energy & Environment, Energy Report, Energy User News, Enhanced Energy Recovery News, Fuels Energy & Power, ESP-Report on Oil Gas & Petrochemicals in the Developing World, European Energy Report, International Coal Report, International Solar Energy Intelligence Report, Utility Reporter*, and *Worldwide Energy*. See Business Database.

Relevant databases on IQuest (see IQuest) include:

- Regarding the energy industry, see: API Energy Business News Index, Apilit, APS Review, Coal & Synfuels Technology, Coal Outlook, EDF-DOC, Electric Power Database, Energy Conservation News, Energy User News, Energyline, Enhanced Energy Recovery News, Financial Times Business Reports: Energy, Georef, Hydrowire, Japan Energy Scan, Nuclear Waste News, Nucleonics Week, Platt's Oilgram News, Platt's Oilgram Price Report, Power Source, PTS Newsletter Database, U.S. Oil Week, Utility Reporter—Fuels, Energy & Power, and Worldwide Energy.

- For energy and science, see Apilit, DAUGAZ, Electric and Magnetic Field Keeptrack, Energy Conservation News, Energyline, Japan Energy Scan, National Technical Information Service, and PTS Newsletter Database.

- *Alternative Energy Digests, Alternative Energy Network Online Today*, and *EC Energy Monthly* (magazines) can be searched through the Business Database Plus (GO BUSDB). See Business Database. Also searchable there is *Eastern European Energy Report*.

- Energy and evironment are discussed in the White House Forum (GO WHITEHOUSE). See White House.

See also Oil, Coal, Earth studies and Geo studies.

Engineering Automation Forum (GO LEAP) is operated by the League for Engineering Automation Productivity. Its mission is to help engineers (and other design professionals) improve their productivity by using automation or computers. You'll find information about new products, technologies, and methods that are of use to engineers and design professionals. The primary sysop is Evan Yares (75300,1771), who is assisted by Joel Orr, Joe MacRae, and Brad Holtz.

Engineering: Computerized Engineering Index (GO COMPENDEX) (GO COMPENDEX) is a Telebase Systems Incorporated gateway that contains abstracts of articles from significant engineering and technological literature, including journals, publications of engineering societies and organizations, papers from the proceedings of conferences, selected government reports, and books from around the world. Related subjects covered include properties and testing of materials, fluid flow, pollution, ocean technology, applied physics, food technology, and measurements.

Surcharges for the database are $5 for the first 10 titles located, $5 for additional titles in groups of 10, and $5 for each full reference retrieved, with abstract where available, and a $1 charge for searches that retrieve no titles. In addition, reprints by normal delivery are $18 each or $42 for express delivery.

For information on other Telebase gateways, see Telebase Systems Incorporated. Also:

- Through IQuest a number of engineering databases are searchable, including Compendex Plus, EI Engineering Meetings, Energy Design Update, Engineered Materials Abstracts, Engineering News Record, IBSEDEX: Mechanical, Machine Design, IHS International Standards and Specifications, and Electrical and ISMEC. See IQuest.

- *Derivatives Engineering & Technology, E-MJ—Engineering & Mining Journal, Engineering Economist, ESP—Report on Engineering Construct & Operations in the Developing World,* and *Machine Design* can be searched through the Business Database Plus (GO BUSDB). See Business Database.

- National Technical Information Service (GO NTIS) is a gateway to a database published by the U.S. Department of Commerce, which contains nearly 1.5 million references to articles from government-sponsored research, development, and engineering reports, usually with corresponding abstracts. See National Technical Information.

See also Electronic and see Electricity.

English   is a topic of the Education Forum (GO EDFORUM) and Students' Forum (GO STUFO). See Education and Students' Forum.

Enhanced Recovery Week (magazine) can be searched through the Business Database Plus (GO BUSDB). See Business Database.

Enhanced Services Outlook (magazine) can be searched through the Business Database Plus (GO BUSDB). See Business Database.

En Route Technology (magazine) can be searched through the Business Database Plus (GO BUSDB). See Business Database.

Enterprise Integration Strategies (magazine) can be searched through the Business Database Plus (GO BUSDB). See Business Database.

Entertainment (movies, books, TV) is covered in various CompuServe services, with the Showbiz Forum (GO SHOWBIZ) central to them. Showbiz is designed for discussions of films and television programs, record albums, celebrity gossip and nightly news shows. See Showbiz.

Other highlights are listed below. For more details, see articles on the specific features.

Television

- Broadcast Professional Forum (GO BPFORUM)
- Consumer Electronics Forum (GO CE FORUM)
- Journalism Forum (GO JFORUM)
- Soap Opera Summaries (GO SOAPS)

Movies

- Hollywood Hotline (GO HOLLYWOOD)
- Hollywood by Marilyn Beck (GO BECK)
- Magill's Survey of Cinema (GO MAGILL)
- Roger Ebert's Movie Reviews database (GO EBERT)

Books

- Book Review Digest (GO BOOKREVIEW)
- Books in Print (GO BOOKS)
- Collectibles Forum (GO COLLECT).
- Literary Forum (GO LITSIG)
- Prentice-Hall Forum (GO PHCP)
- Science Fiction and Fantasy Forum (GO SCIFI)

Music

- All-Music Guide Forum (GO ALLMUSIC)
- Collectibles Forum (GO COLLECT)
- MIDI/Music Forums (GO MIDI)
- Music/Arts Forum (GO MUSICART)
- Music Vendor forum (GO MUSICVEN)
- RockNet (GO ROCK)

Also, see Games and Sports and Recreation. And to reach the main menu for this subject online, enter GO ENTERTAINMENT.

Entertainment Center (GO ECENTER) offers games played with others online in an informal "lobby" atmosphere. Before playing, users need to download the interface software from the Entertainment Center Main Menu for a nominal fee. The games currently require a PC-compatible computer with EGA or better graphics capability. (Connect-time charges are waived while the files are being downloaded). Play in the Entertainment Center Lobby is part of CompuServe's extended services and are billed at regular connect-time rates. But, if you join the CB Club (GO CBCLUB), you can play at special Club rates. At this writing, you can pay a monthly fee of either $85, to access the Entertainment Center at 30 cents per hour, 24 hours a day, or $25 to access the Entertainment Center at $4.30 an hour, 24 hours a day. The baud rate for the discounts can be up to 2400bps. The club rate also allows similar discount access to the

CB Simulator. Instructions for club signup are on the Entertainment Center introductory menu.

Games in the Entertainment Center include:

- Backgammon, where players can compete with others from around the world.
- Chess.
- Go, the classic Oriental board game that dates back nearly 4,000 years.
- With StarSprint, an easy-to-play deep-space flight simulator, you choose a ship depending upon whether you want to protect your bases, intercept enemy ships, or attack enemy bases. You can play head-to-head or in teams. Bases are used for refueling and arming your ships, but if the enemy zaps all your bases, you lose.

See also Games.

Entertainment databases, searchable on IQuest (see IQuest), include Academic Index, Backstage, Broadcasting, Communications Daily, Entertainment Weekly, High Fidelity, Magazine ASAP, Magazine Index, Magill's Survey of Cinema, People Weekly, Public Broadcasting Report, Stereo Review, Television Digest, and Video Week.

Entertainment Encyclopedia is featured in Hollywood Hotline (GO HOLLY-WOOD), offering old TV schedules, award lists, and more. See Hollywood Hotline.

Entertainment Marketing Letter (**magazine**) can be searched through the Business Database Plus (GO BUSDB). See Business Database.

Entertainment Weekly (magazine) can be searched through IQuest. See IQuest.

Entrepreneur Magazine (GO ENT) is available though a kiosk on The Electronic Mall (GO MALL). See Electronic Mall.

Entrepreneur's Business Franchise and Opportunities database (GO EBF) offers a searchable listing of some 2,000 franchise and nonfranchise businesses. The database includes company addresses, phone numbers, contact names, and descriptions of franchising and business opportunities. To access the database, GO ENTMAGAZINE and choose Option 2: "Franchise & Business Opportunities." See also Franchising.

Entrepreneurs' Network, International (GO USEN) operates for people looking for new business opportunities, such as ways to raise investment capital, get management advice, and make contacts with entrepreneurs in other cities. The service is backed by the Entrepreneurship Institute, an international nonprofit organization. Administering the forum is Linda Zupnick (76703,2032).

For a related subject, a category in the CompuServe Classifieds lets you read and post ads regarding business opportunities. See Classifieds Service. For other related features, see Financial and see Employment.

EnviroLeague is represented in the Earth Forum (GO EARTH). See Earth Forum.

Environmental issues are discussed in the Earth Forum (GO EARTH). For details, see Earth.

- Relevant databases on IQuest (see IQuest) include:

Academic Index
Air/Water Pollution Report
AQUALINE
Asbestos & Lead Abatement Report
Business and The Environment
Clean Tech News and Policy
   Outlook
Coal & Synfuels Technology
Energyline
Enviroline
Environmental Bibliography
Environmental Compliance Update
Global Environmental Change
   Report
Golob's Oil Pollution Bulletin
Hazardline
Hazardous Materials Intelligence
   Report
Hazardous Materials
   Transportation
Hazardous Waste News

Hazmat Transport News
Indoor Air Quality Update
Industrial Environment
Medical Waste News
Nuclear Waste News
Oil Spill Intelligence Report
Oil Spill U.S. Law Report
Pollution Abstracts
PTS Newsletter Database
Report on Defense Plant Wastes
Solid Waste Report
Superfund Week
Toxic Materials News
TSCA Chemical Substances
   Inventory
Waste Treatment Technology
   News
Water Resources Abstracts
Waternet
World Environment Outlook

See IQuest.

- Also, *Buzzworm: The Environmental Journal, Conservationist, Environment,* and *Mother Earth News* (magazines) can be searched in the Magazine Database Plus (GO MDP). See Magazine Database.

- *Business & the Environment, Clean Air Network Online Today,* and *E&P Environment* (magazines) can be searched through the Business Database Plus (GO BUSDB), as can *Environment Watch (East Europe, Russia & Eurasia, Latin America, Western Europe), Environment Week, Environmental Business Journal, Environmental Compliance Update, Global Trade, Global Warming Network Online Today, Global Environmental Change Report, Industrial Environment, Louisiana Industry Environmental Alert, Multinational Environmental Outlook, New Jersey Industry Environmental Alert, Ohio Industry Environmental Advisor, Ozone Depletion Network Online Today, Pennsylvania Industry Environmental Advisor, State Environment Report, Texas Industry Environmental Alert,* and *World Environment Report.* See Business Database.

- In the Health Database Plus (GO HLTBD), you can search *Archives of Environmental Health* and *Environmental Nutrition*. See Health.

- In addition to the above, Florida Today NewsLink Forum (GO FLATODAY), a unique link to this Gannett Inc. newspaper on the Florida Space Coast's, includes a section on environment. (See Florida.) Environment also is discussed in the Political Debate Forum (GO POLITICS) and in the White House Forum (GO WHITEHOUSE). See Political and White House. And environmental hygiene is discussed in the Safetynet Forum (GO SAFETY). See Safety.

See also Earth studies, Geo studies, Energy, Hazardous materials, Waste management, VISTA Environmental Profiles, and Gardening.

EPAT (European Patent Registry) database can be searched through IQuest. See IQuest.

Epic MegaGames products are distributed and supported through Epic Online (GO EPIC). The service enables you to get games such as OverKill, Epic Pinball, Jill of the Jungle, Zone 66, and others. For a $3.00 surcharge, you can download the shareware version of Epic's featured "Game-Of-The-Month." Downloads are free of connect-time charges, but communication surcharges, if any, still apply. And, with each "Game-Of-The-Month" you download, you will receive a $3.00 usage credit. You also can visit the Epic MegaGames Forum (GO EPICFORUM) to get the latest tips, hints, and strategies.

Epson Forum (GO EPSON) supports all Epson products, from its line of printers to its MS-DOS computers. Topics identified for discussion include telecommunications, hardware and software, and systems such as the QX-10 and QX-16, the PX-8, HX-20, HX-40, and others.

The forum also gives advice on use of add-ons, such as Titan expansion boards.

The Epson Forum is operated by Epson America Inc. to provide technical assistance and product information. The sysop is Bob Merchant (76711,1247), assisted by and Joe Vanderhoof.

ERIC (GO ERIC) is a database containing abstracts of articles covering all aspects of education, including vocational education, counseling, teacher education, and testing. See Educational Resources Information Center.

Ervin, Bette and Jerry (76703,2063) are sysops of Foreign Language Forum (GO FLEFO). See Foreign Language Forum.

ERwin (database design tools) are supported in the General Computing Forum (GO GENCOM). See General Computing.

ESP is covered in the New Age Forum (GO NEWAGE). For more information, see New Age Forum.

E-Span JobSearch (GO ESPAN) is an employment advertising network that enables organizations to reach more than a million PC-literate professional, technical and managerial candidates nationwide. The database of listings and opportunities, operated as part of the Classified Ads section (GO CLASSIFIED), is updated twice weekly. Usually, ads run for two weeks. Jobs are offered in various fields, including senior executive positions, engineering, architecture, telecommunications, accounting, banking, manufacturing, health care, education, etc.

Those seeking a job can browse opportunities listed by hundreds of Fortune 1,000 companies and can search them by job category and/or geographic region. There are no charges (other than basic connect charges) to view these listings.

To place an ad with E-Span JobSearch or get more information, contact the operators by sending CompuServe Mail to 76702,1771 or by calling 1-800/682-2901.

Past participants in the service include Motorola Corp., Johns Hopkins Hospital, Digital Equipment Corp., MasterCard International, H&R Block, Shearson Lehman, and a number of federal government agencies.

See also Classifieds Service and Employment.

ESP—Business Opportunities (in Africa, the Middle East, Asia, the Pacific, Latin America, and the Caribbean) can be searched through the Business Database Plus (GO BUSDB). See Business Database.

Esperanto is spoken in the Foreign Language Education Forum (GO FLEFO), a service for students and teachers. See Foreign Language.

ESP—Report (on Engineering Construct & Operations in the Developing World, on Mining & Metals in the Developing World, and on Oil Gas & Petrochemicals in the Developing World) can be searched through the Business Database Plus (GO BUSDB). See Business Database.

Esquire (magazine) can be searched in the Magazine Database Plus (GO MDP). See Magazine Database.

ESRI products are supported in the CADD/CAM/CAE Vendor Forum (GO CADDVEN). See CAD/CAM.

Essence (magazine) is searchable through Magazine Database Plus (GO MDP). For details see Magazine Database.

Estvanik, Steve (76703,3046) is the games programmer who created Sniper! (GO SNIPER) and Air Traffic Controller (GO ATCONTROL). He is a regular in the Multi-Player Games Forum (GO MPGAMES).

Ethernet is supported in the Standard Microsystem Forum (GO SMC) and Thomas-Conrad Support Forum (GO TCCFORUM). See Standard Microsystem and Thomas-Conrad.

EtherTwist is supported in the HP Systems Forum (GO HPSYS). See Hewlett-Packard.

Ethics and human rights is a topic in the Issues Forum (GO ISSUESFORUM). See Issues.

E*Trade Securities (GO ETRADE) is a discount stock brokerage firm offering around-the-clock order entry and instantaneous access to account records. See also Stock Brokerages Services.

Europe is a topic in the Travel Forum (GO TRAVSIG). See Travel.

European, called Europe's first national newspaper, is covered in the UK Newspaper Library (GO UKPAPERS). See UK Newspaper.

European Access (GO EUROLOGON). European subscribers can access the system through CompuServe network or through a number of third-party systems, including InfoNet, PSS Dialplus, Telepac, Datex-P, and PTT (Public Packet Switching Network). These networks levy communications surcharge that are billed in addition to applicable connect charges. For details, see Billing Information.

European business news is the subject of databases searchable through IQuest, including ABC Europe, D&B—European Dun's Market Identifiers, EDOC and EPAT patent databases, Europe's Largest Companies, European Directory of Agrochemical Products, European Community: Business Forecast, European Chemical News, Kompass Europe, Spearhead, Spicer's Centre for Europe, and Tenders Electronics Daily. See IQuest for details.

Searchable through Business Database Plus (GO BUSDB) are *EuroBusiness, Euromarketing, Euromoney, European Cosmetic Markets, European Energy Report, European Polymers Paint & Colour Journal, European Report, European Rubber Journal, European Social Policy, European Venture Capital Journal, Europe 2000, Europe Energy, Europe Environment, Europe 92, Market Europe, Market Research Europe, Tech Europe,* and *Transport Europe.* See Business Database.

European Company Library (GO EUROLIB) has databases covering European companies outside England and Germany. See also UK Company Library and German Company Library.

European Community is covered in several IQuest databases (see IQuest), including Celex (computerised Documentation System on Ec Law), European Community: Business Forecast, Spearhead, and Spicer's Centre For Europe.

European Community Telework Forum (GO ECTF) provides information about two community actions initiated by the European Community Directorate General XIII that address telecommunications and telematics. Discussion focuses on new kinds of work enabled by telecommunications, and telematics for small businesses and tourism. The RACE programme (Research into Advanced Communications for Europe) is a research action of the European Community that aims to define an Integrated Broadband Communications Network (IBCN), which will enable a new range of intelligent, multimedia telecommunications services to be offered to organisations and individuals. The ECTF is in Sections 1–7, covering teleworking issues relating to business, traffic, people, technology, legal and regulatory issues, and rural development. The chief sysop David Brain (76703,401), who is assisted by Costas Daskalakis (100137,2553), Jaynie Taylor (100116,563), and Sarah Hewitt (100137,1416).

European Forum (GO EURFORUM), formerly the IBM European Users Forum, supports the online international community and conducts most of its business in the respective languages of the various message board sections, including French, German, Spanish, and Italian. The forum focuses on computing as it applies to European members, with discussion of culture, travel, and more. The sysop is Earle Robinson (76004,1762), assisted by Adrian Godfrey (100012,1762), Marco Garibaldi (100016,2405), and Inga M. Nathhorst (100272,46).

Europe Forum, Microsoft Central (GO MSCE) is conducted in German and allows members to communicate directly with the Microsoft Corp. staff in that language and to exchange messages. See Microsoft Software.

Evans, Larry chess grand master, provides the latest news and commentary on the game in the Chess Forum (GO CHESSFORUM). The syndicated column "Evans on Chess," is available each Friday in the forum's "Ask the GMs" library. See Chess.

Evans-Novak Political Report can be searched through the Business Database Plus (GO BUSDB). See Business Database.

Eventide (products) are supported in the MIDI A Vendor Forum (GO MIDIAVEN). See Music.

Eventline (conference and seminar database) may be searched through the IQuest gateway (GO IQUEST) and through the Knowledge Index (GO KI). See IQuest and see Knowledge Index.

Everyman's Encyclopedia (database) may be searched through the IQuest gateway (GO IQUEST) and through the Knowledge Index (GO KI). See IQuest and see Knowledge Index.

Evolution Computing software is supported in the CADD/CAM/CAE Vendor Forum (GO CADDVEN). See CAD/CAM.

Excel (software) is supported in the Microsoft Excel Forum (GO MSEXCEL). See Microsoft Software.

Excelerator is supported in the Intersolv Forum (GO INTERSOLV). See Intersolv.

Exceptional Child Education Resources (database) may be searched through the IQuest gateway. See IQuest. Also, *Exceptional Children* and *The Exceptional Parent* magazines are searchable in the Health Database Plus (GO HLTBD). See Health.

Exchange (magazine) can be searched through the Business Database Plus (GO BUSDB). See Business Database.

EXE (magazine) can be searched through Computer Database Plus (GO COMPDB). See Computer Database Plus.

Executive Briefing Service (covering Asia and the Pacific, Eastern Europe, Middle East and North Africa, North and Central America, South America, Sub-Saharan Africa, Western Europe) can be searched through the Business Database Plus (GO BUSDB). See Business Database.

Executive Female (magazine) can be searched in the Magazine Database Plus (GO MDP). See Magazine Database.

Executive Health Report is searchable in the Health Database Plus (GO HLTBD). See Health.

Executive News Service (GO ENS): The Executive News Service provides access to current news from various resources, up to 4,000 new stories daily, including those from:

- The Associated Press (national, Washington, sports, and business)
- Deutsche Presse-Agentur (German language reports).
- OTC NewsAlert (press releases from companies)
- Reuter News Service (World, North America, Sports, Financial, and European Community reports.)
- Today's *Washington Post* (selected articles)
- United Press International (national, regional, sports, business).

ENS also automatically can save in personalized electronic *clip folders* any stories containing keywords about subjects that you want to follow. ENS works around the clock, even when you are not online, instantly clipping stories to offer to you the next time you visit the feature. Of course, you also may browse ENS's wires yourself in "real time" as well as search for recent stories about specific companies and corporations.

ENS is surcharged at $15 an hour over the base connect rates.

To use ENS, you first must sign up for the Executive Option (GO EXECUTIVE), which provides access to a number of additional services. (For details, see Executive Option.)

There are three ways to use ENS:

1. Searching for news from specific companies.
2. Browsing current news from the various resources.
3. Collecting future stories in clipping folders.

Search by ticker This gives you access to the hot business news from the last 24 hours, located by stock market ticker symbols. Selecting it causes the system to prompt for "Ticker." Enter the appropriate letters, such as AAPL for Apple Computer Inc. or MSFT for Microsoft Corp. and the system compiles a menu of article titles from Reuter's Financial Report and OTC NewsAlert. Select each article by number from the menu to read the full text of the story. If the corporation in which you are interested has not made the news in the last 24 hours, the system tells you that no stories were found. Ticker symbols may be searched on CompuServe by company name by selecting GO LOOKUP. (For more about ticker searching and other financial information online, see Financial Services.)

Browsing You can browse the ENS system and, using a menu, it will prompt you to identify the wires you wish to scan. The Associated Press offers its national and world news wires, as well as its sports and financial wires. United Press International provides national, business, sports, and regional wires. (For a breakdown of the states in each UPI region, see below.) Reuters is a British wire service with financial reports of an international flavor. OTC NewsAlert is a business wire concentrating on news of companies traded over-the-counter in the stock market. *The Washington Post*, the largest newspaper in the nation's capital, brings selected stories online from that morning's editions.

Folders Also note that ENS also can automatically save in personalized electronic clip folders any stories containing keywords about subjects that you want to follow. In creating a folder, you select its name, expiration date, and the number of days to retain clipped stories. You also specify the news resources to search and the subjects to watch for in the form of keywords.

About UPI's state wires, the regions are:

Central Illinois, Indiana, Iowa, Michigan, Minnesota, Nebraska, Wisconsin, South Dakota

Mid-Atlantic Kentucky, Maryland, Ohio, Pennsylvania, Virginia, West Virginia, New Jersey, Delaware

Northeast Connecticut, Delaware, Maine, Massachusetts, New Hampshire, New Jersey, New York, Vermont, Rhode Island

Southeast Alabama, Florida, Georgia, Mississippi, North Carolina, South Carolina, Tennessee

Southwest Arkansas, Colorado, Kansas, Louisiana, Missouri, New Mexico, Oklahoma, Texas, Wyoming.

Western Arizona, California, Hawaii, Idaho, Nevada, Montana, South Dakota, Oregon, Utah, Washington

(Alaska is not listed in the regional news for UPI.)

About Keywords   ENS folders support up to seven keywords or phrases, such as candidates' names. These are the words and phrases the system will search for in clipping stories for the folder. Phrases may be up to 80 characters long and may be enclosed in parentheses (LEAGUE OF WOMEN VOTERS).

Tips:

- An asterisk (*) is a wildcard, so VOT* clips stories containing "vote," "votes," "voters," and so on.

- You also may qualify your phrase with a plus sign (+) to require that two or more words or phrases be clipped. This means "AND" as in SMITH+VOTERS or SMITH+ELECTION.

- To indicate that a story should be clipped if it contains one keyword but not another, use a minus sign (-), such as ELECTION-NATIONAL.

- To clip a story that matches any of two or more phrases, use the | sign to mean OR, as in ELECTION | VOTE | RUN-OFF.

Other commands are used for narrowing and broadening keywords and phrases in clipping folders. They also can be mixed and matched in some interesting ways, using parentheses to enclose complex concepts. Listed below are some examples that CompuServe has offered online:

APPLE + COMPUT* finds any story containing both the word Apple and any variation of comput. Since both combinations are required, it avoids stories dealing with apple growers and those about computers other than Apple's computers.

COMPUT* + (SECUR* | CRIME | PRIVACY) finds stories containing variations of the word comput, and one or more of the words secur*, crime, and privacy.

COMPUT* + (VIRUS | DISEASE) finds stories containing variations of the word comput and the word virus, but not the word disease.

MERRILL LYNCH | (CAPITAL MARKETS) finds stories on Merrill Lynch but not those regarding the initial public offerings it is underwriting.

MERRILL LYNCH | (DAILY TREASURY INDEX | TELERATE) lets you follow Merrill Lynch announcements, such as initial public offerings it is underwriting and corporate news on itself, but not daily reports on its bond index.

OHIO ST* + FOOTBALL finds stories containing both the phrase Ohio St and the word football.

From the time of a folder's creation until its expiration date, ENS monitors the wires and news categories you have specified, setting aside any stories that contain at least one of your keywords or phrases. You may read the clipped news any time you are online by entering GO ENS.

Also, you may revise or delete a folder by choosing the "Create/Change/Delete" option on the main ENS menu. The option provides an opportunity to add and delete key phrases and news wires and categories. Note the revision option also lets you change the expiration date and the retention days.

In Addition, *News Clips*, a relatively new feature of the Executive News Service, predesignates clipping folders for particular topics:

- Apple News Clips (GO APPLENEWS) is a preestablished clipping folder that anyone can access for stories clipped from various news sources including AP, UPI, and The Washington Post.
- Outdoors News Clips (GO OUTNEWS) is a folder for stories of interest to hunters, campers, and other outdoors enthusiasts.
- UK News Clips (GO UKNEWS) is a folder for stories of interest to British subscribers.

As with folders you create yourself, you may select articles to read by choosing the appropriate number(s) from the News Clips menu. There is a $15.00 an hour surcharge in addition to base-connect rates for accessing News Clips. Other topics are likely to be added later. To see a list of the latest group, enter FIND NEWS CLIPS at a ! prompt.

Meanwhile, sometimes during a major national or international event, CompuServe adds such a prearranged clipping folder to the menu. For example, during the aftermath of the San Francisco earthquake and the Persian Gulf War, additional options for related stories were added to the main ENS main.

For other related features, see News.

Executive Option is a tier of extra features, including financial and news databases, special merchandise offers, discounts, and other special services both online and off. If you subscribe to the Executive Option, you receive:

- Access to exclusive databases and services, including Company Analyzer, Company Screening Executive News Service, Disclosure II, Institutional Broker's Estimate System, Return Analysis, Securities Screening, and SuperSite.
- A 50 percent increase in the amount of online storage along with an opportunity to purchase additional storage space at a reduced weekly rate.
- A six-month storage period for personal files without charge. Thirty days is standard for users who do not subscribe to the Executive Option.
- A 10 percent discount on the purchase of most CompuServe products
- Direct marketing offers for goods and services from CompuServe's affiliated merchants and manufacturers.
- Volume discounts on information retrieval from selected transaction price financial databases.

The costs Those who choose the Executive Option are subject to a $10 monthly minimum usage level. Your $8.95 monthly fee under the Standard Pricing Plan (see Billing) is applied toward this minimum. For related topics, see Billing Information.

Executive Stamper (GO EX) is a store in the Electronic Mall (GO MALL) that offers rubber stamps, engraved gifts, and so on. See Electronic Mall.

Executives Online Forum (GO ZNT:EXECUTIVES) is intended as a place for in-depth discussions with people who set trends and make news in the desktop computing industry. See ZiffNet.

Exercise and fitness is a topic of the Health & Fitness Forum (GO GOODHEALTH). See Health.

Expedition (software) is supported in the PC Vendor B Forum (GO PCVENB). See IBM Computers.

Expenses, CompuServe: Your current billing information and details of CompuServe charges may be examined by entering GO RATES. See Billing Information.

Expert Choice products are supported in the PC Vendor I Forum (GO PCVENI). See IBM Computers.

Exploration (software) is supported in Windows 3rd-Party Forum A (GO WINAPA). See Microsoft Software.

Exporter (database) may be searched through the IQuest gateway. Exports also are covered in the Piers Exports (databases) See IQuest. Also, *Export Control News* can be searched through the Business Database Plus (GO BUSDB). See Business Database. See also Trade.

Express (hDC software) is supported in Windows 3rd-Party Forum A (GO WINAPA). See Microsoft Software.

Express (Javelin software) is supported in the Javelin/EXPRESS Forum (GO IRIFORUM). See Javelin Software.

Express (Lotus software) is supported in the Lotus Words & Pixels Forum (GO LOTUSB). See Lotus Software.

Expressdocs and Truetype for WordPerfect (software) are supported in the Windows 3rd-Party Forum (GO WINAPD). See Microsoft Software.

Extel International Financial Cards and News Cards (databases) may be searched through the IQuest gateway. See IQuest.

Extraterrestrials are a topic in in the Space/Astronomy Forum (GO SPACEFORUM). See Space.

F

Facts on File World News Digest can be searched through the Business Database Plus (GO BUSDB). See Business Database.

Fairbase (trade fair database) may be searched through the IQuest gateway. See IQuest.

Faircom products are supported in the IBM PC Vendor F Forum (GO PCVENF). See IBM Computers.

Fairfield County Business Journal (magazine) can be searched through the Business Database Plus (GO BUSDB). See Business Database.

Falcon (software) by Spectrum-HoloByte is supported in the National Modem-to-Modem Game Players' Challenge Board (GO CHALLENGE). For more information, see Modem-to-Modem Games.

Family Handyman Forum (GO HANDYMAN), sponsored by The Family Handyman Magazine, discusses all kinds of projects for do-it-yourself home-owners, from major remodeling to help with home maintenance and repair. Message sections include those in which you can share your experiences as well as solicit advice from the editors and other professionals on home remodeling, plumbing, electricity, painting, building, and more. Libraries contain articles covering all aspects of home upkeep and repair.

   Also, *Family Handyman* magazine, part of the *Reader's Digest* group of special interest magazines, can be searched in the Magazine Database Plus (GO MDP). See Magazine Database.

Family history is the topic of the Genealogy Forum (GO ROOTS). For more information, see Genealogy.

Family Practice, Journal of is searchable in the Health Database Plus (GO HLTBD). See Health.

Family Resources **(pyschology database)** may be searched through the IQuest gateway. See IQuest.

Fantasy fiction is covered in the Science Fiction & Fantasy Forum (GO HOM-9). For more information, see Science Fiction and Fantasy. Also, *The Magazine of Fantasy and Science Fiction* can be searched in the Magazine Database Plus (GO MDP). See Magazine Database.

Fantasy games **(role-playing games and adventures)** are offered in CompuServe's game section (GO GAMES). Specific games include:

- BlackDragon (GO BLACKDRAGON)
- British Legends (GO LEGENDS)
- Castlequest (GO CQUEST)
- Classic Adventure (GO CLADVENT)
- Enhanced Adventure (GO ENADVENT)
- The Island of Kesmai (GO ISLAND)

For more information, see Games and entries under specific game names.

Farallon Computing products are supported in the IBM PC Vendor E Forum (GO PCVENE). See IBM Computers. They also are supported in the in Macintosh C Vendor Forum (GO MACCVEN). See Apple Computers.

Farmaner, Gary (76703,3050) is administrator of the Commodore Applications Forum (GO CBMAPP). For more information, see Commodore computers.

Farming is covered in several IQuest databases, including Agribusiness U.S.A., Agricola, Agris International, Agrochemicals Databank, and Aquaculture. See IQuest.

Also, *Successful Farming* can be searched through the Business Database Plus (GO BUSDB). See Business Database.

See also Agriculture, Food and Cooking, Pets and Animals, and Gardening Forum.

FastBack **(software)** is supported in the Symantec Fifth Generation Systems Forum (GO SYMFGS). See Symantec.

FastCAD is supported in the CADD/CAM/CAE Vendor Forum (GO CADDVEN). See CAD/CAM.

FastLynx **(software)** is supported in the PC Vendor C Forum (GO PCVENC). See IBM Computers.

FAX **(facsimile machines):** Electronic mail may be sent from CompuServe to Group 3 FAX machines. For details, see Mail, CompuServe.

Fax machine technology is a topic of the Consumer Electronics Forum (GO CEFORUM). See Electronics Forum, Consumer.

Faxy **(telefax board)** is supported in the German-speaking Dr. Neuhaus Forum (GO NEUHAUS). See Dr. Neuhaus.

FBI is discussed in the White House Forum (GO WHITEHOUSE). See White House.

FCC (Federal Communications Commission) is discussed in the Broadcasters and Engineers Forum (GO BPFORUM). For more information, see Broadcasters and Broadcast Engineers.

   Also, FCC Daily Digest and FCC Week databases may be searched through the IQuest gateway (GO IQUEST). See IQuest. The resource also can be searched through the Business Database Plus (GO BUSDB), as can *FCC Report*. See Business Database.

FDA Enforcement Report and **FDA Medical Bulletin** can be searched through the Business Database Plus (GO BUSDB). See Business Database. Also, *FDA Consumer* is searchable in the Health Database Plus (GO HLTBD). See Health.

F-D-C Reports **(drug and medical database)** may be searched through the IQuest gateway. See IQuest.

FDIC Watch can be searched through the Business Database Plus (GO BUSDB). See Business Database.

Fearless Taster **(food database)** may be searched through the IQuest gateway. See IQuest.

   See also Food.

Federal Aviation Administration **(FAA)** rules, regulations, advisories, press releases, and other information are provided and discussed in the Aviation Forum (GO AVSIG). See Aviation.

Federal Computer Week **(magazine)** is searchable (abstracts) through Computer Database Plus (GO COMPDB). See Computer Database Plus.

Federal Employee/Retiree Newsletter, Federal Grants and Contracts Weekly, Federal Index, Federal/Industry Watchdog, Federal Register, Federal Research in Progress, Federal Register Abstracts **(database)** may be searched through the IQuest gateway. See IQuest.

Federal & State Insurance Week can be searched through the Business Database Plus (GO BUSDB). See Business Database.

Federation of International Distributors Forum (GO FEDERATION) supports the association's international Macintosh, OS/2, Windows, NeXT, UNIX, and MS-DOS distributors and republishers. Founded in 1988 to provide open accessibility to a range of resources and educational activities, the federation has continually expanded to address global issues and cover a broader range of country markets. The International Managers' Club (IMC) is intended to bring together people in the computer industry who are involved in international operations and provide them with information resources and various forums in which to network more effectively. The sysop is Lynne Patkin (75300,3070), assisted by Tony Hamwey.

Federationist, American (**magazine**) is searchable in both Magazine Database Plus (GO MDP) and Business Database Plus (GO BUSDB). For details, see Magazine Database and see Business Database.

Feedback to CompuServe (GO FEEDBACK) allows you to write directly to the operators of the service with questions or suggestions. For more information, see Help Online.

Fertilizer International (**magazine**) can be searched through the Business Database Plus (GO BUSDB). See Business Database.

Fiber/Optics News (**database**) may be searched through the IQuest gateway. See IQuest. It also can be searched through Business Database Plus (GO BUSDB). See Business Database.

Fiction is a regular topic in the Literary Forum (GO LITFORUM). For details, see Literature.

Fidonet user can be written to using CompuServe Mail. See Mail, CompuServe, and refer to the discussion about Internet.

Fifth Generation software products are supported in the Symantec Fifth Generation Systems Forum (GO SYMFGS). See Symantec.

Figallo, Cliff (76711,320) is the sysop of the Electronic Frontier Foundation Forum (GO EFFSIG). See Electronic Frontier.

Figi's (GO FG) is a store in the Electronic Mall (GO MALL) specializing in food and gifts. See Electronic Mall.

File Finders are databases that provide file descriptions from the libraries of a group of related forums. Such databases are intended to save users the trouble of having to search the libraries directly. The feature provides you with seven common search criteria for quickly finding the location of a desired file or files. You may search by keyword or keywords, submission date of file, forum name, file type, file extension, filename, or file submitter's user ID number. When a file is located, you are told where the file is located, the library name, and the filename. If you select a file from the menu, you are shown the filename, forum, library name and number, submitter's user ID number, date the file was uploaded, size of the file in characters, the number of times the file was has been accessed, the file's keywords, and a short description of the contents. **NOTE:** If you are using some versions of CompuServe Information Manager, such as DOS CIM 2.0 or higher, Mac CIM 1.6 or higher, or WinCIM, you also can download the files directly from this File Finder display.

CompuServe has launched several of these special databases so far, including:

- Amiga File Finder (GO AMGFF). See Commodore Computers.
- Atari File Finder (GO ATARIFF). See Atari.
- Graphics File Finder (GO GRAPHFF). See Graphics.
- IBM File Finder (GO IBMFF). See IBM Computers.
- Macintosh File Finder (GO MACFF). See Apple Computers.
- ZiffNet File Finder (GO ZNT:FILEFINDER). See ZiffNet.
- ZiffNet/Mac File Finder (GO ZMC:FILEFINDER). See ZiffNet/Mac.

FileMaker (**software**) is supported in the Claris Corp. Forum (GO CLARIS). For more information, see Claris.

Files, Compressed: Many files in forum libraries these days are compressed and "archived" to save space and to allow you to retrieve them faster.

Some background: Software development today is more sophisticated than when this medium started a decade ago. Programs are longer, taking advantage of the larger memories in our machines. Often they are integrated software systems that require several linked programs and data files to interact on the same task. Before archiving utilities became common, this caused problems for beginners, because a single program might have required users to retrieve and install a half dozen different files, each with a different name. If one of the files was overlooked, the program wouldn't run properly, meaning another trip online to find and download the missing file. To solve the problem, the telecomputing community started using programming utilities with two main functions:

1. One function is to pack and unpack a number of related program and text files—installation, documentation, configuration, data—into a single file. It is a lot easier to download one large file than four or five small ones.

2. The second function is to squeeze and "unsqueeze" files. A compressed file takes up to 50 percent less space in the library and requires less time for you to download it.

A file that has been uploaded in a compressed format appears in the data library with a special extension that tells you (a) to download it with error-checking (see Files, Transfer) and (b) to have available the software tools necessary to unpack it and unsqueeze it offline.

Files saved in these special archieved formats have unique extensions on the filenames, such as .ZIP, .ARC, .ZOO, .SIT, and so on. These days, a number of popular packer-unpacker squeezer-unsqueezer utilities are used in the various forums. If in doubt about the archieve utilities used in a particular forum, check the libraries or leave a message for the sysop. Just remember, if the extension of the file you retrieve indicates the file is compressed, you will need a utility for use offline to convert it into something your computer can use. This process is known as de-archiving ("unzipping," "unstuffing," etc.).

In addition, some modern hardware platforms now support a special form of compressed files called "self-extracting" or "self-dissolving." You do not need a decompression utility for this type of compressed file. Just download the file and then load/execute/launch the file; it will decompress itself.

The operators of the CompuServe Help Forum (GO HELPFORUM) and the Practice Forum (GO PRACTICE) maintain lists of the latest archiving tools. Here are the forums, libraries, and file for the type of de-compression utility for the major systems used on CompuServe at this writing:

Amiga Machines

ARC Format	AmigaUser Forum (GO AMIGAU) Library 16 (Archivers/Crunchers) Files: ARC.EXE and ARCHLP.EXE
LZH Format	AmigaUser Forum (GO AMIGAU) Library 16 (Archivers/Crunchers) Files: LHARC.EXE and ARCHLP.EXE
ZIP Format	AmigaUser Forum (GO AMIGAU) Library 16 (Archivers/Crunchers) Files: UNZIP.LZH and ARCHLP.EXE
ZOO Format	AmigaUser Forum (GO AMIGAU) Library 16 (Archivers/Crunchers) Files: ZOO210.EXE and ARCHLP.EXE

Apple Macintosh

ARC Format	Mac Communications Forum (GO MACCOMM) Library 4 (Comm Progs/Utils) File: ARCPOP.BIN
CPT Format	Mac Communications Forum (GO MACCOMM) Library 4 (Comm Progs/Utils) File: COMPAC.SEA Mac Communications Forum (GO MACCOMM) Library 4 (Comm Progs/Utils) File: EXTRAC.BIN

LZH Format	Mac Communications Forum (GO MACCOMM) Library 4 (Comm Progs/Utils) File: LHARC.SIT
	Mac Communications Forum (GO MACCOMM) Library 4 (Comm Progs/Utils) File: EXTRAC.BIN
SIT Format	Mac Communications Forum (GO MACCOMM) Library 4 (Comm Progs/Utils) File: UNSTUF.SEA
ZIP Format	Mac Communications Forum (GO MACCOMM) Library 4 (Comm Progs/Utils) File: ZIPIT1.CPT Mac New Users Forum (GO MACNEW) Library 4 (Comm Progs/Utils) File: UZ201.CPT
ZOO Format	Mac System Forum (GO MACSYS) Library 7 (Utilities) File: BOOZ2.SIT

Apple 128K IIe or IIc Machines

BNY Format	Apple User Forum (GO APUSER) Library 12 (Telecommunications) FILE: SHRINK.EXE
ARC Format	Apple User Forum (GO APUSER) Library 4 (Utilities) File: DEARC2.BQY
ZOO Format	Apple User Forum (GO APUSER) Library 4 (Utilities) File: BOOZ2E.BXY

Apple IIgs Machines

ARC Format	Apple User Forum (GO APUSER) Library 12 (Telecommunications) FILE: SHRINK.EXE
BNY Format	Apple User Forum (GO APUSER) Library 12 (Telecommunications) FILE: SHRINK.EXE
SIT Format	Apple User Forum (GO APUSER) Library 12 (Telecommunications) FILE: SHRINK.EXE

ZOO Format	Apple User Forum (GO APUSER) Library 12 (Telecommunications) FILE: SHRINK.EXE

Atari 8-bit Machines

ARC Format	Atari 8-Bit Forum (GO ATARI8) Library 3 (System Utilities) Files: UNARC.COM and SUPERA.ARC

Atari Machines

ARC Format	Atari Productivity Forum (GO ATARIP) Library 4 (Utility Programs) File: ARC602.TTP
ARJ format	Atari Productivity Forum (GO ATARIP) Library 4 (Utility Programs) File: STUNAR.ARC
LZH Format	Atari Productivity Forum (GO ATARIP) Library 4 (Utility Programs) Files: LHARC.TTP and ARCLZH.PRG
ZIP Format	Atari Productivity Forum (GO ATARIP) Library 4 (Utility Programs) File: STZIP2.TOS
ZOO Format	Atari Productivity Forum (GO ATARIP) Library 4 (Utility Programs) File: ZOO21.TTP

Commodore 8-bit Machines

ARC Format	Commodore Art/Games Forum (GO CBMART) Library 1 (Help/Data Lib Tools) Files: ARC230.BIN and ARCEAZ.HLP
LBR Format	Commodore Applications Forum (GO CBMAPP) Library 2 (ARC/Help/Forum Utilities) Files: ARC230.BIN

IBM and compatibles running DOS systems

ARC Format	IBM Systems Forum (GO IBMSYS) Library 6 (File Utilities) Files: ARC-E.COM and ARC-E.DOC
CPT Format	IBM Systems Forum (GO IBMSYS) Library 6 (File Utilities) File: EXTPC.EXE

LZH Format	IBM Systems Forum (GO IBMSYS) Library 6 (File Utilities) File: LHA213.EXE
	IBM Systems Forum (GO IBMSYS) Library 6 (File Utilities) File: PK204G.EXE
PIT Format	IBM Systems Forum (GO IBMSYS) Library 6 (File Utilities) File: UNPACK.ZIP
SIT Format	IBM Systems Forum (GO IBMSYS) Library 6 (Utilities) File: UNSTUF.ZIP
ZIP Format	PC Vendor C Forum (GO PCVENC) Library 11 (PKWare) File: PK204G.EXE
ZOO Format	IBM Systems Forum (GO IBMSYS) Library 6 (File Utilities) File: ZOO201.EXE

IBM and compatible machines running Windows

ARC Format	IBM Systems Forum (GO BMSYS) Library 6 (File Utilities) File: WINZIP.ZIP
ARJ Format	IBM Systems Forum (GO IBMSYS) Library 6 (File Utilities) File: WINZIP.ZIP
LZH Format	IBM Systems Forum (GO IBMSYS) Library 6 (File Utilities) File: WINZIP.ZIP
ZIP Format	IBM Systems Forum (GO IBMSYS) Library 6 (File Utilities) File: WINZIP.ZIP

NeXT Computers

ARC Format	NeXT Users Forum (GO NEXTFORUM) Library 5 (Applications) File: OPENER.TAZ
LZH Format	NeXT Users Forum (GO NEXTFORUM) Library 5 (Applications) File: OPENER.TAZ

SIT Format	NeXT Users Forum (GO NEXTFORUM) Library 5 (Applications) File: OPENER.TAZ
ZIP Format	NeXT Users Forum (GO NEXTFORUM) Library 5 (Applications) File: OPENER.TAZ
ZOO Format	NeXT Users Forum (GO NEXTFORUM) Library 5 (Applications) File: OPENER.TAZ

OS/2-based IBM and compatible systems

ARC Format	IBM Systems Forum (GO IBMSYS) Library 6 (File Utilities) Files: ARC2.EXE
ARJ Format	IBM OS/2 Users Forum (GO OS2USER) Library 4 (Application Questions) Files: GNUARJ.EXE
ZIP Format	IBM OS/2 Users Forum (GO OS2USER) Library 4 (Application Questions) Files: UNZ50.ZIP
ZIP Format	PC Vendor C Forum (GO PCVENC) Library 11 (PKWare) File: PKZOS2.EXE IBM Systems Forum (GO IBMSYS) Library 6 (File Utilities) File: PKZOS2.EXE
ZOO Format	IBM OS/2 Users Forum (GO OS2USER) Library 4 (Application Questions) Files: ZOO201.ZIP

Unix-based systems

ARC Format	Unix Forum (GO UNIXFORUM) Library 3 (Tools) Files: ARCSRC.TAZ
SIT Format	Unix Forum (GO UNIXFORUM) Library 3 (Tools) File: UNSIT1.SHZ

ZIP Format	Unix Forum (GO UNIXFORUM)
	Library 3 (Tools)
	File: UNZIP4.TAZ
	Unix Forum (GO UNIXFORUM)
	Library 3 (Tools)
	File: ZIP10E.TAZ
ZOO Format	Unix Forum (GO UNIXFORUM)
	Library 3 (Tools)
	File: ZOO.TAZ

Files, extensions: Names of files in forum libraries are assigned by the people who contribute them. Filenames may have up to six letters and a three-letter extension, such as DRGNET.COM. Some other extensions have particular meanings in most forum libraries. Here are some common ones:

.ASC means ASCII format. Sometimes this is used instead of .TXT to indicate text files. Sometimes it also is used to indicate a BASIC program saved in ASCII rather than tokenized BASIC. Like any ASCII file, it can be viewed online by entering the Read command at a Library prompt, or downloaded for reading offline.

.ASM is a source code listing for an editor/assembler.

.BAS means a program written in Basic.

.BIN means this is a program in "binary," a machine-language program; it should be downloaded with error-checking. (.BIN isn't used much in the some forums. The sysops sometimes encourage users to upload files with their "correct" extensions, such as .COM or .EXE in the IBM world, instead of .BIN. Also .IMG, for image, is used in some computer-specific forums.)

.CNF or .CO or .CON, a conference transcript, is for discussions that occurred in the real-time conferencing section of the system, saved in ASCII.

.DOC stands for documentation, that is, the instructions for a particular program. Sometimes used are .MAN for users manual and .INS for instructions. Nearly always .DOC, .MAN, and .INS have been saved in ASCII. Often the extensions are used in connection with another file of a similar name. MEMORY.BAS might be the program, while MEMORY.DOC contains the instructions. Documentation files often contain a general discussion of the program in the first pages, so if you are uncertain about whether a program meets your needs, you might use the REAd command to examine the first part of the file online.

.FIX means a file that corrects an error. It might refer to a specific program (MEMORY.FIX might apply to MEMORY.BAS), or it might be a general article with programming tips.

.HLP, "Help." These usually are ASCII files written by the sysops that contain answers to commonly asked questions.

.INF, "information." Usually, this is an ASCII file containing background information on a topic.

.PAT, "patch," is a bit of programming that can be incorporated in another file to change the program.

.THD or .THR stands for thread. Important discussions from a forum's message board often are stored in the library with an extension like that.

.TXT is for text files, usually in ASCII.

.ZIP, .ARC, .ZOO, .SIT, .LZH, .CPT, .BNY, .PIT, .LBR, and .ARJ are common extensions for *compress files*, that is, those that have been "packed and squeezed" to save online space in the libraries and download for the retrievers. (See Files, Compressed.)

Files, Personal Area (GO FILES) is a section of online space that holds your own files, including your mail, form letters, and so on. See Personal Files Area.

Files, transfer (**downloading, uploading**): Tens of thousands of files—text articles as well as public domain and shareware programs—can be retrieved, saved on your disk, and used when you are offline. In addition, you may contribute text and original programs to the growing online resources, sending them from your disk directly to CompuServe so that others may retrieve them. Similarly, you may transfer electronic letters between your disk and your online electronic mailbox. This process of file transfer also is called *downloading* (receiving) and *uploading* (sending).

If you're using the CompuServe Information Manager software, retrieving and sending files is easy, because the software designed by CompuServe itself directs you throughout the process. To retrieve a forum file with CIM, just visit the library and browse or search the files with the pull-down menu options or icons. When you find something interesting, select the "Retrieve" option and the program takes care of the rest. Or you may mark a file to add it to a group for retrieval later. Similarly, many of the automated terminal programs (See Automated Terminal) customize the downloading process. See the user manual for your specific software for details.

On the other hand, if you use a general, third-party communications program to log on to CompuServe, file transfer is a little trickier. That's because you need to know something about transfer *protocols* and how to choose one that both CompuServe and your software can use.

A protocol is a set of rules that allows computers to send data back and forth without errors caused by static from phone lines. With a protocol, computers carry on a clever little conversation during the file transfer, periodically checking to see if the data received is identical to what was sent.

With CompuServe Information Manager, the computer itself selects a protocol for your data transfer; with most third-party communications programs, you must make that selection yourself. CompuServe offers several different transfer protocols, so check the manual to see if your terminal software also supports any of these:

1. CompuServe's B Protocol and QB ("Quick B") Protocol, developed specifically for CompuServe. This is the protocol automatically supported by the CompuServe Information Manager; it also is included in a number of other communications programs.

2. Kermit is a protocol developed at Columbia University for file transfer that is becoming increasingly popular in communications software.

3. Ymodem is a similar protocol to Xmodem. It sends and receives a larger block of data for verification during the electronic conversation between the computers.

4. Xmodem is a well-known public domain protocol developed in the late 1970s by Ward Christensen of Chicago. If your third-party communications program supports only one transfer protocol, it probably is Xmodem. However, each program may support a slightly different version. In some parts of CompuServe a "Macintosh Xmodem" is listed on protocol menus, indicating a Xmodem installation for the Apple Macintosh computer.

Retrieval (downloading) When you are retrieving file programs other than the CompuServe Information Manager, you are shown a menu from which to select a protocol. It is up to you to have done your homework by studying your software's manual. If the manual tells you that your program supports the Xmodem protocol, you could select that option from the menu. Then, when prompted, initiate the download with whatever command sequences your software requires for an Xmodem transfer.

Most communications programs also pause before the transfer begins to prompt you for the name you want to assign the file as it arrives on your disk. This does not have to be the same name that exists online. The online file may be called BBALL.BAS, but you might have it saved on your disk as BASEBALL.BAS. Just be sure to specify a legal filename for your computer. Also, if you have a hard disk and use directories and subdirectories to organize it, be sure to enter the full path name when specifying the filename.

After this, the actual download begins. CompuServe sends data and your machine captures it, comparing blocks of data to verify what is received and then saving it on your disk.

After the transfer is done, and the file has been transmitted from CompuServe, confirmed, and saved on your disk under the name you specified, the system notifies you. If you download a second file at this point, the system does not prompt you to choose a transfer protocol; it skips that menu, assuming you are using the same protocol you used on the first transfer.

One more note about the file transfer menu. "DC4/DC2 (Capture)," listed on most CompuServe file transfer menus, is *not* an error-checking protocol, meaning it does compare data blocks like B and Quick B Protocol, Xmodem, etc. Instead, DC4/DC2, sometimes called an "ASCII" transfer, is simply an ASCII display of the file. Some communications programs have what an option called "ASCII dump" or "buffer capture." You can use this option for such capturing. But DC2/DC4 should be used only for capturing *text files* where occasional static on the phone line usually can do no more than garble a few characters. In other words, *program files* always should be downloaded only with an error-checking protocol to protect against noisy phone lines.

Contributing (uploading) Uploading can be used in a number of CompuServe features, and the procedure is about the same in each. Once you select the upload option, you are prompted and then asked for a filename.

About filenames Various parts of CompuServe, such as data libraries of forums, the personal file area, and elsewhere, use names to identify files. A name always can be one to six characters with an optional extension (a period and up to three characters), as in NEWONE.TXT. You may use alphabetic or numeric characters and/or hyphens in the name, but the first character must be a letter of the alphabet. When the system prompts for a filename, it means the name under which the data will be stored on CompuServe; what you enter does *not* have to be the same name that exists on your disk. So you might have a file called PROPOSAL.DAT on your disk and upload it to CompuServe to be saved there as NEWONE.TXT.

After you have specified a filename, the system wants to know which transfer protocol you want to use and will display its menu of available protocols (B Protocol, Kermit, Xmodem, etc.) as in downloading. (See above for the list of protocols.) After the protocol is specified, the system needs one other piece of information: the file *type*. When it get this information, it displays a menu asking if the file is ASCII, binary, or graphics. File type means the format in which the file should be *saved* on CompuServe.

Some notes:

- ASCII (the "American Standard Code for Information Interchange") usually means text, including letters, documents, or source code of programs.

- Binary means computer programs, primarily, or files saved in a specific program's unique format, such as some spreadsheet data.

Remember to specify the same file type as is used for the file currently stored on your disk. If the file you are uploading is binary (a program, for instance), you should specify that it be saved in binary format on CompuServe's end of the connection; if it is an ASCII text (perhaps an article or letter), it should be saved in ASCII on the receiving end.

(A confusion about text files sometimes arises because many commercial word processors routinely store documents, not in ASCII, but in a binary format to save space on your disk and to embed commands for printers and so on. It is a mistake to upload one of these *compressed* binary files and have it saved as ASCII on CompuServe. Since it is not ASCII, it will not be readable by those who download it. Fortunately, your word processor itself usually offers the solution. A good word processor usually has an option for saving files in a plain-vanilla ASCII format rather than its own compressed format. Check the users manual of your word processor and use that option to save your text files in true ASCII before uploading them.)

After the file type has been specified, the system prompts you to begin the transmission. Your communication program's manual should outline its command sequence for uploading. Usually, the terminal software prompts for the name of the file on your disk that you want to upload.

In a forum library, after the upload is completed, the system will ask you to enter keywords and a description of the file.

As in downloading, if you were to upload a second file, the system wouldn't prompt again for a file transfer protocol, but rather it would assume you were using the same protocol you used for the first upload.

If for any reason you need to stop an upload (or a download) before it is finished, press Control C or the Escape key several times. Usually, CompuServe displays a message reporting that the transfer is aborted and allows you to return to a menu.

Uploading also is possible in the personal file area and the CompuServe Mail service.

Finally, as noted in the discussion of downloading, DC4/DC2 CAPTURE, which is listed on most upload menus on the system, is *not* an error-checking protocol, meaning it does not compare checksums the way B and Quick B Protocol, Xmodem, and Kermit do. Instead, DC4/DC2, sometimes called an "ASCII" transfer, is simply an ASCII display of the file; if phone-line static occurs during the transfer, it *will* cause garble in the file as it is received. For that reason, it should be used sparingly for uploading material. When you select the DC4/DC2 options from the protocol menu for uploading, the system displays, "This protocol supports ASCII file transfer only. Is this an ASCII file (Y or N)?" In other words, the system is reminding you that an error-checking protocol, rather than DC4/DC2, should be used for uploading binary files.

If you answer this prompt with Y for yes, meaning your file is indeed ASCII, the system then prompts with, "No error detection protocol in use. Do you wish to be prompted for each line (Y or N)?"

If you answer this question with Y, the system asks you to enter the prompt character to use. (For instance, if you enter a question mark, the system will prompt with a ? at the beginning of each new line.)

If you answer N, the system will not prompt you at the beginning of each new line. After that, the system reports, "Begin sending your data. Use a control-Z (1A hex, 032 octal) to indicate the end of your data." Now you may tell your software to begin its ASCII transmission. (Also with the DC4/DC2 option, you can even type in your file directly from your keyboard.) When you are finished, inform CompuServe by pressing Control-Z.

Again, while DC4/DC2 is fine for transmitting text files, it cannot be used for binary files, such as programs. Use a file transfer protocol for binary files.

Also see Mail, CompuServe.

Films are covered in Magill's Survey of Cinema (GO MAGILL), a database that contains descriptions of most major films from 1902 to the present. For more information, see Magill's Survey of Cinema.

Subscribers also might be interested in the ShowBiz Forum (GO SHOWBIZ), designed for discussions of films or television programs, record albums, celebrity gossip, and nightly news shows. For more information, see Show Biz.

Also, science fiction and fantasy movies are discussed in the Science Fiction &

Fantasy Forum (GO SCI-FI). See Science Fiction. And British films are discussed in the UK Forum (GO UKFORUM). See UK Forum.

Finance, Journal of (**magazine**) can be searched through the Business Database Plus (GO BUSDB). See Business Database.

Financial Calculator (**software**) is supported in the Meca Software Forum (GO MECA). See Meca.

Financial Services: A variety of business and financial tools are available. For a general overview online, enter GO MONEY at any prompt.

Four services are provided as part of the Standard Pricing Plan (see Billing), meaning users under the plan have unlimited access to them. These basic services are:

1. Basic Quote (GO BASICQUOTES), which is delayed 15 minutes or so, is for securities traded on the New York, American, Philadelphia, Boston, and National exchanges, as well as over-the-counter. Price and volume information are reported as a composite of the exchanges.

2. FundWatch Online by Money Magazine (GO FUNDWATCH) lets you screen more than 1,900 mutual funds using criteria that reflect your investment philosophy. You also can use the feature to obtain a detailed report on a fund by entering its name or ticker symbol. Screening criteria include investment objective, fees and expenses, return over time, performance ratings and rankings, management company, dividend yield, risk ratings, total assets, and asset allocations. Funds are displayed in menu form, then summarized and ranked by return over one of seven different time periods. FundWatch Online is updated with new ratings, rankings, and performance information each month (normally in the first seven to ten days of the month). Figures for each fund's total assets, asset allocations, sector holdings, and portfolio holdings are reported quarterly. (Since the reporting deadline for each fund varies, each monthly update also updates the quarterly figures for those funds where new information is available.)

3. Issue/Symbol Lookup (GO SYMBOLS or GO LOOKUP) provides several features to determine what securities and indexes are covered in other securities areas as well as to access the symbols needed to make efficient use of most databases. This is one of the system's basic services, meaning those signed up under the Standard Pricing Plan (see Billing) have unlimited access to the feature. You can search for Company Name, Ticker Symbol, and CUSIP (GO LOOKUP), which allows you to search by name, CUSIP number, ticker symbol, CNUM, or SIC code and list all the issues for a company you select. This service finds the ticker symbols or CUSIP numbers that you then may use in other investment services. You also can see a menu of Available Indexes (GO INDICATORS), which gives the ticker and CUSIP number various indexes. They are categorized into manageable groups designated by market/industry

indexes, bonds/yields, exchange rates, volumes, advances and declines, and any issues that are new or that don't fall into other categories. Another option lets you list all the indexes (more than 700) without going through additional menus.

4. **Mortgage Calculator** (GO MORTPAY) allows the user to figure out the amounts of mortgage payments at different rates (that is, the loan amortization table). It determines monthly payments on a loan as well as the total interest to be paid. You enter the loan amount, the annual rate of interest, the number of payments per year, and the number of years. The program generates a payment schedule.

Other major financial services (extended features outside the basic services area) include:

- Brokerage Services (GO BROKERAGE) that allow you to buy and sell stocks online. See Stock Brokerage Services.

- Company Information (GO COMPANY), a collection of financial services that provide the latest information about all aspects of American and foreign corporations and businesses. See Company Reports.

- Earnings/Economic Projections (GO EARNINGS), which provides access to the I/B/E/S Earnings Estimates (GO IBES); a financial service called the Institutional Broker's Estimate System (see Investment Analysis Tools); S&P Online (GO S&P), with data on about 4,700 companies; and InvesText (GO INVTEXT), featuring two years of reports by analysts in more than 50 Wall Street, regional, and international brokerage houses and research firms (see Company Reports); MMS Financial Reports (GO MMS), a multinational corporation specializing in financial and economic research (see Investment Tools); and Cendata demographics (see Census data).

- Market Quotes and Highlights, including Current quotes (GO QQUOTE), on a 15-minute delayed basis for securities traded on major stock exchanges; Historical quotes (GO PRICES); pricing history on tens of thousands of stocks, bonds, warrants, and mutual funds available on a daily basis to the present; and commodity markets (GO COMMODITIES). For more information, see Commodities. Also included is Current Market Snapshot (GO SNAPSHOT), which gives a quick overview of current stock market trends by displaying key indicators in a one-page statistical report. See Current Market Snapshop. Various investment analyis tools also are accessible; see Investment Analysis.

- Personal Finance and Insurance (GO FINANCE). Apart from business and investment services, CompuServe provides some resources to help in the running of the home. Included are the Checkbook Balancer Program (GO CHECKBOOK), providing a way to keep your checkbook accounting system online, entering debits and credits; and the Personal Net Worth Program (GO

HOM-16), which asks you for dollar amounts of your assets and liabilities, then produces a detailed report on net worth and the Loan Amortization Program (GO MORTPAY). For more information, see Personal Finance and Insurance.

Among related services are several business-investment related forums, including the Investors Forum (GO INVFORUM) and the NAIC Forum (GO NAIC). See Investors Forum.

Through the Business Database Plus (GO BUSDB), several relevant magazines are searchable, among them *Financial Management, Financial Market Trends, Financial World, Financial Services Report, The Financial Post*, and *Inside Market Data*. See Business Database.

Relevant databases on IQuest (GO IQUEST) include:

ABI/INFORM	Fortune
American Banker Fulltext	Guarantor
Automated Medical Payments News	High Yield Report
Bank Automation News	Inside Market Data
Bond Buyer Fulltext	Insider Trading Monitor
Business Periodicals Index	International Reports
Business Week	Item Processing Report
California Public Finance	Knight-Ridder/Tribune Business News
Card News	Lloyd's List
Corporate EFT Report	Management Contents
Credit Card News	Money
Credit Risk Management Report	POS News
D&B—Dun's Electronic Business Directory	PTS Newsletter Database
EFT Report	Rategram Online
Financial Services Report	Securities Week
Financial Times Business Reports: Business/Finance	Tokyo Financial Wire
FINIS: Financial Industry Information Service	Trading Systems Technology
	TRW Business Credit Database

See IQuest.

A number of business-related services and products are sold in a store in the Electronic Mall (GO MALL), including Business Incorporating Guide (GO INC) for information on Nationwide incorporating; Checkfree Corporation (GO CF), an electronic payment service; Dreyfus Corporation (GO DR), for mutual funds; H&R Block (GO HRB) for tax preparation; Max Ule Discount Brokerage (GO TKR), for brokerage and financial information; NewsNet (GO NN), an online news service signup; TRW Credentials (GO CRE), for managing credit records; and University of Phoenix (GO UP), business degree programs online. For more information, see Electronic Mall.

Categories in the CompuServe Classifieds let you read and post ads regarding business/investments and business opportunites. For more information, see Classifieds Service.

Some news features have a business orientation. See Executive News Service, Business Wire and News-a-Tron.

Also see Company Reports, Franchising, International Business and Trade, Investment Analysis and Stocks, and Stock Brokerage Services.

Financial Technology Insight can be searched through the Business Database Plus (GO BUSDB). See Business Database.

Financial Times (**newspaper**) is covered in the UK Newspaper Library (GO UKPAPERS). See UK Newspaper.

Finansa products are supported in the UK Computing Forum (GO UKCOMP). See UK Computing.

FIND is a command that helps you locate features on the system. The Find feature is built into the CompuServe Information Manager platforms. It also can be used by those running third-party general terminal programs. Entered at any prompt, FIND followed by a keyword causes the system to list one or more related features. For instance, FIND Apple directs the system to locate any features it has on file that deal with Apple computers and software. FIND builds a special menu for you, from which you can access any of the features found by simply entering a numbered option. For information on other commands, see Commands.

Findex (**business database**) is accessible through the Marketing/Management Research Center (GO MKTGRC). For details, see Marketing/Management. The database also is accessible through IQuest (GO IQUEST). For more information, see IQuest.

Finest House (**software**) is supported in the PC Vendor B Forum (GO PCVENB). For more information, see IBM Computers.

FINIS (**business database**) is accessible through the Marketing/Management Research Center (GO MKTGRC). For details, see Marketing/Management. The database also is accessible through IQuest (GO IQUEST). For more information, see IQuest.

Finland, Finance & can be searched through the Business Database Plus (GO BUSDB), as well as *Finnish Trade Review*. See Business Database.

Finmeccanica News can be searched through the Business Database Plus (GO BUSDB). See Business Database.

Firearms is a topic of the Outdoors Forum (GO OUTDOORFORUM).

Fire fighters and fire safety are discussed in the SafetyNet Forum (GO SAFETYNET). For information, see Safety.

1st Class Peripherals   is supported in the Apple II Vendor Forum (GO APIIVEN). For more information, see Apple Computers.

First Graphics and First Publisher (software) are supported in the Software Publishing Forum (GO SPCFORUM). For more information, see Software Publishing Corporation.

Fish   (tropical) are the subject of the Aquaria and Fish Forum (GO AQUAFORUM), operated by FISHNET. It covers diverse interests centering on aquariums and tropical fish. Included in the group are public aquarium administrators, aquarium product manufacturers, fish farmers and breeders, and especially general aquarium hobbyists. John R. Benn (76703,4256) is FISHNET manager. Daily management of the forum is handed by forum manager Deb Tanaka (76702,1467). Assisting her are Stanley D. Brown, Pam Chin, Paul Cook, Jerry Corcoran, Philip S. Cusimano, Art Deacon, Carl Delfavero, Jay Hemdal, Richard Hendricks, Chris Higgins, Barb Hunter, Doug Hunter, Larry Jackson, John Jankowski, Don S. Johnson, Debbie Kitchin, John Farrell Kuhns, Jeff Lodge, Chris Moler, Steve Szabo, Barry Szakolczay, Ferdi Velasco, Gary Wagner, Mike Wickham, and David Wisniewski.
For related topics, see Pets and Animals Forum.

Fisher, Jerry (76711,22) is sysop in the end-user forums in the Microsoft area of the system (GO MICROSOFT). See Microsoft Software.

Fishing, hunting, and camping   are discussed in the Great Outdoors Forum (GO OUTDOORFORUM). For more information, see Sports and Recreation.

Fitness, AFFA's American   is searchable in the Health Database Plus (GO HLTBD), as is *American Fitness* and *American Health: Fitness of Body and Mind*. Also, abstracts of *Muscle & Fitness* are searchable. See Health.

Fitzgibbons, Patricia,   also known on the system as "Nightshift," 76703,657, is sysop of the game forums (GO GAMERS). For more information, see Games. She also is sysop of the Chess Forum (GO CHESSFORUM). See Chess.

.FIX,   as an extension on filenames in forum libraries, often means a file that corrects an error in another file in the library. For more information, see Files, Extensions.

Flame Retardancy News   can be searched through the Business Database Plus (GO BUSDB). See Business Database.

FlexQL (software) is supported in the Data Access Corp. Forum (GO DACCESS). For details, see Data Access.

Flight Information   is provided in an assortment of online services. For details, see Airlines and Aviation.

Flight International (magazine) can be searched through the Business Database Plus (GO BUSDB). See Business Database.

Flightline (database) may be searched through the IQuest gateway. See IQuest.

Flight simulator software from various publishers is supported in the Flight Simulation Forum (GO FSFORUM). See Gaming Forums for details.

   Also, Microsoft's Flight Simulator software is supported the Microsoft Application Forum (GO MSAPP). For more information, see Microsoft Software.

Floor Covering Business (magazine) can be searched through the Business Database Plus (GO BUSDB). See Business Database.

Florida (news) is covered in the Fort Lauderdale Sun-Sentinel, the Miami Herald, the Orlando Sentinel, the Palm Beach Post, and the St. Petersburg Times, all searchable through Telebase System's News Source USA (GO NEWSUSA). See News Source. Also:

   • Selected reports from Florida are included in the Southeast regional reports from United Press International. See Executive News Service.

   • *Florida Trend* magazine can be searched through the Business Database Plus (GO BUSDB), as can *Jacksonville Business Journal*, *Orlando Business Journal*, *Sarasota Magazine*, and *Tampa Bay Business Journal*. See Business Database.

Florida Forum (GO FLORIDA) is a travel feature operated by Larry Wood (76703,704) with assistance from Dave Shaver, David Pool, John and Pat Mullin, Laura "Pixie" Burns, and Doug Cody. Many of the forum's staff work for the Florida Department of Commerce, Tourism Division, and are ready to answer questions about visiting their state. The forum also provides educational assistance to schools, teachers, students, and parents planning visits to Florida. Also represented in the forum is the Disabled Traveler's Friendship Network, a nonprofit group providing travel information to physically challenged individuals and families. Files in the forum's Library 17 ("Handicap Travel") include phone listings for handicap services and information on handicap parking permits.

   For other travel-related features, see Travel.

Florida Fruit Shippers (GO FFS) is a store in the Electronic Mall (GO MALL) that offers citrus and tropical fruits. For more information, see Electronic Mall.

Florida Today NewsLink Forum (GO FLATODAY) provides a unique link to this Gannett Inc. newspaper on the Florida Space Coast. The forum provides access to articles published in Florida Today, as well as communication with the paper's news staff. Each message section is administered by a newsroom editor or reporter, allowing you to voice opinions or ask questions about Florida Today articles. Sections include The Space Program, Seniors/Snowbirds, Florida Politics, The Environment, and more. The sysop is Kristen Zimman (76711,1111). Assisting are Mark Decotis and Dan Patellis, and section leaders Pam Platt, Jim Banke, Don Wittekin, Tom Squires, Tony Boylan, Wevonneda Minis, Ann Mittman, Cathy Liden, Pat Weiss, Lenore Beecken, Elaine Cartechine, and Tom Kehoe.

Flower & Garden Magazine (magazine) can be searched in the Magazine Database Plus (GO MDP). See Magazine Database. See also Gardening.

Flower and Plants are sold in a number of stores in the Electronic Mall (GO MALL), including 800 Flower and Gift Shoppe (GO GM), The Flower Stop (GO FS), and Walter Knoll Florist (GO WK). For related subjects, see Gardening, Farming, and Agriculture.

FLS users are supported in the ZiffNet Bendata Forum (GO ZNT:BENDATA). See ZiffNet.

Fluidex (engineering database) may be searched through the IQuest gateway. See IQuest.

Focus Connection (GO FOCUS) is operated by Information Builders Inc. and FUSE (FOCUS User's Group) for online support of customers. The Fuse Forum (GO FUSE) provides technical databases and diagnostic aids, as well as educational course schedules and publications. It also offers online discussions with ISI founder/President Gerry Cohen. Operating the service are sysops John Genzano (76702,1703) (who has been developing FOCUS systems since 1981, on VM/CMS, MVS/TSO, and PC/MS-DOS machines), Paul McGee (76444,14), Peter J. Natali, (76702,1704), and Jim Scheef (76702,1654).

Also, FocWizards Forums (GO FOCWIZARD) is operated by Information Builders Inc. to offer direct technical support to users of its software, including FOCUS, LEVEL5, LEVEL5 OBJECT, and FOCCALC. The firm says the "FocWizards" are the primary source of technical help. (Their names and account numbers are listed on the sysop roster announcement.) The forum also provides code and text from the firm's FOCUS Systems Journal. The sysops are Art Greenhaus (76702,1343) and Noreen Redden (76702,1347).

Folio Corp. products are supported in the Novell Vendor Forum A (GO NVENA). See Novell Software.

Folio: The Magazine for Magazine Management (magazine) can be searched through the Business Database Plus (GO BUSDB). See Business Database.

Folk music is a subject of the Music/Performing Arts Forum (GO MUSICARTS). See Music.

FontBank Online (GO FONTBANK) offers more than 1,300 commercial display and text typefaces available on five different font platforms. These fonts are available for immediate purchase and downloading. Also incorporated are a searching mechanism and a GIF graphic file, which gives users a visual representation of the font before making the purchase decision. FontBank Online also features downloadable GIF tutorial files, providing members with a graphical overview of popular font terms and how they affect the look of a font.

Also see Desktop Publishing.

FontBank products are supported in the Desktop Publishing Vendor Forum (GO DTPVENDOR). For details, see Desktop Publishing.

Food and cooking are the subjects of several forums. Of particular note are:

- The Bacchus Wine Forum (GO WINEFORUM), covering all aspects of wine with experts as well as those who simply enjoy wine. For more information, see Wine Forum.

- British eateries are discussed in the UK Forum (GO UKFORUM). See UK Forum.

- Cook's Online Forum (GO COOKS), where favorite recipes, cooking tips, and information on new products are exchanged. For more information, see Cook's Online.

- Diet, herbs, and health are discussed in the New Age Forum (GO NEWAGE). See New Age.

- *Food & Nutrition* magazine is searchable in the Health Database Plus (GO HLTDB). For more information, see Health.

- Restaurant reviews are the topic of the Zagat Survey (GO ZAGAT). See Zagat.

- Searchable through the Business Database Plus (GO BUSDB) are a number of related magazines, including *Food & Beverage Marketing*, *Food & Drink Daily*, *Food Channel*, *Food Chemical News*, *Food Cosmetics & Drug Packaging*, *Food Engineering*, *Food Engineering International*, *Food Labeling News*, *Food Manufacture*, *Food Processing*, *Frozen and Chilled Foods*, *Frozen Food Digest*, *National Food Review*, *Prepared Foods*, *New Food Products in Japan*, *Quick Frozen Foods International*, *Tea and Coffee Trade Journal*, *Milling & Baking News*, and *Food in Canada*. See Business Database.

- Searched through the Knowledge Index (GO KI) is Food Science and Technology Abstracts. See Knowledge Index.

- Through IQuest (GO IQUEST) you may search Food Channels, Food Science and Technology Abstracts, Coffeeline, Fearless Taster, Foods Adlibra, Current Research Information/USDA, Ice Cream Reporter, Washington Beverage Insight, and World Food & Drink Report (databases). See IQuest.

Food and cooking products are sold in a number of Electronic Mall stores (GO MALL), including Adventures in Food (GO AIF), the Chef's Catalog (GO CC), Coffee Anyone ??? (GO COF), Figi's (GO FG), Florida Fruit Shippers (GO FFS), Gimmee Jimmy's Cookies (GO GIM), Green Mountain Coffee Roasters (GO GMR), Honeybaked Hams (GO HAM), Omaha Steaks (GO OS) and, Virginia Diner (GO VA). For more information, see Electronic Mall. See also Restaurants.

Food and Drug Administration is discussed in the White House Forum (GO WHITEHOUSE). See White House.

Football is a regular topic in the Sports Forum (GO FANS) and on the NCAA Collegiate Sports Network (GO NCAA). For more on this and related subjects, see Sports and Recreation.

Footwear News (database) may be searched through the IQuest gateway. See IQuest. It also can be searched through Business Database Plus (GO BUSDB). See Business Database.

For Your Eyes Only (government database) may be searched through the IQuest gateway. See IQuest.

Forbes (business database) may be searched through the IQuest gateway (see IQuest and through News Source USA (GO NEWSUSA); see News Souce USA. Abstracts of the magazine also can be searched through Computer Database Plus (GO COMPDB). See Computer Database Plus.

Ford Cars & Trucks (GO FD) is a kiosk in the Electronic Mall that provides cars and trucks information, dealer locations, and so on. See Electronic Mall.

Ford Motor Co. (GO FMC) has a store in the Electronic Mall (GO MALL) that offers car and truck information, a dealer locator, and so on. For more information, see Electronic Mall. And for other automobile features, see Cars.

Ford, Ric (72511,44) is primary sysop of the MacWEEK Forum (GO ZMC:MACWEEK), part of magazine publisher Ziff-Davis' ZiffNet/Mac services for Apple Macintosh users. See ZiffNet/Mac.

ForeFront Software Inc. products are supported in the OS/2 Vendor Forum (GO OS2AVEN). See IBM Computers.

Foreign Language Education Forum (GO FLEFO) is for teachers and students of all languages. The sysops are Jerry Ervin (76703,2063), who holds a Ph.D in foreign language education from Ohio State University, and Doug Lacey (76702,1245). Ervin's languages are French, Spanish, German, and Russian. Lacey, who holds a Ph.D. in Classics, is interested in modern language focus on French, German, and Italiah.

For other school-related features, see Education.

Forensic Science Database (database) may be searched through the IQuest gateway. See IQuest.

Foresight Incorporated products are supported in the PC Vendor A Forum (GO PCVENA). For more information, see IBM Computers.

Forest industry is covered in several services, including *Forest Industries* and *American Forests*. Both are searchable Magazine Database Plus (GO MDP) and Business Database Plus (GO BUSDB). For details, see Magazine Database and see Business Database. See also Wood Industry.

FormBase (**software**) is supported in the Ventura Software Forum (GO VENTURA). See Ventura.

Forth (**software**) is supported in the CSI Forth Net (GO FORTH). For more information, see Programmers Support.

Fort Lauderdale is a topic of the Florida Forum (GO FLORIDA). See Florida.

Fort Lauderdale (FL) Sun-Sentinel (**newspaper**) is searchable through Telebase System's News Souce USA (GO NEWSUSA) and through the Knowledge Index (GO KI). For more information, see News Source and see Knowledge Index.

FORTRAN (**Microsoft software**) is supported in the Microsoft Languages Forum (GO MSLANG). See Microsoft Software.

Fortune (**magazine**) can be searched through the IQuest gateway (see IQuest) and through News Source USA (GO NEWSUSA); see News Source USA. Abstracts of the magazine can be searched through Computer Database Plus (GO COMPDB). See Computer Database Plus.

Forums (sometimes still called "special interest groups" or "SIGs" as they were called in the early days) are CompuServe's neighborhoods. More than 600 forums now operate, covering subjects ranging from law and medicine to gardening, religion, sports, travel, and every conceivable aspect of personal computing hardware, software, and applications.

The forums are operated by *sysops* (systems operators) and a large forum usually has more than one, a chief sysop and several assistants. Most sysops aren't CompuServe employees, but rather are independent contractors who keep the forums going. Each chief is paid a percentage of the connect-time dollars that subscribers spend in his or her forum. Most forums are public, but not all. The forum software, with its sophisticated message boards, libraries, and real-time conferences, can be a valuable tool for business, so some companies have private forums on CompuServe for their own use.

Forums have five main components:

- Announcements and bulletins from the sysops.
- Conference rooms for immediate real-time online discussions. The conference area has multiple "rooms" where members may type their messages to others in attendance and wait a few seconds for replies.
- Libraries, or databases, filled with a variety of specific information related to the interests of the group. This includes public domain and shareware programs that you may retrieve, as well as text files such as news reports and important threads of conversation from the message board on hot topics of the past.
- Message boards, for the posting of public messages to which all members also may reply.
- Member directories in which forum members may list their interests.

Each forum has its own service name (or address) which can be used with the GO command for direct access. For the latest list of forums, enter FIND FORUMS at any prompt online (see Find). Also there are several broad categories of forums, such as computer-related (including groups interested in specific computers and some more general forums devoted to programming), general-interest (about topics ranging from games to space to music), and professional forums (for the lawyers, doctors, aviators, and so on). You can locate forums by using the FIND command followed by a keyword. In addition, related forums are grouped on some menus, such as GO HARDWARE, for hardware-related forums, and GO SOFTWARE, for software-related forums.

Announcements Eight different kinds of announcements from the forum sysop are on file. It is unnecessary to leave a note on the message board asking a sysop or the membership to explain what the forum is all about. Such information already is on file in the Notice area. The notices, which differ in terms of content from forum to forum, include:

- Conference. This notice tells of regular real-time conferences held in the forum, or reports upcoming special conferences and provides tips.

- General Announcement. This includes information that has more lasting interest to the group than what is contained in the News Flash notice. It usually summarizes functions and operating instructions and give tips on usage and etiquette.

- Library. This one usually summarizes what each library section contains, and may list recently contributed files along with other library news.

- Membership. This notice usually contains additional information about membership and provides general conduct guidelines.

- Messages. This may tell you about the latest hot message topics. It also might outline the various message sections and the subject matter in each.

- New Member. This welcomes first-time visitors to the forum, explains the usage rules, and tells how to get additional information and assistance.

- News Flash. This usually reports recent developments, announces upcoming events, and so on. This notice often automatically is shown as you enter a forum.

- Sysop Roster. It details the sysops' backgrounds, with information on how they came to be here in the first place.

Forum options (available only to users of software other than the CompuServe Information Manager) lets you alter aspects of the individual forums, such as name (the way your name appears in the forums, as in the header of any message you post), message number (the number of the last message you read in the forum), and default sections. This last option lets you specify the message board sections that you routinely access when you Search for messages. You may exclude any message board sections that don't interest you.

Conferencing   Real-time talk is another big part of the forums. Each forum has a number of electronic "conference rooms" that may be used for live chats between forum members. These range from informal gabfests to formal lectures, panel discussions, and interviews. Forum conferencing is similar to several other CompuServe features, including the CB Simulator and the Convention Center. For more information, see CB Simulator.

Libraries   The libraries hold the resources and treasures of a forum. They contain three kinds of data:

1. Public domain and shareware software that you may retrieve on your disk. Once retrieved, the programs may be used over and over again offline.
2. Text files, such as past topics discussed in the forum that may be read online or retrieved for offline reading later. Also the text may include reprints of published articles, reviews and commentaries written by other forum members, how-to articles by sysops and forum regulars, transcripts of important real-time conferences, and message board conversations of note.
3. Graphics files that may be viewed online or retrieved for offline viewing. These sometimes are referred to as ".GIF" files because they usually have that filename extension (such as "BOARD.GIF"). GIF stands for "Graphic Interchange Format," CompuServe's own format for picture files that may be exchanged between different types of computers.

Libraries, like the message boards, are divided into sections, each devoted to a particular aspect of the forum's subjects. One section might contain general utility programs; another might have files relating to word processing; others might have game software and reviews, and programs and articles about computer graphics, and so on. Any of the files in the library—programs or text—may be *retrieved* (or "downloaded"), meaning a copy of it is made on your disk so that you may use it later offline. In addition, you may *contribute* ("upload") copies of your own files, including original programs and text, for others to use. (For more on this, see Files, Transfer.)

As with the message boards, there is more than one way to prowl the forum libraries. You may either browse sections, reading descriptions of recently contributed files, or search for specific files by name, a contributor's user ID, or keywords.

Message boards   The message board is a forum's communications center, where subscribers share ideas, news, gossips, and suggestions. Here are the basics about all forum message boards:

1. The messages are public, both from members and the sysops. Anyone who has joined the forum may (a) read messages and (b) write and post original messages as well as replies to existing messages.

2. Messages can be gathered for you to read in several ways and can be sorted to help you find discussions of interest. You may collect the messages by *topics* and *sections*.

   Topics are the chains of related messages—the originals and their replies (and replies to the replies and so on). Sometimes they are thought of as *threads*, since all messages in the group are connected by the thread of a single idea. Forums call these message chains "topics" because all the messages in a thread have the same words in the subject line. A reply to any message in the group keeps the same subject heading. You usually view the messages by topic, reading one group before moving on to the next, because it makes it easier to follow the discussions.

   Sections: Message boards also usually have specialties, and are divided into multiple sections (sometimes called "subtopics") devoted to specific ideas. These are like the various departments of a magazine or an office. Typically, a computer-related forum might have a section for messages relating to hardware, another to software, another to new products, another to user help, and so on. In addition to topics, the section structure can be used to quickly zero in on new messages of interest. Also, when writing and posting messages, members are asked to put them in the relevant sections. In addition, sysops may decide to make some sections of the message board private, accessible by invitation only.

3. At any time, you may contribute to existing discussions by using the built-in text feature (either online or offline) to reply to messages in current subjects (topics). Also, you may start your own discussion by composing a message with a new topic and posting it on the board. The system asks you to identify the subject and the intended recipient. The receiver can be another forum member, or you may indicate that the message is for ALL or for SYSOP. Note, though, that even messages addressed to other members may be read and replied to by others in the forum. In other words, *all* forum messages between members are public. (Private messages may be sent to the sysops, however, as discussed later.)

4. Besides topics and sections, there are two other ways to find messages on the board. You can search by a specific writer or recipient or about a specific subject. You may search the entire message board or just a specific section.

   You also can search specific message numbers. (Each message on the board automatically is assigned a unique number by the system when it is posted.) This method of retrieval is useful primarily when someone has recommended that you read a particular message.

5. Message boards hold only a limited number of messages. Adding new messages causes the older ones to be automatically deleted by the system. Busier forums have a faster "scroll rate," meaning a message may stay on the board only a day or so.

6. As you begin visiting a specific forum and reading messages, the system makes note of the most recent message posted. When you exit the message board, the

system automatically records the latest posting date as the starting message for your next visit. Then, the next time you read messages, you won't have to see any messages posted before that date.

Many of the messages on the forums make liberal use of abbreviations for standard phrases. For more on this, see Acronyms.

Membership directory This is a voluntary database of forum members' names and interests. The feature also lets you add information about your own interests. For related topics, see Help Online and see Practice Forum.

Fosgate Audionics products are supported in the Consumer Electronics Vendor Forum (GO CEVENDOR). See Electronics Forum.

Foster, Lee is a California travel writer whose Adventures in Travel (GO AIT) and West Coast Travel (GO WCT) have been featured on CompuServe since 1984. On the road approximately one week out of every four, Foster has taken armchair travelers on such sojourns as a bicycle trip across The Netherlands, an inside peak of the Great Wall of China, and close-up looks at places like San Francisco's bustling Chinatown and Upper Michigan's pristine Royale Isle National Park. Foster turned to writing and photographing the world near and far in 1975 after graduating from Stanford with a degree in literature. The author of 15 books, he has written hundreds of feature articles which have graced the pages of over 50 newspapers and magazines including The Los Angeles Times and *Travel & Leisure*. For related topics, see Travel.

FotoMan is supported in the Logitech Forum (GO LOGITECH). See Logitech.

Foundations, associations, and grants are covered in several databases searchable through the IQuest gateway (GO IQUEST), including Corporate Giving Watch, Encyclopedia of Associations, Federal Grants and Contracts Weekly, Foundation Directory, Foundation Giving Watch, Foundation Grants Index, and Grants. See IQuest.

Foundry Management & Technology (magazine) can be searched through the Business Database Plus (GO BUSDB). See Business Database.

4DOS (software) is supported in the UK Shareware Forum (GO UKSHARE). See UK Shareware.

4D Server (software) is supported in the ACIUS Forum (GO ACIUS), as is 4D/4D Compiler, 4D Modules, and 4D DAL/SQL Server. See ACI US.

411 Newsletter can be searched through the Business Database Plus (GO BUSDB). See Business Database.

4PRINT (software) is supported in the PC Vendor B Forum (GO PCVENB). For more information, see IBM Computers.

Foxpro Advisor electronic version is available in the Data Based Advisor Forum (GO DBADVISOR). See Data Based Advisor.

Fox Software is supported in the Microsoft Fox Software Forum (GO FOXFORUM) and the Microsoft Fox Users forum (GO FOXUSER). See Microsoft Software.

Fractal Design products are supported in the Ultimedia Tools Forum A (GO ULTIATOOLS). See Ultimedia.

Fractals graphics are featured in the Graphics Developers Forum (GO GRAPHDEV) and in the Graphics Plus Forum (GO GRAPHPLUS). For more information, see Graphics. They also are supported in the Ultimedia Tools Series A Forum (GO ULTIATOOLS). See Ultimedia.

Frame Technology products are supported in the Desktop Publishing Vendor Forum (GO DTPVENDOR). For details, see Desktop Publishing.

Framework software is supported in the Borland Applications Forum (GO BORAPP). For more information, see Borland.

France is discussed and supported in a number of features. See French news.

Franchising is the topic of a number of online business resources:

- Biz*File (GO BIZFILE) has searchable databases of yellow page listings around the country.
- Business Database Plus (GO BUSDB) provides access to all types of business articles, including those on franchising.
- Business Dataline (GO BUSDATE) tracks trends and the reputation of franchises in 115 regional business publication.
- D&B Dun's Market Identifiers (GO DUBS) and Dun's Electronic Business Directory (GO DYP) provides basic company information.
- *Entrepreneur's* Business Franchise and Opportunities database (GO EBF) offers a searchable listing of some 2,000 franchise and nonfranchise businesses.
- *Entrepreneur's* Small Business Forum (GO USEN) is a discussion group for entrepreneurs.
- TRW Business Profiles (GO TRWREPORTS) enables users to determine a franchise's credit history and financial information.

  See also Financial Services.

Franklin Quest is supported in the Office Automation Vendor Forum (GO OAFORUM). See Office Automation.

Freehand (software) is supported in the Aldus Forum (GO ALDUS). See Aldus.

Freelance Plus (software) is supported in the Lotus Words & Pixels Forum (GO LOTUSB). For more information, see Lotus Software.

Free Trade Advisory can be searched through the Business Database Plus (GO BUSDB), as can *North American Report on Free Trade*. See Business Database. See also Trade.

French is spoken in the Foreign Language Education Forum (GO FLEFO), a service for students and teachers. For more information, see Foreign Language.

French news is the speciality of Agence France Presse, an international news service that is searchable through Comtex Scientific Inc.'s NewsGrid database. For details, see NewsGrid.

Also, several IQuest resources cover French topics, including AFPE, the French Press Agency; AGRA, a general newswire; Adhemix, a glue industry database; AECO, a business database; D&B—France, a business database; EDF-DOC, an economics database; ESSOR, a company database; Francis, a database of history and humanities; FPAT, patent database; Logos, a government database; News From France, updated every two weeks; Oriadoc, about French information services; Questa, with data on legislative sessions; and Telefirm Directory of French Companies. See IQuest.

French issues are also discussed in the European Forum (GO EURFORUM). See European Forum.

Frenster Associates products are supported in the OS/2 Vendor Forum (GO OS2AVEN). See IBM Computers.

Fresno (CA) Bee (newspaper) is searchable through Telebase System's News Source USA (GO NEWSUSA). For more information, see News Source.

Friday Memo (information industry database) may be searched through the IQuest gateway. See IQuest.

Friederich, Brenda (76711,366) is sysop of the Digitalk Forum (GO DIGITALK). See Digitalk.

Frier, David (76702,1417) is sysop of the Software Publishers Association Forum (GO SPAFORUM). He also is sysop of Data Based Advisor Forum (GO DBADVISOR). For more information, see Data Based Advisor.

Frontier scripting system for the Apple Macintosh is supported in the UserLand Software Forum (GO USERLAND). See UserLand.

Frontier Technologies products are supported in the Windows 3rd-Party B Forum (GO WINAPB). See Microsoft Software.

Frost & Sullivan Political Risk Country Reports (database) may be searched through the IQuest gateway. See IQuest.

Frozen and Chilled Foods (magazine) can be searched through the Business Database Plus (GO BUSDB). See Business Database. See also Food.

FTC FOIA Log and **FTC: Watch** (databases) may be searched through the IQuest gateway. See IQuest. The resources also can be searched through the Business Database Plus (GO BUSDB). See Business Database.

Fudpucker, Orville (72241,105) is the sysop of PC Magazine's Editorial Forum (ZNT:EDITORIAL). See PC Magazine.

Fujitsu Peripherals from Fujitsu Australia's Volume Products Group are supported in the Pacific Vendors Forum (GO PACFORUM). See Pacific.

Fujitsu products are supported in the PC Vendor J Forum (GO PCVENJ). See IBM Computers.

Fujitsu Weekly can be searched through the Business Database Plus (GO BUSDB). See Business Database.

FundWatch (GO FUNDWATCH) lets you sort through more than 1,500 funds by entering its ticker symbol or name. For more information, see Financial Services.

Funk Software products are supported in the IBM PC Vendor F Forum (GO PCVENF). See IBM Computers.

FURY modems and others are supported in the Dr. Neuhaus Forum (GO NEUHAUS). See Dr. Neuhaus.

FUSE (FOCUS User's Group) is online in the Focus Connection (GO FOCUS). For more information, see Focus.

Fusion Power Report can be searched through the Business Database Plus (GO BUSDB). See Business Database.

Futurehome Technology News can be searched through the Business Database Plus (GO BUSDB). See Business Database.

Futures: Magazine of Commodities & Options (magazine) can be searched through the Business Database Plus (GO BUSDB). See Business Database.

Future Software Engineering (software products) are supported in Windows 3rd-Party Forum A (GO WINAPA). See Microsoft Software.

Future Trends Software products are supported in the IBM PC Vendor I Forum (GO PCVENI). See IBM Computers.

FutureWave/Banyan products are supported in the Pacific Vendor Forum (GO PACVEN). See Pacific Vendor.

Futurist (magazine) is searchable through Magazine Database Plus (GO MDP). For details see Magazine Database. It also can be searched through Business Database Plus (GO BUSDB). See Business Database.

Futurus products are supported in the PC Vendor G Forum (GO PCVENG). See IBM.

Fuzzy logic is discussed in the AI Expert Forum (GO AIEXPERT). See AI Expert.

FW (magazine) can be searched through Business Database Plus (GO BUSDB). See Business Database.

FX Week can be searched through the Business Database Plus (GO BUSDB). See Business Database.

FYI products are supported in the PC Vendor G Forum (GO PCVENG). See IBM.

G

Gadgets by Small (products) are supported in the Atari Vendors Forum (GO ATARIVEN). See Atari Computers.

Gagliardo, Tony (76711,401) is the sysop of the Meca Software Forum (GO MECA). See Meca Software.

Galileo spacecraft graphic images are available in the Space Forum (GO SPACEFORUM) in GIF format. See also NASA.

Game Publishers Forums (GO GAMPUB) cater to game designers, project co-ordinators, and other technical and managerial staffs from various companies. See Gaming Forums.

Games (GO GAMES) on CompuServe include both human-against-machine and multiplayer contests. Each game provides instructions. Some are lengthy, so you should plan to save them in a disk file for reading or printing later. Also, most have a suggested age limit, indicating the age group for which the game was designed. The complexity and level of challenge of the game are the determinant factors. Here is an overview of CompuServe's games.

> **Basic Services** These allow unlimited access as part of the Standard Price Plan (see Billing), including:
>
> - BlackDragon (GO BLACKDRAGON)
> - Biorhythms (GO BIORHYTHM)
> - CastleQuest (GO CQUEST)
> - Classic Adventure (GO CLADVENT)
> - Enhanced Adventure (GO ENADVENT)
> - Grolier Whiz Quiz (GO WHIZ)

- Hangman (GO HANGMAN)
- Science Trivia (GO SCITRIVIA)
- ShowBiz Quiz (GO SBQ)

Fantasy These include role-playing and adventure games:

- British Legends (GO LEGENDS)
- The Island of Kesmai (GO ISLAND)

War/Simulation Games These test one's ability to out-maneuver an opponent:

- Air Traffic Controller (GO ATCONTROL)
- Megawars I: The Galactic Conflict (GO MEGA1)
- Megawars III: The New Empire (GO MEGA3)
- Sniper (GO SNIPER)

Parlor and Trivia Games

- Astrology Calculator (GO ASTROLOGY)
- The Two-Stage Trivia Game (GO STAGEII)
- The Multiple Choice (GO MULTIPLE)
- You Guessed It (GO YGI)

For more information, see individual game titles. See also Modem Games Forum, Chess, Entertainment Center, and Gaming Forums.

Gametek products are covered in the Game Publishers B Forum (GO GAMBPUB). See Gaming Forums.

Gaming Forums cover various facets of computer entertainment.

- The Gamers' Forum (GO GAMERS) supports conversation about all sorts of online and offline computer games, adventure games, role-playing games, and more. Since 1982, this forum has been the premier online resource for game players and now is the hub of a network of the game-playing forums. The system offers game hints, reviews, and product news about adventure, war/strategy, action/arcade, sports, cartridge games, etc. Some members also participate in online games played in the forum's real-time conference rooms or via the message board. Regulars also include expert gamers, play testers, game designers, and magazine writers and editors. The administrator for this and several other gaming forums is Patricia Fitzgibbons, known on the system as Nightshift. Her user ID is 76703,657. Many of the staff members of the gaming forums use pseudonyms to keep in the spirit of modern gaming fantasy. Nightshift is assisted in the Gamers' Forum by Ms. Wiz, Hercules, Joe Cataudella, and Bob Provencher.

- The Multiplayer Games Forum (GO MPGAMES) is dedicated to the support of CompuServe's online multiplayer games, including MegaWars I, MegaWars III, SeaWAR, Island of Kesmai, British Legends, You Guessed It!, Sniper!, Air Traffic Controller. Members take part in the forum by helping others with questions and by sharing information about their game experiences. Designers of the games, as well as support staff from CompuServe's own entertainment technology department, provide some technical assistance. In running the forum, Nightshift is assisted by Cail (76704,33) and Bonsai (76702,746).

- The Play-By-Mail Games Forum (GO PBMGAMES) offers discussions about games such as Alamzae, Beyond the Stellar Empire, Continental Rails, Droids, Family Wars, Feudal Lords, Heroic Fantasy, Illuminati, It's A Crime, Kings & Things, Midgard, The Next Empire, The Next Empire, Realms of Altair, Spiral Arm, Starweb, and more. Numerous PBM game vendors—including Adventures By Mail, Andon Games, Cyborg Games, Delta Games, Flying Buffalo, Game Systems Inc., Graaf Simulations, King's Guild, Orpheus Publishing Co., Rolling Thunder Games, and Twin Engine Gaming—support their products in the forum. Members form teams and alliances via messages on the message board. Several vendors offer "all-CompuServe" games in which all players are forum members and online turns are accepted. The editors of the major PBM game magazines—Flagship and Paper Mayhem—visit the forum, as do representatives of the Play-By-Mail Game Association. Nightshift's assistants in this forum are William Pegues, James Retief, and Harry Bee.

- The Role-Playing Games Forum (GO RPGAMES) is for discussions and for playing board, paper, dice, and role-playing games including Advanced Dungeons & Dragons, Call of Cthulhu, GURPS, Paranoia, RuneQuest, Star Trek, SuperHeroes, Traveller. Forum members include experts as well as novice game masters and players, game designers, writers, editors, and play testers. The forum hosts many online games played via the forum's message board, as well as real-time conferences. In addition, the forum sponsors weekly help conferences and personalized advice sessions for players and game masters. Monthly workshops, hosted by expert RPG'ers, are offered on a wide variety of topics including scenario design, character creation, combat, and magic. Transcripts of important conferences, copies of significant discussion threads, and advance releases of game errata and play test materials. In addition, a wide variety of GM and player aids are available in the forum's file libraries. Assisting Nightshift in this forum are Janet Naylor, Darius, Dazzler and Matantisi.

- The Game Publishers Forums are where you find designers, project coordinators, and other technical and managerial staffs for assorted publishers. Three forums are available: Game Publishesrs A Forum (GO GAMAPUB), Game Publishers B Forum (GO GAMBPUB), and Game Publishers C Forum (GO GAMCPUB). At this writing, the following were the publishers represented online (followed by the directions to their home forum):

Access (GO GAMBPUB)
Accolade (GO GAMBPUB)
Activision/Infocom (GO GAMBPUB)
Bethesda Softworks (GO GAMAPUB)
Cactus Development (GO GAMCPUB)
Cyberdreams (GO GAMAPUB)
Disney/Buena Vista (GO GAMBPUB)
Dynamix (GO GAMCPUB)
Electronic Arts (GO GAMAPUB)
GameTek (GO GAMBPUB)
Impressions (GO GAMAPUB)
Interplay (GO GAMBPUB)
Intergalactic Development (GO GAMCPUB)
Konami (GO GAMBPUB)
Legend Entretainment (GO GAMCPUB)
LucasArts (GO GAMAPUB)

MacPlay (GO GAMBPUB)
Mallard (GO GAMBPUB)
Masque Publishing (GO GAMCPUB)
Maxis (GO GAMBPUB)
Merit Software (GO GAMAPUB)
MicroProse (GO GAMBPUB)
Mindcraft (GO GAMCPUB)
Omnitrend (GO GAMCPUB)
Origin (GO GAMAPUB)
QQP (GO GAMCPUB)
Sierra On-Line (GO GAMAPUB)
Sir-Tech Software (GO GAMBPUB)
Spectrum Holobyte (GO GAMBPUB)
SSI (GO GAMAPUB)
SubLOGIC (GO GAMAPUB)
Three-Sixty Pacific (GO GAMAPUB)
Westwood Studios (GO GAMBPUB)

- Modem Game Forum (GO CHALFORUM) supports the players of modem games who use CompuServe's Challenge Boards (GO CHALLENGE). The forum provides an area where they can get to know one another, discuss strategy, chat with other players, etc. Administrator of the forum is Mike Schoenbach, (76703,4363). He is primary administrator of the Atari forums as well as the person in charge of maintaining the Modem-to-Modem Game Players' Challenge Board. See Modem-to-Modem Games.

- Flight Simulation Forum (GO FSFORUM) supports all aspects of computerized flying. A variety of flight simulation and air/space combat software is covered, including programs from Microsoft, BAO, subLOGIC, Lucasfilm Games, MicroProse, Spectrum HoloByte, Sierra Online, Electronic Arts, and Origin. Topics range from computerized aviation, air transport, and air traffic control to hardware peripherals and scenery design. Assisting Nightshift in this forum are Rick Lee, Mike Barrs, Jim Ross, Rob Heittman, Bryant Arnett, Terry Carraway, Michael J. Fisher, Charles Gulick, Scott Holtzman, Laemming Wheeler, and Steve Wigginton.

- Sports Simulations Forum (GO SPRTSIMS) hosts discussions and computer-based games on golf, baseball, football, basketball, hockey, boxing, wrestling, motorsports, etc. Each message section is managed by an online "league commissioner." Members exchange tips, opinions, and product information with other forum members, who include gaming designers, programmers, and journalists. The libraries offer shareware games, utilities, courses, replays, team rosters, and league results. Conferences with sports game publishers and designers are regular events. Assisting Nightshift in this forum are Mark Adams, Bill Holmes, Stuart Malis, "commissioners/tour directors" Keith S. Blair and John Grimes (FPSF League), Lane Charnes (Indy 500 Challenge), Terry Clark (JNSE Golf Tour), Gilles Etcheverry (Links CGA Tour), Jim Krumrei and Derm Quinn for (World Circuit Racing/F1SA) and Ben Rousseau (Gretzky Hockey League). See also Sports.

Gaming publications online: *The Electronic Gamer*, also called "TEG" (GO EGAMER) is edited by Patricia Fitzgibbons. Among its features ar the following:

- Walkthrus are step-by-step instructions for solving specific adventure games. Each is divided into two or more sections so you can focus on those that deal with your question. These are full solutions to the games listed, not merely hints. (Each contains just one person's solution, not the *only* solution to a game.)

- Hints: If you want only a nudge, you might prefer the hints rather than complete answers. It displays a menu indicating which hints are available. Choose the game you are playing, and look on the menu for the spot where you are stuck. Not every obstacle is covered for every game, of course, but the section has clues to the most frequently asked questions about the most popular games.

- Reviews: Here you may read about the features of computer or board games before you buy them. The computer game's review area is divided into several sections (computer games, board games, cartridge games, etc.).

- Teg's Gazette: An online mini-magazine of articles, essays, interviews, current events, and so forth from *The Electronic Gamer*.

GammaLink   products are supported in the IBM PC Vendor D Forum (GO PCVEND). See IBM Computers.

Gang, Kelly   (76702,541) manages the Software Publishing Forum (GO SPCFORUM). See Software Publishing.

Gannett Inc.   newspaper publisher sponsored several forums, including the Florida Today NewsLink Forum (GO FLATODAY) and the New York Newslink Forum (GO NEWYORK). See Florida and see New York. Also see USA Today.

GAO Reports and Testimony   (database) may be searched through the IQuest gateway. See IQuest.

Gardening, landscaping,   and related topics are covered in the Gardening Forum (GO GARDEN), managed by the National Gardening Association. The system promises sections for users to exchange hints about planting, pruning, and pest control.

The libraries contain articles from National Gardening Magazine, addresses for seed companies, recipes, tips on organic gardening, and so on. The sysops are Alison Mixter, Howard Maculsay, Virginia Blakelock, Bob Riffle, Tom Tallardy, Warren Schultz, and Judy White.

In addition:

- *Gardening, Better Homes and Gardens, The Magazine of American Horticulture, Organic Gardening*, and *Flower & Garden Magazine* can be searched in the Magazine Database Plus (GO MDP). See Magazine Database. Also, *Lawn & Garden Marketing* magazine can be searched through the Business Database Plus (GO BUSDB). See Business Database.

- Florida Today NewsLink Forum (GO FLATODAY) offers a unique link to this Gannett Inc. newspaper on the Florida Space Coast's, and includes a section on the Florida gardening. See Florida.

See also Agriculture, Farming and Pets, and Animals.

Garrett Wade Co. (GO GW) is a store in the Electronic Mall (GO MALL) that offers tools and supplies. See Electronic Mall.

Gas Daily and **Gas World** can be searched through the Business Database Plus (GO BUSDB) as can *International Gas Report, Octane Week*, and *Oxy-fuel News*. See Business Database. See also Energy.

Gateways: Many of the system's online services are provided on CompuServe's own network of computers. But for some features, CompuServe provides an electronic portal called a *gateway* that automatically links the user to a different network of computers. CompuServe recently established links with Ziff Communications' systems for connection to services by major computer magazines, including *PC Magazine, PC Week*, and *MacUser/MacWEEK*. (See ZiffNet and see ZiffNet/Mac). Ziff's primary networks are ZiffNet and ZiffNet/Mac (also called Ziff-Davis MacUser/MacWeek). When using the GO command, you can reach features of these additional networks faster if you include a three-letter code before the address. ZNT: is the code for ZiffNet, so to reach ZiffNet's suit of *PC Magazine* forums (PCMAGNET), you can get in the fastlane by entering GO ZNT:PCMAGNET. The code for the ZiffNet/Mac features is ZMC:, so entering GO ZMC:MACWEEK is the express lane for the MacWeek forum. Once you have accessed one of these features, you may need to enter GO CIS to return to the regular CompuServe Information Service network.

NOTE: Technically, you can use CIS: as a code before any of the usual CompuServe features, but most users leave out the gateway code to save keystrokes. However, if you are currently at a ZiffNet feature and want to return to a main CompuServe feature, you can save a few keystrokes by preceeding it with the CIS: code. For instance, GO CIS:OLT-90 takes you from the current ZiffNet feature back to CompuServe Information Service and directly to page OLT-90 in the Online Today feature.

Throughout this book, addresses of ZiffNet and ZiffNet/Mac features are preceded by their gateway codes.

CompuServe also has added a few features of the Electronic Engineering Times Network Service. Its gateway code is EET:.

Gateway 2000 Forum (GO GATEWAY) supports customers of a direct marketer and manufacturer of IBM PC-compatible computers. Online are the company's technical support and customer service representatives. The forum libraries contain product updates; pricing and configuration information; feature and specification sheets; utility and support files for local-bus sytems, hard drives, modems, and video drivers; fun files, including Gateway 2000 icons, wallpaper files, and so on. The forum is administered by Neil Roepke (75300,1300), with assistance from Tim Richter, Shawna Ploen, Brian Davies, and Lisa Lukecart.

Gay issues are a topic in the Issues Forum (GO ISSUESFORUM). See Issues. Such issues also are discussed in Human Sexuality Forums (GO HSX). See Sex.

G. Cam Serveur of Paris is a database vendor accessible through the IQuest gateway (GO IQUEST). See IQuest.

GCC Technologies products are supported in the Mac B Vendor Forum (GO MACBVEN). See Apple Computers.

Geffen Records (GO GEFFEN) is represented in the Music Vendor Forum (GO MUSICVEN). See Music.

GEM (software) is supported in the Novell Desktop Forum (GO NDESKTOP). See Novell.

Genealogy Forum (GO ROOTS) is dedicated to family history and related genealogical subjects, particularly the use of personal computers in maintaining genealogy files. Forum members list the surnames in which they are interested in the member directory, thereby creating a quick reference guide for those seeking others working on the same family tree. The forum also has a section devoted to assisting adoptees find their natural parents.

Dick Eastman (76701,263) is forum manager. He is assisted by Gay Spencer, Michael Mac Cannell, Phil DeSilva, Martha Reamy, Michael K. Smith, and Mary Jo Rillera.

General Accounting Office Reports & Testimony can be searched through the Business Database Plus (GO BUSDB). See Business Database.

General Computing Forum (GO GENCOM) was created by different organizations dedicated to the dissemination of news, information, support, software, and discussions relating to the computer industry. The original founders are the Software Entrepreneur's Forum, the Institute for Certification of Computer Professionals, the Association for Customer Support Professionals, IDEF, IYM Software Review, and the National Computer Security Association.

"General Hospital" (television) summaries of the latest shows are available in Soap Opera Summaries (GO SOAPS). See Soap Opera.

Generations (magazine) is searchable in the Health Database Plus (GO HLTBD). See Health.

Genereaux, Tom (76703,4265) is sysop of the DBMS Forum (GO DBMS). See DBMS. He also is the sysop of Dr. Dobb's Journal Forum (GO DDJFORUM). See Dr. Dobb's Journal. He also operates the Lan Magazine Forum (GO LANMAG). See LAN.

Genesis Report can be searched through the Business Database Plus (GO BUSDB). See Business Database.

Genetics News, Applied (database) may be searched through the IQuest gateway. See IQuest. It also can be searched through the Business Database Plus (GO BUSDB), as can *Genetic Technology News*. See Business Database.

Genoa Systems software is supported in the Graphics B Vendor Forum (GO GRAPHBVEN). See Graphics.

Genus products are supported in the Graphics A Vendor Forum (GO GENUS). See Graphics.

Geo studies are the topic of several IQuest databases, including Geoarchive, Geobanque, Geomechanics Abstracts, Georef, Meteorological and Geoastrophysical Abstracts, and Oceanic Abstracts. See IQuest. It also is a topic in the Science/Math Education Forum (GO SCIENCE). See Science.

See also Earth sciences, Life sciences, Environmental issues, and Energy.

GeoGraphix (software products) are supported in Windows 3rd-Party Forum A (GO WINAPA). See Microsoft Software.

Geography is a topic in the Students' Forum (GO STUFO). See Students.

Georgia (news) is covered in the Atlanta Constitution and the Atlanta Journal, both searchable through Telebase System's News Source USA (GO NEWSUSA). See News Source.

Also:

- Selected reports from Georgia are included in the Southeastern regional reports from United Press International. See Executive News Service.

- *Business Atlanta* can be searched through the Business Database Plus (GO BUSDB). See Business Database.

German is spoken in the Foreign Language Education Forum (GO FLEFO), a service for students and teachers. See Foreign Language.

Also:

- Borland Deutschland Forum (GO BORGER). See Borland.
- CA Micro Germany Forum (GO CAMICRO) and CA-Clipper Germany Forum (GO CLIPGER).
- DPA—Kurznachrichtendienst Basic News Services (GO DPANEW), full-text articles in German.
- Deutsches Computer Forum (GO GERNET) invites CompuServe users in Germany to discuss a range of computing and other topics. The forum is conducted in German. See Deutches.
- Dr. Neuhaus Forum (GO NEUHAUS) is a German-speaking forum that supports Dr. Neuhaus modems and other communication products, operated by the Dr. Neuhaus support staff.
- ELSA GmbH Forum (GO ELSA) for German technical support.
- Lotus GmbH Forum (GO LOTGMBH) provides technical support for German-speaking users of German-language products, including Lotus 1-2-3, Ami Pro, Lotus Notes, and cc:Mail. See Lotus.
- Markt & Technik AG Forum (GO MUT) supports readers of that European publication.
- Microsoft Central Europe Forum (GO MSCE), a forum conducted in German, allows members to communicate directly with Microsoft staff in that language and to exchange messages with other users of Microsoft products such as Visual Basic, Microsoft C, Microsoft MASM, MS-DOS, LAN-Manager, and Windows.
- Prisma Deutschland Forum (GO PRISMA).
- Siemens Automatisierungs Forum (GO AUTFORUM).
- Toshiba GmbH Forum (GO TOSHGER) provides technical support for users of Toshiba computers and peripherals. Messages are exchanged with the technical staff at Toshiba's German headquarters in Neuss, Duesseldorf.
- Ziff Windows Forum (GO ZNT:GERWIN) supports the readers of its monthly magazine *Windows Aktiv*. See ZiffNet.

German Company Library (GO GERLIB) offers databases with directory and credit information on 48,000 German companies. BDI German Industry, an English-language database covering nearly 20,000 German exporting companies, includes company names, addresses, phone numbers, product descriptions, ownership, and management information. All databases in the German Company Library have been updated, adding coverage of companies located in the former East Germany.

German news and business are the specialty of Deutsche Presse-Agentur, an international news service that is searchable through NewsGrid (GO NEWSGRID). For details, see NewsGrid. Reports from this resource also are included in the Executive News Service (GO ENS). See Executive News Service.

Also, searchable in the IQuest gateway are these databases BDI German Industry, DIN—German Standards and Technical Rules Database, German Business Press Abstracts, German Business Scope, German Buyers' Guide, Hoppenstedt Austria, Hoppenstedt Directory of German Companies, Week in Germany, and Who Supplies What? See IQuest.

In addition, *German Business Scope* also can be searched through the Business Database Plus (GO BUSDB), as can *Week in Germany*. See Business Database.

Gerontologist (**magazine**) and ***Journals of Gerontology*** (**abstracts**) are searchable in the Health Database Plus (GO HLTBD). See Health.

GFA products are supported in the Windows 3rd-Party C Forum (GO WINAPC). See Microsoft Software.

GIF (Graphics Interchange Format) images are online pictures that can be created and viewed with nearly any type of computer system. A number of forums in the graphics network (GO GRAPHICS) support the technology. For details, see Graphics.

Gifted children are a subject of the Mensa Forum (GO MENSA). For more information, see Mensa. They also are a topic in the Education Forum (GO EDFORUM). See Education.

Gifts & Decorative Accessories (**magazine**) can be searched through the Business Database Plus (GO BUSDB). See Business Database.

Gift Sender (GO GS) is a kiosk in the Electronic Mall (GO MALL) that provides gifts for all occasions. See Electronic Mall.

Also, gifts and toys are sold in other shops in the Electronic Mall, including Americana Clothing (GO AC) carrying exclusively Levi Strauss & Co. products; Breton Harbor Baskets Company (GO BH) for gift baskets, gourmet foods, skin care, and so on, as well as Chef's Catalog (GO CC), Coffee Anyone??? (GO COF), 800 Flower and Gift Shoppe (GO GM), Figi's (GO FG), Florida Fruit Shippers (GO FFS), Flower Stop (GO FS), Gimmee Jimmy's Cookies (GO GIM), Green Mountain Coffee Roasters (GO GMR), Hammacher Schlemmer (GO HS), Honeybaked Hams (GO HAM), Sunglasses, Shavers & More (GO SN) for travel accessories, Virginia Diner (GO VA), and Walter Knoll Florist (GO WK). See Electronic Mall.

Gilbert & Associates products are supported in the Windows 3rd-Party C Forum (GO WINAPC). See Microsoft Software.

Gilmore, Tom (75300,2261) is sysop of the Packard Bell Forum (GO PACKARDBELL). See Packard.

Gimmee Jimmy's Cookies (GO GIM) is a store in the Electronic Mall (GO MALL) that offers homemade gourmet cookies. See Electronic Mall.

Girou, Ed (76702,542) is sysop of the Crosstalk Forum (GO XTALK). See Crosstalk.

Givler, Greg (76702,647) is the sysop of the Commodore Service Forum (GO CBMSERVICE). See Commodore.

Glass-working is a topic of the Crafts Forum (GO CRAFTS). See Crafts.

Global Crisis Forum (GO CRISIS) is devoted to discussion of the world's trouble spots and disasters (sadly, it never seems to go begging for material). The primary sysop is Atlanta writer/software designer Shel Hall (76701,103), a veteran online personality. He was a sysop on the Earthquake Forum, the Persian Gulf Crisis Forum, the Soviet Union Crisis Forum, and the Hurricane Forum. Assisting are Sally Ryce, Mary Beth Finnerty, and Judy G. Russell.

Global Mobility Database contains abstracts of technical papers presented at meetings and conferences of the Society of Automotive Engineers, and the International Federation of Automobile Engineering Societies, the Institute of Mechanical Engineers, and SAE Japan. See IQuest.

Global Report (GO GLOREP), launched by Citibank in 1987, brings together under one roof 12 highly respected financial and news services. These include U.S. suppliers like Standard & Poors, Quotron, Knight Ridder, and MMS International as well as international resources such as Financial Times (UK), Il Sole 24 Ore (Italy), Business International, and AFX News from AFP-Extel. The main menu offers 17 general subject categories ranging from country, company, and industry news and profiles to commodities, bonds, foreign exchange, and stocks.

The feature also has advanced direct access capabilities. Each screen, in the top left-hand corner, contains a code page which, if entered from any Global Report "Selection:" prompt, takes you directly there. Codes certain to be widely used are "GLO/MET/PRC" (world precious metals prices), "TEC/NWS" (telecommunications news), "TRE/YLD" (U.S. Treasury yields), "SPO/NWS" (sports news), and "CPS/MEN," returning you to the main menu from any point from within the service.

Also, the ticker command is an invaluable feature in researching a stock. By entering a period (.) immediately followed by a stock's ticker symbol (i.e., .AAPL for Apple Computer), you'll be shown a menu of available information which includes such things as corporate profiles, earnings, six months of company news, SEC filings, lists of officers and directors, along with descriptions of all its publicly traded securities.

The feature is surcharged at $30 an hour during evening and weekend hours and $60 an hour during prime-time weekly daytime hours.

Global Softworks products are supported in the Graphics A Vendor Forum (GO GSLSUPPORT). See Graphics.

Global Village Communications (modem equipment) is supported by the Modem Vendor Forum (GO MODEMVEN). See Modem Vendor.

Global Warming Network Online Today can be searched through the Business Database Plus (GO BUSDB). See Business Database.

GO is a navigation command. GO followed by a page address or quick reference word takes you directly to another page in the system. For instance, entering GO IBMNEW and G PHONES will transport you from any part of the system to the specified features. For users of the CompuServe Information Manager, the Go... function is available on the Services menu. Check your users manual for shortcuts. For instance, in IBM versions of the program, CONTROL-G is a shortcut to reach the Go... function. For more on navigation commands, see Commands.

Go (game) is played in the Entertainment Center (GO ECENTER). See Entertainment.

GO Corp. (software) is supported in the Pen Technology Forum (GO PENFORUM). For more information, see Pen Technology.

Going Public: The IPO Reporter can be searched through the Business Database Plus (GO BUSDB). See Business Database.

Gold Disk products are supported in the Windows 3rd-Party C Forum (GO WINAPC). See Microsoft software. They also are supported in the Ultimedia Tools Forum A (GO ULTIATOOLS). See Ultimedia.

Golden CommPass (software), a commercial automated program for an IBM OS/2 link with CompuServe, is discussed in the Golden CommPass Support Forum (GO GCPSUPPORT). The program is published by Creative Systems Programming Corp., a Mount Laurel, New Jersey, firm operated by sysop Larry B. Finkelstein, 76702,1354). He is assisted in the forum by Alan Buck, Don Gloistein, and Donna Finkelstein. For details, see Automated Terminal Software.

Gold Hill products are supported in the Windows 3rd-Party C Forum (GO WINAPC). See Microsoft Software.

Golf Guide Online (GO GLF) is a comprehensive listing of great places to play golf. The database—compiled from Lanier Publishing's *Golf Courses: The Complete Guide*, *Golf Resorts*, and *Golf Resorts International*—provides descriptions from golf professionals on par, total yardage, fees, rates, reservation information, and more. The feature is part of the system's basic services (see Billing).

Also, *Golf* magazine can be searched in the Magazine Database Plus (GO MDP). See Magazine Database. In addition, Austad's (GO AU) offers a store in the Electronic Mall (GO MALL) that sells golf equipment and accessories. See Electronic Mall. See also Sports.

Good Housekeeping (magazine) is searchable through Magazine Database Plus (GO MDP). For details see Magazine Database.

Goodin, Shawn   (76703,1034) is a sysop in the Micronetworked Apple Users Groups, (GO MAUG). See Apple Computers.

Goodridge, Duane   (76711,217) is the sysop of the Military Forum (GO MILITARY). See Military.

Gordon, Dawn   (76703,204) is the sysop of the Consumer Electronics Forums (GO CEFORUM). See Electronics Forum, Consumer. Dawn is married to Ron Luks, chief sysop of the Atari forums online.

Goretsky, Aryeh   (76702,1714) is a sysop of McAfee Virus Help Forum (GO VIRUSFORUM). See McAfee.

Government Computer News   **(magazine)** is searchable through Computer Database Plus (GO COMPDB). See Computer Database Plus.

Government contacts and information   are specialties of Matthew Lesko's Information USA (GO INFOUSA), which tells you how to get your questions answered. The feature has a particularly large database of material on selling to the government and on government financing. See Information USA.

Government databases   searchable through IQuest (see IQuest) include:

Academic Index	Federal/Industry Watchdog
Access Reports/Freedom of Information	For Your Eyes Only
	FTC FOIA Log
American Marketplace	FTC: Watch
Antitrust FOIA Log	GAO Reports and Testimony
Bmd Monitor	Hotline
BNA Daily News	Keesing's Record of World Events
Cendata	Labordoc
Commerce Business Daily	Logos
Congressional Activities	Managed Care Outlook
Congressional Information Service (CIS)	Military Space
	NIST Update
Congressional Record Abstracts	PAIS International
Defense & Aerospace Electronics	Political Finance & Lobby Reporter
Defense Daily	Product Safety Letter
DMS/FI Contract Awards	PTS Aerospace/Defence Markets and Technology
Federal Grants and Contracts Weekly	PTS Newsletter Database
Federal Register	U.S. Political Science Documents
Federal Register Abstracts	

See IQuest.

Government Publications (GO GPO) includes a catalog of government publications, books, subscription services, and ordering information. See Personal Finance and Insurance.

GPO Monthly Catalog and **GPO Publications Reference File** (database) may be searched through the IQuest gateway (GO IQUEST). GPO Publications also can be searched through the Knowledge Index (GO KI). See IQuest and see Knowledge Index.

GPS Report can be searched through the Business Database Plus (GO BUSDB). See Business Database.

Grabs (software) is supported by the Office Automation Vendor Forum (GO OAFORUM). See Office Automation.

Grade schools are a topic in the Students' Forum (GO STUFO). See Students.

Gradline (educational database) may be searched through the IQuest gateway (GO IQUEST). See IQuest. See also Education.

Grammy music award winners from 1958 to the present are listed in the Entertainment Encyclopedia, which is part of the Hollywood Hotline (GO HOLLYWOOD). See Hollywood Hotline.

GrandView (software) is supported in the Symantec Forum (Go SYMANTEC). See Symantec Software.

Grapes and winemaking are discussed in the Bacchus Wine Forum (GO WINEFORUM). See Wine.

Graphics (and computer art): The Graphics Net (GO GRAPHICS) consists of a group of forums that discuss the expanding world of CompuServe graphics.

Most online pictures these days are GIF (Graphics Interchange Format) images. GIF (pronounced "jiff") images can be created and viewed with nearly any type of computer system, making them ideal for the exchange of images among users of differing hardware. The forum libraries have thousands of colorful, imaginative GIFs. Support for viewing GIF images is built into the CompuServe Information Manager software and some of the third-party terminal programs. Users of general terminal software may need to obtain separate viewing software to look at online and downloaded GIF images. See the Graphics Support Forum (GO GRAPHSUP) for assistance in finding the viewing software for your equipment.

Also of value to newcomers to the medium is the Graphics Tutorial area (GO INTROGRAPH), set up to make it easy for you to learn more about graphics in general and the Forums in particular. It is intended to answer many commonly asked questions.

The administrator of the forums is Larry W. Wood (76703,704). He is assisted by Richard White, David Shaver, Tom Potocki, Matt Drury, Jenee Burns, Jim Beebe, Jeff Bowermaster, Patty Buckingham, Jim Burton, Stephen Coy, Leann Drury, Kyle

Miller, Tom Mitchell, Lily Owens, John Parker, Vince Pilgrim, Tom Price, Mike Schoenborn, John Swenson, Bert Tyler, Jim Wallace, Chris Young, Doug Wolfgram, Doug Zeffer, and Mark Zimmer.

Supporting the technology are:

- The Graphics Support Forum (GO GRAPHSUP) contains all the programs and utilities necessary for viewing graphics. Libraries offer such choices as computer paint programs, online viewing, video adapters, desktop publishing utilities, and clip art. Novices will find tips on how to download GIF files and view them offline, while experts will enjoy learning more about creating and manipulating images with their computers.

- The Fine Art Forum (GO FINEART), which focuses on high-resolution computer reproductions of world-class art, is dedicated to presenting high-quality images of art from the past and present. Some of modern art's best works as well as the great classics are offered in such media as sculpture, illustration, photography, oil, acrylic, tempera, and more. The works of Salvadore Dali, Penni Ann Cross, R.C. Gorman, Rembrandt, van Gogh, and many others are found in the libraries that are organized by theme or subject, such as panoramic landscape or still life.

- The Computer Art Forum (GO COMART) contains images created by a computer, or those images created on a computer using a paint program or graphics editor. The files here capitalize on the idea of the computer as an art tool and a new medium for the artist. Whether it's a simple cartoon or a complex figure study painted with light, you'll find the images and many of the artists who created them in the Computer Art Forum. The forum is also devoted to the study of fractal images, which are created by the computer (not a human) acting upon a mathematical formula. In addition, a Beginner's Studio offers newcomers to the field a chance to learn computer art skills and trade tips and techniques with other enthusiasts.

- The Graphics Corner Forum (GO CORNER) offers high-resolution, scanned, or digitized images. Images include famous actors and actresses, landmarks, the Earth and solar system, examples of fine architecture, cars, boats, planes, and more. One interesting feature of the forum is its Cartoons & Comics library.

- The Quick Picture Forum (GO QPIC) contains 32-color or less, scanned or digitized images. The thousands of images range from people to animals to star clusters and galaxies. These scanned and digitized images can be found by browsing through the various libraries using the keyword or phrase of the object you wish to find. Each image in this forum was created by using no more than 32 colors, which means the files are smaller and take less time to download than more complex pictures. The Missing Children's Database is also located here, where you'll find images and information about missing children.

- The Graphics Gallery Forum (GO GALLERY) for image collections from such organizations as NASA, USDA, and the Smithsonian.

- Missing Children Forum (GO MISSING) contains descriptions and computerized pictures of missing children.

- The Glamour Graphics Forum (GO GLAMOUR) for images representing fashion, modeling, swimwear, formal wear, business attire, swimsuits, and so on. It also is the graphics community's online gathering place for professional modeling agencies.

- The Graphics Developers Forum (GO GRAPHDEV), home of the Stone Soup workgroups, for fractals, raytracing, and virtual reality.

- The Graphics Plus Forum (GO GRAPHPLUS) for GIF images that are at least 800 X 600 pixels in size.

- Graphics A Vendor Forum (GO GRAPHAVEN) hosts Appian Technology Inc., ATI Technologies (GO ATITECH), Big-D (GO BIGD), ColoRIX/WinRIX (GO RIXSOFT), ComputerEyes/Digital Visual (GO DIGVIS), Genus Microprogramming products (GO GENUS), Global Softworks (GO GSLSUPPORT), Grasp from Paul Mace Software (GO GRASP), Image-In (GO IMAGEIN), Inset Systems (GO INSET), Jovian Inc. products (GO JOVIAN), Metagraphics Inc. (GO METAGR), Pacific Motion (GO PRES), STB Systems and Jovian Inc. with support for their graphics adapter boards for PC- and MS-DOS-compatible computers (GO STBSYS), TEGL Systems (GO TEGL), Tempra from Mathematica Inc. (GO TEMPRA), and VRLI Inc. (GO VRLI).

- Graphics B Vendor Forum (GO GRAPHBVEN) includes support for products from Tseng Labs (GO TSENG), Diamond Computer Systems (GO DMNDONLINE), Animated Software (GO ANISOFT), StereoGraphics Inc. (GO INDEPTH), Sun Country Software (GO SUNSHOW), LEAD Technologies (GO LEADTECH), Hercules Computer Technology (GO HERCULES), Genoa Systems, Volante Inc., CrystalGraphics, and DesignWare.

Also:

- The Graphics File Finder (GO GRAPHFF) is a special database containing information on all important files from the graphics forums. The File Finder allows you to search on a filename or keyword or use a variety of search methods that help you locate files of interest in any of the forums.

- The forums provide many public domain and shareware programs (called *decoders* and *encoders*) for viewing and sharing graphics on CompuServe. To find a program for your specific computer, visit the Graphics Support Forum (GO GRAPHSUP) and see in Library 1 the "Forum Information" called PROGS.TXT.

- CompuServe also has added a full tutorial area to the graphics section, available from the feature's top menu (GO GRAPHICS).

- PRC Database Publishing (GO PRC) is a store in the Electronic Mall (GO MALL) that offers *Best of "GO Graphics"* directory.

Finally, many other forums now have GIF graphics in their database libraries. Here are the online homes of some of the larger specialized collections: Aquaria/Fish Forum (GO FISHNET), Astronomy Forum (GO ASTROFORUM), Automobile Forum (GO CARS), Collectors Forum (GO STAMPS), Earth Forum (GO EARTH), Florida Forum (GO FLORIDA), Military Forum (GO MILITARY), Outdoors Forum (GO OUTDOORS), Photography Forum (GO PHOTOFORUM), Racing Forum (GO RACING), Reuter News Pictures Forum (GO NEWSPIX), Showbiz Forum (GO SHOWBIZ), Space Forum (GO SPACEFORUM), TrainNet Forum (GO TRAINNET), and Travel Forum (GO TRAVESIG).

Grasp (software) is supported in the Graphics A Vendor Forum (GO GRASP). See Graphics.

Gray F/X (software) is supported in the Ventura Software Forum (GO VENTURA). See Ventura.

Great Outdoors Forum (GO OUTDOORFORUM) covers various forums including fishing, hunting, camping, boating, and photography. See Sports and Recreation.

Greatworks (software) is supported in the Symantec Forums (GO SYMANTEC). See Symantec.

Greek is spoken in the Foreign Language Education Forum (GO FLEFO), a service for students and teachers. See Foreign Language.

Greenberg, Ed (76703,1070) is sysop of the Ask3Com Information Service (Go THREECOM). See 3Com Software (in the "T" section).

Greenfield, David (72241,1457) is one of the editors and writers associated with the PC Magazine forums. See PC Magazine.

Greenleaf products are supported in the IBM PC Vendor B Forum (GO PCVENB). See IBM Computers.

Green Marketing Report can be searched through the Business Database Plus (GO BUSDB). See Business Database.

Green Mountain Coffee Roasters (GO GMR) is a store in the Electronic Mall (GO MALL) specializing in coffee. See Electronic Mall.

Greenpeace is discussed in the Earth Forum (GO EARTH). See Earth.

Greenview Data products are supported in the PC Vendor I Forum (GO PCVENI). See IBM Computers.

Gribnif Software products are supported in the Atari Vendors Forum (GO ATARIVEN). See Atari Computers.

GRiD Systems (software) is supported in the Pen Technology Forum (GO PENFORUM). For more information, see Pen Technology.

Grief, dealing with, is a topic in the Seniors Forum (GO SENIORS). See Seniors.

Griffith, Chris (76702,2017) is the primary sysop DataEase International Forum (GO DATAEASE). See DataEase.

Griffith, Georgia (76703,266) has been a CompuServe forum manager since 1981. She is administrator of the Issues Forum (GO ISSUESFORUM). See Issues Forum. She also is sysop of the IBM Special Needs Forum (GO IBMSPEC). See Handicapped Issues for more information. She also manages the Political Debate Forum (GO POLITICS) and the White House Forum (GO WHITEHOUSE). See Political and White House. And she oversees the Religion Forum (GO RELIGION). See Religion.

Grocery Marketing and **Progressive Grocer** (magazine) can be searched through the Business Database Plus (GO BUSDB). See Business Database. Also, *Grocery Marketing* can be searched through the Business Database Plus (GO BUSDB). See Business Database.

Grolier's Academic American Encyclopedia (GO ENCYCLOPEDIA) has more than 31,000 articles, fact boxes, bibliographies, and tables. See Academic American Encyclopedia.

Grolier Whiz Quiz (game) (GO WHIZ) is sponsored by Grolier Electronic Publishing Inc. Up to four people may compete at a time in a quiz. A total of 30 questions are asked for each quiz taken from one of nearly a dozen categories. Players receive a point for each correct answered. Game scores are calculated by subtracting the total number of questions answered incorrectly from the total number of questions answered correctly. The top ten scores for a session are entered in the Whiz Quiz Hall of Fame. This is one of the system's basic services, meaning those signed up under the Standard Pricing Plan (see Billing) have unlimited access to the feature. For information on other games, see Games.

Ground Water Monitor can be searched through the Business Database Plus (GO BUSDB). See Business Database.

Groves, Dave (76703,4223) is sysop of the Diabetes Forum (GO DIABOL). See Diabetes Forum.

Guarantor (financial database) can be searched through IQuest. See IQuest.

Guaranty, Global can be searched through the Business Database Plus (GO BUSDB). See Business Database.

Guardian (newspaper) is covered in the UK Newspaper Library (GO UKPAPERS). See UK Newspaper.

GUI Program News (database) may be searched through the IQuest gateway. See IQuest. The resource also can be searched through the Business Database Plus (GO BUSDB). See Business Database.

Guidance and testing are covered in the Education Forum (GO EDFORUM). See Education.

"Guiding Light" (television) summaries on the latest shows are available in Soap Opera Summaries (GO SOAPS). See Soap Opera.

Gulf Business Report and **Gulf Reconstruction Report** can be searched through the Business Database Plus (GO BUSDB). See Business Database.

Gunn Kristen (72662,1072) coordinates the U.S. News Forum as part of U.S. News & World Report Online (GO USNEWS). See U.S. News & World Report.

Guns for hunters, collectors, competitive shooters, and other enthusiasts are covered in Great Outdoors Forum (GO OUTDOORFORUM). See Outdoors Network.

Gupta Forum (GO GUPTAFORUM) is operated by Gupta Corporation's technical services people to provide support and information about its products. Dave Karow (72662,70) is the primary sysop, assisted by Tim Conway, Dan deGrazia, Marcia Gossard, Matt Miller, Karyn Price, Ellyn Schumacher, Mike Stone, Kuntal Thakore, and Kevin Watts.

Gut abstracts are searchable in the Health Database Plus (GO HLTBD). See Health.

H

Hall, Bill (76707,14) is the sysop of the Symantec Forums (GO SYMANTEC). See Symantec.

Hall, Shel (76701,103) is sysop of the Automobile Forum (GO CARS) (see Automobile) and sysop of the Global Crisis Forum (GO CRISIS). See Global Crisis.

Hammacher Schlemmer (GO HS) has a store in the Electronic Mall (GO MALL) that offers gifts and unique and unusual products. See Electronic Mall.

HamNet (Ham Radio) Forum (GO HAMNET) is one of the older forums on CompuServe and is devoted to amateur radio and related subjects. This includes on-the-air operating, advanced techniques, short wave listening, satellite television, and packet radio. The primary sysop is Scott Loftesness (W3VS) (76703,407), assisted by Dan Ferguson Ken Hoehn, Luck Hurder (KY1T), and Don Stoner (W6TNS).

Handheld computers are supported in a number of forums, including the HP Handhelds Forum (GO HPHANDHELDS), the Newton/PIE Forum (GO NEWTON), and the Palmtop Forum (GO PALMTOP).

Handicapped Issues are addressed in several services; among them are the following:

- The Disabilities Forum (GO DISABILITIES) is open to everyone interested in disabilities, from those with handicapping conditions and their families to those who assist, train, educate, or employ the disabled. The administrator is Dr. David Manning (76703,237), director of the mainstream center at The Clarke School for the Deaf in Northampton, Massachusetts. Assisting are Larry Orloff and Karen Mann.
- IBM Special Needs Forum (GO IBMSPEC) is aimed at finding information and IBM PC-compatible programs for primary and adult students with special

education needs. It addresses education of the handicapped, literacy programs, special education, and so forth. The primary sysop is Georgia Griffith (76703,266).

- The Handicapped Users' Database (GO HANDICAPPED) is a collection of information specifically for those with handicaps. It includes the latest news about handicapped issues, a reference library, rehabilitation research and development, lists of self-help organizations for those with handicaps, sources of special computer software and hardware for the handicapped, and more. This is one of the system's basic services, meaning those signed up under the Standard Pricing Plan (see Billing) have unlimited access to the feature.

- The Disabled Traveler's Friendship Network, a nonprofit group providing travel information to physically challenged individuals and families, is represented in Florida Forum (GO FLORIDA). See Florida.

Also, self-help and handicapped issues are regularly discussed in the Issues Forum (GO ISSUESFORUM). For details, see Issues.

See also Rehabilitation.

Handyman Forum, Family (GO HANDYMAN), discusses all kinds of projects for do-it-yourself home-owners. See Family Handyman Forum.

Hangman (game) (GO HANGMAN) is one of the older games on the system. It is a word-guessing game, intended for children, in which the computer comes up with a word and you try to learn it by picking letters. Each time you enter a correct letter, the computer shows you where it goes in the word. On each incorrect guess, the computer adds a part of your body to the hangman's gallows. This is one of the system's basic services, meaning those signed up under the Standard Pricing Plan (see Billing) have unlimited access to the feature. For information on other games, see Games.

Hansen, Paul E. (76702,475) is sysop of the Practical Peripherals Forum (GO PPIFORUM). See Practical Peripheral Inc. Equipment.

Harbus, Bob, (75050,2014) is sysop of the IBM DB2 Family Forum (GO IBMDB2). See IBM Computers.

Hardcopy (magazine) is searchable (abstracts) through Computer Database Plus (GO COMPDB). See Computer Database Plus.

Hardware Age (magazine) can be searched through the Business Database Plus (GO BUSDB). See Business Database.

Hardware-related computer forums are grouped together for easy finding. To see them, enter GO HARDWARE. Among those operating hardware-oriented forums are APPC Information Exchange Forum, Apple Macintosh Forums, Apple II/III Forums, Artisoft Forum, Ask3Com, Atari Users Network, Cabletron Systems, Inc.,

CADD/CAM/CAE Vendor Forum, Canon Peripherals, Canopus Forum, CDROM Forum, CDROM Vendor Forum, Commodore and Amiga Forums, Compaq Connection, CompuAdd Forum, CompuServe Help Forum, Computer Club Forum, CTOS/Open Forum, Digital Equipment Corporation, Dell Forum, Desktop/Electronic Publishing Forums, Eicon Forum, Engineering Automation Forum (LEAP), European Forum, Gateway 2000 Forum, Graphics Forums, Hewlett-Packard Forums, IBM Forums, Intel Corporation, Kodak CD Forum, Logitech Forum, MIDI Forums, Modem Vendor Forumm, Multimedia Forums, NCR/ATT Forum, NeXT Users Forum, Packard Bell Forum, Palmtop Forum, PCM Online, PC Plug and Play Forum, Pen Technology Forum, Practical Peripherals Forum, Practice Forum, Prisma Forum, Stac Electronics Forum, Standard Microsystems Forum, Tandy Users Network, Telecommunication Issues Forum, Texas Instruments Forum, Thomas-Conrad Forum, 54 Toshiba Forum, Toshiba GmbH Forum, UK Computing Forum, and Zenith Data Systems Forum.

See also Forums and see specific computer types.

Harman Video products are supported in the Consumer Electronics Vendor Forum (GO CEVENDOR). See Electronics Forum.

Harpercollins Online (GO HAR) is a store in the Electronic Mall (GO MALL) featuring general and special interest books. See Electronic Mall.

Harper's Bazaar and **Harper's Magazine** can be searched in the Magazine Database Plus (GO MDP). See Magazine Database.

Harrington, Courtney (72662,155) is the sysop of the Multimedia Vendor Forum. See Multimedia.

Hart, Jim (76702,646) is sysop in the JFK Assassination Forum (GO JFK). See JFK.

Hartmann, Thom (76702,765) is the sysop of the Attention Deficit Disorder Forum (GO ADD). See Attention Deficit. He also is sysop of the International Trade Forum (GO ITFORUM) (see International Trade), the Desktop Publishing Forum (GO DTPFORUM) (see Desktop Publishing), Office Automation Vendor Forum (GO OAFORUM), and the JFK Assassination Forum (GO JFK) (see JFK).

Harvard Business Review Online (database) may be searched through the IQuest gateway (GO IQUEST) and through the Knowledge Index (GO KI). See IQuest and see Knowledge Index.

Harvard Health Letter and **Harvard Medical School Health Letter** are searchable in the Health Database Plus (GO HLTBD). See Health.

Harvard Project Manager and **Harvard Graphics** (software) are supported in the Software Publishing Forum (GO SPCFORUM). See Software Publishing Corporation.

Haskell, E. F. (general ledger/accounting software) is supported by the Office Automation Vendor Forum (GO OAFORUM). See Office Automation.

Hastings Center Report is searchable in the Health Database Plus (GO HLTBD). See Health.

Hawaii (news) is included in the daily Western regional reports from United Press International. See Executive News Service for details. Also, *Hawaii Business* magazine can be searched through the Business Database Plus (GO BUSDB). See Business Database. Hawaii is a topic in the Travel Forum (GO TRAVSIG). See Travel.

Hayden Books computer books are supported in the Prentice Hall Computer Publishing Forum (GO PHCP). See Prentice Hall.

Hayes Microcomputer Products Inc., best known for its modems, operates the Online With Hayes Forum (GO HAYES). The forum provides Hayes customers with additional technical support and helps future customers learn more about Hayes products. Technical support representatives respond to forum messages each business day. New product announcements, press releases, and technical bulletins are available for downloading and are updated on a regular basis. An extensive product description area that details the Hayes product line also is available.

Adminstering the forum is Joey Browning (76702,1365), who has been with Hayes since July 1985. He is responsible for high-level systems support, new product testing, and technical liason with both Sales and Product Development. He is assisted by Grant Porter.

Hazardous materials are the topics of several databases searchable through IQuest (GO IQUEST), including Hazardline, Hazardous Materials Intelligence Report, Hazardous Waste News, Hazmat Transport News, State Regulation Report: Toxics, Toxic Materials News, TOXLINE, and Toxic Materials Transport. See IQuest.

Through the Business Database Plus (GO BUSDB) you can search *Hazardous Waste Network Online Today*, *Hazardous Waste News*, *Hazmat Transport News*, *HazNews*, and *Medical Waste News*. See Business Database. See also Safety.

hDC (software products) are supported in Windows 3rd-Party Forum A (GO WINAPA). See Microsoft Software.

Headmaster (software) is supported in the PC Vendor B Forum (GO PCVENB). See IBM Computers.

Health is covered in hundreds of online services, from forums to the Health Database Plus gateway to magazines and journals. Health/Medical issues are covered in features throughout the system. Here are the major medical services:

- Health Database Plus (GO HLTDB), provided by Information Access Company, covers consumer and professional publications in the areas of health, nutrition, and fitness. The database covers more than 18,000 articles and is updated weekly. It is made up of three kinds of publications, including:

1. Core journals covering health, medical, and nutrition for the lay reader include *Food & Nutrition*, *Health*, and *Psychology Today*. In general, articles include full text, with coverage beginning in January 1989.

2. Technical and professional journals, such as *Patient Care*, *RN*, and *The New England Journal of Medicine* are offered. These generally do not include full text but do offer synopses for the lay reader and authors' abstracts.

3. Consumer publications, selected by topic, beginning in 1987. Articles generally include full text.

*   Health and Fitness Forum (GO GOODHEALTH) discusss such "wellness"-related subjects as nutrition, mental health, child care, aging, and fitness. Professionals (including physicians, optometrists, pharmacists, counselors, physiologists, nurses, and therapists) often join interested nonprofessionals in free-wheeling discussions. In addition, those interested in substance abuse issues may attend online Alcoholics Anonymous meetings in the electronic conference rooms (see the Conference announcement in the forum for specific times). The forum administrator is Allan Stevens (76702,562). Assistants include Chuck Etienne, Dr. Mark Stevens, Tom Koch, Dr. Diego Redondo, Don Goldberg, Benji Durden, Susan Robbins, Mike Janay, and Ed Madara.

*   HealthNet (GO HNT) is one of the older online home medical reference sources for personal computer users. The database is in several parts. The HealthNet Reference Library is a large, menu-driven resource, covering diseases and symptoms with linked topics. Primary groups include drugs, surgeries, tests, procedures, home care and first aid, obstetrics and reproductive medicine, and ophthalmology and eye care. Also included in the resource is Sports Medicine, with data on general aspects of exercise, nutrition, and some specific sports. This is one of the system's basic services, meaning those signed up under the Standard Pricing Plan (see Billing) have unlimited access to the feature.

*   Holistic Health Forum (GO HOLISTIC) discusses various topics, from vitamins and minerals to chiropractic and holistic medicine. See Holistic Health.

*   MedSig (GO MEDSIG) is a health-related forum sponsored by the American Medical Informatics Association. It serves primarily health professionals and people in related technical fields of study, though interested laymen also are welcome. The forum also provides information on the AMIA, which specializes in computer applications in medicine. The forum is administered by Dr. Frank Meissner (71333,3377). He is assisted by Sue Frisch and Dr. John Farrer, and section leaders Dr. Steven A. Reid, James Harp, Frank Block, Dr. Richard G. Spindler, Sylvia Steiger, Dr. Sam Feinstein, Dr. Norman Saba, and Dr. Bertram Warren.

The database connect time is surcharged at $1.50 for each full-text article retrieved. Abstracts are $1.

The database also allows for downloading of articles (as well as displaying them on the screen). Selecting the download option from a menu causes the database to display a File Transfer Protocol list. The first option on the menu is explicitly for users of the CompuServe Information Manager. Users of other terminal programs can select a different protocol. See Files, Transfer.

An electronic users guide is available for downloading in the ZiffNet Support Forum (GO ZIFFHELP) from its Library 10 ("Health Database"). See file HDPUSR.TXT. Also available is a list of the publications (in file HDPPUB.TXT).

Techniques for searching this resource are the same as those used with all of the ZiffNet gateways. For specifics, see ZiffNet Databases.

Full text articles are searchable from the following:

Accent on Living
Addiction & Recovery
The Addiction Letter
AFAA's American
    Fitness
AIDS Alert
AIDS Weekly (for-
    merly CDC AIDS
    Weekly)
AIMplus
Alcohol Health &
    Research World
Alcoholism & Addic-
    tion Magazine
Alcoholism & Drug
    Abuse Week
Alcoholism & Drug
    Abuse Weekly
The Alcoholism
    Report
American Family
    Physician
American Fitness
American Health:
    Fitness of Body and
    Mind
American Journal of
    Cardiology
American Journal of
    Drug and Alcohol
    Abuse
American Journal of
    Medicine

American Journal of
    Ophthalmology
The American Journal
    of Sports Medicine
American Journal of
    Surgery
American Medical
    News
American Rehabilita-
    tion
Archives of Environ-
    mental Health
Arthritis Today
The Back Letter
Bestways
Better Nutrition
Better Nutrition for
    Today's Living
British Medical Journal
Brown University
    Child and Adoles-
    cent Behavior
    Letter
Brown University
    Child Behavior and
    Development
    Letter
Brown University
    Digest of Addiction
    Theory and Appli-
    cation
Brown University
    Long-Term Care
    Letter

Brown University
    Long-Term Care
    Quality Letter
Brown University
    STD Update
Bulletin of the World
    Health Organiza-
    tion
Business & Health
Ca (formerly Ca—A
    Cancer Journal for
    Clinicians)
Cancer News
Cancer Weekly
Chest
Child Health Alert
Clinical Diabetes
Consultant
Consumer Reports
    Health Letter
Current Health 2
Diabetes
Diabetes Forecast
Diabetes in the News
The Doctor's People
    Newsletter
East West
East West Natural
    Health
The Edell Health
    Letter
Environmental
    Nutrition

Exceptional Children
The Exceptional
  Parent
Executive Health
  Report
Executive Health's
  Good Health
  Report
FDA Consumer
Food and Nutrition
Generations
Harvard Health Letter
Harvard Medical
  School Health
  Letter
The Hastings Center
  Report
Health
Health Care Financing
  Review
HealthFacts
Health News
Health News &
  Review
HealthTips
HeartCare
HeartCorps
Hippocrates
Hospital & Health
  Services Adminis-
  tration
In Health
Independent Living
Inside MS
Issues in Law &
  Medicine
Journal of the Ameri-
  can Dietetic
  Association
JAMA
The Journal of the
  American Medical
  Association

Journal of Family
  Practice
Journal of Health Care
  Marketing
The Journal of Reha-
  bilitation
Journal of School
  Health
Journal of Toxicology:
  Clinical Toxicology
The Lancet
Mainstream
Mature Health
Medical SelfCare
Medical Update
Medical World News
Medicine
Men's Health
The Milbank Quar-
  terly
Morbidity and Mortal-
  ity Weekly Report
Mothering
NCAHF Newsletter
NCI Cancer Weekly
The Network News
New Scientist
Newsline
Nursing Homes
Nursing Homes and
  Senior Citizen Care
Nutrition Action
  Healthletter
Nutrition Forum
Nutrition Health
  Review
Nutrition Research
  Newsletter
Nutrition Today
Occupational Hazards
Ostomy Quarterly
PALAESTRA
Paraplegia News

Parents' Magazine
Patient Care
Pediatric Report's
  Child Health
  Newsletter
Pediatrics for Parents
People's Medical
  Society Newsletter
Physical Therapy
The Physician and
  Sportsmedicine
Physician Executive
Population Reports
Postgraduate Medicine
Prevention
Psychology Today
Public Health Reports
RN
Runner's World
Second Opinion
Society News
Solutions for Better
  Health
Special Delivery
Today's Living
Total Health
Tufts University Diet
  & Nutrition Letter
The University of
  California
  Berkeley Wellness
  Letter
Vegetarian Times
Vibrant Life
The Western Journal
  of Medicine
The Women's Letter
Women's Sports and
  Fitness
Worklife
World Health

Also searchable (full text) are pamphlets from scores of health and medical associations.

Abstracts of a number of medical journals and magazines also are searchable in the Health Database Plus, including the following:

Acta Oto-Laryngologica

American Heart Journal

American Journal of Clinical Nutrition

American Journal of Clinical Pathology

American Journal of Diseases of Children

American Journal of Obstetrics and Gynecology

American Journal of Pathology

American Journal of Psychiatry

American Journal of Psychology

American Journal of Psychotherapy

The American Journal of Public Health

American Review of Respiratory Diseases

Annals of Internal Medicine

Annals of Neurology

Annals of Otology Rhinology and Laryngology

Annals of Surgery

Annals of the Rheumatic Diseases

Annals of Thoracic Surgery

Annual Review of Psychology

Archives of Diseases in Childhood

Archives of Internal Medicine

Archives of Neurology

Archives of Surgery

Archives of Toxicology

Arthritis and Rheumatism

Blood

Brain

British Heart Journal

British Journal of Obstetrics and Gynecology

British Journal of Ophthalmology

British Journal of Psychiatry

British Journal of Psychology

British Journal of Surgery

Canadian Medical Association Journal

Cancer

Clinical Pediatrics

Contemporary Psychology

Developmental Medicine and Child Neurology

Developmental Psychology

Digestive Diseases and Sciences

Gerontologist, The

Gut

Health & Safety at Work

Heart and Lung

Holistic Medicine

Hospital Practice

International Journal of Aging & Human Development

Journal of Abnormal Child Psychology

Journal of Abnormal Psychology

JAOA: Journal of the American Osteopathic Association

Journal of Acquired Immune Deficiency Syndromes

Journal of Bone and Joint Surgery: American Volume

Journal of Chiropractic

Journal of Clinical Investigation

Journal of Clinical Pathology

Journal of Experimental Psychology

Journal of Immunology

Journal of Infectious Diseases

Journal of Laryngology and Otology

Journal of Nervous and Mental Disease

Journal of Nuclear Medicine

Journal of Occupational Medicine

Journal of Pathology
Journal of Pediatrics
Journal of the American Academy of Dermatology
Journal of the American Dental Association
Journal of the National Cancer Institute
Journal of Thoracic and Cardiovascular Surgery
Journal of Vascular Surgery

Journals of Gerontology
Laryngoscope
Law
Medicine & Health Care
Medical Letter on Drugs and Therapeutics
Muscle & Fitness
Nature
Neurology
New England Journal of Medicine
Nursing Times

Nutrition & Food Science
Obstetrics and Gynecology
Occupational Safety & Health
Pediatrics
Primary Cardiology
Radiology
Science
Sexually Transmitted Diseases
Shape
Women & Health

Health references elsewhere on the system include:

- Through the IQuest gateway (see IQuest), Health Business, Health Care Competition Week, Health Care Reform Week, Health Devices Alerts, Health Grants and Contracts Weekly, Health Legislation and Regulation, Health News Daily, Health Periodicals Database, Health Planning and Administration, and Health and Psychosocial Instruments.

- Through the Business Database Plus (GO BUSDB), searchable are *Health Business, Health Care Competition Week, Healthcare Financial Management, Health Care Management Review, Healthcare Technology & Business Opportunities, Health & Human Services News, Health Industry Today, Health Legislation & Regulation, Health Manager's Update, Industrial Health & Hazards Update, National Report on Computers & Health*, and *Topics in Health Care Financing*. See Business Database.

- Searched through the Knowledge Index (GO KI) is Health Planning and Administration. See Knowledge Index.

- Health and herbs are discussed in the New Age Forum (GO NEWAGE). See New Age.

- Health and medicine are topics in the Seniors Forum (GO SENIORS). See Seniors.

- Health care is discussed in the Political Debate Forum (GO POLITICS) and in the White House Forum (GO WHITEHOUSE). See Political and White House. The topic also is discussed in the Working From Home Forum (GO WORK). See Working From Home.

To reach CompuServe's main menu on the subject, enter GO HEALTH.

For more health-related services, see Medical References, Cancer, Diabetes, Rare Disease Database, and Medical InfoCenter, IQuest.

Health and beauty products are sold in some stores in the Electronic Mall (GO MALL), including Contact Lens Supply Incorporated (GO CL), Health and Vitamin Express (GO HVE), SDV Vitamins (GO SDV), and Sunglasses, Shavers & More (GO SN). See Electronic Mall.

HeartCare and ***HeartCorps*** are searchable in the Health Database Plus (GO HLTBD), as are abstracts from *American Heart Journal, Heart and Lung, British Heart Journal,* and *Primary Cardiology.* See Health.

Health and Vitamin Express (GO HVE) is a store in the Electronic Mall (GO MALL) that sells thousands of over-the-counter and health-related products at discount prices. See Electronic Mall.

HEAT users are supported in the ZiffNet Bendata Forum (GO ZNT:BENDATA). See ZiffNet.

Heating, Piping, Air Conditioning (**magazine**) can be searched through the Business Database Plus (GO BUSDB). See Business Database.

Heath Co. (GO HEATH) has a store in the Electronic Mall (GO MALL) that offers build-it-yourself kits, etc. See Electronic Mall.

Helicopter News (**database**) may be searched through the IQuest gateway. See IQuest. The resource also can be searched through the Business Database Plus (GO BUSDB). See Business Database.

Helix products are supported in the IBM PC Vendor G Forum (GO PCVENG). See IBM Computers. They also are supported in the Mac D Vendor Forum (GO MACDVEN). See Apple Computers.

Heller Report on Educational Technology & Telecommunications (**database**) can be searched through IQuest. See IQuest.

Help Forum, CompuServe (GO HELPFORUM) is a free forum designed to assist users, especially newcomers, to learn how to use and to take full advantage of CompuServe's hundreds of forums, databases, and other online services. Sixteen sections are offered on the forum message board, including CompuServe Mail, reference services, news services, using File Finders, CB/conferencing, Ask Customer Service, pricing plans, games, online symbols.

Use this forum to debate the advantages and disadvantages of the alternative pricing plan versus the standard pricing plan. Learn about network surcharges and tips on saving money. If you want help in figuring out how to best use any number of research databases from the Executive News Service to Quick Quote, just ask here.

The forum also has has free IQuest directories available for downloading. See IQuest for details.

The sysops are Mike Schoenbach (76703,4363) and Keith Joins (76702,375), assisted by Aaron Dickey and Jim Ness.

See also Practice Forum and CompuServe Information Manager.

Help, offline: CompuServe Customer Service can be reached in the U.S. with a toll-free call to 800/848-8990. The Customer Service office is open from 8 a.m. to midnight, Monday through Friday, and noon to 10 p.m. on weekends. In Ohio, call (614) 457-8650. Call the same number for assistance from outside the U.S. (including Canada). For assistance in the UK, call either 0800-525-5448 (freephone) or 44-272-255-111. In Germany, the number is 0130-86-4643; elsewhere in Europe, the number is 49-89-66-550-222.

Help online (GO HELP) is available in a database of answers to frequently asked questions about billing, forums, electronic mail, logons, real-time conferencing, and so on (GO QUESTIONS). The collection is part of the Feedback area (GO FEEDBACK). If you have a question not addressed in those files, you also may write a letter in Feedback that will be automatically addressed to the Customer Service Department.

Forum help Besides the Q&A material, some forums have as their prime objective to help new users.

- The CompuServe Help Forum (GO HELPFORUM) is a free forum intended for assistance on all aspects of CompuServe.
- A Practice Forum (GO PRACTICE), free of connect-time charges, stands ready to help you learn the commands and procedures used in all CompuServe forums. See Practice.
- Users of CompuServe Information Manager software also may use free forums for support: IBM DOS CIM Support Forum (GO CIMSUPPORT), WinCIM Support Forum (GO WCIMSUP), and Macintosh CIM Support Forum (GO MCIMSUP). See CompuServe Information Manager.
- In addition, most forums have a message board section set aside for "Ask the Sysop" messages.

Tour The system also offers an online "tour" of its major features, a selection from the Help menu, or you can access it directly by entering GO TOUR.

See also Billing Information, Phone, CompuServe access numbers, and Member Directory.

Henley, Ron, chess grand master, provides the latest news and commentary on the game in the Chess Forum (GO CHESSFORUM). See Chess.

Herbs and health are discussed in the New Age Forum (GO NEWAGE). See New Age.

Hercules Computer Technology (GO HERCULES) software is supported in the GraphicsBA Vendor Forum (GO GRAPHBVEN). See Graphics.

Heritage, American (**magazine**) is searchable in Magazine Database Plus (GO MDP). For details, see Magazine Database.

Hewlett-Packard Computers: The Hewlett-Packard PC Forums (GO HP), sponsored by Hewlett-Packard Company, are part of the company's HP/ONLINE service and give customers an online link to its support division. Subtopics include those on data communications, word processing, data management, system utilities, and programming. The forums are:

- HP Handhelds Forum (GO HPHANDHELDS) for support of your HP handheld computer, HP palmtop computer, or HP calculator.
- HP OmniBook Forum (GO HPOMNIBOOK) supports the company's Omnibook line.
- HP Peripherals Forum (GO HPPERIPHER) for discussions and support of all HP peripheral products, including printers, plotters, scanners, fax units, and mass storage devices (disk drives, tape drives, CD-ROMs, and read/write optical disks).
- HP Systems Forum (GO HPSYS) supports PCs, calculators, networking products, mini-computers, workstations, and software, including HP NewWave.

The primary sysop is Ted Dickens (76701,272), assisted by Miles Kehoe, Annie Baxter, and Isaac Blake. They are not HP employees. However, if you need an answer directly from HP, check out the file HP.HLP in the General library (1) of the HP Systems Forum.

Hewlett-Packard Journal and **HP Professional** (magazines) are searchable through Computer Database Plus (GO COMPDB). See Computer Database Plus.

HFD—The Weekly Home Furnishings Newspaper (database) may be searched through the IQuest gateway. See IQuest. It also can be searched through Business Database Plus (GO BUSDB). See Business Database.

Hickey, Thom (70760,2475) is a sysop in the ACI US Forum (GO ACIUS).

High Fidelity (database) may be searched through the IQuest gateway. See IQuest.

Highlights for Previous Day (GO MARKET) analyzes the stock markets most recent history. See Stock Quotes.

High Performance Plastics and ***High Performance Textiles*** can be searched through the Business Database Plus (GO BUSDB). See Business Database.

High school is a topic in the Students' Forum (GO STUFO). See Students.

High Tech Ceramics News (database) may be searched through the IQuest gateway. See IQuest.

High Technology (magazine) is searchable (abstracts) through Computer Database Plus (GO COMPDB). See Computer Database Plus.

High Technology Business (magazine) is searchable through Magazine Database Plus (GO MDP), Computer Database Plus (GO COMPDB), and Business Database Plus (GO BUSDB). For details see Magazine Database, Computer Database, and Business Database.

High Tech Separations News (database) may be searched through the IQuest gateway. See IQuest. The resource also can be searched through the Business Database Plus (GO BUSDB). See Business Database.

Highway & Heavy Construction (magazine) can be searched through the Business Database Plus (GO BUSDB). See Business Database.

High Yield Report (database) can be searched through IQuest. See IQuest. The resource also can be searched through the Business Database Plus (GO BUSDB). See Business Database.

Hiking and camping are discussed in the Great Outdoors Forum (GO OUTDOORFORUM). See Sports and Recreation. Also, *Backpacker* magazine can be searched in the Magazine Database Plus (GO MDP). See Magazine Database.

Hilbert Computing products are supported in the OS/2 Vendor Forum (GO OS2AVEN). See IBM Computers.

Hilgraeve (developer of HyperACCESS/5) products are supported in PC Vendor F Forum (GO PCVENF). For details, see IBM Computers.

Hippocrates magazine is searchable in the Health Database Plus (GO HLTBD). See Health.

HI-Q International (software products) is supported in Windows 3rd-Party Forum A (GO WINAPA). See Microsoft Software.

Hispanic Issues are a topic in the Issues Forum (GO ISSUESFORUM). See Issues.

Historical documents, such as the Declaration of Independence and the U.S. Constitution, can be retrieved in full text in Grolier's Academic American Encyclopedia, Grolier's (GO ENCYCLOPEDIA). See Academic American.

Historical stock market data may be retrieved by entering GO PRICES. Data is provided on tens of thousands of stocks, bonds, warrants, and mutual funds. See Stock Quotes.

History is a favorite topic in the Genealogy Forum (GO ROOTS). See Genealogy. Also, history studies is a topic in the Education Research Forum (GO EDRESEARCH) and in the Students' Forum GO STUFO). See Education and Students. Also "living history," including re-enactments and Renaissance faires, as well as scholarly research and heraldic study, is discussed in the Living History Forum (GO LIVING). See Living History.

Relevant databases such as America: History and Life and Historical Abstracts may be searched through the IQuest gateway (GO IQUEST) and through the Knowledge Index (GO KI). See IQuest and see Knowledge Index.

Also, West Coast history is a topic of California Forum (GO CALFORUM). See California.

Hitachi Weekly can be searched through the Business Database Plus (GO BUSDB). See Business Database.

.HLP, as an extension on filenames in forum libraries, means help. These usually are text files written by the sysops and contain answers to commonly asked questions. See Files, Extensions.

Hobbies of all types are covered by the system's general interest forums. For the main menu on this topic, enter GO HOBBY.

Hockey is a regular topic in the Sports Forum (GO FANS). For more on this and related subjects, see Sports.

HockWare products are supported in the OS/2 Vendor Forum (GO OS2AVEN). See IBM Computers.

Hoffman, John (76703,1036) is sysop of Broadcasters and Engineers Forums (GO BPFORUM). See Broadcasters and Broadcast Engineers.

Holistic Health Forum (GO GO HOLISTIC) has message sections covering vitamins and minerals; plants and herbs; Chinese, Ayurvedic, chiropractic, and holistic medicine; naturopathy; birth and child care; massage and bodywork; health education and politics; the natural products industry, and more. Libraries contain shareware and freeware for PCs and Macs, the latest data from the Natural Products Quality Assurance Alliance, and catalogs and applications from universities offering chiropractic, naturopathy, acupuncture, massage, and holistic health programs. The forum is operated by chiropractic physicians Skye Liniger (76702,1101) and Edward Brown (71154,674), with assistance from Donald Goldberg, Michael Janson, and Kris Keller.

Hollander, Michael F. (76703,771) is sysop of the Motor Sports Forum (GO RACING). See Sports and Recreation.

Hollywood Hotline (news) (GO HOLLYWOOD) is a daily collection of news items from the entertainment world, including TV, films, stage plays, and recordings, and so on. Also featured there is the Entertain Encyclopedia, which offers prime time TV schedules from 1948 to the present, celebrity birthdays, the Beatles tour history, Academy Award, Tony and Grammy Award lists, and pop-rock music singles list. The feature also has celebrity interviews, daily entertainment news, and a showbiz quiz.

This is one of the system's basic services, meaning those signed up under the Standard Pricing Plan (see Billing) have unlimited access to the feature. Other popular newslike features from the entertainment world are:

- Soap Opera Summaries (GO SOAPS), which offers daily summaries, news of prime time soaps, news and gossip from the industry and related features.
- Marilyn Beck's Hollywood (GO BECK) provides reports five days a week from Hollywood, from the inner offices of the studios and from the personalities, producers, and other power players. The reports are prepared by famed columnist Marilyn Beck and her associate Stacy Jenel Smith. See Beck.
- Hollywood Hotline's Movie Reviews (GO MOVIES) provides reviews of current movies and pick hits.

This resource also may be searched through IQuest. See IQuest. See also Entertainment.

Home automation is a topic of the Consumer Electronics Forum (GO CEFORUM). See Electronics.

Homefinder Service (GO HF) is a store in the Electronic Mall (GO MALL) that offers assistance in relocating. See Electronic Mall.

Home Lawyer (**software**) is supported in the Meca Software Forum (GO MECA). See Meca.

Home Media Technology News can be searched through the Business Database Plus (GO BUSDB). See Business Database.

Home Office Computing (**magazine**) can be searched in the Magazine Database Plus (GO MDP). See Magazine Database.

Home remodeling is discussed in the Family Handyman Forum (GO HANDYMAN). See Family Handyman Forum.

Home schooling is a topic in the Education Forum (GO EDFORUM). See Education.

Home Video Publisher (**magazine**) can be searched through the Business Database Plus (GO BUSDB). See Business Database.

Homing Instinct Forum (GO HOMING), operated by Time Warner, is intended for those interested in designing, building, restoring or renovating a home. The forum is run by architect, builder and author John Connell (72662,1370) and other professionals from the Yestermorrow School in Vermont which specializes in design and building. Would-be architects and do-it-yourselfers as well as professional builders and architects can ask questions and exchange views in the message sections. Message sections and libraries cover tools, landscape, "green" architecture, affordable housing, urban dwelling, kitchens and baths, interior design, construction, remodeling and restoration, and more.

See also Family Handyman Forum.

Honeybaked Hams (GO HAM) is a store in the Electronic Mall (GO MALL) that offers specialty ham and gift basket store. See Electronic Mall.

Hooper International products are supported in the PC Vendor C Forum (GO PCVENC). See IBM Computers.

Hoppenstedt Austria, Hoppenstedt Directory of German Companies, and **Hoppenstedt Benelux Database** (database) may be searched through the IQuest gateway. See IQuest.

Horn, Jim (76703,603) is administrator of the Texas Instruments Forum (GO TIFORUM). See Texas Instruments Computers.

Horse racing is a topic of the Sports Forum (GO FANS). See Sports and Recreation.

Horses are regularly discussed in the Pets and Animals Forum (GO PETS). For details, see Pets.

Horticulture (The Magazine of American) (magazine) can be searched in the Magazine Database Plus (GO MDP). See Magazine Database.

Hospitals (database) may be searched through the IQuest gateway. See IQuest. It also can be searched through Business Database Plus (GO BUSDB), as can *Hospital & Health Services Administration* magazine. See Business Database. The resource also can be searched through the Health Database Plus (GO HLTDB). See Health.
     See also Health and Medicine.

Hotel & Restaurant Administration Quarterly, Cornell (magazine) can be searched through the Business Database Plus (GO BUSDB). See Business Database.

Hotels information is available in ABC Worldwide Hotel Guide (GO ABC). It provides descriptions, rates, phone numbers, and facilities for more than 60,000 motels and hotels in the United States and around the globe in a menu-driven, searchable database that is updated quarterly. It also lists miles to airports, local and toll-free phone numbers, Telex machine identification numbers, credit card information, and more. To search the database, select menu choices, using price, location, and facilities to find hotels and other resorts.
     Hotel information also is available in some travel-related features and flight reservation services. See Eaasy Sabre and Official Airline Guides. For other travel-related features, see Travel.

Hotline (political database) can be searched through IQuest. See IQuest.

Housewares (magazine) can be searched through the Business Database Plus (GO BUSDB). See Business Database.

Housing is discussed in the White House Forum (GO WHITEHOUSE). See White House.

Housing Scene, The, (column) is among the syndicated columns provided by United Features (GO COLUMNS). See Colmnists.

Houston Post **(newspaper)** is searchable through Telebase System's News Source USA (GO NEWSUSA). See News Souce.

Also, *Houston Business Journal* magazine can be searched through the Business Database Plus (GO BUSDB). See Business Database.

Howard, Bill (72241,54) is among *PC Magazine*'s editors and contributors who are regulars in the publication's PC-Magnet service. See *PC Magazine*.

Howling Dog products are supported in the MIDI C Vendor Forum (GO MIDICVEN). See Music.

H&R Block (GO HRB), the income tax people, offers a store in the Electronic Mall (GO MALL). See Electronic Mall. H&R Block also owns CompuServe Incorporated. Note that in many of the surcharged financial services, you can see a nonsurcharged sample by searching for a report on H&R Block, using the ticker symbol HRB. See Company Reports and Stock quotes (Historical) for details.

HRMagazine can be searched through the Business Database Plus (GO BUSDB). See Business Database.

HSC Software products are supported in the Multimedia Vendor Forum (GO MULTIVEN). See Multimedia.

HSELine: Health and Safety **(database)** may be searched through the IQuest gateway. See IQuest.

Hubble Space Telescope images are available in Astronomy Forum (GO ASTROFORUM), in Library 13, "Orbiting Scope," which houses the forum's extensive collection of images from NASA's orbiting observatories in GIF format. See also NASA and see Graphics.

Humancad products are supported in the Ultimedia Tools Forum A (GO ULTIATOOLS). See Ultimedia.

Humane Society Forum (GO HSUS), associated with the Humane Society of the United States, is used to educate the public on pet care and to discuss issues ranging from animal experimentation to conservation of wildlife to the environment. Sysop Patrick Preston (76702,2013) is an attorney who also serves as legal advisor to HSUS' executive committee. He is a member of the board of directors of the Chesapeake Wildlife Sanctuary in Mitchellville, Maryland. See also Pets.

Humanism is discussed in the Religion Forum (GO RELIGION). See Religion.

Humanities is the topic of a number of databases on IQuest (see IQuest), including Academic Index, Arts & Humanities Search, Biography Master Index, Book Review Index, Books in Print, Dissertation Abstracts Online, Humanities Index, and Quotations Database. See IQuest.

Human rights is a frequent topic in the Issues Forum (GO ISSUESFORUM). See Issues.

Human Sexuality Forums (GO HUMAN) cover all aspects of sex issues. See Sex.

Hunt, Sue (76711,1100) is sysop of the Intel ACCESS/Real-Time Forum (GO INTELACCESS). See Intel Corp.

Hunting, fishing, and camping are discussed in the Great Outdoors Forum (GO OUTDOORFORUM). See Sports and Recreation.

Hutchison Information Services Ltd. offers CompuServe connections from the Far East and Middle East. See Hong Kong for details.

Hydraulics & Pneumatics (magazine) can be searched through the Business Database Plus (GO BUSDB). See Business Database.

Hydrocarbon Processing (magazine) can be searched through the Business Database Plus (GO BUSDB). See Business Database.

Hydrowire (database) may be searched through the IQuest gateway. See IQuest.

Hydroponics is a topic in Gardening Forum (GO GARDENING). See Gardening.

HyperACCESS/5 is supported in PC Vendor F Forum (GO PCVENF). For details, see IBM Computers.

Hyperactivity is a topic of the Education Forum (GO EDFORUM). See Education.

Hypercard (Apple Macintosh) applications are supported in the Hypertext Forum (GO MACHYPER). HyperCard GS also is supported in Apple II Programmers Forum (GO APPROG). See Apple Computers.

HyperCard (software) is supported in the Claris Corp. Forum (GO CLARIS). For more information, see Claris.

Hyperkinetix products are supported in the IBM PC Vendor D Forum (GO PCVEND). See IBM Computers.

Hyperpress Publishing products are supported in the Mac B Vendor Forum (GO MACBVEN). See Apple Computers.

HyperWare products are supported in the IBM PC Vendor B Forum (GO PCVENB). See IBM Computers.

Hyphen products are supported in the Desktop Publishing Vendor Forum (GO DTPVENDOR). For details, see Desktop Publishing.

Hypoglycemia and related chronic metabolic disorders are discussed in the Diabetes Forum (GO DIABOL). See Diabetes.

Hyundai products are supported in the IBM PC Vendor E Forum (GO PCVENE). See IBM Computers.

I

Ialine **(food and agriculture database)** may be searched through the IQuest gateway. See IQuest.

I/B/E/S Earnings Estimates (GO IBES), available to subscribers of the Executive Option (see Executive Option), is a financial service called the Institutional Broker's Estimate System. It represents a consensus of annual and long-term forecasts from more than 2,500 analysts at 130 brokerage and institutional research firms. See Investment Analysis Tools.

IBM CAD products are supported in the IBM CAD/CAM Information Exchange Forum (GO IBMENG) and in the CADD/CAM/CAE Vendor Forum (GO CADDVEN). See CAD/CAM.

IBM Computers are supported on dozens of CompuServe features.

The IBM Users Network (GO IBMNET), one of the most popular collections of forums on the system, is the core of CompuServe's many IBM-oriented forums. Sysop duties in most of these forums (unless otherwise indicated) are shared by Don Watkins (76703,750), Chris Dunford (76703,2002), Vern Buerg (70007,1212), and Jim McKeown (76702,1102). Scores of volunteers help in various specific areas.

The IBMNET forums are the following:

- Applications Forum (GO IBMAPP), applications software for business, home, school, fun, and more, is the core applications forum for the PC. It includes word processing, database management, business and personal accounting, business graphics, desktop publishing, and educational software.

- BBS Forum (GO IBMBBS) contains bulletin board programs, utilities, door programs, and a discussion of issues concerning bulletin board operators and users.

- Communications Forum (GO IBMCOM) deals with the ins and outs of telecomputing with the IBM, both in hardware and software. You'll find discussions on how to use various communications programs and hardware. In the libraries, you'll see the best public domain and shareware communications software available. This is also the home for the public domain CompuServe-specific Autosig program (see AutoSig).

- Hardware Forum (GO IBMHW) covers everything from the heart of the machine to printers, monitors, hard disks, and other peripherals. In addition to reviews and other comments on hardware, there are hardware diagnostic programs, hardware-specific utilities (printer utilities, disk managers, special video programs, especially for the EGA and VGA), and other hardware-specific software in the libraries. The forum also has special sections for mainframes and for the PCjr that spans both hardware and software.

- Lan Vendor Forum (GO LANVEN) supports providers of systems for local area networks, including Synergy Solutions and Newport Systems.

- New Users/Fun Forum (GO IBMNEW) fields questions from people new to computing, new to IBM computing, and new to computing on CompuServe. It also is the place to find leisure-time software and discussions of recreational computing, such as games and puzzles. If you're just getting started with the PC or with the CompuServe Forum software this is the best place to start.

- PC Vendor A Forum (GO PCVENA) includes the following vendors: ButtonWare Incorporated, creator of PC-File+, PC-Type+, PC-Calc+, Baker's Dozen, PC-Dial, PC-Stylist, PC-Tickle, and XD Extended DOS; Mansfield Software Group, creator of KEDIT and REXX; Enable Software Incorporated, developer of the integrated product ENABLE; Magee Enterprises and its primary product Automenu; Custom Technologies, developer of CheckMate, CheckMate-GL, and Magic Menus; Mustang Software, creator of WILDCAT! Bulletin Board; Sabre, creator of the Saber LAN Workstation and the Saber Menu System; Qualitas, maker of REXX, a complete implementation of the SAA REXX procedure language for DOS and OS/2; Northgate Computer Systems; Quercus Systems; Ctrlalt Associates; Foresight Resources Corp.; PC-Kwik; and DeScribe.

- PC Vendor B Forum (GO PCVENB) includes the following vendors: Powercore; Primavera Systems Incorporated, which offers support for Primavera Project Planner (P3), Primavision, Finest Hour, Parade, and Expedition; Korenthal Associates Incorporated, which KA publishes, 4PRINT, and TAPMARK; Personics Corp, creators of UltraVision, Look&Link, @Base, @Base Option Pac, SeeMore for 1-2-3, SmartNotes, and HeadMaster; Quicksoft Incorporated, developer of PC-Write; Turbopower Software, which specializes in productivity aids for Turbo Pascal programmers, and DacEasy, an independent software firm dedicated to developing software for small businesses; DacEasy; PRO-C Corporation; JP Software; Prolog Development Center; HyperWare; One-Write Plus; Advanced Gravis; INMAGIC Inc.; and Greenleaf.

- PC Vendor C Forum (GO PCVENC) supports these vendors: Interactive Image, which makes Electronics Workbench and Authority; Vericomp, which publishes SoftBytes, Memory Master, and Password; Hooper International, which provides the Cheque-It-Out bookkeeping software; Innovative Data Concepts, which publishes Swap Utilities; Wordtech Systems, with a line of database management products that includes dBXL and Quicksilver; Parsons Technology, which offers the MoneyCounts program; Rupp Corporation, which offers the FastLynx file transfer package; PKWare, which produces popular data compression programs, including PKZIP, PKUNZIP, and PKSFX; TaxCut, which is connected with Legal Knowledge Systems Inc., the developer of the program "Andrew Tobias TaxCut"; NetFRAME Systems, producer of EMU/470 and EMU/220 emulators; and M-USA, which created the Pacioli accounting systems.

- PC Vendor D Forum (GO PCVEND), which provides support for additional third-party vendors, including Above Software, Legato Systems, Brightwork Development, Tech III, Micropolis, Cumulus Corporation, Complementary Solutions Inc., Timeslips, Hyperkinetix, Magma Systems, GammaLink, Procom Technology, Clarion Tech Journal, Pacific Data Products, and BLOC Publishing.

- PC Vendor E Forum (GO PCVENE) supports TurboPower Software—C++ products, XTree Company, Iomega Corporation, Farallon Computing, ZEOS International, SemWare, American Power Conversion, Eiffel OOP, Objects Inc., American Cybernetics Inc., AddStor, DSI Software Systems, Alpha Software, and Hyundai.

- PC Vendor F Forum (GO PCVENF) supports Acer America, manufacturer of computer systems; Storage Dimensions, developer of various storage devices; Pure Data, Ltd., designer and manufacturer of LAN connectivity products; Hilgraeve, developer of HyperACCESS/5; Willies Computer Software Corp., developer of several serial communication products; Funk Software, developer of Sideway; MIP Fund Accounting; Command Software Systems; Peachtree Software; PCMCIA; Avery Dennison; Faircom; and TRIUS.

- PC Vendor G Forum (GO PCVENG) supports Brown Bag Software (PowerMenu Plus, MindReader, and PC-Outline), Reach Software Corp. (WorkMAN 2.0 and Personal MailMAN), Magic Software (Magic), Futurus Corp.(TEAM product line), Identitech Inc. (FYI, AIMS, ISVS, and LOFS), Vertisoft (DoubleDisk and Emulaser), Advanced Logic Research (Ranger notebook, Flyer, Business VEISA, and ProVEISA products) (GO ALRINC), PC Brand Inc., Pinnacle Publishing, Mitchell and Gauthier, SofNet, Cheyenne Software, SunDisk, Helix, Cogent Data Technologies, Swan Technologies, and Madge Networks Ltd.

- PC Vendor H Forum (GO PCVENH) supports Micronetics Design Corporation (MSM); Xircom (Pocket Ethernet Adapter III & CreditCard Ethernet Adapter); PCI SIG (PCI Local Bus Specification); Performance Technology

(POWERLan, POWERsave, POWERfusion, and POWERshare); Alcom (LanFax Redirector); RTA, Ltd. (Modular Languages Compilers); Object Design Inc. (ObjectStore); IQ Technologies (the HyperPAD series and Show Partner F/X 3.7); Lahey Computer Systems (Lahey Personal, Optional Toolkit, F77L, and F77L-EM/32); Reality Technology (WealthBuilder); WATCOM (C, C++ and FORTRAN compilers); Strategic Mapping Inc. (Atlas GIS); Object Design; IQ Technologies; ReferencePoint; Landmark; and Datapoint.

- PC Vendor I Forum (GO PCVENI) includes support from companies such as Expert Choice, Pocket Soft, Greenview Data, Sytron Corporation, Allied Telesis, Kingston Technology, Banner Blue Software, World Software, Sealevel Systems, Future Trends Software, and Norton-Lambert.

- PC Vendor J Forum (GO PCVENJ) supports products from Fujitsu and other companies.

- Programming Forum (GO IBMPROG) devoted to the programming enthusiasts in the MS-DOS and Personal System/2 world. Assemblers, source code in a variety of languages, and help from fellow members are available, as well as hints, tips, and tutorials for those just starting to program.

- Systems/Utilities Forum (GO IBMSYS), for questions and answers about operating systems. Data libraries stocked with handy utility programs and information on the various operating systems and environments available for the PC, including multi-tasking and OS/2.

Some IBM forums specialize in the systems that use the OS/2 operating system. The IBM OS/2 Forums are administered by primary sysop Irv Spalten (76711,175) and Frank Andress (76711,176), with the assistance from Mel Hallerman, Aimee Shapiro, Brian Duquette, Larry Finkelstein and Guy Scharf. They include:

- IBM OS/2 User's Forum (GO OS2USER) for discussions of general hardware topics, from computers to printers.

- IBM OS/2 Support Forum (GO OS2SUPPORT), covering applications issues.

- IBM OS/2 Developer 1 and Developer 2 forums (GO OS2DF1 and GO OS2DF2), for project-oriented discussions.

- IBM OS/2 PSP Beta Forum (GO PSPBETA) for new product topics.

- OS/2 Vendor Forum (GO OS2AVEN), which supports Creative Systems Programming (Golden CommPass), Sourceline Software (SourceLink), Sundial Systems (Relish), Development Technologies (DeskMan/2) and HockWare (HockWare Visual Programming), BocaSoft, Micro Decisionware, CadWare, Canyon Software Corp., Carry Associates, Clear & Simple Inc., ForeFront Software Inc., Frenster Associates, Hilbert Computing, MHR Software and Consulting, Multitask Consulting, New Freedom Data Center, PrOffice, Rightware Inc., The Software Division, Spincode, and Synetik Systems.

- OS/2 B Vendor Forum (OS2BVEN) supports Software Corporation Of America and PCX. It also includes a general shareware section.

Miscellaneous IBM forums include the following:

- Advanced Program-to-Program Communications (GO APPC) is for information about CPI-C (Common Programming Interface Communications) and Advanced Peer-to-Peer Networking (APPN), and is a major enhancement to IBM's Systems Network Architecture (SNA). The forum addresses many of the "hot topics" in networking today, including LAN/WAN integration, client/server development, multivendor networking, downsizing, and rightsizing. The primary sysop is Zeke Crater (76711,773). Assisting him are Lance D. Bader, Tim Hefel, Peter Schwaller, Tim Huntley, and John Walker.

- IBM CAD/CAM Information Exchange Forum (GO IBMENG) links to the IBM CAD/CAM Technical Support team. See CAD/CAM.

- IBM DB2 Family Forum (GO IBMDB2) supports users of DB2/2, DB2/6000, and DB2/VSE & VM and those who are interested in IBM DB2/2 relational database products. The forum is operated by Bob Harbus (75050,2014) with assistance from Randy Schinkel.

- IBM Desktop Software Forum (GO IBMDESK) supports users of IDS products, including the DisplayWrite family, Storyboard, and Current. Primary sysops are Gary Vieregger (76711,35) and R. A. Temple (76711,67). They are assisted by Linda Johnson, Jaynie Shaffer, Mike Pearson, Doug Spath, Jill Randolph, and Anita Holser.

- The IBM File Finder (GO IBMFF) is a special database containing information on all IBMNET and most IBM-related forum files. The IBM File Finder allows you to search on a filename or keyword or use a variety of search methods that help you locate files of interest in any of the forums.

- IBM Lan Management Utilities/2 Forum (GO LMUFORUM) is intended for discussion of topics related to IBM LAN Management Utilities/2 (LMU/2). The forum administrator is Steve Pace (76711,724).

- IBM PowerPC Forum (GO POWERPC) supported systems using the new PowerPC chip developed by IBM, Apple Computer Inc. and Motorola Corp. The sysop is Nori Kato (76711,715), assisted by Maureen Ferraro and Nelly Ng.

- IBM Special Needs Forum (GO IBMSPEC) finds information and IBM PC compatible programs for primary and adult students with special education needs. (See Handicapped Issues.)

- IBM Thinkpad Forum (GO THINKPAD) supports IBM's first pen-based computers and related products. The forum visitors discuss all aspects of ThinkPad brand, including product development, manufacturing, marketing, service, and support, worldwide. The primary sysop is Noriyoshi Kato (76711,715) of Somers, New York, an international assignee from Japan to IBM as assistant to general manager of mobile computing. Assisting are Michael Anderson and Andrew Klausman.

In addition, a category in the CompuServe Classifieds lets you read and post ads regarding MS-DOS computers and software. See Classifieds Service. Also, Tandy/ IBM Science is a topic in the Science/Math Education Forum (GO SCIENCE). See Science.

IBM ImagePlus products are supported in the ImagePlus Forum (GO IBMIMAGE). See ImagePlus.

IBM Lab products are supported in the Software Solutions Forum (GO SOFSOL). See Software Solutions.

IBMLink (GO IL) and **IBM Personal Software Products** (GO IBMPSP) are stores in the Electronic Mall (GO MALL). IBMLink provides electronic connections to IBM data, while IBM Personal Software Products offers software for OS/ 2 and other systems. See Electronic Mall.

IBM Linkway Live, IBM Storyboard Live, and **IBM OS/2 MM Tools** products are supported in the Ultimedia Tools Forum A (GO ULTIATOOLS). See Ultimedia.

IBM, Report on and **SAA—An Inside Look at IBM** (databases) may be searched through the IQuest gateway. See IQuest. Report on IBM also can be searched through the Business Database Plus (GO BUSDB), as can *DataTrends Report on DEC & IBM* and *IBM Japan Weekly*. See Business Database.

IBM Storage Systems Division Forum (GO IBMSTORAGE) supports its products, which include ADSTAR Distributed Storage Manager. The forum is administered by Jacquie Reith (71333,3610), with assistance from Toby Yamagiwa and Gary Archer.

IBM System User (magazine) is available for full-text searching through Computer Database Plus (GO COMPDB). In the same service, abstracts of *IBM Journal of Research and Development* and *IBM Systems Journal* can be searched. See Computer Database Plus.

ICC Key Note Market Research can be searched in the UK Marketing Library (GO UKMARKETING). See UK Marketing.

ICD Incorporated products are supported in the Atari Vendors Forum (GO ATARIVEN). See Atari Computers.

Ice Cream Reporter (database) may be searched through the IQuest gateway. See IQuest. See also Food.

ICEN (magazine) can be searched through the Business Database Plus (GO BUSDB). See Business Database.

ICOM products are supported in the Windows 3rd-Party Forum A (GO WINAPA). See Microsoft Software.

I&CS (Instrumentation & Control Systems)   **(magazine)** is searchable through Computer Database Plus (GO COMPDB). See Computer Database Plus.

Idaho **(news)** is included in the daily Western regional reports from United Press International. See Executive News Service for details.

IDC Japan Report **(magazine)** can be searched through the Business Database Plus (GO BUSDB). See Business Database.

IDD M&A Transactions **(database)** may be searched through the IQuest gateway. See IQuest.

Ideas, Inventions & Innovations Forum (GO INNOVATION) discusses all aspects of inventing—finding a better, quicker, cheaper way to improve on what's out there. The forum seeks to bring inventors and potential inventors together with the people to guide them in taking the right steps to help turn an idea into a new product. Sysop Barbara Burnes (76711,1246) has started six companies and has marketed many consumer products, including several of her own. She is a principal in a consulting company, Burnes & Waldron, which deals with technology transfer and specializes in helping defense manufacturers diversify into open markets. Assisting in the forum operation are Frank Moody, Robert B. Whittridge II, S. Pal Asija, Marguerite Ellen, Jack Breckenridge, and Gerry Elman.

IDEF is a sponsor of the General Computing Forum (GO GENCOM). See General Computing.

Identitech Inc. products are supported in the PC Vendor G Forum (GO PCVENG). See IBM.

IDP Report **(magazine)** is searchable through Computer Database Plus (GO COMPDB). See Computer Database Plus. It also can be searched through Business Database Plus (GO BUSDB). See Business Database.

IEE publications (including abstracts of those on control theory and applications, computer graphics, control systems, design and test, robotics and automation) can be searched through Computer Database Plus (GO COMPDB). See Computer Database Plus.

Illinois **(news)** is covered in the Chicago Tribune, searchable through Telebase System's News Source USA (GO NEWSUSA). See News Source.

   Also, selected reports from Illinois are included in the Central regional reports from United Press International. See Executive News Service. Also, *Illinois Business Review* magazine can be searched through the Business Database Plus (GO BUSDB). See Business Database.

Illustrator, Adobe is supported in the Abode Forum Adobe Forum (GO ADOBE). See Adobe Software.

Image-In products are supported in the Graphics A Vendor Forum (GO IMAGEIN). See Graphics.

ImagePlus Forum, IBM (IMAGEPLUS) supports the line of ImagePlus products. The forum is operated by the firm's customers support department (71333,3704).

Image and Vision Computing (magazine) is searchable (abstracts) through Computer Database Plus (GO COMPDB). See Computer Database Plus.

Imaging Report, Electronic (magazine) can be searched through the Business Database Plus (GO BUSDB), as can *Imaging News* and *Imaging Update*. See Business Database. *Imaging Update* also can be searched through the IQuest gateway. See IQuest.

IMMS Weekly Marketletter (financial database) may be searched through the IQuest gateway. See IQuest.

Immunology, Journal of abstracts are searchable in the Health Database Plus (GO HLTBD). See Health.

Implement & Tractor (magazine) can be searched through the Business Database Plus (GO BUSDB). See Business Database.

Impressions Software products are covered in Game Publishers B Forum (GO GAMBPUB). See Gaming Forums.

Improved Recovery Week can be searched through the Business Database Plus (GO BUSDB). See Business Database.

Impulse products are supported in the Amiga Vendor Forum (GO AMIGAVENDOR). See Commodore Computers.

IMS Marketletter and **IMSWorld R&D Focus Drug News** (pharmacology databases) may be searched through the IQuest gateway. See IQuest.

Inc. (magazine) is searchable through Magazine Database Plus (GO MDP), IQuest (GO IQUEST), and Business Database Plus (GO BUSDB). For details, see Magazine Database, IQuest, and Business Database.

Incider (magazine) is searchable (abstracts) through Computer Database Plus (GO COMPDB). See Computer Database Plus.

Incue Online (GO INCUE) is an electronic magazine published by Broadcasters and Broadcast Engineers Forum (GO BPFORUM). For details, see Broadcasters.

Inmark products are supported in the Windows 3rd-Party D Forum (GO WINAPD). See Microsoft Software.

Independent (newspaper) is covered in the UK Newspaper Library (GO UKPAPERS). See UK Newspaper.

Independent Investors Research, Inc. (GO IIR) is a store in the Electronic Mall (GO MALL) that offers financial earnings and forecast recommendations. See Electronic Mall.

Independent Living is searchable in the Health Database Plus (GO HLTBD). See Health.

Independent Telco News can be searched through the Business Database Plus (GO BUSDB). See Business Database.

Indepth software is supported in the Graphics B Vendor Forum (GO INDEPTH). See Graphics.

Index (GO INDEX) is a database of all current features on CompuServe, searchable by keyword. Another fast way to locate services is with the FIND command. For details, see FIND.

Indiana (news) is covered in selected reports from Indiana, which are included in the Central regional reports from United Press International. See Executive News Service. Also, *Indiana Business Magazine* can be searched through the Business Database Plus (GO BUSDB). See Business Database.

Indianapolis 500 and other auto races are regularly covered in the Motor Sports Forum (GO RACING). See Sports and Recreation.

Indonesian Investment Highlights can be searched through the Business Database Plus (GO BUSDB). See Business Database. See also Pacific.

Indoor Air Quality Update (database) may be searched through the IQuest gateway. See IQuest.
  See also Environmental issues.

Industry is covered in assorted features:

- *Industrial Computing* and *Industrial Engineering* (magazines) can be searched through Computer Database Plus (GO COMPDB). See Computer Database Plus.
- Through the Business Database Plus (GO BUSDB), magazines include *Industrial Bioprocessing, Industrial Communications, Industrial Distribution, Industrial Engineering, Industrial Environment, Industrial Finishing, Industrial Health & Hazards Update, Industrial Management, Industrial Relations, Industrial Specialties News, Industries in Transition*, and *Industry Week*. See Business Database. *Industry Week* also is searchable through Magazine Database Plus (GO MDP). For details see Magazine Database.
- Industry Data Sources database is accessible through the Marketing/Management Research Center (GO MKTGRC). For details, see Marketing/Management.

- Relevant databases on IQuest (see IQuest) include Asbestos & Lead Abatement Report, Business America, Business Periodicals Index, Business Week, Cendata, Chain Store Age, Comline Japan Daily: Industry Automation, Computerized Processes, Consumer Reports, D&B—Dun's Electronic Business Directory, Discount Store News, F-D-C Reports, Financial Times Business Reports: Business/Finance, Reports: Energy, FINIS: Financial Industry Information Service, Footwear News, HFD—The Weekly Home Furnishings Newspaper, Industries in Transition, Industry Week, Manufacturing Automation, Nation's Business, Nation's Restaurant News, Noriane, PIERS Exports, PTS Newsletter Database, Restaurant Business Magazine, Standards & Specifications, Supermarket News, Thomas New Industrial Products, Thomas Register Online, Trade and Industry ASAP, Trade and Industry Index, Transin, and Womens Wear Daily. See IQuest.

Industrial safety is discussed in the SafetyNet Forum (GO SAFETYNET). For information, see Safety. Also Industrial Health & Hazards Update is searchable through IQuest. See IQuest.

Inertia (**software**) is supported in Windows 3rd-Party Forum A (GO WINAPA). See Microsoft Software.

.INF, as an extension on filenames in forum libraries, usually stands for information, meaning it is an ASCII text file containing background information on a topic. See Files, Extensions.

Infectious Diseases, Journal of abstracts are searchable in the Health Database Plus (GO HLTBD). See Health.

Infinite Technologies products are supported in the Novell Vendor Forum A (GO NVENA). See Novell Software.

Inflation indexes, including the Consumer Price Index and Producer Price Index and Gross National Product, is available from CENDATA, the government's online census material (GO CENDATA). To find the indexes, select the "U.S. Statistics at a Glance" option from the main menu, then choose the "Economic Indicators" option from the subsequent menu. See Census data.

InfoAccess products are supported in the Windows 3rd-Party B Forum (GO WINAPB). See Microsoft Software.

Infocheck (**database**) can be searched through IQuest. See IQuest.

Infomat International Business (**business database**) is accessible through the Marketing/Management Research Center (GO MKTGRC). For details, see Marketing/Management.

Infomedia Publisher (**database**) may be searched through the IQuest gateway. See IQuest.

Infonet: Electronic mail may be exchanged between users of CompuServe and InfoPlex. For details, see Mail, CompuServe.

Information Executive is searchable through Computer Database Plus (GO COMPDB). See Computer Database Plus. It also can be searched through Business Database Plus (GO BUSDB), as can *Information Technology and Libraries*, *Information Today*, and *Infosystems*. See Business Database.

Information & Interactive Services Report (database) can be searched through IQuest. See IQuest.

Information/Management for MVS (software) is supported in the Software Solutions Forum (GO SOFSOL). See Software Solutions.

Information Manager, CompuServe (software) is a front-end program CompuServe itself produced for IBM PC and Apple Macintosh users in 1990. See CompuServe Information Manager.

Information Networks (database) can be searched through IQuest. See IQuest.

Information Report, International (database) may be searched through the IQuest gateway. See IQuest.

Information Resources Incorporated products are supported in the Javelin/EXPRESS Forum (GO IRIFORUM). See Javelin Software.

Information Science Abstracts (database) may be searched through the IQuest gateway. See IQuest.

Information Today (magazine) can be searched through the Business Database Plus (GO BUSDB). See Business Database.

Information USA (GO INFOUSA) is produced by author Matthew Lesko, known for his *Information USA*, a 1,250-page reference book from Viking Penguin Books. The online service specializes in illustrating Lesko's techniques for getting questions answered, with tutorials such as "The Art of Obtaining Information from Bureaucrats."

This detailed resource provides phone numbers, addresses, how-to articles, tutorials, and so on. Lesko emphasizes how to get information from the government. Some of the topics covered on the menus are Information Starting Places, Consumer Power, Housing and Real Estate, Education, Careers and Workplace, Arts and Humanities, Your Community, Financial Help to Individuals, Vacations and Business Travel, Investments and Financial Services, Taxes, Free Health and Care, Drugs and Chemical Dependence, Law and Social Justice, Information on People/Companies, Auctions and Surplus Property, Giveaways for Entrepreneurs, Business and Industry, Selling To The Government, International Trade, Economics, Demographics and Statistics, International Relations/Defense, Science and Technology, Patents, Trademarks and Copyrights, Agriculture and Farming, Energy, Weather and Maps,

Environment and Nature, Freedom of Information Act, Information From Law-makers, Books and Libraries, Government Databases/Bulletin Boards, and Odds and Ends.

Information Week (magazine) is searchable (abstracts) through Computer Database Plus (GO COMPDB). See Computer Database Plus. It also may be searched through the IQuest gateway. See IQuest.

Infosystems (magazine) can be searched through the Business Database Plus (GO BUSDB). See Business Database.

InfoWorld can be searched through Computer Database Plus (GO COMPDB). See Computer Database Plus.

Ingram's (magazine) can be searched through the Business Database Plus (GO BUSDB). See Business Database.

In Health is searchable in the Health Database Plus (GO HLTBD). See Health.

INIT Manager (software) is supported in Mac C Vendor Forum (GO MACCVEN). For details, see Apple Computers.

Inline Designs (software) is supported in Mac C Vendor Forum (GO MACCVEN). For details, see Apple Computers.

INMAGIC Inc. products are supported in the IBM PC Vendor B Forum (GO PCVENB). See IBM Computers.

Inn Forum (GO INNFORUM) is operated in conjunction with the Bed & Breakfast Database (GO INNS). See Bed and Breakfast.

Innovation and **Innovator's Digest** can be searched through the Business Database Plus (GO BUSDB). See Business Database.

Innovative Data Concepts products are supported in the PC Vendor C Forum (GO PCVENC). See IBM Computers.

Innovative Quality Software (products) are supported in the MIDI C Vendor Forum (GO MIDICVEN). See Music.

Innovator's Digest and **Inpadoc: Patents** (databases) may be searched through the IQuest gateway. See IQuest.

INOVAtronics Products are supported in the Amiga Vendor Forum (GO AMIGAVENDOR). See Commodore Computers.

Inset Systems products are supported in the Graphics A Vendor Forum (GO IN-SET). See Graphics.

Inside DOT & Transportation Week can be searched through the Business Database Plus (GO BUSDB). See Business Database.

Inside IVHS can be searched through the Business Database Plus (GO BUSDB). See Business Database.

Inside Market Data and **Insider Trading Monitor** (databases) may be searched through the IQuest gateway. See IQuest. *Inside Market Data* also can be searched through the Business Database Plus (GO BUSDB). See Business Database.

Inside R&D can be searched through the Business Database Plus (GO BUSDB). See Business Database.

Insight (magazine) can be searched in the Magazine Database Plus (GO MDP). See Magazine Database.

INSPEC (database) may be searched through the IQuest gateway (GO IQUEST) and through the Knowledge Index (GO KI). See IQuest and see Knowledge Index.

Institute for Certification of Computer Professionals is a sponsor of the General Computing Forum (GO GENCOM). See General Computing.

Institutional Broker's Estimate System (GO IBES), available only to subscribers of the Executive Option, is a financial service reporting annual and long-term forecasts from more than 2,500 analysts at 130 brokerage and institutional research firms. See Investment Analysis Tools.

Institutional Distribution and **Institutional Investor** (magazines) can be searched through the Business Database Plus (GO BUSDB). See Business Database.

Insurance is the topic of Continental Insurance (GO CIC) and Safeware Computer Insurance (GO SAF), which offer insurance through the Electronic Mall (GO MALL). See Electronic Mall.

In addition, IQuest (GO IQUEST) provides a number of related databases, including ABI/INFORM, Federal & State Insurance Week, Financial Services Report, IMMS Weekly Marketeer, Insurance Periodicals Index, Liability Week, Lloyd's List, and Management Contents. See IQuest.

Searchable through the Business Database Plus (GO BUSDB) are *Best's Review Life-Health Insurance Edition* and *Property-Casualty Insurance Edition, Federal & State Insurance Week, Federal Industry Watchdog, Insurance Review, Liability Week, National Underwriter Life & Health, National Underwriter Property & Casualty,* and *Risk & Benefits Management Edition.* See Business Database. On the same database, *East European Insurance Report, World Insurance Corporate Report,* and *World Insurance Report* can be searched.

InTech (magazine) is searchable (abstracts) through Computer Database Plus (GO COMPDB). See Computer Database Plus.

Intel Corp. products (GO INTEL) are supported in several online features:

- The Intel Forum (GO INTELFORUM) for support of Intel Personal Computer Enhancement (PCED) or Development Tools Operation (DT) products. Primary sysop is Paul Crandall (76702,366).
- The Intel ACCESS/Real-Time Forum (GO INTELACCESS), serving software developers and others needing the latest in technical information on Intel chips such as the i386, i486, i750 (DVI), and i960. The forum promises programming tips, benchmarks, literature, and expert advice. Part of the forum is associated with the Intel-sponsored Users'Group (iRUG), which encourages the exchange of ideas in development of iRMX Operating System-based software. Primary sysops are Sue Hunt (76711,1100) and Scott Durrant (76702,2035).

Intellectual property is a topic of several IQuest databases (see IQuest), including Innovator's Digest, Trademarkscan—U.S. Federal, Trademarkscan—U.S. State, and U.S. Copyrights.

Integrated Circuits International and **Intelligent Network News** can be searched through the Business Database Plus (GO BUSDB). See Business Database.

Intelligent Software Strategies (database) may be searched through the IQuest gateway. See IQuest.

Interactive Image Technologies products are supported in the IBM PC Vendor C Forum (GO PCVENC). See IBM Computers.

Interactive System Productivity Facility (software) is supported in the Software Solutions Forum (GO SOFSOL). See Software Solutions.

Intergalactic Development (software) is supported in the Game Publishers C Forum (GO GAMCPUB). See Gaming Forums.

Intergraph/Bentley Systems (software) is supported in the CADD/CAM/CAE Vendor Forum (GO CADDVEN). See CAD/CAM.

Interior Department is discussed in the White House Forum (GO WHITEHOUSE). See White House.

Interior Design (magazine) can be searched through the Business Database Plus (GO BUSDB). See Business Database. See also Decorating.

Internal Auditor (magazine) can be searched through the Business Database Plus (GO BUSDB). See Business Database.

Internal medicine is covered in several publications searchable in the Health Database Plus (GO HLTBD). Abstracts are searchable in *Archives of Internal Medicine* and *Annals of Internal Medicine*. See Health.

International Access Information (GO INTERNATIONAL) includes a database of access phone numbers for logging on to CompuServe from around the world, including from parts of Africa, Asia and the Pacific Rim, Atlantic and the Caribbean Islands, eastern and western Europe, Latin and South America, the Middle East, and Canada. See also Phone, CompuServe Access Numbers.

International business and trade are covered in many IQuest databases. For business, see:

Academic Index
Asia-Pacific
Baltic Business Report
Business Opportunities
Celex (computerized
    Documentation
    System on Ec Law)
Corporate Affiliations
Creditreform
D&B—Asia-Pacific
    Dun's Market
    Identifiers
D&B—International
    Dun's Market
    Identifiers
East Europe Intelli-
    gence Report
Eastern Europe
    Finance
European Community:
    Business Forecast
Exporter
Extel International
    Financial Cards

Extel International News
    Cards
Financial Times (full text)
Financial Times Analysis
    Reports—Europe
Financial Times Analysis
    Reports—UK
FT Mergers & Acquisi-
    tions International
German Business Press
    Abstracts
German Business Scope
Hoppenstedt East
    Germany
INFOCHECK
Infomat International
    Business
International Business
    Climate Indicators
International Reports
Japan Economic
    Newswire Plus
Japan Weekly Monitor
Knight-Ridder/Tribune
    Business News

Lloyd's List
Moody's Corporate News
    International
PAIS International
PTS International
    Forecasts
PTS Newsletter Database
Reuters
Russia Express
Russia Express Contracts
Russia/Cis Intelligence
    Report
Spearhead
Stamm's Xsu Business
Telefirm Directory of
    French Companies
Textline Global News
Thrift Accountant
West Europe Intelligence
    Report
Worldwide Telecom
Worldwide Videotex
    Update

For trade, see:

Asahi News Service
Celex (computerized
    Documentation
    System on Ec Law)
Cendata
Chemical Engineering
    & Biotechnology
    Abstracts (CEBA)
D&B—Asia-Pacific
    Dun's Market
    Identifiers

Exporter
International Stocks
    Database
Knight-Ridder/Tribune
    Business News
Lloyd's List
PIERS Exports
PIERS Imports (U.S.
    Ports)—current
PTS Newsletter Database

Scrip—Current News
Scrip—Daily News
Scrip—Retrospective
Stamm's Xsu Business
Transin
Washington Trade Daily
World Surface Coatings
    Abstracts
World Textiles

International distributors of computers are supported in the Federation of International Distributors Forum (GO FEDERATION). See Federation of International Distributors Forum.

International Entrepreneurs' Network (GO USEN) operates for people looking for new business opportunities. For details, see Entrepreneurs.

International Management (magazine) can be searched through the Business Database Plus (GO BUSDB). See Business Database.

International Market Identifiers, Dun's (GO DII-1) is a database of information on approximately 2.1 million public, private, and government-controlled companies in 120 countries. For details, see Company Reports.

International Reports can be searched through the Business Database Plus (GO BUSDB). See Business Database.

International Trade Forum (GO ITFORUM) is available for discussion of world business. Message sections include topics such as "Starting Out in IT," "Trading in the EEC," "Shipping & Customs," and "IT Banking/Finance." Topics range from government restrictions to trading in the Orient. The primary sysop is Thom Hartmann (76702,765) who has more than 20 years of experience as an international entrepreneur, having started projects on four continents, and having built and sold five companies. He is assisted by Nigel Peacock and Dennis Aruta.

International Trade Forum and **International Trade Finance** can be searched through the Business Database Plus (GO BUSDB). See Business Database.

International travel is the subject of the U.S. Department of State's Travel Advisory Service (GO STATE) and is maintained by the Citizen Emergency Center as a continuously updated information service to Americans traveling abroad. See U.S. Government Information. See also Visa Advisors.

Internet: Electronic mail may be exchanged between users of CompuServe and Internet. For details, see Mail, CompuServe. Internet also is a favorite topic of the Telecommunication Issues Forum (GO TELECOM). See Telecommunication.

Interplay Productions software is regularly discussed in The Game Publishers B Forum (GO GAMBPUB). See Gaming Forums.

Inter Press Service International News (database) may be searched through the IQuest gateway. See IQuest. The resource also can be searched through the Business Database Plus (GO BUSDB). See Business Database.

Intersect Software is supported in the Atari Vendors Forum (GO ATARIVEN). See Atari Computers.

Intersolv Forum (GO INTERSOLV) supports INTERSOLV tools. The primary sysop is Keith Alexander (76711,1223), assisted by Bonita Evans, Ken Barrette, and

Roger Joachim. Products supported include APS/Maintenance Workbench, Excelerator, and PVCS.

InTrec Software products are supported in the Apple II Vendor Forum (GO APIIVEN). See Apple Computers.

Intuit Forum (GO INTUIT) provides technical support and discussion areas for all of the Intuit products, including its famed Quicken series of DOS, Windows, and Macintosh financial programs, as well as Quickpay and Quickbooks for DOS and Windows. Operating the forum is Harry Dreier (72662,1755) with assistance from Rachel Montgomery, Kevin Lojewski, Kathryn Saunders, and Jerry Thornton.

Inventors and those interested in the topic are invited to the Ideas, Inventions & Innovations Forum (GO INNOVATION). See Ideas. See also Patents.

InvesText (GO INVTEXT) is a financial service that features two years of reports by analysts in more than 50 Wall Street, regional, and international brokerage houses and research firms. See Company Reports.

This resource also may be searched through IQuest. See IQuest.

Investment Analysis Tools (GO ANALYSIS) offers databases of various investment data and the screening capabilities of DISCLOSURE II to search for facts on thousands of companies, letting you comparison shop before buying. Additional options let you track purchased securities and gauge their success. All are surcharged and most are updated overnight. These investment analysis tools are the following:

- Company Screening (GO COSCREEN) lets you search the DISCLOSURE II database of information on more than 10,000 companies based on your own guidelines and produces a list of companies that meet your criteria. You select any combination of 39 available selection criteria, including various growth rates and financial ratios as well as industry codes, state, total assets, book value, market value, annual sales, net income, cash flow, latest price, and so on. Those interested in selling or in marketing research can find companies on demographic information such as state, city, area code, or ZIP code, number of employees, annual sales, type of business, etc. The service is surcharged at $15 an hour.
- FundWatch Online by Money Magazine (GO FUNDWATCH) lets you screen more than 1,900 mutual funds. See Financial Services.
- I/B/E/S Earnings Estimates (GO IBES) is available to subscribers of the Executive Option (see Executive Option). It is the Institutional Broker's Estimate System and represents a consensus of annual and long-term forecasts from more than 2,500 analysts at 130 brokerage and institutional research firms, including the top 20 research firms in the country. The database includes information about 3,400 companies and reports the most optimistic and pessimistic EPS estimates, as well as median, mean, and variation. Current share price, earnings per share, and price/earnings ratio are also included. The service is

surcharged at 50 cents for a summary earnings discussion and $2 for a detailed earnings report.

- MMS Financial Reports (GO MMS) is available from MMS International. This is a multinational corporation specializing in financial and economic research. MMS focuses on monetary theory and forecasts central banking policies and operations. More than 50 economists and market analysts in 12 international centers form a network that covers the markets 24 hours a day. MMS market analysts provide economic and technical analysis of the debt, currency, and equity markets to over 20,000 market participants worldwide. It produces a series of economic reports released, including the nonsurchased Calendar of Economic Events, which is divided into three parts: the Economic Calendar, the Treasury Calendar, and the Global Critical Events Calendar. Other reports include the Daily Equity Market Report, the Daily Currency Market Report, The Daily Debt Market Report, the Weekly Economic Summary, and FEDWATCH, which focuses on interest rate trends and Federal Reserve Board activity. All are surcharged at $5 a report. Other nonsurcharged reports include monthly and quarterly forecasts and the biweekly Economic Briefing.

- Portfolio Valuation (GO PORT) finds the value of a portfolio for dates you select, and displays unrealized gains and losses. It figures the weighted value of each item, reporting gains or losses on individual securities and the total portfolio's value. You are charged $1 per report plus costs of the quotes (a nickel for historical quotes, 1.5 cents for current quotes.) Note: Later versions of the CompuServe Information Manager platforms have a Portfolio feature built in and ready to interact with the system. See CompuServe Information Manager.

- RateGram (GO RATEGRAM) lets you search for the best current rates for money market accounts, certificates of deposit, and money market mutual funds, predictions about future rates, and more. See RateGram.

- Return Analysis (GO RETURN) calculates the holding period and annual returns for as many as 30 requested securities. Securities may be entered individually or in a file containing securities. The reported returns may be sorted alphabetically by percent gain or by percent loss. Because you enter the holding period, this product is useful for analyzing historical performances of specific issues such as mutual funds in bull and bear markets. You are charged 50 cents per report plus 15 cents for each return calculated.

- Securities Screening (GO SCREEN), with which you may select a type of investment, screens the database to find securities that meet your demands. For example, if you were considering common stocks, you might search by price, earnings, dividends, risk, capitalization, recent highs and lows, exchange, and industry. Securities Screening is useful for buying into or selling short and for picking bonds with specific maturity dates and yield targets. The service is surcharged at $5 for each screen plus 25 cents for each company displayed.

Also, to reach the main CompuServe menu on this topic, enter GO INVEST-MENTS.

For other money-related features, enter GO MONEY at any prompt. See also Financial Services.

Investment databases searchable through IQuest (GO IQUEST) include ABI/INFORM, Biotechnology Investment Opportunities, Bond Buyer Fulltext, Business Week, High Yield Report, Insider Trading Monitor, International Stocks Database, Investext, Knight-Ridder/Tribune Business News, MPT Review, PTS Newsletter Database, and Trendvest Ratings. See IQuest.

Investment Management Technology can be searched through the Business Database Plus (GO BUSDB). See Business Database.

Investors Forum (GO INVFORUM) is where investors of all kinds meet to discuss their passion. The forum's libraries are filled with computer programs aimed at assisting the investor. The forum is co-administered by Harry Knutowski (76703,4214) and Mike Pietruk (76703,4346). Assisting are Larry Ettelson, Paul Hinrichs, John Yurko, Michael Shapiro, Randy Harmelink, Christopher Worth, and Sven U. Grenander.

You also may be interested in the NAIC Forum (GO NAIC), for value-oriented long-term investors who aren't concerned with day-to-day changes in market prices, but who focus on finding quality companies and buying them at good prices. For more on that, see NAIC Forum.

Iomega Corporation products are supported in the IBM PC Vendor E Forum (GO PCVENE). See IBM Computers. They also can be supported in the Macintosh C Vendor Forum (GO MACCVEN). See Apple Computers.

Iowa (news) is included in the daily Central regional reports from United Press International. See Executive News Service for details.

Also, *Business Record (Des Moines)* is searchable through the Business Database Plus (GO BUSDB). See Business Database.

IQ Technologies products are supported in the PC Vendor H Forum (GO PCVENH). See IBM Computers.

IQ testing is a subject of the Mensa Forum (GO MENSA). For more information, see Mensa.

IQuest (GO IQUEST) is a gateway to hundreds of databases from all the major vendors in the country. IQuest, a joint project by CompuServe and Telebase Systems Incorporated of Wayne, Pennsylvania, came online in 1985, allowing subscribers to link with more than 700 databases that are provided by such major vendors as Dialog, BRS, and NewsNet. With IQuest, you pay your usual CompuServe connect time and also pay for material retrieved through the gateway.

The gateway has three different approaches:

1. IQuest-I, designed for inexperienced subscribers, is menu-driven and actually helps you select an appropriate database by prompting you to (a) make selections from a series of categories listed by menus, then (b) enter your question in the form of a keyword or keywords. IQuest-I then takes you through the gateway to a relevant database, which it chooses, and automatically translates your query into a command language understood by that particular database.

2. IQuest-II, for more experienced searchers, offers a larger selection of databases. It asks you to (a) name the database you wish to search, then (b) to enter the keywords that make up your query. IQuest-II then takes over, making the call to the remote service and, again, translating your question into the database's own language.

3. SmartScan lets you make a preliminary scan of several relevant databases at one time to see which ones contain information on your search topic. It then builds a menu from which you may access specific databases.

Beginners usually choose IQuest-I, letting the system handle more of the work. The system narrows the search to a broad area of interest. The service also keeps a running tab of your charges. Generally, IQuest bills only for the searching and the information actually retrieved from a database.

Costs   There is a charge of $9 for searching and retrieving information from a database. If a search turns up no files that meet your search specifications, the charge may be only $1. Some of the databases carry an additional $2 to $75 in surcharges. These databases are identified online to alert users in advance; you are given an opportunity to back out of a search before incurring such an extra charge. Standard CompuServe communications connect-time charges also are in effect in IQuest. Additional online purchases, such as abstracts of references or full-text articles, are charged on a per-item basis.

IQuest-I uses a series of menus to zero in on a topic of interest. Each menu is more specific about the information for which you are looking, giving the system the background it needs to decide which database to access for you. Surcharges remain zero until after the actual trip through the gateway to a database (however, you are incurring the usual CompuServe connect charges during this time).

Information types   Information in IQuest is available in two forms:

1. Bibliographic, basic information about published material, such as the name of the publication, date, author, and title of the article. Many bibliographic databases also provide abstracts (brief summaries) of the cited articles, for an extra charge.

2. Full-text, the complete text of the articles you have located.

Most of the databases contain only bibliographic reference or only full-text articles. When there is a choice, IQuest asks which you prefer.

After you have made your selections on all the menus, IQuest-I is ready to determine your question with a prompt that says, "Enter your specific topic." (Type H for important examples, or B to back up). At this point, the system is looking for a keyword or keywords to describe what you are looking for. Notice, too, there are other options. You may enter:

- H for Help (which provides examples of search strategies). Some databases have their own syntax for searches, so examples are useful.
- B to back up (return to the previous menu).

H and B may be used at virtually any IQuest prompt. Two other commands are T (for "TOP") which returns you to the main IQuest menu and L (for "Leave") to log off IQuest and return to the main CompuServe system.

After verifying your keyword, IQuest-I reports the name of the database it has selected for the job and makes its way through the gateway. This could take a few minutes as IQuest automatically does the following:

1. Accesses a communications network and dials into the chosen database vendor.
2. Submits a password for admission. (Because IQuest is your representative, the password is sent from the gateway to the host computer; it isn't displayed to you.)
3. Navigates to the database it has selected.
4. Translates your query into a local language that the database understands.

After the search is finished, IQuest reports a number of "hits," that is, the number of references it has found that meet your keyword specifications.

If your destination is a bibliographic database, your $9 charge provides a list of up to ten of the most recent references. Each is displayed with a heading number along with the title of the article, the name of the author, the publication, the publication date, volume number, and usually the page number. For additional charges, you sometimes may see abstracts of selected articles ($3 apiece) and/or the next ten headlines in the haul ($9), or you may order reprints of the selected articles to be mailed to you directly for additional charges.

If your destination is a full-text service, your initial $9 provides up to the latest 15 references. For no extra charge, you may enter a heading number to view the complete text of one article. Usually for extra charges you also may order mailed reprints, display the text of other articles, or see the next 15 references from the search.

After a search, the system reports the amount of your charges so far and provides options for additional services, including the next collection of headings, another search, paper reprints of articles, and so on.

After you become familiar with IQuest-I, you might want to step up to the advanced service, IQuest-II. It is faster, since it provides fewer menus to study, and it offers access to a wider variety of databases. The difference is that you select the database you wish to search, rather than turning that responsibility over to the system. You also may request information on specific IQuest databases at the ->

prompt; just enter DIR followed by a subject, such as DIR MUSIC, to find databases devoted to a specific subject.

When you are ready, select IQuest-II and, when prompted to enter the name of the database to search, enter a name such as MAGAZINE ASAP. IQuest prompts for keywords that describe your subject, then logs on and makes the search. Incidentally, you also may enter DIR LIST at the -> to get a list of IQuest's various search areas.

Also, SmartScan is a convenient way to make a preliminary scan of several relevant databases at one time to determine which ones contain information relevant to your subject. It then lets you choose from a menu of databases from which you want to retrieve the data. To start, select the SmartScan option from the main menu. Subsequent menus narrow the topics, similar to those used with IQuest-I. The system then prompts for keywords and ultimately produces an *occurrence menu*. The "Occurrences" column shows you how many records, relevant to your keywords, may be retrieved from each database, so you know up front where the coverage is—and isn't—for your particular topic. Pressing H (for Help) retrieves database descriptions. Once you have reviewed the menu, you can retrieve references from the databases by making your selection from the menu. The system conducts a standard search, after which, if you choose, you may start a new search. The SmartScan costs $5.

Keywords With IQuest-I, IQuest-II, or SmartScan, the key to successful searching is in defining keywords. The best place to start your search strategies—in IQuest as well as with other extra-cost, keyword-searchable features—is offline. Before you log on, you can save money by giving some thought to what you want to specify at the keyword prompt. Here are some guidelines for entering IQuest keywords:

- Omit common words, like OF, THE, FOR, and AT. (Instead of "the Department of the Interior," make it DEPARTMENT INTERIOR.)

- Come up with words and phrases that are unique to your subject. For example, "convertible" is a more specific term than "automobile."

- Don't worry about capitalization. IQuest views upper- and lowercase letters the same.

- The slash (/) character is a wildcard and may be used at the end of a keyword to retrieve references to text that includes words beginning with specified letters. (COMPUT/ retrieves COMPUTER, COMPUTERS, COMPUTING, COMPUTATIONS, and so on.) The slash also may be used in the middle of words, such as PRACTI/E, to retrieve both "practice" and the British spelling, "practise."

IQuest recognizes three connectors:

1. AND to narrow your search. (APPLE AND IBM to fetch only those files that contain *both* keywords.)

2. OR to expand your search. (APPLE OR IBM retrieves files containing *either* the word "Apple" or the letters "IBM.")

3. NOT to exclude a specified topic. If you are looking for references to the country of Libya that do not deal with political violence, you might enter LIBYA NOT TERRORIS/ to collect files that mention "Libya" but do *not* also mention words that begin with "terroris," such as "terrorism" and "terrorist."

Also, you may combine (or *nest*) searches by using parentheses around groups of words you have connected with AND, OR, or NOT. (LIBYA OR SYRIA OR IRAN) AND TERRORISM retrieves files that contain a mention of at least one of the three countries *and* the word "terrorism."

Major vendors on IQuest include the following:

- BRS (Bibliographic Retrieval Service) of Latham, New York, offers some 80 databases. It was designed in the mid-1970s as a dialup service for research librarians. Since then, it has been expanded to cover science, medicine, business and finance, references, education, and humanities.

- DataSolve of London, a product of the British Broadcasting Corporation, offers summaries of world radio broadcasts from 120 countries and foreign news agencies, as well as BBC news.

- DataTimes of Oklahoma City, Oklahoma, is another newspaper service with full-text of additional papers.

- Dialog Information Services Incorporated of Palo Alto, California, provided by Knight-Ridder Company, offers more than 200 databases. Originally, it was conceived by Lockheed Corporation as a tool for NASA researchers. The databases deal with a wide range of topics from law and government to medicine and science, engineering and technology, and patents and agriculture.

- NewsNet of Bryn Mawr, Pennsylvania, brings together hundreds of newsletters from 34 industry groups, including computing, telecommunications, electronics, as well as medicine, business, education, law, social sciences, and others. Publications are daily, weekly, monthly, and quarterly.

- Questel of Washington, D.C., is a subsidiary of the French Telesystems, containing more than 40 databases, including its best-known DARC chemical files.

- SDC/Orbit of Santa Monica, California is a subsidiary of Burroughs Corporation and is considered to be the oldest modern database vendor. Brought online in 1965, it has about 80 databases, including some not found anywhere else, such as SDC, the provider of Accountant of the American Institute of CPAs; MONITOR, an index of The Christian Science Monitor newspaper; and SPORT, covering sports literature.

In addition, IQuest has added Datastar of Switzerland, G. Cam Serveur of Paris, and QL Systems of Kingston, Ontario, Canada.

In recent years, Telebase Systems has brought online other reference databases that work essentially like IQuest. For a summary, see Telebase.

Also, the CompuServe Help Forum (GO HELPFORUM) has free IQuest directories available for downloading. Updated monthly, these directories provide useful information such as database numbers and update frequencies for all of IQuest's more than 850 databases. To get the free directories, see the Reference Help library and download IQSUBS.TXT (for subject listing) and IQDESC.TXT (for the database descriptions).

Databases searchable through IQuest include the following:

ABC Europe
ABI/INFORM
Abstracts of Tropical
    Agriculture
Academic Index
Access Reports/
    Freedom of Infor-
    mation
ADIS DrugNews
Advanced Wireless
    Communications
AECO
Affiliations
AFPE
Africa News Online
Ageline
AGRA
Agribusiness U.S.A.
Agricola
Agris International
AIDS Articles from
    Comprehensive
    Core Medical
    Library
AIDS Knowledge Base
AIDS Weekly
Air Safety Week
    Newsletter
Air Safety Week
    Accident/Incident
    Log
Air Safety Week
    Regulatory Log
Air/Water Pollution
    Report
Airline Financial News

Airports
Allied & Alternative
    Medicine
Aluminium Industry
    Abstracts
America: History and
    Life
American Banker
    Fulltext
American Business
    Directory
American Business 20
    Plus Companies
American Libraries
American Marketplace
American Metal
    Market
American Statistics
    Index
Analytical Abstracts
Antitrust FOIA Log
API Energy Business
    News Index
Apilit
Applied Genetics
    News
Applied Science and
    Technology Index
APS Diplomat
APS Review
AQUALINE
Aquatic Sciences and
    Fisheries Abstracts
Arab Information Bank
Architecture Database
Artbibliographies
    Modern

Art Index
Arts & Humanities
    Search
Art Literature Interna-
    tional
Asahi News Service
Asbestos & Lead
    Abatement Report
Asian Economic News
Asia-Pacific
Asian Political News
Audio Week
Audiotex Update
Automated Medical
    Payments News
Avery Architecture
    Index
Aviation Week and
    Space Technology
A-V Online

Backstage
Baltic Business Report
Bank Automation
    News
Battery & EV Tech-
    nology
BBC Summary of
    World Broadcasts
BDI German Industry
Biobusiness
Biocommerce Ab-
    stracts
Biography Index
Biography Master
    Index

Biological & Agricultural Index
Biosis Previews
Biotech Business
Biotechnology Investment Opportunities
Biotechnology Newswatch
BMD Monitor
BNA Daily News
BODACC
Bond Buyer Fulltext
Book Review Digest
Book Review Index
Books in Print
Boomer Report
Bowker Biographical Directory
Bowker's International Serials Database
Bowne Digest—Corp/ SEC Article Abstracts
British Medical Association's Press Cuttings
Broadcasting
Business America
Business and the Environment
Business Computer
Business Dateline
Business Opportunities
Business Periodicals Index
Business Publisher
Business Software Database
Business Travel News
Business Week
Businesswire
Buyer's Guide to Micro Software (SOFT)

CAB Abstracts
CAD/CAM Update
California Public Finance
Campaign
Canadian Business and Current Affairs
Cancer Research Weekly
Cancerlit
Cancorp
Card News
Career Placement Registry
CA Search
CASE Strategies
CD Computing News
CD-ROM Databases
Celex (computerized Documentation System on Ec Law)
Cellular Sales and Marketing
Cendata
Chain Store Age
Chapman and Hall Chemical Database
Chemical Abstracts Source Index
Chemical Business Newsbase
Chemical Engineering
Chemical Engineering & Biotechnology Abstracts (CEBA)
Chemical Industry Notes
Chemical Monitor
Chemical Safety Newsbase
Chemname
Chemplant Plus
Chemsearch

Child Abuse and Neglect and Family Violence
Christian Science Monitor
Chronicle of Latin American Economic Affairs
Churchnews International
CIM
Claims/Citation
Compendex Plus
Comprehensive Core Medical Library
Computer ASAP
Computer Database
Computer Decisions
Computergram International
Computerized Processes
Computer News Fulltext
Computer Protocols
Computer Reseller News
Conference Papers Index
Congressional Activities
Congressional Information Service (CIS)
Congressional Record Abstracts
Connect Times
Construction Claims Citator
Consumer Electronics
Consumer Reports
Corporate & Poor's Daily News
Corporate Affiliations

Corporate EFT
Report
Corporate Giving
Watch
Corptech
Credit Card News
Creditreform
Credit Risk Manage-
ment Report
Criminal Justice
Periodical Index
Cuadra Directory of
Online Databases
Current Biotechnology
Abstracts
Current Research
Information/USDA

D&B—Asia-Pacific
Dun's Market
Identifiers
D&B—Canadian
Dun's Market
Identifiers
D&B—Donnelley
Demographics
D&B—Dun's Elec-
tronic Business
Directory
D&B—Dun's Market
Identifiers
D&B—European
Dun's Market
Identifiers
D&B—France
D&B—International
Dun's Market
Identifiers
D&B—Million Dollar
Directory
Daily and Sunday
Telegraph
Data Channels
Data Communications

Database
Datamation
DAUGAZ
Defense & Aerospace
Electronics
Defense Daily
Defense Marketing
International
Department of Health
and Social Security
Derwent World
Patents Index
Diogenes
Disclosure Database
Disclosure/Spectrum
Ownership
Discount Store News
Dissertation Abstracts
Online
DMS/FI Contract
Awards
Druginfo and Alcohol
Use and Abuse
Drug Information
Fulltext
Drug Topics

East European Moni-
tor—The Chemical
Industry Database
(2768)
East Eastern Europe
Finance
Eastern European &
Soviet Telecom
Report
EBIS—Employee
Benefits Infosource
ECOMINE
Econbase
Economic Literature
Index
Economist
EDF-DOC

Edge On and About
AT&T
Edge: Work Group
Computing Report
EDI News
Editors Only
EDOC
Education Daily
Educational Resources
Information Center
Education Index
EFT Report
Electric and Magnetic
Field Keeptrack
Electric Power
Database
Electronic Buyer's
News
Electronic Design
Electronic Engineer-
ing Times
Electronic Materials
Technology News
Electronic Messaging
News
Electronic News
Electronic Services
Update
L'Elite et les Institu-
tions Sovietiques
(evenements)
Embase
Encyclopedia of
Associations
Energy Conservation
News
Energyline
Energy User News
Engineered Materials
Abstracts
Engineering News
Record
Enhanced Energy
Recovery News

Entertainment Weekly
Enviroline
Environmental
  Bibliography
Environmental
  Compliance Update
EPAT

FINDEX: Directory
  of Market Research
  Reports
FINIS: Financial
  Industry Informa-
  tion Service
Flightline
FLUIDEX

Guardian, GUI
  Program News

Harvard Business
  Review Online
Hazardline
Hazardous Materials
  Intelligence Report
Hazardous Materials
  Transportation
Hazardous Waste
  News
Hazmat Transport
  News
HDTV Report
Health Business
Health Care Competi-
  tion Week
Health Care Reform
  Week
Health Devices Alerts
Health Grants and
  Contracts Weekly
Health Legislation and
  Regulation
Health News Daily
Health Periodicals
  Database

Health Planning and
  Administration
Health and
  Psychosocial
  Instruments
Helicopter News
Heller Report on
  Educational Tech-
  nology & Telecom-
  munications
HFD—The Weekly
  Home Furnishings
  Newspaper
High Fidelity
High Tech Ceramics
  News
High Tech Separa-
  tions News
High Yield Report
Historical Abstracts
Holy Bible

Industries in Transi-
  tion
Industry Week
INFOCHECK
Infomat International
  Business
Information & Inter-
  active Svcs. Report
Information Networks
Information Report
Information Science
  Abstracts
Information Week
Innovator's Digest
Inpadoc: Patents
Inpanew: Patents
Inside Market Data
Insider Trading
  Monitor
INSPEC
Insurance Periodicals
  Index

Intelligent Software
  Strategies
Inter Press Service
  International News
International Business
  Climate Indicators
International Informa-
  tion Report
International News
International Pharma-
  ceutical Abstracts
International Reports
International Stocks
  Database
Investext
Iron Age
ISDN News
Ismec: Mechanical
  Engineering
  Abstracts
Item Processing
  Report

Janssen
Japan Computer
  Industry Scan
Japan Consumer
  Electronics Scan
Japan Economic
  Newswire Plus
Japan Energy Scan
Japan Policy and
  Politics
Japan Science Scan
Japan Semiconductor
  Scan
Japan Telecommuni-
  cations Scan
Japan Transportation
  Scan
Japan Weekly Monitor
Japio
Jordans Registered
  Companies

Keesing's Record of World Events
Kirk-Othmer Encyclopedia of Chemical Technology
Knight-Ridder/ Tribune Business News
Kompass Europe
Kompass U.K.
KOSMET
Kreditcchutzverband von 1870
Kyodo News Service

Labordoc
Laborlaw I
Laborlaw II
Lancet
Land Mobile Radio News
LAN Product News
Law Office Technology Review
Lawyers' Micro Users Group Newsletter
LC MARC Books File
Legal Resource Index
Liability Week
Library and Information Science Abstracts
Library Literature
Life
Life Sciences Collection
Linguistics & Language Behavior Abstracts
Liquidation Alert
Lloyd's List
Logos
Long Term Care Management

Lutheran News Service

M & A Filings
Machine Design
Magazine ASAP
Magazine Index
Magill's Survey of Cinema
Managed Care Law Outlook
Managed Care Outlook
Management Contents
Management Matters
Manufacturing Automation
Marketing
Marketing Surveys Index
Market Research Reports from MSI
Marquis Who's Who
Materials Business File
Mathsci
McCarthy Information Company & Industry Press News & Comment
McGraw-Hill Publications Online
Media General Plus
Media Week
Medical Outcomes & Guidelines Alert
Medical Utilization Review
Medical Waste News
Medicine & Health
Mediconf
Medline
Meeting
Membrane & Separation Technology News

Mental Health Abstracts
Mental Measurements Yearbook
Merck Index Online
Metadex
Metals Datafile
Meteorological and Geoastrophysical Abstracts
Microcomputer Index
Microcell Report
Microcomputer Resources
Microcomputer Software Guide
Microsearch
Mid-East Business Digest
Military Robotics 1989 Sourcebook
Military Space
Mobile Data Report
Mobile Phone News
Mobile Satellite News
Mobile Satellite Reports
Modem Users News
Money
Moody's Corporate News International
Moody's Corporate News U.S.
Moody's Corporate Profiles
Morgan Report on Directory Publishing
Mpt Review
Multimedia Monitor
Multimedia Publisher
Music Literature International

National Newspaper
  Index
National Technical
  Information Service
Nation's Business
Nation's Restaurant
  News
Navy News and
  Undersea Technol-
  ogy
NCJRS
Network Management
  Systems & Strate-
  gies
Networks Update
New England Journal
  of Medicine
New Era: Japan
News From France
Newsbytes News
  Network
Newsearch
NewsNet Action
  Letter
Newspaper & Periodi-
  cal Abstracts
Newspaper Abstracts
New York Times
NIST Update
Noriane
Northern Ireland
  News Service
Nuclear Waste News
Nucleonics Week
Nursing & Allied
  Health

Occupational Safety
  and Health
Oceanic Abstracts
Oil Spill Intelligence
  Report
Oil Spill U.S. Law
  Report

Online Libraries and
  Microcomputers
Online Newsletter
Online Products News
OPEN: OSI Product
  and Equipment
  News
Open Systems Com-
  munication
Open Systems Today
Optical Materials &
  Engineering News

Packaging Science and
  Technology
  Abstracts
PAIS International
Paperchem
PASCAL
Patdata
Patent Abstracts of
  China
PC Business Products
PC Magazine
PC Week
People Weekly
Performance Materials
Periscope—Daily
  Defense News
  Capsules
Perspectives
Peterson's College
  Database
Peterson's Gradline
Pharmaceutical News
  Index
Pharmline
Philosopher's Index
Photobulletin
Photoletter
Photomarket
Physician Data Query
PIERS Exports
PIRA Abstracts

Platt's Oilgram News
Platt's Oilgram Price
  Report
Political Finance &
  Lobby Reporter
Pollution Abstracts
POS News
Power Source
PR Newswire
PR Week
Product Safety Letter
PSN News
PsycINFO
PTS Aerospace/
  Defence Markets
  and Technology
PTS F&S Indexes
  (1980 to present)
PTS International
  Forecasts
PTS MARS
PTS New Product
  Announcements
PTS Newsletter
  Database
PTS PROMT
PTS U.S. Forecasts
PTS U.S. Time Series
Public Broadcasting
  Report

Questa10
Questa7
Questa8
Questa9
Quotations Database

Rapra Abstracts
Rategram Online
Readers' Guide
  Abstracts
Rehabdata
Religion Index
Remarc

Report on AT&T
Report on Defense
Plant Wastes
Report on IBM
Report on Literacy
Programs
Restaurant Business
Magazine
Reuters
RNS Daily News
Reports
Rsinews
Russia/Cis Intelligence
Report
Russia Express
Russia Express Con-
tracts

Satellite News
Satellite Week
SciSearch
Scrip—Current News
Scrip—Daily News
Scrip—Retrospective
Searchable Physics
Information
Notices
Securities Week
Security Intelligence
Report
Semiconductor
Industry & Business
Survey
Sensor Business Digest
Small Business Tax
Review
Smoking and Health
SMT Trends
Social Sciences Index
Social SciSearch
Social Work Abstracts
Sociological Abstracts
Solid Waste Report
Sourcemex: Economic
News on Mexico

Space Business News
Space Calendar
Space Daily
Space Exploration
Technology
Space Station News
Spearhead
Spicer's Centre For
Europe
Sport
Stamm's Xsu Business
Standard & Poor's
Register
Standards & Specifica-
tions
State Telephone
Regulation Report
Stereo Review
Super Marketing
Superfund Week
Supermarket News

Tass
Tax Notes Today
Technical Computing
Telecom Data Net-
works
Telecommunications
Reports
Telecommunications
Week
Telefirm Directory of
French Companies
Telephone Engineer
and Management
Telephone Week
Tele-Service News
Television Digest
Telocator Bulletin
Terry Shannon on
DEC
Textile Technology
Digest
Textline Global News

The Spectrum Report
Thomas New Indus-
trial Products
Thomas Register
Online
Thrift Accountant
Time International
Time Magazine
Time Publications
Times and Sunday
Times
Tokyo Financial Wire
Tour & Travel News
Toxic Materials News
TOXLINE
Trade and Industry
ASAP
Trade and Industry
Index
Trademarkscan
Trading Systems
Technology
Transin
Transportation
Research Informa-
tion Service
Trendvest Ratings
TRW Business Credit
Database
TSCA Chemical
Substances Inven-
tory
Turing Institute
Bibliographic
Database

UK News
U.S. Classification
U.S. Copyrights
U.S. News and World
Report
U.S. Oil Week
U.S. Patent Office
U.S. Political Science
Documents

USA Today
Unlisted Drugs
UPI News
Urbamet
Utility Reporter—
    Fuels, Energy &
    Power

Video Marketing
    News
Video Technology
    Newsletter
Video Week
Voice Technology
    News

Wall Street Journal
Washington Beverage
    Insight
Washington Post
Washington Trade
    Daily
Waste Treatment
    Technology News
Waternet
Water Resources
    Abstracts
Week in Germany
Weekly of Business
    Aviation
West Europe Intelli-
    gence Report

Who Supplies What?
Windows Magazine
Womens Wear Daily
World Environment
    Outlook
World Surface Coat-
    ings Abstracts
World Textiles
Worldwide Databases
Worldwide Energy
Worldwide Telecom
Worldwide Videotex
    Update

Zoological Record
    Online

IQuest Business Management InfoCenter (GO IQBUSINESS), a Telebase Systems Incorporated gateway, accesses specific information from databases covering management research, marketing studies, company ownership, mergers and acquisitions, and so on. See Business Management.

IQuest Medical InfoCenter (GO IQMEDICINE) is a Telebase Systems Incorporated gateway to information from and about the medical profession. For details, see Medical InfoCenter.

Iraq is a topic of the Global Crisis Forum (GO CRISIS). See Global Crisis.

Ireland is the topic of Northern Ireland News Service (database) and can be searched through IQuest. See IQuest.

Irish/Celtic heritage is a topic of the Genealogy Forum (GO ROOTS). See Genealogy.

iRMX **(Intel software)** is supported in the Intel forums. For details, see Intel Corp.

Iron Age **(database)** may be searched through the IQuest gateway. See IQuest. See also Metal Industry.

ISD Marketing products are supported in the Atari Vendors Forum (GO ATARIVEN). See Atari Computers.

ISDN News **(database)** may be searched through the IQuest gateway. See IQuest. The resource also can be searched through the Business Database Plus (GO BUSDB). See Business Database.

ISICAD software is supported in the CADD/CAM/CAE Vendor Forum (GO CADDVEN). See CAD/CAM.

Islam is a topic of the Religion Forum (GO RELIGION). See Religion.

Island of Kesmai (game) (GO ISLAND) invites you to search catacombs for riches. You can play the game alone or with others for a group adventure. Veteran explorers on the island say it is best to order the printed Island of Kesmai manual (GO ORDER). When you start the game, the system prompts you to create a character and give it a gender, country of origin, name, and character class (that is, a fighter, martial artist, thief, wizard, or a "thaumaturge"—a magically enhanced fighter with a few wicked spells at his or her command). The system then tells you your character's strength, dexterity, intelligence, wisdom, constitution, and charisma. Some of these characteristics are altered by experience and by spells. Part of the fun is finding that out on your own. You then are set down on a wood dock at the edge of town. You begin your journey by entering a direction (N for North, E for East, etc.). The game is intended for those age 12 and up.

    Incidentally, you might be interested in using a graphics interface with the game. Most of the programs are available in Library 4 ("Island of Kesmai") of the Multi-Player Games Forum (GO MPGAMES). Some of the major programs available there at this writing were GKTerm for IBM and compatibles, KTerm for Apple Macintosh systems, Aterm for Amiga computers. Playing the game via these programs automatically converts the system's rather pedestrian ASCII symbols into easy-to-read graphic displays.

    To find other Kesmai enthusiasts, visit the Multi-Player Games Forum (GO MPFORUM). For information on other games, see Games.

Israel Business and **Israel High-Tech Report** can be searched through the Business Database Plus (GO BUSDB). See Business Database.

Issue and Symbol Lookup (GO SYMBOLS) is a financial service that helps you determine what securities and indexes are covered in other securities areas and access the symbols needed to make efficient use of most databases. See Stock Symbols, Lookup.

Issues Forum (GO ISSUESFORUM) is intended for discussing current issues in the news. Politics, handicapped issues, human rights, and more are all welcome topics. And, as new social issues arise, they are often given their own topic area in this forum. Georgia Griffith (76703,266) is the forum administrator. Assisting are Elvira Casal, David Bush, Ran Talbott, Keir Jones, Kevin H. E. Finch, Scott Place, Ted Markley, Bob Sirianni, Alex Krislov, David Tucker, Bev Sykes, and Frances Bannowsky.

ISVS products are supported in the PC Vendor G Forum (GO PCVENG). See IBM.

Italian issues are discussed in the European Forum (GO EURFORUM). See European Forum.

Item Processing Report (database) may be searched through the IQuest gateway. See IQuest.

It's Legal (software) is supported in the Parsons Technology Forum (GO PTFORUM). See Parsons Technology.

IYM Software Review is a sponsor of the General Computing Forum (GO GENCOM). See General Computing.

J

Jacksonville Business Journal (magazine) can be searched through the Business Database Plus (GO BUSDB). See Business Database.

Jacobs, Lance (76702,1527) is a sysop of the Symantec/Norton Utilities Forum (GO NORUTL). See Symantec Software.

JAMA—The Journal of the American Medical Association (magazine) can be searched through the Business Database Plus (GO BUSDB). See Business Database.

Janssen (database) may be searched through the IQuest gateway. See IQuest.

Japanese Aviation News: Wing (database) may be searched through the IQuest gateway. See IQuest. The resource also can be searched through the Business Database Plus (GO BUSDB). See Business Database.

Japanese news and business reports are the specialty of Kyodo, a Japanese news service that is searchable through Comtex Scientific Inc.'s NewsGrid database. For details, see NewsGrid.

 Also, from IQuest, these databases are searchable; Asahi News Service, Asian Economic News, Japan Computer Industry Scan, Japan Consumer Electronics Scan, Japan Economic Newswire Plus, Japan Energy Scan, Japan Policy and Politics, Japan Science Scan, Japan Semiconductor Scan, Japan Telecommunications Scan, Japan Transportation Scan, Japan Weekly Monitor, Japio (patents), Kyodo News Service, and Tokyo Financial Wire. See IQuest.

 Also, the related resources you can search through the Business Database Plus (GO BUSDB) include:

 Asian Economic News, Asian Political News, IDC Japan Report, COMLINE: Transportation Industry of Japan, Japan Computer Industry Scan, Japan Consumer Electronics Scan, Japan Energy Scan, Japan Policy & Politics, Japan Report Biotechnology, Japan Re-

port Information Technology, Japan Report Telecommunications, Japan Science Scan, Japan Semiconductor Scan, Japan Transportation Scan, Japan Weekly Monitor, Japanese Government Weekly, Japanese New Materials Advanced Alloys & Metals, Japanese New Materials Advanced Plastics, Japanese New Materials Electronic Materials, Japanese New Materials High-Performance Ceramics, as well as *Cosmetics & Toiletries & Household Products Marketing News in Japan, New Era Japan, New Food Products in Japan, New Materials Japan,* and *IBM Japan Weekly.*

See Business Database. For other related databases, see Comline and see Asian news.

Japan Forum (GO JAPAN) offers discussion and information on topics ranging from Japanese business and industry to food and sports. You can find tips on where to eat, what to order, and unique things to do. They also discuss politics, law, sports, entertainment, education, hardware and software issues, and more. Japanese nationals can ask questions in Romaji and get easy-to-understand answers.

Libraries contain information on such things as Japan's commercial ties with Russia, rules for sumo pool, and how to access the Japanese-language information service NIFTY-Serve. Download freeware games and descriptions of aikido, judo, karate, and other sports or compare dollars to yen by reading files on the Japanese economy. The forum is operated by Ken Love (72662,273) (NIFTY: SHB00363), a professional photographer who usually is in four or five times a year on various commercial photo assignments or public relations/marketing assignments. He and a partner have an office in Tokyo and an electronic mall shop on NIFTY-Serve where he has been an active user almost since it started in 1986. He is assisted in the Japan Forum by Yukio Shimoda, Koichi Mori, Hideki Michihata, James Reese, Hiko Fukawa, and Gordon Housworth.

Japanimation is discussed in the Comics/Animation Forum (GO COMICS). See Comics.

Jasik Designs products are supported in the Mac B Vendor Forum (GO MACBVEN). See Apple Computers.

Javelin Software: The Javelin/EXPRESS Forum (Go IRIFORUM) is operated by the staff of Information Resources Incorporated, and supports Javelin and the Express family of products on this forum.

The sysops are Mark Moormans (76702,1547), Beth-Anne Mathews (76702,535), Chris Flockton (76702,1546), and Craig Schiro (76703,4402). The service is geared toward technical support, training, and other online help in taking advantage of Javelin's analytical capabilities as well as using Express products.

Jazz is a subject of the Music/Performing Arts Forum (GO MUSICARTS). See Music.

JC Penney Online Catalog (GO JCP) is a store in the Electronic Mall (GO MALL) that offers apparel, electronics, and merchandise. See Electronic Mall.

JDR Microdevices (GO JDR) is a store in the Electronic Mall (GO MALL) that offers computer products. See Electronic Mall.

Jensen-Jones products are supported in the Windows 3rd-Party Forum A (GO WINAPA). See Microsoft Software.

Jeppesen DUAT is an aviation-related gateway that provides access to an FAA weather database. See Aviation.

Jewelers Circular Keystone **(magazine)** can be searched through the Business Database Plus (GO BUSDB). See Business Database.

Jewelry making is one of the topics discussed in the Crafts Forum (GO CRAFTS). See Crafts.

JFK Assassination Research Forum (GO JFK) invites visitors to share information and discuss theories surrounding the 1963 assassination of U.S. President John F. Kennedy. Regulars talk about political motivations and potential cover-ups and download literature and court transcripts of proceedings surrounding the assassination. The sysops are Thom Hartmann (76702,765) and Jim Hart (76702,646).

Jill of the Jungle **(game software)** is distributed and supported in Epic Online (GO EPIC). See Epic.

JLCooper Electronics **(music software)** is supported in the MIDI A Vendor Forum (GO MIDIAVEN). See Music.

Job hunting is facilitated in several online services. For details, see Employment.

Job number is a user's individual session number while logged onto a CompuServe computer. In some online features, such as the CB Simulator and related real-time conferencing, job numbers can be used with some commands.

JobSearch, E-Span (GO ESPAN) is an employment advertising network that enables organizations to reach more than a million PC-literate professional, technical, and managerial candidates nationwide. See E-Span.

Job training is offered through Careertrack (GO CT) and is a service provided through the Electronic Mall (GO MALL). Also, Macmillan Publishing (GO MMP) offers career development and training books. See Electronic Mall.

Johnson, Andy (75300,1504) is sysop of the UK Computing Forum (GO UKCOMP). See UK Computing. He also is a sysop in the UK Forum (GO UKFORUM). See UK Forum.

Johnson, Lisa (75300,2751) manages the CompuAdd Forum (GO COMPUADD). See CompuAdd.

Johnson, Steve   (76702,1216) is sysop in the Crosstalk Forum (GO TALK). See Crosstalk.

Joins, Keith   (76702,375) is the sysop of the CompuServe Help Forum (GO HELPFORUM). See Help.

Jokes   are collected in the "Comics and Humor" section (Library 8) of the Literary Forum (GO LITFORUM). See Literature. Also, puns, jokes and puzzles are a topic in the Mensa Forum (GO MENSA). See Mensa.

Jones, Mitt   (72241,35) is one of the editors and writers associated with the PC Magazine forums. See PC Magazine.

Journal (software) is supported in Windows 3rd-Party Forum B (GO WINAPB). See Microsoft Software.

Journalism Forum   (GO JFORUM) was established in 1985 by Jim Cameron (76703,3010), who is president of Cameron Communications, Inc., a New York City consulting firm specializing in radio news and program syndication. He also is the anchorman several days a week for newscasts on the United Stations (RKO) Networks. The forum is designed to serve professional journalists, those in related fields, and students considering careers in the profession. Assisting Cameron are Dan Hamilton, Tony Russomanno, Dave Cohen, Lamar Graham, Don Fitzpatrick, John Toon, Mark Loundy, Garry Fairbairn, and Roger Johnson.

> The forum also introduced in 1993 what it touted as the first "truly electronic" newspaper. The 5th annual Electronic Photojournalism of the NPPA produced the online newspaper in PDF format, which the forum made available for viewing (using the Acrobat software). For background, read the LIB12 file ET5PDF.TXT and download any of the dozen or so PDF files in that LIB for viewing.

> Also featured in the forum is MedNews, a searchable database that offers news releases on medical research from 30 universities and nonprofit research institutions, including Columbia University College of Physicians & Surgeons, Duke University Medical Center, Johns Hopkins Medical Institutions, Stanford University Medical Center, Yale University School of Medicine, as well as the American Medical Association, the National Cancer Institute, the National Institutes of Health, and more.

> See also News, Newspaper Library, Broadcasters, and Television.

Journalist (software) is supported in the Windows 3rd-Party Forum (GO WINAPD). See Microsoft Software.

Jovian Inc.   products are supported in the Graphics A Vendor Forum (GO JOVIAN). See Graphics.

JP Software   products are supported in the IBM PC Vendor B Forum (GO PCVENB). See IBM Computers.

Judaism   is regularly discussed in the Religion Forum (GO RELIGION). See Religion.

Juge, Ed   (70007,1365) is the sysop of the Recreational Vehicle Forum (GO RVFORUM). See Recreational Vehicle.

Junk Bond Reporter   can be searched through the Business Database Plus (GO BUSDB). See Business Database.

Just Enough Pascal   (**software**) is supported in the Symantec Forum (Go SYMANTEC). See Symantec Software.

Justice Department and the FBI   are discussed in the White House Forum (GO WHITEHOUSE). See White House.

Justice Records   (GO JR) is a store in the Electronic Mall (GO MALL) that specializes in R&B/jazz artists. See Electronic Mall.

Just-In-Time & Quick Response News   can be searched through the Business Database Plus (GO BUSDB). See Business Database.

JustWrite   (**software**) is supported in the Symantec Forums (GO SYMANTEC). See Symantec.

K

Kamm, David (76711,1031) is the sysop of the Ultimedia software forums. See Ultimedia.

Kansas (news) is covered in the Wichita Eagle-Beacon, searchable through Telebase System's News Source USA (GO NEWSUSA). See News Source.

Also:

- Selected reports from Kansas are included in the Southwest regional reports from United Press International. See Executive News Service.

- *Corporate Report—Kansas City* and *The Kansas City Business Journal* can be searched through the Business Database Plus (GO BUSDB). See Business Database.

Kansas City (news) is covered in *Corporate Report—Kansas City* and *The Kansas City Business Journal*, which can be searched through the Business Database Plus (GO BUSDB). See Business Database.

Kaputa, Bob (76701,300) is sysop in the Aviation Forum (GO AVSIG). See Aviation.

Karow, Dave (72662,70) is the sysop of the Gupta Forum (GO GUPTAFORUM). See Gupta.

Kaseworks (software products), including the Case:W software, are supported in Windows 3rd-Party Forum B (GO WINAPB). See Microsoft Software.

Kato, Noriyoshi (76711,715) is sysop of the IBM Thinkpad Forum (GO THINKPAD) and the IBM Power PC Forum (GO POWERPC). See IBM Computers.

Katt, Spencer F., the catty columnist of *PC Week*, is online (GO ZNT:PCWEEK). See also *PC Week* and see Ziffnet.2.

Katz, Joseph (76703,662) is sysop of Students' Forum (GO STUDENTS). See Students. He also is manager of the Zenith Data Systems Forum (GO ZENITH) and the Symantec Fifth Generation Systems Forum (GO SYMFGS). For details, see Zenith and Symantec.

Kaypro computers are among those supported in the Computer Club Forum (GO CLUB). See Computer Club. Also of possible interest is the CP/M Users Group Forum (GO CPMFORUM). See Programmers Support.

KEDIT (software) is supported in the PC Vendor A Forum (GO PCVENA). See IBM Computers.

Keesing's Record of World Events (database) may be searched through the IQuest gateway. See IQuest.

Kenfield, Dick (76702,1560) is the sysop of the NAIC Forum (GO NAIC), a financial forum. See NAIC.

Kennedy, John F. is the topic of the JFK Assassination Research Forum (GO JFK). See JFK.

Kentucky (news) is covered in the Cincinnati/Kentucky Post and the Lexington Herald-Leader, both searchable through Telebase System's News Source USA (GO NEWSUSA). See News Source.
   Also:

- Selected reports from Kentucky are included in the Mid-Atlantic regional reports from United Press International. See Executive News Service.
- *Business First—Louisville* magazine can be searched through the Business Database Plus (GO BUSDB). See Business Database.

Kermit is a binary protocol supported by CompuServe for sending and receiving files in forums, in electronic mail, and so on. See Files, Transfer.

Kesmai, Island of (game) (GO ISLAND) is an adventure game that challenges you to search catacombs for riches. See Island of Kesmai.

Keuffel, Warren (76702,525) is the sysop of CASE DCI Forum (GO CASEFORUM). See CASE.

Keywords are the search words or phrases for which you are prompted in order to search a library or database. Many major resources use keywords, including Academic American Encyclopedia, American Heritage Dictionary, Computer Database Plus, Business Database Plus, Health Data Plus, IQuest, the Magazine Database Plus, the Newpaper Library, the Knowledge Index, and others. Entries on those features provide specific guidelines to keywords. In addition, here are some general tips for planning a search:

1. Have alternate keywords in mind. If you can't find an entry under FILMS, try MOVIES, CINEMA, or MOTION PICTURES.

2. Include in your plans some broad categorical terms. The resource may have no entry for BALD EAGLE, but information about the bird might be found under EAGLE.

3. If in doubt about spelling, enter only as much of the word as you are sure of. If you enter BRZ, the service finds BRZEZINSKI.

4. Check the spelling before going online. A misspelled keyword is the most common reason for failure to find entries.

Kidasa (**software products**) are supported in Windows 3rd-Party Forum B (GO WINAPB). See Microsoft Software.

Kirk-Othmer Online can be searched through the Knowledge Index (GO KI). See Knowledge Index.

Kingston Technology products are supported in the PC Vendor I Forum (GO PCVENI). See IBM Computers.

Kinsey Report, a syndicated newspaper column by Dr. June M. Reinisch, is a regular feature of the Human Sexuality Information and Advisory Service (GO HSX). See Sex.

Kinsman, Chris (76701,154) is the sysop of the Cobb Applications Forum (GO ZNT:COBBAPP) and the Cobb Group Programming Forum (ZNT:COBBPROG). See Cobb Group Forums.

Kiplinger's Personal Finance Magazine (**magazine**) can be searched in the Magazine Database Plus (GO MDP). See Magazine Database.

Knight, Betty (76703,4037) administers the Seniors Forum (GO SENIORS). See Senior citizens. She also is associated with the Commodore Arts and Games Forum (GO CBMART), serving a variety of Commodore 8-bit machines. See Commodore computers. She also is a sysop of the Practice Forum (GO PRACTICE). For more on that, see Practice.

Knight-Ridder/Tribune Business News (**database**) may be searched through the IQuest gateway. See IQuest.

Knights of the Sky (**modem game**) is supported in the Modem-to-Modem Gaming Lobby (GO MTMLOBBY). See Modem-to-Modem Games.

Knisley, Jonathan (72662,1234) is sysop of the Republican Forum (GO REPUBLICAN). See Republican.

Knitting is one of the topics discussed in the Crafts Forum (GO CRAFTS). See Crafts.

Knowledge Garden Incorporated (**software**) is supported in Windows 3rd-Party Forum B (GO WINAPB). See Microsoft Software.

Knowledge Index (GO KI), offered by Dialog Information Services Inc., enables you to search for more than 100 popular full-text and bibliographic databases. The surcharged service promises affordable reference database searching of Dialog databases during evenings and weekends. Knowledge Index includes databases from more than 50,000 magazines and journals covering all areas of interest, from agriculture to general reference to the social sciences and the arts. The references include more than 4,000 engineering and technical articles and over 720 law journals published worldwide. The system has both menu-based and command-driven options. Three types of databases are supplied:

1. Bibliographic databases with complete reference information for an article in a publication, including title, author, publication date, and pages.

2. Full-text databases which contain the complete text of an article

3. Directory databases which contain the complete text of entries

The service provides both menu- and command-driven search options with online instructions for both.

At this writing, the database is surcharged at $24 per hour and is available only in evening hours (6 p.m. to 5 a.m. local time).

Databases searchable through Knowledge Index include:

ABI/INFORM
Academic Index
Ageline
AGRICOLA
The Agrochemicals
    Handbook
AIDSline
Akron Beacon Journal
American History and
    Life
Analytical Abstracts
Arizona Republic/
    Phoenix Gazette
Art Bibliographies
    Modern
Art Literature International (RILA)
Atlanta Journal/Atlanta
    Constitution
A-V Online
Baltimore Sun
Bible (King James
    Version)

BNA Daily News
Books In Print
Boston Globe
Business Software
    Database
Businesswire
CAB Abstracts 1984–
    present
CAB Abstracts 1972–
    1983
Canadian Business and
    Current Affairs
Cancerlit
Chapman and Hall
    Chemical Database
Charlotte Observer
Chemical Business
    Newsbase
Chemical Engineering
    and Biotechnology
    Abstracts
Chicago Tribune

Christian Science
    Monitor
Columbus Dispatch
Computer Database
Computer News
    Fulltext
Consumer Drug
    Information Fulltext
Consumer Reports
Current Biotechnolgy
    Abstracts
Current Digest of the
    Soviet Press
Daily News of Los
    Angeles
Detroit Free Press
Dissertation Abstracts
    Online
Drug Information
    Fulltext
Economic Literature
    Index
EICOMPENDEX*PLUS

Embase
ERIC
Eventline
Everyman's
   Encyclopaedia
Food Science and
   Technology
   Abstracts
GPO Publications
   Reference File
Harvard Business
   Review
Health Planning and
   Administration
Historical Abstracts
ICC British Company
   Directory
INSPEC
International Pharma-
   ceutical Abstracts
Kirk-Othmer Online
Legal Resource Index
Life Sciences Collec-
   tion
Linguistics & Lan-
   guage Behavior
   Abstracts
Los Angeles Times
Magazine Index
Magill's Survey of
   Cinema
Marquis Who's Who
MATHSCI
MEDLINE
Mental Health Ab-
   stracts

Merck Index Online
Miami Herald
Micro Software
   Directory (SOFT)
Microcomputer Index
Microcomputer
   Software Guide
National Newspaper
   Index
Newsday and New
   York Newsday
Newsearch
NTIS
Nursing and Allied
   Health
Oregonian
Orlando Sentinel
PAIS International
Palm Beach Post
Peterson's College
   Database
Peterson's Gradline
Philadelphia Inquirer
Philosopher's Index
Pittsburgh Press
Pollution Abstracts
PR Newswire
PsycINFO
Public Opinion Online
   (POLL)
Quotations Database
Religion Index
Richmond News
   Leader/Richmond
   Times Dispatch

Rocky Mountain News
Sacramento Bee
St. Louis Post-
   Dispatch
St. Paul Pioneer Press
San Francisco
   Chronicle
San Jose Mercury
   News
Seattle Times
Smoking and Health
Sociological Abstracts
SPORT
Standard & Poor's
   Corporate Descrip-
   tions
Standard & Poor's
   News
Standard & Poor's
   Register—Bio-
   graphical
Standard & Poor's
   Register—Corpo-
   rate
Sun-Sentinel (Fort
   Lauderdale)
Times-Picayune (New
   Orleans)
Trade and Industry
   Index
UPI News (most
   current 6 months)
USA Today
Washington Post
   Online

KnowledgePro (**software**) is supported in Windows 3rd-Party Forum B (GO
   WINAPB). See Microsoft Software.

Knozall Systems products are supported in the Novell Vendor Forum A (GO
   NVENA). See Novell Software.

Knutowski, Harry (76703,4214) an administrator of the Investors Forum (GO
   INVFORUM). See Investors Forum.

Kodak CD Forum (GO KODAK) is devoted to that company's CD products and technology, and closely related products. Information in the libraries is posted and maintained by Kodak. The primary sysop is Paul Wisotzke (70007,6237), who works at Eastman Kodak Co. in the customer assistance center that supports electronic products. For related services, see CD.

Kompass Europe and **Kompass U.K.** **(company financial database)** can be searched through IQuest. See IQuest.

Konami/Ultra products are covered in Game Publishers B Forum (GO GAMBPUB). See Gaming Forums.

Kondrake, Morton, **(column)** is among the syndicated columns provided by United Features (GO COLUMNS). See Columnists.

Koppelman, Mitch (76711,1210) manages the Reuter News Pictures Forum (GO NEWSPIX). See Reuter.

Korea Economic Daily can be searched through the Business Database Plus (GO BUSDB). See Business Database. See also Asia.

Korenthal Associates Incorporated products are supported in the PC Vendor B Forum (GO PCVENB). See IBM Computers.

Kreditcchutzverband von 1870 **(international business database)** may be searched through the IQuest gateway. See IQuest.

Krishnan, Chandrika (70007,4671) is the sysop of the Sybase Forum (GO SYBASE). See Sybase.

Krislov, Alex (76703,243) is sysop of The Literary Forum (GO LITFORUM). See Literature.

Kronman, Jim (76703,431) administers the Wine Forum (GO WINEFORUM). See Wine Forum.

Kurzweil **(products)** are supported in the MIDI A Vendor Forum (GO MIDIAVEN). See Music.

Kyle-DiPietropaolo, Joe (76703,437) administers the LDOS/TRSDOS6 Users Forum (GO LDOS). For details, see Tandy Computers.

Kyodo is a Japanese news service that is searchable through Comtex Scientific Inc.'s NewsGrid database. See NewsGrid. It also can be searched through Business Database Plus (GO BUSDB). See Business Database. And it can be searched through IQuest. See IQuest.

Labor issues are covered in *Monthly Labor Review* magazines, searchable through Magazine Database Plus (GO MDP). For details see Magazine Database.

Also, Labordoc and **Laborlaw I and II (databases)** may be searched through the IQuest gateway. See IQuest. And *Community & Worker Right-To-Know News* can be searched through the Business Database Plus (GO BUSDB). See Business Database.

See also Employment.

LabTech products are supported in the Windows 3rd-Party C Forum (GO WINAPC). See Microsoft software.

LA-C Business Bulletin can be searched through the Business Database Plus (GO BUSDB). See Business Database.

Lace making is one of the topics discussed in the Crafts Forum (GO CRAFTS). See Crafts.

Lacey, Doug (76702,1245) is a sysop in the Foreign Language Education Forum (GO FLEFO). See Foreign Language.

Ladies Home Journal (magazine) can be searched in the Magazine Database Plus (GO MDP). See Magazine Database.

Lagniappe Letter and **Lagniappe Quarterly Monitor** can be searched through the Business Database Plus (GO BUSDB). See Business Database.

Lahey Computer Systems products are supported in the PC Vendor H Forum (GO PCVENH). See IBM Computers.

"L.A. Law" (television) summaries on the latest shows are available in Soap Opera Summaries (GO SOAPS). See Soap Opera.

Lam, Reuben (76703,4357) is the sysop of the Aldus Forum (GO ALDUS). See Aldus Software.

LAN (**local area networks**) are discussed in several forums. Lan Magazine Forum (GO LANMAG) is intended as a vendor-independent venue for network users, installers, and integrators. Topics include discussions of matters such as client/server network, peer-to-peer networks, wiring, topology, etc. Lan Technology Forum (GO LANTECH) is sponsored by an independent monthly magazine and is devoted to the technical issues and problems faced by network specialists. The primary sysop of the forums is Tom Genereaux (76703,4265), assisted by editor Alan Frank.

Among other forums covering LAN issues are Ask3Com Online (GO THREECOM), Banyan Systems Inc. (GO BANFORUM), Cabletron Systems Forum (GO CTRONFORUM), Hayes Forum (GO HAYES), IBM Communications Forum (GO IBMCOM), IBM LMU/2 Forum (GO LMUFORUM), Lan Vendor Forum (GO LANVEN), MAC Communications Forum (GO MACCOMM), McAfee Virus Help Forum (GO VIRUSFORUM), Microsoft Network Forum (GO MSNETWORKS), Novell Netwire (GO NOVELL), Standard Microsystems Corp. Forum (GO SMC), and Thomas-Conrad Corp. Support Forum (GO TCCFORUM).

Also:

- *LAN Product News* can be searched through the Business Database Plus (GO BUSDB). See Business Database.

- LAN Product News, Network Management Systems & Strategies, and Networks Update (databases) may be searched through the IQuest gateway. See IQuest.

- *LAN Magazine*, *LAN Computing*, and *LAN Technology* (magazines) can be searched through Computer Database Plus (GO COMPDB), as can abstracts of *LAN Times*. See Computer Database Plus.

For related topics, see Telecomputing.

Landmark products are supported in the IBM PC Vendor H Forum (GO PCVENH). See IBM Computers.

Land Mobile Radio News can be searched through the Business Database Plus (GO BUSDB). See Business Database.

Landscaping is a topic in Gardening Forum (GO GARDENING). See Gardening.

Lands' End (GO LA) apparel store is represented in the Electronic Mall (GO MALL). See Electronic Mall.

LanFax Redirector is supported in the IBM Vendors H Forum (GO PCVENH). See IBM Computers.

Lance Haffner Games software is supported in the Game Publishers A Forum (GO GAMAPUB). See Gaming Forums.

Lancet (**medical database**) may be searched through the IQuest gateway. See IQuest. It also can be searched through Business Database Plus (GO BUSDB) and the Health Database Plus (GO HLTBD). See Health and Business Database.

Land Mobile Radio News (**database**) can be searched through IQuest. See IQuest.

Lanier Golf Directory (GO GLF) is a comprehensive listing of more than 12,000 U.S. golf courses and 500 golf resorts worldwide. See Golf Guild Online.

LAN Manager (**software**) is supported in the Microsoft Networks Forum (GO MSNETWORKS). See Microsoft Software.

Language studies: The Foreign Language Forum (GO FLEFO) is intended for teachers and students of all languages. See Foreign Language Forum.
    Also, the Linguistics & Language Behavior Abstracts database may be searched through the IQuest gateway. See IQuest.

LANtastic (**software**) is supported by the Artisoft Forum. See Artisoft.

Laptop and notebook computers of all kinds are discussed in various forums, including Canon Support (GO CANON), Compaq Computer Forum (GO CPQFORUM), CompuAdd Forum (GO COMPUADD), Computer Club Forum (GO CLUB), Dell Forum (GO DELL), HP Handheld Forum (GO HPHAND), Tandy Model 100 Forum (GO TANDYLAPTOP), Mac Hardware Forum (GO MACHW), Newton/PIE Forum (GO NEWTON), Palmtop Forum (GO PALMTOP), Texas Instruments Forums (GO TIFORUM). See Texas Instruments, Toshiba Forum (GO TOSHIBA), and Wolfram Research Forum (GO WOLFRAM).

Laryngoscope magazine abstracts are searchable in the Health Database Plus (GO HLTBD). See Health.

Laserdisk Professional (**magazine**) can be searched through the Business Database Plus (GO BUSDB). See Business Database.

Laserjet systems is supported in the HP Peripherials Forum (GO HPPER). See Hewlett-Packard.

Laser's Edge (GO LE) is a store in the Electronic Mall (GO MALL) that offers laser discs and laser disc equipment. See Electronic Mall.

Lasers & Optronics (**magazine**) is searchable through Computer Database Plus (GO COMPDB). See Computer Database Plus. In addition, abstracts of *Lasers and Applications* can be searched in the same feature.

LaserTools   products are supported in the Windows 3rd-Party Forum (GO WINAPD). See Microsoft Software.

Las Vegas entertainment schedules are regularly featured in Lee Forest's West Coast Travel column (GO WCT). Produced in cooperation with the Las Vegas News Bureau, the feature includes a three-month calendar of stage shows. See West Coast.

Latin is spoken in the Foreign Language Education Forum (GO FLEFO), a service for students and teachers. See Foreign Language.

Latin American news is covered in Chronicle of Latin American Economic Affairs. See IQuest. The resource also can be searched through the Business Database Plus (GO BUSDB), which also provides access to ESP-Business Opportunities in Latin America & the Caribbean, *Latin America Opportunity Report*, *Latin American Business News Wire*, and *Latin American Telecom Report*. See Business Database.

Latter Day Saints are discussed in the Religion Forum (GO RELIGION). See Religion.

Law and related issues are discussed in the Legal Forum (GO LAWSIG). For details, see Legal.

    Also, relevant databases on IQuest (GO IQUEST) include Academic Index, BNA Daily News, Bowne Digest—Corp/SEC Article Abstracts, Celex (computerised Documentation System on Ec Law), Child Abuse and Neglect and Family Violence, Construction Claims Citator, Criminal Justice Periodical Index, EBIS—Employee Benefits Infosource, Federal Register Abstracts, Index to Legal Periodicals, Industrial Health & Hazards Update, Labordoc, Laborlaw I, Laborlaw II, Law Office Technology Review, Lawyers' Micro Users Group Newsletter, Legal Resource Index, Managed Care Law Outlook, NCJRS, Trademarkscan—U.S. Federal, and Trademarkscan—U.S. State. See IQuest.

    Law and the federal courts also are discussed in the Political Debate Forum (GO POLITICS). See Poltical. And govenment and law are topics in the Seniors Forum (GO SENIORS). See Seniors. Legal issues also are a topic in the Working From Home Forum (GO WORK). See Working From Home.

Law Brief, Business (magazine) can be searched through the Business Database Plus (GO BUSDB), as can *Law Office Technology Review*. See Business Database.

Law & Medicine, Issues in is searchable in the Health Database Plus (GO HLTBD). See Health.

Law, Medicine & Health Care magazine abstracts are searchable in the Health Database Plus (GO HLTBD). See Health.

Lawn care is discussed in the Gardening Forum (GO GARDEN). See Gardening.

Lawn & Garden Marketing (magazine) can be searched through the Business Database Plus (GO BUSDB). See Business Database.
  See also Gardening.

Lawyer's PC (magazine) is searchable (abstracts) through Computer Database Plus (GO COMPDB). See Computer Database Plus.

Lazear, Susan (76702,1664) is the sysop of the Crafts Forum (GO CRAFTS). See Crafts.

.LBR, as an extension on filenames in forum libraries, usually means the program is in a *compressed/packed* form. See Files, Compressed.

LCSI products are supported in the LOGO Forum (GO LOGOFORUM). See Programmers Support.

LDC Debt Report can be searched through the Business Database Plus (GO BUSDB). See Business Database.

LDOS/TRSDOS (software) is supported by the LDOS/TRSDOS6 Users Forum (GO LDOS). See Tandy Corporation Computers.

LEAD Technologies (GO LEADTECH) software is supported in the Graphics B Vendor Forum (GO GRAPHBVEN). See Graphics.

League for Engineering Automation Productivity Forum (GO LEAP) is also known as CADD/CAM/CAE Vendor Forum (GO CADDVEN). See CAD/CAM. The forum is for discussion of anything related to engineering or design automation.

Learning disability is discussed in the Disabilities Forum (GO DISABILITIES). See Disabilities.

Leeman, Bill (76703,3055) is administrator of the DEC PC Forum (GO DECPC). See Digital Equipment Forums.

Legacy (software) is supported in Windows 3rd-Party Forum B (GO WINAPB). See Microsoft Software.

Legal Forum (GO LAWSIG) is open to lawyers and anyone interested in discussing law issues, ranging from court decisions to United National resolutions. CompuServe veteran Noel D. Adler (76703,264) administers the forum. Adler has been a member of the New York State Bar since 1974 and is principal law assistant of the Suffolk County, New York, Supreme Court. He is assisted in the forum management by Perry Norton, Dan D. Kohane and Larry Halman.
  See also Court Reporters.

Legal Periodicals, Index to (**database**) may be searched through the IQuest gateway. See IQuest.

Legal Publisher can be searched through the Business Database Plus (GO BUSDB). See Business Database.

Legal Research Center (GO LEGALRC) is a gateway to major legal resources, including indices to articles from more than 750 law journals, publications, and studies covering practical and theoretical aspects of criminal justice, law enforcement and related areas. It offers summaries of legislative, regulatory, judicial, and policy documents and covers federal tax issues, legal issues in banking and finance, and more. The information is made available by Dialog Information Services Incorporated.

The surcharge is $5 for the first 10 titles located, $5 for each additional 10 titles, and $5 for each full-text article retrieved. There is a $1 charge for a search that retrieves no titles, except for normal connect-time charges.

Many of the resources also are searchable through IQuest. In addition, searching the research centers is similar to IQuest's procedure. (See IQuest.) For information on other Telebase gateways, see Telebase Systems Incorporated.

Databases accessible through the Legal Research Center are:

- American Banker Full Text (copyright, American Banker-Bond Buyer)
- Child Abuse and Neglect (published by the U.S. Department of Health and Human Services)
- Congressional Information Service (copyright, Congressional Information Service)
- Criminal Justice Periodical Index (copyright, University Microfilms International)
- Legal Resource Index (copyright, Information Access Co.)
- National Criminal Justice Reference Service (published by the U.S. Department of Justice)
- Tax Notes Today (copyright, Tax Analysts)

Legal Resource Index is accessible through the Legal Research Center (GO LEGALRC). For details, see Legal Research Center. This resource also may be searched through IQuest (GO IQUEST) and through the Knowledge Index (GO KI). See IQuest and see Knowledge Index.

Legato Systems products are supported in the IBM PC Vendor D Forum (GO PCVEND). See IBM Computers.

Legend Entertainment software is supported in the Game Publishers C Forum (GO GAMCPUB). See Gaming Forums.

L'Eeggs Hanes Store (GO LEGGS) is a store in the Electronic Mall (GO MALL) that carries L'eggs, Hanes, Bali, and Playtex brand hosiery, activeware, and intimate apparel. See Electronic Mall.

Leibrand, Mike (70006,405) is sysop in the free Navigator Support Forums. See Navigator.

Lesko, Matthew, author of *Information USA* (Viking Penguin Books), also provides Information USA (GO INFOUSA), a service that specializes in techniques for getting questions answered. See Information USA.

LEVEL5 and **LEVEL5 OBJECT** are supported in the FocWizards Forums (GO FOCWIZARD). See FocWizard.

Lewallen, Dale (76000,21) is among the writers and editors assoicated with the PC Magazine forums. See PC Magazine.

Lewis, Howard and Martha (76703,303) administer the Human Sexuality Forums (GO HUMAN). See Sex.

Lexicor Software products are supported in the Atari Vendors Forum (GO ATARIVEN). See Atari Computers.

Lexicon products are supported in the MIDI B Vendor Forum (GO MIDIBVEN). See Music.

Lexington (KY) Herald-Leader (newspaper) is searchable through Telebase System's News Source USA (GO NEWSUSA). See News Source.

Liability Week (database) can be searched through IQuest. See IQuest. The resource also can be searched through the Business Database Plus (GO BUSDB). See Business Database.

Libertarian Party is discussed in the Political Debate Forum (GO POLITICS). See Political.

Library, Computer: Computer Library (GO COMPLIB) is sponsored by Information Access Company in conjunction with magazine publisher Ziff-Davis Company. See Computer Database Plus.

Library of Congress: The MARC Books File and Remarc databases may be searched through the IQuest (GO IQUEST) gateway. (Remarc covers all books cataloged by the Library of Congress from 1897 to 1980. Later records are in LC Marc.) See IQuest.

Library of Science (GO LOS) provides a kiosk in the Electronic Mall (GO MALL). See Electronic Mall.

Library sciences and library work are covered in several resources:

- *Library Hi Tech* magazine is searchable (abstracts) through Computer Database Plus (GO COMPDB). See Computer Database Plus.

- Through Business Database Plus (GO BUSDB), you may search *Library Software Review*, *Online Libraries & Microcomputers*, *Small Computers in Libraries*, *Special Libraries*, and *Library Workstation Report* magazines. See Business Database.

- Through the IQuest gateway (GO IQUEST), you may search a number of relevant databases, including American Libraries, Book Review Digest, CD-ROM Databases, Comprehensive Core Medical Library, Cuadra Directory of Online Databases, Editors Only, Educational Resources Information Center, Friday Memo, IDP Report, Information Science Abstracts, LC MARC Books File, Library and Information Science Abstracts, Library Literature, Morgan Report on Directory Publishing, Multimedia Publisher, NewsNet Action Letter, Online Libraries and Microcomputers, Online Newsletter, Open Systems Today, and Worldwide Videotex Update. See IQuest.

- It also is a topic of the Education Forum (GO EDFORUM). See Education.

See also Books.

Librex (computer products) are supported in the PC Vendor E Support Forum (GO LIBREX). See IBM Computers.

LI Business News (magazine) can be searched through the Business Database Plus (GO BUSDB). See Business Database.

Licensing Letter can be searched through the Business Database Plus (GO BUSDB). See Business Database.

Life (magazine, from 1985 to the present) can be searched through IQuest. See IQuest.

Life Sciences are covered in a collection of databases accessible through IQuest (GO IQUEST), including Academic Index, Applied Genetics News, Aquatic Sciences and Fisheries Abstracts, Biobusiness, Biocommerce Abstracts, Biological & Agricultural Index, Biosis Previews, Biotech Business, CAB Abstracts, COLD, Current Biotechnology Abstracts, Foods Adlibra, High Tech Separations News, Life Sciences Collection, Oceanic Abstracts, PASCAL, PTS Newsletter Database, and Zoological Record Online. See IQuest.

Life Sciences Collection can be searched through the Knowledge Index (GO KI). See Knowledge Index.

See also Science.

Limbaugh, Rush, conservative radio personality, is a regular topic in the Issues Forum (GO ISSUES). See Issues.

Lincoln/Mercury Showroom (GO LM) is a shop in the Electronic Mall that provides car information and dealer locations. See Electronic Mall.

Linguistics & Language Behavior Abstracts (database) may be searched through the IQuest gateway (GO IQUEST) and through the Knowledge Index (GO KI). See IQuest and see Knowledge Index.

Lininger, Skye (76702,1101) is sysop of the Holistic Health Forum (GO GO HOLISTIC). See Holistic.

Link-Up (magazine) can be searched through the Business Database Plus (GO BUSDB). See Business Database.

Liquidation Alert (database) can be searched through IQuest. See IQuest.

Lisp (programming language) is supported in the AI Expert Forum (GO AIEXPERT). See AI Expert.

Literature: The Literary Forum (GO LITFORUM) serves writers and readers of fiction, poetry, and nonfiction. It is open to working writers and aspirants alike. The sysop is CompuServe veteran Alex Krislov (76703,243) of Cleveland, Ohio. Assisting are Janet McConnaughey, Margaret Campbell, Barry Fogden, Karen Pershing, and John L. Myers.

Writing and poetry also is a topic in the Commodore Art/Games Forum (GO CBMART). See Commodore.

Also, some IQuest databases—Academic Index, Business Publisher, Linguistics & Language Behavior Abstracts, and Quotations Database—cover the subject. See IQuest.

Live Sound! products are supported in the MIDI B Vendor Forum (GO MIDIBVEN). See Music.

Livestock is discussed in the Pets and Animals Forum (GO PETS). For details, see Pets.

Living History Forum (GO LIVING) is devoted to the various aspects, as well as groups, related to the "Living History" movement, including historical re-enactments, Renaissance faires, scholarly research, heraldic study, and more. The message sections of this Forum are divided into three main categories: Time Periods (from the ancient past to the distant future), Interests (such as combat, arts, sciences, social studies, costuming, etc.), and Groups (for specific organizations to meet publicly or privately). Operating the forum are Brett Charbeneau, Leann Drury, Matt Drury, Mark Gist, Angela Jones, William Kubeck, Warner Lord, Marilyn Morey, Glenn Overby, Mary Ellen Smith, and Pat Taylor.

Lloyd's List (shipping newspaper) can be searched through IQuest. See IQuest.

Loan Amortization Program (GO MORTPAY) is a quick way to determine monthly payments on a loan as well as the total interest to be paid. You enter the loan amount, the annual rate of interest, the number of payments per year, and the number of years. The program generates a payment schedule.

Local Area Networking (database), see LAN.

Lockwood, Russ (72241,567) is the sysop of the After Hours Forum (GO ZNT:AFTERHOURS) of the PC Magazine feature. See PC Magazine.

Locomotives are a topic in the TrainNet Forum (GO TRAINNET). See TrainNet.

Lodging Hospitality (**magazine**) can be searched through the Business Database Plus (GO BUSDB). See Business Database.

LOFS products are supported in the PC Vendor G Forum (GO PCVENG). See IBM.

Loftesness, Scott (76703,407) is sysop of HamNet (Ham Radio) Forum (GO HAMNET) and assistant sysop of the Telecommunication Issues Forum (GO TELECOM). See HamNet and Telecommunication Issues.

Logitech Forum (GO LOGITECH) provides technical support to owners of Logitech products such as mice, ScanMan family of scanners, and software packages (PaintShow Plus, Finesse, and Logitech Windows). The forum is managed by the Logitech Support Group (76702,1367).

LOGO (**software**) is supported the LOGO Forum (GO LOGOFORUM). See Programmers Support.

Logos (**French government database**) may be searched through the IQuest gateway. See IQuest.

London *Times & Sunday Times* (**newspapers**) are covered in the UK Newspaper Library (GO UKPAPERS). See UK Newspaper.

Long-Distance Letter and **Long Distance Outlook** can be searched through Business Database Plus (GO BUSDB). See Business Database.

Long Term Care Management can be searched through the Business Database Plus (GO BUSDB). See Business Database.

Look&Link (**software**) is supported in the PC Vendor B Forum (GO PCVENB). See IBM Computers.

LooLoo a/k/a Pat Phelps (70006,522) is sysop of the CB Forum (GO CBFORUM). See CB Forum.

Los Angeles Times and **Los Angeles Daily News** (**newspapers**) are searchable through Telebase System's News Source USA (GO NEWSUSA) and through the Knowledge Index (GO KI). See Newspaper Library and see Knowledge Index. Abstracts of The Times can be searched through Computer Database Plus (GO COMPDB). See Computer Database Plus.

Also, *Los Angeles Business Journal* (magazine) can be searched through the Business Database Plus (GO BUSDB). See Business Database. And *Los Angeles Magazine* can be searched in the Magazine Database Plus (GO MDP). See Magazine Database.

Lotus (**magazine**) is searchable through Computer Database Plus (GO COMPDB). See Computer Database Plus.

Lotus (**software**): The Lotus Forums (GO LOTUS), operated by Lotus Development Corporation, offer specific focuses:

- Lotus GmbH Forum (GO LOTGER) provides technical support for German-speaking users of German-language products, including Ami Pro, Lotus Notes, Lotus 1-2-3, and cc:Mail. Support is also provided for all other DOS, OS/2, Windows, and UNIX products. Forum members can ask the technical staff at Lotus' headquarters in Munich, Germany for support. Forum libraries contain software such as Notes applications, drivers, upgrades, and utilities; the message boards are used to post important notes for the German-speaking customers of Lotus.

- The Lotus Spreadsheets Forum (GO LOTUSA) covers Lotus 1-2-3, Symphony, Improv for Windows, and others. The message board covers issues from general information to communications, macro languages, and graphics, listing users groups around the country. The libraries offer utility programs and background articles. Forum administrator is Wayne Heitmann (76711,455), Peter Thompson, John O'Keefe, Dwight Morse, Doug Knowles, Ashley Sands, Jerry Lerman, Nick Delonas, and Claudia Basso.

- Lotus Communications Forum (GO LOTUSCOMM) cover cc:Mail, Lotus Notes, and related programs.

- Lotus Words & Pixels Forum (Go LOTUSB) covers all other Lotus products, including Agenda, Freelance, LotusWorks, Magellan, Metro, Express, One Source, Organizer, and so on. Wayne Heitmann is in charge of this forum as well, along with Peter Thompson, John O'Keefe, Dwight Morse, Mary Santo, Paul Destefanis, Gary Oglesby, Judy Hamner, J. Stephen Yeo, and Mark Cuban.

- Lotus Word Processing Forum (GO LOTUSWP), operated by Lotus's Atlanta-based word processing division support department, covers related products, including Ami, Ami Pro, LotusWrite, Manuscript, Samna Word IV, SmarText, and WinImage. The forum is administered by Beth Dixon (76702,763), Ildiko Nagy, Mike Wentz, Cris Williams, Sandra Wilson, Warren Hall, Elizabeth Swoope, Gerry Kowarsky, and Rich Zaleski.

Enter GO LOTUS for the overview of the World of Lotus. At the menu, company statements are available, as well as a summary of new entries in the data libraries, lists of software and books recommended, descriptions of drivers and add-ons available for downloading, and so forth. The Lotus Technical Library (GO LTL-1), a comprehensive collection of Lotus product information, contains answers to common questions, tips and techniques for using Lotus products more effectively, and troubleshooting guidelines for identifying and resolving technical difficulties.

Also, Lotus 1-2-3 is a topic of the Cobb Applications Forum (GO ZNT:COBBAPP). See Cobb Group Forums.

Louisiana news is covered in the New Orleans Times-Picayune, searchable through Telebase System's News Source USA (GO NEWSUSA). See News Source.
Also:

- Selected reports from Louisana are included in the Southwest regional reports from United Press International. See Executive News Service.
- *Baton Rouge Business Report* and *Louisiana Industry Environmental Alert* magazines can be searched through the Business Database Plus (GO BUSDB). See Business Database.
- *New Orleans Magazine* can be searched in the Magazine Database Plus (GO MDP). See Magazine Database.

Louisville (KY) business news is reported in *Business First-Louisville* magazine, which can be searched through the Business Database Plus (GO BUSDB). See Business Database.

Love, John (71333,1267) is the sysop of the Canopus Research Forum (GO CANOPUS). See Canopus.

Love, Ken (72662,273) is the sysop of the Japan Forum (GO JAPAN). See Japan Forum.

"Loving" (television) summaries on the latest shows are available in Soap Opera Summaries (GO SOAPS). See Soap Opera.

Lowenstein, Judi (76703,4047) is the administrator of the Symantec Forum (GO SYMANTEC). See Symantec Software.

Lucasfilm Games (software) is regularly discussed in The Game Publishers A Forum (GO GAMAPUB) and in the Flight Simulation Forum (GO FSFORUM). See Gaming Forums.

Lucid Corp. products are supported in the Windows 3rd-Party Forum A (GO WINAPA). See Microsoft Software.

Luks, Ron (76703,254) is chief sysop of the Atari forums online (GO ATARINET). See Atari Users Network. He also is sysop of the Palmtop Forum (GO PALMTOP) and the Pen Technology Forum (GO PENFORUM); see Palmtop and see Pen Technology. He is co-sysop of the Apple Newton/PIE Forum (GO NEWTON or GO APPLEPIE). See Apple computers.

Lunar Command (**software**) is supported in the Game Publishers B Forum (GO GAMPUB). See Gaming Forums.

Lung, Heart &, magazine abstracts are searchable in the Health Database Plus (GO HLTBD). See Health.

Lutheran News Service (**database**) may be searched through the IQuest gateway. See IQuest. See also Religion.

Lutz, Brion (76702,1561) is sysop of the Sailing Forum. See Sports and Recreation. He also is associated with the White House Forum (GO WHITEHOUSE). See White House.

Lyall, Pete (76703,4230) is sysop in OS-9 Forum (GO OS9). See Tandy.

Lynd, Chuck (76703,674) is the sysop of the Education Forum. See Education Forum.

Lynx (**video game**) is discussed in the Atari 8-Bit Forum (GO ATARI8). For details, see Atari Users Network.

.LZH, as an extension on filenames in forum libraries, usually means the program is in a *compressed/packed* form. See Files, Compressed.

M

MacAccess (**software**) is supported in the DaVinci Forum (GO DAVINCI). See DaVinci.

Machine Design (**engineering database**) may be searched through the IQuest gateway. See IQuest. It also can be searched through Business Database Plus (GO BUSDB). See Business Database.

Machine Shop, Modern (**magazine**) can be searched through the Business Database Plus (GO BUSDB). See Business Database.

Machinist, American (**magazine**) is searchable through the Business Database Plus (GO BUSDB). See Business Database.

Machrone, Bill (72241,15) is among *PC Magazine*'s editors and contributors who are regulars in the publication's PC-Magnet service. See *PC Magazine*.

Macintosh (Apple) computers are supported in CompuServe's Apple users network (GO MAUG) in several different forums. See Apple Computers.

Mackay, Harvey, (**column**) is among the syndicated columns provided by United Features (GO COLUMNS). See Columnists.

Mackie Designs products are supported in the MIDI B Vendor Forum (GO MIDIBVEN). See Music.

Macmillan Publishing (GO MMP), offering career development and training books, is represented in the Electronic Mall (GO MALL). See Electronic Mall.

MacPlay (**software**) is regularly discussed in The Game Publishers B Forum (GO GAMBPUB). See Gaming Forums.

MacProject/SF **(software)** is supported in the Claris Corp. Forum (GO CLARIS). For more information, see Claris.

Macromedia Forum (GO MACROMEDIA) supports Macromedia products and is operated by the Macromedia technical support staff. Discussions cover the firm's sound products, 3-D modeling software, clipping programs, etc. The primary sysop is Doug Wyrick (75300,2303). See also Multimedia.

MacTech Magazine is supported in the Mac D Vendor Forum (GO MACDVEN). See Apple Computers.

Mac Tools Deluxe **(software)** is supported in the Central Point Software Forum (GO CENTRAL). See Central Point.

Mac User (GO MC) is a discount Macintosh dealer in the Electronic Mall (GO MALL). See Electronic Mall.

MacUser, MacWeek, and **Macworld** **(magazines)** are searchable in Computer Database Plus (GO COMPDB). See Computer Database Plus. In addition, ZiffNet/Mac (GO ZMAC), a collection of services by Ziff-Davis publishing company, has forums operated by the staffs of *MacUser* and *MacWeek*. See ZiffNet/Mac for details.

Mac Warehouse (GO MW) is a store in the Electronic Mall (GO MALL) that offers Macintosh hardware, software, and access. See Electronic Mall.

MacWrite **(software)** is supported in the Claris Corp. Forum (GO CLARIS). For more information, see Claris.

Mac Zone/PC Zone (GO MZ) is a store in the Electronic Mall (GO MALL) that offers PC and Macintosh equipment. See Electronic Mall.

Madge Networks, Ltd. products are supported in the IBM PC Vendor G Forum (GO PCVENG). See IBM Computers.

Madison (WI) Capital Times **(newspaper)** is searchable through Telebase System's News Source USA (GO NEWSUSA). See News Source.

Maestro **(modem maker)** is covered in the Pacific Vendors Forum (GO PACVENDOR). For details, see Pacific.

Magazine topics are discussed in the Literary Forum (GO LITFORUM), an information exchange for writers and readers of fiction, poetry, and nonfiction. See Literature.

   Also, backlogs of magazine articles of all sorts are searchable in Magazine Database Plus (GO MDP) and IQuest (GO IQUEST), while computer magazines can be searched in Computer Database Plus (GO COMPDB). See Magazine Database, IQuest, and Computer Database Plus.

Magazine ASAP and Magazine Index databases may be searched through the IQuest gateway (GO IQUEST). See IQuest. Magazine Index also can be searched through the Knowledge Index (GO KI). See Knowledge Index.

In addition, magazines and newspapers are sold in a number of stores in the Electronic Mall (GO MALL), including Computer Shopper (GO CS), MacUser (GO MC), McGraw-Hill Book Co. (GO MH), Money's Financial Market (GO MFM), PC Computing (GO PCC), and PC Magazine (GO PM). See Electronic Mall.

Magazine Database Plus (GO MDP) is provided by Ziff Communications Company, the same magazine publisher that produces Computer Database Plus and Health Database Plus. The service contains full text of articles from more than 90 general-interest magazines. Topics include current events, business, science, sports, news, people, personal finance, family, arts and crafts, cooking, education, the environment, travel, politics, and consumer opinions. Also available are book and movie reviews. Coverage for most titles begins as of January 1, 1986, and is updated weekly.

Besides the basic connect charge, the service levies of $1.50 for each full-text article retrieved.

The feature's search methods fall into two broad categories:

- General searches, which let you look for articles based on individual words occurring in articles, are useful when you aren't sure exactly where to look in an article for the occurrence of a word.

- Specific searches let you look for articles based on specific kinds of words or phrases, such as a subject heading or publication name. For specific searches, a search term can be composed of letters, numerals, and spaces. Search methods include:

  1. Keywords (in article titles, subject headings, names of featured people, companies, or products)

  2. Subject headings, words, or phrases selected from a controlled list of terms to best describe the primary focus of an article

  3. Publication names, without the word *the* if it occurs at the beginning: You may obtain a complete list by typing ?? when asked for a publication name

  4. Publication dates (as in Feb 8 1993)

  5. Words in the article text

  6. Article by reference number (a unique eight-digit code)

As you search, the feature generates a menu of actual search terms that match the (partial) search term you supply. You then make one or more selections from the menu. Techniques for searching this resource are the same as those used with all of the ZiffNet gateways. For specifics, see ZiffNet Databases.

The database also allows you to download articles (as well as displaying them on the screen). Selecting the download option from a menu causes the database to display a File Transfer Protocol list. The first option on the menu is explicitly for users of the CompuServe Information Manager. Users of other terminal programs can select a different protocol. See Files, Transfer.

A user guide and publication list for the feature is available for downloading in the Ziff Support Forum (GO ZIFFHELP). In Library 11 ("Magazine DB Plus"), see the file called MDPUSR.TXT for the user guide and the file MDPPUB.TXT for the publication list.

Magazines searchable through the database include:

Aging
Alternatives
American Artist
American City &
   County
American Forests
American Imago
American Salesman
American Spectator
Astronomy
The Atlantic
Audio
Audubon
Backpacker
Better Homes and
   Gardens
Bicycling
BioScience
Boating
Bulletin of the Atomic
   Scientists
Business Economics
Business Horizons
Buzzworm: The
   Environmental
   Journal
Car and Driver
Changing Times
Chicago
Children Today
Commentary
Conservationist
Consumer Reports
Consumer Reports
   Travel Letter
Consumers Digest

Consumers' Research
   Magazine
Cosmopolitan
Country Living
Current
Cycle World
Discover
Ebony
The Economist
Electronic Learning
Environment
Esquire
Essence Magazine
Executive Female
Family Handyman
Financial World
Flower & Garden
   Magazine
The Futurist
Gardening
Golf
Good Housekeeping
High Technology
   Business
Home Office
   Computing
Horticulture (The
   Magazine of
   American)
Inc.
Industry Week
Insight
Journal of Small
   Business
   Management
Kiplinger's Personal
   Finance Magazine

Ladies Home Journal
Los Angeles Magazine
The Magazine of
   Fantasy and Science
   Fiction
Management Today
Metropolitan Home
Modern Maturity
Monthly Labor
   Review
Monthly Review
Mother Earth News
Mother Jones
Motor Trend
Minn.-St. Paul
   Magazine
The Nation
Nation's Business
National Review
New Orleans
   Magazine
The New Republic
Occupational Outlook
   Quarterly
Off Road
Omni
Online Magazine
Organic Gardening
Parents' Magazine
Parks & Recreation
Playboy
Popular Mechanics
Popular Science
Premier
The Progressive
Psychology Today
Railway Age

R & D
Real Estate Today
Redbook
Regardie's Magazine
Research & Develop-
ment
Road & Track
Sales & Marketing
Management
Saturday Evening Post
Scholastic Update
Science World
Science'86
Scientific American
Seventeen

Sierra
Sky & Telescope
Smithsonian
Society
Special Libraries
Sport
Sports Afield
Stereo Review
Sunset Magazine
Technology Review
Teen Magazine
Texas Monthly
Town & Country
Monthly
Travel-Holiday

U.S. News & World
Report
UNESCO Courier
USA Today Magazine
US Department of
State Dispatch
Video Magazine
Washington Monthly
Weatherwise
Whole Earth Review
Wilderness
Woman's Day
Working Woman
World Health
World Press Review

Magazine publishing is the subject of *Folio: the Magazine for Magazine Management,* which is searchable through the Business Database Plus (GO BUSDB). See Business Database.

Magee Enterprises (**software**) is supported in the PC Vendor A Forum (GO PCVENA). See IBM Computers.

Magellan (**software**) is supported in the Lotus Words & Pixels Forum (GO LOTUSB). See Lotus Software.

Magic is covered in the New Age Forum (GO NEWAGE). For more information, see New Age Forum.

Magic Menus (**software**) is supported in the PC Vendor A Forum (GO PCVENA). See IBM Computers.

Magic Software products are supported in the PC Vendor G Forum (GO PCVENG). See IBM.

Magical Blend Magazine is represented in the New Age Forum (GO NEWAGE). For more information, see New Age Forum.

Magill's Survey of Cinema (GO MAGILL) is a gateway that contains descriptions of most major films from 1902 to the present. Information on file includes title, release date, running time, country of release, cast and credits, production studio, motion Picture Association of America rating, and references to reviews. In addition, the plot and significant influences on the film are summarized and discussed.

The cost is $2 for the first 10 titles located, $2 for each additional 10 titles, and $2 for each complete text of movie information retrieved. A $1 charge is levied for each search that produces no titles.

This resource also may be searched through IQuest (GO IQUEST) and through the Knowledge Index (GO KI). See IQuest and see Knowledge Index.

For information on other Telebase gateways, see Telebase Systems Incorporated.

Magma Systems products are supported in the IBM PC Vendor D Forum (GO PCVEND). See IBM Computers.

Magnetic Music 76711 (products) is supported in the MIDI A Vendor Forum (GO MIDIAVEN). See Music.

Mail, CompuServe (GO MAIL): Each subscriber has a private mailbox to receive electronic letters online around the clock. Other people can communicate with you by writing messages and having the system deliver them to your user ID number. When letters are posted, they automatically are placed in your private mailbox and only you can read them. Sending an electronic letter for delivery to another person on CompuServe is simply a matter of composing the message and, following the screen prompts, addressing it to that person's user ID number. (The CompuServe Information Manager software has elaborate built-in mail options; see your users manual.)

CompuServe Mail also enables you to forward messages to other subscribers, send messages with "receipts" so that you automatically are informed when the recipients have picked up the letters, send binary files (such as programs and spreadsheet documents), and save names and user IDs of your frequent correspondents in an Address Book for easy mailing in the future. Messages, whether ASCII or binary, may be up to 2 million characters (2MB) in length.

In addition, CompuServe Mail also can forward messages from you to computerists on other electronic mail systems, such as MCI Mail, Sprintmail, AT&T Mail, Internet subscriber, and users of any Telex I or Telex II (formerly TWX) machine. You also may use the features to send messages to any Group 3 Fax machine in the world or to write letters that will be automatically printed and sent by the U.S. Postal Service to designated addresses. CompuServe Mail gives you an easy way to correspond with members of the U.S. Congress. And CompuServe Mail supports the X.400 protocols established for standardization in electronic mail by the International Telegraph and Telephone Consultative Committee (CCITT), as described later in this section.

To send mail beyond CompuServe to remote systems, write your message as you would if you were corresponding with another CompuServe users, then in the To: field in the CIM display (or at the Send To: prompt in the third-party ASCII system display), enter the address of the recipient on the other system, as described in the following sections.

MCI Mail You may send mail from CompuServe to MCI Mail's Global Messaging Services, which consist of MCI MAIL public mailboxes and XChange private mail service. The simplest way to send your message to an MCI Mail address, enter "MCIMAIL:" followed by the MCI address of the intended recipient, such as

```
MCIMAIL:123-4567
```

You also may use an MCI Mail registered name (such as "MCI MAIL:Charles Bowen"), but the MCI user ID number is preferred (because it is unique to the recipient, while there could be several MCI Mail users with the same name).

You also can communicate with users of Private Management Domain (PRMD) mailboxs serviced by MCI XChange 400 by using this format in your addressing:

```
X400:(c=us;a=mci;p=PRMD;o=ORGANIZATION;s=SURNAME;g=GIVEN NAME)
```

So, if an MCI XChange 400 user told you his address was "PRMD of ABCCORP, Organization of XYZORG, Surname of SMITH and Given Name of John" you would address the message as:

```
X400:(c=us;a=mci;p=abccorp;o=xyzorg;s=smith;g=john)
```

For online help on communicating with these systems, enter HELP MCI_MAIL at the Mail feature prompt.

TELEX   You may post a letter to a Telex I or II machine by entering at the To: (or Send to:) prompt the letters TLX and colon (:) and the machine number, such as:

```
TLX: 1234567
```

You also may follow that with an answer-back code, like this:

```
TLX: 1234567 ABCDEF
```

The answer-back code is optional, but if used, it must be complete for the delivery, so if you are not sure, don't use it. Telexes sent to MCI Mail subscribers require a special 650 prefix before the Telex number. Also, those sent to destinations within the continental United States are considered domestic, while those to destinations outside of the U.S. (regardless of point of origin) are international and require a three-digit country code before the Telex machine number. Enter HELP TELEX INTERNATIONAL at the CompuServe Mail Menu for a list of country codes.) Telex messages up to 50,000 characters in length may be sent.

Also, Telex messages can be sent to your CompuServe mailbox. The Telex user needs to send a message to your CompuServe mailbox to your user ID in care of machine number 3762848 which has the answerback of COMPUSERVE. The sender must specify "TO: " on the first nonblank line of the message, followed by your User ID to inform CompuServe Mail where to deliver the message. (The colon after the TO is required.) If a subject is desired, the sender can also add a "RE:" after the "TO:" line in the message. So the format would look like:

```
TO: 71635,1025 (This is Required)
```

```
RE: Your Request (This is optional message subject)
```
This is the information you requested... (etc.)

For more information on Telex delivery, enter HELP TELEX in the Mail feature.

Facsimile (FAX) machines CompuServe Mail may be routed to Group 3 FAX machines. The text cannot exceed 50,000 characters and the lines of the text must be no longer than 80 characters. To send to domestic recipients, enter the letters FAX and a colon (:) and the domestic machine number, that is, a 1 and the area code, followed by the phone number, as in:

```
FAX: 16145551234
```

To send to an international facsimile machine, enter FAX: followed by the country and city codes before the phone number, as in:

```
FAX: 447112345.
```

This example would reach United Kingdom (44), city of London (71). To send multiple fax messages, separate the routing information with semicolons as in FAX:16145551234; FAX:16145554321 etc. All faxes should include a country code even if their destination is within your own country. You will automatically receive a confirmation through CompuServe Mail when your fax message has been delivered. CompuServe Mail will attempt to send a fax message up to 30 times if the line is busy; otherwise, five attempts are made. If after the last attempt the message cannot be delivered, it will be returned.

Messages sent to fax machines have a cover page that includes TO: (the recipient's name), FROM: (your name), DATE: (the date and time in Eastern Time the fax is delivered), and SUBJECT: (information on the fax contents). You also can create a customized fax cover sheet to add additional text. For instructions on setting up a cover sheet, enter HELP FAX COVER at the CompuServe Mail Main Menu.

For more information, enter HELP FAX at the Mail prompt.

Internet To send a message (of up to 50,0000 characters) to an Internet address, enter at the To: (or Send To:) prompt INTERNET: followed by the recipient and the "address@domain" in Internet style, such as:

```
INTERNET:Jdoe@abc.michigan-state.edu
```

In this example, the INTERNET: is required by CompuServe to route the message to the Internet system; "Jdoe" is the valid address used by this recipient on the Internet system; the "@" tells Internet that the domain address is following; and the "abc.michigan-state.edu" is the domain address. The domain address elements must be separated by periods and the domain must be separated from the recipient's address by the "@" character, with no spaces. Also, you may have a space after the "INTERNET:" The amount of time it takes to deliver an Internet message varies from a half hour to two days.

Messages sent to some networks via Internet require special addressing formats, as in the following:

- Bitnet addresses—.BITNET must be appended to the Bitnet address for it to be delivered via Internet. For example:

```
INTERNET:Charlieb@EDUNAB.BITNET
```

- UUNET addresses usually can be in the regular Internet address format. However, occasionally, the more complex form is needed, as in INTERNET:user%organization.domain@UUNET.UU.NET. This results in an address such as:

```
INTERNET:harry%edunab.msu@UUNET.UU.NET
```

- FidoNet can be addressed via Internet in this format:

```
INTERNET:Firstname.Lastname@pPPP.fFFF.nNNN.zZZZ.fidonet.org
```

where PPP = Point Number (if other than 0), FFF = Node Number, NNN = Net Number, ZZZ = Zone Number (1 thru 6 are valid), and ZZZ:NNN/ FFF.PPP is the format used in Fido. So, if you are sending to Charlie Bowen, with an address of 1:114/15, so his FidoNet Internet address is:

```
Charlie.Bowen@p0.f15.n114.z1.fidonet.org
```

If an Internet message is undeliverable, request for notification in your CompuServe mailbox. Sometimes the notification also includes the text of your original message, though this depends on functions at the remote mail system (some don't return the text). Also, you can request a receipt with mail sent via Internet

Note: the receipt is generated *only* when the message leaves CompuServe on its own to Internet. Receipts to indicate whether the user actually receives the messages are not available through Internet.

To *receive* a message from Internet in your CompuServe Mail mailbox, the Internet user needs your correct Internet address. Your address is: (1) Your User ID with the comma changed to a period; (2) the CompuServe domain, which is "compuserve.com", and (3) the correct addressing format to send the message. This format varies from one system to another. Typically, the address is shown as "User ID@compuserve.com" so the address appears as: 71635.1025@compuserve.com.

Note: Usually, users of the Standard Pricing Plan are not charged for the time spent in reading incoming messages; an exception is Internet. For reading or downloading Internet messages, users are charged 15 cents for the first 7,500 characters and 5 cents for each additional 2,500 characters. For more on charges, see Mail Costs below.

For more about Internet and CompuServe Mail, enter HELP INTERNET at the Mail prompt online.

AT&T Mail An AT&T user can be addressed by using a surname and given name, in addition to the country and administrative domain values that are required for all X.400 messages. To ensure uniqueness on the AT&T Mail system, a person's unique ID should also be included, in a style like this:

```
x400:(c=us;a=attmail;s=SURNAME;g=GIVEN;d=id:UNIQUE ID)
```

The information in capitals are the user specific variables that you need to supply.

For example, if an AT&T user told you the address was "Surname of JONES, Given name of BOB, and AT&T ID of BJONES", in CompuServe Mail you would enter:

```
x400:(c=us;a=attmail;s=jones;g=bob;d=id:bjones)
```

For more information, enter HELP AT&T_MAIL at the Mail prompt.

SprintMail   A SprintMail user can be addressed by using an organization name, surname, and a given name, in addition to the country and administrative domain values required for all X.400 messages, such as:

```
x400:(c=us;a=telemail;o=ORGANIZATION;s=SURNAME;g=GIVEN)
```

Note that the information in capitals in the above are the *user specific variables* that you need to supply. So, if a SprintMail user has told you his address is "Organization of BEEZERK, Surname of SMITH, Given name of JOHN," you would enter the following address in CompuServe Mail:

```
x400:(c=us;a=telemail;o=beezerk;s=smith;g=john)
```

The "x400:" must always precede the address, the address must be enclosed in parenthesis, and the elements must be separated by semicolons.

For more information, enter HELP SPRINTMAIL at the Mail prompt.

Western Union 400   A Western Union 400 user can be addressed by using his/her Western Union Number (ELN) along with the country and administrative domain values required for all X.400 messages. The unique ELN should be included as a domain-defined attribute. The Western Union 400 address including the receiver's name could be entered as:

```
x400:(C=US;A=WESTERN UNION;S=surname;G=given;D=ELN:unique id)
```

So, if an Western Union 400 user's address was "surname of SMITH, given name of SAM, and Western Union number of 62044400" in CompuServe Mail you would enter the following address:

```
x400:(C=US;A=WESTERN UNION; S=SMITH;G=SAM;D=ELN:62044400)
```

NIFTY-Serve   (Japan) To send mail to users of NIFTY-Serve, CompuServe's sister information service in Japan, enter NIFTY: followed by the User ID. (NIFTY-Serve User IDs are composed of three alphabetic characters followed by five numbers.)

The NIFTY-Serve link is currently one of eight X.400 connections available to CompuServe members, so you also can address a message in this format:

```
X400:(c=jp;a=nifty;p=svc;s=Nifty Serve ID)
```

So, if a NIFTY-Serve user told you his or her ID was ABC12345 you could enter the address in CompuServe Mail as either NIFTY:ABC12345 or X400:(c=jp;a=nifty;p=svc;s=ABC12345). For more information on X.400 connections, NIFTY-Serve, and how to use the new CompuServe Mail link, GO MAILHELP.

Infonet   To send a message to an Infonet Notice mailbox, address it with this format:

```
X400:(c=us;a=infonet;p=PRMD;o=ORGANIZATION;s=SURNAME;g=GIVEN NAME)
```

So, if the intended recipient's address is "PRMD of ABCCORP, organization of XYZORG, surname of SMITH, and given name of JOHN", you would enter address the message to:

```
X400:(c=us;a=infonet;p=abccorp;o=xyzorg;s=smith;g=john)
```

For more information, enter HELP INFONET at the Mail prompt.

Advantis   To send to a remote user of the Advantis system (a network formerly operated by the IBM Information Network and the Sears Communication Co.), address it with this format:

```
X400:(c=us;a=ibmx400;p=ibmmail;s=SURNAME;g=GIVEN NAME)
```

For more information, enter HELP ADVANTIS at the Mail prompt.

Receiving Mail Via x.400 Connection   Many remote mail systems can route mail through an x.400 interconnection following protocols established for standardization by the International Telegraph and Telephone Consultative Committee (CCITT). This means you can receive mail from SprintMail, AT&T Mail, Western Union, or other such systems through x.400 if you provide the following address information to the party on the remote system:

Country = US
ADMD = CompuServe
PRMD = csmail
DDA Type = id
DDA Value = Your User ID with a period instead of a comma.

So if your user ID number were 71635,1025, a message could be addressed to you as:

```
x400:(c=us;a=CompuServe;p=csmail;d=id:71635.1025)
```

For more information on this, enter HELP X400 at the Mail prompt.

Gateways and Mail Hub   AT&T Mail has defined a gateway named mhs!csmail that can be used in place of the c=, a=, and pd= parameters for a user on the AT&T Mail System.

SprintMail, Lotus cc:Mail, and AT&T Mail users can also send messages to Novell NetWare MHS mailboxes via the CompuServe Mail Hub. The address that you should give in order to be reached at a NetWare MHS mailbox through the CompuServe Mail Hub via X.400 is:

Country = US
ADMD = CompuServe
PRMD = csmail
DDA Type = id
DDA Value = mhs:username(a)workgroup

The "@" symbol normally used in a NetWare MHS address must be replaced by "(a)" when used in a X.400 address.

U.S. Postage Service Letters also can to routed to a printer and sent by U.S. Mail. The lines must not exceed 80 characters in width and the length of message must not exceed 279 lines. At the Send To: prompt (or in CIM's To: box), enter POSTAL. After that, the system prompts you for addresses asking for the name, title/company (optional), street address, city, state or province, and ZIP code. You can enter the state's full name or its two-letter postal code. After entering the address, you will be given the opportunity to edit. Finally, you will be prompted for your return address. For more information, enter HELP POSTAL at the Mail feature prompt.

Congressgrams, SantaGrams, Valentines CompuServe Mail also has extra features, some seasonal in nature. As Christmas nears, the CompuServe Mail menu is expanded to include a "SantaGram" option for sending specialized Christmas greetings to online friends. In February, a similar Valentine option is added for electronic greetings of the season. Other extra e-mail services are on-going. Congressgrams are personalized, hardcopy letters you can send electronically from CompuServe to members of the U.S. Senate, the U.S. House of Representatives, the President or Vice President. Congressgrams are delivered by the U.S. Postal Service and carry a $1 surcharge for each letter.

To use the feature, select the "Send a CONGRESSgram" option from the Mail menu or enter CONGRESS at the prompt. You then are prompted to enter the recipient's name and title (senator, representative, President, or Vice President), the text of your message, the subject, your name, and your postal address. CompuServe Mail will automatically enter the recipient's address, the salutation, and a closing.

A Members of Congress database also is provided to help CompuServe members obtain the names of their congressional representatives, the President, or Vice President. To use the database, enter GO FCC-1 at a prompt. It provides a state-by-state listing of all members in the House of Representatives and the Senate. Each listing includes the name, party affiliation, Washington telephone number, hometown, and committee memberships.

Mail Costs If you use the basic Standard Pricing Plan, your monthly $8.95 membership fee includes an electronic mail allowance of $9. With this allowance you can send up to the equivalent of 60 three-page messages per month with no additional charge (each 2,500 characters being calculated to be about one double-spaced page). This monthly allowance applies to both ASCII and binary messages. Your remaining message allowance expires at the end of each month. Here is what is included in your monthly allowance:

- Send Mail (per message):
    First 7500 characters, 15 cents
    Additional 2500 characters, 5 cents
- Receipt Requested: 15 cents per recipient

- Read/Download Internet Messages:
    First 7500 characters, 15 cents
    Additional 2500 characters, 5 cents

Regarding the Send Mail allowance, note that the charge per message is multiplied by the number of recipients you have chosen to receive your message. Surcharged messages, such as Congressgrams, fax, telex, and postal are not included in the $9.00 monthly allowance.

If Internet messages are deleted without reading, or if they are automatically deleted by the system after 30 days, no charges are incurred.

The following special mail items are *not* included in your monthly allowance:

- Congressgrams ($1), CandidateGrams ($1.50), SantaGrams ($2), CupidGrams ($2), Postal letter with a U.S. destination (first page, $1.50, additional page, 20 cents), Postage letter outside the U.S. (first page, $2.50, additional page, 20 cents), TELEX and TWX messages with U.S. Destination ($1.15 per 300 characters sent), and FAX messages (costs vary depending upon the destination). The worldwide fax prices and country codes can be found by typing HELP FAX PRICES at the CompuServe Mail Main Menu.

    If you are using the Alternative Pricing Plan, your CompuServe Mail useage is billed an hourly connect-time charge (see Billing). In addition to connect-time charges, the following items have additional premium charges:

- Receipt Requested (15 cents per recipient), Multiple send feature (10 cents for each after the first recipient, up to 10 per message), Congressgrams ($1), CandidateGrams ($1.50), SantaGrams ($2), CupidGrams ($2), Postal letter with a U.S. destination (first page, $1.50, additional page, 20 cents), Postage letter outside the U.S. (first page, $2.50, additional page, 20 cents), TELEX and TWX messages with U.S. Destination ($1.15 per 300 characters sent), and FAX messages (cost varying depending upon the destination).

Mail, U.S. Postal: Letters can be sent from CompuServe Mail to a laser printer for delivery via the U.S. Postal Service. See Mail, CompuServe. Also street addresses throughout the country can be searched through the surcharged Phonefile database. For details, see Phone Directories.

MailMAN, Personal (software) is supported in the PC Vendor G Forum (GO PCVENG). See IBM.

Maine (news) is included in the daily Northeast regional reports from United Press International. See Executive News Service for details.

Mainframe Computing can be searched through the Business Database Plus (GO BUSDB). See Business Database.

Mainstay software is supported in the Mac A Vendor Forum (GO MACAVEN). See Apple Computers.

Mainstream (**magazine**) is searchable in the Health Database Plus (GO HLTBD). See Health.

Maki, Jim   (76701,33) is a sysop in the MIDI/Music Forum (GO MIDI), the Music Vendor Forum (GO MUSICVEN), the All-Music Guide Forum (GO AMGPOP), and the Music/Arts Forum (GO MUSICART). See Music. He also administers the Sight and Sound Forum (GO SSFORUM). See Multimedia.

Mallard Software products, supporting Microsoft's Flight Simulator, are supported in the Game Publishers B Forum (GO GAMBPUB). The firm's products include Tower, Lunar Command, Air Traffic Controller, Pilot's Power Tools, and Aircraft & Adventure Factory. Mallard Software also is represented in the Flight Simulations Forum (GO FSFORUM). See Gaming forums.

Mammoth Micro Productions products are supported in the Ultimedia Tools Forum B (GO ULTIBTOOLS). See Ultimedia.

Manaccom products are supported in the Pacific Vendor Forum (GO PACVEN). See Pacific Vendor.

Managed Care Outlook and **Managed Care Law Outlook** (**health business databases**) may be searched through the IQuest gateway. See IQuest. The resources also can be searched through the Business Database Plus (GO BUSDB), as well as *Managed Care Week*. See Business Database.

Management is the topic of a large collection of databases on IQuest (see IQuest), including: ABI/INFORM, Agribusiness U.S.A., Biobusiness, Biotech Business, Business Periodicals Index, Business Week, Businesswire, Chemical Business Newsbase, D&B— Dun's Electronic Business Directory, Economist, ESSOR, Forbes, Harvard Business Review Online, Inc., Management Contents, Management Matters, McGraw-Hill Publications Online, Network Management Systems & Strategies, PTS F&S Indexes, PTS PROMT, Trade and Industry ASAP, and Trade and Industry Index.
   Also:

   • *Management Review* and *Management Matters* can be searched through the Business Database Plus (GO BUSDB). See Business Database.

   • *Management Today* magazine is searchable through Magazine Database Plus (GO MDP). For details see Magazine Database. It also can be searched through Business Database Plus (GO BUSDB). See Business Database.

   See also Industry, Business, and Ecomonics.

Manager's Organizer (**software**) is supported in the Meca Software Forum (GO MECA). See Meca.

ManageWare/400 (**software**) is supported in the Software Solutions Forum (GO SOFSOL). See Software Solutions.

Managing the Market (software) is supported in the Meca Software Forum (GO MECA). See Meca.

Managing Your Money (software) is supported in the Meca Software Forum (GO MECA). See Meca.

Manitoba Business (magazine) can be searched through the Business Database Plus (GO BUSDB). See Business Database.

Mankins, Marty (75300,1770) is the sysop of the Palmtop Forum (GO PALMTOP). See Palmtop. He also is associated with the Pen Technology Forum (GO PENFORUM). See Pen Technology.

Manners, Steve (70007,4737) is sysop of the UK Computing Forum (GO UKCOMP). See UK Computing. He also is sysop of the UK Forum (GO UKFORUM). See UK Forum.

Manning, David (76703,237) is sysop of the Disabilities Forum (GO DISABILI-TIES). See Handicapped Issues.

Mansfield Software is supported in the PC Vendor A Forum (GO PCVENA). See IBM Computers.

Manufacturing Automation (database) may be searched through the IQuest gateway. See IQuest. The resource also can be searched through the Business Database Plus (GO BUSDB). See Business Database.

Manufacturing Technology, Advanced and **Electro Manufacturing** (magazines) can be searched through the Business Database Plus (GO BUSDB). See Business Database.

Manuscript (software) is supported in the Lotus Word Processing Forum (GO LOTUSWP). See Lotus Software.

MapLinx (products) are aupported in the Windows 3rd-Party Forum (GO WINAPD). See Microsoft Software.

Marine life is discussed in the Aquaria and Fish Forum (GO AQUAFORUM). See Fish.

Marketing is discussed in the Public Relations and Marketing Forum (GO PRSIG). See Public Relations and Marketing. For other business-oriented subjects, see Financial Services and see Investment Analysis Tools.
Also:

- American Marketplace , Database Marketing, Marketing, Market Research Reports From MSI, and Marketing Surveys Index may be searched through the IQuest gateway. See IQuest.

- Magazines searchable through the Business Database Plus (GO BUSDB) are *Affluent Markets Alert, Aftermarket Business, Frohlinger's Marketing Report, Green Marketing Report, Grocery Marketing, Journal of Marketing, Journal of Marketing Research, Market Asia Pacific, Market Europe, Marketing, Marketing & Media Decisions, Marketing Computers, Marketing News, Marketing Research Review, Marketing to Women, Marketletter, Market Research Europe, Minority Markets Alert, OTC Market Report Update USA,* and *OTC News & Market Report.* See Business Database.

- For British marketing information, see the UK Marketing Library (GO UKMARKETING). See UK Marketing.

Marketing/Management Research Center (GO MKTGRC) is a Telebase Systems Incorporated gateway to indices and full text of major U.S. and international business, management, and technical magazines; market and industry research reports; market studies and statistical reports; and U.S. and international company news releases. The information is made available by Dialog Information Services Incorporated.

The surcharge is $5 for the first 10 titles located, $5 for each additional 10 titles, and $5 for each full-text article retrieved. There is a $1 charge for a search that retrieves no titles.

Many of the papers also are searchable through IQuest. In addition, search of the research centers is similar to IQuest's procedure. See IQuest. And for information on other Telebase gateways, see Telebase Systems Incorporated.

Databases accessible through the research center are:

- ABI/INFORM by UMI/Data Courier.
- Findex by National Standards Association, Inc.
- FINIS by Bank Marketing Association.
- Industry Data Sources by Information Access Company.
- Infomat International Business by Infomat Ltd.
- McGraw-Hill Publications Online.
- PTS MARS, PTS New Product Announcements, and PTS PROMT by Predicasts Inc.

Marketing Surveys Index can be searched in the UK Marketing Library (GO UKMARKETING). See UK Marketing.

Market Snapshot (GO SNAPSHOT) gives a quick overview of current stock market trends by displaying key indicators in a one-page statistical report. See Current Market Snapshot.

Market, stock: Stock market quotes are available on a 15- or 20-minute delayed basis. Those signed up for the Standard Pricing Plan (see Billing) can get free market quotes by enter GO BASICQUOTES. This provides data on securities traded on the New York, American, Philadelphia, Boston, and National exchanges, as well as over-the-counter. Price and volume information are reported as a composite of the exchanges. See Stock Quotes, Current, and Stock Quotes, Historical. And for information on other money-related features, see Financial Services and see Investment Analysis Tools.

Mark IV Pro Audio products are supported in the MIDI B Vendor Forum (GO MIDIBVEN). See Music.

Markt & Technik AG Forum (GO MUT) supports readers of that European publication. Messages are in German.

Mark of the Unicorn products are supported in the MIDI C Vendor Forum (GO MIDICVEN). See Music.

Marquis Who's Who (GO BIOGRAPHY) is a Telebase Systems Incorporated gateway to Marquis Who's Who, which includes biographical information describing key North American professionals. Most information is obtained directly from the profiled individuals. Included are name, occupation, date and location of birth; parents, spouse, and children's names; education; positions held during career; civic, military and political activities; memberships; awards; and other organizational affiliations. You may retrieve biographies by entering the subject's name, birth (year, city, or country), occupation, research specialty, creative works, awards/honors, or military service as your search criteria. The feature provides "Search Guidelines" that are similar to those used with IQuest. The material is made available by Dialog Information Services Incorporated.

Who's Who carries transaction charges in addition to CompuServe's basic connect rates. A running total of transaction charges is displayed on Marquis Who's Who menu pages. Connect charges are not included in the displayed total. Searches (retrieving up to 10 names) are charged at $5, with additional names (in groups of 10) costing an additional $5. Each full biography retrieved is charged at $5. There is a $1 for each search that retrieves no titles.

For information on other Telebase gateways, see Telebase Systems Incorporated.

Marquis Who's Who also may be searched through the IQuest gateway (GO IQUEST) and through the Knowledge Index (GO KI). See IQuest and see Knowledge Index.

Martial arts is a topic of the Health & Fitness Forum (GO GOODHEALTH). See Health.

Maryland news is covered in selected reports from Maryland are included in the Mid-Atlantic regional reports from United Press International. See Executive News Service.

Also, the Baltimore Sun (newspaper) is searchable through Telebase System's News Source USA (GO NEWSUSA). See News Source. And *Baltimore Business Journal* can be searched through the Business Database Plus (GO BUSDB). See Business Database.

Masie, Elliott (76703,4375) is a sysop in the Computer Training Forum (GO DPTRAIN). See Computer Training.

MASM (software) is supported in the Microsoft Languages Forum (GO MSLANG). See Microsoft Software.

Masonry Forum (GO MASONRY) serves members of the world's fraternal order of Masons. The forum grew out of a section in the New Age Forum (GO NEWAGE). The Mason Forum is open to the public, with sections dedicated to Masonry history and books, Blue Lodge management, The Shrine, the Philalethes Society, and other Masonic orders.

Forum libraries offer graphic images in GIF and other formats, special programs for Lodge and Masonic use, as well as articles, poems, and newsletters written by past and present Masons.

The Masonry Forum is managed by Neil Shapiro (76703,401). He is assisted by Scott M. Sherman and William N. Wine.

Masque Publishing (software) is supported in the Game Publishers C Forum (GO GAMCPUB). See Gaming Forums.

Massachusetts news is covered in the Boston Globe, searchable through Telebase System's News Source USA (GO NEWSUSA). See News Source.

Also:

- Selected reports from Massachusetts are included in the Northeast regional reports from United Press International. See Executive News Service.
- *Boston Business Journal* can be searched through the Business Database Plus (GO BUSDB). See Business Database.

Material sciences are covered in *Material Handling Engineering*, *Materials Engineering*, and *Modern Materials Handling* magazines, which can be searched through the Business Database Plus (GO BUSDB). See Business Database.

Also, relevant databases on IQuest (GO IQUEST) include Aluminium Industry Abstracts, American Metal Market, Coal Outlook, Compendex Plus, Engineered Materials Abstracts, High Tech Ceramics News, Iron Age, Materials Business File, Metadex, Metals Datafile, Paperchem, PIRA Abstracts, PTS Newsletter Database, Rapra Abstracts, World Surface Coatings Abstracts, and World Textiles.

See also Energy, Chemistry, Industry and Metal industry.

Matesys Software products are supported in Windows 3rd-Party Forum C (GO WINAPC). See Microsoft Software.

Math studies: The Science/Math Forum (GO SCIENCE) is a gathering place for teachers, students, and other subscribers with an interest in science and math. See Science/Math Forum. It also is a topic in the Students' Forum (GO STUFO). See Students.

These topics also are searchable through the IQuest gateway (GO IQUEST),

Mathsci and Academic Index (GO IQUEST), and through the Knowledge Index (GO KI). See IQuest and see Knowledge Index.

In Computer Database Plus (GO COMPDB), you can search abstracts of *The Journal of Computers in Mathematics and Science Teaching*. See Computer Database Plus.

See also Science.

Mathematica (**software**) is supported in the Wolfram Research Forum (GO WOL-FRAM). See Wolfram Research Software.

Mathematica Inc. products are supported in the Graphics A Vendor Forum (GO GRAPHVEN). See Graphics.

Matsushita Weekly can be searched through the Business Database Plus (GO BUSDB). See Business Database.

Mature Health is searchable in the Health Database Plus (GO HLTBD). See Health.

Maturity, Modern (**magazine**) is searchable through Magazine Database Plus (GO MDP).

Max Ule's Tickerscreen (GO TKR-1) is an online stock brokerage service. See Stock Brokerages. It also operates a store in the Electronic Mall (GO MALL). See Electronic Mall.

Maxis products are covered in Game Publishers B Forum (GO GAMBPUB). See Gaming Forums.

Maxwell CPU products are supported in the Atari Vendors Forum (GO ATARIVEN). See Atari Computers.

McAfee Virus Help Forum (GO VIRUSFORUM) covers the growing problems caused by computer viruses and related rogue programs. The forum is operated by McAfee Associates and supports the firm's virus scan software, such as VIRUSCAN, NETSCAN, CLEAN-UP, VSHIELD, and WSCAN. This release adds detection for 70 new viruses including the 644 and Tabulero, bringing the total number of viruses detected to 755, and counting strains, to 1,471. The CLEAN-UP program has also been updated to remove several viruses.

The National Computer Security Association has put together a comprehensive list of information about its various resources, including membership, publications, and conferences. For more information, download file NCSA.ZIP from Library 6, "NCSA."

Note, the forum is not restricted to McAfee Associates customers, nor is it limited to discussions of McAfee Associates products. Questions about all aspects of viruses and other antivirus packages are encouraged.

The primary sysops are Aryeh Goretsky (76702,1714) and Spencer Clark (76702,1713), assisted by Robert Bales, Charles Rutstein, Richard Ku, and Patricia Hoffman.

See also Virus.

McCarthy Information Co. **(databases)** may be searched through the IQuest gateway. See IQuest.

McCarthy, Steve (71333,1570) is the sysop of the Sun Select Forum (GO SUNSELECT). See Sun Select.

McClellan, Gary (76702,1440) is sysop of the BASIS International Forum (GO BASIS). See BASIS International Software.

McCormack, Lisa, (72662,1235) is sysop of the Republican Forum (GO REPUB-LICAN). See Republican.

McCoy, John (75300,3634) is sysop of the Thomas-Conrad Corp. Support Forum (GO TCCFORUM). See Thomas-Conrad.

McGrath, Scott (72241,325) is sysop of the UTILFORUM/TIPS Forum (GO ZNT:UTILFORUM) of the PC Magazine Forum. See PC Magazine.

McGraw-Hill Book Co. (GO MH) offers a store in the Electronic Mall (GO MALL) for book orders. See Electronic Mall.

McGraw-Hill Publications Online **(business database)** is accessible through the Marketing/Management Research Center (GO MKTGRC). See Marketing/Management. This resource also may be searched through IQuest (GO IQUEST). See IQuest.

MCI Mail: Electronic mail may be exchanged between users of CompuServe and MCI Mail. For details, see Mail, CompuServe.

McKeown, Jim (70007,3441) is a sysop in the IBM Users Network (GO IBMNET). See IBM Computers.

McNamara, Tony (76702,1454) sysop of the Symantec/Norton Utilities Forum (GO NORUTL). See Symantec Software.

M.D. Computing **(magazine)** is searchable (abstracts) through Computer Database Plus (GO COMPDB). See Computer Database Plus.

Meca Software Forum (GO MECA) supports a variety of programs, including Managing Your Money, Checkwrite Plus, Home Lawyer, TaxCut, Managing the Market, Financial Calculator, and the Manager's Organizer.

The forum is administered by Dan Vener (76711,402) and Tony Gagliardo (76711,401), assisted by Mel Masuda.

Mechanical engineering is the subject of *Mechanical Engineering—CIME* magazine, searchable through the Business Database Plus (GO BUSDB). See Business Database.

Also, relevant databases on IQuest (GO IQUEST) include CIM, Compendex Plus, FLUIDEX (Fluid Engineering Abstracts), Global Mobility Database, Ismec:

Mechanical Engineering Abstracts, Machine Design, and Sensor Business Digest. See also Engineering.

Media General Plus (database) may be searched through the IQuest gateway. See IQuest.

Media Industry Newsletter, MIN, can be searched through the Business Database Plus (GO BUSDB). See Business Database.

Media Markets, New, can be searched through the Business Database Plus (GO BUSDB). See Business Database.

Media Newsletters (GO MEDIANEWS) are searchable through a gateway to PTS/Newsletter Database. See PTS Newsletter Database. For media-related topics, see News.

Media Vision products are supported in the MIDI B Vendor Forum (GO MIDIBVEN) and Multimedia Vendor Forum (GO MULTIVEN). See Music and Multimedia.

Media Week (database) may be searched through the IQuest gateway. See IQuest.

Medical Advisor, The, (column) is among the syndicated columns provided by United Features (GO COLUMNS). See Columnists.

Medical InfoCenter, IQuest (GO IQMEDICINE) is a Telebase Systems Incorporated gateway to information from and about the medical profession.

This is a surcharged gateway to major medical databases covering various aspects of medicine, including medical practice and research, pharmaceutical news, and allied health studies. These databases contain information from journals, books, government publications, special reports, and many other published sources.

Many of the references also are searchable through IQuest. In addition, search of the research centers is similar to IQuest's procedure. (See IQuest.) And for information on other Telebase gateways, see Telebase Systems Incorporated.

The surcharge is $9 for the first 10 titles located, $9 for each additional 10 titles, and $2 for each abstract retrieved. A "SmartScan" for the databases costs $5. There is a $1 for each search that retrieves no titles. Note, though, that some of the databases carry additional surcharges. The system notifies you in advance if you are requesting information from a surcharged database.

Medical references, available through the system, include a database of material from medical journals and health reports. For details, see Health Database Plus (GO HLTDB), PaperChase (GO PCH-1), Rare Disease Database (GO NORD), Physicians Data Query (GO PDQZ), Medical InfoCenter, IQuest (GO IQMEDICINE), and Journalism Forum's (GO JFORUM) MedNews. See Journalism. Medicine also is a topic in the Scuba Forum (GO DIVING). See Sports and Recreation.

For related topics, see Health.

Medicine also is the topic of a number of magazines and databases, including the following:

- Through the Business Database Plus (GO BUSDB), *American Medical News*, *Business & Health*, *The Journal of the American Medical Association*, *Medical Economics*, *Medical Laboratory Observer*, *Medical Research Funding News*, *Medical Textiles*, *Medical Utilization Review*, *Medical Waste News*, *Medical World News*, and *Medicine & Health*, as well as *FDA Enforcement Report* and *FDA Medical Bulletin*. See Business Database.

- Relevant databases on IQuest (GO IQUEST) include Academic Index, Ageline, AIDS Articles from Comprehensive Core Medical Library, AIDS Database, AIDS Knowledge Base, AIDS Weekly, Allied & Alternative Medicine, Biosis Previews, Biotechnology Investment Opportunities, British Medical Association's Press Cuttings, Cancer Research Weekly, Cancerlit, Combined Health Information Database, Comprehensive Core Medical Library, Department of Health and Social Security, Embase, Forensic Science Database, Hazardline, Health and Psychosocial Instruments, Health Care Competition Week, Health Care Reform Week, Health Devices Alerts, Health Grants and Contracts Weekly, Health Periodicals Database, Health Planning and Administration, Hospitals, Lancet, Medical Waste News, Medline, New England Journal of Medicine, Nursing & Allied Health, Occupational Safety and Health, PASCAL, Pharmaceutical News Index, Physician Data Query: Cancer Information File, Physician Data Query: Directory File, Physician Data Query: Patient Information File, Physician Data Query: Protocol File, Rehabdata, Rsinews, Smoking and Health, Sport, TOXLINE, and Unlisted Drugs.

- Searchable through the Knowledge Index (GO KI) are Medline, Cancerlit, Health Planning and Administration, Embase, SPORT, Nursing and Allied Health, Smoking and Health, and AIDSLine. See Knowledge Index.

See also Drugs, Health and Medicine, and Pharmaceuticals.

Medicine, American Journal of is searchable in the Health Database Plus (GO HLTBD), as is *American Medical News*, *Issues in Law & Medicine*, *Medical SelfCare*, *Medical Update*, *Medical World News*, *Medicine*, and *Postgraduate Medicine*. See Health.

Meditation is discussed in the New Age Forum (GO NEWAGE). See New Age.

MEDLINE (GO PCH-1) is the National Library of Medicine's database of references to the biomedical literature, at your fingertips. The service is surcharged at $24 an hour during weekday business hours, and $18 an hour during evenings and on weekends. See PaperChase.

   This resource also may be searched through IQuest (GO IQUEST) and through the Knowledge Index (GO KI). See IQuest and see Knowledge Index.

MedSig (GO MEDSIG) is a health-related forum sponsored by the American Medical Informatics Association. For details, see Health.

Meeting (**conference database**) may be searched through the IQuest gateway. See IQuest.

Mefford, Michael (72241,161) is one of the editors and writers associated with the PC Magazine forums. See PC Magazine.

Megahertz Corp. products are supported in the Modem Vendor Forum (GO MODEMVEN). See Modem Vendor.

Megawars (**games**) are the earliest multi-player computer games, developed by Kelton Flinn and John Taylor. MegaWars is a real-time space battle to be played by one to ten persons.

　　The mission in MegaWars I: The Galactic Conflict (GO MEGA1) is to destroy the enemy, capture planets, stay away from black holes and Archerons, rise in rank from cadet to admiral, and avoid getting zapped by other players.

　　Megawars III: The New Empire (GO MEGA3) gets more complex. It involves building spaceships to seek new planets, establishing colonies on them, building defenses, creating economic systems, and ruling the people.

　　The games are intended for those age 12 and up.

　　To find other Megawars enthusiasts, visit the Multi-Player Games Forum (GO MPFORUM). For information on other games, see Games.

Meier, Wilma (76701,274) administers the Science Fiction & Fantasy Forum (GO HOM-9). See Science Fiction & Fantasy Forum.

"Melrose Place" (**television**) summaries on the latest shows are available in Soap Opera Summaries (GO SOAPS). See Soap Opera.

Member Assistance (GO HELP): CompuServe maintains a database of answers to frequently asked questions about billing, forums, electronic mail, logons, real-time conferencing, and so on. See Help Online.

Member Directory (GO DIRECTORY) is a free database of CompuServe subscribers that is searchable by name. The state and city may be used as search criteria to narrow a name search. You may omit the first name, state, or city responses by entering a blank line (that is, by pressing RETURN). However, if you omit any of these, there is a good chance the resulting list will be too large to be displayed and, if that happens, you will be prompted again for the omitted information. You may use /START to terminate any current search and begin a new one. Inclusion in the directory is voluntary. The feature itself provides an option that lets you include or exclude your own user ID number in the directory. Any change you request will take a week to be effective.

Member Recommendation Program (GO FRIEND) rewards current members for signing up new CompuServe subscribers, giving each $25 in free online usage. In addition, the newcomer gets a $5 bonus credit not available in any other way except through the recommendation. There also are regular recommend-a-member contests. Details are available online.

Members of Congress database (GO FCC-1) provides the names of congressional representatives, the President, and Vice President. To use the database, enter GO FCC-1 at a prompt. This service provides a state-by-state listing of all members in the House of Representatives and the Senate. Each listing includes, the name, party affiliation, Washington telephone number, hometown and committee memberships. For related information, see Mail, CompuServe.

Membrane & Separation Technology News (science database) may be searched through the IQuest gateway. See IQuest. The resource also can be searched through the Business Database Plus (GO BUSDB). See Business Database.

Memory Management (software) is supported in the Quarterdeck Office Systems Forum (GO QUARTERDECK). For details, see Quarterdeck.

Memory Master (software) is supported in the PC Vendor C Forum (GO PCVENC). See IBM Computers.

Memphis Business Journal (magazine) can be searched through the Business Database Plus (GO BUSDB). See Business Database.

Memphis (TN) Commercial Appeal (newspaper) is searchable through Telebase System's News Source USA (GO NEWSUSA). See News Source.

Mendelson, Edward (72241,41) is among *PC Magazine*'s editors and contributors who are regulars in the publication's PC-Magnet service. See *PC Magazine*.

Mens, Joe R. (76711,1165) is the sysop of the Powersoft Forum (GO POWERSOFT). See Powersoft.

Mensa Forum (GO MENSA) operates with the theme "Intelligence—Its Development and Application." Message sections of the forum include Mensa's scholarship program, literacy and education, gifted children, IQ testing and research, mind to mind, the arts, and so on. Mensa is for anyone with a score in the 98th percentile or above on an acceptable I.Q. test or equivalent. The file BROCH.TXT from forum Library 1 has general information on Mensa.

The forum, which is open to Mensa members and nonmembers alike, is operated by David L. Van Geest (76711,330), assisted by Bill Horton, Geoff Smith, Jean Cooper, Alan Gore, Lana Mountford, and Laura Hathaway.

Men's Health is searchable in the Health Database Plus (GO HLTBD). See Health.

Men's issues is a topic in the Issues Forum (GO ISSUESFORUM). See Issues.

Mental Health Abstracts and **Mental Measurements Yearbook** **(databases)** may be searched through the IQuest gateway. See IQuest. Mental health also is a topic of the Health & Fitness Forum (GO GOODHEALTH) and in the MedSIG Forum (GO MEDSIG). See Health. Mental Health Abstracts also can be searched through the Knowledge Index (GO KI). See Knowledge Index.

Menu, Personal is an option in the logon/service area of Terminal Settings section (GO TERMINAL) that allows you to create your own top menu of favorite features. (Note: This is a feature of value only to those not using the CompuServe Information Manager software from CompuServe.) For details, see Personal Menu.

Merchant, Bob (76711,1247) is the sysop of the Epson Forum (GO EPSON). See Epson.

Merck Index Online can be searched through the Knowledge Index (GO KI). See Knowledge Index.

Mercury Systems products are supported in the Mac D Vendor Forum (GO MACDVEN). See Apple Computers.

Merger Law, International **(database)** may be searched through the IQuest gateway. Also accessible there are FT Mergers & Acquisitions International and M & A Filings. See IQuest.

For related topics, see Legal.

Mergers & Acquisitions Report can be searched through the Business Database Plus (GO BUSDB). See Business Database.

Meridian Data products are supported in the CD-ROM Vendors Forum (GO CDVEN) and the Multimedia Vendor Forum (GO MULTIVEN). See CD-ROM and Multimedia.

Merit Software products are covered in Game Publishers A Forum (GO GAMAPUB). See Gaming Forums.

Metagraphics, Inc. products are supported in the Graphics A Vendor Forum (GO METAGR). See Graphics.

Metal industry is covered in several IQuest databases, including Aluminium Industry Abstracts, American Metal Market, Iron Age, Materials Business File, Metadex, Metals Datafile and Nonferrous Metals Abstracts. See IQuest.

Also, related magazines searchable through the Business Database Plus (GO BUSDB) include *Advanced Metals Technology, ESP—Report on Mining & Metals in the Developing World, Metallurgia,* and *Metalworking News,* as well as *Japanese New Materials Advanced Alloys & Metals.* See Business Database.

Meteorological and Geoastrophysical Abstracts (database) may be searched through the IQuest gateway. See IQuest.

Metro (software) is supported in the Lotus Words & Pixels Forum (GO LOTUSB). See Lotus Software.

MetroNet sponsors a service called Phonefile (GO PHONEFILE) that lists more than 80 million households nationwide. It is a 25-cent-a-minute, surcharged feature that allows users to search by last name, phone number, ZIP code, and other means. See Phone Directories.

Metropolitan Home (magazine) can be searched in the Magazine Database Plus (GO MDP). See Magazine Database.

Metropolitan Museum of Art (GO MMA) is a store in the Electronic Mall (GO MALL) that offers artistic reproductions. See Electronic Mall.

METZ Software products are supported in the Windows 3rd-Party C Forum (GO WINAPC). See Microsoft Software.

Mexico is a topic in the Travel Forum (GO TRAVSIG). See Travel.
  Also, Mexico: Sourcemex, Economic News on Mexico database may be searched through the IQuest gateway (GO IQUEST). See IQuest. The resource also can be searched through the Business Database Plus (GO BUSDB), as can *Mexico Business Monthly* and *Mexico Service*. See Business Database.

Meyer, Arnie (76004,2500) administers the WealthBuilder Forum. See Wealth Builder.

MHR Software and Consulting products are supported in the OS/2 Vendor Forum (GO OS2AVEN). See IBM Computers.

Miami Herald (newspaper) is searchable through Telebase System's News Source USA (GO NEWSUSA) and through the Knowledge Index (GO KI). See News Source and see Knowledge Index.

Michigan news is covered in the Detroit Free Press, searchable through Telebase System's News Source USA (GO NEWSUSA). See News Source.
  Also:

  - Selected reports from Michigan are included in the Central regional reports from United Press International. See Executive News Service.
  - *Michigan Business* magazine can be searched through the Business Database Plus (GO BUSDB). See Business Database.

Michtron products are supported in the Atari Vendors Forum (GO ATARIVEN). See Atari Computers.

MicroBiz (**accounting software**) is supported by the Office Automation Vendor Forum (GO OAFORUM). See Office Automation.

MicroBotics products are supported in the Amiga Vendor Forum (GO AMIGAVENDOR). See Commodore Computers.

Microcell Report (**database**) may be searched through the IQuest gateway. See IQuest. The resource also can be searched through the Business Database Plus (GO BUSDB). See Business Database. See also PSN News.

Microcomputer Index, Microcomputer Resources, Microcomputer Software Guide, and **Microsearch** (**databases**) may be searched through the IQuest gateway. See IQuest. Micro Software Directory (SOFT), Microcomputer Index, and Microcomputer Software Guide can be searched through the Knowledge Index (GO KI). See Knowledge Index.

Micro Decisionware products are supported in the OS/2 Vendor Forum (GO OS2AVEN). See IBM Computers.

Micro Focus products are supported in the Micro Focus Forum (GO MICROFOCUS). The message sections cover areas for support of Micro Focus product, as well as discussion areas for COBOL-related authors and educators, for Micro Focus User Groups, and an area on the COBOL Language itself. The Library sections contain areas for product updates, product information, technical bulletins, program examples, training information, and announcements. Operating the forum is Alan Wheeler (71333,2247), assisted by Jon Harrison and Bill Weiregna.

Micrografx (**software products**) are supported in Windows 3rd-Party Forum A (GO WINAPA). See Microsoft Software.

MicroLink: Former subscribers of this British system might be interested in the UK Computing Forum (GO UKCOMP). For details, see UK Computing.

Micro Marketworld (**magazine**) is searchable (abstracts) through Computer Database Plus (GO COMPDB). See Computer Database Plus.

MicroMat products are supported in the Macintosh A Vendor Forum (GO MACAVEN). See Apple Computers.

Micronesian Investment Quarterly can be searched through the Business Database Plus (GO BUSDB). See Business Database.

Micronetics Design Corp. products are supported in the IBM Vendors H Forum (GO PCVENH). See IBM Computers.

MicroNet Technology products are supported in the Mac D Vendor Forum (GO MACDVEN). See Apple Computers.

Micronetworked Apple Users Groups (GO MAUG) is the official name of CompuServe's collection of Apple forums. See Apple Computers.

Micropolis products are supported in the IBM PC Vendor D Forum (GO PCVEND). See IBM Computers.

Microprocessors and Microsystems (magazine) is searchable through Computer Database Plus (GO COMPDB). See Computer Database Plus.

MicroProse software is regularly discussed in The Game Publishers B Forum (GO GAMBPUB) and in the Flight Simulation Forum (GO FSFORUM). See Gaming Forums.

Microrim Forum (GO MICRORIM) is operated by the software publisher's technical support staff to provide information about the company's flagship database management program, R:BASE 3.1 and higher versions. Managing the forum is Paul T. Scheiner (767111,1354), assisted by Aaron Carta and Dave van de Sompele.

Microseeds Publishing products are supported in the Mac B Vendor Forum (GO MACBVEN). See Apple Computers.

Microsoft Press (GO MSP), providing Windows and programming books, operates a kiosk in the Electronic Mall (GO MALL). See Electronic Mall.

Microsoft Software: Microsoft Connection (GO MICROSOFT) is operated by Microsoft Corporation's retail division product as the online gathering place for users of Microsoft programs. Microsoft is the company that created IBM's BASIC programming language and its PC-DOS/MS-DOS operating system.

Microsoft Product Support Services runs the forums. Jerry Fisher (76711,22) is sysop of the end-user forums, while Ridge Ostling (75300,3307) is sysop of the developer forums.

The desktop applications forums are the following:

- Access Forum (GO MSACCESS) supports Access users. The software enables the building of a database containing text, numbers, pictures, sound, and full-motion video.
- Application Forum (GO MSAPP): Here is where you can get help for DOS applications such as Word, Works, Chart, Project, MultiPlan, Flight Simulator, and for Macintosh applications such as Works, File, Word, Chart, Powerpoint, and Multiplan.
- Excel Forum (GO MSEXCEL) supports the publisher's spreadsheet system for IBM and Apple Macintosh computers.
- Fox Software Forum (GO FOXFORUM) provides online support for Fox Software's FoxBase+, FoxBase+/Mac, FoxPro, FoxGraph, and other products.
- Microsoft Fox Users Forum (GO FOXUSER) is for Fox "user-community" topics and discussions, generally less technical than those covered in the Fox Software Forum (GO FOXFORUM).
- Microsoft Sales and Information Center Forum (GO MSIC), monitored by the firm's sales staff, replies to product and pricing questions.

- Programming Applications Forums (GO PROGMSA) are intended for discussions of tips and techniques for programming various Microsoft Applications.
- Word Forum (GO MSWORD) supports Microsoft's word-processing package. The forum is divided into two main components, support and discussion. Forum section leaders will focus their attention on the support sections to ensure that questions are answered quickly. The discussion sections are available for nontechnical questions or thoughts on Word. The forum also includes a Project Worktable section for those involved in Word projects such as macros and templates.

Operating system forums are the following:

- MS-DOS 5.0 Forum (GO MSDOS) covers the features and uses of the June 1991 release of Microsoft's popular operating system for IBM PC and compatibles. The forum supports sections that feature setup and installation, hardware issues, compatibility, networks, command usage, the newest feature of the DOS shell, BASIC conversions, shareware, and the developers exchange.
- Microsoft Windows Forum (GO MSWIN) provides technical support from the Microsoft support team.
- Wordgroup Forum (GO MSWRKGRP) offers discussions of workgroup application techniques.

Development tools forums are the following:

- Languages Forum (GO MSLANG), with technical support for the Microsoft Language and Quick Language products. The forum includes sections for Assembler/Microsoft Editor, BASIC/QuickBASIC, COBOL, FORTRAN, Mac QuickBASIC, Microsoft C, QuickC, and QuickPascal/Pascal.
- 32-Bit Languages Forum (GO MSLNG32)
- Windows Extensions Forum (GO WINEXT), for information on the Windows SDK extensions.
- Microsoft Windows NT SNA Forum (GO MSSNA) is designed to exchange information on Windows multimedia products.
- Windows Multimedia Forum (GO WINMM)
- Windows Objects Forum (GO WINOBJECTS)
- Windows SDK Forum (GO WINSDK)

Advanced Systems Forums:

- Network Forum (GO MSNETWORKS) (also called Client Server Computing Forum) supports customers using Microsoft's LAN Manager and SQL Server products. The forum helps visitors with installation and configuration, LAN Manager internals, transports, SQL Server, as well as network management and developer relations. Managing the forum are Jerry Fisher and Ridge Ostling, assisted by Liz McDaniel, Kelly Elliot, and Kara McKenzie.

- SQL Server Forum (GO MSSQL) offers information on various Microsoft SQL products.
- Windows NT Forum (GO WINNT) discusses the new Windows NT system.

Windows Forums are:

- Windows Fun Forum (GO WINFUN) is designed to allow Windows users to discuss and obtain entertaining Windows programs such as games, screen savers, and graphics.
- Windows Shareware Forum (GO WINSHARE) lets Windows users talk about and download Windows applications, utilities, and tools.
- Windows 3rd-Party Forums A, B, C, D, and E (GO WINAPA, GO WINAPB, WINAPC, WINAPD, and WINAPE) are for non-Microsoft Windows applications. Third-party software companies producing applications for the highly successful Windows have their representatives in this forum to answer questions about their products. The companies (and products) supported:

  1. In WINAPA are Access Softek (Prompt!), Arabesque Software, Asymetrix, Future Software Engineering (DynaComm), GeoGraphix (Exploration), hDC (Express), HI-Q International (APE), ICOM, Jensen-Jones, Lucid Corp., Micrografx (Designer), Playroom, Premia, 3-D Visions, and WilsonWare (CommandPost).

  2. In WINAPB are Connect Software, Comp Presentations (ColorLab), Frontier Technologies, InfoAccess, Kaseworks (Case:W), Kidasa (Milestones), Knowledge Garden (KnowledgePro), NBI (Legacy), Nu-Mega Technologies, Ocean Isle Software, Softbridge (Bridge), SoftCraft (WYSIFonts), WindowCraft, WonderWare, and Zenographics (SuperPrint).

  3. In WINAPC are Abacus, Aristosoft, Berkeley Systems (After Dark), Campbell Services, GFA, Gilbert & Associates, Gold Disk, Gold Hill, LabTech, Matesys (ObjectScript), METZ Software, Protoview, Saros, Stirling Group (SHIELD tools), Thinx Software, and Wall Data.

  4. In WINAPD are ABC Systems, Automated Design, Avantos, Baseline Publishing, DeltaPoint, Inmark, Okna Corp., Peachtree Software, Q+E Software, ShapeWare Corp., SWFTE International, and Wextech Systems.

  5. In WINAPE are Andyne Computing Ltd. (Andyne Graphical Query Language), Archimedes Software (BugBase for Windows), Calera Recognition Systems Inc. (Caleras WordScan and WordScan Plus), CyberCorp (Cyberdesk), LaserTools (Expressdocs and Truetype for WordPerfect), MapLinx, PED Software (Journalist), Scitor (Project Scheduler 6 for Windows), SPSS Inc., and Systems Compatibility Corp. (Software Bridge).

Also, Microsoft's international services have been rapidly growing. At this writing, CompuServe provides access to the following:

- Benelux Developers Forum (GO MSBEN) offers information in English and Dutch about the company's Benelux services. It supports all of Microsoft's products, including BASIC, C/C++, Client Service Computing, Windows SDK, and database products based in the Benelux countries.

- Central Europe Forum (GO MSCE), a forum conducted in German, allows members to communicate directly with Microsoft staff in that language and to exchange messages with other users of Microsoft products such as LAN-Manager, Microsoft C, Microsoft MASM, MS-DOS, Visual Basic, and Windows. The forum libraries offer numerous files including drivers, samples, and updates for the various localized Microsoft products. Microsoft will also host periodic online conferences within the forum to discuss product-related topics.

- Microsoft Italy Forum (GO MSITALY) features messages and data library files, mostly in Italian, for assorted Microsoft products.

- Microsoft Spain/Latin America Forum (GO MSSPAIN), a Spanish-language service, features representatives from Microsoft Spain and Latin America who frequent the forum to answer questions about MS-DOS, Windows, Windows NT, applications, multimedia, programming tools, and more. The libraries contain help files, patches, technical notes, source codes, and Spanish shareware.

- Microsoft Sweden (GO MSSWEDEN) offers a suite of services of interest to Swedish users of Microsoft products.

In addition, Microsoft provides the Microsoft Knowledge Base online (GO MSKB), a database of 20,000 documents about Microsoft products. It allows you to search for specific information via a full text search application. It provides CompuServe users with the same database that Microsoft's support staff uses.

Also, the Microsoft Developer Network Technical Library (GO MSDNLIB) is part of the Microsoft Developer Services area. The library contains downloadable technical articles and application code samples to aid developers programming in Windows. These newly created technical articles are written by experts from the Microsoft Developer Network. New articles are added daily.

Microsoft Software Library (GO MSL), a keyword-searchable library contains downloadable text, graphics, sample code, and utilities files.

Technet (GO TECHNET) is available to everyone at no additional charge and is a component of a larger Microsoft program, Microsoft TechNet, which is an annual subscription service for support professionals and systems administrators. Microsoft TechNet includes a monthly CD-ROM disc that is packed with technical information, the Microsoft Services Directory, a customized version of WinCIM for accessing CompuServe, a discount on a CD-ROM disc drive, and much more. Microsoft TechNet is available at a special introductory price of $295 (U.S.). For more information about the TechNet program, a datasheet (TECHNT.EXE) can be downloaded from the Gen/Admin library of the TechNet forum.

Microsoft Systems Journal (**magazine**) is searchable through Computer Database Plus (GO COMPDB). See Computer Database Plus.

Microstation Forum (GO MSTATION) supports users of the CAD/CAM products of Bentley Systems Inc. Operating the forum are Mike Capuzzi and Phil Chouinard.

Micro Warehouse (GO MCW) is a store in the Electronic Mall (GO MALL) that offers hardware, software, and accessories for personal computers. See Electronic Mall.

Microware Software is the subject of the Microware Online Support Service (GO MICROWARE), designed to aid users of Microware software and introduce Microware products to CompuServe users. The service is divided into nine separate areas from a single menu, including new products, press releases, product specifications and prices, OS-9/68000 application notes and software problems, OS-9/6809 application notes, direct support from Microware, addresses, phone, telex, CompuServe Mail IDs of Microware distributors, and an area to send messages Microware.

Microwave Journal (**magazine**) can be searched through the Business Database Plus (GO BUSDB). See Business Database.

Mid-Atlantic Journal of Business (**magazine**) can be searched through the Business Database Plus (GO BUSDB). See Business Database.

Middle East news is provided in several IQuest databases, including APS Diplomat, APS Review, Arab Information Bank, and Mid-East Business Digest. See IQuest.
　Also:

- APS Diplomat and APS Review can be searched through the Business Database Plus (GO BUSDB), as can *ESP—Business Opportunities in Africa & the Middle East, Executive Briefing Service Middle East & North Africa, MEED Middle East Business Weekly, MEED Middle East Economic Digest, Mid East Business Digest, Middle East News Network,* and *Mideast Markets.* See Business Database.

- Middle East also is a topic of the Global Crisis Forum (GO CRISIS) (see Global Crisis), and in the International Trade Forum (GO TRADE) and the Travel Forum (GO TRAVSIG). See Travel and International Trade.

MIDI (Musical Instrument Digital Interface) is the subject of the MIDI/Music Forum (GO MIDI). See Music.

Midiman products are supported in the MIDI B Vendor Forum (GO MIDIBVEN). See Music.

MIDRANGE Systems (**magazine**) can be searched through Computer Database Plus (GO COMPDB). See Computer Database Plus.

Milbank Quarterly (magazine) can be searched through the Business Database Plus (GO BUSDB). See Business Database. The resource also can be searched through the Health Database Plus (GO HLTDB). See Health.

Milestones (software) is supported in Windows 3rd-Party Forum B (GO WINAPB). See Microsoft Software.

Military Forum (GO MILITARY) serves military veterans and those who want to exchange views about military topics, including military history and politics and the military adventure. Duane Goodridge (76711,217), the sysop, served two tours in Vietnam as an artillery forward observer with the 3rd Marines and has attended Capital University School of Journalism. Assisting him are Alex Humphrey, Jim Sorensen, John Paul, Jim Hubbard, Jack Hammond, Frank Tansey, Shawn Forney, David Woodbury, and Bill Smith.

Military subjects covered through the IQuest gateway (GO IQUEST) include Military Robotics 1989 Sourcebook and Military Space. See IQuest.

Also, *Military & Commercial Fiber Business*, *Military Robotics*, and *Military Space* can be searched through Business Database Plus (GO BUSDB). See Business Database.

Military also is a topic in in the Space/Astronomy Forum (GO SPACEFORUM). See Space. See also Defense.

Miller, Andrew (72662,1120) is sysop of the Polaris Software Forum (GO PO-LARIS). See Polaris.

Miller, Michael (72241,352) is one of the editors and writers associated with the PC Magazine forums. See PC Magazine.

Miller, Paul (76702,756) is sysop of the Music Arts Forum (GO MUSICART). See Music.

Milling & Baking News (magazine) can be searched through the Business Database Plus (GO BUSDB). See Business Database.

Milwaukee business news is reported in *The Business Journal-Milwaukee*, which can be searched through the Business Database Plus (GO BUSDB). See Business Database.

Minard, Kevin (72662,736) is sysop of the Dvorak Development Forum (GO DVORAK). See Dvorak Development.

Mindcraft Software is regularly discussed in The Game Publishers C Forum (GO GAMCPUB). See Gaming Forums.

MindReader (software) is supported in the PC Vendor G Forum (GO PCVENG). See IBM.

Mindscape Inc. software is regularly discussed in The Game Publishers Forum (GO GAMPUB). See Gaming Forums.

Miniatures   is one of the topics discussed in the Crafts Forum (GO CRAFTS). See Crafts.

Mini-Micro Software   **(magazine)** is searchable (abstracts) through Computer Database Plus (GO COMPDB). See Computer Database Plus.

Mini-Micro Systems   **(magazine)** can be searched through the Business Database Plus (GO BUSDB). See Business Database.

Mining Journal, E-MJ—Engineering & **(magazine)** can be searched through the Business Database Plus (GO BUSDB), as well as *ESP—Report on Mining & Metals in the Developing World* and *Mine Regulation Reporter*. See Business Database.

Also, ECOMINE, a mining information database, may be searched through the IQuest gateway. See IQuest.

Minnesota news   is covered in the St. Paul Pioneer Press Dispatch and the Minneapolis Star Tribune, and is searchable through Telebase System's News Source USA (GO NEWSUSA). See News Source.

Also:

- *CityBusiness—Minneapolis-St. Paul* and *Corporate Report—Minnesota* magazines can be searched through the Business Database Plus (GO BUSDB). See Business Database.
- *Minneapolis-St. Paul City Business* can be searched in the Magazine Database Plus (GO MDP). See Magazine Database. The resource also can be searched through the Business Database Plus (GO BUSDB). See Business Database.
- Selected reports from Minnesota are included in the Central regional reports from United Press International. See Executive News Service.

Minority Markets Alert   can be searched through the Business Database Plus (GO BUSDB). See Business Database.

Mintel Research Reports and **Mintel Special Reports** can be searched in the UK Marketing Library (GO UKMARKETING). See UK Marketing.

MIP Fund Accounting   products are supported in the IBM PC Vendor F Forum (GO PCVENF). See IBM Computers.

Miracom modems   and others are supported in the U.K. Computing Forum (GO UKCOMP). See UK Computing.

Mirror Technologies   products are supported in the Macintosh C Vendor Forum (GO MACCVEN). See Apple Computers.

MISOSYS Incorporated   products are supported in the LDOS/TRSDOS6 Users Forum. See Tandy Corporation Computers.

Missing Children Database, an effort by the National Child Safety Council, the oldest and largest U.S. nonprofit organization entirely dedicated to the safety of children, this database is supported in the Missing Children Forum (GO MISSING). See Children, Missing.

Mission Control Software (GO MCS) is a store in the Electronic Mall (GO MALL) that offers software and accessories. See Electronic Mall.

Mississippi news is included in the daily Southeast regional reports from United Press International. See Executive News Service for details.

Also, *Mississippi Business Journal* can be searched through the Business Database Plus (GO BUSDB). See Business Database.

Miss Manner (column) is among the syndicated columns provided by United Features (GO COLUMNS). See Columnists.

Missouri news is covered in the St. Louis Post-Dispatch, searchable through Telebase System's News Source USA (GO NEWSUSA). See News Source.

Also:

- Selected reports from Missouri are included in the Southwest regional reports from United Press International. See Executive News Service.

- *St. Louis Business Journal, Corporate Report—Kansas City,* and *The Kansas City Business Journal* can be searched through the Business Database Plus (GO BUSDB). See Business Database.

MIS Week (magazine) is available for full-text searching through Computer Database Plus (GO COMPDB), which also has abstracts of *MIS Quarterly.* See Computer Database Plus.

Mitchell and Gauthier products are supported in the IBM PC Vendor G Forum (GO PCVENG). See IBM Computers.

MMS Financial Reports (GO MMS) is a financial service specializing in economic research. See Investment Analysis Tools.

Mobile Data Report, Mobile Phone News, Mobile Satellite News and **Mobile Satellite Reports** (databases) may be searched through the IQuest gateway. See IQuest.

Searchable through the Business Database Plus (GO BUSDB) are *Land Mobile Radio News, Mobile Communications, Mobile Data Report, Mobile Phone News, Mobile Satellite News,* and *Mobile Satellite Reports.* See Business Database.

Mobile Office magazine editors frequent the Consumer Electronics Forum (GO CEFORUM). See Electronics.

Mobility Impaired is discussed in the Disabilities Forum (GO DISABILITIES). See Disabilities.

Model 100 (Tandy Corp.): CompuServe has forums that support this Tandy Corp. machine (GO TANDYLAPTOP). See Tandy Corp. Computers.

ModelNet Forum (GO MODELNET) is for model builders of airplanes, cars, boats, and rockets to share their experiences on this hobby forum. Doug Pratt (76703,3041) is the administrator of the forums. He is special projects director of the Academy of Model Aeronautics, the model airplane fliers' national organization. Assisting are Tom Caldwell, Keir Jones, Don Edberg, Bill McCall, Melvin Schuette, Gary Kato, Gary Underwood, John Atchley, Sheldon Markesteyn-Smith, and Bob Andrews.

See also TrainNet (GO TRAINNET).

Modem Games Forum (GO MODEMGAMES) serves those interested in one of the more exciting recent innovations in computer gaming, the ability to play computer games with and against other people who are located in different areas. This forum brings gamers together from around the world to discuss computer games that are capable of using telecommunications and/or networking technology for play and competition. This includes (but is not limited to) games which support a direct modem-to-modem connection, null-modem connections, LAN-based games, turn/scenario-based games—where uploading and downloading can be utilized for competition, and BBS door games. Also known as the "Game Challenge" Forum, the Modem Games Forum is committed to organizing tournaments for game competitions that can be integrated with CompuServe's Forum environment. The sysops are Mike Schoenbach (76703,4363), Sara Howard (76702,543), and Linda Lindley (76702,1504). Assisting are Steve Schafer, Randy Michal, Rick Moscatello, Lorna Anton, and Roger White.

Modem-to-modem games are supported in the National Modem-to-Modem Game Players' Challenge Board (GO CHALLENGE), which was created to allow owners of modem-to-modem computer games to find one another. This lets you find opponents in your local calling area. In addition, the challenge board allows players to put together nationwide tournaments.

The games listed on the Challenge Board are not playable on CompuServe nor via the network. Modem-to-modem games that the Challenge Board supports include BattleChess by InterPlay; Empire by Interstel; Falcon by Spectrum-HoloByte; Flight Simulator 3 by Microsoft; Modem Wars by Electronic Arts; and 3-D Helicopter by Sierra Online.

Each game has its own area on the CHALLENGE menu. Each game menu has the following areas:

- A database where you can find other players of the game. You are shown the names only of other users who live in the telephone area code selected. The default is your own area code. You may narrow this search by the telephone prefix (first three digits). You are shown a list of potential opponents matching the search criteria. By entering the number next to the user's name, you see a summary screen about that user. You may then use the INVITE command to send a CompuServe Mail challenge to the user.

- A menu selection where you may submit or revise your own entry. Use this option to enter your own information so that other players may contact you.
- A news bulletin area where notices are posted by representatives of the game publishers.

Another menu selection takes you to forums that support the modem-to-modem challenge game concept.

CompuServe also has added the Modem-to-Modem Gaming Lobby (GO MTMLOBBY), which enables players to connect their modem-capable games and play opponents at reduced CompuServe connect-time charges. The lobby supports the most popular game titles, including Command HQ, Flight Simulator 4, Knights of the Sky, Stunt Driver, Tank, 3D Helicopter, 'Vette, and so on. Live interactive help is available from 7 p.m. to 12 a.m. EDT daily.

For information on other games, see Games. For more on modem use, see Telecomputing.

Modem Users News (database) may be searched through the IQuest gateway. See IQuest. The resource also can be searched through the Business Database Plus (GO BUSDB). See Business Database.

Modem Vendor Forum (GO MODEMVEN) offers product support, product updates, announcements, and reviews, plus utilities, drivers, and script files for an assortment of modem makers. Among the companies represented in the forum are Boca Research, The Complete PC, Computer Peripherals, Global Village Communcations, Megahertz, Multi-Tech, National Semiconductor, PSI Integration, Supra Corp., Telebit, U.S. Robotics, Zoom, and ZyXEL.

Also, DataPort fax modems are offered through AT&T Online Store (GO DP) in the Electronic Mall (GO MALL). See At&T Online.

Modem Wars (software) by Electronic Arts is supported in the National Modem-to-Modem Game Players' Challenge Board (GO CHALLENGE). See Modem-to-Modem Games.

Modern Brewery Age See Brewery Age, Modern.

Modular Languages Compilers are supported in the IBM Vendors H Forum (GO PCVENH). See IBM Computers.

Modula-2 (software) is discussed in CODEPORT, The Portable Programming Forum (GO CODEPORT), sponsored by the UCSD Pascal System Users' Society. See Programmers Support.

Modula-2 and **Modula-3** are supported in the Portable Programming Forum (GO CODEPORT). See Programmers Support.

Moen, Rick (76711,243) is sysop of the Blyth Software Forum (GO BLYTH). See Blyth.

Money (**magazine**) can be searched through the IQuest gateway (GO IQUEST). See IQuest. It also can be searched in News Source USA (GO NEWSUSA). See News Source.

MoneyCounts (**software**) is supported in the Parsons Technology Forum (GO PTFORUM). See Parsons Technology.

Money Laundering Alert can be searched through the Business Database Plus (GO BUSDB). See Business Database.

Moneyline (**software**) is supported in the Monogram Software Forum (GO MONOGRAM). See Monogram Software.

Money Magazine (GO MONEYMAG) provides FundWatch (GO FUND WATCH), which lets you research more than 1,900 funds by entering ticker symbols or names. This is one of the system's basic services, meaning that those signed up under the Standard Pricing Plan (see Billing) have unlimited access to the feature. For details, see Financial Services.

Monitor Information Services products are supported in the CD-ROM Vendors Forum (GO CDVEN). See CD-ROM.

Monopoly (**game**) enthusiasts gather in the Play-by-Mail Games Forum (GO PBMGAMES). See Games.

Monotype products are supported in the Desktop Publishing Vendor Forum (GO DTPVENDOR). For details, see Desktop Publishing.

Montage Group Ltd. products are supported in the Ultimedia Tools Forum B (GO ULTIBTOOLS). See Ultimedia.

Montana news is included in the daily Western regional reports from United Press International. See Executive News Service for details.

Also, *Montana Business Quarterly* can be searched through the Business Database Plus (GO BUSDB). See Business Database.

Monthly Review (**magazine**) is searchable through Magazine Database Plus (GO MDP). For details see Magazine Database.

Moody's Corporate News U.S., Moody's Corporate News International, and **Moody's Corporate Profiles** (**databases**) may be searched through the IQuest gateway. See IQuest.

Morbidity and Mortality Weekly Report is searchable in the Health Database Plus (GO HLTBD). See Health.

MORE and **MORE II** (**software**) are supported in the Symantec Forum (Go SYMANTEC). See Symantec Software.

Morgan Report on Directory Publishing (database) may be searched through the IQuest gateway. See IQuest.

Morgret, Kathy (76702,1665) is the sysop of the Crafts Forum (GO CRAFTS). See Crafts.

Mormonism is a topic in the Religion Forum (GO RELIGION). See Religion.

Morphing, a computer graphics technique by which images are reshaped by a computer to resemble other objects while still keeping the colors and shades of the original image, is covered in the Graphics Developers Forum (GO GRAPHDEV). See Graphics. See also the Comic/Animation Forum (GO COMICS).

Morse code is a topic in the HamNet <Ham Radio> Forum (GO HAMNET). See HamNet.

Mortgage Banking (magazine) can be searched through the Business Database Plus (GO BUSDB), as can *Mortgage Marketplace* and *Mortgage-backed Securities Letter*. See Business Database.

Mortgage Calculator (GO MORTPAY) allows the user to figure out the amounts of mortgage payments at different rates. This is one of the system's basic services, meaning those signed up under the Standard Pricing Plan (see Billing) have unlimited access to the feature.

Moskowitz, David (76701,100) is chief sysop of the Computer Consultant's Forum (GO CONSULT). See Computer Consulting. He also is associated with the Unix Forum (GO UNIXFORUM). For details, see Unix.

Mother Earth News and **Mother Jones** (magazines) can be searched in the Magazine Database Plus (GO MDP). See Magazine Database.

Mothering magazine is searchable in the Health Database Plus (GO HLTBD). See Health.

Motor Age and **Motor Report International** (magazines) can be searched through the Business Database Plus (GO BUSDB). See Business Database. See also Cars.

Motorcycle racing is covered in the Motor Sports Forum (GO RACING). See Sports and Recreation. Also, see Cars.

Motor homes are a topic of the Recreational Vehicle Forum (GO RVFORUM). See Recreational Vehicle.

Motor Sports Forum (GO RACING) covers all kinds of car racing. See Sports and Recreation.

Motor Trend (magazine) can be searched in the Magazine Database Plus (GO MDP). See Magazine Database.

Movies are covered in Roger Ebert's Movie Reviews (GO EBERT), a database of 20 years worth of reviews, (see Roger Ebert) and in Magill's Survey of Cinema (GO MAGILL), a database that contains descriptions of most major films from 1902 to the present. See Magill's Survey of Cinema.

Moving is the topic of Relo (GO RL) and Homefinder Service (GO HF), stores in the Electronic Mall (GO MALL). See Electronic Mall.

MPT Report (**investment database**) may be searched through the IQuest gateway. See IQuest.

MS-DOS/PC-DOS (**software**) is supported in the MS DOS Forum (GO MSDOS). See Microsoft Software.

MSI Market Reports: Market Research Reports (**database**) may be searched through the IQuest gateway. See IQuest. It also can be searched in the UK Marketing Library (GO UKMARKETING). See UK Marketing.

Muller, Jim (76703,3005) is sysop (and "Chief Turtle") in the LOGO Forum (GO LOGOFORUM). See Programmers Support.

Multichannel News (**magazine**) can be searched through the Business Database Plus (GO BUSDB). See Business Database.

Multimate (**software**) is supported in the Borland Applications Forum (GO BORAPP). See Borland.

Multimedia is the topic of several forums, including the following:

- Multimedia Forum (GO MULTIMEDIA) is operated by Multimedia Computing Corporation, and covers video, audio, animation, interface design, music, hypertext, entertainment, and more. Many files are available for downloading. There also are discussion areas for Macintosh, Windows/DOS/OS-2, and Amiga; application areas are covered for education/training, sales/marketing, technical documentation, simulations and visualizations, and entertainment, as well as sections for talking about legal issues and marketing. The forum is operated by Nick Arnett (75300,1324), who is president of Multimedia, and Jim Ogilvie (76247,741). They are assisted by Eric Moody, Julian Thomas, Ian Martin, and Courtney Harrington.

- Multimedia Vendor Forum (GO MULTIVEN) supports the leading multimedia hardware and software vendors. The sysops are Jim Ogilvie (75300,2253) and Courtney Harrington, (72662,155). They are assisted by Bob Hoskins, Nick Arnett, Dan Ryder, and Tim Bajarin. Suppliers supported include AimTech, Asymetrix, Authorware, BCD Associates, The Center for Electronic Art, Cognetics, HSC Software, Media Vision, Meridian Data, New Media Graphics, nTergaid, Owl International, Specular International, Truevision, Turtle Beach, VideoLogic, and The Voyager Company.

- Sight and Sound Forum (GO SSFORUM) serves those interested in computer graphics, animation, and sound files and their integration. Participants talk about and share files that involve digital sound, sampling, multimedia, GIF images, animation, and all other forms of computer images accompanied by sound and music. Message sections and libraries cover various hardware platforms, MIDI, sound cards, applications, etc. Administering the forum is Jim Maki (76701,33). Assisting him are Mike Ward, Dan McKee, Gary Maddox, K.K. Proffitt, Tom LeCompte, Bruce Johnson, James Chandler Jr., Dominick Fontana, Frank Marousek, John Hays, Paul Miller, James Port, Dan Sevush, Larry Wood, Dave Shaver, Matt Drury, Jenee Burns, Tom Price, Bill Hinkle, Tom Mitchell, Jim Beebe, Patty Buckingham, Tom Potocki, Jacqui Kinnie, and Jamie O'Connell.

See also Amiga Arts Forum (GO AMIGAARTS) (see Commodore), CDROM Forum (GO CDROM) (see CD), CompuAdd Forum (GO COMPUADD) (see CompuAdd), Education Forum (GO EDFORUM) (see Education), Gamer Forum (GO GAMERS), IBM OS/2 Developer's Forum #1 (GO OS2DF1) (see IBM Computers), Microsoft Applications Forum (GO MSAPP) (see Microsoft Software), Macintosh Multimedia Forum (GO MACMULTI) (see Apple Computers), NeXT Forum (GO NEXTFORUM) (see NeXT), Packard Bell Forum (GO PACKARDBELL) (see Packard Bell), Windows Support Forum (GO MSWIN), and Windows Users Network Forum (GO WUGNET) (see Microsoft Software).

- Searchable through IQuest (GO IQUEST) are Multimedia Monitor and Multimedia Publisher. Through the Business Database Plus (GO BUSDB), related resources include *Multimedia & Videodisc Monitor*, *Multimedia Publisher*, and *Multimedia Week*. See Business Database.

See also Ultimedia Tool Forums and Macromedia Forum, as well as Graphics and Music.

Multimedia Monitor (Future Systems Inc.) is supported at the CD-ROM Vendor Forum (GO CDVEN). See CD.

MultiModem II and other modems are supported in the Modem Vendor Forum (GO MODEMVEN). See Modem Vendor.

Multinational Environmental Outlook and **Multinational Service** can be searched through the Business Database Plus (GO BUSDB). See Business Database.

Multiplan (software) is supported Microsoft Application Forum (GO MSAPP). See Microsoft Software.

Multiplayer Games Forum (GO MPGAMES) is dedicated to the support of CompuServe's online multi-player games. See Gaming Forums.

Multiple Choice (game) (GO MULTIPLE) gives a menu that includes trivia for kids (ages 7 to 12), trivia for teens (ages 13 to 18), relaxing games, achievement challenges, trivia for everyone, a personality profile test, and serious brain challenges. For information on other games, see Games.

Multiple Sclerosis is covered in *Inside MS*, which is searchable in the Health Database Plus (GO HLTBD). See Health. The the topic also is discussed in the Disabilities Forum (GO DISABILITIES). See Disabilities.

Multiscope is supported in the Symantec Development Forum (GO SYMDEVTOOL). See Symantec.

Multitask Consulting products are supported in the OS/2 Vendor Forum (GO OS2AVEN). See IBM Computers.

Multi-Tech products are supported in the Modem Vendor Forum (GO MODEMVEN). See Modem Vendor.

Multi-User DOS products are supported in the Novell Vendors Forum A (GO NVENA). See Novell.

Municipal planning is a topic of the Legal Forum (GO LAWSIG). See Legal Forum.

M-USA products are supported in the IBM PC Vendor C Forum (GO PCVENC). See IBM Computers.

Museum of Art, Metropolitan (GO MMA) is a store in the Electronic Mall (GO MALL) that offers artistic reproductions. See Electronic Mall.

Music is the topic of a collection of services, including the following:

- All-Music Guide (GO ALLMUSIC), is a database that promises information on more than 200,000 albums, covering most known forms of music. It is said to be the largest collection of music albums, ratings, and reviews open to public comment. The All-Music Guide is also a 1,200-page book (Miller-Freeman), a CD-ROM (Compton's NewMedia), and an online service licensed by Phonolog, Muze Systems (Tower records), Musicland, and other music retailers. AMG represents the combined effort of over 200 experienced music writers who point out the most important artists and their best music. Most are well-known reviewers. Operating the forum (GO AMGPOP) is Jim Maki (76701,33), with the assistance of Mike Ward, Paul Miller, and Michael Erlewine.

- MIDI A Vendor Forum (GO MIDIAVEN) supports products from Animotion, Barefoot/Hybrid, Big Noise, E-mu Systems, Eventide, JLCooper, Magnetic Music, Music Quest, Opcode, PG Music, REP Magazine, Turtle Beach, Twelve Tone, and YC/Kurzweil.

- MIDI B Vendor Forum (GO MIDIBVEN) supports products from Coda Music Technology, Cool Shoes Software, Covox, Lexicon, Live Sound!, Mackie Designs, Mark IV Pro Audio, Media Vision, Midiman, Passport Designs, Sweetwater Sound, and Temporal Acuity.

- MIDI C Vendor Forum (GO MIDICVEN), provides support for Asystem, Blue Ribbon, Dr. T's, DrumTrax, Howling Dog, Innovative Quality Software,

Mark of the Unicorn, OSC, Roland Corp., Soundcraft, Sound Deals, Steinberg/Jones, and Thought processors.

- The MIDI/Music Forum (GO MIDIFORUM) is devoted to the use of the Musical Instrument Digital Interface, a way for synthesizers, samplers, and other electronic equipment to communicate. Forum features include highlights of interviews, columns, and synthesizer sound banks and patches, as well as online support from MIDI manufacturers and software developers. The sysops include Jim Maki (76701,33), a composer and musician. He is assisted by Mike Ward, Paul Miller, Frank Marousek, John Hays, James Port, James Chandler Jr., Tom LeCompte, Dominick Fontana, Dan McKee, K.K. Proffitt, Bruce Johnson, and Gary Maddox.

- Music/Performing Arts Forum (GO MUSICARTS) supports budding performers and accomplished artists, as well as those who simply enjoy the work of others. Operated by sysops Jim Maki (76701,33) and Paul Miller (76702,756), the forum features message sections and libraries spanning the musical gamut from classical, nostalgic, and folk, to country, rock and New age, along with special areas covering theater, dance and spoken-word recordings. Assisting in the management of the forum are K. K. Proffitt and section leaders Steve Ledbetter (classical music), Les Line (jazz/blues music), Mike Lawson and Glenn Smith (the music industry), Carol McAlpine (the blues), John Egenes (country/folk), Paula Kay Williams (pop/rock/techno/rap), Bruce A. Johnson (instruments/sound), Mike Sullivan (world/new age), and David Coste (religious music).

- Music Vendor Forum (GO MUSICVEN) brings you the latest industry news from major recording labels and music companies. The forum allows you to find out about new album releases before they arrive in stores, join online fan clubs, obtain tour schedules, read artists' biographies, and participate in live conferences with popular artists and groups. Among the participants are Warner Bros. Records (GO WARNER), which has sections of the message board and a library for its news and lists; Geffen Records, providing information on such artists as Nirvana, Aerosmith, Guns 'N' Roses, Primus, and Rickie Lee Jones (GO GEFFEN); and RCA (GO RCA), with information on artists such as Bruce Hornsby, ZZ Top, SWV, Freddie Jackson, and Wu-Tang Clan; and CMC. The forum is managed by Jim Maki (76701,33) and Mike Ward (76703,2013).

- ROCKNET Forum (GO ROCKNET) features live discussions of the latest rock 'n roll. It is part of a forum-database area set aside for popular music. Administrator of the area is Les Tracy (76703,1061), who co-founded the service with Jim Palozola (76703,3027). They are assisted by Gina, Sheila Rene, and a group of reviewers who spend their time at rock concerts and report back on the latest happenings. The database (GO ROCK) contains late-breaking ROCKNET news, reviews, and commentary, as well as rumors, the top charts, and lists and reports on rock radio and video.

Subscribers also might be interested in the ShowBiz Forum (GO SHOWBIZ), designed for discussions of films, television programs, record albums, celebrity gossip, and nightly news shows. See Show Biz.

Also, music collectables—records, sheet music, tapes, promotional material—are discussed in the Collectibles Forum (GO COLLECT). See Collectibles.

MIDI/music also is a topic in Amiga Arts Forum (GO AMIGAARTS), Atari ST Arts Forum (GO ATARIARTS), Mac Fun/Entertainment Forum (GO MACFUN), OS-9 Forum (GO OS9), PC Plus/PC Answers Forum (GO PCPFORUM), Sight & Sound Forum (GO SSFORUM), Students' Forum (GO STUFO), and UK Computing Forum (GO UKCOMPUTING).

Music products also are for sale in some shops in the Electronic Mall (GO MALL), including BMG Compact Disc Club (GO CD), Columbia House Music (GO CH), The Laser's Edge (GO LE), Justice Records (GO JR), and Music Alley Online (GO MAO). See Electronic Mall.

Also:

- *Audio* and *Stereo Review* magazine is searchable through Magazine Database Plus (GO MDP). For details see Magazine Database. *Stereo Review* also may be searched through IQuest. See IQuest.

- The IQuest gateway (GO IQUEST) provides searching of Academic Index, Magazine ASAP, Magazine Index, and Music Literature International. See IQuest.

- *The Music Trades* magazine can be searched through the Business Database Plus (GO BUSDB). See Business Database.

Music Alley Online (GO MAO) is a store in the Electronic Mall (GO MALL) that offers mixers, synthesizers, keyboards, and so on. See Electronic Mall.

Music Quest products are supported in the MIDI A Vendor Forum (GO MIDIAVEN). See Music.

Mustang Software is supported in the PC Vendor A Forum (GO PCVENA). See IBM Computers.

Mutual Funds are the topic of FundWatch (GO FUNDWATCH), a feature that lets you sort through more than 1,900 funds by entering its ticker symbol or name. For details, see Financial Serivices.

Also, Dreyfus Corp. (GO DR) and Twentieth Century Investors (GO TC) are stores in the Electronic Mall (GO MALL) that offer investment opportunities information, including information on mutual funds. See Electronic Mall.

MWave System products are supported in the Ultimedia Hardware Plus Forum (GO ULTIHW). See Ultimedia.

N

NAIC Forum (GO NAIC) is a financial forum for value-oriented long-term investors. It caters to those who aren't concerned with day-to-day changes in market prices, but who focus on finding quality companies and buying them at good prices. It is sponsored by National Association of Investors Corporation which supports both Individual investors and those who belong to clubs. The group's concepts focus on investing in common stocks for the long term, from three to five years at a time. Forum administrators are Dick Kenfield (76702,1560) and Liz Hart, assisted by Bill Bentley.

   Also of possible interest is the Investors Forum (GO INVFORUM). For more on that, see Investors Forum.

NAPLPS art is supported in the Quick Pictures Forum (GO QPICS). See Graphics.

Narada Productions (GO NP) is a store in the Electronic Mall (GO MALL), offering compact discs and cassettes. See Electronic Mall.

NASA is the favorite topic in the Space Forum (GO SPACE). For background, see Space. Also, graphic images from NASA and the Jet Propulsion Laboratory are available in the Astronomy Forum (GO ASTROFORUM). The forum's Library 13, "Orbiting Scope," houses the forum's extensive collection of images from NASA's orbiting observatories in .GIF.

NASCAR and **stock car racing** is discussed in the Motor Sports Forum (GO RACING). See Sports and Recreation.

Nashville Business and Lifestyle (magazine) can be searched through the Business Database Plus (GO BUSDB). See Business Database.

Nation, Nation's Business, and **National Review** (magazines) articles are searchable through Magazine Database Plus (GO MDP). For details, see Magazine Database. Nation's Business also can be search on IQuest. See IQuest.

On the Business Database Plus (GO BUSDB) are *Nation's Business* and *Nation's Cities Weekly*. See Business Database.

National Association of Investors Corp. supports a financial forum (GO NAIC). See NAIC Forum.

National Modem-to-Modem Game Players' Challenge Board (GO CHALLENGE) was created to allow owners of modem-to-modem computer games to find one another so that they may find opponents in their local calling area. See Modem-to-Modem Games.

National Rifle Association has a section in the Outdoors Forum (GO OUT-DOORS) for discussing issues. See Outdoors.

National Semiconductor products are supported in the Modem Vendor Forum (GO MODEMVEN). See Modem Vendor.

National Technical Information Service (GO NTIS) is a gateway to a database published by the U.S. Department of Commerce, which contains nearly 1.5 million references to articles from government-sponsored research, development, and engineering reports, usually with corresponding abstracts. Coverage goes back to 1970, and the database is updated every two weeks.

Available in most articles are the titles, authors, corporate sources, sponsors, report numbers, publication years, contract numbers, and abstracts. You may retrieve abstracts by entering subject words, author names, or the publication year.

The cost is $2 for the first 10 titles located, $2 for each additional 10 titles, and $2 for each listing retrieved. There is a $1 for each search that retrieves no titles.

For information on other Telebase gateways, see Telebase Systems Incorporated.

This resource also can be searched through the Knowledge Index (GO KI). See Knowledge Index.

National Weather Service (GO WEATHER) provides local, state, and national weather forecasts and summaries for the nation. See Weather.

Native American crafts is among the topics discussed in the Crafts Forum (GO CRAFTS). See Crafts. Also, Native Americans is a topic in the Issues Forum (GO ISSUESFORUM). See Issues.

Nature magazine abstracts are searchable in the Health Database Plus (GO HLTBD). See Health.

Nautilus (**magazine on disk**) is supported in the CDROM Forum (GO CDROM). See CD.

Navigator, CompuServe (**software**) is a program by Mike O'Connor for Apple Macintosh and for Windows-based computers that allows automated interaction with the forums, CompuServe Mail, and other areas of the system. CompuServe distributes the software online (GO CISSOFT). The Macintosh program also is supported in a free Navigator Support Forum (GO MNAVSUP). This is one of the system's basic services, meaning those signed up under the Standard Pricing Plan (see Billing) have unlimited access to the feature. The forum's libraries offer many scripts that further expand Navigator's functionality. Recent additions include scripts for reading the Associated Press' hourly news update, forwarding stories from an Executive News Service clipping folder to CompuServe Mail, and a tool that simplifies the retrieval of local weather forecasts. The forum's sysops are Shelley Myers (70006,275) and Mike Leibrand (70006,405), both of whom work for CompuServe in the Customer Service Department and specialize in Macintosh support for Navigator.

The newer Windows-based version of Navigator also has online information and distribution (GO CSNAV), and technical assistance in the WinNav Support Forum (GO WNAVSUPPORT). Like the Mac forum, it is free of connect-time charges. The forum is operated by Paul Oakes (70006,401), Mike Liebrand (70006,405), David Nedrow (70006,207), and Ed Wahl (70000,1131).

For related subjects, see Automated Terminal Software.

NavCIS SE (**communication software**) is supported online in the Dvorak Development Forum (GO DVORAK). See Dvorak Development.

Navy News and **Undersea Technology** (**database**) may be searched through the IQuest gateway. See IQuest. It also can be searched through Business Database Plus (GO BUSDB). See Business Database.

See also Military.

NBI software products are supported in Windows 3rd-Party Forum B (GO WINAPB). See Microsoft Software.

NCAA Collegiate Sports Network (GO NCAA) provides menu collections of sports statistics, scores, men's and women's basketball schedule information, assorted news releases, and sports polls, as well as information on the NCAA visitors center and news from the college sports world. See also Sports and Recreation.

NCAHF Newsletter is searchable in the Health Database Plus (GO HLTBD). See Health.

NCJRS (**law database**) may be searched through the IQuest gateway. See IQuest.

NCR/ATT Forum (GO NCRATT) is the place to find the latest information on computers and add-ons from AT&T subsidiary, NCR Corporation. Also available are the latest drivers and patches for existing systems. Supported in the forum is NCR's Windows NT Global Support Center. The sysops are John Bruckmann, Dan Dremann, and Gerald Mimms.

NDIS is supported in the Microsoft Network Forum (GO MSNETWORKS). See Microsoft Software.

NDT Update can be searched through the Business Database Plus (GO BUSDB). See Business Database.

Nebraska news is included in the daily Central regional reports from United Press International. See Executive News Service for details.

NEC Weekly can be searched through the Business Database Plus (GO BUSDB). See Business Database.

Needham, Rick (76703,627) is administrator of the Science/Math Forum (GO SCIENCE). See Science/Math Forum.

Neighborhood Reports (GO NEIGHBOR) is a demographics service that lets you find age, income, occupation, and household statistics, searching by ZIP code, county, or state. The reports are available to all CompuServe subscribers, while the *full* set of demographic reports that comprise SuperSite is available to Executive Service Option subscribers only. (See SUPERSITE.) The Neighborhood Report provides the demographics for a ZIP code area. The surcharge for each report is $10. A sample report is available online for view. At this writing, available are the Neighborhood Civic Report, the Neighborhood Demographic Report, the Neighborhood Gift Report, and the Neighborhood Sports/Leisure Activities Report.
    See also Demographics.

Nervous and Mental Disease, Journal of abstracts are searchable in the Health Database Plus (GO HLTBD). See Health.

NetComm (**modem maker**) is covered in the Pacific Vendors Forum (GO PACVENDOR). For details, see Pacific.

NetFRAME Systems products are supported in the IBM PC Vendor C Forum (GO PCVENC). See IBM Computers.

Netherlands computer issues are covered in Personal Computer Mag (Netherlands) Online (GO PCNL). See Personal Computer Mag.

Netline Network Management Systems & Strategies and **Networks Update** (**databases**) may be searched through the IQuest gateway. See IQuest. The resources also can be searched through the Business Database Plus (GO BUSDB), as can *Network Monitor*. See Business Database.

Netprint is supported in the **SunSelect Forum** (GO SUNSELECT). See SunSelect.

Netscan (**software**) is supported in the McAfee Virus Help Forum (GO VIRUSFORUM). See McAfee.

Netware (**software**) is supported by the Novell Netware and Forums (GO NOVELL). See Novell Software.

NetWare SunLink is supported in the **SunSelect Forum** (GO SUNSELECT). See SunSelect.

NetWare Technical Journal (**magazine**) is searchable (abstracts) through Computer Database Plus (GO COMPDB). See Computer Database Plus.

Network Access Information (GO NETWORK) is a free database that can find various access numbers around the world. The CompuServe Network Services Assistance area can be reached on any CompuServe access number or by dialing 1-800-848-4480. For more details, see Phone, CompuServe access numbers.

Network File Server is supported in the SunSelect Forum (GO SUNSELECT). See SunSelect.

Networking Management (**magazine**) is available for full-text searching through Computer Database Plus (GO COMPDB), while abstracts of *Network World* can be searched in the same service. See Computer Database Plus.

Network News is searchable in the Health Database Plus (GO HLTBD). See Health.

Network surcharges: Besides basic connect charges, users are billed for network communication surcharges (e.g., CompuServe Network, SprintNet) for each session on the Information Service. See Billing Information.

Network Technology products are supported in the Ultimedia Tools Forum B (GO ULTIBTOOLS). See Ultimedia.

NetWorth products are supported in Novell Vendors Forum B (GO NVENB). See Novell.

Net Worth Program, Personal (GO HOM-16) asks you for dollar amounts of your assets and liabilities, then produces a detailed report on net worth.

Neural networks are discussed in the AI Expert Forum (GO AIEXPERT). See AI Expert.

Neurology magazine abstracts are searchable in the Health Database Plus (GO HLTBD), as are abstracts of *Annals of Neurology*, *Archives of Neurology*, and *Developmental Medicine and Child Neurology*. See Health.

Nevada news is included in the daily Western regional reports from United Press International. See Executive News Service for details.

New Age Forum (GO NEWAGE) covers spiritual growth, Eastern philosophy, "earthmanship" and ecology, ESP and mind powers, tarot and astrology, magic and shamanism, pagan and wiccan beliefs, New Age sciences, and books.

   Also, *Magical Blend Magazine* is represented in the forum in Section and Library 16, "Magazine Corner."

The forum is managed by Neil Shapiro (76703,401), who has operated the system's highly successful Micro-Networked Apple Users Groups (MAUG) forums for more than a decade. He is assisted by Rilla Moulden and Brad Hill. Also in the forum are section leaders are Ernest Ramsey (spiritual growth), Dick Kaser (tarot and oracles), Theresa Kinney (astrology), Tony Alicea (esoteric societies), Alain Beaulieu (New Age sciences), Helen Stewart (channeled thought), Jeff Wiley (ESP/mind/dreams), Dennis Mahlmeister (pagan/wicca), and David C. Brune (UFOlogy/contacts).

See also Masonry Forum (GO MASONRY).

New age music is a subject of the Music/Performing Arts Forum (GO MUSICARTS). See Music.

New Car/Truck Showroom (GO NEWCAR) lets users view and compare features of passenger cars, vans, and trucks to help with buying decisions. The database has information on more than 850 cars, vans, special-purpose vehicles, and light-duty trucks. The feature is surcharged; you may look at models one at a time for 90 cents, or two at a time in a side-by-side comparison format for $1.20. An auto selector feature is surcharged at 40 cents.

See also Cars and Shopper Features.

New England Business (magazine) can be searched through the Business Database Plus (GO BUSDB). See Business Database.

New England Journal of Medicine (magazine) articles are searchable in the Health Database Plus (GO HLTDB). See Health Database. This resource also may be searched through IQuest (GO IQUEST).

New Era Japan can be searched through the Business Database Plus (GO BUSDB). See Business Database.

New Freedom Data Center products are supported in the OS/2 Vendor Forum (GO OS2AVEN). See IBM Computers.

New Hampshire news is included in the daily Northeast regional reports from United Press International. See Executive News Service for details. Also, BNH (Business of New Hampshire) can be searched through the Business Database Plus (GO BUSDB). See Business Database.

New Horizons products are supported in the Amiga Vendor Forum (GO AMIGAVENDOR). See Commodore Computers.

New Jersey Record (newspaper) is searchable through Telebase System's News Source USA (GO NEWSUSA). See News USA.

Also:

- Selected reports from New Jersey are included in the Northeast regional reports from United Press International. See Executive News Service.

- *Business Journal of New Jersey Magazine* and *New Jersey Industry Environmental Alert* can be searched through the Business Database Plus (GO BUSDB). See Business Database.

New Media Graphics products are supported in the Multimedia Vendor Forum (GO MULTIVEN). See Multimedia.

New Mexico news is included in the daily Southwest regional reports from United Press International. See Executive News Service for details. Also *New Mexico Business Journal* can be searched through the Business Database Plus (GO BUSDB). See Business Database.

New Orleans Times-Picayune **(newspaper)** is searchable through Telebase System's News Source USA (GO NEWSUSA) and through the Knowledge Index (GO KI). See News Source and see Knowledge Index. Also, *New Orleans Magazine* can be searched in the Magazine Database Plus (GO MDP). See Magazine Database.

Newport Systems products are supported in the Lan Vendor Forum (GO LANVEN). See IBM Computers.

New Republic **(magazine)** is searchable through Magazine Database Plus (GO MDP). For details see Magazine Database.

New Riders Publishing computer books are supported in the Prentice Hall Computer Publishing Forum (GO PHCP). See Prentice Hall.

News: CompuServe has a multitude of news, weather, and sports services. This is a rapidly growing portion of the system where you may retrieve up-to-the-minute reports from the nation's top news organizations. Among the major news resources are the following:

- AP Online is a menu-driven resource from the Associated Press that also is available at standard connect charges. See Associated Press.
- The Business Wire (GO TBW) provides a daily diet of press releases and company statements. See Business Wire.
- Executive News Service (GO ENS), an extra-cost feature of the Executive Option, provides access to a wide range of news services, including the Associated Press, the Reuter financial news wires, United Press International, and more. It provides for *electronic clipping folders* for the automatic retrieval of future news displays. See Executive News Service.
- Hollywood Hotline (GO HOLLYWOOD) is a daily collection of news items from the entertainment world. See Hollywood Hotline and see Entertainment.
- News-A-Tron (GO NAT) is a surcharged service that provides business news. For details, see News-A-Tron.
- NewsGrid (GO NEWSGRID) offers a searchable database of selected news stories from a number of resources at no extra cost. See NewsGrid.

- Textline Global News is searchable on IQuest (see IQuest). It covers international business news and comments from hundreds of publications, including newspapers, newswires, magazines, and trade journals. The file has been divided into three chronological subfiles: the last 12 to 24 months, 1990 to the beginning of the current file, and 1980 to 1989 inclusive.
- Time International databse and Time Magazine can be searched through IQuest. See IQuest.
- U.S. News & World Report Online (GO USNEWS) provides access to the news magazines articles and enables visitors to interact with the magazine's editors and writers. See U.S. News & World Report.

Also, a number of forums concentrate on news and news coverage, including the Broadcasters and Engineers (GO BPFORUM), the Issues Forum (GO ISSUESFORUM), the Journalism Forum (GO JFORUM), the Literary Forum (GO LITFORUM), the Reuter News Pictures Forum (GO NEWSPIX), the Public Relations and Marketing Forum (GO PRSIG).

To reach the main menu on this topic, enter GO NEWS.

News-A-tron (GO NAT) is a daily surcharged service that provides business news, analytical features, and cash quotes for selected commodities, market indices, and financial instruments. The feature, which is a service of News-A-Tron Corporation, is updated throughout the business day and includes quotes giving high, low, and last trade for the major commodities. News-A-tron Market Reports are surcharged at $1.25, which allows you to read one or all of the reports. Reports average two minutes read time. See also Commodities.

Newsbytes News Network, founded in 1983 by current editor-in-chief Wendy Woods (72241,337), covers computer news, with 19 reporters based in bureaus in the following cities: Atlanta, Denver, Hongkong, London, Los Angeles, Moscow, New Delhi, New York, Oslo, San Francisco, Sydney, Tokyo, Toronto, and Washington. It estimates it has 4.5 million readers on major online networks, via magazines, newspapers, and newsletters. The feature is published Monday through Friday, with the exception of Christmas and New Year's Day. The resource may be searched through the IQuest gateway (see IQuest) and through the Business Database Plus (see Business Database). Abstracts also are accessible through the Computer Database Plus (See Computer Database Plus). In addition, Newsbytes is distributed through various printed and online sources including ZiffNet (GO ZNT:NEWSBYTES), and magazine publisher Ziff Communications' electronic link with its readers. See ZiffNet.

See also News, Computer.

News, computer: A number of features provide computer-specific news on a regular basis, among them:

- Newsbytes News Network may be searched through the IQuest gateway (GO IQUEST). See IQuest. It also can be searched through Computer Database

Plus (GO COMPDB). See Computer Database Plus. It also is provided by ZiffNet (GO ZNT:NEWSBYTES). See Newsbytes.

- Online Today (GO OLT), a daily electronic publication by CompuServe itself, provides computer news as well as stories of events around the system. For direct access to the daily news menu, enter GO OLT-90. See Online Today.

- PC Week Extra (GO ZNT:PCWEEK), maintained by editors of PC Week newspaper, includes a searchable database of products and vendors and the Corporate Buyers' Forum. See PC Week.

- PC World Online (GO PCWORLD) includes the publication's monthly departments, hardware and software reviews, feature articles, etc. See PC World.

News databases: The IQuest gateway (see IQuest) offers a number of databases provided to news from around the world. For general international news, see AFPE, Asahi News Service, Guardian, International News, Life, Reuters, Textline Global News, Time International, Time Magazine, Time Publications, Times and Sunday Times, UK News, UPI News, and Washington Post.

For IQuest news resources from specific countries:

- Canada: Canadian Business and Current Affairs.

- France: AFPE, AGRA and News From France.

- Japan: Asahi News Service, Asian Economic News, International News, Japan Economic Newswire Plus, Kyodo News Service, PTS Newsletter Database, and Tokyo Financial Wire.

- Russia: International News, Perspectives, and Tass.

- United Kingdom: BBC Summary of World Broadcasts, Daily and Sunday Telegraph, Financial Times & The Economist, Guardian, Times and Sunday Times, and UK News.

- United States: Christian Science Monitor, International News, National Newspaper Index, Newsearch, Newspaper & Periodical Abstracts, Newspaper Abstracts, New York Times, UPI News, USA Today, and Wall Street Journal.

Also, *World Press Review* can be searched in the Magazine Database Plus (GO MDP). See Magazine Database. And the National Newspaper Index can be searched through the Knowledge Index (GO KI). See Knowledge Index.

Newsday (NY)   (newspaper) is searchable through Telebase System's News Source USA (GO NEWSUSA) and through the Knowledge Index (GO KI). See News Source and see Knowledge Index.

Newsearch can be searched through the Knowledge Index (GO KI). See Knowledge Index.

Newsearch (database) may be searched through the IQuest gateway. See IQuest.

NewsGrid (GO NEWSGRID), offered by Comtex Scientific Corporation of Stamford, Connecticut, is compiled from major wire services throughout the world. It is searchable with a main menu that provides detailed tips and how to search it.

Each business day, NewsGrid's editors capture thousands of stories from the world's major wire services, including Agence France Presse (France), The Business Wire, Deutsche Presse-Agentur (West Germany), Kyodo (Japan), PR Newswire, TASS (Russia), United Press International, Xinhua (China), and more. During business hours, a new story is added to the database about every two minutes.

NewsGrid offers two ways to view its reports, by scanning the headlines of stories the editors have selected and by searching the current database with a keyword.

Two options on the main NewsGrid menu—US/World headline news and US and World business headline news—represent the first of the two approaches. The headline news is updated continuously throughout the day as news breaks. Stories are selected by NewsGrid editors. Also, as stories fall off the Headline News lists, they still are available in the keyword-searched database for seven days.

Another option—Market Update—is a variation on the headline feature. Each market update story appears on a regular basis, some updated every half hour, others updated daily, weekly, monthly, or quarterly. Only the most current stories are available in the Market Update section, with all Market Update stories from the past seven days available in the Keyword Search database.

NewsGrid's most power feature is its search capabilities. All NewsGrid stories, including headline and market update stories for the previous seven days are in the keyword-search database. NewsGrid editors assign each story five to ten keywords. If you entered a keyword that matches one an editor assigned, that story is included on the list of stories found.

NewsGrid automatically searches for keywords that begin with the string of letters you specify. This is indicated by an asterisk (*) succeeding the word when it is redisplayed to you. To instruct NewsGrid to match only the exact word or string you specified, end your keyword with an exclamation point. If you enter DOG at the search prompt, the system looks for keywords that *begin* with those three letters; if you enter DOG!, it looks only for the keyword "dog."

Keywords most often used by NewsGrid editors are proper names (Clinton, Gore, Dole), country names (U.S., Russia, England), regions of the world (Middle East, Caribbean), industry names (financial services, autos), company names (Sony Corp., Eastman Kodak Co.), ticker symbols (IBM, GM), or any of the following category-type words: sports (or the name of a particular sport), feature, election, capitol (for congressional stories), annual report, earnings, market, or weather. Ordinary words may be used but less frequently than these.

Industry groups used as NewsGrid keywords are: advertising, aerospace, agriculture, autos, aviation, banking, beverages, biotechnology, broadcasting, building material, business services, chemicals, computers, construction, consumer products, defense contracting, education, electronic publishing, electronics, entertainment, environmental service, financial services, food, forestry products, freight, health care, industrial products, insurance, machinery, metals, mining, nuclear energy, office equipment, personal care, petroleum products, pharmaceuticals, photography, plastics, precious metals, publishing, railroads, real estate, restaurants, retail, rubber, ship building, telecommunications, textiles, tobacco, toys, travel services, trucks, and utilities.

Newsletter Database, PTS: Telebase Systems Incorporated offers a gateway to data-processing and telecommunications newsletters (GO DPNEWS) and to broadcast and publishing newsletter (GO MEDIANEWS). See PTS Newsletter Database.

Newsline is searchable in the Health Database Plus (GO HLTBD). See Health.

NewsNet (GO NN), the online information service, offers a kiosk in the Electronic Mall (GO MALL) for signups. See Electronic Mall. NewsNet also is a major database vendor accessible through the IQuest gateway (GO IQUEST). See IQuest.

Newspaper Library: See News Source USA.

Newspapers are discussed in the Journalism Forum (GO JFORUM). See Journalism Forum and for related features, see News, General.

Also, newspapers and magazines are sold in a number of stores in the Electronic Mall (GO MALL), including Computer Shopper (GO CS), Data Based Advisor (GO DB), MacUser (GO MC), McGraw-Hill Book Co. (GO MH), PC Computing (GO PCC), PC Magazine (GO PM) and PC Publications (GO PCB). See Electronic Mall.

News Source USA (GO NEWSUSA) is a Telebase Systems Incorporated gateway to selected full-text articles from major U.S. magazines and about 50 newspapers from across the United States. (Classified ads are not included.) The database (formerly called the Newspaper Library) is updated daily, but there is a two-day delay in making today's newspapers available and a month's delay on magazines articles.

The resource incorporates a Scan feature intended as a quick way to locate articles from several sources at the same time. It also provides a Search Specialist (SOS) feature to provide research assistance online. (At this writing, SOS is available Monday through Friday, from 8 a.m. to 10 p.m. Eastern Time and Saturday and Sunday from 10 a.m. to 8 p.m. Eastern Time.)

The surcharge is $3 for the first five titles located, $3 for each additional five titles, $3 for each full-text newspaper article retrieved, and $5 each for full-text articles from magazines and business publications. There is a $1 charge for each search that retrieves no titles. For all scans, the charges are $2 to see the basic Results Menu, $3 to select a database from Results Menu and retrieve up to five titles, a $1 for scans that produce no titles.

Many of the papers and other publications here also are searchable through IQuest. (See IQuest.) For information on other Telebase gateways, see Telebase Systems Incorporated.

Magazines searchable in this service include People Weekly, Sports Illustrated, Time, and U.S. News & World Report.

Searchable business publications include Business Week, Forbes, Fortune, and Money.

The papers searchable in the Newspaper Library include:

Akron (OH) Beacon
Journal
Albany (NY) Times-
Union
Allentown (PA)
Morning Call
Anchorage (AK) Daily
News
Arizona Republic/
Phoenix Gazette
Atlanta (GA) Constitu-
tion/Atlanta Journal
Baltimore (MD) Sun
Boston (MA) Globe
Buffalo (NY) News
Charlotte (NC)
Observer
Chicago (IL) Tribune
Christian Science
Monitor
Cincinnati (OH)/
Kentucky Post
Cleveland (OH) Plain
Dealer
Columbia (SC) State
Columbus (OH)
Dispatch
Dayton (OH) Daily
News
Denver (CO) Rocky
Mountain News

Detroit (MI) Free
Press
Ft. Lauderdale (FL)
Sun-Sentinel
Fresno (CA) Bee
Houston (TX) Post
Lexington (KY)
Herald-Leader
Los Angeles (CA)
Daily News
Los Angeles (CA)
Times
Memphis (TN)
Commercial Appeal
Miami (FL) Herald
Minneapolis (MN)
Star Tribune
New Jersey Record
New Orleans (LA)
Times-Picayune
Newsday (NY)
Norfolk (VA) Ledger-
Star & Virginian-
Pilot
Orlando (FL) Sentinel
Palm Beach (FL) Post
Philadelphia (PA)
Daily News
Philadelphia (PA)
Inquirer
Pittsburgh (PA) Press

Portland (OR)
Oregonian
Richmond (VA) News
Leader/Richmond
Times-Dispatch
Sacramento (CA) Bee
San Francisco (CA)
Chronicle
San Francisco (CA)
Examiner
San Jose (CA) Mercury
News
St. Louis (MO) Post-
Dispatch
St. Paul (MN) Pioneer
Press
St. Petersburg (FL)
Times
Seattle (WA) Post-
Intelligencer
Seattle (WA) Times
USA Today
Washington (DC)
Post
Washington (DC)
Times
Wichita (KS) Eagle-
Beacon
Wisconsin State
Journal & Madison
Capital Times

Also of interest are several IQuest databases, including National Newspaper Index, Newspaper & Periodical Abstracts, and Newspaper Abstracts. See IQuest.

NewTek products are supported in the Amiga Vendor Forum (GO AMIGAVENDOR). See Commodore Computers.

Newton, Apple, the MessagePad pen-based personal communicator, is discussed in the Apple Newton/PIE Forum (GO NEWTON). See Apple Computers.

Newwave software is supported in the HP Systems Forum (GO HPSYS). See Hewlett-Packard.

New York news is covered in the Albany Times-Union, Buffalo News, Knickerbocker News, and Newsday, all searchable through Telebase System's News Source USA (GO NEWSUSA). See News Source.

Also:

- Selected reports from New York are included in the Northeast regional reports from United Press International. See Executive News Service.
- *Business First of Buffalo* and *LI Business News* magazines can be searched through the Business Database Plus (GO BUSDB). See Business Database.
- New York Times, selected abstracts, is searchable through Computer Database Plus (GO COMPDB). See Computer Database Plus.

New York Newslink Forum (GO NEWYORK) is operated as an electronic extension of a dozen of Gannett Inc.'s suburban New York newspapers, serving Westchester, Rockland, and Putnam counties (including coverage of New York City sports, entertainment, and cultural scene). The feature provides news and comments from editors and writers of the publications and an opportunity to communicate with them on a variety of New York topics, from news and sports to restaurants and recreation. Libraries contain feature articles and background information covering sports, business, entertainment, health, family living, and more. The primary sysop is Barry Abisch (71333,3066), systems editor at Gannett Suburban Newspapers. He also is an associated editor of the newspaper group and has been in the newspaper business 25 years.

New Zealand topics are discussed in the Pacific Forum (GO PACFORUM). For details, see Pacific Forum. Also of possible interest is the Australian/New Zealand Company Library (GO ANZCOLIB).

NextBase/Automap products are supported in the UK Computing Forum (GO UKCOMP). See UK Computing.

NeXT Computers are supported in the NeXT Forum (GO NEXTFORUM), an independently operated service designed to help users learn more about the machines. Sections cover NeXT computing issues such as connectivity, utilities, applications, sound, and graphics. Administering the forum is David Bowdish (76711,143), who also owns a Denver desktop publishing firm. Assisting him is Paul Lynch.

Nibble (**magazine**) is searchable (abstracts) through Computer Database Plus (GO COMPDB). See Computer Database Plus.

NICCY is supported in the German-speaking Dr. Neuhaus Forum (GO NEUHAUS). See Dr. Neuhaus.

Nicholas Direct (GO ND) provides marketing and advice on self-publishing through a kiosk in the Electronic Mall (GO MALL). See Electronic Mall.

Nicholson, Lydia (76004,1614) is the sysop of the Claris Corp. forums (GO CLARIS). See Claris.

Nifty-Serve, the Japanese installation of CompuServe, is one of the remote computer services that CompuServe Mail can forward messages to. See Mail, CompuServe for details. Also, Nifty-Serve is a regular topic in the Japan Forum (GO JAPAN). See Japan Forum.

Nightshift, a/k/a Patricia Fitzgibbons (76703,657) is sysop of the game forums (GO GAMERS). For more information, see Games.

Nimbus products are supported in the CD-ROM Vendors Forum (GO CDVEN). See CD-ROM.

Nist Update (**government database**) may be searched through the IQuest gateway. See IQuest.

__Nitrogen__ (**magazine**) can be searched through the Business Database Plus (GO BUSDB). See Business Database.

Node Patrol (**software**) is supported in the Software Solutions Forum (GO SOFSOL). See Software Solutions.

Nodes and their abbreviations (GO NODES): A node is a specialized communications computer that allows many terminals to communicate through the same line to CompuServe's computer complex in Columbus. In some features, such as the CB Simulator, users sometimes look at abbreviations for nodes to see from where various visitors are calling. A list of node codes is available online.

Nonprofit organizations is a topic in the Issues Forum (GO ISSUESFORUM). See Issues.

__Nonwovens Industry__ (**magazine**) can be searched through the Business Database Plus (GO BUSDB). See Business Database.

Norfolk (VA) Ledger-Star and **Virginian-Pilot** are searchable in the News Source USA (GO NEWSUSA). See News Source.

Norfolk, David (71333,1462) is the sysop of the PC PLUS Online (GO PCPLUS). See PCPlus.

Noriane (**international business database**) may be searched through the IQuest gateway. See IQuest.

North Carolina news is covered in the Charlotte Observer, searchable through Telebase System's News Source USA (GO NEWSUSA). See News Source.
   Also:

- Selected reports from North Carolina are included in the Southeast regional reports from United Press International. See Executive News Service.

- *Business North Carolina* and *The Business Journal Serving Charlotte and the Metropolitan Area* magazine can be searched through the Business Database Plus (GO BUSDB). See Business Database.

"Northern Exposure" (television) summaries on the latest shows are available in Soap Opera Summaries (GO SOAPS). See Soap Opera.

Northern Ireland News Service (database) can be searched through IQuest. See IQuest.

Northgate (computer equipment) is supported in the PC Vendor A Forum (GO NORTHGATE). See IBM Computers.

North Sea Letter can be searched through the Business Database Plus (GO BUSDB). See Business Database.

Norton (software) is supported in the Symantec Forums (GO SYMANTEC). See Symantec Software.

Norton-Lambert products are supported in the IBM PC Vendor I Forum (GO PCVENI). See IBM Computers.

Notebook computers of all kinds are discussed in various forums. See Laptop.

Note It (software) is supported in the Symantec Forum (Go SYMANTEC). See Symantec Software.

Notes (software) is supported in the Lotus Communication Forum (GO LOTUSCOMM). See Lotus.

Notework products are supported in the Novell Vendor Forum A (GO NVENA). See Novell Software.

Novell NetWare MHS mailboxes can receive SprintMail electronic messages via the CompuServe Mail Hub. See the SprintMail entries under Mail.

Novell Software: Novell Netware and Forums (GO NOVELL) are operated by the company to provide customer support information and services. At this writing, Novell's forums include:

- Novell Client Forum (NOVCLIENT), talking about IPX/ODI, NETX, VLM, ODINSUP and NetBios
- Novell Connectivity Forum (GO NCONNECT), covering assorted LANs topics
- Novell Desktop Forum (GO NDESKTOP) for discussions on Digital Research applications, such as DRDOS and the DRI GEM collection
- Novell Developer Support (GO NDEVSUPP), discussing Btrieve, NetWare SQL and SDK, and related topics
- Novell Information Forum (GO NGENERAL) for information on Novell applications and utilities
- Novell NetWare 4.x Forum (GO NETW4X), for discussing relating to NetWare v4.x

- Novell Network Management (GO NOVMAN) for related discussions
- Novell NETW2X Forum (GO NETW2X) for questions relating to NetWare v2.x
- Novell NETW3X Forum (GO NETW3X), for questions relating specifically to NetWare v3.x
- Novell OS/2 Forum (GO NOVOS2), covering OS/2 topics and Novell software
- Novell User Forum (GO NOVUSER) for general question and answers
- Novell UnixWare Forum (GO UNIXWARE), for topics relating to Novell's Unix software (see Unix)
- Novell Vendors Forum A (GO NVENA) supporting products from AST Research, Best Power, BindView, Blue Lance, Computer Tyme, Dell Computer, Folio, Infinite Technologies, Knowzall Systems, Multi-User DOS, Notework, RoseWare, SynOptics, and TriCord
- Novell Vendors Forum B (GO NVENB) with information on products from Ontrack Data Recovery and NetWorth

In addition, the Novell Library Forum (GO NOVLIB) is intended for downloading files, patches, etc. (Messages may be posted in section 1 of the NOVLIB Forum. The sysops request that you do not post technical questions on NOVLIB; only library-related questions should be posted there.) The sysops are Rich Adams, Mickey Applebaum, Dennis Beach, Andrew Burbank, Don Crawford, Allen Harris, Dave Kearns, David Kirsch, Les Lovesee, Deborah Schmidt, Brett Warthen, Peter Kuo, and Richard Hornbaker.

Netwire also includes a technical bulletin database (GO NTB) which provides technical information about Novell software and hardware. You may access technical bulletins about NetWare, communications, hardware, and development products, and search the database by title, keywords, technical bulletin number, or product division.

The Compatibility Database is a keyword-searchable database that provides information about the compatibility of various software packages with Novell's local area network solutions.

Also available is the Novell Directory of Independent NetWare Support Providers, which lists companies that support NetWare users helping you to choose a NetWare provider. The listings include information about the services provided and the products supported. In addition, listings contain a company description about each support provider that will help you differentiate the type of service. You can search by the company name or geographic location.

nTergaid   products are supported in the Multimedia Vendor Forum (GO MULTIVEN). See Multimedia.

NTIS   (GO NTIS) stands for National Technical Information Service. It is a Telebase Systems Incorporated gateway to a database published by the U.S. Department of Commerce. For details, see National Technical Information.

NTIS Alert Foreign Technology and **NTIS Foreign Technology Newsletter** can be searched through the Business Database Plus (GO BUSDB). See Business Database.

NTT Topics and **NTT Weekly** can be searched through the Business Database Plus (GO BUSDB). See Business Database.

Nuclear Medicine, Journal of abstracts are searchable in the Health Database Plus (GO HLTBD). See Health.

Nuclear Waste News and **Nucleonics Week** (**databases**) may be searched through the IQuest gateway. See IQuest. *Nuclear Waste News* also can be searched through the Business Database Plus (GO BUSDB). See Business Database. See also Hazardous.

Nudism is a topic of the Outdoors Forum (GO OUTDOORFORUM).

Nu-Mega Technologies products are supported in the Windows 3rd-Party B Forum (GO WINAPB). See Microsoft Software.

Nursing and Allied Health databases may be searched through the IQuest gateway, including Automated Medical Payments News, Health Business, Health Legislation and Regulation, Health News Daily, Medical Outcomes & Guidelines Alert, Medical Utilization Review, and Medicine & Health. See IQuest.

Nursing and Allied Health also can be searched through the Knowledge Index (GO KI). See Knowledge Index.

See also Health/Medicine and Medicine.

Nursing Homes and **Nursing Homes and Senior Citizen Care** (**magazines**) can be searched through the Business Database Plus (GO BUSDB). See Business Database. The resources also can be searched through the Health Database Plus (GO HLTDB). See Health.

Nursing Times abstracts are searchable in the Health Database Plus (GO HLTBD). See Health.

Nutrition, Better and **Better Nutrition for Today's Living** are searchable in the Health Database Plus (GO HLTBD), as is *Environmental Nutrition, Food and Nutrition, Nutrition Action Healthletter, Nutrition Forum, Nutrition Health Review, Nutrition Research Newsletter, Nutrition Today,* and *Tufts University Diet & Nutrition Letter*. Also searchable are abstracts from the *American Journal of Clinical Nutrition* and *Nutrition & Food Science*. Nutrition also is a topic of the Health & Fitness Forum (GO GOODHEALTH). See Health.

Oakes, Rudy (75300,2515) is sysop of the DiagSoft Forum (GO DIAGSOFT). See DiagSoft.

Oakland Business Monthly (magazine) can be searched through the Business Database Plus (GO BUSDB). See Business Database.

Oberon is supported in the Portable Programming Forum (GO CODEPORT). See Programmers Support.

Object Design Inc. products, including ObjectStore, are supported in the PC Vendor H Forum (GO PCVENH). See IBM Computers.

Objects Inc. products are supported in the IBM PC Vendor E Forum (GO PCVENE). See IBM Computers.

Object-Oriented Programming, Journal of is searchable in Computer Database Plus (GO COMPDB). See Computer Database Plus.
    See also Programmers Support.

ObjectScript (software) is supported in Windows 3rd-Party Forum C (GO WINAPC). See Microsoft Software.

Obstetrics and Gynecology magazine abstracts are searchable in the Health Database Plus (GO HLTBD), as can those of *American Journal of Obstetrics and Gynecology*, *British Journal of Obstetrics and Gynecology*, and *JAOA: Journal of the American Osteopathic Association*. See Health.

Ocean Isle Software products are supported in the Windows 3rd-Party B Forum (GO WINAPB). See Microsoft Software.

Occupational Hazards and **Occupational Health & Safety Letter** can be searched through the Business Database Plus (GO BUSDB). See Business Database. *Occupational Hazards* also can be searched through the Health Database Plus (GO HLTDB). See Health. See also Safety.

Occupational Outlook Quarterly (magazine) articles are searchable through Magazine Database Plus (GO MDP). For details see Magazine Database.

Occupational Safety & Health abstracts are searchable in the Health Database Plus (GO HLTBD), as are those of *Journal of Occupational Medicine*. See Health. *Occupational Safety and Health* also can be searched through the IQuest gateway. See IQuest.

Oceanic Abstracts   (database) may be searched through the IQuest gateway. See IQuest.

Ocean Industry (magazine) can be searched through the Business Database Plus (GO BUSDB). See Business Database.

O'Connor, Mike is the Long Island, New York, programmer who created the popular CompuServe Navigator communications program for Apple Macintosh computers, which allows automated interaction with the forums, CompuServe Mail, and other areas of the system. A few years ago, CompuServe also realized the potential of O'Connor's efforts and began distributing the program through the online CompuServe Store (GO ORDER) merchandise area. It also supports free Navigator Support Forums where O'Connor talks with those who use his program.
   See also Navigator.

Octane Week can be searched through the Business Database Plus (GO BUSDB). See Business Database.

Odell, Jerry (72662,74) is the sysop of the IBM CAD/CAM Information Exchange Forum (GO IBMENG). See CAD/CAM.

OECD Economic Outlook (magazine) can be searched through the Business Database Plus (GO BUSDB). See Business Database.

Office, Office Technology Management, and **Today's Office** are searchable (abstracts) through Computer Database Plus (GO COMPDB), as are *Advanced Office Technologies Report* and *Modern Office Technology*. See Computer Database Plus. And *Electronic Office* can be searched through the Business Database Plus (GO BUSDB). See Business Database.

Office Automation Vendor Forum (GO OAFORUM) is dedicated to office automation issues. It offers software support from such vendors as Advanced Support Group (distributors and support for various office automation software tools), CU Services (credit union software), Dayo Software, Franklin Quest, E. F. Haskell (general ledger/accounting software), MicroBiz (a point-of-sale/accounting software package designed for retail stores), Open Systems, XP Systems, ZIPKEY ZIP codes, and ZPAY Payroll Systems (producers of ZPAY payroll software, Grab and WinGRAB). Administering the forum is Thom Hartmann (76702,765), assisted by Ann Linden.

Office supplies are sold at some Electronic Mall shops (GO MALL), including Direct Micro (GO DM), Executive Stamper (GO EX), Omron (GO OMRON), and Penny Wise Office Products (GO PW). See Electronic Mall.

Office Technology, Modern (magazine) can be searched through the Business Database Plus (GO BUSDB). See Business Database.

OfficeWriter is supported in the Software Publishing Forum (GO SPCFORUM). See Software Publishing.

Official Airline Guides (GO OAG), the longest running electronic airline information service, supplies schedule data from almost all of the 415 airlines in the world that use automated reservation systems. It is not affiliated with any specific airline. It also offers low far finders, performance ratings, data on hotels and car rentals, and allows users to book flights from the keyboard. In addition to flight information, OAG offers access to several databases on matters such as travel news and tours, cruises, and discount travel packages to frequent flyer and frequent lodger award programs. Also accessible online are Country and Traveler's Information, U.S. State Department Travel Advisories, ZapoDel's Adventure Atlas, Vacation Florida, Nationwide Intelligence, The Official Recreation Guide, CruiseStar Worldwide Cruises, All Cruise Travel, Cruise Marketplace, Ski Resort Information, Star Rated Restaurants & Hotels, and actual Arrival/Departure Information for Chicago's O'Hare International Airport.

OAG EE is a surcharged service at $10 an hour during evenings (from 7 p.m. to 8 a.m. local time) and all day on weekends and holidays, and $28 an hour during daytime business hours. The service also uses short-cut commands that are preceded by a slash (/). A "Command summary" on the introductory menu provides the details.

Inside OAG itself, the main menu offers these major areas:

- Accu-Weather Forecasts, with reports for selected cities around the world.
- Airport Arrivals, Departures, and Gate Information, including arrival and departure information for major U.S. airports, including Washington's Dulles and National, San Francisco International, New York's JFK and La Guardia, and more.
- Cruises, with data on a number of full-service cruise agencies that offer their tours online, many at a substantial discount.
- Flight Information and Reservations, with a listing of airline fares as well as such information as fuel/terminal surcharges, smoking ban facts, U.S. government fare details, etc.

- Frequent Traveler Programs, including a quick-reference listing of minimum award levels and bonuses.

- General and How-to-Use, with database access commands, user terms, and conditions and more.

- Leisure and Discount Travel, featuring information on discounts for last-minute tours and cruises.

- Lodging and Dining, featuring seven databases of worldwide hotels, restaurants, tours, conferences, cruises, and recreational activities.

- Travel Industry News, with tips on how to maximize your frequent traveler miles and points.

- User Comments & Suggestions.

- What's New, about new OAG features.

- Worldwide Travel Facts, with such tidbits as U.S. document requirements, local currency and climate, advisories for U.S. citizens traveling abroad, exchange rates for countries, and key business and economic facts about every country.

The system also operates a Help Disk. The numbers are 800/323-4000 in the U.S. and 708/574-6414 outside the U.S.

See also Airlines, Aviation, and Travel.

Off Road (**magazine**) can be searched in the Magazine Database Plus (GO MDP). See Magazine Database.

Ogilvie, Jim   (75300,2253) is the sysop of Multimedia Forum (GO MULTIMEDIA) and the Multimedia Vendor Forum (GO MULTIVEN). See Multimedia.

Oklahoma news   is included in the daily Southwest regional reports from United Press International. See Executive News Service for details.

Okna Corp.   products are supported in the Windows 3rd-Party D Forum (GO WINAPD). See Microsoft software.

Ohio news   is covered in the Akron Beacon Journal, the Cincinnati/Kentucky Post, Cleveland Plain Dealer, Columbus Dispatch, and Dayton (OH) Daily News; all searchable through Telebase System's News Souce USA (GO NEWSUSA). See News Source.

Also:

- Selected reports from Ohio are included in the Mid-Atlantic regional reports from United Press International. See Executive News Service.

- Searchable through the Business Database Plus (GO BUSDB) are *Ohio Business* and *Ohio Industry Environmental Advisor*, as well as *Business First-Columbus*, *Cincinnati Business Courier*, and *Crain's Cleveland Business*. See Business Database.

Ohio Scientific Instruments: One of the computer systems supported in CompuServe's Computer Club Forum (GO CLUB). See Computer Club.

Oil industry is covered in several magazines accessible through Business Database Plus (GO BUSDB), including *Oil Express, The Oil and Gas Journal, Oil Price Information Service, Oil Spill Intelligence Report, Oil Spill US Law Report, Oilweek, World Oil,* and *US Oil Week*. See Business Database. Also U.S. Oil Week database may be searched through the IQuest gateway. See IQuest.
See also Energy, Gas, and Coal.

Oil Spill Intelligence Report and **Oil Spill U.S. Law Report** (**databases**) may be searched through the IQuest gateway. See IQuest.

Olduvai Corporation products are supported in the Mac B Vendor Forum (GO MACBVEN). See Apple Computers.

Omaha Steaks (GO OS) is a store in the Electronic Mall (GO MALL) that offers gourmet food. See Electronic Mall.

Omni (**magazine**) can be searched in the Magazine Database Plus (GO MDP). See Magazine Database.

Omnibook computers are supported in the HP OmniBook Forum (GO HPOMNIBOOK). See Hewlett-Packard.

Omnis 5 and 7 (**software**) is supported in the Blyth Software Forum (GO BLYTH). For details, see Blyth Software.

Omnitrend Software products are supported in the Game Publishers C Forum (GO GAMCPUB). See Gaming Forums.

Omron (GO OMRON) provides office automation products through features in the Electronic Mall (GO MALL). See Electronic Mall.

"One Life To Live" (**television**) summaries on the latest shows are available in Soap Opera Summaries (GO SOAPS). See Soap Opera.

One-Off CD Shops products are supported in the CD-ROM Vendors Forum (GO CDVEN). See CD-ROM.

One Source (**software**) is supported in the Lotus Words & Pixels Forum (Go LOTUSB). See Lotus.

One-Write Plus products are supported in the IBM PC Vendor B Forum (GO PCVENB). See IBM Computers.

Online (**magazine**) articles are searchable through Magazine Database Plus (GO MDP). For details see Magazine Database. It also can be searched through Business Database Plus (GO BUSDB). See Business Database.

Online Computer Systems products are supported in the CD-ROM Vendors Forum (GO CDVEN). See CD-ROM.

Online Inquiry (GO OLI) lets you request general information about an advertisement displayed in *CompuServe Magazine*. You may leave your name and address(es) at the prompts supplied and further information will be sent to you. You may also add specific comments or special requests to the inquiry if you like. The requests are filed electronically and are accessible only by the advertisers you specify.

Online Libraries and Microcomputers, Online Newsletter, and **Online Products News** **(databases)** may be searched through the IQuest gateway. See IQuest. The resources also can be searched through the Business Database Plus (GO BUSDB). See Business Database.

Online Today **(magazine)** (now called *CompuServe Magazine*) is searchable (abstracts) through Computer Database Plus (GO COMPDB). See Computer Database Plus. It also can be searched through Business Database Plus (GO BUSDB). See Business Database.

Online Today **(news)** (GO OLT): CompuServe's daily electronic publication, *Online Today* is produced by the editors and staff of *CompuServe Magazine*. It provides daily stories from the computer world as well as reviews of hardware, software, books, reports from the activities around the system, and more. Like many publications, *Online Today* is made up of a number of separate sections, including the latest news about the happenings in the system's forums as well as daily news from the computer industry as a whole ("Monitor Daily News"). Here is a guide to direct page numbers for some of the services: "Behind the Screens" (a humor column by John Edwards) GO OLT-130, Book Reviews GO OLT-240, Earlier Daily Reports GO OLT-20, Hardware Reviews GO OLT-220, Software Reviews OLT-230, and Today's Computer News GO OLT-90.

See also News, Computer.

OnTarget **(software)** is supported in the Symantec Forums (GO SYMANTEC). See Symantec.

Ontario information is provided in *Northern Ontario Business* magazine, which can be searched through the Business Database Plus (GO BUSDB). See Business Database.

Ontrack Data Recovery products are supported in Novell Vendors Forum B (GO NVENB). See Novell.

On Three Inc. products are supported in the Apple II Vendor Forum (GO APIIVEN). See Apple Computers.

Opcode Systems products are supported in the Mac B Vendor Forum (GO MACBVEN). See Apple Computers. They also are supported in the MIDI A Vendor Forum (GO MIDIAVEN). See Music.

Open Systems is supported in the Office Automation Vendor Forum (GO OAFORUM). See Office Automation.

Open systems computing information is provided in a number of databases that can be searched through the IQuest gateway, including Open Systems Communication, Open Systems Today, and Open: OSI Product and Equipment News. See IQuest. Searchable through the Business Database Plus (GO BUSDB) are *Open OSI Product & Equipment News*, *Open Systems Communication*, and *Open Systems Report*. See Business Database.

Operating rules, CompuServe's (GO RULES) are displayed online, along with an elaboration on the policy (GO COPYRIGHT). For a copy of the operating rules agreement that all subscribers sign, see Rules, CompuServe Operating.

Ophthalmology, American Journal of is searchable in the Health Database Plus (GO HLTBD). Also *British Journal of Ophthalmology* abstracts are searchable there. See Health.

Optical and Magnetic Report (database) may be searched through the IQuest gateway. See IQuest.

Optical Information Systems (magazine) is searchable through Computer Database Plus (GO COMPDB). See Computer Database Plus.

It also can be searched through Business Database Plus (GO BUSDB), as can *Optical Materials & Engineering News* and *Optical Memory News*. See Business Database.

Optical scanners are discussed in various forums, including Canon Support Forum (GO CANON), Desktop Publishing Forum (GO DTPFORUM), HP Peripherials Forum (GO HPPER), Logitech Forum (GO LOGITECH), and Mac Hardware Forum (GO MACHW).

Optima modem and others are supported in the Online with Hayes Forum (GO HAYES). See Hayes.

Options, Users (GO DEFALT) (screen sizes and characteristics for your CompuServe account) may be set in the Terminal Settings area of the system. See Terminal.

Options Profile (GO OPRICE) is a financial feature that lists all options currently trading on a given common stock or market index. See Stock Quotes (Historical).

Oracle Software: The Oracle Forum (GO ORACLE) supports SQL*Forms, SQL*Plus, and Pro*C. It offers tips and solutions to common questions, software patches, and programs. The primary sysop is Chris Wooldridge (76711,1014). Assisting are members of the company's technical department, including Michael Abbey, Michael Corey, Jeff Jacobs, Buff Emslie, and Dave Kreines.

Orange County Business Journal (**magazine**) can be searched through the Business Database Plus (GO BUSDB). See Business Database.

Ordering, CompuServe products (GO ORDER): CompuServe offers its own online ordering service for a variety of products, from books and manuals to T-shirts, coffee mugs, and posters. As with other shopping features, you may browse without ordering. Items you do order are charged to your monthly CompuServe bill. There are no connect charges while you are in the Online Ordering Service area. You aren't charged for connect time while viewing descriptions or placing an order. When you complete your order, the entire list is displayed for verification. At that point, you may change it or confirm it. Then you are given an order number to jot down so you may check on the order later if necessary.

See also Shopper Features.

Oregon (**news**) is covered in the Portland Oregonian, searchable through Telebase System's News Source USA (GO NEWSUSA) and through the Knowledge Index (GO KI). See News Source and see Knowledge Index.

Also:

- Selected reports from Oregon are included in the Western regional reports from United Press International. See Executive News Service.
- *Oregon Business* and *Business Journal—Portland* magazines can be searched through the Business Database Plus (GO BUSDB). See Business Database.

Organic Gardening (**magazine**) can be searched in the Magazine Database Plus (GO MDP). See Magazine Database.

Organizer (**software**) is supported in the Lotus Words & Pixels Forum (Go LOTUSB). See Lotus.

Origin software is regularly discussed in The Game Publishers A Forum (GO GAMAPUB) and in the Flight Simulation Forum (GO FSFORUM). See Gaming Forums.

Orlando is a topic of the Florida Forum (GO FLORIDA). See Florida.

Orlando (FL) Sentinel (**newspaper**) is searchable through Telebase System's News Source USA (GO NEWSUSA) and through the Knowledge Index (GO KI). See News Source and see Knowledge Index.

Also, *Orlando Business Journal* can be searched through the Business Database Plus (GO BUSDB). See Business Database.

Osborne computer problems can be discussed CP/M Users Group Forum (GO CPMFORUM). See Programmers Support.

OSC **(products)** are supported in the MIDI C Vendor Forum (GO MIDICVEN). See Music.

OS/2 **(software)** is supported in a collection of IBM forum devoted specifically to the software. See IBM Computers.

OS/2 Monthly **(magazine)** editors are accessible in in the OS/2 Vendor Forum (GO OS2AVEN). See IBM Computers.

OS-9-based Computers: CompuServe has a forum that supports this Tandy Corp. machine (GO OS9). See Tandy Corp. Computers. Also, the Microware Online Support Service (GO MICROWARE) has OS-9/68000 and OS-9/6809 application notes and software problems. See Microware Software.

Ostling, Ridge (75300,3307) sysop of the developer forums in the Microsoft area of the system (GO MICROSOFT). See Microsoft Software.

Ostomy Quarterly is searchable in the Health Database Plus (GO HLTBD). See Health.

OTC Market Report Update USA and *OTC News & Market Report* can be searched through the Business Database Plus (GO BUSDB). See Business Database.

OTC NewsAlert is a database of press releases and statements from various business and companies. It is searchable through the Executive News Service. See Executive News Service.

Otology, Rhinology and Laryngology, Annals of, and *Journal of Laryngology and Otology* abstracts are searchable in the Health Database Plus (GO HLTBD). See Health.

Outdoors Network (GO OUTNET) features resources for planning camping trips. The network includes:

- Outdoor Forum (GO OUTDOORFORUM) covers many interests, including fishing, hunting, camping, scouting activities, and more. For details, see Sports and Recreation.

- Outdoors News Clips (GO OUTNEWS). Articles are clipped from various sources, including the Associated Press, United Press International, and The Washington Post. Recent articles covered a change in Yellowstone National Park's camping regulations and a look at the problems faced by first-time campers. There is a $15 per hour surcharge in addition to base connect rates for accessing News Clips. For related features, see News.

See also:

- CompuServe Classifieds (GO CLASSIFIEDS), where the "Travel" section has a "Hotels/Camping" area.
- The Florida Forum (GO FLORIDA), which has created Message Section 8, "Florida Camping."
- The Travel Forum (GO TRAVSIG), which helps members arrange camping trips in both the U.S. and abroad.

Outdoor Writers Association of America meetings in the Great Outdoors Forum (GO OUTDOORFORUM). See Sports and Recreation.

OverKill **(game software)** is distributed and supported in Epic Online (GO EPIC). See Epic.

Owl International products are supported in the Multimedia Vendor Forum (GO MULTIVEN). See Multimedia.

OXXI/Precision Software is supported in the Atari Vendors Forum (GO ATARIVEN). See Atari.

Oxy-fuel News can be searched through the Business Database Plus (GO BUSDB). See Business Database.

OzCis **(terminal software)** an IBM-compatible auto-navigator program for CompuServe Mail, forums, and other services by Steve Sneed of Colorado Springs, Colo., is supported in the OzCIS forum (GO OZCIS). For additional information and system requirements, access file OZCIS2.BRO in library 1 (General Library) and OZCIS1.BRO in library 9 (OzCIS V1). These text files will give you an overview of the software. The OzCIS program files also are in the forum. At this writing, version 2 files were located in library 2 (OzCIS Ver. 2) and version 1.2a files were available in library 9 (OzCIS V1). Administering the forum are Mike Bessy, Cam Castiglia, Steve Sneed, and Don Watkins. See also Automated terminal software.

Ozone Depletion Network Online Today can be searched through the Business Database Plus (GO BUSDB). See Business Database.

P

Pace, Steve (76711,724) is sysop of the IBM LMU/2 Forum (GO LMUFORUM). See IBM.

Pace Micro Technologies products are supported in the UK Computing Forum (GO UKCOMP). See UK Computing.

Pacific Business News (**magazine**) can be searched through the Business Database Plus (GO BUSDB). See Business Database.

Pacific Data Products products are supported in the IBM PC Vendor D Forum (GO PCVEND). See IBM Computers.

Pacific Forum, CompuServe (GO PACFORUM) is in operation to discuss Australian and New Zealand topics, and is intended for subscribers living in that region or interested in it. Discussion usually covers a range of cultural topics, which now includes Sports, Politics, Entertainment, and Business. The chief sysop in the Pacific Forum is Tony Williams (75300,3644). The forum also has a New Zealand section. See also the Australian/New Zealand Company Library (GO ANZCOLIB).

Pacific Motion (GO PRES) software is supported in the Graphics A Vendor Forum (GO GRAPHAVEN). See Graphics.

Pacific Vendors Forum (GO PACVENDOR) offers visitors support from Australian and New Zealand manufacturers and distributors of computer products. The companies represented include Banksia, Fujitsu Peripherals, FutureWave/Banyan, Information Technologies, Maestro, Manaccom, NetComm, Reckon Software, SealCorp, SoundBlaster, Wizard Works, and SystemBuilder. The sysop is Tony Williams (75300,3644).

Pacioli (**accounting software**) is supported in the IBM PC Vendor C Forum (GO PCVENC). See IBM Computers.

Packaging and ***Packaging Week*** **(magazines)** can be searched through the Business Database Plus (GO BUSDB). See Business Database.

Also, Packaging Science, Technology Abstracts, and SMT Trends, packaging business databases, may be searched through the IQuest gateway. See IQuest.

Packard Bell Forum (GO PACKARDBELL) supports Packard Bell computer equipments. The primary sysop is Tom Gilmore (75300,2261), assisted by Franklin Starnes.

Packet radio is a topic in the HamNet (Ham Radio) Forum (GO HAMNET). See HamNet.

PackRat **(software)** is supported in Polaris Software Forum (GO POLARIS). See Polaris.

PageMaker **(software)** is one of the programs supported in the Aldus Forum (GO ALDUS). See Aldus Software.

Paging equipment is a topic in the Telecommunication Issues Forum (GO TELECOM). See Telecommunication.

Paige, Chip (76270,2131) is a sysop in the ACI US Forum (GO ACIUS).

Paint and Coatings, Modern, Polymers Paint & Colour Journal, and ***American Paint & Coatings Journal*** **(magazines)** can be searched through the Business Database Plus (GO BUSDB), as well as *European Polymers Paint & Colour Journal*. See Business Database. See also Coatings and Surface Technology.

PAIS International **(economic database)** may be searched through the IQuest gateway (GO IQUEST) and through the Knowledge Index (GO KI). See IQuest and see Knowledge Index.

PALAESTRA is searchable in the Health Database Plus (GO HLTBD). See Health.

Palm Beach (FL) Post **(newspaper)** is searchable through Telebase System's News Source USA (GO NEWSUSA) and through the Knowledge Index (GO KI). See News Source and see Knowledge Index.

Palmtop Forum (GO PALMTOP) serves as a clearinghouse for palmtop computer users. It's a place where members—newcomers and experts—can meet, exchange ideas and advice, and find out the latest developments in the palmtop field. Several palmtop PC manufacturers also maintain a presence in the forum.

Among the systems and software supported are Poqet Computers, Sharp Wizard, Casio B.O.S.S., and Traveling Software. Forum Manager Marty Mankins (75300,1770) recently offered forum members his analysis of several popular palmtop systems for users interested in word processing. The primary sysop is Ron Luks (76703,254).

See also Hand-held.

Palozola, Jim   (76703,3027) is a sysop in the ROCKNET Forum. (GO ROCKNET). See Music.

Panasonic: One of the computer systems supported in CompuServe's Computer Club Forum (GO CLUB). See Computer Club.

PaperChase health database (GO PAPERCHASE) connects with MEDLINE, the National Library of Medicine's database of references to the biomedical literature. Also in the resource are reports from AIDSLine (the National Library of Medicine's database of clinical, research, and health care policy information on AIDS) and CancerLit (the National Cancer Institute's database of cancer information, which includes more than 950,000 references and abstracts about cancer). Paperchase combines all references so that one search can access all databases simultaneously. At this writing, MEDLINE has more than 7 million references to articles from 4,000 journals. Paperchase has all the references indexed for MEDLINE since its inception in 1966. Each week, some 8,000 new referecnes are added. Paperchase also includes the Health Planning and Administration (HEALTH) database, which includes nonclinical literature on health care planning, facilities, insurance, management, personnel, licensure, and accreditation.

The service is surcharged at $24 an hour during weekday business hours and $18 an hour in the evenings and on weekends.

Each month some 25,000 more references are indexed and abstracted. The service is provided by Boston's Beth Israel Hospital, a teaching hospital of Harvard Medical School. Monday through Friday, the system provides a customer support line at 800/722-2075 (within Massachusetts, call 617/278-3900).

Searching commands are quite powerful and you are advised to read the help sections available on the main menu online before accessing the database.

See also Medical References, Health, and Drugs.

Paper industry is the subject of the Paperchem database, which may be searched through the IQuest gateway. See IQuest.

Also, related magazines are searchable through the Business Database Plus (GO BUSDB). They include *American Papermaker, Paper, Film and Foil Converter, Paper, Party and Paper Retailer,*and *Pulp & Paper, Pulp and Paper International*. See Business Database.

Parade (**software**) is supported in the PC Vendor B Forum (GO PCVENB). See IBM Computers.

Paradigm Software products are supported in the LOGO Forum (GO LOGOFORUM). See Programmers Support.

Paradox **(software)** is supported in the Borland International Forums (GO BORLAND), as is Paradox for Windows. See Borland Software. Also, *Paradox Users' Journal* and *Paradox Developers' Journal* are among the journals supported in the Cobb Group Programming Forum (ZNT:COBBPROG). See Cobb Group. Paradox also is a topic in the DBMS Magazine Forum (GO DBMSFORUM). See DBMS Magazine.

Paragon Concepts products are supported in the Macintosh Vendor A Forum (GO MACAVEN). See Apple Computers.

Paramount Interactive is represented in the Prentice Hall Computer Publishing Forum (GO PHCP). See Prentice Hall.

Paraplegia News is searchable in the Health Database Plus (GO HLTBD). See Health.

Parapsychology is discussed in the New Age Forum (GO NEWAGE). See New Age.

Parenting is a topic in the Issues Forum (GO ISSUESFORUM). See Issues.

Parents' Magazine **(magazine)** is searchable through Magazine Database Plus (GO MDP). For details see Magazine Database. The resource also can be searched through the Health Database Plus (GO HLTDB). See Health.

Park Service, U.S., is discussed in the White House Forum (GO WHITE HOUSE). See White House.

Parks & Recreation **(magazine)** can be searched in the Magazine Database Plus (GO MDP). See Magazine Database.

Parlor and Trivia Games are supported on the system, and include:

- Astrology Calculator (GO ASTROLOGY)
- Biorhythms (GO BIORHYTHM)
- Grolier Whiz Quiz (GO WHIZ)
- Hangman (GO HANGMAN)
- The Multiple Choice (GO MULTIPLE)
- Science Trivia (GO SCITRIVIA)
- ShowBiz Quiz (GO SBQ)
- The Two-Stage Trivia Game (GO STAGEII)
- You Guessed It (GO YGI)

For more, see Games.

Parsons Technology Forum (GO PTFORUM) supports various software packages from that publisher, including MoneyCounts, It's Legal, QuickVerse, and

Personal Tax Edge. The forum is administered by Paula Weber (72662,1425), assisted by Trish Tenney.

Also, Parsons Technology (GO PA) is a store in the Electronic Mall (GO MALL) that offers financial/productivity software. See Electronic Mall.

PARTICIPATE (GO PARTI) is an electronic messaging system that is provided and supported by The Point Information Network Inc. PARTICIPATE (or "PARTI" as it often is called by its regulars) became best known in the mid-1980s as the primary conferencing feature of The Source, a McLean, Virginia, information service that merged with CompuServe several years ago.

Users of PARTI (which sometimes also is called "The Point" on CompuServe) may start topics or read and write to any of several hundred existing topics. Topics can be open or private. While many of its visitors are hobbists, PARTI has other applications too. Businesses, associations, and government agencies effectively use its capabilities for planning, for projects, for confidential communications between individuals, and/or groups and for numerous other applications.

For free online brief instructions, GO PARTICIPATE. CompuServe's usual charges apply. There is no surcharge. Also there is an online instruction area that you can reach by entering GO FRE-99.

PASCAL (science database) may be searched through the IQuest gateway. See IQuest.

Pascal (software) is supported in the Microsoft Languages Forum (GO MSLANG). See Microsoft Software. Also it is supported in the Borland PASCAL Forum (GO BPASCAL). See Borland. Also *Inside Turbo Pascal* is among the journals supported in the Cobb Group Programming Forum (ZNT:COBBPROG). See Cobb Group.

See also Programmers Support.

Pascal programmers might enjoy CODEPORT, The Portable Programming Forum (GO CODEPORT), sponsored by USUS, the UCSD Pascal System Users' Society for discussion of topics related to Pascal, Apple Pascal, Modula-2, and similar software systems. Apple Macintosh programmers might want to check into the Mac Developers' and Programmers' Forum (GO MACDEV); see Apple Computers.

For related topics, see Programmers Support.

Passport Designs products are supported in the MIDI B Vendor Forum (GO MIDIBVEN). See Music. They also are supported in the Ultimedia Tools Forum B (GO ULTIBTOOLS). See Ultimedia.

Passport and visa information is available in Visa Advisors and Electronic Visaguide (GO VISA). See Visa Advisors.

Passwords are the keys to users CompuServe accounts online. Never discuss your password on the system, either in forum messages, CompuServe Mail, or real-time conferencing. Never make your password anything easily associated with you (such as your name or nickname.)

Also, change your password regularly. To do that, enter GO PASSWORD at any prompt. The system will ask you to confirm your present password and then type in your new password. Good passwords are two unrelated words connected with a symbol. After you have typed in the new password, the system confirms that the change has been made.

If you ever forget your password or think it has been stolen, contact the customer service people immediately (800/848-8990 or in Ohio, 614/457-8650). The representative won't be able to give you a new password over the phone, but he or she can mail it to you at the address on file with your account number.

See also Help Online.

.PAT, as an extension on filenames in forum libraries, often stands for "patch," which is a bit of programming that can be incorporated in another file to change the program. See Files, Extensions.

Patagonia (GO PG) offers a kiosk in the Electronic Mall (GO MALL) selling sports clothing for mountaineers, sailors, kayakers, backcountry skiers, and fly fishermen. See Electronic Mall.

Patent Research Center (GO PATENT) is a gateway to summaries of U.S. patents granted in chemical, mechanical, electrical, and design categories and gives summaries of patents granted internationally since the mid-1970s. The information is made available by Dialog Information Services Incorporated. The databases accessible here include Claims/U.S. Patent Abstracts (1950 to date) from IFI/Plenum Data Corp., and World Patents Index (1963 to date) from Derwent Inc.

The surcharge is $4 for the first 10 titles located, $4 for each additional 10 titles, and $4 for each full-text article retrieved. There is a $1 for each search that retrieves no titles.

Many of the papers also are searchable through IQuest. In addition, search of the research centers is similar to IQuest's procedure. (See IQuest.) And for information on other Telebase gateways, see Telebase Systems Incorporated.

Also:

- On IQuest (see IQuest) are: Claims/Citation (1971 to present), Claims/Compound Registry, Claims/Reassignment & Reexamination, Claims/Reference, Claims/U.S. Patent Abstracts, Claims/U.S. Patent Abstracts Weekly, Derwent World Patents Index, EDOC, EPAT (European Patent Registry), Foods Adlibra, FPAT, Index to Legal Periodicals, Innovator's Digest, Inpadoc: Patents, Inpanew: Patents, Japio, Paperchem, Patdata, Patent Abstracts of China, Textile Technology Digest, U.S. Classification, U.S. Copyrights, and U.S. Patent Office. See IQuest.

- Patents, trademarks, and copyrights are topics in Information USA (GO INFOUSA). See Information USA.

- Trademarkscan (GO TRADERC) is a gateway to major sources of information on national and international trademarks, including all textual-numeric (nongraphic) federal trademarks active in the United States. See Trademarkscan.

- Searchable through the Business Database Plus (GO BUSDB) are *Innovation* and *Innovator's Digest*. See Business Database.

Pathology, American Journal of Clinical, American Journal of Pathology, Journal of Clinical Pathology, and **Journal of Pathology** abstracts are searchable in the Health Database Plus (GO HLTBD). See Health.

Patient Care (magazine) is searchable in the Health Database Plus (GO HLTDB). See Health.

Patkin, Lynne (75300,3070) is sysop of the Federation of International Distributors Forum (GO FEDERATION). See Federation.

Paul Fredrick Shirt Co. (GO PFS) is a store in the Electronic Mall (GO MALL) that offers men's shirts. See Electronic Mall.

Paul Mace Software is supported in the Graphics A Vendor Forum (GO GRAPHVEN). See Graphics.

Payne, Linda (76004,3107) is sysop of the ChipSoft Support Forum (GO CHIPSOFT). See ChipSoft.

pcAnywhere (software) is supported in the Symantec Forums (GO SYMANTEC). See Symantec.

PC Brand Inc. products are supported in the IBM PC Vendor G Forum (GO PCVENG). See IBM Computers.

PC Business Products (database) may be searched through the IQuest gateway. See IQuest. The resource also can be searched through the Business Database Plus (GO BUSDB). See Business Database.

PC Catalog (GO PCA) is a store in the Electronic Mall (GO MALL) that offers mail order PC products. See Electronic Mall.

PC/Computing (magazine) also has a kiosk in the Electronic Mall (GO MALL) that offers online magazine subscriptions. To access it, enter GO PCC. See Electronic Mall. Articles from the magazine are searchable through Computer Database Plus (GO COMPDB). See Computer Database Plus.

PC/Contact Forum (GO ZNT:PCCONTACT) has message sections devoted to various computing topics. Visitors find discussions of issues and products that affect the computer industry. The data libraries contain debug scripts, utility files, and shareware products. The forum is operated under Ziff Communications' ZiffNet structure and is administered by sysop John Taschek (76000,21), assisted by Sally Neuman and Paul Friedman.

See also ZiffNet.

PC-DOS/MS-DOS (software) is supported in the Microsoft Operating MSDOS Forum (GO MSDOS). See Microsoft Software.

PC-File+, PC-Type+, and **PC-Calc+** (software) are supported in the PC Vendor A Forum (GO PCVENA). See IBM Computers.

PCI SIG products are supported in the IBM Vendors H Forum (GO PCVENH). See IBM Computers.

PC-Kwik products are supported in the IBM PC Vendor A Forum (GO PCVENA). See IBM Computers.

PC Logo products are supported in the LOGO Forum (GO LOGOFORUM). See Programmers Support.

PC Magazine (GO PM) has a kiosk in the Electronic Mall (GO MALL) that offers online magazine subscription signup. See Electronic Mall.

Also, articles from the magazine are searchable in Computer Database Plus (GO COMPDB). See Computer Database Plus.

And the resource is searchable through the IQuest gateway. See IQuest.

PC Magazine's PC MAGNET: The PC MAGNET forums (GO PCMAGNET) are operated by Ziff Communications as part of its ZiffNet features. The forums are:

- After Hours Forum (GO ZNT:AFTERHOURS), a forum for informal chatter about everything from music and games to politics and science fiction. The sysop is Russ Lockwood (72241,567).

- Editorial Forum (GO ZNT:EDITORIAL), supporting the magazine's feature stories and editorial content, such as "First Looks," and the regular columnists. The primary sysop is Orville Fudpucker (72241,105).

- Programming Forum (GO ZNT:PROGRAMMING), covering environments, power programming, and computer languages. The sysop is Sheryl Canter (72241,510).

- UTILFORUM/TIPS Forum (GO ZNT:UTILFORUM), an extension of the magazine's utilities, advisor, and tutorial offerings. The sysop is Scott McGrath (72241,325).

Some of *PC Magazine*'s editors and columnists can be reached through this forum, among them Chris Barr (72241,13), Douglas Boling (72241,217), John Clyman (72241,1365), Joel Dreyfuss (72241,264), Ray Duncan (72241,52), John Dvorak (72241,47), David Greenfield (72241,1457), Bill Howard (72241,54), Mitt Jones

(72241,35), Dale Lewallen (72241,1773), Bill Machrone (72241,15), Michael Mefford (72241,161), Edward Mendelson, (72241,41), Michael Miller (72241,352), Charles Petzold, (72241,56), Alfred Poor (72241,1301), Jeff Prosise (72241,44), Robin Raskin (72241,12), Sal Ricciardi (72241,33), Winn Rosch (72241,107), Neil Rubenking (72241,50), Jim Seymour (72241,45), Richard Shaw (72241,155), Barry Simon (76004,1664), Craig Stinson (72241,216), M. David Stone (72241,361), Gus Venditto (72241,42), and Ethan Winer (72657,3070).

In addition, the PC MagNet offers a program that allows you to search the libraries of all the PC MagNet forums. You can type and send a letter to the editor of the magazine. You can even upload a submission to PC Magazine in the PC MagNet area.

Articles from *PC Magazine* also are featured in Computer Database Plus (GO COMPDB). See Computer Database Plus.

See also ZiffNet and *PC/Computing*.

PC Magazine UK Editorial Forum (GO ZNT:PCMAGUK) supports the British version of PC Magazine. The sysop is Rupert Goodwins (72241,476), assisted by Nicola Berry and Dave Rigler.

PCMCIA (Personal Computer Memory Card Association) products are supported in the IBM PC Vendor F Forum (GO PCVENF). See IBM Computers.

PCM Online (GO PCMONLINE) and the associated PCM Forum support readers of the Personal Computer Magazine, the leading Dutch computing journal published by VNU Business Publications in Amsterdam. PCM Online provides the latest news in Dutch on the computing industry in Belgium and The Netherlands, listings of the top files available for download, etc.

PCN News can be searched through the Business Database Plus (GO BUSDB). See Business Database.

PC-Outline (software) is supported in the PC Vendor G Forum (GO PCVENG). See IBM.

PC PLUS Online (GO PCPLUS) is operated by major British computing magazines, *PC Plus* and *PC Answers*, as a new support service for their readers and PC enthusiasts worldwide. The service includes the PC PLUS Forum (GO PCPFORUM), Top Ten Downloads, latest news, Letters to the Editor, and more.

The service enables visitors to download reviewed programs, upload programs, chat with other readers in many professions, swap hints and tips, ask for advice, and talk with the editorial team.

The primary sysop is David Norfolk (71333,1462), assisted by Wilf Hey, Steve Townsley, and Nick Thompson.

PC Publications (GO PCB) is a store in the Electronic Mall (GO MALL) that offers *PC Today* and *PC Novice* subscriptions. See Electronic Mall.

PCS News can be searched through the Business Database Plus (GO BUSDB). See Business Database.

PC Sources (magazine) (GO PC) has a kiosk in the Electronic Mall (GO MALL). It is a guide to direct computer buys, with comparisons, Q&As, and so on. Also the online service offers signups for subscriptions. For related information, see Electronic Mall. Also the resource can be searched through Computer Database Plus (GO COMPDB). See Computer Database Plus.

PC Tech Journal (magazine) is searchable through Computer Database Plus (GO COMPDB). See Computer Database Plus.

PC Tools Deluxe (software) is supported in the Central Point Software Forum (GO CENTRAL). See Central Point.

PC User (magazine) is searchable through Computer Database Plus (GO COMPDB). See Computer Database Plus.

PC Week: PC Week Extra (GO ZNT:PCWEEK) is maintained by the editors of PC Week newspaper and includes a searchable database of products and vendors and the Corporate Buyers' Forum. Product information is compiled from reviews, buyers' guides, news stories, and analysis of the PC Week Poll of Corporate Satisfaction by the editors. Users may download guides and polls and full text of reviews. The service is owned and operated by Ziff Communications.

The products database is updated weekly and contains one year's worth of articles. You may search on products or product categories. Buyers' guides and poll charts may be optionally downloaded to your PC in Lotus 1-2-3 format or viewed as regular text. The Vendor Information Service contains nearly 1,800 vendors. This service helps you quickly find a vendor's telephone number, FAX number, complete address, and a brief description of the company.

The forum is maintained by Joe Salemi (72631,23), with the assistance of Becky J. Campbell (76247,1761).

See also ZiffNet.

Also, articles from the magazine are searchable through Computer Database Plus (GO COMPDB). See Computer Database Plus.

And the resource is searchable through IQuest. See IQuest.

See also ZiffNet.

PC World Online (GO PCWORLD) includes that famed computer publication's monthly departments, hardware and software reviews, feature articles, etc., along with articles from the current issue. It also offers material from previous *PC World* issues, a shareware library, industry news, and magazine subscription services.

The PC World Forum (GO PWOFORUM) offers message boards and conferencing facilities for communicating with the magazine's staff. You can leave messages for the editors, send consumer watch reports, and so on. Here are some direct addresses you might find handy: For a quick update see what's special this week by looking at This Week in PC WORLD Online (GO PWONEW). If you'd like to look through the current PC WORLD issue, select menu choice Current Issue (GO PWOISSUE). GO PWOEXCLUSIVE will take you to the Online Exclusive area, featuring special articles and reviews found only on PC WORLD Online. Enter GO PWOPRESS for press releases from major vendors. Operating the forum is Dennis Sheridan (71154,362), with assistance from Mike Schmitt, Mike Callahan, and Jim Moody.

Also, *PC World* is searchable (abstracts) through Computer Database Plus (GO COMPDB). See Computer Database Plus.

PC-Write **(software)** is supported in the PC Vendor B Forum (GO PCVENB). See IBM Computers.

PCX products are supported in the OS/2 B Vendor Forum (OS2BVEN). See IBM computers.

PDP-11 Forum (GO PDP11) covers using one of Digital Equipment Corporation's major systems. For details, see Digital Equipment.

Pea, Bruce (76702,1400) is sysop of the Wolfram Research Forum (GO WOLFRAM). See Wolfram Research Software.

PeachPit Press (GO PPP) offers books through a kiosk in the Electronic Mall (GO MALL). See Electronic Mall.

Peachtree Software products are supported in the IBM PC Vendor F Forum (GO PCVENF). See IBM Computers. They also are supported in the Windows 3rd-Party D Forum (GO WINAPD). See Microsoft Software.

Pediatrics for Parents is searchable in the Health Database Plus (GO HLTBD). Also abstracts of *Pediatrics*, *Clinical Pediatrics*, and *Journal of Pediatrics* are searchable there. See Health. Pediatrics also is a topic in the MedSIG Forum (GO MEDSIG). See Health.

PED Software **(products)** are supported in the Windows 3rd-Party Forum (GO WINAPD). See Microsoft Software.

PenCentral is supported in the SunSelect Forum (GO SUNSELECT). See SunSelect.

Pen pals is a topic in the Students' Forum (GO STUFO). See Students.

Penney (JC) Online Catalog (GO JCP) is a store in the Electronic Mall (GO MALL) that offers apparel, electronics, and merchandise. See Electronic Mall.

Pennsylvania news is covered in the Allentown Morning Call, the Philadelphia Daily News, the Philadelphia Inquirer, and the Pittsburgh Press, all searchable through Telebase System's News Source USA (GO NEWSUSA). See News Source.

Also:

- Selected reports from Pennsylvania are included in the Mid-Atlantic regional reports from United Press International. See Executive News Service.
- *Philadelphia Business Journal* and *Pittsburgh Business Times* can be searched through the Business Database Plus (GO BUSDB), as can *Pennsylvania Industry Environmental Advisor*. See Business Database.

Penny Wise Office Products (GO PW) and **Penny Wise Custom Print Shop** (GO PWP) are stores in the Electronic Mall (GO MALL) that offer office products and printing services. See Electronic Mall.

Pension World (**magazine**) can be searched through the Business Database Plus (GO BUSDB). See Business Database.

Pen Technology Forum (GO PENFORUM) is dedicated to the emerging pen-based computing technology.

The forum covers topics related to pen-based hardware and software, new communication systems including satellite and cellular links, and the latest news and trade show reports. Company representatives from CIC, GO Corp., GRiD Systems, Slate Corp., PenWorld, and many other companies participate in the forum to provide technical support, information on product enhancements, new product announcements, and more. The primary sysop is Ron Luks (76703,254), assisted by Randy Parker, Mike Schoenbach, and Marty Mankin.

See also Palmtop Forum (GO PALMTOP) and IBM Thinkpad Forum (GO THINKPAD); see IBM.

PenWorld products are supported in the Pen Technology Forum (GO PENFORUM). See Pen Technology.

People's Medical Society Newsletter is searchable in the Health Database Plus (GO HLTBD). See Health.

People Weekly (**magazine**) can be searched through News Source USA (GO NEWSUSA) and through IQuest (GO IQUEST). See News Source and see IQuest.

PerFORM (**software**) is supported in Delrina Technology Forum (GO DELRINA). See Delrina.

Performance Technology products are supported in the IBM Vendors H Forum (GO PCVENH). See IBM Computers.

Periscope—Daily Defense News Capsules (**database**) may be searched through the IQuest gateway. See IQuest. The resource also can be searched through the Business Database Plus (GO BUSDB). See Business Database. See also Defense.

Perkins, C. Cash (71333,1673) is the sysop of the UnixWare Forum (GO UNIXWARE). See Unix.

Personal Computer Enhancement products (Intel Corporation software) is supported in the Intel Forum (GO INTELFORUM). For details, see Intel.

Personal Computer Magazine (Netherlands) Online (GO PCNL) supports readers of that European publication. See also Personal Computer Magazine Europe Forum (GO PCMFORUM).

Personal Computer Markets can be searched through the Business Database Plus (GO BUSDB). See Business Database.

Personal Computing (magazine) is searchable in Computer Database Plus (GO COMPDB). See Computer Database Plus.

Personal Entertainment Guide, called the world's first computerized television guide, is available in CompuServe's Consumer Electronics Forum (GO CEFORUM). For details, see Television and Broadcasting.

Personal File Area (GO FILES) is an area of the system in which you may store your own files. A menu enables you to catalog the files already stored there, edit the files, rename them, change their protection level, or delete them. Other options let you upload and download files to and from the area. For users of the CompuServe Information Manager platform, the PER area is somewhat redundant, since CIM's built-in Filing Cabinet feature serves most storage needs offline.

Personal Finance and Insurance (GO FINANCE): CompuServe provides some resources to help in the running of the home. For instance:

- FundWatch Online by Money Magazine (GO FUNDWATCH) lets you screen more than 1,900 mutual funds using criteria that reflect your investment philosophy. See Financial Services.

- Information USA/Finance (GO IUS) is a specific area of the larger Information USA database that provides a list of government publications on finance and how to order them. You can learn about banking, consumer credit laws, safeguarding your investments, and bill collection. Borrowing money is explained in publications on credit, types of loans, loan applications, and interest rates.

- RateGram (GO RATEGRAM) is a financial service that lets users search for the best current rates for money market accounts, certificates of deposit, money market mutual funds, and so on. See Rategram.

- U.S. Government Publications (GO GPO) comes in two parts. The first part is a catalog of government publications, books, and subscription services. In addition to obtaining ordering information, any CompuServe subscriber with a valid MasterCard or VISA may order online any publication handled by the Government Printing Office. The orders are compiled and forwarded directly to the Government Printing Office at least once a week and more frequently as volume dictates. The second part has online consumer information articles from government publications including articles on personal finance. The entire database is updated weekly or as important changes occur.

For other money-related features, see Financial Services and Investment Analysis Tools.

Personal Manager (Personal Developer) (software) is supported in the Clarion Software Forum (GO CLARION). See Clarion.

Personal menu is an option in the logon/service area of the Terminal Settings section (GO TERMINAL) that allows you to create your own top menu of favorite features. (This is similar to what users of the CompuServe Information Manager are accustomed to with their built-in menu of "Favorite Places.")

The personal menu may contain up to 10 choices and for each; you are prompted to enter the system page number you wish to access and a description of the feature. After you have the selections the way you want them, the system sets up the personal menu and places in your personal file (PER) area a new file called MENU.CTL. You then may use the Terminal Settings area to indicate the personal menu as your first service. Then the next time you log in, you are greeted by your own customized top menu, which works like any other menu on CompuServe. To return to your personal menu from elsewhere in the system, enter GO MENU.

When you are creating your menu, you occasionally might receive a message that says, "That page is empty," even though you know it is an active page. The customer service people can provide you with a page number which will work in the menu for that particular service. Just send a message, via FEEDBACK, that includes the page address you have had trouble with.

To disable the personal menu, simply return to the First Service menu in TERMINAL/OPTIONS and pick something other than personal menu, such as MAIN or COMMAND.

See also Terminal Settings.

Personal Tax Edge (software) is supported in the Parsons Technology Forum (GO PTFORUM). See Parsons Technology.

Personal Workstation (magazine) can be searched through Computer Database Plus (GO COMPDB). See Computer Database Plus.

Personics Corporation products are supported in the PC Vendor B Forum (GO PCVENB). See IBM Computers.

Personnel (magazine) can be searched through the Business Database Plus (GO BUSDB). See Business Database.

Perspectives (**Eastern European financial database**) can be searched through IQuest. See IQuest. The resource also can be searched through the Business Database Plus (GO BUSDB). See Business Database.

Persuasion (software) is supported in the Aldus Forum (GO ALDUS). See Aldus.

Pesticide & Toxic Chemical News can be searched through the Business Database Plus (GO BUSDB). See Business Database.

Petaccia, Tom (76702,563) is the sysop of the MacUser Forum (GO ZMC:MACUSER) on the ZiffNet/Mac network. See ZiffNet/Mac.

Peterson's College Database (GO PETERSON) contains descriptions of more than 3,400 accredited or approved U.S. and Canadian colleges that grant associate and/or bachelor's degrees. It is provided by the same company that published the printed *Peterson's Guide to Four-Year Colleges* and *Peterson's Guide to Two-Year Colleges*. This is one of the system's basic services, meaning those signed up under the Standard Pricing Plan (see Billing) have unlimited access to the feature.

The database lets you search for colleges based on more than 500 characteristics, arranged in 19 primary categories, including: location, coed/single sex, size, level of study, public/private, campus setting, entrance difficulty, majors, sports, housing, costs, campus life and activities, special programs, freshman data/enrollment patterns, ethnic/geographic mix, admissions requirements, admissions policies, application deadlines, and entrance/transfer difficulty. After you have chosen all of the characteristics that are important to you, the system displays your final list of colleges and you may choose some for in-depth profile.

Some abbreviations are used in the profiles including Degree levels (A for associate, B for bachelor's, C for master's, and D for doctorate), Athletics (S after a sport indicates availability of grants-in-aid; Roman numerals indicate NCAA divisions), Majors (A means associate and B means bachelor).

This resource as well as Peterson's Gradline, also can be searched through IQuest (GO IQUEST) and through the Knowledge Index (GO KI). For details, see IQuest and see Knowledge Index.

See also Education.

Petroleum and gas industries are covered in *National Petroleum News*, *Petroleum Economist*, *Petroleum Independent*, and *Petroleum Times* magazines which can be searched through the Business Database Plus (GO BUSDB). See Business Database.

Also searchable in the IQuest gateway (see IQuest) are API Energy Business News Index, Apilit, APS Review, DAUGAZ, Energy Conservation News, Enhanced Energy Recovery News, Geoarchive, Georef, Golob's Oil Pollution Bulletin, Oil Spill Intelligence Report, Platt's Oilgram News, Platt's Oilgram Price Report, U.S. Oil Week, and Utility Reporter—Fuels, Energy & Power.

See also Energy.

Pets and Animals Forum (GO PETS) offers advice from the professionals. It also caters to your favorite pet stores. Heading up the forum is John R. Benn (76703.4256), who also heads the Aquaria and Fish Forum (GO AQUAFORUM). Assisting him are managers Martha Ashley, Mark Miller, Doug Hunter, and Lenny Southam, as well as support staff members Debbie Gates, Marci McKim, Doug Hart, Eric Johnson, Kris Moler, Chuck Clark, and Felisha Gaetz.

See also Fish and see Humane Society.

Pets-Supplies-Marketing (magazine) can be searched through the Business Database Plus (GO BUSDB). See Business Database.

Petzold, Charles (72241,56) is among *PC Magazine*'s editors and contributors who are regulars in the publication's PC-Magnet service. See *PC Magazine*.

PFS:Write, PFS:File, and **PFS:Plan** (software) are supported in the Software Publishing Forum (GO SPCFORUM). See Software Publishing Corporation.

PG Music (products) are supported in the MIDI A Vendor Forum (GO MIDIAVEN). See Music.

Pharmaceuticals and Pharmacology are covered in a variety of databases searchable through the IQuest gateway (GO IQUEST), including ADIS DrugNews, AIDS Knowledge Base, Diogenes, Druginfo and Alcohol Use and Abuse, Drug Information Fulltext, Drug Topics, Embase, IMS Marketletter, IMSWorld R&D Focus Drug News, International Pharmaceutical Abstracts, Kirk-Othmer Encyclopedia of Chemical Technology, Merck Index Online, Pharmaceutical News Index, Pharmline, Scrip—Current News, Scrip—Daily News, Scrip—Retrospective, and Unlisted Drugs. See IQuest.

   Also, *Chain Drug Review, Diagnostics Business Matters,* and *Pharmaceutical Business News* can be searched through the Business Database Plus (GO BUSDB). See Business Database.

   See also Drugs and Pharmacy.

Phelps, Pat (70006,522) is sysop of the CB Forum (GO CBFORUM). She is known to her CB buddies as LooLoo. See CB Forum.

Philadelphia Daily News and **Philadelphia Inquirer** (newspapers) are searchable through Telebase System's News Source USA (GO NEWSUSA). See News Souce. Also the Inquirer can be searched through the Knowledge Index (GO KI). See Knowledge Index.

   Also, *Philadelphia Business Journal* can be searched through the Business Database Plus (GO BUSDB). See Business Database.

Philosopher's Index (database) may be searched through the IQuest gateway (GO IQUEST) and through the Knowledge Index (GO KI). See IQuest and see Knowledge Index.

Phoenix, University of (GO UP) has a service in the Electronic Mall (GO MALL) that offers business degree programs online. See Electronic Mall.

Phoenix business news is reported in *The Business Journal—Serving Phoenix & the Valley of the Sun*, which can be searched through the Business Database Plus (GO BUSDB). See Business Database.

Phone, CompuServe access numbers (GO PHONES): Access numbers for hundred of locations can be found in the phone number database, which lets you list all the numbers accessible from anywhere in the U.S., Canada, and countries around the world. You can search for specific CompuServe network numbers and/or supplemental network numbers and specify the search for all baud rates or only specific baud rates (2400-, 9600-, or 14400-baud). Also, you can search by either state/province or by area code.

In addition, CompuServe has set up a free network that can find various access numbers around the world. The CompuServe Network Services Assistance area can be reached on any CompuServe access number or by dialing 1-800-848-4480. After dialing the number, enter CPS at the Host Name: prompt. When asked for a User ID, enter 74,74 with the password NETWORK. The system is a menu-driven database that permits you to list and search for CompuServe direct access phone numbers and other network gateways by state or area code. Enter BYE at a prompt to log off the system.

Phone Directories: CompuServe's powerful searching capabilities are being used to provide massive interstate telephone directories. Phonefile (GO PHONEFILE) lists more than 80 million U.S. households and contains consumer data such as name, home address, phone number, and length of residence. You can retrieve listings by searching by name with address, by name with ZIP code, city and/or state, and by phone number.

Phone*File, a 25-cent-a-minute ($15 an hour) surcharged feature, is offered by MetroNet, which already has provided businesses with access to the database. MetroNet is part of Metromail, which in turn is a subsidiary of R. R. Donnelley, the directory publishing company that sells mailing list information to direct marketing firms. The service is available Monday through Saturday from 6 a.m. til 2:30 a.m. and on Sundays from 10 a.m. to 8 p.m. Eastern Time.

Backers of the venture noted that, rather than being dependent solely on telephone books, data in Phonefile comes from white-page directories as well as published birth announcements, real estate transactions, and other data from public sources. (The length of residence information is determined by the number of years a household record remains unchanged in the database.)

Phonefile offers three types of searches:

- Name and address
- Phone number
- Surname and geographical area

(CompuServe notes these types of restricted search methods are designed to retrieve individual names and discourage use of their compilation for mailing or telephone solicitation.)

An opening menu informs users of surcharges, then provides the three search options, plus directions for use and for the exit command. A search by name and address prompts for the person's name, street address, city/state, and ZIP code. For a surname search, the system gives users a choice of searching by city and state, by state only, or by ZIP code, then asks a last name.

This means the service could be used to look up every person with a specific last name in any city or state. The phone search option asks users to enter either the three-digit area code or five-digit ZIP code. In addition to address and telephone information, the database can include the name of a spouse and the length of residence at the address listed.

Phone Directories, Yellow Pages: An online "yellow pages" installation, Biz*File (GO BIZFILE), provides access to names, addresses, and phone numbers for more than 10 million U.S. and Canadian business listings, and contains data including business name, address, phone number, and length of time each business has been listed in its source directory. Listings can be retrieved through searches by company name, by company phone number, and by the type of business. Also, the feature has added Boolean operators. Using AND, OR, and NOT lets you search more specific companies. The service is available around the clock seven days a week except for a three-hour period beginning at 8 p.m. Eastern Time on the last Friday of each month. The database is surcharged at $15 an hour.

Also, to search for business phone numbers, you might check out Dun's Electronic Yellow Pages (GO DYP), a surcharged a gateway that contains directory information on nearly 8 million businesses and professionals in the United States. See Dun's Electronic Yellow Pages.

Phonefile (GO PHONEFILE) lists more than 80 million households nationwide. It is surcharged at $15 an hour (25 cents a minute) and allows users to search by last name, phone number, ZIP code, and other means. See Phone Directories.

Phones, government numbers: Information U.S.A. (GO INFOUSA) reports many contact phone numbers for government agencies. See Information U.S.A.

Phosphorous and Potassium (magazine) can be searched through the Business Database Plus (GO BUSDB). See Business Database.

Photography is the topic of the Photography Forum (GO PHOTOFORUM), a gathering place for amateur and professional photographers alike. Mike Wilmer (76703,4400), a graduate of Brookings Institute of Photography and a professional portrait photographer, is the administrator. Assistants include Scott Hughes, Jon Jacobs, Len Wilcox, Lloyd O'Daniel, Katherine Miller, Lara Hartley, Joel Albert, and William Safford. Also assisting are a number of equipment specialists and photo mentors who offer considerable expertise in a photographic specialization, and who have offered to share their knowledge with others.
Also:

- British pictures are offered in the UK Forum (GO UKFORUM). See UK Forum.

- Computer art and photography: visit Graphics Net (GO GRAPHICS). For more on that, see Art, Computer.

- The IQuest gateway gives access to several photography databases, including Photobulletin, Photoletter, Photomarket, and Iconos. See IQuest.
- Nature photography is a topic in the Great Outdoors Forum (GO OUTDOORFORUM). See Sports and Recreation.
- Photo CD technology is discussed in the MultiMedia Forum (GO MULTI-MEDIA). See Multimedia.
- Photography also is a topic in the TrainNet Forum (GO TRAINNET). See Trainnet.
- Reuter News Pictures Forum (GO NEWSPIX) provides actual news images from around the world, available in both GIF and JPEG formats.
- 35mm cameras and lenses are discussed in the Cannon Support Forum (GO CANON). See Canon.
- Underwater photography is discussed in the Scuba Forum (GO DIVING). See Sports and Recreation.

Photonics Spectra (magazine) can be searched through the Business Database Plus (GO BUSDB). See Business Database.

Photoshop is supported in the Adobe Forum (GO ADOBE). See Adobe Software.

PhotoStyler (software) is supported in the Aldus Forum (GO ALDUS). See Aldus.

Photoview products are supported in the Windows 3rd-Party C Forum (GO WINAPC). See Microsoft Software.

Physical Therapy is searchable in the Health Database Plus (GO HLTBD). See Health.

Physician Executive is searchable in the Health Database Plus (GO HLTBD). See Health.

Physicians Data Query (GO PDQ) is a collection of surcharged databases copyrighted and published by the National Cancer Institute. See Cancer Information. The resource also can be search on IQuest. See IQuest.

Physics is a topic in the Science/Math Education Forum (GO SCIENCE). For details, see Science/Math.

   Also available in IQuest (see IQuest) are Academic Index, INSPEC, Meteorological and Geoastrophysical Abstracts, National Technical Information Service, and Searchable Physics Information Notices. See IQuest.

"Picket Fences" (television) summaries on the latest shows are available in Soap Opera Summaries (GO SOAPS). See Soap Opera.

Pictor (software) is supported in the Graphics A Vendor Forum (GO GRAPHVEN). See Graphics.

PicturePro (software) is supported by the Ventura Software Forum (GO VENTURA). See Ventura.

Pictures on computers and computer art are discussed and displayed in the forums of Graphics Net (GO GRAPHICS). See Graphics (and Art, Computer).

Pierce, Jean W. (76703,445) administers the Education Research Forum (GO EDRESEARCH). See Education Research Forum.

Piers Exports (databases) covers virtually all maritime movements into and out of the continental U.S. and Puerto Rico. The databases are searchable on IQuest. See IQuest.

Pietruk, Mike (76703,4346) is an administrator of the Investors Forum (GO INVFORUM). See Investors Forum.

Pike, Jeffrey (76702,531) is administrator of the Autodesk Forum (GO ADESK). See Autodesk Software.

Pilgrim, Debbie (76701,245) is a sysop in the Microsoft forums (GO MICROSOFT). For details, see Microsoft Software.

Pilots frequent the Aviation Forum (GO AVSIG). See Aviation.

Pilot's Power Tools (software) is supported in the Game Publishers B Forum (GO GAMPUB). See Gaming Forums.

Pinball (game software) is distributed and supported in Epic Online (GO EPIC). See Epic.

Pinnacle Publishing products are supported in the IBM PC Vendor G Forum (GO PCVENG). See IBM Computers.

Pioneer Electronics products are supported in the Consumer Electronics Vendor Forum (GO CEVENDOR). See Electronics Forum.

Pipe smoking is discussed in a section of the message board in the Bacchus Wine Forum (GO WINEFORUM). See Wine.

Pipeline and ***Pipe Line Industry*** (magazines) can be searched through the Business Database Plus (GO BUSDB). See Business Database.

PIRA Abstracts (paper industry database) may be searched through the IQuest gateway. See IQuest.

Piracy, software is a regular topic in the Software Publishers Association Forum (GO SPAFORUM). See Software Publishers.

.PIT, as an extension on filenames in forum libraries, usually means the program is in a *compressed/packed* form. See Files, Compressed.

Pittsburgh (PA) Press (newspaper) is searchable through Telebase System's News Source USA (GO NEWSUSA) and through the Knowledge Index (GO KI). See News Source and see Knowledge Index. Also, Pittsburgh Business Times (magazine) can be searched through the Business Database Plus (GO BUSDB). See Business Database.

PKWare software products, including the popular data compression programs PKZIP, PKUNZIP, and PKSFX, are supported in the PC Vendor C Forum (GO PCVENC). See IBM Computers.

Planet graphics from NASA in GIF format are featured in the Graphics Gallery Forum (GO GALLERY) in data library 9, "The Planets." See Graphics.

Planning and ***The Journal of the American Planning Association*** can be searched through the Business Database Plus (GO BUSDB). See Business Database.

Planning League, American has a section of the Legal Forum (GO LAWSIG) for discussion of its issues. See Legal Forum.

PlanPerfect (software) is supported by the WordPerfect Support forums. See WordPerfect Software.

Plant Engineering (magazine) can be searched through the Business Database Plus (GO BUSDB). See Business Database.

Plastics industry is cover in several magazines that can be searched through Business Database Plus (GO BUSDB), including *High Performance Plastics*, *Plastics Engineering*, *Plastics Technology*, and *Plastics World*, as well as *Japanese New Materials Advanced Plastics*. See Business Database.

Platt's Oilgram News and **Platt's Oilgram Price Report** (newsletters) can be searched through IQuest. See IQuest.

Play-By-Mail Games Forum (GO PBMGAMES) is devoted to discussions about a wide variety of games that can be played by electronic mail or by conventional postal service delivery. See Gaming Forums.

Playboy (magazine) articles are searchable through Magazine Database Plus (GO MDP). For details see Magazine Database.

Playthings (magazine) can be searched through the Business Database Plus (GO BUSDB). See Business Database.

Playroom products are supported in the Windows 3rd-Party Forum A (GO WINAPA). See Microsoft Software.

Plug and Play Forum (GO PLUGPLAY) is operated by several hardware and software manufacturers for discussion of issues relating to implementing plug and play technology. ("Plug and Play" refers to the automatic identification and configuration of computer systems, peripherals, and operating systems. A set of hardware and software interfaces are being defined to enable such operation.) In addition to general discussion and information, the forum provides technical support for the Plug and Play ISA Specifications to members of the Plug and Play ISA Association. Managing the forum are Bob Taniguchi, Carl Stork, Mike Flora, and Moshe Lichtman.

Pocket Soft products are supported in the PC Vendor I Forum (GO PCVENI). See IBM Computers.

Poetry is a regular topic in the Literary Forum (GO LITFORUM). For details, see Literature.

Point, an electronic messaging system also called PARTICIPATE. For details, see PARTICIPATE.

Polaris Software Forum (GO POLARIS) provides support for that San Diego, Calif., firm's programs, including various versions of its PackRat system. The forum is administered by Andrew Miller (72662,1120), with assistance from James Boyd, Anita Johnson, and Sal Viveros.

Police and law enforcement are discussed in the SafetyNet Forum (GO SAFETYNET). For information, see Safety.

Policy, CompuServe's operating rules (GO RULES) are displayed online, along with an elaboration on the policy (GO COPYRIGHT). For a copy of the operating rules agreement all subscribers sign, see Rules, CompuServe Operating.

Political Debate Forum (GO POLITICS) is intended as a platform for major political parties and Ross Perot's "United We Stand, America" organization. Its message sections focus on topics of interest to all U.S. citizens, including health care, the economy, defense, and the environment. Included in the forum is a section devoted to Empower America, a nonpartisan political advocacy committee whose codirectors are William Bennett, Jack Kemp, and Jeane J. Kirkpatrick. Manager of the forum is Georgia Griffith (76703,266), assisted by Ran Talbott, David Bush, Keir Jones, David Rogers, Scott Place, Steve Davis, Les Prus, Joe Balsamo, Steve Dasbach, Al Goggins, Jackie G. Howell, Stephen Katsurinis, and Alex Krislov.

Also politics is a favorite subject in:

- The White House Forum (GO WHITEHOUSE) and the Issues Forum (GO ISSUESFORUM). For details, see White House and see Issues.
- British politics is discussed in the UK Forum (GO UKFORUM). See UK Forum.
- Computer-oriented political and legal issues are discussed in Computer Consultant's Forum (GO CONSULT). See Computer Consulting.

- Democratic Party Forum (GO DEMOCRATS) overseen by the Democratic National Committee. See Democratic.
- Republican Forum (GO REPUBLICAN) is a clearinghouse for GOP news and information. See Republican.
- Florida politics is discussed in the Florida Today NewsLink Forum (GO FLATODAY). See Florida.
- Pacific Rim politics is discussed in CompuServe Pacific Forum (GO PACFORUM). See Pacific Forum.
- Political issues also are discussed in the Space/Astronomy Forum (GO SPACEFORUM). See Space.
- Politics and economics are topics in the Mensa Forum (GO MENSA). See Mensa.
- West Coast politics is a topic in the California Forum (GO CALFORUM). See California.

Political Finance & Lobby Reporter (database) can be searched through IQuest. See IQuest.

Political Risk Letter can be searched through the Business Database Plus (GO BUSDB). See Business Database.

Political Science Documents, U.S. (database) may be searched through the IQuest gateway. See IQuest.

Pollution Abstracts (database) may be searched through the IQuest gateway (GO IQUEST) and through the Knowledge Index (GO KI). See IQuest and see Knowledge Index.

See also Environment.

Poor, Alfred (72241,1301) is one of the editors and writers associated with the PC Magazine forums. See PC Magazine.

Popular Mechanics and **Popular Science** (magazines) can be searched in the Magazine Database Plus (GO MDP). See Magazine Database.

Population Reports is searchable in the Health Database Plus (GO HLTBD). See Health.

Poqet computers are supported in the Palmtop Forum (GO PALMTOP). See Palmtop.

Portable Programming Forum (GO CODEPORT) is covered in the Programming section.

Portfolio Systems products are supported in the Macintosh Vendor A Forum (GO MACAVEN). See Apple Computers.

Portfolio Valuation (GO PORT) is a financial service that finds the value of a portfolio for dates you select and displays unrealized gains and losses. See Investment Analysis Tools.

Portland Oregonian (**newspaper**) is searchable through Telebase System's News Source USA (GO NEWSUSA). See News Source.

Also, *Business Journal—Portland* magazine can be searched through the Business Database Plus (GO BUSDB). See Business Database.

Portuguese is spoken in the Foreign Language Forum's (GO FLEFO). See Foreign Language.

POS News (database covering the use of debit and credit cards for payment at the Point of Sale) can be searched through IQuest. See IQuest. The resource also can be searched through the Business Database Plus (GO BUSDB). See Business Database.

PostScript (**software**) is supported in the Aldus Forum (GO ALDUS). See Aldus Software.

Potato Markets can be searched through the Business Database Plus (GO BUSDB). See Business Database.

PowerBASIC products are supported in the IBM PC Vendor B Forum (GO PCVENB). See IBM Computers.

Power boating is a topic of the Outdoors Forum (GO OUTDOORFORUM). See Sports and Recreation.

PowerBuilder, **PowerMaker,** and **PowerViewer** (**software**) are supported in the Powersoft Forum (GO POWERSOFT). See Powersoft.

Powercore products are supported in the IBM PC Vendor B Forum (GO PCVENB). See IBM Computers.

POWERLan, POWERsave, POWERfusion, and **POWERshare** are supported in the IBM Vendors H Forum (GO PCVENH). See IBM Computers.

PowerMenu Plus (**software**) is supported in the PC Vendor G Forum (GO PCVENG). See IBM.

PowerModem and others from PSI Integration are supported in the Modem Vendor Forum (GO MODEMVEN). See Modem Vendor.

Powerpoint (**software**) is supported in the Microsoft Application Forum (GO MSAPP). See Microsoft Software.

Powersoft Forum (GO POWERSOFT) is administered by employees of software publisher Powersoft Corporation to support its programs, such as PowerBuilder,

PowerMaker, and PowerViewer. Managing the forum is Joe R. Mens (76711,1165), with assistance from Eric Bulock.

Power Source (database) can be searched through IQuest. See IQuest.

Power Systems, Modern (magazine) can be searched through the Business Database Plus (GO BUSDB). See Business Database.

POW/MIA (prisoners of war/missing in action) is an issue discussed regularly in the Military Veterans Forum (GO MILITARY). See Military Forum.

PR (public relations) is discussed in the Public Relations and Marketing Forum (GO PRSIG). See Public Relations and Marketing. For other business-oriented subjects, see Financial Services and see Investment Analysis Tools.

PR Newswire (news) is searchable through Comtex Scientific Inc.'s NewsGrid database. For details, see NewsGrid. The database also is accessible through IQuest (GO IQUEST), Business Database Plus (GO BUSDB), and Knowledge Index (GO KI). See IQuest, Business Database, and Knowledge Index.

PR Week (database) may be searched through the IQuest gateway. See IQuest.

Practical Peripherals Inc. Equipment: The Practical Peripherals Forum (GO PPIFORUM) is sponsored by the company as technical support for users of PPI products. The sysop is Paul E. Hansen (76702,475), an independent computer consultant and technical writer. He is assisted by Mark Young.

Practice Forum (GO PRACTICE) is a free forum intended to help visitors learn to navigate and use a typical CompuServe Forum environment. This is one of the system's basic services, meaning those signed up under the Standard Pricing Plan (see Billing) have unlimited access to the feature. Because the forum is a training ground, it uses its message board heavily. At the same time, it is designed not to support a few features available in most CompuServe forums, such as real-time conferencing and private mail. The forum is staffed by veteran forum administrators who have volunteered their time. The primary sysop is Mike Schoenbach (76703,4363), who is an administrator in several Atari forums (GO ATARI) and maintains CompuServe's National Modem-to-Modem Game Players' Challenge Board (GO CHALLENGE) and the Game Challenge Forum (GO CHALFORUM). He is assisted by Sara Howard, Betty Knight, Steve McCoy, Bill Walp, and Sue Thornburg.
    See also Forums and see Help.

Pratt, Doug (76703,3041) is administrator of the ModelNet Forum (GO MODELNET). See ModelNet. He also is a sysop in the Comics and Animation Forum (GO COMICS). See Comics.

PRC Database Publishing (GO PRC) is a store in the Electronic Mall (GO MALL) that offers *Best of "GO Graphics"* directory, considered to be the guide to the "stars" of the world's largest online collection of computer artwork. See Electronic Mall. Also see Graphics.

Precision Software products are supported in the Atari Vendors Forum (GO ATARIVEN); see Atari Computers.

Predicasts Inc. publishes the PTS Newsletter Database, carried as a gateway from Telebase Systems. For details, see PTS Newsletter.

Premia products are supported in the Windows 3rd-Party Forum A (GO WINAPA). See Microsoft Software.

Premier (**magazine**) can be searched in the Magazine Database Plus (GO MDP). See Magazine Database.

Premiere (**software**) is supported in the Adobe Forum (GO ADOBE). See Adobe Software.

Prentice Hall Computer Publishing Forum (GO PHCP) provides information and technical support for the company's computer books and software. Members can access disk updates and information on books published by PHCP's imprints, including Que Publishing, Sams Publishing, New Riders Publishing, Alpha Books, Brady Books, and Hayden Books. The forum also offers information on Que Software products. In addition, Paramount Interactive, a division of Paramount Technology Group, has representatives visiting the forum. Message sections allow members to share tips, tricks, and techniques. The sysops are Al Bruner (72662,102) and Jon McCormick (71333,3270).

PrePrint (**software**) is supported in the Aldus Forum (GO ALDUS). See Aldus.

Presentation Manager (**software**) is supported in the Microsoft Developer Relations Forum (GO MSDR). See Microsoft Software.

President and the presidency are discussed in the White House Forum (GO WHITEHOUSE). See White House.

Presidio Software products are supported in the Graphics A Vendor Forum (GO GRAPHVEN). See Graphics.

Press: The news business is discussed in the Journalism Forum (GO JFORUM). See Journalism. TV/radio news is the focus of the Broadcasters and Engineers Forum (GO BPFORUM). See Broadcasters and Broadcast Engineers. For other related features, see News, General.

Preston, Patrick (76702,2013) is the sysop of the Humane Society Forum (GO HSUS). See Humane.

Prevention magazine is searchable in the Health Database Plus (GO HLTBD). See Health.

Price histories, stock market: Enter GO PRICES for market histories on tens of thousands of stocks, bonds, warrants, and mutual funds available on a daily basis. See Stock Quotes (Historical) and for an overview of other money-related features, see Financial Services and see Investment Analysis Tools.

Pricing Statistics (GO PRISTATS) gives a quick look at the performance price and volume performance for a stock market issue over a given period. See Stock Quotes (Historical).

Primaversa Systems Incorporation Software is supported in the PC Vendor B Forum (GO PCVENB). See IBM Computers.

Printer, American (**magazine**) is searchable through the Business Database Plus (GO BUSDB). See Business Database.

Printers: Several forums provide technical support for specific computer printers, including:

- Canon Forum (GO CANON). See Canon.
- Compaq Computer Forum (GO CPQFORUM). See Compaq.
- Desktop Publishing Vendors Forum (GO DTPVENDOR). See Desktop Publishing.
- Epson Forum (GO EPSON). For details, see Epson.
- Hewlett-Packard PC Forums (GO HP). See Hewlett-Packard.
- Kodak CD Forum (GO KODAK). See Kodak.
- Practical Peripherals Forum (GO PPIFORUM). See Practical.
- TandyNet forums (GO TANDYNET). See Tandy.
- Texas Instruments Forums (GO TIFORUM). See Texas Instruments.

Also, some forums cover hardware commonly used with specific computers. For details, see the entries for those computers.

Prisma Deutschland Forum (GO PRISMA) is available for support of German-speaking computerists.

Private Placement Reporter can be searched through the Business Database Plus (GO BUSDB). See Business Database.

Privatisation International can be searched through the Business Database Plus (GO BUSDB). See Business Database.

Pro*C (**software**) is supported in the Oracle Forum (GO ORACLE). See Oracle Software.

PRO-C Corporation products are supported in the IBM PC Vendor B Forum (GO PCVENB). See IBM Computers.

Process Engineering (magazine) can be searched through the Business Database Plus (GO BUSDB). See Business Database.

ProComm (communications software) is supported in the Datastorm Forum (GO DATASTORM). The forum supports ProComm and ProComm Plus communication programs as well as the new ProComm Plus Network version and Hot Wire programs. The forum is operated by Mike Robertson (76702,1130) assisted by Dick Cravens, Nick Witthaus, Jim Pointer, Jody Cooper, Susan Reid-Pfau, and Larry Dorman.

   Also, the British edition of ProComm Plus is supported in the UK Shareware Forum (GO UKSHARE). See UK Shareware.

   See also Telecomputing.

Procom Technology products are supported in the IBM PC Vendor D Forum (GO PCVEND). See IBM Computers.

Product Alert, International can be searched through the Business Database Plus (GO BUSDB). See Business Database. The resource also can be searched through the Business Database Plus (GO BUSDB). See Business Database.

Production can be searched through the Business Database Plus (GO BUSDB). See Business Database.

Productivity Software can be searched through the Business Database Plus (GO BUSDB). See Business Database.

Products, Ordering CompuServe (GO ORDER): CompuServe offers its own online ordering service for a variety of products, from books and manuals to T-shirts, coffee mugs, and posters. See Ordering, CompuServe Products.

Product Safety Letter (database) can be searched through IQuest. See IQuest.

Professional File, Professional Write, and **Professional Plan** (software) are supported in the Software Publishing Forum (GO SPCFORUM). See Software Publishing Corporation.

PrOffice products are supported in the OS/2 Vendor Forum (GO OS2AVEN). See IBM Computers.

Profile, User screen sizes and characteristics for your CompuServe account, may be recorded in the Terminal Settings area of the system. See Terminal.

Program Development Facility (software) is supported in the Software Solutions Forum (GO SOFSOL). See Software Solutions.

Programmers Support: Some forums cater to programmers; and the word *development* or *developers* in the name often is a tipoff.

- Amiga programmers ought to look in on the Amiga Technical Forum (GO AMIGATECH). See Commodore Computers.

- Apple programmers should check out the Mac Developers' and Programmers' Forum (GO MACDEV) and the Apple II Programmers' Forum (GO APPROG). See Apple Computers.

- Commodore 8-bit programmers will be interested in the Commodore Application Forum (GO CBMAPP). See Commodore.

- IBM-compatible programmers might want to look in on the IBM Programming Forum (GO IBMPROG). See IBM Computers.

If your system is not listed here, visit the general forums supporting that hardware. Other programmers also are likely to be there.

Here are some other forums for programmers and serious computer hobbyists:

- CODEPORT, The Portable Programming Forum (GO CODEPORT), is sponsored by USUS, the UCSD Pascal System Users' Society for discussion of topics related to Pascal, Apple Pascal, Modula-2, and similar software systems. Primary sysop is Harry Baya (76702,513). He is assisted by Tom Cattral.

- CP/M: One of the oldest forums on the system, CP/M Users Group Forum (GO CPMFORUM) (originally CP-MIG Forum) is devoted to users of the CP/M operating system on various computers. Running the show are John Ross (76703,551) and John Deakin (76702,310). The forum is one of the few resources any owner of an Osborne 1 or Kaypro 2 can turn to in order to seek help for a thorny operating system problem.

  CP/M also is discussed in the Commodore Applications Forum (GO CBMAPP), Computer Club Forum (GO CLUB), and Epson Forum (GO EPSON).

- FORTH: The Forth Forum (GO FORTH), has operated since October 1984 by Creative Solutions Incorporated, providing online support for its Forth language products. The primary sysop is CSI president/founder Don Colburn (76703,4160), who implemented the first Forth system on the 68000 processor in 1979. He is assisted by Zach Zachariah, Ward McFarland, Jon Bryan, Greg Guerin, John Baxter, and John Jepson.

- LOGO: The Young Peoples' Logo Association provides the LOGO Forum (GO LOGOFORUM) for students of any age. The sysop (and "Chief Turtle") is Jim Muller (76703,3005), who says that while the group's main interest is the many versions of Logo, there are other languages and other technologies discussed in the forum. The forum also offers technical support for products from Terrapin Inc., Paradigm Software, Schemers Inc., PC Logo, and LCSI.

In addition:

- PC MAGNET has a programmer's forum (GO ZNT:PROGRAMMING); for more information, see PC Magazine's PC MAGNET.

- Borland Programming Forum A (GO BPROGA) is for Turbo Pascal and Turbo Basic programmers. Also, Borland Programming Forum B (GO BPROGB) is devoted to the new artificial intelligence system, Turbo Assembler, Turbo C, Turbo Debugger, and Turbo Prolog. See Borland.

- The Cobb Group Programming Forum (GO ZNT:COBBPROG) provides code listings from Cobbs Group journals, including *The DOS Authority, Inside Microsoft BASIC, Inside QuickBASIC, Inside Turbo C++, Inside Turbo Pascal, Inside Turbo C, Inside Visual BASIC, Microsoft C, C++ Developers' Journal, Paradox Developers' Journal,* and *Paradox Users' Journal.* See Cobb Group.

- Computer Database Plus (GO COMPDB) offers access to full-text and abstracts of many computer publications. See Computer Database Plus.

- Computer Language Magazine also is represented online (GO CLMFORUM), and offers discussions of languages such as C and FORTH, uploading and downloading of utilities, swapping of programming tips and techniques, and so on. See Computer Language Magazine.

- The dBASE Forum (GO DBASE) is devoted entirely to topics related to dBASE. See Borland.

- Dr. Dobb's Journal Forum (GO DDJFORUM) offers discussions on C, CP/M, ALGOL, FORTH, 68000 programming, artificial intelligence, and so on. See Dr. Dobb's Journal.

- LISP, Turbo Prolog, expert systems in general, and other topics relating to artificial intelligence are discussed in the AI Expert Forum (GO AIEXPORT). See AI Expert Magazine.

- Microsoft Languages Forum (GO MSLANG) provides technical support for the Microsoft Language and Quick Language products. The forum includes sections for Assembler/Microsoft Editor, BASIC/QuickBASIC, COBOL, FORTRAN, Mac QuickBASIC, Microsoft C, QuickC, and QuickPascal/Pascal. See Microsoft Software.

See also Telecomputing, Word processors, and Spreadsheets. Also, see entries for specific programming products.

Progressive (magazine) can be searched in the Magazine Database Plus (GO MDP). See Magazine Database.

Progressive Solutions products are supported in the Zenith Data Systems Forum (GO ZENITH). For details, see Zenith.

Project (software) is supported in the Microsoft Application Forum (GO MSAPP). See Microsoft Software.

Project Scheduler 6 for Windows (software) is supported in the Windows 3rd-Party Forum (GO WINAPD). See Microsoft Software.

Prolog (**software**) is supported in the Borland Programming Forum B (GO BPROGB); see Borland. Also, see AI Expert magazine.

Prolog Development Center products are supported in the IBM PC Vendor B Forum (GO PCVENB). See IBM Computers.

Promotion is discussed in the Public Relations and Marketing Forum (GO PRSIG). See Public Relations and Marketing. For other business-oriented subjects, see Financial Services and see Investment Analysis Tools.

Prompt (**software**) is supported in Windows 3rd-Party Forum A (GO WINAPA). See Microsoft Software.

Prosise, Jeff (72241,44) is one of the editors and writers associated with the PC Magazine forums. See PC Magazine.

ProWrite and **ProScript products** are supported in the Amiga Vendor Forum (GO AMIGAVENDOR). See Commodore Computers.

PRS Automotive Service can be searched through the Business Database Plus (GO BUSDB). See Business Database.

PSA Journal (**magazine**) articles are searchable through Magazine Database Plus (GO MDP). For details see Magazine Database. It also can be searched through Business Database Plus (GO BUSDB). See Business Database.

PSI Integration products are supported in the Modem Vendor Forum (GO MODEMVEN). See Modem Vendor.

Psion Dacom products are supported in the UK Computing Forum (GO UKCOMP). See UK Computing. Psion Inc. products are supported in the Palmtop Forum (GO PALMTOP). See Palmtop.

PSN News (**database**) covers news and analysis of the personal communications networks (microcell) industry, and can be searched through IQuest. See IQuest.

PS/2 (**IBM computers**) are supported in the IBM Users Network (GO IBMNET). See IBM Computers for addition information.

Psychic topics are discussed in the New Age Forum (GO NEWAGE). See New Age.

Psychology and psychiatry are the topics of the PsycINFO (GO PSYCINFO), a database that contains abstracts of articles from international literature in psychology and the behavioral sciences. The database is published and copyrighted by the American Psychological Association and provided by Telebase Systems Inc. Abstracts are available from 1967 to the present and include the fields of applied, developmental, general and experimental psychology, communication systems, education, personnel and professional issues, psychometrics, treatment and prevention, social processes and issues, etc. The information available in each article may include authors, title, journal name, language, date of publication, and an abstract. You can retrieve abstracts of articles by entering subject words, author names, language, or publication year as your search criteria. The database is surcharged at $5 for the first 10 titles found, $5 for the next 10 titles, and $5 for each full abstract selected from the search lists. There is a $1 for each search that retrieves no titles. For information on other Telebase gateways, see Telebase Systems Incorporated.

This resource also can be searched through the Knowledge Index (GO KI). See Knowledge Index.

In addition:

- Abstracts of *American Journal of Psychiatry*, *American Journal of Psychology*, *American Journal of Psychotherapy*, *Annual Review of Psychology*, and *Developmental Psychology* are searchable in the Health Database Plus (GO HLTBD), as are those from *British Journal of Psychiatry*, *British Journal of Psychology*, *Contemporary Psychology*, *Journal of Abnormal Child Psychology*, *Journal of Abnormal Psychology*, and *Journal of Experimental Psychology*. See Health.

- Through the IQuest gateway (GO IQUEST), databases that are searchable include Academic Index, Ageline, Child Abuse and Neglect and Family Violence, Family Resources, Mental Health Abstracts, Mental Measurements Yearbook, PsycINFO, and Rehabdata. See IQuest.

- *Psychology Today* magazine is searchable in the Health Database Plus (GO HLTDB). See Health Database. The magazine also is searchable through Magazine Database Plus (GO MDP) and through Health Database Plus (GO HLTDB). See Health and see Magazine Database.

See also Health.

PTS MARS, PTS New Product Announcements, and PTS PROMT

(business databases) are accessible through the Marketing/Management Research Center (GO MKTGRC). For details, see Marketing/Management. These databases also are accessible through IQuest (GO IQUEST), as are PTS F&S Indexes, PTS International Forecasts, PTS U.S. Forecasts, PTS U.S. Time Series, and PTS Aerospace/Defence Markets. See IQuest.

PTS Newsletter Database/Communications

(GO DPNEWS), a Telebase Systems Incorporated gateway, is the computer and telecommunications section of PTS Newsletter Database, which includes the full text of articles from several of the leading newsletters covering the computer, electronics, and telecommunications industries. They are seen as good sources of facts, figures, analyses, and current information in that market.

Surcharges for the database are $5 for the first 10 titles located, $5 for additional titles in groups of 10, and $5 for each full reference retrieved, along with the abstract where available. There is a $1 charge for each search that retrieves no titles.

PTS Newsletter Database/Media (GO MEDIANEWS) is the broadcast and publishing section of PTS Newsletter Database. It includes full text of articles from several major newsletters covering the broadcasting and publishing industries.

Surcharges for the database are $5 for the first 10 titles located, $5 for additional titles in groups of 10, and $5 for each full reference retrieved, along with the abstract where available. There is a $1 charge for each search that retrieves no titles.

For information on other Telebase gateways, see Telebase Systems Incorporated.

P296FMV modems and others from Megahertz are supported in the Modem Vendor Forum (GO MODEMVEN). See Modem Vendor.

Public Brand Software, a major distributor of shareware products, operates two forums on the ZiffNet system (see ZiffNet). They are the Public Brand Software Arcade (GO ZNT:PBSARCADE) and the Public Brand Software Applications Forum (GO ZNT:PBSAPPS). Both feature extensive libraries of downloadable programs, text files, newsletters, etc. The forums are operated by Sue Ayre (72241,234), with the assistance from Bob Ostrander, Al Thompson, Dave Burton, Reed Butler, Jim Edwards, and Rich Holler.

See ZiffNet and see Shareware.

Public Broadcasting Report can be searched through IQuest. See IQuest. The resource also can be searched through the Business Database Plus (GO BUSDB). See Business Database.

Public Finance Washington Watch can be searched through the Business Database Plus (GO BUSDB). See Business Database.

Public Health Reports is searchable in the Health Database Plus (GO HLTBD). See Health.

Public Opinion Online (POLL) can be searched through the Knowledge Index (GO KI). See Knowledge Index.

Public Relations and Marketing: The Public Relations and Marketing Forum (GO PRSIG) began in January 1984 as a medium for electronic dialogue between professional publicists and students in the communications field. The founding sysop is Ron Solberg (76703,575), who owns and operates his own Chicago-area public relations, marketing, and consulting agency, specializing in productive communication through technology. Assisting him are John Baker, Mike Bayer, Fred Ennis, Jon Hoornstra, Daniel Janal, Ken Love, Bill Lutholtz, and Bill Weylock.

Also:

- Searchable through Business Database Plus (GO BUSDB) are *Public Relations Journal* and *Public Relations Review*. See Business Database.
- PR Newswire is searchable through Comtex Scientific Inc.'s NewsGrid database. For details, see NewsGrid. The database also is accessible through IQuest

(GO IQUEST) and through Business Database Plus (GO BUSDB). See IQuest and Business Database.

- PR Week **(database)** may be searched through the IQuest gateway. See IQuest.

Publish! **(magazine)** is searchable (abstracts) through Computer Database Plus (GO COMPDB). See Computer Database Plus.

Publisher, Ventura **(software)** is supported in the Ventura Software Forum (GO VENTURA). See Ventura.

Publishing services are provided by Nicholas Direct (GO ND) in the Electronic Mall (GO MALL). See Electronic Mall.

Publishing Magazine, Personal, is supported in the Desktop Publishing Vendor Forum (GO DTPVENDOR). For details, see Desktop Publishing.

Puget Sound Business Journal **(magazine)** can be searched through the Business Database Plus (GO BUSDB). See Business Database.

Pure Data, Ltd. **(local area network)** products are supported in PC Vendor F Forum (GO PCVENF). For details, see IBM Computers.

Purchasing and **Purchasing World** **(magazines)** can be searched through the Business Database Plus (GO BUSDB). See Business Database.

PVCS Production Gateway is supported in the Intersolv Forum (GO INTERSOLV). See Intersolv.

Q&A **(software)** is supported in the Symantec Forum (Go SYMANTEC). See Symantec Software.

QAPlus **(software)** is supported in the DiagSoft Forum (GO DIAGSOFT). See DiagSoft.

QBlazer transportable modems are supported in the Modem Vendor Forum (GO MODEMVEN). See Modem Vendor.

QEMM **(software)** is supported in the Quarterdeck Office Systems Forum (GO QUARTERDECK). For details, see Quarterdeck.

Q+E Software products are supported in the Windows 3rd-Party D Forum (GO WINAPD). See Microsoft Software.

QL Systems of Canada is a major database vendor accessible through the IQuest gateway (GO IQUEST). See IQuest.

QMS Inc. products are supported in the Desktop Publishing Vendor Forum (GO DTPVENDOR). For details, see Desktop Publishing.

Qualitas products are supported in the IBM PC Vendor A Forum (GO PCVENA). See IBM Computers.

Quality Paperback Book Club (GO QPB) offers a store in the Electronic Mall (GO MALL) for book buying. See Electronic Mall.

Quantum Quality Productions products are supported in the Game Publishers C Forum (GO GAMCPUB). See Gaming Forums.

Quarterdeck Office Systems Software, including DESQview, is supported in the Quarterdeck Office Systems Forum (GO QUARTERDECK).

The forum has message sections and libraries dedicated to areas including the Memory Management, QEMM, and DESQview products.

The DESQview/X C libraries and the Gnu C Compiler, which are used in DESQview/X development, are now available on CompuServe (GO DVXTOOLS). Documentation for these files can be purchased directly from Quarterdeck Office Systems. Experienced representatives in the Quarterdeck Forum are supporting these files, in addition to Quarterdeck's line of products. The primary sysop is Michael Chapman (76004,2310).

Quattro Pro   (software) is supported in the Borland International Forums (GO BORLAND). See Borland Software.

Que Publishing computer books are supported in the Prentice Hall Computer Publishing Forum (GO PHCP). See Prentice Hall.

Quercus Systems   products are supported in the IBM PC Vendor A Forum (GO PCVENA). See IBM Computers.

Questa (databases) contain questions, oral and written, raised in the French National Assembly of Ministers or asked of the Parliamentary Government during various legislatures. See IQuest.

Questel   of Washington, D.C., is a major database vendor accessible through the IQuest gateway (GO IQUEST). See IQuest.

Questions & Answers, CompuServe   (GO QUESTIONS) is a database of answers to frequently asked questions about billing, forums, electronic mail, logons, real-time conferencing, and so on. For details, see Help Online.

QuickBASIC and **QuickPascal**   (software) are supported in the Microsoft Languages Forum (GO MSLANG). See Microsoft Software.

Quick B Protocol   is a binary protocol supported by CompuServe for sending and receiving files in forums, in electronic mail, and so on. See Files, Transfer.

QuickCIS   (software) is a public domain automated terminal program that runs on Atari ST computers. It was written by Jim Ness and is available in the Atari Productivity Forum (GO ATARIPRO). For related subjects, see Automated Terminal Software.

Quicken, Quickpay, Quickbooks   and other financial programs from Intuit are supported in the Intuit Forum (GO INTUIT). See Intuit.

Quick Response News   can be searched through the Business Database Plus (GO BUSDB). See Business Database.

QuickScan   products are supported in the CD-ROM Vendors Forum (GO CDVEN). See CD-ROM.

Quicksilver (software) is supported in the PC Vendor C Forum (GO PCVENC). See IBM Computers.

QuickSoft Incorporated products are supported in the PC Vendor B Forum (GO PCVENB). See IBM Computers.

QuickTime INIT (software) and associated support programs from Apple Computer are supported in the Mac Developer Support Area (GO SYSTEM7). See Apple Computers.

QuickVerse (software) is supported in the Parsons Technology Forum (GO PTFORUM). See Parsons Technology.

Quick Way Online Brokerage Service (GO QWK) is an online stock brokerage service. See Stock Brokerages.

Quilting is one of the topics discussed in the Crafts Forum (GO CRAFTS). See Crafts.

Quotations are the topic of the Classic Quotes game (GO TMC-45) part of the Multiple Choice trivia games. For information on other games, see Games.

Quotations Database (database) may be searched through the IQuest gateway (GO IQUEST) and through the Knowledge Index (GO KI). See IQuest and see Knowledge Index.

Quotes (stock market) are available on a 20-minute delayed basis. For daily quotes, enter GO QQUOTES for data on securities traded on the American, Boston, National exchanges, New York, and Philadelphia, as well as over-the-counter price and volume information are reported as a composite of the exchanges. See Stock Quotes, Current. And for information on other money-related features, see Financial Services and see Investment Analysis Tools.

QX-10 and QX-16 computers are supported in the Epson Forum (GO EPSON). See Epson.

R

Radio is discussed in the Broadcasters and Engineers Forum (GO BPFORUM). See Broadcasters and Broadcast Engineers. Radio news also is discussed in the Journalism Forum (GO JFORUM). See Journalism and for other related features, see News, General.

Also of interest:

- HamNet (Ham Radio) Forum (GO HAMNET) is devoted to amateur radio. See HamNet.
- RockNet (GO ROCKNET) has a section is devoted to rock music radio. For details, see Music.
- *Radio News, Land Mobile,* and *Spectrum Report* can be searched through the Business Database Plus (GO BUSDB). See Business Database.
- ShowBiz Forum (GO SHOWBIZ): see ShowBiz.
- Spectrum Report (database on global radio frequency allocation) can be searched through IQuest. See IQuest.

Radiology magazine abstracts are searchable in the Health Database Plus (GO HLTBD). See Health.

Radius products are supported in the Mac B Vendor Forum (GO MACBVEN). See Apple Computers.

Railroads and model-building are discussed in the TrainNet Forum (GO TRAINNET). For details, see Trainnet.

Rail travel is a topic in the Travel Forum (GO TRAVSIG). See Travel.

Railway Age (magazine) is searchable through Magazine Database Plus (GO MDP). For details see Magazine Database. It also can be searched through Business Database Plus (GO BUSDB), as can *US Rail News.* See Business Database.

Rainbow   (magazine) is searchable through Computer Database Plus (GO COMPDB). See Computer Database Plus.

Rainbow computers are supported in the DEC PC Forum (GO DECPC). See Digital Equipment Forums.

Ranger notebook is supported in the Advanced Logic Research section (GO ALRINC) in the PC Vendor G Forum (GO PCVENG). See IBM.

RapidFile (software) is supported in the Borland Applications Forum (GO BORAPP). See Borland.

Rapra Abstracts (rubber and plastics industry database) may be searched through the IQuest gateway. See IQuest.

Rare Disease Database (GO NORD) is made up of the online reports by the National Organization for Rare Disorders, a nonprofit, voluntary health agency dedicated to the identification, control, and cure of rare "Orphan Diseases." Each entry has a "Resources" section containing names and addresses of other agencies, organizations, and clinics that provide further assistant to those with each rare disorder.

The database is funded by the Generic Pharmaceutical Industry Association and receives additional aid from the Pharmaceutical Manufacturers Association, REVCO Drug Stores Foundation, the Robert Leet and Clara Guthrie Patterson Trust, the March of Dimes Birth Defects Foundation, and the Hugh J. Anderson foundation. In addition to the database, it provides access to newsletters, information on prevalent health conditions and concerns, and an AIDS Update.

For related topics, see Medical References and see Health.

Raskin, Robin (72241,12) is one of the editors and writers associated with the PC Magazine forums. See PC Magazine.

RateGram (GO RATEGRAM) is a financial service that lets users search for the best current rates for money market accounts, certificates of deposit, money market mutual funds, and so on.

The weekly RateGram newletter is produced by Martin Bradshaw, who has been providing consumer financial analysis since 1982. Its listings of the highest-paying federally insured bank and saving and loan accounts have been divided into several main sections:

- CDs and small minimum balance accounts
- Jumbo certificates of deposit
- Liquid Money Markets Accounts

The last two have been further subdivided for accounts of different maturities ranging from 90 days to five years.

The publication also surveys Money Market Mutual Funds and the Rate Almanac summarizes interest rates in general. Figures for the current and previous week as well as one year ago are shown for a variety of indicators and instruments. These include the prime, discount, and federal fund rates along with broker call money, commercial paper, and home mortgages. Individual reports are surcharged at $1 each.

This resource also may be searched through IQuest. See IQuest.

See also Investment Analysis Tools.

Rates, CompuServe (GO RATES) provides a multifunction menu that allows you to look at your own latest charges, to check news on surcharges, and so on. See Billing Information.

Raytrace graphics and animations are featured in the Graphics Plus Forum (GO GRAPHPLUS) and the Graphics Developers Forum (GO GRAPHDEV). For more information, see Graphics.

R:BASE (**database software**) is supported in the Microrim Forum (GO MICRORIM). See Microrim.

RBOC Update can be searched through the Business Database Plus (GO BUSDB). See Business Database.

RCA (GO RCA) is represented in the Music Vendor Forum (GO MUSICVEN). See Music.

R & D (**magazine**) can be searched in the Magazine Database Plus (GO MDP). See Magazine Database.

Reach Software Corp. products are supported in the PC Vendor G Forum (GO PCVENG). See IBM.

Readers' Guide Abstracts (**database**) may be searched through the IQuest gateway. See IQuest.

Reading and literacy are topics in the Mensa Forum (GO MENSA). See Mensa.

Ready! (**software**) is supported in the Symantec Forum (Go SYMANTEC). See Symantec Software.

Real Estate is a category in the CompuServe Classifieds. With it, you may read and post ads regarding buying and selling land. See Classifieds Service. Real estate also is discussed in the Investors Forum (GO INVFORUM). For details, see Investors.

Also, *Real Estate Today* (magazine) can be searched in the Magazine Database Plus (GO MDP) and the Business Database Plus (GO BUSDB), which also provides access to *National Real Estate Investor*. See Magazine Database and see Business Database.

Related databases on IQuest (see IQuest) include Liquidation Alert and PTS Newsletter Database.

Reality Technology products are supported in the PC Vendor H Forum (GO PCVENH). See IBM Computers.

Real Time Computing, World of (GO REALTIME) supports the iRMX Operating System-based software. For details, see Intel Corp.

Recipes are the subject of much of the discuss in Cook's Online Forum (GO COOKS). For details, see Cook's Online. Cooking also is a topic in Gardening Forum (GO GARDENING). See Gardening.

Reckon Software products are supported in the Pacific Vendors Forum (GO PACVENDOR). See Pacific.

Recommendation Program, Member (GO FRIEND) rewards current members for signing up new CompuServe subscribers. See Member Recommendation.

Records are discussed and covered in a number of features. For related services, see Music.

Recreational Vehicle Forum (GO RVFORUM) is the online gathering spot for those who enjoy (or would like to) camping in tent trailers, travel trailers, fifth-wheels, and motor homes. Experienced RVers exchange opinions and experiences on where to go, where to stay, and what to do when they get there. Visitors also share expert opinions on which RV to buy, where to get it serviced, and what accessories are best for their needs. Also RV clubs exchange information on events and campouts and the forum offers a classified section. Managing the forum is Ed Juge (70007,1365), a Fort Worth, Texas, consultant/writer. He and his wife have owned four travel trailers, one pickup camper, and have recently purchased their first motor home.

Recreational vehicles also are a topic of the Outdoors Forum (GO OUTDOORFORUM).

See also Travel, Sports and Recreation, and Cars.

Recycling is discussed in the Earth Forum (GO EARTH). See Earth Forum.

Redbook (magazine) articles are searchable through Magazine Database Plus (GO MDP). For details see Magazine Database.

Re-enactments and Renaissance faires, as well as scholarly research and heraldic study, are discussed in the Living History Forum (GO LIVING). See Living History.

ReferencePoint products are supported in the IBM PC Vendor H Forum (GO PCVENH). See IBM Computers.

Reflection (software) is covered in the WRQ/Reflection Forum (GO WRQFORUM). See WRQ.

Reflex **(software)** is supported in the Borland International Forums (GO BORLAND). See Borland Software.

Regardie's Magazine can be searched in the Magazine Database Plus (GO MDP). See Magazine Database.

Regattas are discussed in the Sailing Forum (GO SAILING). See Sports and Recreation.

Regulation Report: Toxics, State **(database)** may be searched through the IQuest gateway. See IQuest.

Regulatory Compliance Watch can be searched through the Business Database Plus (GO BUSDB). See Business Database.

Rehabdata **(database)** may be searched through the IQuest gateway. See IQuest.

Rehabilitation, American is searchable in the Health Database Plus (GO HLTBD), as is *The Journal of Rehabilitation*. See Health.

Rehabilitation Database, Veterans Administration (GO REHAB) is a collection of information on rehabilitation research and technology provided by the Veterans Administration's Office of Technology Transfer as a public service. The material is not copyrighted and may be reproduced with appropriate acknowledgment of source and author(s). At this writing, the database includes Rehabilitation R&D Progress Reports, Journal of Rehab R&D Online, Publications of Interest, and a calendar of events. Other data is expected to be added.

See also Handicapped Issues, and see Health and Medicine.

Reinisch, Dr. June M., author of the syndicated column "The Kinsey Report," is featured in the Human Sexuality Information and Advisory Service (GO HSX). Reinisch is director of the Kinsey Institute for Research in Sex, Gender, and Reproduction. She also is a professor in the Departments of Psychology and Psychiatry at Indiana University. See Sex.

Reith, Jacquie (71333,3610) is the sysop of the IBM Storage Systems Division Forum (GO IBMSTORAGE). See IBM Storage Systems.

Release 1.0 **(magazine)** can be searched through Computer Database Plus (GO COMPDB). See Computer Database Plus.

Religion is the subject of the Religion Forum (GO RELIGION), which aims to serve people of nearly every religious belief and conviction. The forum is not affiliated with any specific religious organization. Discussions center on aspects of religious, spiritual, or ethical beliefs. The forum administrator is Georgia Griffith (76703,266), assisted by Dave Caplan (75300,761), Keir Jones (76004,101), Tom Sims (73142,2735), and Michele Chavez (71301,437). Section leaders include Robert Archer (Christianity),

Michael Lerner and Nigel Blumenthal (Judaism), Carolyn Blasdel (eastern religions), Aisha Musa (Islam), Tim Musgrove (interfaith dialog), Jon K. Miller (Limbo), Steven Craig Miller (scholarship), Kare Ahlschwede (religion and science), Patrick McLaughlin (religion and world affairs), Chris Plourde (liturgy and ecclesiastical issues), Keith Irwin (Mormonism), Bill Potts (free thought), Bob Burns (ethics and debate), and Richard Gross (youth line).

Also, several databases accessible through IQuest (GO IQUEST) are relevant to the subject, including Academic Index, Churchnews International, Holy Bible (King James Version), Lutheran News Service, Quotations Database, Religion Index, and RNS Daily News Reports. See IQuest. Also Religion Index can be searched through the Knowledge Index (GO KI). See Knowledge Index.

Relish (software) is supported in the OS/2 Vendor Forum (GO OS2AVEN). See IBM Computers.

Remarc (database) carries references to all books cataloged by the Library of Congress from 1897 to 1980. (Later records in LC MARC.) See IQuest.

Remote (software) is supported in the Crosstalk Forum (GO XTALK). See Crosstalk (software).

Repetitive stress injury is the topic of the RSINews database, which can be searched through IQuest. Covered are Cumulative Trauma Disorders such as carpal tunnel syndrome, stress, and back pain. See IQuest.

REP Magazine (products) are supported in the MIDI A Vendor Forum (GO MIDIAVEN). See Music.

Report on Defense Plant Wastes (database) may be searched through the IQuest gateway. See IQuest.

Report on Literacy Programs (database) may be searched through the IQuest gateway. See IQuest.

Report Writer (software) is supported in the Clarion Software Forum (GO CLARION). See Clarion.

Reptiles are regularly discussed in the Pets and Animals Forum (GO PETS). For details, see Pets.

Republican Forum (GO REPUBLICAN) is a clearinghouse for GOP news and information. Besides press releases and talking points, forum provides in its libraries "Rising Tide" (the Republican National Committee's new bimonthly magazine), the RNC's Monday Briefing (a weekly briefing for party leaders and activists), reports from Capitol Hill and more. The sysops are Lisa McCormack (72662,1235) and Jonathan Knisley (72662,1234), both of whom work at the Republican National Committee in the Publications and Electronic Communications Department. See also Political Debate.

Research Alert can be searched through the Business Database Plus (GO BUSDB). See Business Database.

Research & Development (magazine) articles are searchable through Magazine Database Plus (GO MDP). For details see Magazine Database.
   Also:

- Federal Research in Progress databases may be searched through the IQuest gateway (GO IQUEST). See IQuest.

- National Technical Information Service (GO NTIS) is a gateway to a database published by the U.S. Department of Commerce, which contains nearly 1.5 million references to articles from government-sponsored research, development, and engineering reports, usually with corresponding abstracts. See National Technical Information.

Research Funding News, Medical can be searched through the Business Database Plus (GO BUSDB). See Business Database.

Resolve (software) is supported in the Claris Corp. Forum (GO CLARIS). For more information, see Claris.

Respiratory Diseases, American Review of abstracts are searchable in the Health Database Plus (GO HLTBD). See Health.

Restaurant Business Magazine and **Nation's Restaurant News** (databases) may be searched through IQuest (GO IQUEST) and through the Business Database Plus (GO BUSDB). See IQuest and see Business Database.
   In addition, these magazines also are searchable through Business Database Plus (GO BUSDB): *Restaurant Hospitality*, *Restaurant-Hotel Design International*, *Restaurants & Institutions*, and *Cornell Hotel & Restaurant Administration Quarterly*. See Business Database Plus.
   For related subjects, see Food.

Restaurant reviews are the topic of the Zagat Survey (GO ZAGAT). See Zagat.

Retailing, Journal of (magazine) can be searched through the Business Database Plus (GO BUSDB). See Business Database.

Retirement is a topic in the Seniors Forum (GO SENIORS). See Seniors.

Return Analysis (GO RETURN) is a financial service that calculates the holding period and annual returns for as many as 30 requested securities. See Investment Analysis Tools.

Reunions is a category in the CompuServe Classifieds. With it, you may read and post ads regarding upcoming events. Also, you may use it to try to locate old friends and missing people. See Classifieds Service.
   And for family history, see Genealogy.

Reuter News Pictures Forum (GO NEWSPIX) provides actual news images from around the world, available in both GIF and JPEG formats. The photos are uploaded continuously from Reuters, a worldwide news agency, with most news and sports photos appearing online within hours of their occurrence. Also available are selected historical news photos from the Bettmann Archives, the world's largest storehouse of such images. See also Graphics and News. The forum is managed by Mitch Koppelman (76711,1210).

Reuters also is accessible through IQuest. See IQuest.

Reuter News Service (news wire) is searchable through the Executive News Service. See Executive News Service.

Revelation Technologies Inc. Products are covered in the Revelation Tech Forum (GO REVELATION). The system offers update disks in its database libraries. The sysop is Thom Dieterich (75300,2270), assisted by Hal Wyman.

Reviews, computer products: Several online features offer original and reprinted reviews of software, hardware, and related computer products, including:

- Online Today (GO OLT) has a section for hardware/software/book coverage in its Reviews section. See Online Today.
- PC Magnet's Editorial Forum (GO ZNT:EDITORIAL). See PC Magazine.
- PC Week Extra (GO ZNT:PCWEEK) is maintained by editors of PC Week newspaper. See PC Week.
- PC World Online (GO PCWORLD) is an electronic version of the print magazine. See PC World.
- Working from Home Forum (GO WORK) has a library section for reviews of personal finance or small business management packages.
- ZiffNet/Mac Reviews (GO ZMC:INDEX) is a similar database of Apple-oriented products, searchable from the files of MacUser and MacWEEK. See ZiffNet/Mac.
- ZiffNet Reviews (GO ZNT:INDEX) is a database of product reviews from Ziff publications, searchable by product name, company naume, topic in the citation, and/or magazine. See also ZiffNet.

Reviews of entertainment: Movie reviews are featured in the Hollywood Hotline (GO MOVIES) and in Magill's Survey of Cinema (GO MAGILL). Music and record reviews are part of RockNet (GO ROCK) and the MIDI/Music Forum (GO MIDI). For more on these and related topics, see Entertainment.

REXX (software) is supported in the PC Vendor A Forum (GO PCVENA). See IBM Computers.

Reynolds, Joe (76704,37) administers the Earth Forum (GO EARTH). See Earth. He also administers the Great Outdoors Forum (GO OUTDOORFORUM). See Sports and Recreation.

Rheumatic Diseases, Annals of the abstracts are searchable in the Health Database Plus (GO HLTBD). See Health.

Rhintek Inc. products are supported in the IBM PC Vendor C Forum (GO PCVENC). See IBM Computers.

Rhode Island news is included in the daily Northeast regional reports from United Press International. See Executive News Service for details.

Ricciardi, Sal (72241,33) is one of the editors and writers associated with the PC Magazine forums. See PC Magazine.

Richmond (VA) News Leader and **Richmond Times-Dispatch (newspapers)** are searchable through Telebase System's News Source USA (GO NEWSUSA) and through the Knowledge Index (GO KI). See News Souce and see Knowledge Index.

Ridley, Regina Starr (76703,4323) is a sysop in the Computer Language Magazine Forum (GO CLMFORUM). See *Computer Language Magazine*.

Rifle Association, National, has a section for discussion of issues in the Outdoors Forum (GO OUTDOORS). See Outdoors.

Rightware Inc. products are supported in the OS/2 Vendor Forum (GO OS2AVEN). See IBM Computers.

Rig Market Forecast can be searched through the Business Database Plus (GO BUSDB). See Business Database.

Riopel, Jacques (75300,3455) is the sysop of the Eicon Forum (GO EICON). See Eicon.

Risk Management (magazine) can be searched through the Business Database Plus (GO BUSDB). See Business Database.

RIX Softworks products are supported in the Graphics A Vendor Forum (GO (GO RIXSOFT). See Graphics.

RN (magazine) is searchable in the Health Database Plus (GO HLTDB). See Health Database.

RNS Daily News Reports (religious database) can be searched through IQuest. See IQuest.

Road & Track (magazine) can be searched in the Magazine Database Plus (GO MDP). See Magazine Database.

Roads, Public (magazine) can be searched through the Business Database Plus (GO BUSDB). See Business Database.
   See also Construction.

Robertson, Mike (76702,1130) is sysop of the Datastorm Forum (GO DATASTORM). See Procomm (communications software).

Robinson, Earle (76004,1762) is the sysop of the European Forum (GO EURFORUM). See European Forum.

Robotics Today (**magazine**) is searchable through Computer Database Plus (GO COMPDB). See Computer Database Plus. Also *Military Robotics* can be searched through the Business Database Plus (GO BUSDB). See Business Database.

Robotics also is discussed in the AI Expert Forum (GO AIEXPERT). See AI Expert.

Rocknet Forum (GO ROCKNET) covers all facets of rock and roll music. See Music.

Rocky Mountain News, Denver (CO) (**newspaper**) is searchable through Telebase System's News Souce USA (GO NEWSUSA) and through the Knowledge Index (GO KI). See News Source and Knowledge Index.

Roepke, Neil (75300,1300) is the sysop of the Gateway 2000 Forum (GO GATE-WAY). See Gateway.

Roger Ebert's Movie Reviews (GO EBERT) offers reviews by this Pulitzer Prize winner whose work appears in more than 200 newspapers, including the Chicago Sun-Times and New York Daily News, and whose TV show, "Siskel & Ebert," is seen by millions. Main menu options include "Most Recent Movie Reviews" and "Search All Reviews," which together enable you to find any critique Ebert has written in his more than 20 years of reviewing.

Other options offer celebrity interviews as well as Ebert's tongue-in-cheek glossary of movie terms (such as "Ali MacGraw's Disease," which is a "movie illness in which the only symptom is that the sufferer grows more beautiful as death approaches.") An "Essays and News" section provides movie commentary, and "A Movie Lover's Source List" answers frequently asked questions. Ebert also offers his lists of the top ten movies of the year going back to 1990, as well as his picks for the ten greatest films of all time. Another feature is "Video Alert," which tracks new releases on tape and disc. Also provided is a suggestion-box feature for writing to the reviewer.

See also Showbiz.

Rogers, Jennifer (76662,671) is the sysop of Time Warner's Author of the Week Forum (GO TWEP). See Time Warner.

Rohrer, Jim (76702,1300) is a sysop of the Toshiba Forum (GO TOSHIBA). See Toshiba.

Roland Corp. products are supported in the MIDI C Vendor Forum (GO MIDICVEN). See Music.

Role-Playing Games Forum (GO RPGAMES) is for discussions and play of board, paper, and dice role-playing games. See Gaming Forums.

Romania is the topics of *Business Tech Romania*, searchable through the Business Database Plus (GO BUSDB). See Business Database.

Rosch, Winn (72241,107) is one of *PC Magazine*'s editors who regularly contributes to the publication's PC-Magnet service. See *PC Magazine*.

Rosenberger, Rob (70007,4004) is the primary sysop of the ASP Shareware Forum (GO ASPFORUM). See Shareware.

Rosenbluth Vacations (GO CRUISE) is a store in the Electronic Mall (GO MALL) that provides hundreds of cruise vacation packages from Carnival, Premier Cruise Line, Princess Cruises, Royal Caribbean Cruises, and others.

RoseWare products are supported in the Novell Vendor Forum A (GO NVENA). See Novell Software.

Ross, John (76703,551) is administrator of CP-MIG (GO CPMFORUM) and the Cancer Forum (GO CANCER). See Programmers Support and Cancer Information, respectively.

Rotarians Online Forum (GO ROTARY) is operated by the International Computer Users Fellowship of Rotary for fellowship members and interested nonmembers. The forum provides information on the Rotary Foundation and how to become a Rotary Club member, as well as the latest news on club, vocational, community, and international service projects. Managing the forum is Skip Turner (71640,3306), assisted by Tom Smith, Mike Kan, and Bill Herr Jr.

Roth, Rick (75600,1377) is sysop of Artisoft Forum (GO ARTISOFT). See Artisoft.

RQ **(magazine)** articles are searchable through Magazine Database Plus (GO MDP). For details see Magazine Database.

RTA Ltd. products are supported in the IBM Vendors H Forum (GO PCVENH). See IBM Computers.

RTC Watch can be searched through the Business Database Plus (GO BUSDB). See Business Database.

Rubber World **(magazine)** can be searched through the Business Database Plus (GO BUSDB). See Business Database.
    See also Plastics.

Rubenking, Neil (72241,50) is one of *PC Magazine*'s editors who regularly contributes to the publication's PC-Magnet service. See *PC Magazine*.

Rules, CompuServe Operating   (GO RULES) are displayed online. Here are the operating rules and the agreement all new users sign at their first logon:

CompuServe Information Service Operating Rules

The CompuServe Information Service (the "Service") consists of computing and information services and software, information, and other content provided by CompuServe Incorporated ("CompuServe"). In addition, third parties provide information, software, and other content (collectively, "Third Party Content") which may be accessed over the Service. These Operating Rules are provided to make online information usage and communications a positive and secure experience for members.

Members agree during the online sign-up procedure to the terms and conditions outlined in the Operating Rules.

Introduction

These Operating Rules are part of the terms of your Service Agreement with CompuServe, and you are bound by them. CompuServe may modify these rules at any time by publishing the modified rule(s) over the Service.

CompuServe Copyright

The entire contents of the Service are copyrighted as a collective work under the United States Copyright laws. The copying, redistribution, or publication of any part of the Service is prohibited, except as expressly provided below.

Each member who places information, software or other content, in the public areas of the Service grants CompuServe the right to edit, copy, publish, distribute, and translate such information, software, or other content. Subject to this grant, each member who places information, software, or other content on the Service retains any rights a member may have in such information, software, or other content.

Copyrighted Material

Copyrighted material must not be placed on the Service without the permission of the owner(s) or person(s) they specifically authorize. Only the owner(s) or such authorized person(s) may upload copyrighted material to the Service.

Members may download copyrighted material for their own use. Except as expressly provided by copyright law, copying, redistribution, or publication must be with the express permission of CompuServe and the owner(s) or such authorized person(s), if other than CompuServe. Permission must be specified in the document, on the Service, or must be obtained directly from CompuServe and the owner(s) or such authorized persons(s), if other than CompuServe. In any copying, redistribution, or publication of copyrighted material, any changes to or deletion of author attribution or copyright notice are prohibited.

Public Domain Material

Any member may upload public domain programs to the Service. Any member may download public domain programs for their own use or noncommercially redistribute a public domain program. Member assumes all risks regarding the determination of whether a program is in the public domain.

Content & Uses of the Service

Member agrees not to publish on or over the Service any information, software, or other content which violates or infringes upon the rights of any others or which would be abusive, profane, or sexually offensive to an average person, or which, without the approval of CompuServe, contains any advertising or any solicitation of other members to use goods or services. This paragraph, however, shall not be interpreted to restrict member from utilizing CompuServe Mail in the conduct of a legitimate business except that member may not, without the approval of CompuServe, send unsolicited advertising or promotional material to other CompuServe members.

Member agrees not to use the facilities and capabilities of the Service to conduct any business or activity or solicit the performance of any activity which is prohibited by law or to solicit members to become members of other competitive information services.

Editing and Deleting Content

CompuServe reserves the right in its sole discretion to edit or delete any information, software, or other content appearing on the Service, regardless of whether it violates the standards for content.

Service Termination

CompuServe reserves the right in its sole discretion to suspend or terminate Service to any member at any time.

Indemnification

Member agrees to indemnify and hold CompuServe harmless from any claims and expenses, including reasonable attorney's fees, related to member's violation of the Service Agreement, including these rules or any information, software, or other content placed on the Service by the member.

Standard Pricing Plan

Multiple members of the same household may share a single User ID Number. However, only one person is authorized to access the Service at any given time on one User ID Number.

CompuServe Information Service Agreement Terms

1. The CompuServe Information Service (the "Service") consists of computing and information services and software, information and other content provided by CompuServe Incorporated ("CompuServe"). In addition, third parties provide information, software, and other content (collectively, "Third Party Content") which may be accessed over the Service. These terms and any Operating Rules published over the Service constitute the entire and only agreement (collectively, the "Agreement") between CompuServe and member (including its designated users) with respect to the Service and supersede all other communications and agreements with regard to the subject matter hereof.

2. Upon notice published over the Service, CompuServe may modify this agreement, the Operating Rules or prices, and may discontinue or revise any or all other aspects of the Service at its sole discretion and without prior notice.

3. Unless otherwise agreed, member's right to use the Service or to designate users is not transferable and is subject to any limits established by CompuServe, or by member's credit card company if billing is through a credit card.

4. Member agrees to indemnify CompuServe against liability for any and all use of member's account.

5. Member is responsible for and must provide all telephone and other equipment and services necessary to access the Service.

6. Member shall pay, in accordance with the provisions of the Billing Option selected by member, any registration or monthly fees, connect-time charges, minimum charges, and other charges incurred by member or its designated users at the rates in effect for the billing period in which those charges are incurred, including but not limited to charges for any purchases made through the Service and any surcharges incurred while using any supplemental networks or services other than the Service. Member shall pay all applicable taxes relating to use of the Service by member or its designated users. Member shall be responsible for all use of the Service accessed through member's or its designated users' password(s).

7. MEMBER EXPRESSLY AGREES THAT USE OF THE SERVICE IS AT MEMBER'S SOLE RISK. NEITHER COMPUSERVE NOR ANY OF ITS INFORMATION PROVIDERS, LICENSORS, EMPLOYEES, OR AGENTS WARRANT THAT THE SERVICE WILL BE UNINTERRUPTED OR ERROR FREE; NOR DOES COMPUSERVE OR ANY OF ITS INFORMATION PROVIDERS, LICENSORS, EMPLOYEES, OR AGENTS MAKE ANY WARRANTY AS TO THE RESULTS TO BE OBTAINED FROM USE OF THE SERVICE. THE SERVICE IS DISTRIBUTED ON AN "AS IS" BASIS WITHOUT WARRANTIES OF ANY KIND, EITHER EXPRESS OR IMPLIED, INCLUDING BUT NOT LIMITED TO WARRANTIES OF TITLE OR IMPLIED WARRANTIES OF MERCHANTABILITY OR FITNESS FOR A PARTICULAR PURPOSE, OTHER THAN THOSE WARRANTIES WHICH ARE IMPLIED BY AND INCAPABLE OF EXCLUSION, RESTRICTION, OR MODIFICATION UNDER THE LAWS APPLICABLE TO THIS AGREEMENT. NEITHER COMPUSERVE NOR ANYONE ELSE INVOLVED IN CREATING, PRODUCING, OR DELIVERING THE SERVICE SHALL BE LIABLE FOR ANY DIRECT, INDIRECT, INCIDENTAL, SPECIAL, OR CONSEQUENTIAL DAMAGES ARISING OUT OF USE OF THE SERVICE OR INABILITY TO USE THE SERVICE OR OUT OF ANY BREACH OF ANY WARRANTY. MEMBER EXPRESSLY ACKNOWLEDGES THAT THE PROVISION OF THIS PARAGRAPH SHALL ALSO APPLY TO THE THIRD PARTY CONTENT.

8. Except as expressly permitted in the Operating Rules, neither member nor its designated users may reproduce, redistribute, retransmit, publish, or otherwise transfer, or commercially exploit, any information, software, or other content which they receive through the Service.

9. The provisions of paragraphs 7 and 8 are for the benefit of CompuServe and their respective Information Provider, Licensors, Employees, and Agents; and each shall have the right to assert and enforce such provisions directly on their own behalf.

10. Subject to the terms of this Agreement, CompuServe grants to member a personal, nonexclusive, nonassignable, and nontransferable license to use and display the CompuServe Information Manager software ("Software") on any machine(s) of which member is the primary user. Unauthorized copying of the Software, including software that has been modified, merged, or included with the Software, or the written materials associated therewith is expressly forbidden. Member may not sublicense, assign, or transfer this license or the Software. Any attempt to sublicense, assign, or transfer any of the rights, duties, or obligations under this license is void.

11. This agreement is, and shall be governed by and construed in accordance with the law of the State of Ohio applicable to agreements made and performed in Ohio. Any cause of action of member or its designated users with respect to the Service must be instituted within one year after the claim or cause of action has arisen or be barred.

12. If Member's account is a qualified business account and approved by CompuServe for corporate billing, charges for the services provided under this Agreement will be accumulated and identified by User ID Number and will normally be invoiced following the end of the month in which the service is provided. Terms of payment on all charges are net, ten (10) days in the currency in which billed. If any payment due hereunder is not made by the member within thirty (30) days after the invoice date, late charges of one and one-half percent (1 1/2%) per month shall be due and payable with respect to such payment, and CompuServe may, in addition, at its sole discretion and without notice to the member, (a) suspend its performance under this agreement and the member's and its designated users' access to and use of the Service, or (b) terminate this agreement and member's and its designated users' access to and the use of the Service. For accounts not approved by CompuServe for corporate billing, member must provide payment by credit card or direct debit.

13. Notwithstanding any acknowledgement of a member purchase order by CompuServe, any provision or condition in any purchase order, voucher, or other memorandum of the member which is in any way inconsistent with, or adds to, the provisions of this agreement is null and void. Neither the course of conduct between parties nor trade practice shall act to modify the provisions of this Agreement. If any provision of this Agreement is determined to be invalid,

all other provisions shall remain in full force and effect. The provisions of paragraphs 7, 9, and 13 and all obligations of and restrictions on member and its designated users shall survive any termination of this Agreement.

Runner's World is searchable in the Health Database Plus (GO HLTBD). See Health.

Running and racing are topics of the Health & Fitness Forum (GO GOODHEALTH). See Health.

Rupp Corporation products are supported in the PC Vendor C Forum (GO PCVENC). See IBM Computers.

Russian news and information is provided in several IQuest databases, including Russia Express, Russia Express Contracts, and Russia/CIS Intelligence Report. See IQuest.

Also searchable through the Business Database Plus (GO BUSDB) are *Russian Aerospace & Technology, Russia Express Contracts, Russia Express-Perestroika: Executive Briefing,* and *USSR Economics & Foreign Trade.* See Business Database.

RVs are a topic of the Recreational Vehicle Forum (GO RVFORUM). See Recreational Vehicle.

S

Sabre products are supported in the IBM PC Vendor A Forum (GO PCVENA). See IBM Computers.

Sacramento (CA) Bee (newspaper) is searchable through Telebase System's News Source USA (GO NEWSUSA) and through the Knowledge Index (GO KI). See News Source and see Knowledge Index.

Also, *The Business Journal Serving Greater Sacramento* magazine can be searched through the Business Database Plus (GO BUSDB). See Business Database.

Sadoian, Chuck (76703,414) is chief sysop of the PDP-11 Forum (GO PDP11). See Digital Equipment Forums.

Safety is the subject of SafetyNet (GO SAFETYNET), which discusses all aspects of safety, from occupational health and engineering to fire protection and law enforcement. Safety professionals and others interested in some aspect of safety are welcome. The forum is administered by Dr. Charles M. Baldeck, an industrial hygiene consultant (76703,2005). He is assisted by Sgt. Bruce Williams, who runs the police officer/volunteer firefighter sections, as well as Michael Blotzer, Bill Clede, and Mike Ward. Also:

- Aviation Safety Institute (GO ASI) covers hazards to aviation. See Aviation.
- HSELine: Health and Safety, Air Safety Week Accident/Incident Log, Air Safety Week Newsletter, Air Safety Week Regulatory Log, and Product Safety Letter databases may be searched through the IQuest gateway. See IQuest.

For more related topics, see Health/Medicine.

Safeware Computer Insurance (GO SAF) is a store in the Electronic Mall (GO MALL) that offers high-tech equipment insurance. See Electronic Mall.

Sailing Forum (GO SAILING) exists for sailing enthusiasts of all experience levels. See Sports and Recreation.

St. Louis Business Journal (magazine) can be searched through the Business Database Plus (GO BUSDB). See Business Database.

St. Louis (MO) Post-Dispatch, St. Paul (MN) Pioneer Press Dispatch, and **St. Petersburg (FL) Times** (newspapers) are searchable through Telebase System's News Source USA (GO NEWSUSA). See News Source. Also the St. Louis (MO) Post-Dispatch and the St. Paul (MN) Pioneer Press Dispatch can be searched through the Knowledge Index (GO KI). See Knowledge Index.

Salemi, Joe (72241,216) is sysop of the PC Week Corporate Buyers' Forum (GO PCWEEK). See *PC Week*.

Sales & Marketing Management (magazine) is searchable through Magazine Database Plus (GO MDP). See Magazine Database. It also can be searched through Business Database Plus (GO BUSDB). See Business Database.

Salesman, **American** (magazine) is searchable through the Business Database Plus (GO BUSDB) and in the Magazine Database Plus (GO MDP). See Magazine Database and Business Database.

Salesmanship is discussed in the Public Relations and Marketing Forum (GO PRSIG). See Public Relations and Marketing. For other business-oriented subjects, see Financial Services.

Sales Prospector can be searched through the Business Database Plus (GO BUSDB). See Business Database.

Samna Corporation products are supported in the Lotus Word Processing Forum (GO LOTUSWP). For details, see Lotus Software.

Sams Publishing computer books are supported in the Prentice Hall Computer Publishing Forum (GO PHCP). See Prentice Hall.

San Antonio Business Journal (magazine) can be searched through the Business Database Plus (GO BUSDB). See Business Database.

San Diego and **San Francisco** are among the topics in the California Forum (GO CALFORUM). See California.

San Diego Business Journal (magazine) can be searched through the Business Database Plus (GO BUSDB). See Business Database.

San Francisco Business Times (magazine) can be searched through the Business Database Plus (GO BUSDB). See Business Database.

San Francisco Chronicle and San Francisco Examiner (newspapers)
are searchable through Telebase System's News Source USA (GO NEWSUSA).
See News Source. The San Francisco Chronicle also can be searched through the
Knowledge Index (GO KI). See Knowledge Index.

San Jose (CA) Mercury News (newspaper) is searchable through Telebase
System's News Source USA (GO NEWSUSA) and through the Knowledge Index
(GO KI). See News Source and see Knowledge Index. Also, *The Business Journal—
San Jose* can be searched through the Business Database Plus (GO BUSDB). See
Business Database. And abstracts can be searched through Computer Database Plus
(GO COMPDB). See Computer Database Plus.

Santa Cruz Operation Forum (GO SCOFORUM) invites SCO end users,
resellers, developers, partners, and all interested parties. There are files available for
downloading, online conferencing, and message areas dedicated to the discussion of
SCO products, as well as services with other SCO users and experts in the Unix field.
The products include SCO Open Desktop, the SCO Unix Operating System, and
the SCO MPX multiprocessor extension. The sysops are Tim Ruckle (76711,742),
Rhonda Powers (76711,743), and John Esak (76703,746).

Sanyo computers are among the computer systems supported in CompuServe's
Computer Club Forum (GO CLUB). See Computer Club.

Saros products are supported in the Windows 3rd-Party C Forum (GO WINAPC).
See Microsoft Software.

Sarasota Magazine (magazine) can be searched through the Business Database
Plus (GO BUSDB). See Business Database.

Satellite communications is discussed in the Consumer Electronics Forum (GO
CEFORUM). See Electronics.
Also:

- Amateur satellites is a topic in the HamNet (Ham Radio) Forum (GO
  HAMNET). See HamNet.
- Satellite News and Satellite Week (databases) may be searched through the
  IQuest gateway. See IQuest. The resource also can be searched through the
  Business Database Plus (GO BUSDB), as can *Satellite Communications* and
  Satellite TV Finance. See Business Database.
- Satellites also are discussed in the Space/Astronomy Forum (GO
  SPACEFORUM). See Space.
- Satellite TV technology is a topic discussed in the Consumer Electronics Fo-
  rum (GO CEFORUM). See Electronics Forum, Consumer.

Saturday Evening Post (magazine) is searchable through Magazine Database
Plus (GO MDP). For details see Magazine Database.

SBTerm, SBOpen, and other software for SystemBuilder Corporation's systems are supported in the Pacific Vendors Forum (GO PACVENDOR). See Pacific Vendors.

ScanMan and related products are discussed in the Logitech Forum (GO LOGITECH). See Logitech.

Scheiner, Paul T. (76711,1354) is sysop of the Microrim Forum (GO MICRORIM). See Microrim.

Schemers Inc. products are supported in the LOGO Forum (GO LOGOFORUM). See Programmers Support.

Schindler, Esther (72241,1417) is the sysop of ZiffNet's Executives Online Forum (GO ZNT:EXECUTIVES). See ZiffNet.

Schneiderman, Jerry (76702,667) is sysop in the Travel Forum (GO TRAVSIG). For details, see Travel.

Schoenbach, Mike (76703,4363) is sysop of the CompuServe Help Forum (GO HELPFORUM) and of the Modem Games Forum (GO MODEMGAMES); see Help and see Modem Games. He is involved with several of the Atari forums. See Atari Computers. He also is sysop of the Practice Forum (GO PRACTICE). For more on that, see Practice. In addition, he is associated with the Pen Technology Forum (GO PENFORUM). See Pen Technology.

Scholastic Update (**magazine**) is searchable through Magazine Database Plus (GO MDP). For details see Magazine Database.

Schomaker, Paul (76711,1034) is a sysop in the Clarion Software Forum (GO CLARION). See Clarion.

School Health, Journal of is searchable in the Health Database Plus (GO HLTBD). See Health.

Science is the topic of many services. Some of them are:

- IQuest databases (GO IQUEST), Academic Index, American Statistics Index, Applied Science and Technology Index, Books in Print, COLD, Compendex Plus, Conference Papers Index, Dissertation Abstracts Online, Federal Research in Progress, General Science Index, High Tech Ceramics News, HSELine: Health and Safety, IHS International Standards and Specifications, Mediconf, Membrane & Separation Technology News, National Technical Information Service, Optical Materials & Engineering News, Packaging Science and Technology Abstracts, PASCAL, SciSearch, and Spicer's Centre For Europe. See IQuest.

- Magazines: *Bulletin of the Atomic Scientists, Discover, Omni, Popular Science, Scientific American, Science'86, Science World,* and *Smithsonian,* searchable through Magazine Database Plus (GO MDP). For details see Magazine Database.

- *New Scientist* is searchable in the Health Database Plus (GO HLTBD). Also, abstracts of *Science* magazine can be searched there. See Health.
- Science and technology are topics in the Mensa Forum (GO MENSA). See Mensa. Science also is a topic in the Students' Forum (GO STUFO). See Students.

See also Earth Science, Geo studies, Life Sciences, and Math.

Science of Computer Programming (magazine) is searchable (abstracts) through Computer Database Plus (GO COMPDB). See Computer Database Plus.

Science Fiction & Fantasy Forum (GO SCI-FI) offers news from the sci-fi fields, including reviews, and discussions of books and movies, and contact with more fans of Star Trek and Dr. No than you will find anyplace else online. Regulars include a number of published science fiction and fantasy authors. Administrator of the forum is Wilma Meier (76701,274). Assistants include Jim Schneider, Jim S. Lyon, Ilene Schneider, Georgia (Sasha) Miller, and Roger MacBride Allen, along with section leaders Mary Taylor and Jane R. Hansen.

Also, *The Magazine of Fantasy and Science Fiction* can be searched in the Magazine Database Plus (GO MDP). See Magazine Database.

Sci-fi also is a topic in in the Space/Astronomy Forum (GO SPACEFORUM). See Space.

Science/Math Forum (GO SCIENCE) is operated by Rick Needham (76703,627), chairman of the Science Department of the Mercersburg Academy in Mercersburg, Pennsylvania. It serves as a gathering place for teachers, students, and other subscribers with an interest in science and math. Among the items in the data libraries is an extensive collection of practice problems for students studying for college board achievement tests in math, physics, chemistry, and biology.

For other school-related features, see Education.

Science Trivia (game) (GO SCITRIVIA) is a collection of questions in the areas of biology, chemistry, physics, and mathematics. Its questions match the style and complexity of those found on the College Board's Achievement and Advanced Placement Tests. This is one of the system's basic services, meaning those signed up under the Standard Pricing Plan (see Billing) have unlimited access to the feature. For information on other games, see Games.

Scitex/SGAUA products are supported in the Desktop Publishing Vendor Forum (GO DTPVENDOR). For details, see Desktop Publishing.

Scitor products are supported in the Windows 3rd-Party Forum (GO WINAPD). See Microsoft Software.

SCORE (software) by Ashlar Inc. is supported in the CADD/CAM/CAE Vendor Forum (GO CADDVEN).

SCO software products (SCO Open Desktop, the SCO Unix Operating System, and the SCO MPX multiprocessor extension) are supported in the Santa Cruz Operation Forum (GO SCOFORUM). See Santa Cruz.

Scotland Review*, *Royal Bank of (magazine) can be searched through the Business Database Plus (GO BUSDB). See Business Database.

Scottish Rites are discussed in the Masonry Forum (GO MASONRY). See Masonry.

Scouting activities are discussed in the Great Outdoors Forum (GO OUT DOORFORUM). See Sports and Recreation.

Screen Digest and ***Screen Finance*** can be searched through the Business Database Plus (GO BUSDB). See Business Database.

Screenwriters are served in the ShowBiz Forum (GO SHOWBIZ). See also Writers and Writing.

Scrip—Current News, Daily News, and **Retrospective** (pharmaceutical industry databases) may be searched through the IQuest gateway. See IQuest. See also Pharmaceuticals.

Scuba Forum (GO SCUBA) supports experienced divers and beginners. See Sports and Recreation.

SDC/Orbit of Santa Monica, Calif., is a major database vendor accessible through the IQuest gateway (GO IQUEST). See IQuest.

SDI Monitor (database) can be searched through Business Database Plus (GO BUSDB). See Business Database.

SDV Vitamins (GO SDV) operates a store in the Electronic Mall (GO MALL). See Electronic Mall.

SealCorp products are supported in the Pacific Vendor Forum (GO PACVEN). See Pacific Vendor.

Sealevel Systems products are supported in the PC Vendor I Forum (GO PCVENI). See IBM Computers.

Sears (GO SR) provides a shop-at-home service through the Electronic Mall (GO MALL). See Electronic Mall.

Seamanship is the topic of the Sailing Forum (GO SAILING). For more on this and related topics, see Sports.

Seattle Post-Intelligencer and **Seattle Times** (newspapers) are searchable through Telebase System's News Source USA (GO NEWSUSA). See News Source. Seattle Times also can be searched through the Knowledge Index (GO KI). See Knowledge Index.

Second Opinion is searchable in the Health Database Plus (GO HLTBD). See Health.

Sectra is supported in the Thomas-Conrad Support Forum (GO TCCFORUM). See Thomas-Conrad.

Securities Screening (GO SCREEN) is a financial service that lets you screen a database to find securities that meet your demands. See Investment Analysis Tools.

Securities and stocks are supported in a number of features. For an online overview, enter GO MONEY; for more information, see Financial Services and see Investment Analysis Tools.

Securities Week and **Security Intelligence Report** (databases) may be searched through the IQuest gateway. See IQuest.

Security Association, National Computer is a sponsor of the General Computing Forum (GO GENCOM). See General Computing.

Security Management (magazine) can be searched through the Business Database Plus (GO BUSDB). See Business Database.

Security Journal, Computer (magazine) is searchable (abstracts) through Computer Database Plus (GO COMPDB). See Computer Database Plus. Also, *Computer Fraud & Security Bulletin* (magazine) can be searched through the Business Database Plus (GO BUSDB). See Business Database.

SelfCare, Medical is searchable in the Health Database Plus (GO HLTBD). See Health.

Self-defense is a topic of the Health & Fitness Forum (GO GOODHEALTH). See Health.

Semiconductor Industry & Business Survey (database) may be searched through the IQuest gateway. See IQuest. The resource also can be searched through the Business Database Plus (GO BUSDB). See Business Database.

SemWare products are supported in the IBM PC Vendor E Forum (GO PCVENE). See IBM Computers.

Senior citizens are the subject of the Seniors Forum (GO SENIORS). Visitors include the "chronologically advantaged" and others interested in issues related to the "second half of life." Topics range from computers, social security, "eldercare," health and medicine, retirement, the grieving process, and lifelong memories. Among newer sections is "Corporate Retirees," devoted to the retired executive or worker, which lets these individuals reminisce and exchange information on retirement plans, pensions, health care, and other subjects. Members still in the work force may also seek advice from retirees with experience in their fields. Also, the "For Our Boomers" section was opened at the request of "fortysomething" members who are sharing ideas about their own retirement, pensions, health care, and care of their parents and relatives. The forum's libraries contain information on many topics from relationships to government legislation affecting seniors. Administering the forum is Betty Knight (76703,4037), a CompuServe member since 1983. Betty also has served in both the Commodore Arts and Games Forum and the Practice Forum. She was a programmer and systems analyst on mainframe computers for 27 years before retiring. Assisting are Barbara J. Holt and Betty Clay.

Also, *Modern Maturity* can be searched in the Magazine Database Plus (GO MDP). See Magazine Database. *Gerontologist*, *Journals of Gerontology*, and *International Journal of Aging & Human Development* abstracts are searchable in the Health Database Plus (GO HLTBD). See Health.

And Florida Today NewsLink Forum (GO FLATODAY), a unique link to this Gannett Inc. newspaper on the Florida Space Coast, includes a section on seniors issues. See Florida.

Sensor Business Digest (database) may be searched through the IQuest gateway. See IQuest. The resource also can be searched through the Business Database Plus (GO BUSDB), as can *Sensor Technology*. See Business Database.

High Tech Separations News can be searched through the Business Database Plus (GO BUSDB). See Business Database. It also can be search through IQuest (GO IQUEST). See IQuest.

Seven Hills Software products are supported in the Apple II Vendor Forum (GO APIIVEN). See Apple Computers.

Seventeen (magazine) can be searched in the Magazine Database Plus (GO MDP). See Magazine Database.

Sewing is one of the topics discussed in the Crafts Forum (GO CRAFTS). See Crafts.

Sex is the subject of the Human Sexuality Forums (GO HUMAN). Howard and Martha Lewis (76703,303), which began years ago with a single forum devoted to the issues of human sexuality. Today, there are two, the Human Sexuality Open Forum (GO HSX100) and the Human Sexuality Adult Forum (GO HSX200), as well as a database filled with information presented in article form, including question-and-answer features and "tutorials." The Lewises call on experts in sex-related medical fields to answer question and counsel those who make use of this very active area of CompuServe. Among the regular features in the Human Sexuality Information and Advisory Service are excerpts from the newspaper columns of nationally recognized sex expert, Dr. Ruth Westheimer.

Sex education also is discussed in the Education Forum (GO EDFORUM). For details, see Education.

Sexually Transmitted Diseases magazine abstracts are searchable in the Health Database Plus (GO HLTBD). See Health.

Seybold's Outlook on Professional Computing and **Seybold Report on Publishing Systems** (**magazines**) are searchable through Computer Database Plus (GO COMPDB). See Computer Database Plus. Seybold publications also are accessible through the Seybold/ZiffNet Information Connection (GO ZNT:SEYBOLD). See ZiffNet.

Seymour, Jim (72241,45) is one of the editors and writers associated with the PC Magazine forums. See PC Magazine.

Shahamatdoust, Michael (76704,21) is sysop of the Adobe Forum (GO ADOBE). See Adobe Software.

Shannon on DEC, Terry (**database**) can be searched through IQuest. See IQuest.

Shape magazine abstracts are searchable in the Health Database Plus (GO HLTBD). See Health.

ShapeWare Corp. products are supported in the Windows 3rd-Party D Forum (GO WINAPD). See Microsoft Software.

Shapiro, Neil (76703,401) is chief sysop of the Micronetworked Apple Users Groups, (GO MAUG). See Apple Computers. He also operates the New Age Forum (GO NEW AGE), the Masonry Forum (GO MASONRY), and CyberForum (GO CYBERFORUM).

Shareware is an innovation of the online world. These programs are yours to try free of charge, except for the price of the download. You can evaluate the software, and if you decide to continue using it, the shareware honor system calls on you to pay the program's author the indicated fee. Most CompuServe forum libraries have shareware offerings. In addition, some features deal specifically with the shareware:

- ASP Shareware Forum (GO ASPFORUM) is operated in conjunction with the Association of Shareware Professionals for the support of shareware programs for all systems, including IBM, Apple Macintosh, Unix, and others. Shareware is a computer-world phenomenon in which commercial programmers allow potential customers to try out their programs before deciding whether to actually buy or license them. ASP is a nonprofit group dedicated to educating computer users about the "try before you buy" software marketing concept. The forum libraries don't contain any shareware programs, but visitors can check the General Info library (Library 0) for files describing such programs. The files should tell you what forum on CompuServe contains the actual ASP program files. The primary ASP sysop is Rob Rosenberger (70007,4004). Assisting him is IBMNET sysop is Don Watkins (76703,750).

- Freeware and shareware are discussed in other forums as well, including the Artisoft Forum (GO ARTISOFT), Ask3Com Forum (GO ASKFORUM), Banyan Forum (GO BANFORUM), Cannon Support Forum (GO CANON), the Computer Language Forum (GO CLMFORUM), Computer Shopper Forum (GO ZNT:COMPSHOPPER), CTOS/Open Forum (GO CTOS), DBMS Magazine Forum (GO DBMSFORUM), the LOGO Forum (GO LOGOFORUM), Lotus Word Processing Forum (GO LOTUSWP), Mac New Users/Help Forum (GO MACNEW), MECA Software Forum (GO MECA), Microsoft DOS Forum (GO MSDOS), NAIC Investor Education Forum (GO NAIC), Novell Library Forum (GO NOVLIB), Packard Bell Forum (GO PACKARDBELL), PC MagNet: Utilities Forum (GO ZNT:UTILFORUM), PC Plus/PC Answers Forum (GO PCPFORUM), PC Sources Forum (GO ZNT:SOURCES), UK Share Forum (GO UKSHARE), and WinNT Pre-Release Forum (GO WINNT).

- Public Brand Software (GO ZNT:PBS) is operated by one of the older and larger distributors of shareware. This is part of the ZiffNet system. See Public Brand.

- Shareware Depot (GO SD) is a store in the Electronic Mall (GO MALL) that offers shareware software. See Electronic Mall.

- Software Registration (GO SWREG) is a service for shareware authors, who may submit their software for inclusion in the database by selecting the "Submit Shareware" option from the menu. Thereafter, whenever someone chooses to have his or her CompuServe account directly billed to pay for a program by choosing the "Register Shareware" option, notification is sent immediately to the author's CompuServe Mail (GO MAIL) box.

- UK Shareware Forum (GO UKSHARE) is operated by Shareware Publishing of Devon, England, a leading British shareware distributor. For details, see UK Shareware.

- Windows Shareware Forum (GO WINSHARE) supports a variety of shareware for the Windows environment. See Microsoft Software.

Sharp Wizard and **Sharp PC-3000** computers are supported in the Palmtop Forum (GO PALMTOP). See Palmtop.

Shaw, Richard (72241,155) is one of the editors and writers associated with the PC Magazine forums. See PC Magazine.

Shepard, Susan (76703,4326) is the sysop of the Cadence Forum (GO CADENCE). See Cadence. She also is sysop in the AI Expert Forum (GO AIEXPERT). See AI Expert.

Sheridan, Dennis (71154,362) is the sysop of the PC World Forum (GO PWOFORUM). See PC World Online.

Sherman, Richard A. (71154,61) is the sysop of the Court Reporters Forum (GO CRFORUM). See Court Reporters.

SHIELD Tools (**software**) is supported in Windows 3rd-Party Forum C (GO WINAPC). See Microsoft Software.

Shipper, American   (magazine) is searchable through the Business Database Plus (GO BUSDB). See Business Database.

Shipping   is covered in Piers Exports databases, with databases on virtually all maritime movements into and out of the continental U.S. and Puerto Rico. The databases are searchable on IQuest. See IQuest. Shipping and customs also are topics in the International Trade Forum (GO TRADE). See International Trade.

Shooting   as a recreation is a topic of the Outdoors Forum (GO OUTDOORS). See Sports and Recreation.

Shooting Industry   (magazine) can be searched through the Business Database Plus (GO BUSDB). See Business Database.

Shopper features   abound on CompuServe, from individual shopping clubs to the system's own, ever-changing electronic shopping center. The main shopping area is the Electronic Mall (GO MALL), a registered CompuServe trademark. Here you find about 100 merchants offering online ordering and product information. For more on that, see Electronic Mall.

Other shopping features include:

- Classifieds Service (GO CLASSIFIEDS) is CompuServe's classified advertisement section, where users of the system may buy, sell, swap, or give away goods and services. See Classifieds.

- CompuServe Ordering (GO ORDER) is the system's own online ordering service for a variety of products, from books and manuals to T-shirts, coffee mugs, and posters. See Ordering, CompuServe Products.

- Consumer Reports (GO CSR) allows you to search reports prepared by the Consumers Union staff. The reports are similar to what you find in *Consumer Reports* magazine; they are modified slightly for placement in this electronic database. See Consumer Reports.

- The New Car/Truck Showroom (GO NEWCAR) lets you view and compare features of passenger cars, vans, and trucks to help you make buying decisions. See New Car/Truck Showroom.

- Online Inquiry (GO OLI) lets you request general information about an add displayed in *CompuServe Magazine*. You can leave your name and addresses at the prompts supplied and further information will be sent to you. See Online Inquiry.

- Shoppers Advantage Club (GO SAC) is a discount shopping club formerly called Comp-U-Store. It is considered the first of the online shopping services. See Shoppers Advantage Club.

- Softex (GO SOFTEX) is CompuServe's own software catalog, from which you can purchase programs online and retrieve them immediately. See Softex.

Shopper Report   can be searched through the Business Database Plus (GO BUSDB). See Business Database.

Shoppers Advantage Club (GO SAC) is a discount shopping club formerly called Comp-U-Store. This is one of the system's basic services, meaning those signed up under the Standard Pricing Plan (see Billing) have unlimited access to the feature.

This is considered the first of the online shopping services, now boasting more than 3 million members (about 1 percent of the U.S. population). All CompuServe subscribers may browse and order directly from the store. If you like what you see, you might want to sign up as a member of the service to receive further discounts on prints (at this writing, the membership was a $1 for three months). Options on the main menu give details of membership. An advantage of Shoppers Advantage is that you can comparison-shop for more than a quarter million brand name products. Products are available from manufacturers such as Panasonic, GE, JVC, Nikon, Sony, Pioneer, AT&T, Nintendo, Whirlpool, Quasar, Jordache, Hoover, Pentax, Timex, Memorex, Rayban, Radio Shack, Pierre Cardin, Singer, Magnavox, and others.

Shoppers report ordering products for 10 to 50 percent off the regular list price. Generally, the discount prices are available because Shoppers Advantage keeps no inventory. The club arranges for shipping and delivery directly from the manufacturers and distributors, enabling members to save money. The club offers a guarantee: If within 30 days of buying something through Shoppers Advantage, you find the same piece of merchandise being sold for a lower price by a manufacturer's authorized dealer, you can send the operators a copy of the ad and they will send you the difference.

Shoppers Advantage is largely menu-driven, but also provides special commands for advanced users; these are listed with the "All About Us" option from the main menu.

The store operates a staff hotline (1-800/843-7777) to handle questions and provide assistance with the system. The hotline opens at 9:00 a.m. and operates to 11:00 p.m. Monday through Friday and to 7:00 p.m. on Saturday and Sunday. Or you can send questions on CompuServe to 70007,1530.

ShortCut (**software**) is supported in Mac C Vendor Forum (GO MACCVEN). For details, see Apple Computers.

Short wave radio is a topic of HamNet (GO HAMNET). See HamNet.

Showbiz Forum (GO SHOWBIZ) discusses films, television programs, record albums, celebrity gossip, and nightly news shows.

The forum is administered by Don Devich (76711,725). Also associated with the forum is Eliot Stein (76703,305), a longtime editor of the entertainment news and features service "Hollywood Hotline." Assisting are Kim Brant, Diana Cantu, and John Hill.

ShowBiz invites visitors to air their views and read reviews of the latest films, music releases, and TV shows. It also has message sections on cable viewing, radio programming, theater, the regular and "infotainment" media, and show-business collecting.

See also Entertainment.

ShowBiz Quiz (game) (GO SBQ) is a collection of more than 70 trivia quizzes on different aspects of show business. This is one of the system's basic services, meaning those signed up under the Standard Pricing Plan (see Billing) have unlimited access to the feature. For information on other games, see Games.

Showroom, The New Car/Truck (GO NEWCAR) lets you view and compare features of passenger cars, vans, and trucks to help you make buying decisions. See New Car/Truck Showroom.

Shuttle is discussed in the Space/Astronomy Forum (GO SPACEFORUM). See Space.

Sidekick (software) is supported in the Borland International Forums (GO BORLAND). See Borland Software.

Sideways (software) is supported in the IBM PC Vendor F Forum (GO PCVENF). See IBM Computers.

Siemens Automatisierungs Forum (GO AUTFORUM) is a German-speaking forum for users of Siemens products.

Sierra (magazine) can be searched in the Magazine Database Plus (GO MDP). See Magazine Database.

Sierra Online software is regularly discussed in the Game Publishers A Forum (GO GAMAPUB) and in the Flight Simulation Forum (GO FSFORUM). See Gaming Forums.

   Also, Sierra Online has a store in the Electronic Mall (GO SI) that sells computer games and accessories. See Electronic Mall.

Sight and Sound Forum (GO SSFORUM) serves those interested in computer graphics, animation, and sound files and their integration. See Multimedia.

Sigma Designs products are supported in the Desktop Publishing Vendor Forum (GO DTPVENDOR). For details, see Desktop Publishing.

Silveira, Ted (72511,166) is sysop of the Ziff Help Forum (GO ZNT:ZIFFHELP). See ZiffNet.

Silverwood, Steve (76703,3035) is the sysop of the CA Clipper Forum (GO CLIPPER). See CAI.

Simon, Barry (76004,1664) is one of the editors and writers associated with the PC Magazine forums. See PC Magazine.

Simply software, such as Simply Tax and Simply Accounting, from Computer Associates is supported in the CA-Simply Forum (GO CASIMPLY). See CAI Forums.

Simulation (magazine) is searchable (abstracts) through Computer Database Plus (GO COMPDB). See Computer Database Plus.

Simulation/War Games are offered in CompuServe's game section (GO GAMES). Specific games include:

- Air Traffic Controller (GO ATCONTROL)
- Megawars I: The Galactic Conflict (GO MEGA1)
- Megawars III: The New Empire (GO MEGA3)
- Sniper (GO SNIPER)

See Games, Gaming Forums, and entries under specific game names.

Sinclair (Timex/Sinclair) Computers is one of the computer systems supported in CompuServe's Computer Club Forum (GO CLUB). See Computer Club.

Sir-Tech Software is regularly discussed in The Game Publishers B Forum (GO GAMBPUB). See Gaming Forums.

"Sisters" (television) offers the latest shows available in Soap Opera Summaries (GO SOAPS). See Soap Opera.

.SIT, as an extension on filenames in forum libraries, usually means the program is in a *compressed/packed* form. See Files, Compressed.

Sitka (TOPs) products are supported in the Macintosh Vendor A Forum (GO MACAVEN). See Apple Computers.

Ski reports are available from the Associated Press. Use AP Online to check reports daily, in season. To access the ski report, use GO APO and choose Sports from the menu, then look under the Olympics and Other Sports subheading for the day's report. AP Online is a part of CompuServe's basic services (see Billing).
Also:

- The National Weather Service's Weather Reports (GO WEATHER) offers specialized sports and recreational summaries for major national park and resort areas. See Weather.
- Outdoor News Clips (GO OUTNEWS) offers daily regional ski reports, such as the New England Ski Guide, as well as the National Ski Report. Compiled by Morrie Trumble & Associates and distributed through the Associated Press, the National Ski Report lists conditions for hundreds of U.S. and Canadian slopes. Organized by state and province, you'll find information on general ski conditions, as well as comments for specific resorts. A typical report surveys 23 Colorado areas, 20 in Michigan's Upper and Lower Peninsula, 11 in Vermont, 10 Quebec locations, and even one as far south as Tennessee's Smoky Mountains, Ober Gatlinburg. See Outdoors.
- Ski information also is in the Travel Forum (GO TRAVSIG). See Travel.
- *Skiing Trade News* (magazine) can be searched through the Business Database Plus (GO BUSDB). See Business Database. For related topics, see Sports.

Sky & Telescope (magazine) maintains a regular presence in the Astronomy Forum (GO ASTROFORUM). Editors upload the computer programs that appear in their magazine, and provide timely news updates between issues. You also can enter GO SKYTEL to access a number of special features the editors share in addition to their forum contributions. Also the magazine's articles can be searched in the Magazine Database Plus (GO MDP). See Magazine Database.

Slanguage is what some users call the abbreviations often used in the daily conversations in the real-time conferencing and message boards. For details, see Acronyms.

Slate Corp. (software) is supported in the Pen Technology Forum (GO PENFORUM). For more information, see Pen Technology.

Sludge (magazine) can be searched through the Business Database Plus (GO BUSDB). See Business Database.

Small Business Management, Journal of (magazine) is searchable through Magazine Database Plus (GO MDP). For details see Magazine Database.

Small Business Tax Review (database) can be searched through IQuest. See IQuest.

Small Computer Book Club (GO BK) is a store in the Electronic Mall (GO MALL) that offers computer books. See Electronic Mall.

Smalltalk (software) is supported in the Digitalk Forum (GO DIGITALK). See Digitalk.

Small Computers in Libraries (magazine) is searchable (abstracts) through Computer Database Plus (GO COMPDB). See Computer Database Plus.

SmarText (software) is supported in the Lotus Word Processing Forum (GO LOTUSWP). See Lotus Software.

Smartcom (software) and **Smartmodems** are supported in the Online With Hayes Forum (GO HAYES). See Hayes Microcomputer Products Inc.

SmartNotes (software) is supported in the PC Vendor B Forum (GO PCVENB). See IBM Computers.

Smith, Jennifer (72662,1602) is sysop of the Creative Labs' User Support Forum (GO BLASTER). See Creative Labs.

Smith, Norm, the award-winning wildlife and nature photographer, is featured in Earth Forum (GO EARTH). See Earth.

Smith, Stacy Jenel assists in the writing of Hollywood by Marilyn Beck (GO BECK). See Beck.

Smith, William (73007,173) is a sysop in CODEPORT, The Portable Programming Forum (GO CODEPORT). For details, see Programmer's Support.

Smithsonian (magazine) is searchable through Magazine Database Plus (GO MDP). For details see Magazine Database.

Smithsonian art work and artifacts are the subjects of a collection some 500 graphics files in the Art Gallery Forum (GO ARTGALLERY). See Graphics.

Smoking is discussed in the Bacchus Wine Forum (GO WINEFORUM). See Wine.

Smoking and Health (database) may be searched through the IQuest gateway (GO IQUEST) and through the Knowledge Index (GO KI). See IQuest and Knowledge Index.

See also Health and Medicine and Medical References.

SMT Trends (packaging business database) may be searched through the IQuest gateway. See IQuest. The resource also can be searched through the Business Database Plus (GO BUSDB). See Business Database.

Snapshot, Current Market (GO SNAPSHOT) is a surcharged area that gives a quick overview of current stock market trends by displaying key indicators in a one-page statistical report. See Current Market Snapshot.

Sniper (game) (GO SNIPER) is a multi-player infantry combat game, created by Steve Estvanik of Seattle. Set in the battlegrounds of World War II, the game puts you in command of a squad of soldiers against another squad in a simulation of wartime conditions, recreating the geography and weaponry of the time and place. You might engage in brief skirmishes or in full-scale fire fights. The game is intended for those age 13 and up.

If you use an IBM/compatible system with EGA/VGA graphics, you might be interested in "Scope," a graphic interface Estvanik created in the early 1990s. Enter GO SCOPE and retrieve the self-extracting program, SCOPEX.EXE, a 213K file that contains program, documentation, a glossary, and more. If run offline, the program automatically unpacks its files. After reading the documentation, enter SCOPE to run the program. The program costs $2 to download, but users aren't charged for the connect time used in the retrieval.

To find other Sniper enthusiasts, visit the Multi-Player Games Forum (GO MPFORUM). And for information on other games, see Games.

Snorkeling is a topic in the Scuba Forum (GO SCUBA). See Sports and Recreation.

Snow sports is a topic of the Outdoors Forum (GO OUTDOORFORUM). See Sports and Recreation.

Soap box racing is discussed in the Motor Sports Forum (GO RACING). See Sports and Recreation.

Soap Opera Summaries (GO SOAPS) is a service from All My Features Inc., which offers daily summaries, news, and gossip about the prime-time and daily soaps. This is one of the system's basic services, meaning those signed up under the Standard Pricing Plan (see Billing) have unlimited access to the feature.

The daily soaps summarized include "All My Children," "Another World," "As the World Turns," "The Bold and the Beautiful," "Days of Our Lives," "General Hospital," "Guiding Light," "Loving," "One Life To Live," and "The Young and the Restless." The feature also carries summaries of prime-time soaps such as "Beverly Hills 90210," "L.A. Law," "Melrose Place," "Northern Exposure," "Picket Fences," and "Sisters."

See also Showbiz, Hollywood Hotline, and Entertainment.

Social Security (GO SSA) is a topic in the Seniors Forum (GO SENIORS). See Seniors. It also is discussed in the White House Forum (GO WHITEHOUSE). See White House.

Social Science is covered in a variety of databases through IQuest (GO IQUEST), including Academic Index, American Statistics Index, Book Review Index, Books in Print, Cendata, Conference Papers Index, D&B—Donnelley Demographics, Dissertation Abstracts Online, Francis, PAIS International, Social Sciences Index, Social SciSearch, and Social Work Abstracts. See IQuest.

It also is a topic of the Education Forum (GO EDFORUM). See Education.

See also Sociology.

Society (magazine) can be searched in the Magazine Database Plus (GO MDP). See Magazine Database.

Society of Broadcast Engineers (GO SBENET) newsletters and bulletins are offered in conjunction with the Broadcasters and Broadcast Engineers Forum (GO BPFORUM). See Broadcasters.

Sociology is the topic of several IQuest databases, including Child Abuse and Neglect and Family Violence, Family Resources, Linguistics & Language Behavior Abstracts, Sociological Abstracts, and Urbamet. See IQuest. Sociological Abstracts also can be searched through the Knowledge Index (GO KI), as well as PAIS International, Philosopher's Index, and Ageline. See Knowledge Index.

SofNet products are supported in the IBM PC Vendor G Forum (GO PCVENG). See IBM Computers.

Softbridge Software products are supported in Windows 3rd-Party Forum B (GO WINAPB). See Microsoft Software.

SoftBytes (software) is supported in the PC Vendor C Forum (GO PCVENC). See IBM Computers.

SoftCraft Software products are supported in Windows 3rd-Party Forum B (GO WINAPB). See Microsoft Software.

Softdisk Publishing (GO SP) is a store in the Electronic Mall (GO MALL) that offers software by subscription. See Electronic Mall.

Softex (GO SOFTEX) is CompuServe's own software catalog. Through it, you may purchase programs online and retrieve them immediately. The charges are placed on your CompuServe bill. A database lets you search from hundreds of titles for software by computer type, publisher, title, or Softex catalog number. You may examine descriptions of programs, including details of equipment requirements. After you indicate that you want a specific program, CompuServe tells you what, if anything, you need to do to prepare your computer to receive the file. (See Files, Transfer.) The system then copies the software to the disk location you specify.

  See also Shopping.

SoftKlone products are supported in the Zenith Data Systems Forum (GO ZE-NITH). For details, see Zenith.

Soft-Letter   (magazine) is searchable through Computer Database Plus (GO COMPDB). See Computer Database Plus. It also can be searched through Computer Database Plus (GO COMPDB). See Computer Database Plus.

SoftLogik products are supported in the Atari Vendors Forum (GO ATARIVEN). See Atari Computers.

Softsync Inc. products are supported in the Macintosh C Vendor Forum (GO MACCVEN). See Apple Computers.

Software Bridge (software) is supported in the Windows 3rd-Party Forum (GO WINAPD). See Microsoft Software.

Software Corporation of America products are supported in the OS/2 B Vendor Forum (GO OS2BVEN). See IBM Computers.

Software Division products are supported in the OS/2 Vendor Forum (GO OS2AVEN). See IBM Computers.

Software Entrepreneur's Forum is a sponsor of the General Computing Forum (GO GENCOM). See General Computing.

Software Industry Report and **Software Markets** can be searched through the Business Database Plus (GO BUSDB). See Business Database.

Software Magazine (formerly *Software News*) **(magazine)** is searchable through Computer Database Plus (GO COMPDB). See Computer Database Plus. Abstracts of *Software News* can be searched through the same feature.

Software Publishers Association Forum (GO SPAFORUM) is operated by the principal trade group of the personal computer software industry. The SPA launched a forum on CompuServe to provide information about its services and programs.

The 700-member group says software developers, publishers, and information systems managers may be interested in SPA's activities. Forum members discuss software piracy, upcoming conferences, publications, press releases, and special interest group activities.

The forum is managed by sysop David Frier (76702,1417). A regular in the forum is SPA executive director Ken Wasch (76004,3021). Assisting is Peter Beruk (76004,3111), litigation manager for SPA.

Software Publishing Corporation:
The Software Publishing Forum (GO SPCFORUM) was opened for users of its products, including First Graphics, First Publisher, Harvard Graphics, Harvard Project Manager, Professional File, Professional Plan, and Professional Write.

The forum is run by Kelly Gang (76702,541), assisted by Jayne Butterbrodt, Cheri Stephens, Dave Somers, David Cruikshank, Marj Lohse, Raymond Glosser, Shameem Ibrahim, Rik Temmink, and Tim Peterson.

Software-related forums
are grouped together for easy finding. To see them, enter GO SOFTWARE. Among the software-related forums listed at this writing are the following:

ACI US Forum
Adobe Forum
AI Expert Forum
Aldus Corporation
APPC Information
    Exchange Forum
Apple Macintosh
    Forums
Artisoft Forum
Ask3Com
Autodesk Forums
Banyan Forums
BASIS International
    Forum
Blyth Forum
Borland International
CADD/CAM/CAE
    Vendor Forum
Canopus Forum
CASE—DCI Forum
CDROM Forum
Central Point Forums
ChipSoft Forum
Clarion Software
    Forum

Claris Information
    Center
CompuServe Help
    Forum
Computer Associates
Computer Consultants
    Forum
Computer Language
    Forum
Corel Forums
CP/M Forum
Crosstalk Forum
CTOS/Open Forum
Data Access Corpora-
    tion Forum
Data Based Advisor
DataEase International
    Forum
DATASTORM
    Forum
Da Vinci Forum
DBMS Forum
Delrina Forum
Desktop Publishing
    Forum

Deutsches Computer
    Forum
DiagSoft Forum
Digital Equipment
    Corporation
Digitalk
Dr. Dobb's Journal
Dr. Neuhaus
DTP Forums
Dvorak Development
    Forum
ELSA GmbH Forum
Engineering Automa-
    tion Forum (LEAP)
Fed. of Int'l Distribu-
    tors Forum
Forth Forum/Creative
    Solutions
Fox Software Forum
Graphics Forums
Gupta Forum
Hayes
IBM Corp
IBM LMU/2 Forum
IBM OS/2 Forums

Intel Access/iRUG
　Forum
Intersolv Forum
Intuit Forum
IRI Software Forum
Japan Forum
Lan Magazine Forum
Lan Technology
　Forum
LDOS/TRSDOS
　Forum
Logitech Forum
Logo Forum
Lotus Development
　Corporation
Macromedia Forum
Markt & Technik
　Forum
McAfee Virus Help
　Forum
MECA Software
　Forum
Micro Focus Forum
Microrim Forum
Microstation Forum
Microsoft
　Connection(W)
MIDI Forums
Multimedia Forums
NCR/ATT Forum
Newton/PIE Forum
NeXT Users Forum

Norton/Symantec
　Forums
Novell Desktop
　Systems Group
　Forum
Novell NetWire (W)
Office Automation
　Forum
Oracle Forum
OS9 Operating
　System
OzCIS Forum
Palmtop Forum
Parsons Technology
　Forum
PC Plus / PC Answers
　Forum
PCM Online
Pen Technology
　Forum
Polaris Software
　Forum
Portable Programming
　Forum
Powersoft Forum
Practice Forum
Prisma Forum
Quarterdeck Forum
Revelation Tech.
　Forum
Santa Cruz Operation
　Forum

Siemens AG Forum
Software Publishers
　Assoc. Forum
SPC Forum
Spinnaker Software
　Forum
Stac Electronics
　Forum
SunSelect Forum
Sybase Forum
Symantec Forums
TAPCIS Forum
Thomas-Conrad
　Forum
UK Computer
　Shopper Forum
UK Computing
　Forum
UKSHARE Forum
UNIX Forum
UnixWare Forum
Userland Forum
Ventura Software Inc.
　Forum
Wolfram Research
　Forum
WordPerfect Forums
WordStar Forum
World of Lotus
WRQ/Reflection
　Forum
WUGNET Forum
ZiffNet Forums

See also Forums and see specific software publishers and products.

Software Solutions Forum (GO SOFSOL) supports products developed by the IBM Lab in Cary, North Carolina, including BookManager, Cross System Product, Distributed Application/2, Information/Management for MVS, Interactive System Productivity Facility, ManageWare/400, Node Patrol, Program Development Facility, Software Installer for OS/2 and Windows, and VisualAge. The forum is managed by Raymon Kent (72172,742), with assistance from Wilton Tom, Jim Stewart, Bob Crenshaw, and Willis Ward.

Software Ventures is supported in the Mac B Vendor Forum (GO MACBVEN). See Apple Computers.

Softwood computer products are supported in the Amiga Vendor Forum (GO AMIGAVENDOR). See Commodore Computers.

Solar Energy Intelligence Report, International can be searched through the Business Database Plus (GO BUSDB). See Business Database. See also Energy.

Solberg, Ron (76703,575) administers the Public Relations and Marketing Forum (GO PRSIG). See Public Relations and Marketing.

Solid State Technology (magazine) can be searched through the Business Database Plus (GO BUSDB). See Business Database.

Solid Waste Report (database) may be searched through the IQuest gateway. See IQuest. The resource also can be searched through the Business Database Plus (GO BUSDB). See Business Database.

Solutions for Better Health is searchable in the Health Database Plus (GO HLTBD). See Health.

Solutions Forum (software) (GO SOLUTIONS) is available on CompuServe Pacific to support to both developers and end users of Solutions products, Asymetrix ToolBook (and related products), and Lotus (formerly Threadz) Organizer. The forum also offers general support for all Macintosh and Windows applications (where possible), and provides a center for discussing these products.

Somalia is a topic of the Global Crisis Forum (GO CRISIS). See Global Crisis.

Sound Blaster products are supported in the Creative Labs' User Support Forum (GO BLASTER). See Creative Labs.

Soundcraft and **Sound Deals** products are supported in the MIDI C Vendor Forum (GO MIDICVEN). See Music.

Soundtracks are discussed in the Music/Arts Forum (GO MUSICARTS). See Music.

Sourceline Software products, including SourceLink, are supported in the OS/2 Vendor Forum (GO OS2AVEN). See IBM Computers.

Sourcemex: Economic News on Mexico (database) can be searched through IQuest. See IQuest. The resource also can be searched through the Business Database Plus (GO BUSDB). See Business Database.

Sourcerer's Apprentice (software) is supported in the Borland Development Tools Forum (GO BDEVTOOLS). See Borland.

South America is covered in *Executive Briefing Service South America* and can be searched through the Business Database Plus (GO BUSDB), as can *NOTISUR—*

South American & Caribbean Political Affairs. See Business Database. This also is a topic in the International Trade Forum (GO TRADE). See International Trade. South America is a topic in the Travel Forum (GO TRAVSIG). See Travel.

South Carolina news is covered in the Columbia State, searchable through Telebase System's News Souce USA (GO NEWSUSA). See News Source.

Also, selected reports from South Carolina are included in the Southeast regional reports from United Press International. See Executive News Service.

South Dakota news is included in the daily Western and Central region reports from United Press International. See Executive News Service for details.

Also, *South Dakota Business Review* can be searched through the Business Database Plus (GO BUSDB). See Business Database.

Southern California Business (magazine) can be searched through the Business Database Plus (GO BUSDB). See Business Database.

Southern Economic Journal can be searched through the Business Database Plus (GO BUSDB). See Business Database.

Southwest Journal of Business & Economics (magazine) can be searched through the Business Database Plus (GO BUSDB). See Business Database.

South Magazine can be searched through the Business Database Plus (GO BUSDB). See Business Database.

Soviet Union, through documents and other materials, is the topic of a number of IQuest databases, including Perspectives, Russia Express, Russia Express Contracts, Soviet Aerospace and Technology, Stamm's XSU Business, Soviet Science and Technology, Tass, and USSR Business.

See IQuest.

Also, *Soviet Aerospace* can be searched through Business Database Plus (GO BUSDB). See Business Database.

And Current Digest of the Soviet Press can be searched through the Knowledge Index (GO KI). See Knowledge Index.

S&P Online (GO S&P) is a financial service that offers data on about 4,700 companies, including business summaries, earnings outlooks, historical earnings and dividends, and summaries of product lines. See Company Reports.

Space combat is featured in Flight Simulator Forum (GO FSFORUM). See Gaming Forums.

Space Forum (GO SPACEFORUM) serves those interested in any facet of space, including exploration and space development, U.S. and foreign space operations, space technology, the politics of space exploration, science fiction, military space operations, and more. Administrator of the forum is Dick DeLoach (76703,303), who has been a NASA research scientist for over 20 years. He is assisted by Steve Mastellotto (in charge of graphics and animation) and Alan Higgins (handling library files).

For related topics, see Astronomy.

Also:

- Related databases searchable through the IQuest gateway (GO IQUEST) include Space Business News, Space Calendar, Space Daily, Space Exploration Technology, and Space Station News. See IQuest.
- Florida Today NewsLink Forum (GO FLATODAY), a unique link to this Gannett Inc. newspaper on the Florida Space Coast, includes a section on the space program. See Florida.
- Searchable through the Business Database Plus (GO BUSDB) are *Space Business News*, *Space Commerce Week*, *Space Exploration Technology*, and *Space Station News*. See Business Database.

See also Defense and Aviation.

- NASA graphics are downloadable from the libraries of Graphics Gallery Forum (GO GALLERY). See Graphics.
- Technology and space are discussed in the White House Forum (GO WHITEHOUSE). See White House.

Spalten, Irv (76711,175) is sysop in the IBM OS/2 forums. See IBM Computers.

Spanish is spoken in the Foreign Language Education Forum (GO FLEFO), a service for students and teachers. See Foreign Language. Also serving the Spanish-speaking community is Microsoft Spain/Latin America Forum (GO MSSPAIN). See Microsoft Software.

Spanish issues are discussed in the European Forum (GO EURFORUM). See European Forum.

Sparc/SS-2 is supported in the CompuAdd Forum (GO COMPUADD). See CompuAdd.

Spearhead **(European financial database)** can be searched through IQuest. See IQuest.

Special education is a topic of the Educational Research Forum (GO EDRESEARCH) and Education Forum (GO EDFORUM). See Education.

Special Libraries **(magazine)** is searchable through Magazine Database Plus (GO MDP). For details see Magazine Database.

Spectrum HoloByte **(software)** is regularly discussed in The Game Publishers B Forum (GO GAMBPUB) and in the Flight Simulation Forum (GO FSFORUM). See Gaming Forums.

Spectrum Report, a database on global radio frequency allocation, can be searched through IQuest. See IQuest. The resource also can be searched through the Business Database Plus (GO BUSDB). See Business Database.

Specular International products are supported in the Multimedia Vendor Forum (GO MULTIVEN). See Multimedia.

Spicer's Centre for Europe (**European business database**) can be searched through IQuest. See IQuest.

Spincode products are supported in the OS/2 Vendor Forum (GO OS2AVEN). See IBM Computers.

Spinnaker Forum (GO SPINNAKER) supports Spinnaker products. The sysops are Douglas Smith (75300,1164), Jennifer Bubriski (75300,1163), and Ann-Marie Manna (76711,162).

Spinning is one of the topics discussed in the Crafts Forum (GO CRAFTS). See Crafts.

Spooler (**software**) is supported in the Symantec Fifth Generation Systems Forum (GO SYMFGS). See Symantec.

Sport and **Sports Afield** (**magazines**) can be searched in the Magazine Database Plus (GO MDP). See Magazine Database.

Sports cards, trading is discussed in the Collectibles Forum (GO COLLECT). See Collectibles.

Sports Illustrated (**magazine**) can be searched through News Source USA (GO NEWSUSA) and through IQuest (GO IQUEST). See News Souce USA and see IQuest.

Sports medicine is the topic of Sport, a database that may be searched through the IQuest gateway (GO IQUEST) and through the Knowledge Index (GO KI). See IQuest and see Knowledge Index.

   In addition, *The American Journal of Sports Medicine* and *The Physician and Sportsmedicine* are searchable in the Health Database Plus (GO HLTBD). See Health.

   Also, *Physician and Sportsmedicine* magazine can be searched through the Business Database Plus (GO BUSDB). See Business Database.

   And sports medicine is a topic in HealthNet (GO HNT) and in the Scuba Forum. See Health and see Sports and Recreation.

Sports memorabilia is covered in the Collectibles Forum (GO COL-LECTIBLES). See Collectibles.

Sports products are sold in some shops in the Electronic Mall (GO MALL), including Hammacher Schlemmer (GO HS), JC Penney Online Catalog (GO JCP), and Patagonia (GO PG). Also Austad's (GO AU) sells golf equipment and accessories. See Electronic Mall.

Sports and recreation are supported in various online services:

- Great Outdoors Forum (GO OUTDOORFORUM) covers fishing, hunting, camping, scouting activities, cycling, birding, climbing, skiing, boating, photography, as well as environmental and conservation issues. The forum also is the electronic home of the Outdoor Writers Association of America (OWAA). Joe Reynolds (76704,37), northeast regional editor for *Field & Stream* magazine is forum administrator. Assisting are Bill Clede, Tony Mandile, Rich Emmings, and Les Line.

- Motor Sports Forum (GO RACING) invites visitors to talk about past races and learn about upcoming races. Major motor races in America often have forum members and administrators live at races who provide up-to-the-minute reports. Administrator of the forum is Michael F. Hollander (76703,771). He is assisted by George D. Ryerson, Larry Sullivan, Dave Kutilek, Paul Dewey, and Keith Patti.

- Sailing Forum (GO SAILING) is regularly visited by people who want to discuss and learn about sailing and get the latest information on yacht racing. Forum administrators are Brion Lutz (76702,1561) and Keith Taylor (76702,1533), assisted by Roger Honkanen, George Dinwiddie, Mike Hughes, Al Golden, John B. Bonds, Russ Werner, and Mame Reynolds.

- Scuba Forum (GO SCUBA) is administered by experienced divers and diving professionals. The forum discusses all aspects of SCUBA with novice and experienced divers and snorklers. Richard C. Drew (76701,123), a SCUBA diving instructor, is forum administrator. He is assisted by Carl Powell III and Dick Jacoby.

- The Sports Forum (GO FANS) features sports talk of all kinds. It also sponsors contests for its members and conducts fantastic games based on real sporting events including fantasy football leagues, rotisserie-style baseball leagues, college and professional football handicapping contests, and a Super Bowl contest. Harry Conover (76701,220) is the primary forum administrator. He is assisted by Carol Calhoun-Mock, Owen Mock, Paul Clements, Joe Feinstein, Bob Hazlewood, William McNeary, Jeff Sacks, Adam Stein, Steven Rubio, Chuck Wright, Jim Fowler, Rob MacArthur, Tom Naelon, and Gary Reiser.

Also:

- The NCAA Collegiate Sports Network (GO NCAA) provides menu collections of sports statistics, scores, men's and women's basketball schedule information, assorted news releases and sports polls, as well as information on the NCAA visitors center and other news from the college sports world.

- Sports news also is available from The Associated Press (GO APO), including reports on baseball, football, basketball, hockey, soccer, tennis, golf, colleges, and scoreboards. This is an extra cost service from The Associated Press that is surcharged at $15 an hour. Enter GO APN-1 to see the sports menu.

- West Coast sports are a topic in the California Forum (GO CALFORUM). See California.

- Sports in the Pacific area are discussed in the CompuServe Pacific Forum (GO PACFORUM). See Pacific.

- Sports Simulations Forum (GO SPRTSIMS) hosts discussions and play of computer-based games. See Gaming.

- Outdoors News Clips (GO OUTNEWS) is a surcharged clipping folder for retrieving news stories of interest to hunters, campers, and other outdoors enthusiasts. See Executive News Service for details.

- Recreational Vehicle Forum (GO RVFORUM) discusses camping in tent trailers, travel trailers, fifth-wheels, and motor homes. See Recreational Vehicle.

- British sports are discussed in the UK Forum (GO UKFORUM). See UK Forum. Also, you can reach a clipping folder of the latest British sports news by entering GO UKSPORTS.

- To reach the main menu on this topic, enter GO SPORTS.

See also News, General.

Sportster modems and other from U.S. Robotics are supported in the Modem Vendor Forum (GO MODEMVEN). See Modem Vendor.

Spotts, Stan (76004,2053) is a sysop in the Datastorm Forum (GO DATASTORM). See Procomm (communications software).

Spreadsheets by specific publishers are covered in some forums:

- Excel is supported in the Microsoft Excel Forum (GO MSEXCEL). See Microsoft Software for details.

- Improv for Windows is supported the Lotus Spreadsheets Forum (GO LOTUSA). See Lotus.

- Lotus 1-2-3 is supported the Lotus Spreadsheets Forum (GO LOTUSA). See Lotus.

- Multimate is supported in the Borland Applications Forum (GO BORAPP). See Borland.

- PC-Calc+ from Buttonware is supported in the PC Vendor Forums (GO PCVENA). For details, see IBM Computers.

- Symphony is supported the Lotus Spreadsheets Forum (GO LOTUSA). See Lotus.

- 20/20 is supported in the CA—Simply Forum (GO CASIMPLY). See CAI Forums.

See also Designer Template Collections (GO ZNT:FORMS), intended for use with popular word-processing and spreadsheet programs. See Ziffnet.

Sprint (**software**) is supported in the Borland International Forums (GO BORLAND). See Borland Software.

Sprint mail interconnection is supported in CompuServe Mail. See Mail.

Sprintnet (Telenet) logon instructions (GO LGN-212): If you are using the CompuServe Information Manager, select SETTINGS and then select SPRINTNET for the network. You can then proceed with access. If you are not using CIM, follow these directions to logon to CompuServe using the Sprintnet (formerly Telenet) system:

1. Dial the Sprintnet (Telenet) network telephone access number, listen for the modem tone, and connect your communications equipment.
2. Once a connection is established, press the Return key twice if you are connecting at 300 or 1200 baud. If you are connecting at 2400 baud, type a @ then press Enter.
3. SprintNet's TERMINAL= prompt will then be displayed. At this prompt, enter in the characters D1 and press Return.
4. An "@" prompt will then be displayed. At this prompt, enter one of CompuServe's destination addresses, such as

```
C 614227  or  C 202202
```

and press Return. You will then be connected to CompuServe and the User ID: prompt will be displayed. Enter your User ID and log on as usual.

Costs Sprintnet (Telenet) surcharges (rates charged in addition to CompuServe's basic rates) are $1.70 per hour on evening and weekends, and $11.70 per hour daytime for the contiguous U.S. The nonprime-time rate for Alaska and Hawaii is $11.70.

SPSS Inc. products are supported in the Windows 3rd-Party Forum (GO WINAPD). See Microsoft Software.

SQLBase (**software**), as well as SQLNetwork and SQLWindows, are supported in the Gupta Forum (GO GUPTA). See Gupta.

SQL*Forms and **SQL*Plus** (**software**) are supported in the Oracle Forum (GO ORACLE). See Oracle Software.

SQL Server (**software**) is supported in the Microsoft Operating Systems and Development Forum (GO MSOPSYS). See Microsoft Software.

SQZ (**software**) is supported in the Symantec Forums (GO SYMANTEC). See Symantec Software.

Stac Electronics Forum (GO STACKER) is operated by Stac Electronics, which is known for its data compression hardware and software. Perhaps best known is its Stacker software. The primary sysop is Keith Dunlea (75300,2755).

Stage II: The Two-Stage Trivia Game (GO STAGEII) allows you to earn points by first answering a series of trivia questions and then discovering what the answers have in common. You win by scoring enough points to add your name to the "Stage II Spotlight" of high scorers. The game is intended for those age 12 and up. For information on other games, see Games.

Stamm's XSU Business (**Eastern European/Soviet database**) can be searched through IQuest. See IQuest.

Stamp collecting is covered in the Collectibles Forum (GO COLLECT). See Collectibles.

Standard Microsystems Corp. Forum (GO SMC) is sponsored by this supplier of PC LAN systems products for 10BASE-T, coaxial and fiber network interface cards, concentrators, and network management products.

The forum offers information for Arcnet, Ethernet, and Ethernet Elite (formally Western Digital) products. This includes the latest available driver files. The sysops are Cheryl Langone (75300,2647), Pam Shoemaker (76300,2517), and Brian Stramler (75300,2773).

Standard & Poor's Register—Biographical, Descriptions—Corporate, News and Register—Corporate, Daily News (**databases**) are searchable through IQuest (GO IQUEST) and through the Knowledge Index (GO KI). See IQuest and see Knowledge Index.

Standards & Specifications (**industry database**) may be searched through the IQuest gateway. See IQuest.

STAR (Shareware Trade Asscociation and Resource) is represented in the UK Shareware Forum (GO UKSHARE). See UK.

Star-gazing is the subject of the Astronomy Forum (GO ASTROFORUM), devoted to studying the heavens both for professionals and hobbists. For details, see Astronomy.

StarSprint (**game**) is deep-space flight simulator. You choose a ship depending upon whether you want to protect your bases, intercept enemy ships, or attack enemy bases. Play head-to-head or in teams. The game currently requires an IBM PC-compatible computer with EGA or better graphics capability. Members can download the software to play either of these games from the Entertainment Center Main Menu (GO ECENTER) for a nominal fee. See also Games and see Entertainment Center.

Star Trek, in all its various published and broadcast forums, is a favor topic of the SF & Fantasy Forum. For details, see Science Fiction.

State Capitol Quiz (game) (GO TMC-89) is a trivia game that tests your knowledge of U.S. geography. For other recreations, see Games.

State Department, U.S. documents are included in Travel Advisory Service (GO STATE). It is maintained by the Citizen Emergency Center as a continuously updated information service to Americans traveling abroad. See U.S. Government Information.

State Environment Report can be searched through the Business Database Plus (GO BUSDB). See Business Database.

State Telephone Regulation Report (database) covers telephone regulations at the state level. See IQuest. The resource also can be searched through the Business Database Plus (GO BUSDB). See Business Database.

Statistics Index, American (database) may be searched through the IQuest gateway. See IQuest.

STB Systems products are supported in the Graphics A Vendor Forum (GO STBSYS). See Graphics.

STD Update, Brown University is searchable in the Health Database Plus (GO HLTBD). See Health.

Stein, Eliot (76703,305) is a long-time editor of Hollywood Hotline (GO HOLLYWOOD) and a sysop in the ShowBiz Forum (GO SHOWBIZ). See Show Biz.

Steinberg/Jones products are supported in the MIDI C Vendor Forum (GO MIDICVEN). See Music.

StereoGraphics (computer graphics products) is supported in the Graphics B Vendor Forum (GO INDEPTH). See Graphics.

Stereo Review (magazine) is searchable through Magazine Database Plus (GO MDP). For details see Magazine Database. This resource also may be searched through IQuest. See IQuest.

See also Music.

Stevens, Allan (76702,562) administers the Health and Fitness Forum (GO GOODHEALTH). See Health and Fitness Forum.

Stinson, Craig (72241,216) is one of the editors and writers associated with the PC Magazine forums. See PC Magazine.

Stirling Group Software products are supported in Windows 3rd-Party Forum C (GO WINAPC). See Microsoft Software.

Stitchery is one of the topics discussed in the Crafts Forum (GO CRAFTS). See Crafts.

Stock Brokerage Services (GO BROKERAGE) allow you to buy and sell stocks online. They not only afford their customers substantial cost savings, but also offer the additional benefits of around-the-clock order entry and instantaneous access to account records. The system supports these firms:

- E*Trade Securities (GO ETRADE) is a discount stock brokerage firm offering around-the-clock order entry and instantaneous access to account records. It promises quotes on stocks, options, market indices, mutual funds, as well as on commodities and futures. Also featured are news alerts on stocks the moment the news hits the wires. Users receive automatic confirmations when their orders are executed. You can review your portfolio's value, income, and unrealized gains and losses valued with prices delayed at least 15 minutes. See the introductory menu for background on the company.

- Max Ule's Tickerscreen (GO TKR-1): Members may use PC-Venture Capital, Max Ule's program for pairing entrepreneurs with individuals interested in venture capital enterprises. "Mergersource" provides a register of company profiles for individuals or companies interested in acquiring companies. Companies may add a listing in "Mergersource" for review by others. Tickerscreen also offers order placement and confirmation, margin accounts, IRAs, options trading, and pre-authorized electronic funds transfers for securities purchases. The service also provides a stock market summary and NYSE closing price quotations. The system charges 2 cents per issue.

- Quick Way Online Brokerage Service (GO QWK): Orders are executed as they are received when the market is open. Orders placed during the evening or on weekends are executed when the market opens the next business day. Quick Way enables 24-hour access to your account and provides account monitoring capabilities. You may place stock and option orders; review; change or cancel your orders; check your portfolio value, income, unrealized gains, and losses; and check year-to-date realized gains and losses. Quick Way also provides quotes on stocks, options, indexes, and mutual funds with optional real-time quotes on these items. The service is surcharged at $14 an hour during daytime/prime hours and $4 an hour during in the evenings and on weekends. This is most experienced of the online brokers. Established in 1974, it became the first New York Stock Exchange member firm to pass on discounts to the public. Serving 350,000 customers through its 60 branch offices, it has grown to become one of the U.S.'s largest discount brokers and among the few with its own clearing operations, which provides for complete control of all aspects of each order placed.

See also Financial Services and see Investment Analysis Tools.

Stock market overview: Highlights for Previous Day (GO MARKET), analyzes the markets most recent history. See Stock Quotes (Historical)

Stock market reports are available in a number of different forms. For an online overview for the features, enter GO FINANCIAL. For more information, see Financial Services and see Investment Analysis Tools.

Stock quotes (Current) are available as part of the basic services (GO BASICQUOTES), meaning that those who have signed up under the Standard Pricing Plan have unlimited access to the service. Those using the Alternate Pricing Plan can reach the same service by entering GO QQUOTES; for them, the charge is 1.5 cents per quote. (See Billing for background on the Standard and Alternate Pricing plans.) The Current Quotes feature provides daily data on 9,000 securities traded on national and regional exchanges and the over-the-counter national market. The quotes are over 15 minutes delayed (which is as soon as the exchanges will allow you to receive them without paying a monthly fee.) The information includes volume, high, low, last, change, and the time of the last trade or quote. Each time you access the feature, you get the latest Dow Jones stock average report. The CompuServe Information Manager platforms have their own interface for using the quotes feature; see your manual for details. If you are using a generic third-party terminal program, enter a ticker symbol or a series of ticker symbols for quotes. Instructions for using the service are built-in online. Also, company news is available. If there is an asterisk by one or more of the quotes, it means that there is current news about the company. At the next Issue: prompt, enter /CONEWS to go to a surcharged news area where the current news of that company or companies will be displayed. Company News is surcharged at $15 an hour.

Also, Highlights for Previous Day (GO MARKET) analyzes the market's most recent history, including the New York Stock Exchange, American Stock Exchange, over-the-counter markets, and the preparation of 19 different reports. Included are the most active stocks, the largest gainers and losers, stocks for which the price has risen or dropped over the past three, four, or five trading days, stocks with new six-month highs or lows, stocks with a low above yesterday's high or a high below yesterday's low, and stocks that have traded twice their average volume. The feature is surcharged at $15 an hour.

See also Financial Services and Investment Analysis Tools.

Stock quotes (Historical) (GO SECURITIES): Several stock pricing tools are listed by menu. All are surcharged features (the rates are listed in the following paragraphs). Note, though, that quotes for H&R Block, CompuServe's parent company, are not surcharged, so using the HRB ticker symbol is a good way to see a sample of how any of the following features work:

- Detailed Issue Examination (GO EXAMINE) describes a single issue, including trading status, risk measures, capitalization, and descriptive data. The feature offers information about any type of quotable security, with reports varying for bonds, options, and equities. Each issue is surcharged at $1.25.

- Dividends, Splits, and Bond Interest (GO DIVIDENDS) gives historical information about these items for an issue over a given period. Mutual fund distributions also are available. Specify the number of dividends you wish to view. The report includes the ex-date, record date, payment date, distribution type, and the rate or amount of each distribution. Each quote displayed is surcharted at 15 cents.

- Multiple Issues/1 Day (GO QSHEET) gives volume, close/average, high/ask, low/bid, and CUSIP number for several issues for a single trading day. Up to 500 ticker symbols can be entered. The surcharge is 5 cents per quote, unless the data is the most recent trading data, which is surcharged at 1.5 cents per quote.

- Options Profile (GO OPRICE) lists all options currently trading on a common stock or market index, covering more than 10,000 put and call options traded on major U.S. and Canadian exchanges, listing the name, closing price, pricing date, ticker symbol, and exchange code for the company. The system maintains old options data for about three months after the option has expired. Each issue is surcharged at $1.25.

- Price/Volume Graph (GO TREND) provides both the traded price and the trading volume for the requested days, weeks, or months in chart form. Current earnings, price, dividend, and risk information for common stocks are displayed with a graph. It provides a graphic snapshot of a security's performance over any period from 15 to 70 days, weeks, or months. You also can enter a series of ticker symbols. One helpful feature is that when you select for a time series of prices on a particular issue, the price/volume chart is automatically adjusted for stock splits (so that when you look at a price range, for example, you aren't seeing the artificial effect of a split but the actual change in value). In order to display the Price/Volume graph, your terminal must have graphics capabilities, such as those built into the CompuServe Information Manager. The charts are surcharged at $1 each.

- Pricing History/1 issue (GO PRICES) for data on tens of thousands of securities is available on a daily basis, going back 12 years. Data is available for a variety of exchanges. Displayed are historical prices for a single issue by day, week, or month for the requested number of years, including dates, volumes, high/ask, low/bid, and close/average for the given security. You have the option of choosing the beginning and ending date or a number of time periods. All the quotes are adjusted for stock splits and stock dividends to bring the prices into agreement with the current one. The data is surcharged at 5 cents for each quote displayed and 1.5 cents for the most recent closing quote. So, if you request the last five days of quotes for a security, the surcharge would be 20 cents for the first four days and 1.5 cents for the latest quote. Retrieval of weekly and monthly prices are similarly surcharged at 5 cents per quote displayed.

- Pricing Statistics (GO PRISTATS) gives a quick look at the performance price and volume performance for stocks, bonds, options, mutual funds, market indexes, warrants, and more. Exchanges include national and regional in the U.S., and the Toronto and Montreal exchanges in Canada. Each display costs $1.25 in surcharges.

See also Financial Services, Investment Analysis Tools, and Commodities.

Stock quotes (Historical), UK (GO UKPRICE) offers pricing information for more than 5,000 British equity issues and about 350 market indexes. Most securities in the service have data from as far back as July 1, 1990. The update times will vary, but generally the service will offer updated UK equity issues by 9:00 p.m., Eastern Time. Market Indexes are updated by 12:00 a.m., Eastern Time. However, it is wise to refer to the last update (which is displayed when you first enter the service) to ensure that prices have been updated prior to using the service. A quote typically consists of a closing price and the security's volume. In some situations, a security may also offer a high and low price. The surcharge is 5 cents per quote.

Stock symbols, lookup: Issue and Symbol Lookup (GO SYMBOLS) provides several features to determine what securities and indexes are covered in other securities areas and to access the symbols needed to make efficient use of most databases. This is one of the system's basic services, meaning those signed up under the Standard Pricing Plan (see Billing) have unlimited access to the feature. The Symbols menu includes:

- List Bonds for Company (GO BONDS) displays all active bonds for a company. The report displays the ticker symbols, CUSIP numbers, issue descriptions, yield, and current selling price for each bond. In addition, a quality rating is provided, expressed by both Standard & Poor's and Moody's. Each bond displayed is surcharged at 5 cents.

- Menu of Available Commodities (GO CSYMBOL) covers such available commodity groups as foods, grains, metals, financial, petroleum, fibers, currencies, and indexes. Access symbols, active contracts, exchange (where traded), and commodity description are shown for each commodity. No surcharge.

- Menu of Available Indexes (GO INDICATORS) gives the ticker and CUSIP number various indexes. They are categorized into manageable groups designated by market/industry indexes, bonds/yields, exchange rates, volumes, advances and declines, and any issues that are new or that don't fall into one other categories. Another option lets you list all the indexes without going through additional menus. Each index is updated daily. No surcharge is levied in this feature.

- Search for Company Name, Ticker Symbol, and CUSIP (GO LOOKUP) allows you to search by name, CUSIP number, ticker symbol, CNUM or SIC code, and lists all the issues for a company you select. Displayed are the number of equity, debt, option mutual fund, and market index found, and a report that shows the codes and symbols for each. This feature is not surcharged.

Stone, David M. (72241,361) is one of the editors and writers associated with the PC Magazine forums. See PC Magazine.

Stone Edge Technology products are supported the Apple II Vendor Forum (GO APIIVEN). See Apple Computers.

Storage Dimensions storage device products are supported in PC Vendor F Forum (GO PCVENF). For details, see IBM Computers.

Storyboard (**IBM software**) is supported in the IBM Desktop Software Forum (GO IBMDESK). See IBM Computers.

Strategic Mapping Inc. products are supported in the PC Vendor H Forum (GO PCVENH). See IBM Computers.

Strategic Simulations Inc. software is supported in the Game Publishers A Forum (GO GAMAPUB). See Gaming Forums.

Students' Forum (GO STUDENTS) is for students of all ages, from early grades to college. Teachers also are welcome. The sysop is Joseph Katz (76703,662) of the University of South Carolina. Assisting are Janet Stimson, Al Kuntzler, Ruth B. Patterson, Daniel J. Gray, Janet Katz, Richard Gross, Howard Dinin, Mary Lord, Norman L. Reitzel Jr., Tamsin Hekala, Mark Gist, and David VanMeter.
  For other school-related features, see Education.

StuffIt (**software**) is supported in Mac C Vendor Forum (GO MACCVEN). For details, see Apple Computers.

Stunt Driver (**modem game**) is supported in the Modem-to-Modem Gaming Lobby (GO MTMLOBBY). See Modem-to-Modem Games.

SubLOGIC software is regularly discussed in The Game Publishers A Forum (GO GAMAPUB) and in the Flight Simulation Forum (GO FSFORUM). See Gaming Forums.

Subscriber Assistance (GO HELP): CompuServe maintains a database of answers to frequently asked questions about billing, forums, electronic mail, logons, real-time conferencing, and so on. See Help Online.

Subscriber Directory (GO DIRECTORY) is a database of CompuServe subscribers that is searchable by name. For details, see Member Directory.

Substance abuse is discussed in the Health and Fitness Forum (GO GOODHEALTH). See Health.

Suitcase (**software**) is supported in the Symantec Fifth Generation Systems Forum (GO SYMFGS). See Symantec.

Sullivan, Larry (76702,501) is a sysop in the Motor Sports Forum (GO RACING). For details, Sports.

Sulphur (**magazine**) can be searched through the Business Database Plus (GO BUSDB). See Business Database.

SUM   (**software**) is supported in the Symantec Forums (Go SYMANTEC). See Symantec Software.

Sun Country Software (**compter graphics products**) is supported in the Graphics B Vendor Forum (GO SUNSHOW). See Graphics.

Sundial Systems   products are supported in the OS/2 Vendor Forum (GO OS2AVEN). See IBM Computers.

SunDisk   products are supported in the IBM PC Vendor G Forum (GO PCVENG). See IBM Computers.

Sunglasses, Shavers & More (GO SN) is a store in the Electronic Mall that specializes in travel accessories and sunglasses. See Electronic Mall.

SunPC   is supported in the SunSelect Forum (GO SUNSELECT). See SunSelect.

Sun Select Forum (GO SUNSELECT) supports the SunSelect networking and interoperability product line of the Sun Microsystems Inc. business, including Network File Server, NetWare SunLink, Tops, Netprint, PenCentral, SunPC, and Advanced Telenet. The sysop is Steve McCarthy (71333,1570). Also involved in the forum is SunSoft, the system software subsidiary of Sun Microsystems and a supplier of 32-bit operating systems programs.

Sunset Magazine (**magazine**) articles are searchable through Magazine Database Plus (GO MDP). For details see Magazine Database.

SuperCalc (**spreadsheet software**) is supported in the CAI Forums (GO CAI) operated by Computer Associates International. See CAI.

Super Collider News can be searched through the Business Database Plus (GO BUSDB). See Business Database.

Superconductor Week can be searched through the Business Database Plus (GO BUSDB). See Business Database.

Superfund and **Superfund Week** can be searched through the Business Database Plus (GO BUSDB). See Business Database.

SuperGroup Magazine (**magazine**) can be searched through Computer Database Plus (GO COMPDB). See Computer Database Plus.

Super Marketing (**UK database**) may be searched through the IQuest gateway. See IQuest. It also can be searched through Business Database Plus (GO BUSDB). See Business Database.

Supermarket News (**database**) can be searched through IQuest. See IQuest.

Superfund Week (**database**) may be searched through the IQuest gateway. See IQuest. It also can be searched through Business Database Plus (GO BUSDB). See Business Database.

Superkey (**software**) is supported in the Borland International Forums (GO BORLAND). See Borland Software.

SuperLaserSpool (**software**) is supported the Symantec Fifth Generation Systems Forum (GO SYMFGS). See Symantec.

SuperMac Technology products are supported in the Mac B Vendor Forum (GO MACBVEN). See Apple Computers.

Supermarket Business Magazine and ***Supermarket News*** (**magazines**) can be searched through the Business Database Plus (GO BUSDB). See Business Database.

SuperPrint (**software**) is supported in Windows 3rd-Party Forum B (GO WINAPB). See Microsoft Software.

SUPERSITE (GO SUPERSITE) provides demographics for the United States as a whole, as well as every individual state, county, Standard Metropolitan Statistical Area (SMSA), Arbitron TV Market (ADI), Nielsen TV Market (DMA), census tract, minor civil division (MCD), and ZIP code area. Available reports cover general demographics, income, housing, education, employment, and current and projected-year forecasts. In addition, it offers sales potential reports for major types of retail stores and consumer potential reports for three types of financial institutions. ACORN (A Classification of Residential Neighborhoods), available as part of SuperSite, classifies all households in the U.S. into 1 of 44 market segments based upon the demographic, socioeconomic, and housing characteristics of the neighborhood. To use it, indicate the kind of geography and report you need and turn on your printer for an 80-column printout. (In the event of a printer problem, the reports may be redisplayed immediately at no additional charge.)

Most charts give the latest actual census information, a current update based on interim figures gleaned from several sources, a forecast for future dates, the percentage of change expected between now and the projection, and the annual growth or decline predicted in the various categories.

SuperSite reports, surcharged from $25 to $45 depending on the information, include:

- ACORN Target Marketing Reports for population profile, household profile, financial services, investment services, a convenience store, restaurant, shopping center retail, as well as media analysis and media.
- Demographic Reports for housing, ethnic population, education, energy, employment, income, component area, forecast summaries, housing value by age, combined demographic and income forecast, age by sex, and age by income.
- Sales potential reports for various businesses, including an appliance store, consumer finance institution, dry cleaner, hair salon, ice cream store, optical center, photo outlet, retail bakery, savings and loan firm, apparel store, automotive aftermarket, commercial bank, department store, drug store, footwear store, grocery store, home improvement, restaurant, and shopping center.

An option on the main SuperSite menu provides the current costs for specific reports.

SuperSite is accessible to subscribers who have signed up for the Executive Option (See Executive Option).

See also Demographics, Economics, and Neigbhorhood Reports.

Support On Site (GO ZNT:ONSITE) is a database of technical support information on more than three dozen popular PC environment and applications software products. For details, see ZiffNet.

Supra Corporation products are supported in the Atari Vendors Forum (GO ATARIVEN). See Atari Computers. They also are supported in the Modem Vendor Forum (GO MODEMVEN). See Modem Vendor.

Supreme Court is a topic of the Legal Forum (GO LAWSIG). See Legal.

Surface Coatings Abstracts, World (database) may be searched through the IQuest gateway. See IQuest.

Surface Modification Technology News can be searched through the Business Database Plus (GO BUSDB). See Business Database.

Surgery, American Journal of is searchable in the Health Database Plus (GO HLTBD). Also, *Annals of Surgery, Annals of Thoracic Surgery, British Journal of Surgery, Archives of Surgery, Journal of Bone and Joint Surgery: American Volume, Journal of Thoracic and Cardiovascular Surgery,* and *Journal of Vascular Surgery* abstracts are searchable in the Health Database Plus (GO HLTBD). See Health. See Health.

Survey of Cinema, Magill's (GO MAGILL) contains descriptions of most major films from 1902 to the present. See Magill's Survey of Cinema.

Survey of Current Business (magazine) can be searched through the Business Database Plus (GO BUSDB). See Business Database.

Survivor Software is supported in the Mac A Vendor Forum (GO MACAVEN). See Apple Computers.

Swan Technologies products are supported in the IBM PC Vendor G Forum (GO PCVENG). See IBM Computers.

Swapping is a favorite pastime in many forums. See Bartering.

Swap Utilities (software) is supported in the PC Vendor C Forum (GO PCVENC). See IBM Computers.

Swedish computing is supported in Microsoft Sweden Forum (GO MSSWEDEN). See Microsoft Software.

Sweetwater Sound (products) are supported in the MIDI B Vendor Forum (GO MIDIBVEN). See Music.

SWFTE International products are supported in the Windows 3rd-Party D Forum (GO WINAPD). See Microsoft Software.

swissBusiness (magazine) can be searched through the Business Database Plus (GO BUSDB). See Business Database.

Sybase Forum (GO SYBASE) supports all that firm's products, such as the Sybase SQL Server, Data Workbench, and SQR Workbench. Administering the forum is Chandrika Krishnan (70007,4671), assisted by Dave Peterson, Wayne Hong, David Brenegan, Mike Butler, and Daniel Scanlan.

Sybex Publishing Forum (GO SYBEX) is operated by a major independent publisher of computer books, an international company with affiliates in France, Germany and the Netherlands. Sybex authors regularly visit the forum and the company's technical support staff promises to monitor the message boards to assist in accuracy. The sysops are Alicia Abramson (72662,2507) and Gary Masters (72662,1741).

Symantec Software: The Symantec Forums (GO SYMANTEC) has areas set aside for the best-known programs operated by the firm's customer service representative (76376,2450). The forums, operated by Bill Hall (76707,14) are:

- The Symantec AntiVirus Forum (GO SYMVIRUS) offers AntiVirus product support. Assisting the forum operations are Craig Morton, David Perry, and Duncan Morrison.

- The Symantec Applications Forum (GO SYMAPPS) supports Symantec's applications, productivity, and project management tools, including Symantec Q&A, MORE, TimeLine, OnTarget, GrandView, Greatworks, and JustWrite. Assisting in running the forum are Bill Chever, Chris Stehlik, Paul Bishop, and Ginger Stephens.

- The Symantec Development Tools Forum (GO SYMDEVTOOL) supports development tools and languages. Forum management is facilitated by Kevin Irlen, Brian Weed, Oliver Vogel, Jeff Gould, and Philip Davis.
- The Symantec Fifth Generation Systems Forum (GO SYMFGS) supports Fifth Generation software, including FastBack, Untouchable, Suitcase, and SuperLaserSpool. The forum is operated Joesph Katz (76703,662).
- Symantec/Norton Forum (GO SYMUTIL) for discussion of all Symantec utility products including all Peter Norton products as well as the Symantec utilities for the Macintosh and Symantec AntiVirus program. Helping in forum management are Mark Perkins, Robert Stones, David Perry, Ted Sadler, James Whitted, Jim Ferguson, Rich Zaleski, Donald Whytock, Jimi Vigotty, and John Boyd.
- The Symantec Utilities Forum (GO SYMUTIL) supports Norton Utilities, including Norton Desktops, Commanders, backups, utilities, Symantec utilities for the Mac, and pcAnywhere.

The forums are administered by Judi Lowenstein (76703,4047), who is Living Videotext's director of technical services and also an expert on making third-party software compatible with Symantec products.

Symphony (**software**) is supported in the Lotus Spreadsheets Forum (GO LOTUSA). See Lotus Software.

Syndesis products are supported in the Amiga Vendor Forum (GO AMIGAVENDOR). See Commodore Computers.

Synergy Solutions products are supported in the Lan Vendor Forum (GO LANVEN). See IBM Computers.

Synetik Systems products are supported in the OS/2 Vendor Forum (GO OS2AVEN). See IBM Computers.

SynOptics products are supported in the SynOptics Communications Inc. Forum (GO SYNOPTICS). SynOptics makes LAN hubs, LAN management software and associated products. Operating the forum is Vince Watkins (72262,2767).

SystemBuilder products are supported in the Pacific Vendor Forum (GO PACVEN). See Pacific Vendor.

System 5000 is supported in the CADD/CAM/CAE Vendor Forum (GO CADDVEN). See CAD/CAM.

Systems Compatibility Corp. products are supported in the Windows 3rd-Party Forum (GO WINAPD). See Microsoft Software.

System 7.0 (**Apple Macintosh operating system**) is supported in the Mac System 7.0 Forum (GO MACSEVEN). See Apple Computers.

Systems Integration and **Systems Integration Business** (magazines) are searchable through Computer Database Plus (GO COMPDB). See Computer Database Plus. In the same feature, abstracts of *Systems & Network Integration* can be searched.

Systems Management, Journal of and **The Journal of Systems and Software** (magazine) are available for searching through Computer Database Plus (GO COMPDB). See Computer Database Plus.

Sytron Corp. products are supported in the PC Vendor I Forum (GO PCVENI). See IBM Computers.

T

Tactical Technology can be searched through the Business Database Plus (GO BUSDB). See Business Database.

TACTIC Software products are supported in the Macintosh Vendor B Forum (GO MACBVEN). See Apple Computers.

Talking Moose (**software**) is supported in Mac C Vendor Forum (GO MACCVEN). For details, see Apple Computers.

Tampa Bay Business Journal (**magazine**) can be searched through the Business Database Plus (GO BUSDB). See Business Database.

Tampa and **St. Petersburg** are topics of the Florida Forum (GO FLORIDA). See Florida.

Tanaka, Deb (76702,1467) is forum manager of Aquaria and Fish Forum (GO AQUAFORUM), operated by FISHNET. See Fish.

Tandy Corp. computers: TandyNet (GO TANDYNET) is the name for several forums that support Tandy Corporation products. They are associated with a national organization, the independent Tandy Users Network, sponsored by Golden Triangle Corporation of Watauga, Texas, near the home of Tandy Corporation. These include:

- Color Computer Forum (GO COCO)
- Model 100/Portables Forum (GO TANDYLAPTOP)
- OS-9 Forum (GO OS9)
- Tandy Professional Forum (GO TANDYPRO)

Heading up the Tandy network is Wayne Day (76703,376) who has been prominent in the Tandy and the CompuServe communities for many years. In the Coco forum, Day is assisted by Mike Ward, Steve Wegert, and Dave Jenkins. Running the Model 100 forum are Tony Anderson (76703,4062), Eiji Miura, and Wilson Van Alst. OS-9 sysops include Pete Lyall (76703,4230) and Kevin Darling (76703,4227), assisted by Mark Griffith and Bill Dickhaus.

The Tandy Pro forum supports most of that company's computers and peripherals, including the more recent IBM-compatibles, such as the Models 1000, 1200, and 3000, as well as the older systems, such as the Models I, III, and 4.

The Color Computer is devoted for the earliest as well as the more recent versions of that home system.

The Model 100 Forum actually is intended for the users of the TRS-80 Model 100, Tandy 200, NEC portables, Olivetti M-10, Tandy 600, and compatible portables.

The OS-9 Forum is dedicated to users of the multiuser, multitasking OS-9 Operating System that is available for most 6809 and 68000 computers.

Another forum also supporting Tandy equipment, but not operated by the Golden Triangle Corporation, is the LDOS/TRSDOS6 Users Forum (GO LDOS). Long-time Tandy computer users know LDOS as an outstanding alternative to the standard TRSDOS operating system for the company's 8-bit machines. The sysop for this forum, serving users of LDOS/TRSDOS6, is Joe Kyle-DiPietropaolo (76703,437). The forum is sponsored by MISOSYS Incorporated of Sterling, Virginia, for users of MISOSYS and Logical Systems products.

Also part of Tandynet is the Tandy Newsletter (GO TRS-1), which is designed to offer Tandy Computer users a convenient way to keep abreast of activities on CompuServe which may be of interest to them, and to keep informed of current development from within Tandy Corporation. The newsletter is an electronic publication of the Tandy Corporation.

In addition, Tandy/IBM Science is a topic in the Science/Math Education Forum (GO SCIENCE). See Science.

Tank (**modem game**) is supported in the Modem-to-Modem Gaming Lobby (GO MTMLOBBY). See Modem-to-Modem Games.

TAPCIS: is a popular communications program for IBM and compatible computers that automates much of the online operations for its users. The software was written by the late Howard Benner and has been taking a certain segment of the CompuServe community by storm ever since.

Benner opened the TAPCIS Forum (GO TAPCIS) in 1988 as an online support system for his users. The sysops are Joan Friedman, Marilyn Ratcheson, Richard P. Wilkes, Sandy Wilkes, George Sherman, Jeff Gulliford, Loren Jenkins, Dick Kahane, and John Wexler.

See also Benner and Automated Terminal.

TAPMARK (**software**) is supported in the PC Vendor B Forum (GO PCVENB). See IBM Computers.

Tarot cards are discussed in the New Age Forum (GO NEWAGE). See New Age.

Taschek, John (76000,21) is the sysop of the PC/Contact Forum (GO ZNT:PCCONTACT). See PC/Computing.

Tass **(the official Russian news agency)** may be searched through the IQuest gateway. See IQuest. It also is among the resources in NewsGrid (GO NEWSGRID). See Newsgrid.

Tax is covered in Tax Notes Today and is accessible through the Legal Research Center (GO LEGALRC). For details, see Legal Research. This resource also may be searched through IQuest, as is Small Business Tax Review. See IQuest. Taxes and accounting also are discussed in the Working From Home Forum (GO WORK). See Working From Home.

Also, relevant databases on IQuest (GO IQUEST) include Index to Legal Periodicals, Small Business Tax Review, and Tax Notes Today. *World Tax Report* can be searched through the Business Database Plus (GO BUSDB). See Business Database.

See also Accounting.

TaxCut **(software)** is supported in Meca Software Forum (GO MECA). See Meca.

Tax Hotline (GO THL) is a service in the Electronic Mall (GO MALL) operated by H&R Block for tax information. See Electronic Mall.

Taylor, Keith (76702,1533) is sysop of the Sailing Forum. See Sports and Recreation.

TCNS is supported in the Thomas-Conrad Support Forum (GO TCCFORUM). See Thomas-Conrad.

Teacher Education is a topic of the Educational Research Forum (GO EDRESEARCH). See Education.

TEAM products are supported in the PC Vendor G Forum (GO PCVENG). See IBM.

Tech Europe can be searched through the Business Database Plus (GO BUSDB). See Business Database.

Tech III products are supported in the IBM PC Vendor D Forum (GO PCVEND). See IBM Computers.

Technical Computing **(database)** may be searched through the IQuest gateway. See IQuest.

Technology is discussed in the White House Forum (GO WHITEHOUSE). See White House.

Technology Review **(magazine)** is searchable through Magazine Database Plus (GO MDP). For details see Magazine Database. It also can be searched through

Business Database Plus (GO BUSDB), as can *New Technology Week*, *Technology Access Report*, *Technology Alert*, and *Technical Computing*. See Business Database.

Tech PC User, TECH Specialist, Tech Street Journal, and **Technology & Learning** (magazines) are searchable through Computer Database Plus (GO COMPDB). See Computer Database Plus.

Teen Magazine (magazine) can be searched in the Magazine Database Plus (GO MDP). See Magazine Database.

TEGL Systems products are supported in the Graphics A Vendor Forum (GO TEGL). See Graphics.

Teknosys Inc. products are supported in the Mac D Vendor Forum (GO MACDVEN). See Apple Computers.

Telebase Systems Incorporated provides a number of gateway services on CompuServe. Best known is the massive IQuest service (see IQuest), but the Wayne, Pennsylvania, company also provides a number of smaller, specialized gateways. For more information on them, see Books in Print (GO BOOKS), British Trade Marks (GO UKTRADEMARKS), Commerce Business Daily (GO COMBUS), Computerized Engineering Index (GO COMPENDEX), D&B Dun's databases (GO DUNS), Dun's Electronic Yellow Pages (GO DYP), Dissertation Abstracts (GO DISSERTATION), Educational Resources Information Center (GO ERIC), IQuest Business Management InfoCenter (GO IQBUSINESS), IQuest Medical InfoCenter (GO IQMEDICINE), Legal Research Center (GO LEGALRC), Magill's Survey of Cinema (GO MAGILL), Marketing/Management Research Center (GO MKTGRC), Marquis Who's Who (GO BIOGRAPHY), National Technical Information Service (GO NTI), News Source USA (GO NEWSUSA), Patent Research Center (GO PATENT), PTS Newsletter Database/Communications (GO DPNEWS), PTS Newsletter Database/Media (GO MEDIANEWS), Trademarkscan (GO TRADERC), and UK Newspaper Library (GO UKPAPERS).

Telebit Corporation is supported the Modem Vendor Forum (GO MODEMVEN). See Modem Vendor.

Telecom, Worldwide (database) may be searched through the IQuest gateway. See IQuest. The resource also can be searched through the Business Database Plus (GO BUSDB) as can *Global Telecom Report*. See Business Database.

Telecommunication Issues Forum (GO TELECOM) is devoted to discussing events impacting the telecommunication industry and its carriers and networks.

Topics include regulatory affairs, international standards, tariffs, PBXs and other customer premise equipment, network protocols, the Electronic Frontier Foundation's efforts to insure First Amendment rights for electronic communication, and enhanced services such as fax and cellular technology.

The sysop is Marilyn DePaoli (76702,1626). The assistants are Scott Loftesness and Wally Roberts.

See also Electronics.

Telecommunications is covered in *Telecommunications* magazine, available for full-text searching through Computer Database Plus (GO COMPDB). And abstracts of *Telecommunication Journal* may be searched in the same feature. See Computer Database Plus. It also can be searched through Business Database Plus (GO BUSDB). See Business Database.

Also, relevant databases on IQuest (GO IQUEST) include Advanced Wireless Communications, Audiotex Update, Comline Japan Daily: Telecommunications, Common Carrier Week, Communications Daily, Communications Week, Communications Week International, Compendex Plus, Computer Protocols, Connect Times, Eastern European & Soviet Telecom Report, Edge On and About AT&T, Edge: Work Group Computing Report, Electronic Messaging News, Electronic Services Update, FCC Daily Digest, FCC Report, Fiber/Optics News, Heller Report on Educational Technology & Telecommunications, Information Networks, Information Week, ISDN News, Japan Telecommunications Scan, Land Mobile Radio News, Microcell Report, Mobile Data Report, Mobile Phone News, Mobile Satellite Reports, Modem Users News, Multimedia Publisher, OPEN: OSI Product and Equipment News, PSN News, PTS Newsletter Database, Report on AT&T, Satellite News, The Spectrum Report, State Telephone Regulation Report, Tele-Service News, Telecommunications Reports, Telecommunications Week, Telephone News, Telephone Week, Telocator Bulletin, Trading Systems Technology, and Worldwide Telecom. See IQuest.

Searchable through the Business Database Plus (GO BUSDB) are *Technology Access Report*, *Technology Alert*, *Technology Review*, *Tele-Service News*, *Telecom Markets*, *Telecommunications*, and *Telecommunications Alert*. See Business Database.

See also Telecomputing and Telephone industry.

Telecommuting issues are covered in the Working From Home Forum (GO WORK). See Working From Home Forum. For a European spin, visit the European Community Telework Forum (GO ECTF). See European Community.

Telecommuting Review: The Gordon Report (magazine) is searchable through Computer Database Plus (GO COMPDB). See Computer Database Plus.

Telecomputing, or communicating via computers through services like CompuServe, private bulletin board services, and local area networks, is discussed in many services on the system. To see an overview online, select the Connectivity Services option from the Communications menu, GO COMMUNICATE.

The telecomputing services are:

- *Local Area Network forums*, including Ask3Com Online (GO THREECOM), Banyan Systems Inc. (GO BANFORUM), Hayes Forum (GO HAYES), IBM Communications Forum (GO IBMCOM), MAC Communications Forum

(GO MACCOMM), Microsoft Networks Forum (GO MSNETWORKS), and Novell Netwire (GO NOVELL).

- *Modem Communications forums*, including Crosstalk Forum (GO XTALK), Datastorm Forum (GO DATASTORM), Hayes Forum (GO HAYES), Practical Peripherals Forum (GO PPIFORUM), TAPCIS Forum (GO TAPCIS), The Microphone II section of Macintosh Vendor B Forum (GO MACBVEN), the Microsoft Works section of the Microsoft Applications Forum (GO MSAPP), The Autosig section of the IBM Communications Forum (GO IBMCOM), The MacTerminal section of the Macintosh Communications Forum (GO MACCOMM), and Modem-To-Modem Game Support (GO CHALLENGE)

- *The Telecommunications Forum* (GO TELECO) which discusses regulatory affairs and communications services offered by large public carriers and their networks. Regular topics include cellular, FAX, ISDN, and PBX technology, as well as tariffs, FCC rulings and international standards. See Telecommunications.

See also Unix and Telecommunications.

Teleconnect (**magazine**) is searchable through Computer Database Plus (GO COMPDB). See Computer Database Plus.

Telefirm Directory of French Companies (**database**) can be searched through IQuest. See IQuest.

Telegraph, Daily and Sunday (**newspaper**) is covered in the UK Newspaper Library (GO UKPAPERS). See UK Newspaper.

Telenet (Sprintnet) logon instructions are accessible by entering GO LOG-20. See Sprintnet.

Telephone, Access numbers (GO PHONE) provides numbers for hundreds of locations. The database lets you list all the numbers accessible from anywhere in the U.S. and Canada by a specific baud rate, or locate a number in a specific city or area code. See Phone, CompuServe Access.

Telephone Directories of several kinds are supported through CompuServe's powerful searching capabilities. See Phone Directories.

Telephone and telecommunications industry are covered in various IQuest databases, including Common Carrier Week, Communications Daily, Communications Week, Edge On and About AT&T, Information Networks, Japan Telecommunications Scan, Mobile Phone News, State Telephone Regulation Report, Tele-Service News, Telecommunications Reports, Telephone Engineer and Management, Telephone News, and Telephone Week. See IQuest.

Also, through Business Database Plus (GO BUSDB), several related magazines can be searched, including *Advanced Wireless Communications, Electronic Services Up-*

date, *Independent Telco News*, *RBOC Update*, *Telephone IP News*, *Telephone News*, *Telephone Week*, and *Telephony*. See Business Database. *Telephony* also is searchable through Computer Database Plus (GO COMPDB). See Computer Database Plus.

Telephone technology is a topic of the Consumer Electronics Forum (GO CEFORUM). See Electronics Forum, Consumer.

Teleport modems and others from Global Village Communications are supported in the Modem Vendor Forum (GO MODEMVEN). See Modem Vendor.

Telescopes and star-gazing are discussed in the Astronomy Forum (GO ASTROFORUM). For details, see Astronomy.

Television and broadcasting are covered in the Broadcasters and Engineers Forum (GO BPFORUM). See Broadcasters and Broadcast Engineers. TV news also is discussed in the Journalism Forum (GO JFORUM). See Journalism and for other related features, see News, General.

Subscribers also might be interested in the ShowBiz Forum (GO SHOWBIZ), designed for discussions of films or television programs, record albums, celebrity gossip, and nightly news shows. See Show Biz.

And what is being touted as the world's first computerized television guide is available in the Consumer Electronics Forum (GO CEFORUM). PEG (the Personal Entertainment Guide) is a database of more than 12,000 downloadable program and movie listings and can store up to two weeks of listings. Files are available for such U.S. cities as Atlanta, Boston, Chicago, Dallas, Washington D.C., Denver, Houston, Los Angeles, Miami, New York, Philadelphia, and San Francisco. Users may create their own personal TV schedule by searching the listings by date and time and by subject matter. For details, see Section and Library 16, "P.E.G.-T.V. Listings."

British TV is discussed in the UK Forum (GO UKFORUM). See UK Forum.

Prime time TV schedules from 1948 to the present are recorded in the Entertainment Encyclopedia, which is part of the Hollywood Hotline (GO HOLLYWOOD). See Hollywood Hotline.

Also, the IQuest gateway offers a number of related databases, including Academic Index, Broadcasting, HDTV Report, Linguistics & Language Behavior Abstracts, Magazine ASAP, Magazine Index, Public Broadcasting Report, The Spectrum Report, Television Digest, and Video Week. See IQuest. *Television Digest* also can be searched through the Business Database Plus (GO BUSDB), as can *Cable Television Business* and *HDTV Report*. See Business Database.

See also Satellite.

Telex: Electronic mail may be sent from CompuServe to users of Telex machines. For details, see Mail, CompuServe.

Telelocator Bulletin (**database on wireless communications**) can be searched through IQuest. See IQuest.

Template Collections, Designer (GO ZNT:FORMS) are intended for use with popular word-processing and spreadsheet programs. See ZiffNet.

Temple, R. A. is the sysop in the IBM Desktop Software Forum (GO IBMDESK). See IBM Computers.

Templin, Ben (72511,35) is manager of Ziff-Davis' ZiffNet/Mac services for Apple Macintosh users. See ZiffNet/Mac and see ZiffNet.

Temporal Acuity products are supported in the MIDI B Vendor Forum (GO MIDIBVEN). See Music.

Tempra graphics, painting, and desktop publishing software is supported in the Graphics A Vendor Forum (GO TEMPRA). See Graphics.

Tennessee news is included in the daily Southeast regional reports from United Press International. See Executive News Service for details.

Also, the *Memphis Business Journal* and *Nashville Business and Lifestyle* can be searched through the Business Database Plus (GO BUSDB). See Business Database.

Tennis is a topic of the Sports Forum (GO FANS). See Sports and Recreation.

TENpointO products are supported in the Mac A Vendor Forum (GO MACAVEN). See Apple Computers.

Terminal Settings or *defaults* are controlled in the Terminal Type area (GO TERMINAL). You need not visit this area if you are using the CompuServe Information Manager, since that software regulates all your terminal settings automatically. But if you are using a third-party program to communicate with CompuServe, you may need to visit Terminal Settings to coordinate your program with the system. Consult your software users manual. Some 25 options are controlled in this part of the system, including those listed below:

Display options

- **Blank Lines Sent** can be YES (the normal mode) or NO. Note: Not sending blank lines can save space but may make output more difficult to read.
- **Brief Prompts** can be YES for expert mode (you receive abbreviated prompts such as ! or More!) or NO for novice/intermediate mode (you receive full prompts such as Enter choice! or Enter <CR> for more!).
- **Clear Screen Between Pages** can be either YES or NO. The latter suppresses screen clear and use of cursor positioning.
- **Line Feeds Sent** with which the normal setting is YES: Choose NO *only* if your terminal or software always adds a line feed to a carriage return. Not sending line feeds may result in text writing over itself.
- **Paged Display** can be set to YES (output is presented in pages; you are asked to enter <CR> after each page) or NO (output is scrolled continuously to the end of the article).

Logon/service options

- **CompuServe Mail Waiting** can be set to Go to CompuServe Mail (takes you to Mail when you have messages waiting) or to notify only (notifies you that you have messages waiting, then takes you to your first service).

- **First Service** can be set to either MAIN menu (Normal setting), a designated first service (you specify which one), a personal MENU (a menu you have constructed) or to COMMAND mode in the personal file area (PER).

- **Forum Presentation Mode** determines the type of presentation you normally receive in each forum you visit. You may change this for a specific forum via the forum options. The settings are MENU mode (novice/intermediate), COMMAND mode (expert), or DEFAULT (no preference).

- **Online Editor Preference** determines the word editor you will normally use. You may change this for a specific forum via the forum options or for CompuServe Mail via the Mail options. The possible settings here are EDIT (which doesn't use line numbers), LINEDIT (uses line numbers), or DEFAULT (no preference). See Writing.

- **Personal Menu Established** can be set to YES (which you select to *create* or *change* your personal menu) or NO (when you haven't created a personal menu or to delete an existing personal menu). See Personal Menu.

- **TOP Goes To** can be set to MAIN menu, a designated top page, a Personal MENU you have constructed, or COMMAND mode in the personal file area.

SET command for temporary settings

The system supports a powerful SET command that lets you make quick adjustments to your screen display without having to go into the Terminal Settings area. At nearly any prompt on the system, you may enter SET and the system prompts you with "SET sub-command:" The changes are in effect *during that session only*. After you log off and back on again, all defaults automatically are reset to the values saved in the Terminal Settings area.

Several options may be temporarily adjusted with the SET command, including the following:

- **BRIef** turns on and off brief mode. New subscribers automatically receive full menus (or "verbose" prompts) at all features. However, at any ! prompt, you may enter SET BRI ON to turn off the menu for the current session. SET BRI OFF turns the menu back on.

- **LINe** changes the number of lines the system thinks your screen can accommodate. You can use the SET command to quickly change that. With SET LIN you can enter a number between zero and 63. Entering SET LIN 16 at a ! prompt would tell the system you want pages of no more than 16 lines at a time.

- **PAGe** turns on or off paging. If you decide that you temporarily *don't* want your text interrupted by the messages like "Press <CR> for more !" you can enter SET PAG OFF. That means for the current session, the system would avoid paging, no matter how your defaults were set in the TERMINAL/OP-TIONS area. To turn paging back on—you got it, SET PAG ON.

- **WIDth** adjusts the screen width default to a number between 16 and 255 characters.

Also controlled by SET are BLANK (YES/NO) to send blank lines, CAPS (YES/NO) to send characters in CAPS, DELAY (0-255) to output delay, ERASE (YES/NO) to set erase when backspacing, FEEDS (YES/NO) to set automatic line feeds, FORM (REAL/SIM) to set form feeds—real or simulated, PARITY (EVEN/ODD/ONE/ZERO) to change the parity setting, and TABS (REAL/SIM) to set horizontal tabs—real or simulated.

Terminal type/parameters

- **Characters Sent in CAPS** can be NO—the normal mode (meaning that whatever you input is in the case you send it) or YES (whatever you input is always in CAPS regardless of how you send it).
- **Characters Received (CAPS)** can be set to U/L—the normal mode (the output to you is in upper- or lowercase depending on how it is sent by CompuServe), UPPER only (you receive only uppercase output), or LOWER only (you receive only lowercase output.)
- **Erase when backspacing** can be set to YES, the normal setting (when a backspace is received, CompuServe sends a space and another backspace which has the effect of erasing the last character typed) or NO (with which no special processing when a backspace is received).
- **Form Feeds** can be either REAL (uses your terminal software to do new page form feeds) or SIMULATED (prints out 8 blank lines between pages).
- **Horizontal Tabs** can be either REAL (uses your terminal software to move to tab stops across the page) or SIMULATED (uses spaces to simulate tabs).
- **Lines Per Page** determines the number of lines per screen for your system.
- **Output Delays** normally is set to 1, but can be increased if your printer operates at a slower speed than your modem and characters are lost at the beginning of each line. (Delays aren't recognized, however, if you are accessing through a supplemental network such as Tymnet, Datapak, etc.)
- **Parity** can be either EVEN, ODD, or ZERO.
- **Screen Width** determines the number of characters per line on your screen.
- **Send Micro Inquiry Sequence at Logon** should be set to YES if your software is *The Professional Connection* or another of CompuServe's own communications programs.
- **Terminal Type** can be either VIDTEX (Professional Connection and related CompuServe software products), ANSI, VT100, VT52, Heath (Zenith), ADM, CRT, or other.

Transfer protocols/graphics support

- **File Transfer Protocol Preference** can be set to record a preferred transfer protocol—B Protocol, Quick B protocol, Xmodem, Ymodem, Kermit—or set to SHOW MENU (which causes the system to present a menu of available protocols when you request a file transfer).
- **GIF Support** should be set to YES only if your communication software supports CompuServe's Graphic Interchange Facility.
- **NAPLPS Support** should be YES if your terminal software supports NAPLPS, the North American Presentation Level Protocol Syntax.
- **RLE Support** should be YES if your terminal software supports RLE, that is, Run-Length Encoded graphics.

Terrapin Inc. products are supported in the LOGO Forum (GO LOGOFORUM). See Programmers Support.

Terrorism and **political unrest** are topics of the U.S. Department of State's Travel Advisory Service (GO STATE), maintained by the Citizen Emergency Center as a continuously updated information service to Americans traveling abroad. See U.S. Government Information.

Terry Shannon on DEC (database) analyzes the latest technology and market strategies of Digital Equipment Corp. and IBM; it can be searched through IQuest. See IQuest.

Tesserae (software) is supported in Mac C Vendor Forum (GO MACCVEN). For details, see Apple Computers.

Testing Technology can be searched through the Business Database Plus (GO BUSDB). See Business Database.

Texas news is covered in the Houston Post, searchable through Telebase System's News Source USA (GO NEWSUSA). See News Source.

Also:

- Selected reports from Texas are included in the Southwest regional reports from United Press International. See Executive News Service.
- Searchable through the Business Database Plus (GO BUSDB) are *Austin Business Journal, Dallas Business Journal, Dallas-Fort Worth Business Journal, Houston Business Journal, San Antonio Business Journal, Texas Business Review*, and *Texas Industry Environmental Alert*. See Business Database.
- *Texas Monthly* can be searched in the Magazine Database Plus (GO MDP). See Magazine Database.

Texas Instrument computers are covered in the Texas Instruments Forum (GO TIFORUM), including the 99/4A, the TI Professional, CC-40, TI Semiconductors, and so on.

At the helm are forum coordinators Jim Horn (76703,603) who has been sysop since the creation of the forum in 1983, and Jonathan Zittrain (76703,3022), who is the editor of *TINEWS* and a regular columnist in computer publications. Assisting are Steve Davis, Mack McCormick (European sysop), Barry Traver, Paul Charlton, Thor M. Firing, Tom Kennedy, and Warren Agee.

Also in the forum is the Expert Member Board, on which participants write newsletter articles and lend a helping hand to forum visitors. At this writing, the EMB roster includes Matt Beebe, Jerry Coffey, Marty Kroll Jr., Steve Baute, Wayne Stith, Walt Howe, and Jim Reiss.

Textile Technology Digest and **World Textiles Abstracts** (databases) may be searched through the IQuest gateway. See IQuest. *High Performance Textiles* can be searched through the Business Database Plus (GO BUSDB), as can *Medical Textiles*. See Business Database.

Textline Global News (database) can be searched through IQuest. See IQuest.

.THD or **.THR,** as extensions on filenames in forum libraries, often stand for "thread," that is, transcripts of important discussions from a forum's message board. See Files, Extensions.

Theatre is a subject in the ShowBiz Forum (GO SHOWBIZ). For related topics, see Entertainment. Also, the IQuest gateway allows access to the Academic Index, Backstage, Linguistics & Language Behavior Abstracts, Magazine ASAP, and Magazine Index. See IQuest.

T H E Journal (Technological Horizons in Education) (magazine) is searchable through Computer Database Plus (GO COMPDB). See Computer Database Plus.

Theoretical Computer Science (magazine) is searchable (abstracts) through Computer Database Plus (GO COMPDB). See Computer Database Plus.

ThinkTank, THINK C, and **THINK Pascal** (software) are supported in the Symantec Forum (Go SYMANTEC). See Symantec Software.

Thinx (software) is supported in Windows 3rd-Party C Forum (GO WINAPC). See Microsoft Software.

Thomas Companies and Products Online (GO THOMAS) offers searching of two database: Thomas New Industrial Products and Thomas Register Online, a financial service that has data about almost 150,000 U.S. and Canadian manufacturers and service providers. See Company Reports. Both resources also can be searched through the IQuest gateway. See IQuest.

Thomas-Conrad Corp. Support Forum (GO TCCFORUM) provides support for local area network users wanting technical support, the latest adapter drivers, adapter and network diagnostics software, or to inquire about Thomas-Conrad product availability and information. Topic and file library areas include ARCNET, Ethernet, Sectra, Token Ring, TCNS, TXD, and more. The lead sysop is John McCoy (75300,3634), assisted by Kurt Hey and Chris Albright.

Thomson's International Banking Regulator can be searched through the Business Database Plus (GO BUSDB). See Business Database.

Thoughtprocessors products are supported in the MIDI C Vendor Forum (GO MIDICVEN). See Music.

3Com Software: The Ask3Com Information Service (Go THREECOM) is operated by 3Com Corporation, a major supplier of computer networking software. Operated by the company's customer support organization, the forum provides user-to-user communications and idea exchange.

Sysop is Darryl Perry. Also participating in the forum are Mike Kouri, Tony George, Michael Shorts, Ray Quinto, and Bob Driver. All are volunteers from 3Com Technical Support. These and other 3Com employees can be recognized by User IDs beginning with 44124, 44133, and 44134 (as in 44124,13).

3D (magazine) is searchable through Computer Database Plus (GO COMPDB). See Computer Database Plus.

3-D Helicopter (software) by Sierra Online is supported in the National Modem-to-Modem Game Players' Challenge Board (GO CHALLENGE). See Modem-to-Modem Games.

3-D Visions products are supported in the Windows 3rd-Party Forum A (GO WINAPA). See Microsoft Software.

Three-Sixty Pacific (software) is supported in the Game Publishers A Forum (GO GAMAPUB). See Gaming Forums.

Thrift Accountant (newsletter on thrift institutions) can be searched through IQuest. See IQuest.

Thrift Liquidation Alert and **Thrift Regulator** can be searched through the Business Database Plus (GO BUSDB). See Business Database.

Ticker lookup: is for finding stock symbols for other financial services,. See Issue and Symbol Lookup (GO SYMBOLS). See Stock Symbols, Lookup.

Tickerscreen, Max Ule's (GO TKR-1) is an online stock brokerage service. See Stock Brokerages.

TidBITS Magazine products are supported in the Mac D Vendor Forum (GO MACDVEN). See Apple Computers.

Time Arts products are supported in the Ultimedia Tools Forum B (GO ULTIBTOOLS). See Ultimedia.

Time International (news database) can be searched through IQuest. See IQuest.

Time Line (software) is supported in the Symantec Forum (Go SYMANTEC). See Symantec Software.

Time Magazine (from 1985 to the present) can be searched through IQuest. Also searchable is the Time Publications database, with full text of Time Inc. publications, including *Entertainment Weekly*, *Fortune*, *Life*, *Money*, *People Weekly*, *Sports Illustrated*, and others. See IQuest. The publication also can be searched through News Source USA (GO NEWSUSA). See News Source.

Timeslips products are supported in the IBM PC Vendor D Forum (GO PCVEND). See IBM Computers.

Time Warner's Author of the Week Forum (GO TWEP) features weekly visits with authors published by Time Warner Trade Publishing, the home of Little, Brown and Company, and of Warner Books, Inc. You can send messages to those authors, discuss their works, and from time to time meet them in one of the forum's real-time conference rooms. The forum's libraries include files with pictures, autographs, information, and related programs for downloading. Administering the forum is Jennifer Rogers (72662,671), assisted by Thorne Sparkman and Andy Lerner.

Timeworks products are supported in the Desktop Publishing Vendor Forum (GO DTPVENDOR). For details, see Desktop Publishing.

Timex/Sinclair computers is one of the computer systems supported in CompuServe's Computer Club Forum (GO CLUB). See Computer Club.

TI Professional (computer) is supported in Texas Instruments Forum (GO TIFORUM). See Texas Instrument Computers.

Tire industry is covered in *Modern Tire Dealer* magazine, which can be searched through the Business Database Plus (GO BUSDB). See Business Database.

TK Solver Plus is supported in the CADD/CAM/CAE Vendor Forum (GO CADDVEN). See CAD/CAM.

T/MAKER (software) is supported in the Mac B Vendor Forum (GO MACBVEN). See Apple Computers.

TMS Peripherals products are supported in the Apple II Vendor Forum (GO APIIVEN) and in the Macintosh C Vendor Forum (GO MACCVEN). See Apple Computers.

Today (newspaper) is covered in the UK Newspaper Library (GO UKPAPERS). See UK Newspaper.

Today's Living is searchable in the Health Database Plus (GO HLTBD). See Health.

Today's Office (magazine) is searchable (abstracts) through Computer Database Plus (GO COMPDB). See Computer Database Plus.

Tokyo Financial Wire (database) may be searched through the IQuest gateway. See IQuest.

Tony theater award winners from 1947 to the present are listed in the Entertainment Encyclopedia, which is part of the Hollywood Hotline (GO HOLLYWOOD). See Hollywood Hotline.

Tooling & Production (magazine) can be searched through the Business Database Plus (GO BUSDB). See Business Database.

TOPs (Apple software) is supported in the Mac A Vendor Forum (GO MACAVEN). See Apple Computers.

Tops (Sun software) is supported in the SunSelect Forum (GO SUNSELECT). See SunSelect.

TopSpeed Compilers (C, C++, Modula 2, and Pascal software) are supported in the Clarion Software Forum (GO CLARION). See Clarion.

Toshiba Forum (GO TOSHIBA) supports a variety of equipment from that manufacturer. The forum, administered by the Computer System Division of Toshiba America, began as a message section and library in one of the IBM Vendor Support forums. Among the five libraries is "Demo Files" (library 3). This unique area contains actual demonstrations used by Toshiba sales representatives at trade shows, such as Comdex. The forum sysop is Jim Rohrer (76702,1300), assisted by Valerie Luckett, James Doody, James Doody, Kurt Gebauer, and Don Singleton.

Toshiba GmbH Forum (GO TOSHGER) is a German language forum that provides technical support for users of Toshiba computers and peripherals. Messages are exchanged with the technical staff at Toshiba's German headquarters in Neuss, Duesseldorf. The libraries contain drivers, upgrades, and utilities, and the message boards list important notes for Toshiba's German-speaking customer base.

Toshiba Weekly can be searched through the Business Database Plus (GO BUSDB). See Business Database.

Total Health is searchable in the Health Database Plus (GO HLTBD). See Health.

TouchVision Systems products are supported in the Ultimedia Tools Forum B (GO ULTIBTOOLS). See Ultimedia.

Tour & Travel News (database) can be searched through IQuest. See IQuest. See also Travel.

Tourette's Syndrome and other "neurobehavioral disorders" are discussed in the Attention Deficit Disorder Forum (GO ADD). See Attention Deficit.

Tower (software) is supported in the Game Publishers B Forum (GO GAMPUB). See Gaming forums.

Town & Country Monthly (magazine) can be searched in the Magazine Database Plus (GO MDP). See Magazine Database.

Townsley, Steve (70007,4725) is sysop of the UK Shareware Forum (GO UKSHARE). See UK Shareware.

Toxicology is covered in *Journal of Toxicology: Clinical Toxicology*, which is searchable in the Health Database Plus (GO HLTBD). Also, *Archives of Toxicology* abstracts are searchable in the the same resource. See Health.

Toxic Materials News, TOXLINE and **Toxic Materials Transport** (databases) may be searched through the IQuest gateway. See IQuest. *Toxic Materials News* also can be searched through the Business Database Plus (GO BUSDB). See Business Database.

See also Hazardous Materials and Waste Management.

Toys and hobbies are the specialty of some stores in the Electronic Mall (GO MALL), including Concord Direct (GO CA), Garrett Wade Co. (GO GW), Hammacher Schlemmer (GO HS), Heath Co. (GO HTH), and Laser's Edge (GO LE). See Electronic Mall for more information.

TPT-Networking Management Magazine (magazine) is searchable through Computer Database Plus (GO COMPDB). See Computer Database Plus.

Tracy, Les (76703,1061) is sysop of the ROCKNET Forum (GO ROCKNET). See Music.

Trade and Industry ASAP III, Trading Systems Technology, and **Trade, Washington Trade Daily and Industry Index** (databases) may be searched through the IQuest gateway. See IQuest. See also Free Trade. Also Trade and Industry Index can be searched through the Knowledge Index (GO KI). See Knowledge Index.

Trade Commission, Federal is covered in several IQuest databases (GO IQUEST), including FTC FOIA Log and FTC: Watch. See IQuest. Trade also is discussed in the White House Forum (GO WHITEHOUSE). See White House.

Trade, **Global** (magazine) can be searched through the Business Database Plus (GO BUSDB), as can *Free Trade Advisory* and *US ITC Update*. See Business Database.

Trademarks can be researched through Trademarkscan, a service that provides two major databases of information on national and international trademarks, including all textual-numeric (nongraphic) federal trademarks active in the United States. Databases accessible are:

- Trademarkscan—U.S. Federal contains more than a million records representing all active trademark registrations and pending applications filed with the United States Patent and Trademark Office as well as inactive registrations and applications from 1984 forward. The database is updated twice weekly to add new applications and make status changes to existing records.

- Trademarkscan—U.S. State includes trademark registration information obtained from the Secretary of States' offices in all 50 U.S. states and Puerto Rico. Tradenames, assumed names, and fictitious names are generally not included, but may be identified for some states. Corporate name records are not covered.

Telebase Systems Inc., which provides the gateway, suggests that a search for a specific trademark in the U.S. State database may obtain more than one record, since the mark may be registered in many states. Therefore, a search in the State database should complement one in the U.S. Federal file, which should be searched previous to the State file.

Note: If a trademark is not found in the databases, you should not assume it is available for use. Telebase notes online, "In the U.S. it is not mandatory to register a trademark; there are many unregistered (common law) trademarks rightfully in use. Neither of the Trademarkscan databases include common law trademarks. Trademarkscan should be used as a preliminary screening method for a new product or service name to avoid conflicts or confusion with a trademark that is already registered. Further searching by a professional searcher, including searches of common law marks, is always recommended before a trademark is adopted.

The surcharge is $5 for the first 10 titles located, $5 for each additional 10 titles, and $5 for each full-text article retrieved. There is a $1 for each search that retrieves no titles.

Many of the documents also are searchable through IQuest. In addition, search of the research centers is similar to IQuest's procedure. (See IQuest.) For information on other Telebase gateways, see Telebase Systems Incorporated.

And for British trademark information, see UK Trademark Library (GO UKTRADE), which contains registration information. See UK Trademark.

See also Patent Research.

Trading is a favorite pastime in many forums. See Bartering.

Trading Systems Technology can be searched through the Business Database Plus (GO BUSDB). See Business Database.

Traffic Management (magazine) can be searched through the Business Database Plus (GO BUSDB). See Business Database.

Trailers are a topic of the Recreational Vehicle Forum (GO RVFORUM). See Recreational Vehicle.

Training, Computer Forum (GO DPTRAIN) is sponsored by the Association for Computer Training & Support and the Masie Institute for Technology & Training Inc. For details, see Computer Training.

Training & Development Journal and **Training: The Magazine of Human Resources Development** (magazines) can be searched through the Business Database Plus (GO BUSDB). See Business Database.

TrainNet Forum (GO TRAINNET) is for model railroaders and railroad fans, once a section of ModelNet (GO MODELNET). Subjects include such diverse things as operating a scale model railroad, layout construction, tinplate trains, and railroad motive power rosters. Dorr Altizer (76702,402) is the sysop. Assistants are Corbett Price, Bernd Fanghanel, Dick Knisely, Dean Davis, Robert Pinksy, Mike Bettiol, Ray Peeler, Jerry Hoare, and Tom Pinkerton.

See also Railroad.

Transactor products are supported in the Amiga Vendor Forum (GO AMIGAVENDOR). See Commodore Computers.

Transin (products database) may be searched through the IQuest gateway. See IQuest.

Transportation is the subject of a number of IQuest databases (GO IQUEST), including Air Safety Week Accident/Incident Log, Air Safety Week Newsletter, Air Safety Week Regulatory Log, Airline Financial News, Battery & EV Technology, Business Travel News, Comline Japan Daily: Transportation, Commuter/Regional Airline News, Commuter/Regional Airline News International, Flightline, Global Mobility Database, Hazardous Materials Transportation, Japan Transportation Scan, Lloyd's List, PTS Newsletter Database, Tour & Travel News, and Transportation Research Information Service. See IQuest.

Also, *Inside DOT & Transportation Week*, *Urban Transport News*, and *Japan Transportation Scan* can be searched through the Business Database Plus (GO BUSDB). See Business Database.

And transportation safety is discussed in the Safetynet Forum (GO SAFETY). See Safety. The topic also is discussed in the White House Forum (GO WHITEHOUSE). See White House.

Transporter (software) is supported in the Crosstalk Forum (GO XTALK). See Crosstalk (software).

Transport Europe can be searched through the Business Database Plus (GO BUSDB). See Business Database.

Trantor products are supported in the CD-ROM Vendors Forum (GO CDVEN). See CD-ROM.

Travel   (GO TRAVEL) is covered in an assortment of online features, allowing you to plot your business and pleasure trips. Often you can use these services to reserve airline seats, hotel rooms, even rental cars. Major travel-oriented features include the following:

- ABC Worldwide Hotel Guide (GO ABC) provides descriptions, rates, phone numbers, and facilities for 34,000 domestic and international hotels. See Hotel Information.

- Adventures in Travel (GO AIT) is a single travel article that runs for two weeks. Earlier articles also may be reviewed. See Adventures in Travel.

- Air France (GO AF) offers tour booking and information on sights and scenery, and the Travel Club + TWA Service are kiosks in the Electronic Mall (GO MALL). See Electronic Mall.

- Bed & Breakfast Database (GO INNS) from Lanier Publishing provides access to data on more than 9,000 inns in the United States and Canada.

- The Disabled Traveler's Friendship Network, a nonprofit group providing travel information to physically challenged individuals and families, is represented in Florida Forum (GO FLORIDA). See Florida.

- Eaasy Sabre (GO SABRE) is a flight reservation service by American Airlines. See Eaasy Sabre.

- Official Airline Guides/Electronic Edition (GO OAG) is the oldest airline information service of its kind and still is praised by many as the most extensive air schedule database around. See Official Airline Guides.

- Outdoors Network (GO OUTNET) features resources for planning camping trips. See Outdoors.

- Rosenbluth Vacations (GO CRUISE) is a store in the Electronic Mall (GO MALL) that provides hundreds of cruise vacations and packages from Carnival, Premier Cruise Line, Princess Cruises, Royal Caribbean Cruises, and others.

- Travel Britain Online (GO TBOL) is a database that contains information about festivals, concerts, theatre, and sporting events. This is one of the system's basic services, meaning those signed up under the Standard Pricing Plan (see Billing) have unlimited access to the feature. See UK Travel.

- Travelshopper (GO PARS) features a discount fare finder, has information for the frequent flight bonus programs, and offers national and international scheduling. See Travelshopper.

- The U.S. Department of State's Travel Advisory Service (GO STATE) is maintained by the Citizen Emergency Center as a continuously updated information service to Americans traveling abroad. See U.S. Government Information.

- The Visa Advisors and Electronic Visaguide (GO VISA) is a Washington, D.C., passport and visa expediting firm that provides applications and information on travel requirements for more than 200 countries. See Visa Advisor.

- West Coast Travel (GO WESTCOAST) is a consumer guide to travel destinations in the western half of the United States as well as Canada and Mexico. See West Coast Travel.
- Several additional forums are also available, including the Aviation Forum (GO AVSIG), the California Forum (GO CALIFORNIA), the Florida Forum (GO FLORIDA), Florida Today NewsLink Forum (GO FLATODAY), the New York Newslink Forum (GO NEWYORK), Photography Forum (GO PHOTOFORUM), the Recreational Vehicle Forum (GO RVFORUM), the Travel Forum (GO TRAVSIG), the UK Forum (GO UKFORUM), and Worldwide Car Network Forum (GO WWCAR).

In addition, a category in the CompuServe Classifieds lets you read and post ads regarding travel topics. See Classifieds Service.

Business travel and vacations are discussed in Information USA; see Information.

And among the databases of IQuest are International Travel Warning Service, Tour and Travel News, and Business Travel News. See IQuest.

Travel Forum (GO TRAVSIG) is offered by Jerry Schneiderman (76702,667). Assisting him are James Vancouver (Sufi) and Sandy Elson and Makiko Itoh (Maki). Section leaders include Lan Sluder (Caribbean), Harry O'Neill (Oceania), Mireille (Mimi) Petit (Europe), Mike Endres (Hawaii), Dennis Larson and Max Wyss (rail travel), and Marla Baer-Peckham (the travel business). The forum is devoted to all travel questions. For other travel-related features, see Travel.

Travel-Holiday (**magazine**) can be searched in the Magazine Database Plus (GO MDP). See Magazine Database.

Traveling Software is supported in the Palmtop Forum (GO PALMTOP). See Palmtop.

Travelshopper (GO PARS) is a service provided by Worldspan Travel Agency Information Services. This is one of the system's basic services, meaning those signed up under the Standard Pricing Plan (see Billing) have unlimited access to the feature.

Flight availability and fares are updated on an "as needed" basis through a complex communications link operated by the airline industry. Using the service is simple. By providing your destination cities and date of travel, you can have Travelshopper display virtually every airline's available flights starting with the "best" flights for the time you requested. This means you don't have to scroll through screens of flights that don't meet your needs.

The service's fare display provides more than 3 million domestic and international fares that can be updated on a daily basis. You can look at a display of all fares or one airline's fares in a specific market. After determining which fare is applicable to your personal itinerary, you can check the travel restrictions to be sure you fit within that fare's rule.

Travelshopper also offers information on the frequent flier bonus programs, national and international scheduling, provides a currency conversion service, weather information for cities around the world, and offers information on theaters shows, ski areas, and so on.

All CompuServe members are authorized to browse Travelshopper's lists of flight schedules. Later, if you decide to enroll as a member, you also can book flight reservations through the system. When enrolling, you are asked to fill out an online application, including name, address, telephone number, and credit card information (which is to be used only to check your credit.)

When navigating the system, a main menu lets you browse lists of available flights, find out about fares and fare restrictions, enter "book" mode to book flights, enroll as a member in order to make online reservations, learn about the low-fare finder services, look for a rental car and hotel availability, and more.

Note: CompuServe also has introduced a Travelshopper interface for its CompuServe Information Manager software to simplify much of the features. Enter GO WORLDCIM to use the CIM interface to Travelshopper. See CompuServe Information Manager for related information.

See also Airlines and Travel.

Travel Weekly (**magazine**) can be searched through the Business Database Plus (GO BUSDB). See Business Database.

TreeView (**software**) is supported in the UK Shareware Forum (GO UKSHARE). See UK Shareware.

Trendline Information and Communication Services Ltd. offers CompuServe connections from Israel. For details, see Israel, CompuServe.

Trend Micro Devices Inc. is represented in the McAfee Virus Help Forum (GO VIRUSFORUM). See McAfee.

Trendvest Ratings (**investment database**) may be searched through the IQuest gateway. See IQuest.

TriCord products are supported in the Novell Vendors Forum A (GO NVENA). See Novell.

TRIUS products are supported in the IBM PC Vendor F Forum (GO PCVENF). See IBM Computers.

Trivia games (and parlor games) are offered in CompuServe's game section (GO GAMES). Specific games include:

- Astrology Calculator (GO ASTROLOGY)
- Biorhythms (GO BIORHYTHM)
- Grolier Whiz Quiz (GO WHIZ)
- Hangman (GO HANGMAN)
- The Multiple Choice (GO MULTIPLE)

- Science Trivia (GO SCITRIVIA)
- ShowBiz Quiz (GO SBQ)
- The Two-Stage Trivia Game (GO STAGEII)
- You Guessed It (GO YGI)

See Games and entries under specific the game's name.

TRS-80 computers: CompuServe has several forums supporting Tandy Corp. equipment (GO TANDYNET). See Tandy Corp. computers.

Truevision   products are supported in the Multimedia Vendor Forum (GO MULTIVEN). See Multimedia.

TRW Business Credit Profiles (GO TRWREPORT) is a financial service that includes credit and business information on more than 13 million organizations. See Company Reports. This resource also is searchable through IQuest. See IQuest.

TRW Credentials (GO CRE) is a kiosk in the Electronic Mall for managing your credit records. See Electronic Mall.

TSCA Chemical Substances Inventory (database) may be searched through the IQuest gateway. See IQuest.

Tseng Labs   (compter graphics products) is supported in the Graphics B Vendor Forum (GO TSENG). See Graphics.

Tune in Tonight   (column) is among the syndicated columns provided by United Features (GO COLUMNS). See Columnists.

Turbo C, Turbo Pascal, Turbo Lightning, and **Turbo Basic** (software) are supported in the Borland International Forums (GO BORLAND). See Borland Software. Also they are topics of the Cobb Group Programming Forum (ZNT:COBBPROG). See Cobb Group.

Turbopower Software products are supported in the PC Vendor B Forum (GO PCVENB). See IBM Computers.

TurboPower Software—C++ products are supported in the IBM PC Vendor E Forum (GO PCVENE). See IBM Computers.

TurboTax products are supported in the ChipSoft Forum (GO CHIPSOFT). See ChipSoft.

Turing Institute Bibliographic Database   (database) may be searched through the IQuest gateway. See IQuest.

Turner, Skip (71640,3306) is the sysop of the Rotarians Online Forum (GO ROTARY). See Rotarians.

Turtle Beach products are supported in the MIDI A Vendor Forum (GO MIDIAVEN), in the Multimedia Vendor Forum (GO MULTIVEN), and in the Ultimedia Tools Forum B (GO ULTIBTOOLS). See Music, Multimedia, and Ultimedia.

TV and broadcasting are covered in the Broadcasters and Engineers Forum (GO BPFORUM). See Broadcasters and Broadcast Engineers. TV also is discussed in the Journalism Forum (GO JFORUM). See Journalism and for other related features, see News, General.

TWA Services, Travel Club (GO TTC) is a store in the Electronic Mall (GO MALL) that offers travel plans. See Electronic Mall.

Twelve Tone products are supported in the MIDI A Vendor Forum (GO MIDIAVEN). See Music.

Twentieth Century Investors (GO TC) is a store in the Electronic Mall (GO MALL) that offers investment opportunities information. See Electronic Mall.

20/20 spreadsheet is supported in the CA—Simply Forum (GO CASIMPLY). See CAI Forums.

TXD is supported in the Thomas-Conrad Support Forum (GO TCCFORUM). See Thomas-Conrad.

.TXT, as an extension on filenames in forum libraries, means a text file, usually in ASCII. See Files, Extensions.

Tymnet logon instructions (GO LGN-211): To log on to CompuServe using the BT Tymnet system:

1. Dial the Tymnet network telephone access number, listen for the modem tone, and connect your communications equipment.
2. At the "PLEASE ENTER YOUR TERMINAL IDENTIFIER" prompt, enter A. Do *not* press the Enter or Return key afterward. (Note: The PLEASE ENTER YOUR TERMINAL IDENTIFIER prompt may appear to be garbled if you are not accessing at 300 baud. After you enter A, the next prompts will not appear garbled.)
3. At the "PLEASE LOG IN" prompt, enter CML05 and press Return.
4. When the network displays "Host Name:" enter CIS and press Return.
5. At the "User ID:" prompt, enter your User ID number; you will next be prompted for your password.

Costs Tymnet network surcharges (rates charged in addition to CompuServe's basic rates) are $1.70 an hour on evenings and weekends; $11.70 an hour daytime for contiguous U.S. The nonprime rate for Alaska and Hawaii is $11.70.

U

UFOs and extraterrestrials are among the topics discussed in the Space Forum (GO SPACEFORUM). For details, see Space. Also, UFOlogy is discussed in the New Age Forum (GO NEWAGE). See New Age.

UK Company Library (GO UKLIB) contains financial and business information on companies in the United Kingdom. InfoCheck UK Company Financial Datasheets provides financial details, news, and industry sector comparisons for more than 400,000 companies in the United Kingdom. See also British business reports and news.

UK Computer Shopper Forum (GO UKSHOPPER), operated by Dennis Publishing Ltd., provides discussion areas for topics such as hardware, software, new technology, and industry news and gossip. The forum also provides an extension to the latest news and reviews from U.K. Computer Shopper, as well as libraries containing interesting utility files. Forum members can communicate directly with other U.K. Computer Shopper readers and the editorial staff of the magazine. The sysops are Steve Baxter (70007,5571), Mark Jeavons (100111,3254), and Paul Mullen (75300,263).

UK Computing Forum (GO UKCOMP) is a feature for British subscribers, especially former subscribers of the "MicroLink" service. The forum is intended to help them make a transition to CompuServe. The sysops are Steve Manners (70007,4737) and Andy Johnson (75300,1504), with assistance from Terry Love, Paula Payne, and John Rawnsley.

   Also in the forum is support for products from UK computer manufacturers Western Systems, Creative Labs UK (distributor for Soundblaster, Videoblaster, and Portblaster), Amstrad Plc, Datasoft, NextBase/Automap, Psion Dacom, Finansa, Pace Micro Technologies, US Robotics (UK), and WigWam/TeePee.

   See also British business reports and news, PC Plus Online, and PC Magazine UK Editorial Forum.

UK Forum (UKFORUM) is a meeting place for those planning to travel to Britain. Sections include discussion of food and drink, pubs, politics, law and crime, hobbies, health and education, UK travel, sports, music, Brits in the U.S., and Americans in the UK. The primary sysops are Steve Manners (70007,4737) and Andy Johnson (75300,1504). Assisting are Terry Love, David Moore, John Rawnsley, Cliff Lawson, Paula Payne, and Lew Lewis.

UK Marketing Library (GO UKMARKETING) provides market research reports from top British analysts. Resources include ICC Key Note Market Research, Marketing Surveys Index, Mintel Research Reports, Mintel Special Reports, and MSI Market Research Reports. Surcharges for the Marketing Surveys Index are $5 for the first five title retrieved, $5 for each additional five titles, and $7.50 for each full-text article selected from the search lists. The charges for MSI Market Research Reports, ICC Key Note Market Research, Mintel Research Reports, and Mintel Special Reports are $4 for the first five titles retrieved, $4 for each additional five titles, and $11 for each full-text article selected from the search lists. There is a $1 charge for each search that retrieves no titles.

UK Newspaper Library (GO UKPAPERS) provides full text of articles from leading British newspapers. Available are reports on business, finance, people, and current affairs from the last 12 months. The service is charged at $5 for the first five titles retrieved, $5 for each additional five titles, and $7.50 for each full-text articled selected from the search lists. There is a $1 charge for each search that retrieves no titles.

Available papers include:

- The Daily and Sunday Telegraph are a source of strong coverage of British and international news, as well as business news and events, politics, and current affairs. It is updated daily. Court, society, arts, and sports sections are not included.

- The European, called Europe's first national newspaper, is updated weekly. It provides coverage of global and European events from a European perspective. It offers strong coverage of European political and business news. Also provides sports, "lifestyle," and cultural reporting.

- The Financial Times provides financial and corporate information on British and international companies with special coverage of topics, such as management, marketing, industrial relations, economics, politics, world trade, industry information, and technology. One of the world's most highly regarded business newspapers. Updated daily.

- The Guardian for information on social services, education, health, and local government, as well as international coverage that includes third-world economics, civil liberties, and human rights. Updated daily.

- The Independent, updated daily from the newest national newspapers, covers the UK and international news in addition to strong coverage of business, the arts, health, education, sports, and the media. An excellent source for news from the British parliament and current litigation. Specializes in providing in-depth features on major issues of the day.

- The Times & Sunday Times, Britain's oldest and best known newspapers, provide coverage of the UK and international news, business, finance, law, cultural affairs, travel, and sports. Also known for its strong editorial coverage. It does not include articles from the Sunday Times Magazine, news entertainment listings, or letters to the editor.

- Today, a tabloid, is updated daily and provides general news and social news. It offers strong coverage of sports, the arts and entertainment, the royal family, and stories from the U.S. media.

- UK News offers a collection of the most recent two years of the United Kingdom's premier newspapers, providing full-text coverage of topics, ranging from British politics and business to world affairs and the arts.

See also British business reports and news.

UK News/Sports (GO UKNWS) provides, by menu, access to specially created clip folders of the latest general news, sports, and weather from the United Kingdom.

UK Shareware Forum (GO UKSHARE) is operated by Shareware Publishing of Devon, England, a leading British shareware distributor. The forum offers technical support for the software distributed by Shareware Publishing, including As-Easy-AS, Draft Choice, 4DOS, Procomm Plus (UK Edition), TreeView, and others. The forum also reviews popular shareware programs and offers members the opportunity to meet the programs' authors.

The sysop is Steve Townsley (70007,4725), Jon Woodward, and Steve Lee, who is the owner of Shareware Publishing. Assisting are Nick Thompson, Adrian Mardlin, Tony Bryer, and Jerry Olsen.

See also Shareware.

UK stock quotes can be searched (GO UKPRICES). See Stock Quotes (Historical), UK for details.

UK trademarks can be researched in the British Trade Marks database (GO UKTRADE) which contains information on technical standards and registered, lapsed, and pending trademarks since 1976 that have been filed with the Patent Office of the United Kingdom's Trade Marks Registry. Records include trademark name and design description, owner name and address, the types of goods or services trademarked, international class numbers, and the date and status of the application. Graphical displays of marks are not available. The resource is updated weekly. The library is surcharged at $4 for the first 10 titles retrieved, $4 for each addition 10 titles, and $6 for each full-record selected from the search lists. There is a $1 charge for each search that retrieves no titles.

See also British business reports and news.

UK Travel is the topic of the Travel Britain Online (GO TBOL), a database that contains information about festivals, concerts, theatre, and sporting events. Those heading for London can search for London-only events, plus access a listing of some of London's best pubs. Travel Britain Tourist News, from the British Tourist Authority, also is useful for U.K. residents interested in country-wide event listings. See also Travel.

Ultimedia Software, particularly the Ultimedia Tools Series, is supported in a suite of forums administered by David Kamm (76711,1031). The forums offer a full range of authoring, content creation, and capture and editing facilities for video, audio, animation, graphics, and music. See also Multimedia. The forums are:

- Ultimedia Tools Forum A (GO ULTIATOOLS) supporting AimTech, Allen Communications, Asymetrix, Autodesk, Fractal Design, Humancad, Gold Disk, IBM Linkway Live, IBM Storyboard Live, IBM OS/2 MM Tools, and Ultimedia Tools Series.

- Ultimedia Tools Forum B (GO ULTIBTOOLS) supports Mammoth Micro Productions, Montage Group Ltd., Network Technology, Passport Designs, Time Arts, Turtle Beach, Wordstar International, DigiVox, TouchVision Systems, Vision Imaging, Voyetra, Videomedia, and Virtus Corp.

- Ultimedia Hardware Plus Forum (GO ULTIHW) supports products from MWave System, ActionMedia, and V-Lan.

Ultra modems and others are supported in the Online With Hayes Forum (GO HAYES). See Hayes.

UltraVision (software) is supported in the PC Vendor B Forum (GO PCVENB). See IBM Computers.

Ultrix-32 and Ultrix-32m, Digital Equipment Corp.'s version of the Unix operating system, are supported in the VAX Forum (GO VAXFORUM). For details, see Digital Equipment.

UNESCO Courier (magazine) articles are searchable through Magazine Database Plus (GO MDP). For details see Magazine Database.

Unicef, The United States Committee for (GO UC) has a kiosk in the Electronic Mall (GO MALL) in which you can buy UNICEF greeting cards, purchase products in an online catalog, or make a donation.

Unisys Corp. operates the CTOS/Open Forum (GO CTOS). See CTOS.

United Nations is discussed in the White House Forum (GO WHITEHOUSE). See White House.

United Press International (news wire) is searchable through the Executive News Service (GO ENS) and through the Knowledge Index (GO KI). See Executive News Service and see Knowledge Index.

United We Stand America (organization) is discussed in the Political Debate Forum (GO POLITICS). See Political debate.

Universal Technical Systems (software) is supported in the CADD/CAM/CAE Vendor Forum (GO CADDVEN). See CAD/CAM.

Universities: Peterson's College Database (GO PETERSON) contains descriptions of more than 3,400 accredited or approved U.S. and Canadian colleges that grant associate and/or bachelor's degrees. See Peterson's.
　See also Education.

University of California, Berkeley Wellness Letter is searchable in the Health Database Plus (GO HLTBD). See Health.

University of Phoenix (GO UP) has a service in the Electronic Mall (GO MALL) that offers business degree programs online. See Electronic Mall.

Unix: The Unix Forum (GO UNIXFORUM) discusses issues relating to the multiuser, multitasking operating system that was created by AT&T. Topics include Unix in any and all of its forms, UNIX Basics, communication, UUCP, Usenet, protection, file systems, process scheduling, and tools such as C, emacs, make, mail, etc. Running the forum are David Moskowitz (76701,100), Noel Bergman (76704,34), John James, and Don Gloistein.
　Also:

- UnixWare Forum (GO UNIXWARE) is for topics relating to Novell's Unix software, part of the Novell software network (see Novell). The forum is designed to be a meeting place where people who are interested in or use UnixWare can share ideas, techniques, and experiences. The sysop is C. Cash Perkins (71333,1673).

- *UNIX Update* can be searched through the Business Database Plus (GO BUSDB). See Business Database.

- The VAX Forum (GO VAXFORUM) supports Digital's version of Unix known as Ultrix-32 and Ultrix-32m. For details, see Digital Equipment.

- Unix also is a topic of other forums, including Amiga Tech Forum (GO AMIGATECH), Computer Association VAX/UNIX Forum (GO CAIMINI), Corel Support Forum (GO COREL), DBMS Magazine Forum (GO DBMSFORUM), Dr. Dobbs Journal Forum (GO DDJFORUM), Lan Magazine Forum (GO LANMAG), Lan Technology Forum (GO LANTECH), Microsoft WIN32 Forum (GO MSWIN32), Novell User Library Forum (GO NOVUSER), Oracle Support Forum (GO ORACLE), PDP-11 Forum (GO

PDP11), Santa Cruz Operation Forum (GO SCOFORUM), Symantec Fifth Generation Systems Forum (GO SYMFGS), Wang Support Forum (GO WANGFORUM), WordPerfect Corp. Files Forum (GO WPFILES), and Zenith Data Systems Forum (GO ZENITH).

See also Telecomputing.

UNIX Review (magazine) is searchable through Computer Database Plus (GO COMPDB). See Computer Database Plus.

Untouchable (software) is supported in the Symantec Fifth Generation Systems Forum (GO SYMFGS). See Symantec.

Uploading sends a file (a program or a text file, such as a letter or article) from your computer to be stored on CompuServe in a library of a forum, as letter to CompuServe mail, and so on. For more on this, see Files, Transfer.

Urbamet (database) is searchable on IQuest (see IQuest), and contains French- and English-language abstracts from periodicals and other sources on all aspects of urban and regional planning and development.

Urban Development Department is discussed in the White House Forum (GO WHITEHOUSE). See White House.

Urban Transport News can be searched through the Business Database Plus (GO BUSDB). See Business Database.

USA Today (newspaper) is searchable through Telebase System's News Source USA (GO NEWSUSA) and through the Knowledge Index (GO KI). See News Source and see Knowledge Index. The USA Today Magazine can be searched in the Magazine Database Plus (GO MDP). See Magazine Database.

US Department of State Dispatch can be searched in the Magazine Database Plus (GO MDP). See Magazine Database. State Department documents also are included in Travel Advisory Service (GO STATE), maintained by the Citizen Emergency Center as a continuously updated information service to Americans traveling abroad. See U.S. Government Information.

Used car prices are among the topics in the Automobile Information Center (GO AI), a store in the Electronic Mall (GO MALL). See Automobile.

UserLand Software Forum (GO USERLAND) is operated by the developer and publisher of the Frontier scripting system for the Macintosh. Administering is Dave Winer (76244,120), co-author of Frontier and president/founder of UserLand Software. Also in the forum is Doug Baron (76067,214), co-author of UserLand Frontier, and Judi Lowenstein (76703,4047), manager of UserLand's developer services.

U.S. Government Information (GO GPO) includes a catalog of government publications, books, subscription services, and ordering information. See Personal Finance and Insurance.

Also:

- The National Technical Information Service (GO NTI), published by the U.S. Department of Commerce, contains nearly 1.5 million references to articles from government-sponsored research, development, and engineering reports, usually with corresponding abstracts. See National Technical Information Service.

- The U.S. Department of State's Travel Advisory Service (GO STATE) is maintained by the Citizen Emergency Center as a continuously updated information service for Americans traveling abroad. The database includes advisories and warnings covering such conditions as warfare, political unrest, hotel/motel shortages, currency regulations, and other information of interest to the American traveler. To locate a travel advice about a particular country, select a country from an alphabetical menu.

- U.S. Classification (database of patents) and U.S. Copyrights database can be searched through IQuest. See IQuest. See also Patents.

U.S. News & World Report Online (GO USNEWS) provides access to the news magazines articles, and enables visitors to interact with the magazine's editors and writers. As a part of CompuServe's basic service, services include the current week's magazine, complete with text and images. Users can view the text and image files of the latest issue online or download them.

The U.S. News Forum, a part of CompuServe's extended services, is devoted to discussions with U.S. News staff members and other readers. Forum libraries contain public documents, information on current events, and back issues of the magazine's College Ratings and Mutual Fund Ratings. Operating the forum is Kristen Gunn (72662,1072), with assistance from Bill Allman, a senior writer covering science and anthropology; Amy Bernstein, an associate editor interested in social trends; Bill Cook, a senior writer specializing in technology; and Vic Sussman, a senior editor covering cyberspace.

In addition, members can access a searchable, surcharged database of U.S. News articles from the last seven years. The charge for viewing or downloading the full text of an article is $1.50 per article.

U.S. News & World Report also is searchable through Magazine Database Plus (GO MDP). For details see Magazine Database. It also may be searched through the IQuest gateway (GO IQUEST). See IQuest. And it can be searched in News Source USA (GO NEWSUSA). See News Source.

U.S. Robotics (**modem equipment**) is supported the Modem Vendor Forum (GO MODEMVEN). See Modem Vendor. U.S. Robotics (UK) products are supported in the UK Computing Forum (GO UKCOMP). See UK Computing.

Utah news is included in the daily Western regional reports from United Press International. See Executive News Service for details.

Utility Reporter—Fuels, Energy & Power (database) can be searched through IQuest. See IQuest. The resource also can be searched through the Business Database Plus (GO BUSDB). See Business Database. See also Energy.

UUNet users can receive mail from CompuServe. See Mail, CompuServe, under the Internet section.

V

Valvo, Mike, a chess master, provides the latest news and commentary on the game in the Chess Forum (GO CHESSFORUM). See Chess.

van der Linden, Scott (76702,533) is the sysop of the Autodesk Retail Products Forum (GO ARETAIL). See Autodesk.

Van Geest, David L. (76711,330) is the sysop of the Mensa Forum (GO MENSA). See Mensa.

VAX Forum (GO VAXFORUM) supports discussion of the VAX 32-bit systems. For details, see Digital Equipment.

VAX Professional (magazine) can be searched through Computer Database Plus (GO COMPDB). See Computer Database Plus.

Vectra computers is supported in the HP Systems Forum (GO HPSYS). See Hewlett-Packard.

Vegetarian Times is searchable in the Health Database Plus (GO HLTBD). See Health. The topic also is covered in the Cooks Online Forum (GO COOKS). See Cook's.

Vellum software by Ashlar Inc. is supported in the CADD/CAM/CAE Vendor Forum (GO CADDVEN).

Venditto, Gus (72241,42) is among *PC Magazine*'s editors and contributors who are regulars in the publication's PC-Magnet service. See PC Magazine.

Vener, Dan (76711,402) is the sysop of the Meca Software Forum (GO MECA). See Meca Software.

Venettozzi, Tim (76702,1473) is a sysop in the Canon Forum (GO CANON). For details, see Canon.

Ventura Software Forum (GO VENTURA) is managed by Ventura Software Inc. (VSI) to provide support and information about Ventura Publisher and Ventura FormBase, as well as Ventura Database Publisher, Ventura AdPro, ColorPro, and PicturePro. The forum also includes information about software packages produced by two organizations within Xerox. One is The Analyst, a product of Xerox Special Information Systems (XSIS). The other is Gray F/X, a product of Xerox Imaging Systems (XIS). The sysop is Karl Anthony (76702,1206), who has been with Ventura Software since 1990. He is assisted by Byron Canfield, Cleve Garvin, Jim Hart, John Murdoch, and David Satz.

Venture Capital Journal can be searched through the Business Database Plus (GO BUSDB). See Business Database.

Vericomp products are supported in the PC Vendor C Forum (GO PCVENC). See IBM Computers.

Vermont news is included in the daily Northeast regional reports from United Press International. See Executive News Service for details.

Vertisoft products are supported in the PC Vendor G Forum (GO PCVENG). See IBM.

Veterans Administration's Rehabilitation Database (GO REHAB) is a collection of information on rehabilitation research and technology. See Rehabilitation.

Veterans issues are discussed in the Military Forum (GO MILITARY). See Military Forums. Veterans affairs also is discussed in the White House Forum (GO WHITEHOUSE). See White House.

Veterinarians regularly meet in the Pets and Animals Forum (GO PETS). For details, see Pets.

'Vette (modem game) is supported in the Modem-to-Modem Gaming Lobby (GO MTMLOBBY). See Modem-to-Modem Games.

VFXV.32bis, VFPV.32bis modems and others from Zoom Telephonics are supported in the Modem Vendor Forum (GO MODEMVEN). See Modem Vendor.

Vibrant Life is searchable in the Health Database Plus (GO HLTBD). See Health.

Vickery, Michelle (76702,1054) is the sysop of the DaVinci Forum (GO DAVINCI). See DaVinci.

Victor 9000 computers are supported in the Computer Club (GO CLUB). See Computer Club.

Video is covered in a number of databases searchable through the IQuest gateway (GO IQUEST), including Video Marketing News, Videonews International, Video Technology Newsletter, and Video Week. See IQuest.

Also, *Home Video Publisher* magazine can be searched through the Business Database Plus (GO BUSDB), as can *Video Marketing News*, *Video Marketing Newsletter*, *Video Technology News*, and *Video Week*. See Business Database. And *Video Magazine* can be searched in the Magazine Database Plus (GO MDP). See Magazine Database.

Also, Critics' Choice Video (GO CCV) is a store in the Electronic Mall (GO MALL) that features videos of all kinds. See Electronic Mall.

VideoLogic products are supported in the Multimedia Vendor Forum (GO MULTIVEN). See Multimedia.

Videomedia products are supported in the Ultimedia Tools Forum B (GO ULTIBTOOLS). See Ultimedia.

Videonews International can be searched through the Business Database Plus (GO BUSDB). See Business Database.

Videotex Update, Worldwide (database) may be searched through the IQuest gateway. See IQuest. The resource also can be searched through the Business Database Plus (GO BUSDB). See Business Database.

Vieregger, Gary (76711,35) is primary sysop of the IBM Desktop Software Forum (GO IBMDESK). See IBM.

Vietnam veterans are regulars in the Military Forum (GO MILITARY). See Military Forums.

Viewtext (database) can be searched through Business Database Plus (GO BUSDB). See Business Database.

VINES (software) is supported in the Banyan Forum (GO BANFORUM). See Banyan. The software also is discussed in the Lan Technology Forum (GO LANTECH). See Lan.

Virginia news is covered in the Richmond News Leader and the Richmond Times-Dispatch, as well as the Norfolk Ledger-Star & Virginian-Pilot, searchable through Telebase System's News Source USA (GO NEWSUSA). See News Source.

Also, selected reports from Virginia are included in the Mid-Atlantic regional reports from United Press International. See Executive News Service.

Virginia Diner (GO VA) is a store in the Electronic Mall (GO MALL) featuring nutes, candies, hams, and other foods. See Electronic Mall.

Virtual reality is a regular topic of the Computer Art Forum (GO COMART). See Graphics,. It also is one of the topics in the CyberForum (GO CYBERFORUM). See CyberForum.

Virtus Corp. products are supported in the Macintosh C Vendor Forum (GO MACCVEN). See Apple Computer. They are supported in the Ultimedia Tools Forum B (GO ULTIBTOOLS). See Ultimedia.

Viruscan (software) is supported in the McAfee Virus Help Forum (GO VIRUSFORUM). See McAfee.

Viruses, computer are covered and discussed in the McAfee Virus Help Forum (GO VIRUSFORUM). See McAfee. They also are the topic of the Symantec AntiVirus Forum (GO SYMVIRUS) and the Symantec Fifth Generation Systems Forum (GO SYMFGS). See Symantec. See also Central Point (GO CENTRAL), Macintosh New Users/Help Forum (GO MACNEW), and Packard Bell Forum (GO PACKARDBELL).

Visa Advisors and Electronic Visaguide (GO VISA) is a Washington, D.C., passport and visa expediting firm that provides applications and information on travel requirements for more than 200 countries. It even offers same-day service for passports to persons able to submit copies of their round trip tickets. This is one of the system's basic services, meaning those signed up under the Standard Pricing Plan (see Billing) have unlimited access to the feature.

Vision Imaging products are supported in the Ultimedia Tools Forum B (GO ULTIBTOOLS). See Ultimedia.

Vision Impairments are discussed in the Disabilities Forum (GO DISABILI-TIES). See Disabilities.

VisualAge (software) is supported in the Software Solutions Forum (GO SOFSOL). See Software Solutions.

Vitamins are sold by several stores in the Electronic Mall, including Health and Vitamin Express (GO HVE) and SDV Vitamins (GO SDV). See Electronic Mall.

V-Lan products are supported in the Ultimedia Hardware Plus Forum (GO ULTIHW). See Ultimedia.

VNR Bookstore Cafe (GO VNR) offers an online bookstore in the Electronic Mall (GO MALL). See Electronic Mall.

Voice Technology News (database) may be searched through the IQuest gateway. See IQuest. The resource also can be searched through the Business Database Plus (GO BUSDB). See Business Database.

Volante Inc. (software) is supported in the Graphics B Vendor Forum (GO GRAPHBVEN). See Graphics.

Voyager Company products are supported in the Multimedia Vendor Forum (GO MULTIVEN). See Multimedia.

Voyetra products are supported in the Ultimedia Tools Forum B (GO ULTIBTOOLS). See Ultimedia.

VRLI Inc. products are supported in the Graphics A Vendor Forum (GO VRLI). See Graphics.

Vshield **(software)** is supported in the McAfee Virus Help Forum (GO VIRUSFORUM). See McAfee.

VT-180 computers are supported in the DEC PC Forum (GO DECPC). See Digital Equipment Forums.

Walker Richer & Quinn Inc. software is supported in the WRQ Reflection Forum (GO WRQFORUM). See WRQ.

Wall Data products are supported in the Windows 3rd-Party C Forum (GO WINAPC). See Microsoft Software.

Wall Street Computer Review and **Wall Street & Technology (magazines)** are searchable through Computer Database Plus (GO COMPDB). See Computer Database Plus.

Wall Street Journal **(newspaper)** offers selected abstracts are searchable through Computer Database Plus (GO COMPDB). See Computer Database Plus.

Wall Street Network News and **Wall Street Transcript Digest** can be searched through the Business Database Plus (GO BUSDB). See Business Database.

Walrod, Brad (76702,1043) is a sysop in the Desktop Publishing Forum (GO DTPFORUM). For more, see Desktop Publishing.

Walter Knoll Florist (GO WK) is a store in the Electronic Mall (GO MALL) that offers plants, flowers, fruits, and balloons. See Electronic Mall.

Wang Support Forum (WANGFORUM) supports computers produced by Wang Laboratories. The sysops are Ben Little (76711,420), Alan Eisen (76711,464), Tracy McDonald (76711,431), Wayne McWhorter (76711,430), and Jim Demeusy (76702,1632). If you are a user of Wang products, you also are encouraged to contact the company's WangWIDE Support Service department (800-323-WANG) for information on how to access online technical databases.

Warner Bros. Records (GO WARNER) is a participant in the Music Vendor Forum (GO MUSICVEN). See Music.

War/Simulation Games are offered in CompuServe's game section (GO GAMES). Specific games include:

- Air Traffic Controller (GO ATCONTROL)
- Megawars I: The Galactic Conflict (GO MEGA1)
- Megawars III: The New Empire (GO MEGA3)
- Sniper (GO SNIPER)

See Games and entries under specific game names.

Wasch, Ken (76004,3021) is sysop of the Software Publishers Association Forum (GO SPAFORUM). See Software Publishers Association.

Washington (state) is covered in the Seattle Post-Intelligencer and the Seattle Times, both searchable through Telebase System's News Source USA (GO NEWSUSA). See News Source.

Also:

- Selected reports from Washington are included in the Western regional reports from United Press International. See Executive News Service.
- *Puget Sound Business Journal* can be searched through the Business Database Plus (GO BUSDB). See Business Database.

Washington Beverage Insight (database) may be searched through the IQuest gateway. (see IQuest) and through the Business Database Plus (GO BUSDB). See Business Database.

Washington Business Journal (magazine) can be searched through the Business Database Plus (GO BUSDB). See Business Database.

Washington Monthly (magazine) is searchable through Magazine Database Plus (GO MDP). For details see Magazine Database.

Washington Post (newspaper) is searchable through Telebase System's News Source USA (GO NEWSUSA) and through the Knowledge Index (GO KI). See News Source and see Knowledge Index. Selected stories from the Post also may be view in the Executive News Service. See Executive News Service.

Washington Trade Daily (newsletter) can be searched through IQuest. See IQuest.

Washington (DC) Times (newspaper) is searchable through Telebase System's News Source USA (GO NEWSUSA). See News Source.

Wasson, Gregory (72511,36) is sysop of the Download & Support Forum (GO ZMC:DOWNTECH), part of magazine publisher Ziff-Davis' ZiffNet/Mac services for Apple Macintosh users. See ZiffNet/Mac.

Waste treatment is covered in several IQuest (GO IQUEST) databases, including Solid Waste Report, Waste Treatment Technology News, and Water Resources Abstracts. See IQuest.

    Also, *Management of World Wastes* magazine can be searched through the Business Database Plus (GO BUSDB), as can *Medical Waste News, Waste Information Digests,* and *Waste Treatment Technology News*. See Business Database.

    And see Hazardous Material.

WATCOM products are supported in the PC Vendor H Forum (GO PCVENH). See IBM Computers.

Water Resources Abstracts, Oceanic Abstracts, and **Waternet (databases)** may be searched through the IQuest gateway. See IQuest. Also, *Ground Water Monitor* can be searched through the Business Database Plus (GO BUSDB). See Business Database.

Watkins, Don (76703,750) is a chief sysop of the IBM Users Network (GO IBMNET). See IBM Computers. He also is associated with the ASP/Shareware Forum (GO ASPFORUM). For details see Shareware.

Watkins, Vince (72262,2767) is sysop of the SynOptics Communications Inc. Forum (GO SYNOPTICS). See SynOptics.

WealthBuilder **(financial software)** from Reality Technologies is supported in in PC Vendor H Forum (GO PCVENH). See IBM Computers.

Weapon systems are discussed in the Military Forum (GO MILITARY). See Military.

Weather: Up-to-date weather information for your own locality as well as for other towns and cities around the country or around the world is available from CompuServe's own weather center. In addition, more than a dozen national and international weather maps (including radar maps, satellite pictures, and forecast maps) are provided for on-screen viewing. The weather features are among the system's basic services, meaning those signed up under the Standard Pricing Plan (see Billing) have unlimited access to the feature.

International Weather CompuServe also provides weather reports and maps for regions outside the U.S., including Australia/New Zealand, Canada, continental Europe, United Kingdom/Ireland, and Japan/Far East.

Text reports National Weather Service forecasts are available for your local area as well as locations across the country and abroad. (CompuServe provides forecasts for some 85 cities aboard.) Reports offered include short-term forecast, state extended forecast, severe weather alert, precipitation probability, regional summary, daily climatological report, as well as sports, recreation, and marine forecast. (Not all reports are available for all locations.)

Weather maps are the exciting new addition to CompuServe weather. If you are using one of the CompuServe Information Manager software packages (or a third-party program that incorporates a GIF graphics viewer), you can see the weather maps instantly. They are automatically shown to you in high-resolution graphics and you also are given an option to save them on disk for later reviewing. On the other hand, if you are not using a GIF-oriented terminal program such as CIM, CompuServe can automatically transmit selected maps to your computer for offline viewing with decoders, which are available in the Graphics Support Forum (GO PICS). (See Graphics.)

Maps available include:

- About a dozen **Accu-Weather forecast maps** for the U.S. include Current Weather for the nation, Tomorrow's Weather, the 48-Hour Weather forecast, the Current Temperatures, Tonight's Lows, Tomorrow's Highs, and the Wake-Up Weather Maps for the Northeast, Southeast, North Central, South Central, Northwest, and Southwest.

- **Depiction maps,** for which the system takes information from surface reports to create a graphic representation of flight conditions throughout the United States; every 15 minutes a new map is created, and a range of the report times used for that map is shown after the menu selection.

- The latest **radar map**, which shows precipitation echo intensities recorded at radar stations. Each time a map is created, information from radar locations across the country is gathered to create a comprehensive graphic. Each echo intensity is shown as either solid white or shaded, or in a different color if viewed on a color monitor. The upper-left corner of the map shows the maximum and minimum observation times of those radar reports used for the map. A menu item tells the time the map was assemblied; it is usually within a few minute of the current time.

- **Satellite maps** for the continental U.S. and the Pacific, showing the current cloud formations and the high and low fronts.

- **Temperature maps,** which are updated around the clock, show the *current* temperature bands across the country.

Another weather database available is Meteorological and Geoastrophysical Abstracts database, which can be searched through the IQuest gateway. See IQuest.

Weather, Aviation: For pilots, CompuServe offers a surcharged aviation weather database with information defined by the federal aviation regulations. Data includes hourly reports, terminal forecasts, wind data, radar summaries, and more. For more information, enter GO AWX. See also Aviation and see Airlines.

Weatherwise (magazine) can be searched in the Magazine Database Plus (GO MDP). See Magazine Database.

Weaving is one of the topics discussed in the Crafts Forum (GO CRAFTS). See Crafts.

Weber, Paula (72662,1425) is the sysop of the Parsons Technology Forum (GO PTFORUM). See Parsons Technology.

Welfare is discussed in the White House Forum (GO WHITEHOUSE). See White House.

Westchester County Business Journal (magazine) can be searched through the Business Database Plus (GO BUSDB). See Business Database.

West Coast Travel (GO WESTCOAST) is a guide to travel destinations in the western half of the United States, as well as Canada and Mexico. The articles are personal travel research in the field. More than 100 major destinations now are online, covering the 13 western states. For other travel-related features, see Travel.

Western Journal of Medicine is searchable in the Health Database Plus (GO HLTBD). See Health.

Western Systems computers are supported in the UK Computing Forum (GO UKCOMP). See UK Computing.

West Europe Intelligence Report (database) can be searched through IQuest. See IQuest.

Westheimer, Dr. Ruth, nationally known sex advisor, is featured in the Human Sexuality Information and Advisory Service (GO HUMAN). See Sex.

West Virginia news is included in the daily Mid-Atlantic region reports from United Press International. See Executive News Service for details.

Westwood Studios products are covered in Game Publishers B Forum (GO GAMBPUB). See Gaming Forums.

We the People (organization) is discussed in the Political Debate Forum (GO POLITICS). See Political.

Wextech Systems products are supported in the Windows 3rd-Party D Forum (GO WINAPD). See Microsoft Software.

Whap! (software) is an automated terminal program for Commodore Amiga written by Jim Nangano and Steve Ahlstrom. The $39.95 shareware program is available in the Amiga Tech Forum (GO AMIGATECH). For related subjects, see Automated Terminal Software.

What's New (GO NEW) provides news about new additions and upcoming events on CompuServe. Twice a week, the What's New This Week menu is automatically displayed at logon. It is updated every Thursday and the new menu appears the first two times you connect to the system after an update. What's News lists events and other news in a menu of headlines. If you want to read a complete article, select the headline from the menu by number.

Wheeler, Alan   (71333,2247) is sysop of the Micro Focus Forum (GO MICROFOCUS). See Micro Focus.

Which Computer?   (**magazine**) is searchable through Computer Database Plus (GO COMPDB). See Computer Database Plus.

Whitaker, Greg   (76711,1035) is a sysop in the Clarion Software Forum (GO CLARION). See Clarion.

White House Forum   (GO WHITEHOUSE) is devoted to the discussion of the President's administration and its policies and activities. The only files permitted in the forum's libraries are those provided directly by the Office of Media Affairs for the White House. Message sections exist for each cabinet post and responsibility, and allow members to exchange information and opinions with each other on a broad range of topics, including international and United Nations activities, the budget deficit, housing and urban development, and education and national service. The White House is managed by Georgia Griffith (76703,266) and Brion Lutz (76702,1561). Assisting them are Nate Lenow and section leaders Tom Cafesjian (technology/space and justice/FBI), David Bush (internationalism/UN and health care), Les Prus (defense), Tom Sims (education/national service), Al Goggins (commerce/trade and economy/deficit), Steve Davis (environment), Steven J. Murphy (Social Security/welfare), Steven Parker (transportation), Dori Steckley (agriculture), and John Paul (veterans affairs).
See also Political.

Whiz Quiz   (**game**) (GO WHIZ) is a trivia game sponsored by Grolier Electronic Publishing Inc. and is based on the online Academic American Encyclopedia. See Grolier's Whiz Quiz.

Who's Who, Marquis'   (GO BIOGRAPHY) includes biographical information describing key North American professionals. See Marquis' Who's Who.

Whole Earth Review (**magazine**) is searchable through Magazine Database Plus (GO MDP). For details see Magazine Database.

Wichita (KS) Eagle-Beacon   (**newspaper**) is searchable through Telebase System's News Source USA (GO NEWSUSA). See News Source.

Wigwam is a Windows-based automated navigation program from Ashmount Research Ltd. of London. It can be downloaded in Library 10, "WigWam/TP," of the

UK Computing Forum (GO UKCOMP). For details, see Automated Terminal Software.

Wildcat BBS (software) is supported in the PC Vendor A Forum (GO PCVENA). See IBM Computers.

Wilderness (magazine) can be searched in the Magazine Database Plus (GO MDP). See Magazine Database.

Wildlife issues and pictures are available in the Earth Forum (GO EARTH). See Earth.

Wiley Professional Books (GO JW) provides technical and professional books through the Electronic Mall (GO MALL). See Electronic Mall.

Wilkes, Richard and Sandy (76701,23) and (76701,22) are associated with the WordPerfect Support Group Forums (GO WPSG). See WordPerfect Software. They also are associated with the TAPCIS Forum (GO TAPCIS). See TAPCIS.

Williams, Tony (75300,3644) is the sysop of the CompuServe Pacific Forum (GO PACFORUM) and the Pacific Vendor Forum (GO PACVEN). See Pacific.

Willies Computer Software Corp. products are supported in PC Vendor F Forum (GO PCVENF). For details, see IBM Computers.

Wilmer, Mike (76703,4400) is sysop of the Photography Forum (GO PHOTOFORUM). See Photography Forum.

Wilson Co., H. W., publisher of *Book Review Digest*, also has an electronic edition. Book Review Digest (GO BRD) is available directly or through IQuest. See Book Review Digest.

WilsonWare (software products) are supported in Windows 3rd-Party Forum A (GO WINAPA). See Microsoft Software.

WinCIS is a Windows-based terminal program for automating access of CompuServe. See Automated Terminal.

WindowCraft products are supported in the Windows 3rd-Party B Forum (GO WINAPB). See Microsoft Software.

Windows (software) is supported in the Microsoft Windows User Forum (GO MSWIN) and in the Windows Third-Party Vendors Forums (GO WINAPA, GO WINAPB, GO WINAPC and GO WINAPD). See Microsoft Software.

Windows Aktiv (magazine) is supported in the German-language Ziff Windows Forum (GO GERWIN). See ZiffNet.

Windows Magazine can be searched through IQuest. See IQuest. See also Microsoft.

Windows Sources Forum (GO ZNT:WINSOU) is a ZiffNet resource intended as the electronic extension of print magazine *Windows Sources*. Operating the forum is Ron Anderson (72241,113). See ZiffNet. *Windows Sources* can be searched through Computer Database Plus (GO COMPDB), as can *Windows-DOS Developer's Journal*. See Computer Database Plus.

Windows Sources (GO WS) also operates a kiosk in the Electronic Mall (GO MALL). See Electronic Mall.

Windows Users Group Network (GO WUGNET) is operated as the electronic extension of the principal technical user group and association for Windows professionals. WUGNET says they are committed to promoting the exchange of technical information and resources on the Windows environment. Topics include the Windows Advisor, new Windows products, Windows applications support, system configurations, connectivity, programming, development, industry trends, electronic publishing, WUGNET support, etc. See also Microsoft.

Windsurfing is discussed in the Sailing Forum (GO SAILING). See Sports and Recreation.

Wine Forum (GO WINEFORUM) hosts discussions on all aspects of wine with experts and others. A special feature is online wine tasting held in the forum's conference area. Participants purchase the same wines and taste them together during scheduled real-time conferences. Transcripts of these real-time gatherings are available in the forum's libraries for others to view later.

Administrator of the forum is Jim Kronman (76703,431), a systems engineer in the aerospace industry who also publishes a wine newsletter. He is assisted by wine experts and writers from across the country, including several newspaper and magazine columnists. Among the associates are Robin Garr, Emily Johnston, and Ed Flinn. Also helping are Steve Reiss, Charlie Papazian, James Spence, Steve Downey, and Deven Black.

See also Food.

Winer, Dave (76244,120), president and founder of UserLand Software, administers the UserLand Software Forum (GO USERLAND). See UserLand.

Winer, Ethan (72657,3070) is one of the editors and writers associated with the PC Magazine forums. See PC Magazine.

Wines & Vines (magazine) can be searched through the Business Database Plus (GO BUSDB). See Business Database.

WINFAX PRO (software) is supported in Delrina Technology Forum (GO DELRINA). See Delrina.

Wing Newsletter (Japan's Aerospace & Aviation Weekly) can be searched through the Business Database Plus (GO BUSDB). See Business Database.

WinImage (software) is supported in the Lotus Word Processing Forum (GO LOTUSWP). See Lotus Software.

WinRIX for Windows (software) is supported in the Graphics A Vendor Forum (GO GRAPHVEN). See Graphics.

Wisconsin State Journal and **(Madison) Capital Times** (newspapers) are searchable through Telebase System's News Source USA (GO NEWSUSA). See News Source.

> Also:
>
> - Selected reports from Wisconsin are included in the Central regional reports from United Press International. See Executive News Service.
> - *The Business Journal—Milwaukee* can be searched through the Business Database Plus (GO BUSDB). See Business Database.

Wisotzke, Paul (70007,6237) is the sysop of the Kodak CD Forum (GO KODAK). See Kodak.

Witchcraft is covered in the New Age Forum (GO NEWAGE). For more information, see New Age Forum.

Wizard Works products are supported in the Pacific Vendor Forum (GO PACVEN). See Pacific Vendor.

Woeltjen, Linda (76711,1142) manages the California Forum (GO CALFORUM). See California.

Wolfram Research (software) is supported in the Wolfram Research Forum (GO WOLFRAM). The main product is its mathematical calculation software, Mathematica, which handles numerical, graphical, and symbolic calculations, and generates 2-D/3-D plots, contour plots, and shaded-color 3-D images. The forum is operated by Bruce Pea (76702,1400).

Women, Marketing to can be searched through the Business Database Plus (GO BUSDB). See Business Database.

Women & Health magazine abstracts are searchable in the Health Database Plus (GO HLTBD). See Health.

Woman's Day (magazine) is searchable through Magazine Database Plus (GO MDP). For details see Magazine Database.

Women's issues are discussed in the Issues Forum (GO ISSUESFORUM). See Issues.

Women's Letter is searchable in the Health Database Plus (GO HLTBD). See Health.

Women's Sports and Fitness is searchable in the Health Database Plus (GO HLTBD). See Health.

Women's Wear Daily (**database**) may be searched through the IQuest gateway. See IQuest. It also can be searched through Business Database Plus (GO BUSDB). See Business Database.

WonderWare products are supported in the Windows 3rd Party B Forum (GO WINAPB). See Microsoft Software.

Wood carving is one of the topics discussed in the Crafts Forum (GO CRAFTS). See Crafts.

Wood industry issues are covered in *World Wood* and *American Forests* magazines, which can be searched through Business Database Plus (GO BUSDB). See Business Database.

   See also Forest Industry.

Wood, Larry (76703,704) is the primary sysop of the Graphics Net forums (GO GRAPHICS). See Graphics. He also administers the Florida Forum (GO FLORIDA) and the Cook's Online Forum (GO COOKS). See Florida Forum and Cook's Online.

Woods, Wendy (72241,337) is editor/founder of Newsbytes News Network. See Newsbytes.

Wooldridge, Chris (76711,1014) is sysop of the Oracle Forum (GO ORACLE). See Oracle.

Word (**software**) is supported in the Microsoft Application Forum (GO MSAPP). See Microsoft Software.

Word processors are discussed and supported in a number of forums. Here is an overview:

- Ami Pro, Ami, and related programs are supported in Lotus Word Processing Forum (GO LOTUSWP).
- DisplayWrite the IBM Desktop Software Forum (GO IBMDESK). See IBM Computers.
- LotusWrite, Lotus Manuscript, and Lotus Word Processing Forum (GO LOTUSWP). See Lotus.
- PC-Write, the PC Vendor B Forum (GO PCVENB). See IBM Computers.
- Professional Write, the Software Publishing Forum (GO SPCFORUM). For details, see Software Publishing.
- Samna Word IV and SmarText are supported in Lotus Word Processing Forum (GO LOTUSWP). See Lotus.

- Sprint, Borland Applications Forum (GO BORAPP). For details, see Borland.
- WinImage, Lotus Word Processing Forum (GO LOTUSWP). See Lotus Software.
- Word, Microsoft Word Forum (GO MSWORD). See Microsoft Software.
- WordPerfect, the WordPerfect Users Forum (GO WPUSERS), and the WordPerfect Files Forum (GO WPFILES). See WordPerfect.
- WordStar, the WordStar Forum (GO WORDSTAR). See WordStar.

See also Designer Template Collections (GO ZNT:FORMS), which is intended for use with popular word-processing and spreadsheet programs. See Ziffnet.

WordPerfect Software: Two WordPerfect forums are operated, one by WordPerfect Corp. itself and another by an independent support group, WordPerfect Users Forum.

- The WordPerfect Files Forum (GO WPFILES) is managed by the company's customer support department; it promises product information, handles questions and answers, downloadable printer drivers, product announcements, and more to WordPerfect users. A menu of other choices lets you select articles about WordPerfect's DOS, Windows, Macintosh, and Unix products, plus company news, other customer support services, and more. The sysops are Jolene Fincher (71022,3004) and Lynn Crabb (71022,3005).
- WordPerfect Users Forum (GO WPUSERS) is an independent group sponsored by Support Group, Inc., a private company independent of WordPerfect Corp. It supports users of the WordPerfect word processor for various computers and other WordPerfect products. Operating the forum are Guerri Stevens, John Liebson, Joan Friedman, Richard Wilkes, Ralph Alvy, John Filshie, John McAdams, Gordon McComb, Bruce Rodgers, Marilyn Claff, Mark Schaeffer, and Jack Waananen.

For a general menu of WordPerfect features, enter GO WORDPERFECT.

Also, *Wordperfect Magazine* can be searched through Computer Database Plus (GO COMPDB). See Computer Database Plus.

WordStar Software: The WordStar Forum (GO WORDSTAR) supports this famed word processor and other products from WordStar International Corporation for IBM and Apple compatible systems. Its subtopics cover WordStar 2000 and other members of the WordStar family, questions dealing with specific printers, other add-ons, etc. Library files contain utilities and information that add value to WordStar packages.

The forum is operated by Tracy Bruce (76702,1051), who also is the team leader for WordStar's Technical Support Group. Assisting are Chris Hughes, Lief Ashley, Ed Zollars, Julie Rosenberg, and Jane Moore.

Wordstar also is supported in the Ultimedia Tools Forum B (GO ULTIBTOOLS). See Ultimedia.

Wordtech Systems products are supported in the PC Vendor C Forum (GO PCVENC). See IBM Computers.

Workbench (software) is supported in the Sybase Forum (GO SYBASE). See Sybase.

Workgroup Computing Report (formerly Patricia Seybold's Office Computing Report) (magazine abstracts) can be searched through Computer Database Plus (GO COMPDB). See Computer Database Plus.

Working From Home Forum (GO WORK) has a standing invitation to those who work full-time or part-time at home or who are part of the growing number of salaried telecommuters who hold jobs in businesses and industries but who do their work at home. Regulars use it to exchange information, make contacts, share resources and solutions to problems, or just to meet and enjoy each other's company. You can find home/office management tips on resources, laws, tax issues, benefits, and marketing approaches. The sysops are Paul and Sarah Edwards (76703,242). The Edwards', who began working from home in 1974, are the authors of *Working From Home: Everything You Need To Know About Living and Working Under the Same Roof*. The couple started the forum in January 1983, and are assisted by Jerry Fitzgibbon and Don Singleton, along with section leaders Laura Douglas (getting business), Douglas Perreault (accounting/tax), Gerry J. Elman (legally speaking), Debbie Dewey (virtual corporation), and Marguerite L. Ellen (networking/associations).

Working Software products are supported in the Mac B Vendor Forum (GO MACBVEN). See Apple Computers.

Working Woman (magazine) is searchable through Magazine Database Plus (GO MDP). For details see Magazine Database.

Worklife is searchable in the Health Database Plus (GO HLTBD). See Health.

WorkMAN 2.0 (software) is supported in the PC Vendor G Forum (GO PCVENG). See IBM.

Works (software) is supported in the Microsoft Application Forum (GO MSAPP). See Microsoft Software.

World Affairs can be researched in a wide variety of databases through the IQuest gateway (GO IQUEST). They include Academic Index, Africa News Online, APS Diplomat, Arab Information Bank, Asahi News Service, Asian Political News, BBC Summary of World Broadcasts, Business Travel News, Chronicle of Latin American Economic Affairs, EDF-DOC, L'Elite et les Institutions Sovietiques (evenements), ESSOR, International Information Report, International News, Japan Policy and Politics, Logos, Mid-East Business Digest, New Era: Japan, Noriane, Northern Ireland News Service, PAIS International, Perspectives, PTS Newsletter Database, Security Intelligence Report, and Week in Germany. See IQuest.

WorldBlazer modems, carried by Telebit Corporation, are supported in the Modem Vendor Forum (GO MODEMVEN). See Modem Vendor.

Worldfront modems and others from Global Village Communications are supported in the Modem Vendor Forum (GO MODEMVEN). See Modem Vendor.

World Health (**magazine**) can be searched in the Magazine Database Plus (GO MDP). See Magazine Database. The resource also can be searched through the Health Database Plus (GO HLTDB). See Health.

World Health Organization, Bulletin of the is searchable in the Health Database Plus (GO HLTBD). See Health.

World Press Review (**magazine**) can be searched in the Magazine Database Plus (GO MDP). See Magazine Database.

World Software products are supported in the PC Vendor I Forum (GO PCVENI). See IBM Computers.

Worldwide Car Network Forum (GO WWCAR) is a joint venture of European and American concerns where car enthusiasts can share their knowledge and love of automobiles. The forum accommodates virtually every type of car and truck ever made, from pre-1950 vehicles to modern, sport, and exotic cars. The forum's message sections and libraries also cover such topics as motorcycles, car clubs, and model cars. Also offered in the forum is the Worldwide Car Network's Gold Book of car values. It is operated by editor Richard D. Bailey (76702,1637) as well as by Richard Carey (auctions and racing), Parker Converse III (exotic and sports cars), John F. Hribal (trucks and restorations), Chris Makynen (motorcycles), Christian Meyer (rare cars and motorcycles), Marc Meyer (U.S. cars and airplanes), Bob Messershmidt (new technology and micro cars), and Alain Wicki (European car market).

Also see Cars.

Writers and Writing: The Literary Forum (GO LITFORUM) is an information exchange for writers of fiction, poetry, and nonfiction. See Literature. Also, the Journalism Forum (GO JFORUM) is designed to serve professional journalists, those in related fields, and students considering careers in the profession. See Journalism. For screenwriters, see the ShowBiz Forum (GO SHOWBIZ). Science fiction and fantasy writing is discussed in the ScienceFiction & Fantasy Forum (GO SCI-FI). See Science Fiction. Independent writers also are discussed in the Working From Home Forum (GO WORK). See Working From Home.

Writing Online in CompuServe Mail, forum messages, Classified Ads and elsewhere is easy if you are using the CompuServe Information Manager. That's because the software, designed by CompuServe itself, provides a built-in editor that is compatible with the system and can be used offline as well as online. Some third-party communications programs also provide built-in writing programs for preparing messages for online delivery or to link with your favorite word processor.

On the other hand, if you are using communications software that does not include writing/editing facilities, you can use one of CompuServe's own word processors online. Two text editors are in use throughout the system: LINEDIT, a line-numbered editor, and EDIT, an unnumbered editor.

In many features, such as the forums and CompuServe Mail, you may choose which editor you want to use. Also, a preference for editors can be specified in the Profile area of the system (see Terminal). In the forums, a preference can be specified in the OPTIONS area of individual forums. In Mail, you can choose an editor with the SET options on the main menu.

Here are characteristics that both editors share:

- You must press the RETURN key at the end of each screen line.

- You cannot use your computers cursor-positioning arrow keys to edit the document.

- To close a document and leave the editor, use the command /EXIT.

Here are some things unique to each editor:

LINEDIT, the line-numbered editor

For newcomers, LINEDIT is easier than EDIT because it prompts for each line with a new line number and it uses menus for editing changes. The menus list options to CHANGE characters in a line, REPLACE a line, DELETE a line, INSERT new lines, etc. One option, TYPE, is recommended as your first step, because it lets you first see the numbered lines of your message. This is useful because all the other commands, such as REPLACE, DELETE, and so on, will ask for a line number as a reference.

EDIT, the unnumbered editor

Every command begins with a slash (/). If a line does not begin with a slash, the computer assumes it is text. It is helpful to think in terms of an invisible pointer that marks the position of the current line. You can direct the line pointer to move up or down your file. The pointer can be directed to move downward line-by-line from the first line of your text file and search for information to be displayed, changed, or erased.

/EX is used to exit the writing/editing service and return to Command Mode. Incidentally, you don't have to be at the bottom of the file to close with this command.

/T positions the line pointer at an imaginary line just before the first line of the file. This allows you to insert new lines above the current first line of the file.

/P*n* displays a specified number (*n*) of lines in the file. If *n* is omitted, only the current line will be displayed. For example, "/P3" will display three lines starting with the current line. (Tip: /T followed by a carriage return and "/P1000" will display the entire contents of the file, unless it is more than 1,000 lines long.)

/L/*string* scans the lines following the current line one-by-one until the first occurrence of the specified string is located. To display the line located, give the /P command. (If you terminate the /L/*string* command with an ESCAPE key, the located line will be displayed immediately.) Your pointer must be on a line *above* the line you are searching for in order to use /L/. It always searches downward in the file. (Tip: If you give the "/T" command just before the "/L/String command," you will be able to locate a string above the current line.)

/C/*oldstring*/*newstring*. This command replaces any specified string in the current line with a new string, where *oldstring* equals the string to be replaced and *newstring* equals the replacement string. If omitted, then *oldstring* will be erased.

/(GC/*oldstring*/*newstring* means "global change," and is the same as the /C command, except that all occurrences of the old text are changed to the specified new text. If *newstring* isn't specified, the command removes all occurrences of *oldstring*.

/A/*string* adds the specified string to the end of the current line. The line pointer will remain on that line after the command is executed.

/D*n* deletes the number of lines (*n*) specified starting with the current line. The pointer will be positioned at the line following the last line erased. If omitted, only the current line is erased.

/B moves the line pointer to the last line of your file.

/N*n*, meaning Next, moves your line pointer down the file a specified number of lines from its current position. If you enter *n* as a positive number (/N2), the line pointer advances down your file *n* (2) lines. If you enter *n* as a negative number (/N-3), the line pointer retreats up the file *n* (-3) lines.

/TYPE displays the contents of the work space.

/HELP gives more information about editing commands.

Also, even if you are not using CompuServe Information Manager or another program that supports an editor, you still can write letters offline for online delivery. Use your own offline word processor and save the document *in* ASCII. For more on this, see Mail, CompuServe.

WRQ/Reflection Forum (GO WRQFORUM) answers questions about the Reflection series of terminal emulation, networking, office automation, and development applications for DOS, Windows, and Macintosh. The systems are used to connect to DEC, HP, and IBM hosts. Representatives from WRQ (Walker Richer & Quinn Inc.) are online. Operating the forum is Paul Cullen (76711,1117), technical support, and Doyle B. Myers (76703,4403), Macintosh/DEC development.

WScan (software) is supported in the McAfee Virus Help Forum (GO VIRUSFORUM). See McAfee.

Wyoming news is included in the daily Southwest regional reports from United Press International. See Executive News Service for details.

Wyrick, Doug (75300,2303) is primary sysop of the Macromedia Forum (GO MACROMEDIA). See Macromedia.

WYSIFonts (software) is supported in Windows 3rd-Party Forum B (GO WINAPB). See Microsoft Software.

XC is an automated terminal program designed for Unix and Xenix systems. It is available for downloading from the Library 4 of the Unix Forum (GO UNIXFORUM). See Automated Terminal Programs for details.

XChange products are supported in the Desktop Publishing Vendor Forum (GO DTPVENDOR). For details, see Desktop Publishing.

Xenix/UNIX software is of interest to the Unix Forum (GO UNIXFORUM). See Unix.

X.400 protocols established for standardization in electronic mail by the International Telegraph and Telephone Consultative Committee (CCITT) are supported in CompuServe Mail. See Mail, CompuServe.

Xinhua is a Chinese news service that is searchable through Comtex Scientific Inc.'s NewsGrid (GO NEWSGRID). See NewsGrid.

Xircom products are supported in the IBM Vendors H Forum (GO PCVENH). See IBM Computers.

Xmodem is a binary protocol supported by CompuServe for sending and receiving files in forums, in electronic mail, and so on. See Files, Transfer.

XP Systems is supported in the Office Automation Vendor Forum (GO OAFORUM). See Office Automation.

XTree Company products are supported in the IBM PC Vendor E Forum (GO PCVENE). See IBM Computers.

Yares, Evan (75300,1771) is the sysop of the Engineering Automation Forum (GO LEAP). See Engineering.

YC/Kurzweil (products) are supported in the MIDI A Vendor Forum (GO MIDIAVEN). See Music.

Yellow Pages, Dun's Electronic (GO DYP) contains directory information on nearly 8 million businesses and professionals in the United States, covering both public and private companies of all sizes and types. See Dun's Electronic Yellow Pages and see Phone Directories, Yellow Pages.

Ymodem is a binary protocol supported by CompuServe for sending and receiving files in forums, in electronic mail, and so on. See Files, Transfer.

Yoga is discussed in the New Age Forum (GO NEWAGE). See New Age.

You Be the Critic (column) is among the syndicated columns provided by United Features (GO COLUMNS). See Columnists.

You Guessed It (game) (GO YGI) is an online quiz show built around trivia questions. It allows you to watch a game in progress and learn by being part of the "studio audience." The game also offers a "lobby," where potential players may meet and form teams to play the game. The game is intended for those age 18 and up.

    For information on other games, see Games.

"Young and the Restless, The" (television) summaries on the latest shows are available in Soap Opera Summaries (GO SOAPS). See Soap Opera.

Young Peoples' Logo Association gathers in the LOGO Forum (GO LOGOFORUM). See Programmers Support.

Youth Markets Alert can be searched through the Business Database Plus (GO BUSDB). See Business Database.

Z

Zachmann, William F. (76004,3657), president of Canopus Research, manages the Canopus Research Forum (GO CANOPUS). For details, see Canopus.

Zagat Survey (GO ZAGAT), published by Tim and Nina Zagat, is an electronic version of a series of regional restaurant reviews from major U.S. cities and regions. This is one of the system's basic services, meaning those signed up under the Standard Pricing Plan (see Billing) have unlimited access to the feature.

More than a million copies of the restaurant guide have been sold in printed forum. Online, the resource is searchable. Reviews are updated annually, either with a new survey or by editors who update existing reviews, as well as significant chef and management changes. Users begin by selecting a city or region of interest, then, following prompts, refine the search in terms of restaurant name, neighborhood, type of cuisine, price range, or newness of restaurant.

Zagat annually compiled surveys provided by regular restaurant patrons. The participants dined out an average of three or four times per week and completed extensive questionnaires.

Currently, the guide covers the following cities and regions: Atlanta, Baltimore (including Annapolis), Boston (including surrounding areas in New Hampshire, Rhode Island, Maine, plus Cape Cod, Martha's Vinyard, and Nantucket), Chicago (including surrounding areas in Indiana, Michigan, and Wisconsin, plus Milwaukee), Connecticut (western and southern parts of state), Dallas/Fort Worth Area (including the Mid-Cities), the Hawaiian Islands, Houston (including Galveston), Kansas City, Long Island, Los Angeles and Southern California (including Orange County, Palm Springs, San Diego, and Santa Barbara), Miami and Southern Florida (including Ft. Lauderdale, Palm Beach, and the Keys), New Orleans, New York City, New York State (north of the city), Northern New Jersey, Orlando and Central Florida (including Tampa, Daytona, and St. Petersburg), Philadelphia (including Atlantic

City, Bucks County, South New Jersey, and the Wilmington Area), Portland, St. Louis, San Francisco and surrounding area (including the Wine Country, San Jose, and the Monterey Peninsula), Seattle, Vancouver, and Washington D.C.

Z Best (GO ZB) is a store in the Electronic Mall (GO MALL) that offers discount electronics. See Electronic Mall.

ZCI Inc. is supported by the CD-ROM Vendor Forum (GO CDVEN). See CD.

Zenith Data Systems Forum (GO ZENITH) is an independent user group that focuses on the products from Zenith Data Systems, a Groupe Bull company. While the forum is not company operated, a number of Zenith employees volunteer time to field questions.

The group also is the CompuServe home for several independent companies, including Progressive Solutions and SoftKlone. The forum is managed by Joseph Katz (76703,662). Assisting are Al Kuntzler, Norm Reitzel, John Sawyer, Brian Hansen, Chuck Santose, and Vasil Balbay.

Zenographics Software products are supported in Windows 3rd-Party Forum B (GO WINAPB). See Microsoft Software.

Zeos International Ltd. (computer equipment) is supported in the PC Vendor E Forum (GO ZEOS). See IBM Computers.

ZiffNet (GO ZIFFNET) is a major collection of databases and forums provided by magazine publisher Ziff Communications. It includes features from *PC Magazine*, as well as features from *PC/Computing* and *PC Week*. ZiffNet is a part of CompuServe's extended services and has an additional membership fee (GO ZIFFMEM for details). At this writing, a monthly fee of $2.50 provides access to ZiffNet, ZEUS, and ZiffNet/ Mac (see ZiffNet/Mac). The chief sysop of ZiffNet is Rick Ayre (72241,215).

The ZiffNet services include:

- ASSIST Journal Online Forum (GO ZNT:ASSIST) for corporate communicators, instructors, and documentation specialists who are interested in the use of interactive media. The primary sysop is Bill Brandon (72241,1354), assisted by Julie Brown-Haworth and Rhonda Rosenof.

- Benchmark Operations Forum (GO ZNT:ZDBENCH) brings members a large set of Ziff-Davis benchmarks, including PC Bench 8.0, the newest version of the industry standard for measuring the performance of DOS PCs; MacBench 1.0, a subsystem-level Macintosh benchmark; and support for WinStone 94, Version 1.0, an exciting new benchmark that uses 12 top-selling applications to measure overall PC performance in Windows.

- Cobb Applications Forum (GO ZNT:COBBAPP) and Cobb Group Programming Forum (GO ZNT:COBBPROG) provide technical support for assorted computing applications. See Cobb Group.

- Computer Shopper Forum (GO ZNT: COMPSHOPPER) is an online companion to the print publication for direct buyers. See Computer Shopper.

- Executives Online (GO ZNT:EXECUTIVES), the "special events" area of ZiffNet, a place for in-depth discussions with people who set trends and make news in the desktop computing industry. Each week, the forum enables visitors to exchange comments, ask questions, and discuss products with invited guest executives. The libraries offer transcripts of earlier visits. Esther Schindler (72241,1417) is the sysop.

- The German-language Ziff Windows Forum (GO ZNT:GERWIN) supports the readers of its new monthly magazine Windows Aktiv.

- NewsBytes (GO ZNT:NEWSBYTES), covering computer news Monday through Friday, provides new issues each day by 5 p.m. East Coast time. See Newsbytes. Back issues can be read through Computer Database Plus. See Computer Database.

- PC/Contact (GO ZNT:PCCONTACT) hosts discussions of computer topics between readers and the magazine's staff, as well as files and programs for downloading. See PC/Contact.

- The PC Magazine UK Forum (GO ZNT:PCUKFORUM): The flagship of the new service is the PC Magazine UK Editorial Forum, which gives members unique access to the *PC Magazine* staff and information from the magazine. See PC Magazine.

- PC MAGNET (GO ZNT:PCMAGNET) from *PC Magazine* is home to forums such as Editorial, Utilities and Tips, and Programming and After Hours. See PC Magazine.

- PC Week (GO ZNT:PCWEEK) provides weekly news summaries, buyer's information, and more. See PC Week.

- Public Brand Software Arcade (GO ZNT:PBSARCADE) and the Public Brand Software Applications Forum (GO ZNT:PBSAPPS) providing shareware. See Public Brand.

- Seybold Newsletters (GO ZNT:SEYBOLD) includes three newsletters (Digital Media—A Seybold Report, Seybold Report on Desktop Publishing, and Seybold Report on Publishing Systems), as well as conferences and events and consulting services.

- Windows Sources Forum (GO ZNT:WINSOU), the electronic extension of print magazine, *Windows Sources*. See Windows Sources.

- ZiffNet Bendata Forum (GO ZNT:BENDATA) supports its HEAT and FLS products. The primary sysop is Tammy Connolly (72241,1650), assisted by Robert Minneman and David Hicks.

- ZiffNet File Finder (GO ZFILEFINDER or GO ZMC:FILEFINDER), a keyword searchable database of file descriptions from related forums, provides quick and easy reference to major programs and files available in these ZiffNet forums: Editorial, Utilities & Tips, Programming, After Hours, Computer Shopper, PC/Contact, PC Week Extra, PBS Applications, and PBS Arcade. As with other File Finder installations (see File Finder), you can use up to seven common search criteria to quickly find the location of a desired file or files.

- ZiffNet Reviews (GO ZNT:INDEX) is a database of product reviews from Ziff publications, searchable by product name, company naume, topic in the citation, and/or magazine.

Also, Ziff Communications operates the following services:

- Booknet (GO ZNT:BOOKNET) offers computer and technical books from Ziff-Davis Press at a 20 percent discount. See Booknet.
- Designer Template Collections (GO ZNT:FORMS), provided by KMT Software Inc., are intended for use with popular word-processing and spreadsheet programs. The word-processing template collections include those for sales and marketing, administrative forms, employee management, small businesses, job hunting, and a sampler pack of forms. The kits work with systems such as Ami Pro, Microsoft Word (PC and Mac), and WordPerfect for DOS 5.1 and 6.0, WordPerfect for Windows. The spreadsheet template collections include those for home buyers, for personal and company finance, small business forms, and a sampler collection that includes a variety from all of the collections. The spreadsheet collections work with all major spreadsheets including Lotus 1-2-3, Microsoft Excel (PC & Mac), and Quattro Pro for DOS and Windows. Each collection includes 6 to 12 different templates and forms. The cost per collection is $9.95 plus download time. Sampler packs are free of additional charge.
- Some major online gateways include Business Database Plus (GO BUSDB), Computer Database Plus (GO COMPDB), Health Database Plus, and Magazine Database Plus (GO MDP).
- Support On Site is a database of technical support information on more than three dozen popular PC environment and applications software products. It offers a resource base that includes software publishers' manuals and technical notes, reference books by Que and Ziff-Davis Press, and tech notes from industry sources. The applications covered in Support On Site include all the leading word processors, spreadsheets, databases, utilities, and graphics packages, plus MS-DOS, Windows, and OS/2. Powerful search software makes the material in the more than 88,000 documents within Support On Site easily accessible. To access it, enter GO ONSITE on CompuServe or from within ZiffNet and ZiffNet/Mac. It carries a $15 per hour surcharge in addition to standard connect rates.
- ZiffNet/Mac, a service for Macintosh users (GO ZMAC), includes forums operated by the staffs of *MacUser* and *MacWeek* magazines. See ZiffNet/Mac.
- The Ziff Support Forum (GO ZNT:ZIFFHELP) provides help for other Ziff features. The sysop is Ted Silveira (72511,166).

ZiffNet databases include some major gateways, such as Computer Database Plus (GO COMPDB), Magazine Database Plus (GO MDP), Health Database Plus and Business Database Plus (GO BUSDB). Each is searched in the same way. Here are the databases' key tools for creating keyword searches:

Wildcard lets you match variations on your search terms, such as alternate spellings or word endings.

Operator: *
Description: Matches all terms with zero or more characters in the position where the * is placed.
Usage: Type an asterisk (*) between or after characters.
Examples: RECYCL*; VOT*; COLO*R
Notes: Search terms must have at least two characters prior to the * for general search methods.
Operator: ?
Description: Matches all terms that have one character in the position where the ? is placed.
Usage: Type a question mark (?) between or after characters.
Examples: REC?CLE; VOT?; DEFEN?E

Proximity Operator allows you to specify a distance greater than one word as well as to specify the order in which you want the words found.

Operator: NEAR*n* (or N*n*)
Description: Specifies that the search terms on *either side* of the operator and within *n* words of each other in either direction.
Usage: Place the operator, with a numeric value, between search terms.
Example: COMPUTER NEAR5 COMMUNICATIONS finds articles in which the word "computer" occurs in five *or fewer* words in either direction from the word "communications."

Operator: WITHIN*n* (or W*n*)
Description: Specifies that the words on both sides of the operator occur within *n* words of each other in *a forward direction* only. (Contrast this with the NEAR operator above.)
Usage: Place the operator between two words.
Examples: TEST WITHIN10 METHODOLOGY; GULF W5 MEXICO

AND, OR, and NOT Operators can be specified to match articles containing or not containing several specific terms.

Operator: AND
Description: Specifies that the search terms on both sides of the operator match the area you are searching (article, subject heading, etc.).

| Usage: | Place the operator between search terms. |
| Examples: | MORTGAGE AND INTEREST; DEMOCRAT AND RE-PUBLICAN. (These find only articles that contain *both* keywords, that is, articles that contain both "mortgage" and "interest," or those that contain both "Democrat" and "Republican.") |

Operator:	OR, |
Description:	Specifies that *one or both* of the search terms on both sides of the operator matches the search area.
Usage:	Place the operator between search terms.
Examples:	SMOG OR POLLUT*; RUNNING OR JOGGING

Operator:	NOT
Description:	Lets you search for articles that *do not* contain the search term or expression to which the operator applies.
Usage:	Precede the search term or expression with the operator.
Example:	DIGITAL NOT EQUIPMENT, which finds all articles in which the word "digital" occurs as long as the word "equipment" does not also occur.

| Note: | You cannot start a search expression with the NOT operator unless you are narrowing on a search method already in use. |

Range Operators

Operator:	TO (or -)
Description:	Specifies that matching terms must lie within a range of values.
Usage:	Place the operator between two date values.
Examples:	JUL 1 1990 TO DEC 15 1990 finds articles published between July 1, 1990, and December 15, 1990, inclusive.
Note:	The range operator can only be used in the publication dates search method.
Operator:	BEFORE (or <)
Description:	Specifies that matching terms must lie before the value.
Usage:	Place the operator before a date value.
Examples:	BEFORE FEB 11 1990 (or < FEB 11 1990) which will find articles published before (but not *on*) February 11, 1990.

Operator:	AFTER (or SINCE or >)
Description:	Specifies that matching terms must lie on or after the value.
Usage:	Place the operator after a date value.
Examples:	AFTER DEC 1 1989 (or SINCE DEC 1 1989 or > DEC 1 1989) to find articles published on or after December 1, 1989.
Note:	The range operators can only be used in the publication dates search method.

Nesting Operators are used to change the order in which portions of a search expression are evaluated. Parts within parentheses are evaluated first, and the results merged with parts outside the parentheses.

Operator: ()
Description: The nesting operators are used to change the order of the portions evaluated for a search expression. The left parenthesis begins a nesting and the right parenthesis ends a nesting. The most deeply nested part of the expression is evaluated first.
Usage: Place parenthesis around the portion of the expression to evaluate first.
Example: MORTGAGES AND LOANS AND (BANKS OR CREDIT UNIONS)

Remember, keeping a search simple is the most effective approach. The less complex the search strategy, the more likely the success. The design of the feature requires these rules for forming search expressions:

1. AND, OR, and NOT operators must connect either two search terms, a search term and a nested search expression, or two nested search expressions.

2. The NEAR and WITHIN operators can connect only two words, not nested expressions. So, while COMPUSERVE NEAR10 FOOTBALL GAME is a legal expression, COMPUSERVE NEAR10 (FOOTBALL AND GAME) is not.

3. A nested expression must be connected to another word or nested expression by an operator. Therefore, FRIENDS (ROMANS AND COUNTRYMEN) is not a legal expression, but FRIENDS AND (ROMANS AND COUNTRYMEN) is.

ZiffNet/Mac (GO ZMAC) is a collection of services from magazine publisher Ziff Davis Company for Apple Macintosh users, and is part of its massive ZiffNet gateway. Ben Templin (72511,35) is the ZiffNet/Mac Manager. This is a part of CompuServe's extended services and has an additional membership fee (GO ZIFFMEM for details). At this writing, a monthly fee of $2.50 provides access to ZiffNet/Mac, ZiffNet, and ZEUS. The service's features include the following:

• MacWEEK News Beat (GO ZMC:MACBEAT) has top stories in the next week's issue of *MacWEEK*. Important stories that appear in Monday's paper edition are posted on ZiffNet/Mac the Friday beforehand.

• MacUser Power Tools, databases of downloadable files, includes all of the scripts, templates, programming code, and utilities mentioned and developed by the editors of *MacUser*.

• The MacUser Forum (GO ZMC:MACUSER) enables users to interact with editors, writers, and columnists of *MacUser* magazine. The forum is managed by Tom Petaccia (76702,563), with assistance from Joseph Holmes, Louise Kohl Leahy, and Jim Bradbury.

- The *MacWEEK* Forum (GO ZMC:MACWEEK) is hosted by *MacWEEK* magazine and its editors, writers, and contributors. Ric Ford (72511,44) is the primary sysop. He is assisted by Jonathan Oski, Brian Hall, Henry Norr, Rick LePage, and Stephen Howard.

- The Download & Support Forum (GO ZMC:DOWNTECH) is where *MacUser* and *MacWEEK* join forces to offer shareware and freeware plus an open area to help solve technical problems. The primary sysop is Gregory Wasson (72511,36). Helping him are Kevin Norris, Sherry London, and Robert Gibson.

- ZMac Reviews (GO ZMC:INDEX) is a database of product reviews from Ziff publications, searchable by product name, company naume, topic in the citation, and/or magazine. Data is from the files of MacUser and MacWEEK.

- Reference Databases (GO ZMC:REFERENCE) are tools to help users locate, buy, and use products, including:

1. The Buyer's Guide, which lists every product reported on by *MacWEEK* and *MacUser* with company contact information.

2. Tech Support Database indexes all of the tips and hints that have appeared in the magazines' help columns.

3. *MacUser/MacWEEK* Index catalogs every article which has appeared in these two publications since 1987.

ZiffNet/Mac also includes a new expert system series comprised of a set of downloadable HyperCard stacks intended to help users make smarter purchase decisions. The material is based on analysis from MacUser Labs, including benchmarks, product testing, and product reviews. It "lets users quickly and easily find the Macintosh products that are right for them, without having to sift through piles of complicated information," a company statement says. ZiffNet, which is hosted on the CompuServe network as a private service, defines their two expert systems as "Which Mac Should I Buy?" and "Which Storage System Should I Buy."
See also ZiffNet.

Zimman, Kristen, (76711,1111) is the sysop of the Florida Today NewsLink Forum (GO FLATODAY). See Florida Today.

.ZIP, as an extension on filenames in forum libraries, usually means the program is in a *compressed/packed* form. See Files, Compressed.

ZIPKEY ZIP code products are supported in the Office Automation Vendor Forum (GO OAFORUM). See Office Automation.

Zittrain, Jonathan   (76703,3022) administers the Texas Instruments Forum (GO TIFORUM) and is editor of the electronic *TINEWS*. See Texas Instruments Computers.

ZMac (GO ZMAC) is a collection of services from magazine publisher Ziff Davis Company for Apple Macintosh users. See ZiffNet/Mac.

Zone 66 **(game software)** is distributed and supported in Epic Online (GO EPIC). See Epic.

.ZOO, as an extension on filenames in forum libraries, usually means the program is in a *compressed/packed* form. See Files, Compressed.

Zoological Record Online   **(database)** may be searched through the IQuest gateway. See IQuest. See also Life Sciences.

Zoom products are supported in the Modem Vendor Forum (GO MODEMVEN). See Modem Vendor.

Zoos are the topic of the Humane Society Forum (GO HSUS). See Humane Society.

Zortech   **(software)** is supported in the Symantec Development Forum (GO SYMDEVTOOL). See Symantec.

ZPAY Payroll Systems   (producers of ZPAY payroll software, Grab and WinGRAB) is supported by the Office Automation Vendor Forum (GO OAFORUM). See Office Automation.

Zsoft is supported in the WordStar Forum (GO WORDSTAR). See Wordstar.

Zupnick, Linda (76703,2032) is sysop of the International Entrepreneurs' Network (GO USEN). See Entrepreneurs' Network.

ZyXEL products are supported in the Modem Vendor Forum (GO MODEMVEN). See Modem Vendor.